Acclaim for Melvin Patrick Ely's
ISRAEL ON THE APPOMATTOX

"*Israel on the Appomattox* [is one of] the first works that attempts to describe with precision the texture of day-to-day interaction across the color line. . . . A remarkably rich story."   —*The Atlantic Monthly*

"[An] absorbing story. . . . The value of this book lies in the many stereotypes the author has debunked."   —*St. Louis Post-Dispatch*

"Previous historians have described the limits of free blacks' freedom. But none has examined the quality of their lives in the detail or with the sophistication of Melvin Patrick Ely in *Israel on the Appomattox*. . . . A striking portrait. . . . Ely hopes to shift the emphasis in the study of free blacks from disempowerment to accomplishment, and he goes a long way toward reaching this goal."   —*Los Angeles Times*

"A remarkable civics lesson in hope, strength, endurance and quiet courage that most will find important and uplifting."
     —*Rocky Mountain News*

"Compelling, well-written, and thoroughly researched. The author knows Israel Hill and Prince Edward County inside and out, and his study is clearly a labor of love. . . . [Ely] challenges many of our assumptions concerning white and black Southern life in the antebellum period."
     —*Civil War Book Review*

"Ely brings to life the black personages who demonstrated that self-determination was possible in the South prior to the Civil War. . . . A rare slice of history recounted by an uncommonly fastidious historian who is as passionate about the Hill as he is about the Israelites who dwelled there."   —*Black Issues Book Review*

"[Ely] explores as few others have done the meaning of independence . . . and the role of faith and brotherly love."   —*The Decatur Daily*

"An astonishing act of historical research and imagination. Ely has given us the fullest and most humane account we have ever had of free black people."—Edward L. Ayers, author of *In the Presence of Mine Enemies: War in the Heart of America, 1859–1863*

Melvin Patrick Ely

ISRAEL ON THE APPOMATTOX

Melvin Patrick Ely, a native of Richmond, Virginia, took under-graduate and graduate degrees in history at Princeton University, studied linguistics at the University of Texas at Austin, and served as a postdoctoral fellow at the Carter G. Woodson Institute for African American and African Studies, University of Virginia. He has taught in public high schools in Virginia and Massachusetts, at Yale University, and at the Hebrew University of Jerusalem. Since 1995 he has taught at the College of William and Mary, where he is currently Newton Family Professor of History and Black Studies. He is the author of *The Adventures of Amos 'n' Andy: A Social History of an American Phenomenon,* and cotranslator, with Naama Zahavi-Ely, of *The Handicap Principle: A Missing Piece of Darwin's Puzzle,* by Amotz and Avishag Zahavi.

As Author

*The Adventures of Amos 'n' Andy: A Social History
of an American Phenomenon*

As Translator, with Naama Zahavi-Ely

The Handicap Principle: A Missing Piece of Darwin's Puzzle
by Amotz and Avishag Zahavi

ISRAEL ON THE APPOMATTOX

ISRAEL ON THE APPOMATTOX

A SOUTHERN EXPERIMENT IN
BLACK FREEDOM FROM THE 1790S
THROUGH THE CIVIL WAR

Melvin Patrick Ely

VINTAGE BOOKS
A Division of Random House, Inc.
New York

FIRST VINTAGE BOOKS EDITION, OCTOBER 2005

Copyright © 2004 by Melvin Patrick Ely

All rights reserved. Published in the United States by Vintage Books,
a division of Random House, Inc., New York, and in Canada by Random House of
Canada Limited, Toronto. Originally published in hardcover in the United States
by Alfred A. Knopf, a division of Random House, Inc., New York, in 2004.

Vintage and colophon are registered trademarks of
Random House, Inc.

The Library of Congress has cataloged the Knopf edition as follows:
Ely, Melvin Patrick.
Israel on the Appomattox : a southern experiment in Black freedom from the 1790s
through the Civil War / Melvin Patrick Ely.—1st ed.
p. cm.
Includes bibliographical references and index.
1. Free African Americans—Virginia—Prince Edward County—History—19th
century. 2. Free African Americans—Virginia—Prince Edward County—Social
conditions—19th century. 3. Land grants—Virginia—Prince Edward County—
History. 4. Prince Edward County (Va.)—History—19th century. 5. Prince
Edward County (Va.)—Race relations. 6. White family. 7. Free African
Americans—Virginia—Prince Edward County—Biography. 8. Prince Edward
County (Va.)—Biography. 9. Randolph, Richard, 1770–1796. I. Title.
F232.P83E49 2004
75.5'63200496073—dc29
2003065976

Vintage ISBN-10: 0-679-76872-6
Vintage ISBN-13: 978-0-679-76872-2

Author photograph © Gene W. King
Book design by Anthea Lingeman

Maps by George Colbert

www.vintagebooks.com

Printed in the United States of America
10 9 8 7 6 5 4 3 2 1

For

Vivien King Ely

my mother, my teacher

CONTENTS

Black Slavery, Black Freedom

Many years ago, thumbing through an old textbook, I noticed a brief reference to Virginia aristocrat Richard Randolph, his decision in the 1790s to liberate his slaves, and his highly unusual plan to grant them four hundred acres of his land in a place later known as Israel Hill. What became of the freed men and women who settled there? I wondered. What kind of lives did they manage to build so near the scene of their former bondage, surrounded by plantations still tended by their enslaved brothers and sisters?

More than a decade later, I read Richard Randolph's will—the most heartfelt indictment of slavery I had encountered this side of Frederick Douglass. On that same day, I learned that a prominent white neighbor of Israel Hill had described the settlement to a national readership in 1836 as a failure, its free black residents having supposedly degenerated into layabouts, thieves, and harlots. But I also saw quotations from a brief reminiscence by another local white man who praised the Hill colony of antebellum days as the home of "many good free negroes."

Clearly, a remarkable and controversial story surrounded the people, and the idea, of Israel Hill; I resolved to pursue that story. I did not yet know whether this experiment in black freedom before the Civil War had "succeeded" or "failed." I was ready to narrate the throttling of the community by hostile whites, or its success against the odds, or its decline through its residents' own misfortunes and missteps—whatever the record might reveal.

I was *not* fully prepared for what I learned over the next few years about freedom, bondage, and the relationship between the two. Earlier histories had shown in detail how Southern defenders of slavery branded free blacks as walking contradictions—a threat to the South's peculiar institution and to social order. Yet in dusty nineteenth-century documents, I found an additional story—one not of legislation or ideology but of everyday life.

Slavery's long shadow darkened the landscape that surrounded Israel Hill. At the very same time, human bondage played another role that I had not truly understood before: many Southern whites felt secure enough to deal fairly and even respectfully with free African Americans partly because slavery still held most blacks firmly in its grip. That paradox helped make room for a drama of free black pride and achievement to unfold in an Old South where ties of culture, faith, affection, and economic interest could span the barrier between black and white.

ISRAEL ON THE APPOMATTOX

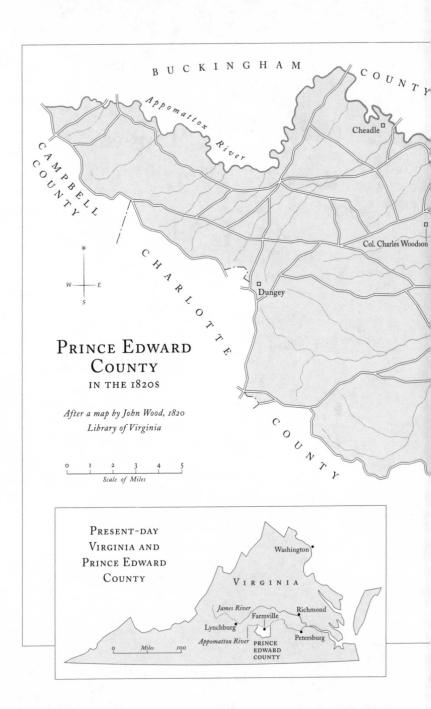

BUCKINGHAM COUNTY

Appomattox River

CAMPBELL COUNTY

CHARLOTTE

Cheadle

Col. Charles Woodson

Dungey

W — E
N
S

PRINCE EDWARD
COUNTY
IN THE 1820S

After a map by John Wood, 1820
Library of Virginia

0   1   2   3   4   5
Scale of Miles

COUNTY

PRESENT-DAY
VIRGINIA AND
PRINCE EDWARD
COUNTY

Washington

VIRGINIA

James River   Richmond
            Farmville
Lynchburg   Petersburg
Appomattox River   PRINCE
            EDWARD
            COUNTY

0   Miles   100

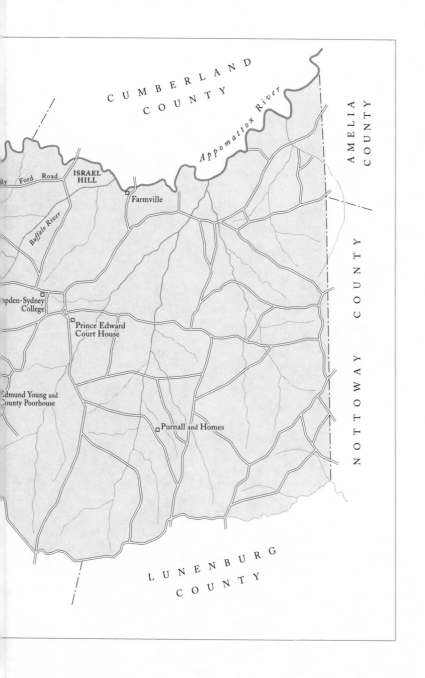

CUMBERLAND COUNTY

AMELIA COUNTY

Appomattox River

y Ford Road

ISRAEL HILL

□ Farmville

Buffalo River

NOTTOWAY COUNTY

mpden-Sydney College □

□ Prince Edward Court House

Edmund Young and County Poorhouse

□ Purnall and Homes

LUNENBURG COUNTY

CHAPTER I

The View from Israel Hill, 1863

I n the winter of his ninety-ninth year, Sam White looked out from his Virginia farmhouse by the railroad tracks, across the gentle slope of Israel Hill, his home of five decades, and onto a world that was reminding him yet again what a remarkable life he had led. White was one of the few Americans left who personally remembered the Revolution that his fellow Virginians had championed and the first years of the Republic they had built. Now, early in 1863, the grandsons of those same Virginians were killing and dying by the tens of thousands to break up that Union.

The once glorious, now tragic history of his state and his country formed only the latest chapter in a life of paradox. On the one hand, Sam White was in many ways a typical Southerner of his time, if there was such a thing. He owned a farm, but only a small one; he, his father, and his three brothers had cleared their own land and built unpretentious but comfortable houses on it. Like two thirds of the households in the South, White and his neighbors farmed their tracts with little or no help from slaves.

Sam White's sons and daughters, nephews, nieces, and grandchildren could grow, raise, hunt, or catch much of the food they needed; they cut timber from the back sections of their hundred acres to construct houses and outbuildings, repair their fences, cook their meals, and keep warm during the winter. They earned cash to satisfy their other wants by raising tobacco and vegetables.

Like many other small landowners in the South, some of the men in the White family had found ways besides farming to earn money. A few worked at carpentry, coopering, or other crafts. Two of Sam White's brothers, one of his sons, and a nephew or two had poled cargo boats, or batteaux, filled with hogsheads of tobacco and barrels of wheat down the nearby Appomattox River to market at Petersburg. In more recent years, some Whites had taken work in the small tobacco factories of nearby Farmville, a growing center of trade for the area. Just now, though, there were fewer men than usual on Israel Hill, as almost everywhere else in the South. For by 1863, the Civil War had become what Abraham Lincoln had warned of: a remorseless revolutionary struggle, consuming American citizen-soldiers in staggering numbers.

Sam White could not guess that the war's final drama would unfold on the very ground he looked out upon in 1863. General Robert E. Lee would fight his last major battle a day's march east of Israel Hill in April 1865. Lee would hold one final, urgent meeting with the Confederate secretary of war just two miles from the White farm before he set out toward neighboring Appomattox Court House, and Ulysses S. Grant would write to Lee later that day from the same place suggesting that the Confederate general surrender. Nothing so dramatic had happened in the neighborhood up to 1863. But even by then, the war had hit White and his friends hard: the Confederate Army had called perhaps a dozen men into its service from the little settlement of Israel Hill alone.[1]

Sam White's experience of peace and war reflected that of his society and his time—yet in some ways he had lived a different sort of life than most other small farmers in the South. For one thing, he and Phil White, his kinsman and neighbor, had made enough money to buy and sell a number of lots and buildings in Farmville. In an overwhelmingly agricultural South, White had played his part in the rise of a would-be boomtown.

But there was another, deeper reason White saw the world from a different angle than other Southerners of his economic level. In a society where most landowners, and most free people, were white, and where most African Americans lived out their lives as slaves, Sam White was both free and black. Apparently of purely African ancestry, a tall man in a family of tall men, he still carried his century-old frame erect as he visited the houses of his neighbors[2]—all of them, like him, former slaves or children and grandchildren of former slaves—to talk about developments in a Southern world that Lincoln and his armies were now struggling to change forever.

White's life journey from slave to free man, from property to proprietor and entrepreneur, had been channeled by the great changes his country had gone through since his childhood. The Revolution that liberated America had belatedly freed Sam White as well. His master, Richard Randolph, wealthy son of a great Virginia planter family and brother of the future statesman John Randolph of Roanoke, had become notorious at twenty-two: accused of impregnating his wife's sister and killing the newborn baby, Randolph had been acquitted in a spectacular court hearing with the help of his attorneys, Patrick Henry and John Marshall. But that generation of patriots had given Randolph something grander than a defense of his good name: the legacy of the American Revolution and its Declaration of Independence.

Citizen Richard Randolph, as he called himself in the style of the French Revolutionaries, had unwillingly inherited Sam White and scores of other slaves from his father. When Randolph died at twenty-six in the year 1796, he left a will, written in his own hand, that assumed the form of a ringing abolitionist manifesto. Randolph took special care to "beg[,] *humbly* beg[,] [his slaves'] forgivness" for his part in the "infamous practice of usurping the rights of our fellow creatures, equally entituled with ourselves to the enjoyment of Liberty and happiness." And he called for Sam White and the others to go free.[3]

Richard Randolph was not the only Virginia emancipator of his era; George Washington left a will at about the same time providing that his slaves be liberated at his widow's death. Contemplating the inhumanity of slavery, Randolph's cousin Thomas Jefferson once wrote, "I tremble for my country when I reflect that God is just." Scores of white Virginians set slaves free during the years that followed the Revolution.

But Jefferson and most others who admitted slavery was morally indefensible never pressed for a sweeping emancipation, for they had no idea what would become of liberated African Americans. Jefferson suspected that Africans were intellectually and physically inferior to Europeans; once emancipated, he believed, they would have difficulty surviving among whites. Even worse, Jefferson feared, generations of grievances between master and bondman would lead to race war if slavery ceased to exist as a system of social control. Many whites believed that blacks who did become free should be removed from Virginia.

Sam White's master, Richard Randolph, had offered a radical answer to Jefferson's moral dilemma: he denied that any dilemma existed. Randolph was not content to restore to his slaves their God-given freedom; he also called for them to receive four hundred acres of his land on which to build new lives as independent men and women. When Randolph's family carried out his will in 1810 after years of delay, his ex-slaves gave the name Israel Hill to their new home in the rolling terrain of Prince Edward County, and they called themselves "Israelites." This was their Promised Land, to which they had been delivered out of bondage.

But Israel Hill amounted to more than a personal promise fulfilled; it was a visionary Southern experiment in black freedom. In building this community of free, self-supporting black landowners in the very neighborhood where the Israelites had grown up as slaves, Richard Randolph and some ninety African Americans had launched a small but audacious attempt to demonstrate that a harmonious society containing free people of both races could exist.

Randolph conceived the idea that became Israel Hill, and his widow, Judith, overcame many obstacles to make his wishes come true. But the community's success over the decades had depended squarely on Sam White and his black fellow settlers. Their path, though arduous, had lain clearer before them because other Afro-Virginians had established themselves as free people in earlier years.

By the time Richard Randolph wrote his will, Prince Edward County already had a small free black population; that group would grow noticeably during the period before Randolph's germ of an idea came to fruition on Israel Hill. At least three local black or mixed-race families had bought land in the 1780s and 1790s, and a couple more would do so about the time Richard's former slaves settled on their new acreage. Other pioneering free blacks in Prince Edward owned no ground, yet by the 1790s were already developing strategies to make the most of their freedom.

The central figure on Israel Hill during the settlement's founding years had been Sam White's father, the aptly named Hercules White, a man esteemed by the Randolphs and the emancipated slaves alike for his strength of body, mind, and spirit. By the time Israel Hill was settled in 1810–11, it seemed that the Hill's new residents might in fact need the strength of a Hercules, and not only because there were houses to build, land to clear, and crops to cultivate. Though no longer in bondage, the men and women of Israel Hill lived in a land where both law and custom limited the rights of free blacks and ensured that relatively few African Americans became free in the first place.

In 1806, the state passed a new law requiring any blacks who received their liberty to leave the state within a year. Authorities did not apply that law to Richard Randolph's freedpeople, whose emancipation had been ordained long before. Still, neither Sam White nor any other free Afro-Virginian could vote, serve on juries, or join the militia; the law had required White to secure a license from the county court to possess a gun, and later prohibited black ownership of firearms outright. The people of Israel Hill owned land, but many of their fellow free blacks did not and therefore had to work for whites to earn their bread. White people rarely addressed or referred to an Israelite as "Mr.," "Mrs.," or "Miss"—titles that even the humbler whites felt entitled to.

Great events—the rise of natural rights philosophy, the American Revolution and its aftermath—had brought Sam White his liberty, and momentous developments had continued to shape his life as a free man. A Virginia slave, Nat Turner, led a rebellion in 1831 that killed at least fifty-five whites. In the days after Turner's revolt, a major of militia in Farmville worried that the blacks of Israel Hill might be considering a local replay of Turner's rising. Cooler heads averted any extreme repression of the Israelites and other blacks of Prince Edward County, but the county court did confiscate free Afro-Virginians' weapons.

In the years after the Turner rebellion, a small but vociferous abolitionist movement had arisen in the North. The abolitionists accused white Southerners—who considered themselves industrious, Christian sons and daughters of the founding fathers—of living parasitically off the labor of others in a violently anti-Christian, antidemocratic slaveholding society.

The indignant response of the white South had yet again complicated the lives of Sam White and the people of Israel Hill. Some influential white Virginians now told themselves and the outside world that slavery was just and godly—the most beneficial arrangement for the slaves themselves. Blacks, the argument went, would live in a state of civilization only so long as whites ruled and guided them; free blacks, white Southern apologists insisted, lived miserable, depraved lives.

Even a Southern proslavery hawk might utter the occasional good word about a free African American. Sam White himself had had a rare experience for a free black in the South, winning praise in publications from New Orleans to New York as one of the "honorable . . . original settlers" of his community, "a venerable patriarch . . . as highly respected for tried and well sustained character as any man."[4] The bad news for him and his fellow Israelites was the context in which White received those accolades.

Colonel James Madison—not the former president, but rather a leading entrepreneur in Prince Edward County—had written a defense of the Southern way of life in 1836 in the form of a brief, highly inaccurate history of Israel Hill, which other proslavery propagandists later elaborated upon. Defenders of slavery asserted that Sam White's upright character had been molded during his half century as the favored bondman of a refined white family; they used the attainments of White and some of his peers to set in sharp relief the degeneracy they said had overtaken more recent generations of black Israelites, deprived of the supposedly civilizing framework of slavery.

The younger residents of Israel Hill had become "idle and vicious," Madison wrote in the *Farmers' Register,* a magazine read throughout the South; the Hill's women, he said, had turned to prostitution. The editor of the *Register,* the famous agricultural reformer and Southern nationalist Edmund Ruffin, added an improbable swipe of his own at the men of Israel Hill: they preferred to pole heavily laden boats up the Appomattox River, he wrote, because of all occupations that one was "nearest to idleness."[5]

Madison, Ruffin, and people like them held one belief that their ideological opposite, Richard Randolph, had apparently shared: if a community of liberated blacks could flourish, it would challenge white people's basic assumptions about the black race and about the organization of Southern society. This Madison and his like could not accept. The bleak picture they drew of Israel Hill in the 1830s proved durable, despite a whole series of achievements by the Whites and their black neighbors; proslavery writers had revived and elaborated on the legend in the press as the North-South struggle deepened during the 1850s. The free black community of Israel Hill, a product of the first American Revolution, had become a potent and tenacious symbol in the great conflict that produced the second.

Sam White had seen many whites in Prince Edward struggle, in a way that Colonel Madison never did, to sort out the dissonance between their desire to defend slavery and their free black neighbors' obvious fitness to function as free people. According to the county's oral tradition, after a series of thefts on neighboring plantations, suspicion had fallen on the free blacks of Israel Hill. White men searched homes on the Hill for stolen goods. Finding none, many Prince Edward whites came to admit, and repeated for years afterward, that the black Israelites were honest and decent even as men like Colonel Madison proclaimed the opposite.[6]

When the need to justify the South's institutions grated against the realities of day-to-day life, race relations became more complex and fluid rather than more uniformly rigid. One historian has written that "the generation preceding the Civil War [saw] the drive against the free Negro . . . so intense that he was branded as the pariah of society"[7]—but that verdict leaves part of the story of race in antebellum Virginia untold.

Sam White and the other Israelites had indeed faced their share of obstacles and insults. Still, having lived the first half of his life as a slave and a second half century as his own man, White knew how much even his imperfect freedom was worth. No one could buy or sell him or separate him from his wife and children. A slave could not buy, sell, bequeath, or inherit property. Sam White had fed his family on his own farm, inherited land from his father, Hercules, and earned enough on his own to buy additional real estate. Most free blacks did not become slaveholders, but occasionally White or a free black neighbor did work a slave, either hired from a white person or purchased outright.

The law barred black testimony against whites in court, but free Afro-Virginians in Prince Edward sued white neighbors and defended themselves against suits by whites; the blacks typically received a full hearing and sometimes won their cases. Farmville and its environs suffered their share of crime, involving both races and all classes; a free black defendant invariably faced an all-white court or jury. But Sam White knew that acquittals of blacks were very common. Local courts had found free African Americans not guilty even when the charge was a sensational one—burning down the house of a public official, for example.

When the first Baptist church in Farmville had formed—at the very time Colonel James Madison of that town published his attack on the Israel Hill experiment—the white pastor welcomed Sam White and his kinsman Phil as the congregation's first members. The presence in the church of free, ambitious, successful black entrepreneurs and landowners did not stop white men and women from joining the congregation. More than a few whites in Prince Edward recognized Sam White and his relatives as "proud" residents of Israel Hill and—Colonel Madison notwithstanding—considered the black settlement "prolific . . . of many good free negroes" of "ability" and "integrity . . . very much respected and trusted by all classes of citizens."[8]

Most of the things people did in Prince Edward County, blacks and whites at least sometimes did together. People of both colors who had money transacted business with one another. Two families seeking their fortune, one white and the other free black, moved west together. Men of both races labored shoulder to shoulder on construction sites and along the Appomattox River. Even in this color-conscious society, free blacks and whites of modest means worked together as hired harvesters on wealthier people's plantations, and men of both races earned the same wages.

Sam White knew, too, that whites and blacks in Prince Edward found themselves side by side in places more intimate than the county's wheat fields or the mercantile houses of Farmville. A white Revolutionary War veteran approached the county court in 1818 to petition for a federal pension that would help him support himself, his daughter, and the mulatto grandchildren she had borne him. One of Prince Edward's solid white citizens revealed during a court proceeding a few years later that his wife's sister had become pregnant by a black man. About the time Richard Randolph died, a comfortable white farmer nearby gave his daughter in marriage to a free mulatto; the couple bought a farm next door to the bride's father and named one of their sons after him. That brown grandson himself took a white wife, as did several of his free Afro-Virginian contemporaries. These interracial unions drew complaints from some whites, but neither authorities nor ordinary citizens broke them up.

Sam White, like other free blacks, had good reason to rejoice that he was not a slave. But he knew that even the relationship between slave and master, and between slave and Southern society at large, was not nearly as simple as Colonel Madison and the Northern abolitionists, each in their own way, depicted it.

The abolitionists did understand that slavery was full of horrors. Prince Edward and Virginia's other tobacco counties struggled through economic depressions during many of Sam White's years as a free man. Land and possessions were frequently forfeited and auctioned off by the sheriff, or sold in desperation—and slaves constituted the main category of personal property. Most whites preferred not to break up black families, for reasons of humanity and of economy—demoralized slaves did not produce as much. Yet black men, women, and children were often moved about, families split apart, and children as young as three or four separated from their mothers. Countless groups of manacled slaves trudged down Prince Edward County's main road toward the cotton states.

Sam White lived in a place and had known a time, as late as his own middle age, in which a slave who stole bacon or whiskey might find himself sentenced to have both ears nailed to a pillory and then cut off, and to be burned on the hand with a hot iron, and to receive thirty-nine lashes. Masters and overseers whipped slaves without any due process at all. The law denied bondpeople the right to own property, and it was exceedingly difficult for them to own themselves by purchasing their freedom.

At the same time, White had seen the local courts exonerate many enslaved men and women charged with serious crimes against whites. On the very eve of the Civil War, a panel of justices in neighboring Nottoway County had acquitted a slave of an assault on his mistress with a rock, despite the two-by-four-inch gash in her head that the white woman pointed to as she made her complaint. And White could recall the acquittal in his own county a few years before the war of an enslaved youth whom a white woman had accused of raping her. Almost until the first shots of the War of Secession were fired, some slaveowners in Prince Edward and neighboring counties had recognized the injustice of human bondage in the way Richard Randolph had: by emancipating slaves.

Sam White took for granted something that the escaped slave and abolitionist Frederick Douglass had noted in the 1840s: that complex human relationships were part and parcel of American slavery, inhumane though that system was. The realities of daily life led whites in Prince Edward to admit the humanity of blacks routinely in myriad ways. And blacks, free and slave alike, successfully laid claim to rights and considerations that the theory of racial slavery denied them.

White would have been surprised by some propositions about values and behavior in the Old South that many Americans of our own time accept as fact. White people had displayed their worries about Israel Hill during the weeks after Nat Turner's slave revolt of 1831, requiring free blacks to turn in their guns to county authorities. But other responses to the Turner rebellion had shown how little Prince Edward resembled the martial society that Yankees of Sam White's time, like some Americans today, believed the South to be.

White's county was one of dozens in Virginia where the scramble to defend against slave rebellion in 1831 revealed not a militarized culture of bold, well-armed, dead-eye marksmen born on horseback, but rather a land of frightened, often befuddled white men milling around in ragtag militia musters. Those men often discovered to their shock that they had no guns to fight off the anticipated tide of vengeful slaves—or that the few arms they did have lay rusted in caches nearly forgotten over years when militia drill consisted of an occasional afternoon of drinking and socializing.

Sam White would also have chuckled at the popular romantic notion that an archaic code of honor rigidly and ritualistically ordered the society he lived in. Southerners did guard their personal honor zealously. Yet White understood that conflicts in Prince Edward, whether they involved blacks or whites, rarely ended with a brace of dueling pistols and two men firing at thirty paces; much more often, a brace of lawyers fired off subpoenas to friends, relatives, and associates of the antagonists. White knew, too, that when men did resort to violence in Prince Edward, a challenge to meet on the field of honor was vastly less common than the spectacle of two neighbors—both white, both black, or occasionally one of each color—carping, then shouting, until one picked up a stick and whacked the other over the head (after which, often enough, the customary brace of lawyers was brought to bear).

Above all, White knew something that many people today find difficult to believe—that his world, in spite of its discriminations against him and other free Afro-Virginians, had never become one in which "whites would not tolerate free Negroes living among them," where most white people treated the free black as "an incorrigible subversive" to be "almost uniformly feared and despised," or where the purchase of property and other steps free blacks took toward self-improvement "enraged" their white neighbors.[9] In reality, the liberties one could secure as a free African American, though circumscribed, were substantial—hence the exertions of many to buy their own freedom and that of their relatives, and to acquire some ground to live on in their Southern homeland.

Of course, Sam White knew only what he himself had seen and heard, and his life had not been "typical." But the more we learn about the South, the better we understand that no one Southern experience and no single landscape typify any era.

As a free black man, Sam White was an exception, but not a rarity: one in eight Afro-Virginians during the generation before the Civil War was a free person, and one in ten free people in his home county was black. White's neighborhood could lay no stronger claim to typicality than anyplace else, but it was thoroughly, unmistakably Southern. Prince Edward was a slaveholding, tobacco-growing, rural, black-majority county in a state that had more slaves than any other and more free African Americans than any save Maryland—a state in which most free blacks, like White himself, lived in the countryside, not in the cities on which many modern studies focus. The view from Israel Hill was finite, but it took in a range of experience that included a goodly portion of what Southern life was before and during the Civil War.

Sam White's liberation as part of a large group, and the Randolphs' grant of land to him and his fellow freedpeople, had indeed been unusual. But White's day-to-day experience as a slave and then as a free man illustrates the span of possibilities in the rural Old South. After all, "to define" means, literally, to trace the bounds or limits of something. The boundaries of life in the slaveholding South encompass the loopholes, the "give," the deeply human interactions, the occasional dramatic acts of conscience, and the African American achievements within that system—all of which, paradoxically, were of the essence in a society at whose core lay white supremacy and economic exploitation.

Richard Randolph may have seen himself as the initiator of a unique experiment in black freedom. But in fact, the people who came to call themselves Israelites, along with their black and white neighbors, help us define what was *normal*—for the venerable Sam White, for Prince Edward County, and for the Southern society in which White lived his century of life.

❈

CHAPTER 2

Liberty and Happiness

CITIZEN RICHARD RANDOLPH AND HIS SLAVES

Dickey Randolph took a fright one summer day when he saw a man leading two horses up the lane toward his parents' plantation house. The boy was only eleven, but he knew what a riderless horse could mean in time of battle, and one of this pair belonged to his father, who had gone off to fight in the Revolutionary War. Dickey had already lost one father to illness when he was only five. Now, in July 1781, he concluded that a British bullet had taken his stepfather, St. George Tucker—the man he called "Papa," and whose "most dutyfull son" young Richard Randolph felt himself to be.

A moment later, though, something struck Dickey as "very odd" in the frightening scene now before him: the man approaching the house was, after all, leading not one but two horses. If Tucker were dead, then Syphax, the black personal servant who had accompanied him to the military encampment, should now be astride that second horse, returning home to bring the sad news and leading Papa's mount behind him. But Syphax had apparently remained in camp—something he would have done, Dickey concluded, only if Tucker were still alive to enjoy the black man's services. The boy soon learned with relief that his deduction was correct. Tucker's horse, Hob, had gone slightly lame; Tucker, alive and unhurt, had sent Hob and a sorrel horse back to Bizarre, the Randolph plantation where Dickey and his family had moved to escape the British menace in his mother's native Tidewater section. For the time being, at least, the family still had a father.[1]

The incident crystallized in one anxious moment three of the interlocking elements that molded young Richard Randolph's view of the world. The war—both as a personal drama and as a crusade for revolutionary ideals—formed many of Richard's most indelible childhood memories. A second essential factor in the day of the riderless horses was Syphax, the Afro-Virginian valet. Sy's presence or absence at that moment, and at others during the war, literally embodied the difference between life and death to young Dickey; fears about Tucker's fate could be instantly "dispell'd by a Grin" from the black man.[2] Syphax and other black figures affected Richard Randolph in ways that proved as abiding as Dickey's moment of panic in the closing weeks of the Revolution was fleeting.

Finally, Richard's character was shaped profoundly by Tucker himself, and by the older man's circle of friends. An intellectual, a young paladin of Revolutionary Virginia, and later an influential political figure, Tucker thought deeply about American liberty, American slavery, and the dissonance between the two. The education he gave Dickey ensured that the boy would think about those things, too.

Dickey Randolph was a deep-dyed patriot with a boy's cordial loathing for the rogues on the other side. "I wish the british may meet with destruction & their attempts be baffled in every instance," he wrote to Tucker. "Which I make no doubt they would if the Tory's did not give them such good intellig[e]nce." "I wish I was big enough to turn out" for battle, the eleven-year-old added, "if I was I woud not stay at home long." A precocious boy, Richard followed the military campaigns in detail, and he was not shy about sharing his own tactical and strategic judgments with Tucker.[3]

By the summer of 1781, when Richard Randolph feared for his stepfather's life, the neighborhood had sent many soldiers into the conflict, and local men had helped guard some two hundred British prisoners in Cumberland, the Randolphs' home county. The military had made heavy demands on the area for guns, foodstuffs, and clothing—"all . . . we could spare," as some leading men put it; an installation not far away at the village of Prince Edward Court House produced gunpowder and ammunition.[4] Now the struggle with the British entered what turned out to be its closing act, in Randolph's own Virginia. General Nathanael Greene, commander of the Continental Army in the South, had retreated into the state from the Carolinas at the beginning of 1781 and sent his heavy weaponry and baggage to Prince Edward Court House for safekeeping. In February, the militia in Cumberland, Prince Edward, and half a dozen neighboring counties had been mustered and sent to reinforce Greene, and St. George Tucker had been called to lead militia troops with the Marquis de Lafayette.[5]

The British commander Charles Cornwallis and his army moved from North Carolina into southeastern Virginia; on the same Monday in early July 1781 that Richard Randolph spied the riderless horses, Cornwallis sent Colonel Banastre Tarleton with a detachment of cavalry and mounted infantry to raid Prince Edward County and other strategic areas. By Friday, Tarleton and his men began burning, looting, and carrying away some local men as prisoners.[6]

On Saturday, with nine hundred British troops only seven miles away, Dickey Randolph's mother, Frances, wrote to tell St. George Tucker of her "utmost distress"; she was preparing to evacuate Bizarre with the three Randolph boys, sons of her late first husband, and with two babies she had borne by Tucker. Frances was a strong, determined woman; her son John remembered how she "flung my deceased father's most valuable papers into a pillow case & put his steel hilted dagger into her stays" as she made ready to leave. Yet Dickey was perceptive enough to detect his mother's fear, and to know what the bustle of slaves packing up the family's belongings meant. Frances knew it would take her slave wheelwright until Monday morning to repair the one wagon, "so very weak," then available at Bizarre. At any moment the mounted British force might decide to wheel back eastward through the Randolph-Tucker plantation before the family could get away.[7]

In the end, Frances, Dickey, and the others apparently did not flee; by the time they were ready to go on Monday, Tarleton had turned south—away from Bizarre—and then east to return to Cornwallis. Still, long weeks of hardship for the neighborhood followed as yet more men, supplies, wagons, and horses were rounded up from an exhausted countryside for an offensive in the east.[8] Finally, three months after the days of fear at Bizarre, Cornwallis, trapped between Continental land forces and a French fleet, surrendered at Yorktown, and the war was over.

During those fearful times, Frances Tucker had found support and stability in her slaves—a boon no master or mistress could take for granted. Slavery robbed blacks of liberty but not of will, and the Revolution had presented some new options to bondpeople. Early in the war, the British had offered freedom to slaves who would join them, and thousands fled from their masters during the conflict. The Tuckers themselves acknowledged that slavery was tyranny and that blacks had good reason *not* to stand by those who owned them. Thus Fanny was expressing relief, and not a mistress's blind assumption of black servility, when she wrote, as she prepared to flee Tarleton's raiding party, "My faithful Servants are every thing I cou'd wish them, & are willing to follow my fortune."[9]

Enslaved African Americans—especially house servants and skilled craftspeople—stood out in the minds of the Tuckers and other slaveholders as vivid personalities, their lives intertwined with those of the whites among whom they lived. Even as Frances prepared to flee the British, she followed the custom of her class, taking time to send her husband news about the health and welfare of several black individuals.

No slave figured more prominently in the letters of the Randolphs and the Tuckers than Syphax, personal servant first to Richard's father, then to his stepfather. As Richard grew into manhood, he, too, would come to depend on a body servant called Syphax—probably the same man who had attended his two fathers. The Randolphs and St. George Tucker trusted Syphax absolutely. He traveled alone back and forth between the several Randolph-Tucker homes and Tucker's military camp, sometimes carrying his master's money and other valuables. Mounted on a good horse, Syphax could easily have ridden off to the British, got his freedom, and sold useful intelligence about the American forces with whom he was living—but it never entered anyone's mind that he might do so.[10]

The family's trust in Syphax did not arise from any fawning submissiveness on the black man's part, however. The Randolphs doubtless assumed that Syphax's family connections—he had a wife and children—would bring him back home. Still, only a fool sends a person into a war zone with vital goods and information unless that man, besides being attached to the homeplace, is also known to be strong of will, brave, and resourceful in the face of unexpected perils. Syphax exuded dignity and ability. Many years after the Revolution, Richard Randolph's brother John, by then a famous politician, described Sy as the ultimate measure of young Dick himself. "You might see in the old Attendant Syphax whom [Richard] had carried with him to [college in] New York that his master was a gentleman," John recalled.[11]

Syphax, the most significant black figure in the life of future emancipator Richard Randolph, was proud to work as the personal servant of genteel, even great, men—and that makes it all too easy to misjudge him utterly. A long-standing stereotype depicts the loyal valet as a mentally tyrannized figure gratefully wearing a white man's castoff clothes and looking down on the lowly field hand. Then there is the modern notion that serving is not a skilled occupation—a snobbish bias that working one shift as a waiter will permanently correct.

Syphax was a slave, and he may have been reared to be a valet. But when Richard Randolph's will set him free, the old man would prove more than ready to defend his interests against white aggression. In the meantime, Syphax Brown, as he was known by the early 1800s, would spend his early years of freedom working in one of the local inns as "a

Waiter on Gentlemen."[12] That was a title that one could claim proudly. During Syphax's hostling days, a master from nearby advertised for a runaway slave who had "a pert walk, good countenance, [and was] very active and fond of waiting on gentlemen."[13] For that proud, even cocky man, escape had been yet another act in a life of black assertiveness; his "fondness" for serving men of quality was no mark of servility, but rather an element in the runaway's self-esteem—as it was in Syphax Brown's.

The natural father whom Richard barely knew, John Randolph Sr., had mortgaged nearly all his slaves—that is, presented them as collateral when taking out loans. But to risk losing Syphax to creditors was unthinkable, so Richard's father had avoided including him in the mortgage.[14] Syphax exerted a direct, active personal influence on the younger Randolph. The black man certainly acted as a source of family history and lore, and probably of wisdom acquired through an eventful life.[15] The time that Syphax spent serving Richard during months of study at Columbia College—leavened for both men by socializing and political stargazing in New York and Philadelphia—not only gave the servant an opportunity to enhance his considerable experience and sophistication, but also may well have deepened the bond between the two men.

As advantaged as Richard was—wealthy, tall, handsome, intelligent, socially prominent—he experienced the culture shock that has affected Southern youth attending Northern schools from that day to this. Yankees seemed less warm and hospitable than Southerners, and all the Virginia students seemed to take ill upon their arrival in the North. Richard won acclaim at Princeton as a public speaker yet quickly grew discontented with the teaching and course of study there.[16] Randolph, barely eighteen, could experience a bit of home in the person of his two younger brothers, who also studied at Princeton and Columbia—and in New York, he had the companionship of Syphax as well.

Other slaves, too, took important places in the Randolphs' lives. That the family called Billy Ellis, one of their slave carpenters, by both a given name and a surname already suggests that he stood out. Indeed, John Randolph later accused Dick's sister-in-law Nancy of having been scandalously intimate with Ellis when she lived at Bizarre. That accusation does not ring true; among other things, Jack alleged that Nancy Randolph had written a love letter to Ellis, who in fact did not know how to read or write. Even so, this skilled slave—a short, black-skinned man whom John indignantly referred to as "this dusky Othello"—had qualities that made him seem to Jack a plausible if illicit paramour for a beautiful, wealthy young white woman.[17] Nancy did feel warmly toward Ellis, but in a manner typical of the more open-minded slaveowners of the period. "Poor Billy," she wrote to a friend after John's outburst; "he does not deserve to be slandered—his fidelity to his Master when living—and his veneration for his memory always made me feel a regard for him such as I had for [her brother] William's Johnny and many of my Father's blacks."[18]

Hercules, a slave born around the midpoint of the eighteenth century, became a Randolph family favorite while filling a prodigious variety of roles much different from those of Syphax. Hercules may have worked at times in the family mansions, but he also knew how to plow a field, grow tobacco and corn, slaughter and dress hogs, drive a wagon or cart, and do cooper's and carpenter's work. Years later, Hercules would become the central figure in the settlement of Israel Hill.[19]

Richard Randolph's view of the world, and of slavery, crystallized not only in conversation with Syphax Brown and other African Americans but also at the feet of St. George Tucker and a couple of the most famous teachers in America's best schools. Richard's mother, Frances Tucker, was conventionally pious: she invoked God's protection for her husband off at war, and she led her sons in reciting the Lord's Prayer and the Credo on going to bed and waking up. Stepfather St. George Tucker, by contrast, looked skeptically at anything that—as Jefferson put it—might exercise tyranny over the mind of man. John Randolph later said that "the conduct and conversation" of Tucker and his friends had persuaded young Jack "early in life . . . to regard Religion as the imposture of priestcraft."[20]

In overthrowing the political tyranny of Great Britain and the mental tyranny of tradition and superstition, Jefferson, Tucker, and others like them exalted the liberty of the individual. But these men believed that a person could defend freedom only by cultivating the mind and avoiding dependence on others for his livelihood. Liberty demanded hard work and extraordinary self-discipline—qualities that we seldom attribute to the wealthy planter, who by definition depended on slave labor.

Richard Randolph's mother and both his fathers unrelentingly exhorted him to mental, moral, and economic self-improvement. In the will that John Randolph Sr. left when Dickey was five, the father insisted that his sons not be allowed to grow up "without learning either trade or profession." Frances Randolph Tucker gave Richard no peace whenever she suspected that the young student was indulging himself with clothing too abundant or too fine, by attendance at "balls," or in "correspondence with licentious young men." St. George Tucker's ambitions for the

Randolph boys equaled those of their natural parents. In a single letter, Dickey could both banter playfully and apologize to Tucker for having slacked off in his study of grammar. "Be assured, I shall have my Syntax at my fingers ends when you return," he wrote to his stepfather.[21]

Mother and stepfather alike required "Improvement" of their boys, meaning education, moral growth, and increased usefulness; that last word became the family motto. There is a certain well-rehearsed obsequiousness in Jack's and Dickey's boyhood pledges to "improve" themselves, yet their parents' puritanical demands shaped Richard as an emancipationist. He came to see that slavery exacted labor by force rather than by appeals to character and internal motivation; that realization in turn apparently led Randolph to admire all the more those slaves who evinced good character and a work ethic in spite of the degradation imposed on them.

St. George Tucker's Enlightenment worldview proclaimed that unfettered reason could and should comprehend all of nature. As a teenaged student at the College of William and Mary in Williamsburg, Richard took special pleasure in witnessing experiments with electricity.[22] Over the years, he acquired books on natural history, mathematics, and astronomy, as well as an account of Captain Cook's famous voyages of discovery. By the time he reached his mid-twenties, Richard owned more than 300 volumes and nearly 120 titles, an impressive private library for the time. Randolph read both Latin and Greek, but his interest in modern history was no less keen, and he considered the New World to be as worthy of study as the Old; American history, and especially that of the Revolution, held his particular interest. One book of sermons and the family Bible occupied a lonely space on shelves stocked with works by Locke, other British writers, the French *philosophes,* Beccaria, and Machiavelli. Volumes of English poetry and prose from Shakespeare to Swift and Fielding and a copy of *Don Quixote* rounded out Richard's library.[23]

Randolph met the great teacher of his life before he ever reached Princeton at age seventeen: George Wythe, signer of the Declaration of Independence, reformer of the Virginia legal code, and teacher of law and other subjects at William and Mary. Wythe pronounced his name like the preposition "with"; he was sixtyish when he instructed young Randolph in Greek, Latin, and mathematics in 1786 and 1787 and oversaw Dick's graduation from grammar school to college.[24] He was a legendary figure in Virginia and beyond—a remarkable fact not only because of Wythe's obscurity today but also because he gained his renown largely as a teacher.

No man in Virginia except George Washington had a name as lustrous as Wythe's. One of Randolph's contemporaries wrote that "nothing would advance me faster in the world, than the reputation of having been educated by Mr. Wythe, for such a man as he, casts a light upon all around him." Richard Randolph himself called Wythe "that best of Men!"—"the brightest ornament of human nature." Richard became one of many students and friends—Thomas Jefferson had been another—for whom meetings at Wythe's house were "not [to] be deferred," and who would go out of their way not to be seen by their teacher as guilty of "neglect."[25]

Enlightenment demanded that every social assumption and institution be subjected to the cold light of reason—and reason told Jefferson, Wythe, St. George Tucker, and Richard Randolph that all men are endowed by their Creator with certain inalienable rights. Reason also left no doubt in their minds that blacks were human; both reason and morality therefore prohibited their enslavement. But slaveowners had a massive investment to protect, slavery underlay Virginia's entire social and economic structure, and most thought a biracial society of free people would be unsustainable. George Washington ordained freedom for his own slaves, yet for society at large he advocated emancipation only by "slow, sure, and imperceptible degrees."[26]

St. George Tucker himself published a detailed plan in 1796 for gradual emancipation. Even as he and other white Americans made their Revolution, he proclaimed, "we were imposing upon our fellow men, who differ in complexion from us, a *slavery*, ten thousand times more cruel than the utmost extremity of those grievances and oppressions, of which we complained." Tucker declared slavery "perfectly irreconcilable . . . to the principles of a democracy," and he opposed any forcible expulsion of blacks, "our fellow men, and equals." Yet his own plan was scarcely more humane. Generations of slavery had instilled in blacks habits of "submission" and in whites "arrogance and assumption of superiority," Tucker believed; the two races were unfitted to live together in freedom. Tucker therefore would cause freedpeople to emigrate "voluntarily" by denying them the right to own property, bring lawsuits, make wills, or otherwise expand their liberty to encompass much beyond the simple absence of chattel slavery and security in life and limb.[27]

George Wythe, Richard Randolph's mentor, acted on the principle of racial equality that Tucker espoused in theory. Wythe declared that, even under existing Virginia law, when the status of a person of color was in doubt, the burden of proof lay on the individual who alleged that the party in question was a slave. Some feared that that principle, should it become established law, could lead to freedom for many enslaved blacks, and the state supreme court soon overruled Wythe's doctrine. Wythe also rejected the idea that freed blacks must be deported, a prominent former student of his recalled: "Mr. Wythe, to the day of his death, was for *simple abolition,* considering the objection to color as founded in prejudice." Wythe reared a mulatto boy named Michael Brown almost as a son, though there was probably no blood relationship between the two. He taught young Brown Latin and Greek, and wrote a will in which he left the young man a large part of his estate and placed him under the protection of Thomas Jefferson.[28] Richard Randolph thus took as his hero a man who carried the doctrine of human equality considerably further than Randolph's "greatest Benefactor," St. George Tucker. Randolph's "brightest ornament of human nature" eventually paid for his racial open-mindedness with his own life: ten years after Richard Randolph died, George Wythe and Michael Brown were poisoned to death by Wythe's grandnephew, who apparently resented the old man's love for and legacy to Brown.[29]

St. George Tucker, Jefferson, and Wythe had carried out their Revolution. Now came another revolution for Richard's generation, the sons and daughters of 1776—in France. For Randolph, as for Jefferson, the French Revolution constituted the next great step in a train of progress, a fulfillment both of the philosophical treatises that filled Richard's bookshelves and of the American Revolutionary struggle. Richard found the teachings of Tucker and Wythe reiterated in the French view that everything old, everything customary, was overdue for reappraisal by reasoning people. The French Revolutionaries declared for the first time that France consisted not of estates or interests, but rather of free individuals who merited the title "Citizen"; they scrapped the old calendar, inventing twelve new months, abolishing the seven-day week, and numbering the years from the onset of the Revolution rather than from the birth of Christ. Accordingly, Richard Randolph, his brother John, and others in their circle of friends began addressing each other as "Citizen" rather than "Mr.," "Mrs.," and "Miss"; when Citizen Richard Randolph wrote a will, he dated it in the traditional month of February—but in "the twentieth year of american Independance" rather than A.D. 1796.[30]

Dick's future wife, Judith, had been born to the same heritage as Richard—in fact, into the Randolph clan itself. The Randolphs included Thomas Jefferson, John Marshall, first president of the Continental Congress Peyton Randolph, and other luminaries. In marrying Richard,

Judy Randolph was following a family custom; Richard's own father had married his first cousin's daughter. The couple wed during the Christmas holiday of 1789, when Dick was nineteen and Judy just turned seventeen; her parents were second cousins to each other, and cousins of Richard Randolph as well.[31]

Judith was as bright and urbane, and at least as wealthy and socially prominent, as Richard. She grew up at Tuckahoe, a plantation on the north bank of the James River a few miles west of Richmond; the family mansion, a stately clapboarded structure laid out in the shape of a letter H, still stands today. Thomas Jefferson, second cousin to both of Judy's parents, had lived there for a time as a boy. A steady stream of the great and near great from Virginia and beyond became a part of young Judy's day-to-day life.[32] By the time she reached her mid-teens, she had become widely known for her "virtues and accomplishments" as well as her beauty. After a visit to Tuckahoe, one cousin called Judy "the most perfect of her sex"; he wrote of her "lovely face," her "angelic majesty," and the "incomparable musick . . . [that she] played as if she had been inspired by some diety [sic]." There was surely a physical chemistry between Judy and her equally blessed and accomplished cousin, Richard. The two were intellectually and ideologically compatible as well: Judy could quote from the classics, she followed politics, and she addressed Richard's stepfather Tucker and other friends as "Citizen."[33]

But nothing could have prepared either for the crisis that beset them in the fall of 1792, when they had been married less than three years. Judy's younger sister Anne Cary (Nancy) Randolph, an attractive girl of seventeen, lived with Richard and Judy at Bizarre plantation, and everyone knew she and Richard were close. On October 1, 1792, those three young people gathered with a group of twentyish Randolph cousins and their spouses at a still-unfinished house in Cumberland County that belonged to one of the group. That night, screams from Nancy's bedroom wakened others in the house. The idea that Nancy had cried out during a miscarriage, an induced abortion, or the birth of a baby, and that a fetus or a murdered infant body had been secretly disposed of in the night, circulated within the mansion and from there to the world at large. The talkers further reported that the man who had gotten Nancy pregnant and hidden the evidence of the birth or abortion was Richard Randolph.[34]

Here again, relationships between black and white played a critical role. The constant physical closeness of personal servants to masters and mistresses sick and healthy, dressed and undressed, positively promoted discussion between slave and owner of the most intimate and sensitive topics; so did some white people's emotional dependence on favored bondpeople. Some slaves even felt free to volunteer derogatory information about one white person to another: Randolph Harrison and his wife, Mary, the Randolphs' hosts that tumultuous night, supposedly had no suspicions about Nancy Randolph's illness until a female servant told one of them that Nancy had miscarried. Harrison's brother also heard the shocking news from a slave. Still other bondpeople later told Harrison that the aborted fetus or newborn corpse had been laid outdoors on a pile of shingles. Harrison did little or nothing to investigate those charges, but apparently he also did not chastise the blacks for making such grave allegations about his relative.[35]

Judith Randolph—who herself seems to have lost a baby during the same period—protested the innocence of her husband and her sister. By March 1793, Richard concluded that "a public enquiry into [the accusations against him] is now *more* than *ever* necessary."[36] The affair ended up in a courtroom, apparently on Richard's initiative. But he, and not any of his accusers, stood as defendant before the fourteen justices of Cumberland County Court late in April. The testimony was almost as graphic and sensational as the gossip on the subject had been, revolving largely around details of Nancy's body, its most intimate functions, and the substances that had supposedly emanated from it on the fateful night. Richard Randolph had used his connections and money to hire as formidable a team of lawyers as anyone ever assembled in those times.[37] Richard's cousin John Marshall, later the pathbreaking chief justice of the United States, joined two other attorneys, one of them Patrick Henry, who had called for "liberty or death" at the dawn of the Revolution and served as first governor of independent Virginia.

The big-name attorneys probably helped; they certainly mounted an effective defense. No one had produced a dead body or an aborted fetus, and the law barred enslaved witnesses, if there were any, from testifying against a white person. Moreover, Richard's lawyers argued that Nancy would not likely have selected a houseful of people as the place to bear or abort the fruit of an affair with her sister's husband. Judith deposed that it was she who had sent Richard in to attend the indisposed Nancy, and that he had not gone downstairs that entire night. Though no one said so in court, any pregnancy of Nancy's could plausibly be blamed on Richard's brother Theodorick, to whom Nancy had been engaged over her father's objections, and who had died less than eight months before the events at issue. Many years later, Nancy would essentially admit Theo's paternity of a baby which, she implied, had been stillborn.[38]

Richard Randolph's exoneration brought some relief to the family.[39] The couple's devotion to each other, which leaps out from their writings, must have helped them recover from the scandal. That mutual understanding had to be deep if the pair were to tackle the second great challenge of Richard's young life: his inheritance of human property despite his opposition to slavery. Dick received a share of his long-dead father's land and slaves upon turning twenty-one in 1791. He had already stated, according to one chronicler, that he wanted to inherit "not a single negro for any other purpose than his immediate liberation." Yet Richard's father, like many other Virginia gentlemen, had incurred huge debts to British creditors before the Revolution. Until Richard paid those obligations, the slaves his father had mortgaged to secure the debts were not legally his to liberate.[40]

Randolph wrestled with this quandary in a will that he wrote at his mahogany desk less than three years after his trial. He was only twenty-five years old; his devoted brother John noticed no sign of ill health. Yet much of Richard's will reads like the testament of a man half-expecting to die any day—a confession, a withering indictment of his society, and an ethical testament to his two children, "that they may know something of their fathers heart when they have forgotten his person."[41]

Randolph devoted the greater part of his will to a long and passionate essay on the evils of slavery. In the spirit of the French Revolutionary left, he embraced his "first and greatest duty"—"to befriend the miserable & persecuted of whatsoever nation[,] colors or degree." Jefferson, in his original draft of the Declaration of Independence, had disingenuously indicted the British crown for kidnapping innocent Africans. Richard Randolph noted that many of the mortgages under which he and other Virginians groaned lay in the hands of "british Harpies"—"rapacious creditors" whose claims prevented him from emancipating his slaves.[42]

But Randolph spread the blame for slavery more widely than Jefferson had: he castigated his fellow Americans, too, for having "exercised the most lawless and monstrous tyranny" over Africans and African Americans for many decades "in contradiction of their own declaration of rights." The excuse that human bondage was a necessary evil Richard denounced as a transgression "of every principle of moral & political honesty"—a threadbare cover for "sordid . . . avarice, and the lust of power."

Randolph—the child of the Revolution who had studied under sign-
ers of the great Declaration—felt betrayed. American slaveholders practiced the very exploitation they had rebelled against twenty years earlier,
and Randolph responded "with an indignation too great for utterance at
the tyrants of the Earth—from the throned Despot of a whole nation, to
the more despicable [and] not less infamous petty tormentor of single
wretched Slaves, whose torture constitutes his wealth and enjoyment."
No abolitionist of the antebellum period would ever put the point more
powerfully.

Richard wrote his will partly to declare that ownership of slaves had
been "forced on me by my father" and "to exculpate myself, to those who
may perchance to think or hear of me after death, from the black
crime . . . of voluntarily holding the . . . miserable beings in the same
state of abject slavery in which I found them." Yet Randolph also took
personal responsibility for the tyranny in which he participated, and pronounced himself determined "to make retribution . . . to an unfortunate
race of bondmen." Though not a conventionally religious man, Richard
well knew that atonement involves admitting guilt, asking for pardon,
and making restitution, and he did, or proposed to do, all three. He confessed that he had been "driven reluctantly to violate [his slaves] in a general degree, (tho' I trust far less than others have done)." He went on to
"beg[,] *humbly* beg [his slaves'] forgivness, for the manifold injuries I
have too often inhumanly, unjustly, & mercilessly inflicted on them."[43]

Randolph saw only one form of restitution as appropriate: to find a
way to liberate his bondpeople after all, mortgages or no. Though he
wrote in the tones of a man anticipating death, he hoped he would not
"be so unfortunate as to die possessed of any slaves"; "I shall surely
[emancipate them] the first moment possible" under the law, he promised. Should he die a slaveholder, though, he ordained that all those
bondpeople whom the law did not bar from going free should do so; if
the courts ordered any of his people sold to satisfy his father's debts, then
£500 should be raised from the rest of his estate and used to purchase and
liberate the "most worthy."

Freedom itself—even if it came to every one of the Randolph slaves—
would not make a just recompense, Richard realized. And here he parted
company with his peers in the planter class—including his stepfather
Tucker—who conditioned emancipation on black emigration, or who
actually liberated slaves but did not offer them the means to sustain
themselves. Randolph owned about two thousand acres on both banks of
the Appomattox River;[44] he called for those slaves he might succeed in

liberating to receive four hundred acres of that land as their own property. Richard Randolph's will thus became a statement not only about slavery and freedom but also about race. One can abhor the enslavement of people one considers inferior—but Randolph insisted that Africans and African Americans were "our fellow creatures, equally entituled with ourselves to the enjoyment of Liberty and happiness." Even if the races were equally endowed, nothing guaranteed that whites would permit emancipated blacks to live and thrive in their midst. Yet Randolph rejected that kind of pessimism when he ordained the land grant; he envisioned his former slaves as self-sustaining members of the very society that had held them in bondage.[45]

Richard Randolph based his opinions of black ability not on blind idealism, but rather on his own experience with people of both races. He had ample reason to view whites—perhaps especially the most "refined" ones—as fallible, often perverse beings. The white slaveholding elite had betrayed the Revolutionary ideals they professed, and some in Richard's own family had nearly wrecked his life with lurid, whispered accusations.

Richard neither disparaged nor idealized blacks. Some slaves at the time of the scandal had been as petty and as quick as their masters to believe the worst of him; he knew other Afro-Virginians, such as Syphax, to be as honest and as dignified as any whites. Where Thomas Jefferson suspected that blacks were inferior, Richard Randolph apparently discerned a span of initiative, talent, and morality among blacks that resembled the range found in any race. Richard assumed that his slaves in general were clever and industrious enough to support themselves on the land he left them; some had special "merits," however, and these people Randolph wanted to save first if the law should require the auctioning of his estate. He called on his wife "to lend every assistance . . . in her power" to the resettled ex-slaves after his death—not because they needed spoonfeeding, but rather because Virginia's "illiberal laws" would place obstacles in their path.

Richard's confidence in his wife exceeded even the faith he invested in his slaves. The eighteenth and nineteenth centuries saw the rise of "companionate marriage"—motivated by love more than by calculation, and characterized by mutual respect and shared decision making. Richard's own mother had been an affectionate, demonstrative, if demanding parent; she had proved during the last months of the Revolutionary War that a woman could be as decisive and effectual as a man, and she had deftly handled plantation crises when her own husband, St. George, had business elsewhere.[46] Judith Randolph, too, had married a man who was often away from home; she rued her "lonely hours" without him, even though her sister, her slaves, and a succession of guests surrounded her. Still, Dick and Judy loved and admired each other, and together they had weathered unimaginable stresses.[47] Judith's strength in the face of scandal equaled that of Richard's mother, Frances Tucker, in time of invasion.

Richard named Judy executor of his emancipatory will. If slaves should have to be auctioned off to pay Richard's father's debts, Judith alone was to decide how to raise £500 from the rest of his estate, and she would determine which slaves were to be bought with the fund and freed. The four-hundred-acre land grant to Richard's ex-slaves, he wrote, was "to be laid off as my wife shall direct, and . . . given to the heads of families . . . as my said wife shall judge for the best." Richard was asking Judy not only to give up part of their land and all their slaves but also to invest months or years of effort to make it happen. Only a man certain that his wife respected his principles could make such a request. Richard's confidence in Judith, he declared later in the will, rested on "the estimation and ardent love which I have always uniformly felt for her, & which must be the [last] acting impulse of my heart."

Richard Randolph's Revolutionary upbringing and the character and achievements of his slaves may not fully account for his actions as a liberator. Most who declared that all men were created equal—including the author of the Declaration of Independence himself—did not free their slaves, while some Federalists who detested the French Revolution did liberate bondpeople. The factors that could turn a Southern democrat into an emancipator and defender of racial equality could be highly personal, even idiosyncratic. Richard Randolph had a powerful sense of guilt, and not only toward the slaves from whom he "*humbly* begged" forgiveness. The Randolph boys early on began offering their stepfather Tucker regular, almost unctuous thanks for pressing them relentlessly to seek personal "improvement." Richard's mother hammered during Dick's student years at his supposed appetite for extravagant clothes, parties, and questionable friends, and for "read[ing] love tales continually." At one point she warned him that she "might look for peace in a better place"—and then, after Richard begged abjectly for pardon in six tightly packed pages, she made good on her threat by dying. Though Richard did resent his mother's strictures, it would have been difficult for him to spend his formative years trying to please Fanny Tucker without largely becoming the penitent he presented himself to be.[48]

The modern observer may be tempted to see Richard Randolph's emancipatory will as one last, dramatic expression of displaced guilt. But if Richard felt he had fallen short of his youthful ambition "to be a great & conspicuous character,"[49] creating a community of free blacks in Cumberland or Prince Edward County was as likely to win him suspicion as approbation among other white Virginians, even if it bolstered his opinion of himself. There is no evidence that Randolph's confession of "manifold injuries" to his slaves referred to any specific crimes against them for which he sought absolution. Neither is it at all clear that Richard used his will to grasp at redemption in the wake of the scandal he had endured. Richard was very possibly innocent of unfaithfulness to Judy, and probably not guilty of infanticide. Besides, his act of emancipation would not affect the opinion of either side in the debate about the scandal—of the immediate family and loyal friends, or of those who wanted to believe the gossip about him and Nancy.

The will Richard wrote does sound gloomy flowing from the pen of a twenty-five-year-old, and he did die only a few months after writing it, unexpectedly enough that his brother Jack later accused Nancy of poisoning him.[50] But there is no compelling evidence that he committed suicide. On the contrary, his will declared a determination to live at least long enough to liberate his slaves.

All in all, Richard Randolph's will expressed not *displaced* guilt, but rather straightforward guilt based on principle and profound disappointment. Randolph was a dyed-in-the-wool moralist, nearly as hard on himself as he ever was on others, capable sometimes of extenuating the guilt he felt, but in the end taking his principles to their logical conclusions. At times he may have carried punctiliousness to a fault, unable to see that doing justice in one sphere could create injustice in another. Some accounts say that Randolph insisted on paying even debts that by law had died with his father, because he considered it "iniquitous" to allow any of the elder Randolph's "just creditors" to go unsatisfied.[51] But honoring those obligations would have raised still higher the financial and legal hurdle that barred Richard from liberating his slaves. It was that same moralism, however, that forced Randolph to face head-on the guilt he felt over owning those slaves, and he felt mortified by it. His principles came through most clearly in the portion of his will where he discussed his little sons, the elder of whom was only four years old. Randolph left the young ones to his wife's "affectionate love—desiring . . . that they be instructed in virtue, and in the most Zealous principles of Liberty & manly independance . . . of which I conjure them to be indefatigable and incorruptible supporters [thro'] life." "Let them be virtuous & free," he concluded; "the rest is vain."

Richard preached incorruptible virtue and freedom mainly out of the despair he felt at belonging to a people that was corrupted and unfree. The enslavement of Africans was the worst corruption, a betrayal of the Revolution that had shaped both Randolph's country and his consciousness. But that evil was magnified because it partook of a broader rot. Richard's father had mortgaged his slaves to bail out a brother, Richard's uncle, a wastrel who had squandered his own money on rakish pursuits; in doing so, John Randolph Sr. tightened the chains on his own slaves "for money to gratify pride & pamper sensuality." Judith Randolph's father had taken on similar mortgages to bail out Judy's grandfather, and many other Virginia planters had done the same.[52]

Here, as nowhere else in the will, Richard may unconsciously have spoken in the voice of one who himself had been accused by many, including his own mother, of indulging in "sensuality." Dick had sometimes bristled at his parents' preachings, but the Tuckers' values had largely become those that he himself professed. Only through self-control, thrift, and hard work could one achieve "improvement" and attain the "manly independance" Richard wanted to instill in his sons. Rather than sequester his first boy, a deaf-mute, in a life of gilded uselessness, Randolph insisted in the will that his sons learn a "trade if they be incapable of a liberal profession."

By these standards, slavery and white supremacy corrupted everyone they touched: they made hypocrites of the nation's founders and their children, helped seduce masters like Richard's uncle into vice and parasitism, fed base impulses to tyrannize and torture other human beings, and put manly independence forever beyond the reach of the blameless black victims and their indolent masters alike. American patriots had won the war against the British and the Tories—only to become Tories themselves.

Richard's hatred of self-indulgence and hypocrisy was the more intense precisely because he considered himself self-indulgent and hypocritical. His letters from school radiate thinly veiled disgust at the apple polishing and exaggerated contrition he felt compelled to adopt in his relationship with his parents. More important, while Richard made the antislavery case as eloquently as anyone of his generation, he went on leading the life of a great Virginia planter until his dying day, a fact he said he despised but did little or nothing to change. He did not even liberate the handful of slaves who were not under mortgage, though he may have allowed them considerable latitude to do as they wished.[53]

Yet whatever his shortcomings, Richard Randolph did at least recognize that his society's many failings, and his own, were all of a piece, and he wrote a will that held true to the principles he professed. He had chosen as his icon the great, now unjustly forgotten George Wythe, whom Richard called in his will, that diatribe against corruption, "the most virtuous & incorruptible of mankind." Wythe was the most consistent champion of the universal rights of humankind Randolph had ever known in Virginia, or probably anywhere else. For Wythe and for Richard, freedom and virtue were inseparable, universal values. The lack of personal virtue led to slavery for whites and blacks alike, and denial of freedom stood as society's greatest sin.

Randolph resolved to become one of the few true Wythians of his day. He would set free, he said, those men and women he might gain the power to liberate. He would requite their years of labor with the means to sustain their liberty in their own native land rather than on some foreign shore. And in doing so, he would give those people the opportunity to achieve the dignity and independence he trusted they were capable of. In the end, the success of Randolph's experiment in black freedom would lie in the hands of the people in whom he had such faith: his widow, Judith, and the Afro-Virginians he believed were as deserving of liberty and happiness as he himself.

SUBORDINATION WAS ENTIRELY OUT OF THE QUESTION

Richard Randolph had not left Judith in a situation that would incline most people to launch an idealistic—and expensive—social experiment. The widow faced not only the mortgages Richard's father had left but also "very considerable" debts of Dick's own. Richard had spent a large sum defending himself and Nancy in time of scandal and, it seems, helping his sister-in-law further in the aftermath.[54]

Judith had been complaining about "severe attacks" of "nervous affections" even before Richard died. Her physical complaints worsened in the months and years that followed; brother-in-law John Randolph came to consider her "a confirmed hypochondriack." "Hope[,] the sweetest soother of a wounded spirit, leaves me," Judith wrote to a friend at the end of the summer after Richard's death. ". . . I have nothing to wish for, no flattering prospect to cheat my senses with, none."[55]

Judith did manage to hold on to the plantation, but at a heavy cost to some of the slaves her husband had wanted to liberate. Richard's brother, John Randolph, had moved in with Dick, Judy, and Nancy at Bizarre in 1794. After his brother's death, John managed the family's finances, and he later took credit for a compromise that Richard's estate struck with those to whom it stood in debt. The latter demanded a partial payment in return for deferring the rest of the family's obligation; an unrecorded number of the Randolph slaves were sold not long after Richard's death in order to raise the money. Although seventy-two other blacks escaped that fate, the forced sale was just the event Richard Randolph had feared. Even most of those slaves who were not sold off remained under mortgage. Until those debts, too, were paid, only five of Richard's slaves could legally go free.[56]

Judith proceeded to emancipate at least one relatively soon after Richard's will was proved in 1797. Syphax Brown, the esteemed valet, appears as a free man on the earliest surviving list of free blacks in Prince Edward County, from 1801, and another former Randolph bondman later recalled that Old Sy had been liberated considerably earlier than that. By 1801, Brown had moved to a spot near the new town of Farmville on the south bank of the Appomattox with his second wife, Betty, and her son. Betty Brown washed clothes and delivered babies to supplement the income her husband earned as a "Waiter on Gentlemen."[57] The other four Randolph slaves not under mortgage were Rose Johnston, about thirty years old when Richard Randolph died, and her small children Jacob, George, and Rachel; it is not clear whether Judy liberated the Johnstons quickly.[58]

Even some of the Randolph slaves who remained under mortgage began a slow transition toward the liberty that had been promised them. In 1799 at the latest, Judith sent Hercules, the jack-of-all-trades whom the Randolphs particularly respected, to live on the land she owned across the Appomattox River in Prince Edward. Hercules took his family with him: his wife Molly, his sons Tony, Dick, and Hercules Junior, as well as another youngster named Guy Howard, who may have been an orphan. The four boys ranged in age from about eight to teenage in 1799. Judith put as many as half a dozen horses under the care of Hercules and company; they must have used the animals in part to farm a portion of the Buffalo tract, as Judith's Prince Edward land was called. Over the next ten years, Judith sent several other slaves to live near Hercules.[59] The black family across the river were allowed to farm for themselves as well as for Judith, and they probably sold some of what they grew. Small transactions between whites and slaves were common at the time, and Hercules' own name begins to show up regularly in such accounts by 1805.

The issue of the seventy-odd still mortgaged slaves lingered. In an age when greedy would-be heirs often contested emancipatory wills, Judith did not question whether the act of liberation Richard had desired should take place. To embrace that assumption was more difficult than it might seem to people today who have been taught that a liberal, emancipationist wave swept the Upper South during the generation or so following the American Revolution. The "wave," though real, might better be called a substantial ripple when it is measured by the fraction of slaves who actually went free; Virginia remained by far the largest slaveholder among the states until bondage itself ended in 1865.

Some Virginia planters had begun expressing antislavery feelings years earlier, at least in private. Robert Beverley wrote in 1761 that human bondage was "something so very contradictory to Humanity, that I am really ashamed of my Country whenever I consider of it." After the Revolution, the young Thomas Jefferson unsuccessfully proposed gradual emancipation for the newly independent state of Virginia. In 1782, the state legislature for the first time passed a law allowing masters to manumit (liberate) slaves at their own discretion. More sweeping measures were at least open to public discussion; the Rhetorical Society in Richmond in 1795 debated "whether . . . the slaves in Virginia should [be] emancipated at present." (The society decided in the negative.)[60]

The last will and testament became the instrument of choice for liberating slaves. Yet fully sixteen years passed after the liberal manumission law took effect before any slaveholder in Prince Edward County, future home of Israel Hill, left a will emancipating even a few bondpeople. Many masters did at least take some account of black family ties as they parceled out slaves among their heirs. Yet dozens of others writing wills unblinkingly mandated that all their slaves and other property be disposed of "at publick sale to the highest bidder" and the proceeds divided among those slaveholders' survivors. Still other masters in the Randolphs' neighborhood, not content to keep the slaves they already owned, left wills requiring that money from their estates be used to buy additional blacks lest any of their children find themselves slaveless.[61] Even a citizen of Prince Edward who recognized his "trusty Slave Lewis" in his last testament left the black man to his widow rather than recognize years of "trusty" service by setting even that one slave free. When the biggest slaveholder in Prince Edward County moved to the free state of Rhode Island in about 1810, he liberated not a single black; instead, he advertised all eighty-nine of his slaves for sale locally.[62]

Religious convictions, especially in the evangelical churches, stirred white misgivings about slavery. Yet by the time Richard Randolph died, the churches had already begun moderating their criticism of human bondage in a region where more than a few of their members, and many of their prospective converts, were slaveholders. In Prince Edward, Cumberland, and other counties, some congregations actually acquired slaves and earned money for the church by hiring those blacks out to others.[63]

Judith Randolph, then, was departing from the norm the minute she freed even the five slaves whom Richard's father had not mortgaged. To carry out her husband's plan for a wholesale emancipation, even at some remote date, would be far more radical. As late as 1810, only 149 free blacks lived in the entire county in which she expected her freedpeople to settle; for every Afro-Virginian in Prince Edward who had his or her liberty, 48 blacks still toiled as slaves.[64] The group Judith planned to liberate would instantly swell the county's free black population by nearly two thirds.

Still, Judith's determination to carry out Richard's will did not leave her wholly isolated. Most slaveholders who expressed humanitarian concerns did so entirely within the existing system, specifying that favored slaves choose which of the master's heirs they would live with, or that their bondpeople be sold only "to those that the said Negroes would wish to go to as Masters."[65] Other neighbors took bolder steps down the road that Richard Randolph had asked his wife to walk. Those 149 free black people who lived in Prince Edward County by 1810, and several score others who resided in Cumberland, had come from somewhere, after all. Some descended from white women who bore free children by black men—a child's status as bond or free followed its mother's—but most apparently were former slaves or children of former bondpeople.

One local master, Jesse Johnson, had liberated four slaves almost as soon as the law of 1782 permitted him to do so.[66] Fifteen years later, not long after Richard Randolph died, Nancy Jackson had concrete reasons not to emancipate her slaves: a person of modest estate, apparently non-literate, she had four siblings and two nieces who stood to inherit the few human beings she did own. Yet Jackson ordained that her female slave Lett "be in the full possession of Freedom and at Lib[erty] to act for herself." Lett's three daughters were to be bound out "to good places," where they would learn occupations (the law required emancipators to provide support for liberated males under age twenty-one and females under eighteen). When Lett's girls reached the appointed age, they were to go free.[67]

Robert Goode, devout Christian owner of twenty-two black persons, specified in 1804 that all slaves born after his widow died were to be "born free," though they would remain in service until age twenty-five. Goode wanted to use that time to prepare the coming generation of blacks for freedom: he commanded his children to "learn them to read and write." "In case any [Goode son or daughter] should refuse to educate them as much as that," the same heir was to lose his or her servants' labor four years early, when those blacks turned twenty-one.[68]

In offering liberty exclusively to people yet unborn, or to those who first endured many years of unfree toil, slaveholders such as Nancy Jackson and Robert Goode did no worse than the laws that abolished slavery in several states north of the Mason-Dixon line. Other slaveholders offered still more to their slaves during the years Judith struggled to pay her inherited debts. Andrew Baker Sr.—a former officer in the Revolution, active Presbyterian layman, and promoter of schooling for the poor—decreed that several of his slaves be hired out for four to six years, to masters of their own choosing if possible; they were to receive part of the proceeds from their hire and go free at the end of their terms.

Baker designated another slave to help his widow run the plantation for a period of years and then to go free after being paid fairly for his services. All children of Baker's bondwomen were to be bound out to people who would teach them to ply good trades and to "read distinctly and well"; at twenty-one, each child was to go free. If Virginia law by that time should pose any obstacle to their remaining in the state, Baker provided that his executors send the freedpeople "to the North western Teritory where they will be entitled by law to that freedom to which they are entitled by nature."[69] Here, at last, Prince Edward County saw a will that echoed Richard Randolph's brand of antislavery. Joseph Mettauer, a physician who lived in Prince Edward, also offered his slaves compensation as well as freedom. He liberated several during his own lifetime and, remarkably, bequeathed $1,000 each to four of his bondpeople—though the latter would still be complaining years later that Mettauer's sons had withheld the money.[70]

The diversity of attitudes among Judith Randolph's neighbors reflected differences within the political realm. Some defenders of slavery had petitioned early on for repeal of the manumission law of 1782.[71] Then, in 1800, a slave named Gabriel had tried to organize a massive rebellion, whose objective was to conquer Richmond and kill proslavery whites. Some citizens saw in free blacks a threat as potent as that from slaves themselves. Virginia's legislature passed a law in 1806 stating that any emancipated black who remained in the Commonwealth for more than one year after liberation forfeited his or her freedom. The act doubtless was aimed in part to discourage manumissions; it told masters who cared about their slaves' welfare that to liberate those people would be to separate them forever from home and friends.

Even so, the law of 1806 did not represent a signal victory for those who opposed manumissions, but rather a compromise between them and those white Virginians who vociferously defended the right of slaveholders to set bondpeople free. This discord among whites helps explain why no change in manumission law passed the General Assembly for half a dozen years after Gabriel's attempted revolution. Moreover, the new ordinance did not forbid private emancipations, nor did these cease after the law was adopted.[72]

But the legislation did have a chilling effect. Andrew Baker saw it coming in 1804, and he provided for the resettlement of his ex-slaves should that become necessary—but the expulsion law apparently dissuaded his widow, who had defended his views on slavery, from manumitting her own bondpeople. John Nash Sr., one of Prince Edward's most respected citizens, freed two slaves in 1800 and retroactively paid at least one of the pair for her services. Ten years later, reflecting the spirit that in the meantime had produced the antimanumission law, Nash's son wrote the opposite of an emancipatory will. He directed that his executor apply many of the assets he left behind to purchase additional "young negroes . . . to be immediately divided" among his children.[73]

The strivings of enslaved people themselves and their long-standing desire for freedom reinforced the antislavery inclinations of individuals such as Judith Randolph both before and after 1806. Blacks remained central figures in Judy's life. She and her brother-in-law dispatched personal servants to deliver valuable property, and slaves served as essential links in the family "grapevine," especially after Jack went off to serve in Congress at the end of the century. Jack and Judy shared their concern over "poor Johnny," Jack's valet, when he suffered an injury, and Judith "rejoiced" to hear that Johnny was "prov[ing] a good nurse" when Jack himself fell ill not long afterward.[74]

All the while, slaves asserted their personalities and exercised their will in big ways and small. Tony, Richard's coachman and stableman, figures as prominently in Judith Randolph's letters as Syphax had in those of Richard's parents. In the old days, Tony had chatted freely, even banteringly, with the white owners he knew so well. As time passed, however, the delay in carrying out Richard's legacy of freedom complicated the stableman's relationship with Judith. When two horses under Tony's care went missing in 1798, Judy did not blame him, and not long thereafter she acknowledged the essential work he continued to do breaking "frolicsome" and sometimes "vicious" young animals. Within a few months, however, she was complaining that Tony's "neglect" had caused harm to St. George Tucker's own mount.[75]

Tony's supposed lapses belonged to what Judith saw as a general problem. By 1800, she lamented to Tucker that "the servants here are . . . extremely inattentive." The reason was obvious to her: the slaves at Bizarre were "fully acquainted" with Richard Randolph's hopes for them. When their situation did not change for months, then for several years after his death, Judith began hearing from her overseer of the blacks' "discontents & murmurings at being detained in what they considered an unjust bondage."

By the winter of 1800–01, Judy complained to Tucker, "it required my continual mediation, & temporizing offices, to keep even tolerable peace between the Negroes & their Overseer; subordination was entirely out of the question, & my mind was perpetually harrassed by his complaints of their ill conduct." Judith thought she detected among the slaves "some remains of respect" for her and a degree of "awe" toward John Randolph that made them less prone to assert their will when he was present at Bizarre. But on one occasion when Jack was away, a group of the Bizarre slaves addressed her neighbor and friend, the planter-lawyer Creed Taylor, in what Judy called "a rude manner, & demanded" to be set free. Some months afterward, when Judith wanted to hire or lend some of her slaves to Taylor, they let her know they were "very averse from [her] wish"; she sent one protester to a different temporary master after he "declared he *would live with no one else*," and she warned Taylor not to expect much cooperation from the rest.[76]

Judith Randolph, though upset by her slaves' assertiveness, does not seem to have been shocked by it. She may even have known that the slaves of Bizarre had mounted a group protest long before they were promised and then denied their freedom. In 1787, the year before Richard and Judith married, Judy's prospective mother-in-law, Frances Tucker, had been summoned urgently to Bizarre from another family plantation. "The extreem, & repeated cruelty of the Overseer," Fanny wrote to St. George, had led "many of the most valuable Negroes" to walk off the plantation. One slave had taken a horse and brought word of the crisis to her, and she did not blame him, or the others either.[77]

Where the Tuckers' slaves had called on their mistress to ameliorate their life in bondage, Judith's now demanded that they cease to be slaves at all. Such pressure from blacks was not unique in Judy's neighborhood: even bondpeople who belonged to antislavery masters were determined to play an active part in their own liberation. Andrew Baker, who lived up Buffalo River from the future site of Israel Hill, was not content to have written the will conveying eventual freedom to most of his slaves and schooling to their children. He decided to give special consideration to Aaron, a favorite bondman: he hired Aaron out to work for four years, and then set him free. Baker wanted to do even more for Aaron, but he concluded that "if he gave him land he would have to give the rest [of his slaves] land also, which would not do."[78] By law and custom, Andrew Baker could favor one slave over others at his own whim. But as Baker well knew, enslaved Afro-Virginians believed they had rights; the protests lodged by Judith Randolph's slaves at nearby Bizarre took place at the very time he was deciding what to do about Aaron. Baker had no doubt that his other bondpeople would invoke a moral right to receive land upon their emancipation if Aaron got any. Baker paid little heed to those whites who opposed manumissions; the public opinion that did constrain his options was that among his slaves.[79]

Aaron, for his part, must have appreciated Baker's liberality, but he, too, asserted his rights. When the black man, now free, took a job on a neighboring plantation, Baker asked the new employer to sign a contract promising to treat Aaron fairly. But that intervention, ironically, looked too much like the behavior of a slaveholder for Aaron's taste, and he said so. Far from accusing his former slave of impertinence, Baker felt he owed Aaron an explanation, followed by a request to the employer to deal directly with the freedman in the future.[80]

All slaveowners had to navigate the politics between master and slave, but that politics took on a special cast when the master professed ideals like those of Andrew Baker and Judith Randolph. Judy might consider her slaves' protests "rude," but like Baker, she remained convinced of their right to liberty, and to good treatment as long as they remained her property.

Judith's bondpeople still brought some of their day-to-day concerns to her. When the chills of late fall one year caught her without adequate clothing for the blacks, the slaves, as usual, protested. Judith recognized their "miserable plight" and admitted that their complaints were "well founded." She decided to send her boat down the Appomattox to Petersburg to pick up warm clothes for them, even though she had no flour or other freight ready to ship downriver to raise money for the clothing. Despite the slaves' assertiveness and impatience to become free people,

Judith seems to have believed, as in earlier years, that "fears for my personal safety were too groundless & absurd for me to entertain."[81]

In the meantime, the few slaves Judith did set free were building active, independent lives. A number of free blacks in the area up to that time had remained with their former masters, performing much the same work—often at skilled trades—that they had done as slaves. The Randolphs' Hercules took a different path: he operated as a free agent, doing skilled tasks for various whites without tying himself down to any one of them. A local partnership called Allen & Fowler set up a grain-milling operation in 1804 on the Cumberland side of the Appomattox. Soon Hercules was applying his varied talents at the mill, plowing the land on which it stood, hauling poles, carting wood, slaughtering hogs, salting meat, and doing various errands.

The typical mill in the area was manned by a miller, a cooper, and perhaps a few helpers; most were either engaged by the year or stationed more or less permanently at the mill. Hercules worked ad hoc and was paid by the day. At the time, 90 cents or $1.00 a day could readily attract young white men of the yeoman farmer class to harvest grain for their planter neighbors; Hercules did a good deal better than that, often earning $1.50 to $2.00 a day. He also sold corn to Allen & Fowler, which he probably grew on the Buffalo land he lived on. Like Judith and John Randolph, Hercules bought flour from the mill.[82]

Hercules plied other skills as well: one nearby plantation hired him to do occasional carpenter's work, and he made tobacco hogsheads for another as early as 1804, apparently receiving the same pay as white coopers in the area. By 1810, Hercules—now probably approaching sixty—was too old and earned too much by other means to be attracted to wheat-cutting, but at least one of his now grown sons supplemented the family income that way.[83] Hercules brought in additional money by growing tobacco, the area's principal cash crop, with another black man named Peter. The two men raised four hundred pounds of leaf in 1805, perhaps on the Randolph lands. Like other small growers, they sold their harvest to a planter neighbor at the going rate or close to it; he would have packed the tobacco in a hogshead with part of his own crop to be inspected at a local warehouse and then shipped downriver.

Minor producers Hercules and Peter were, but not negligible ones: they had harvested a quarter to a third of a hogshead in a region where many white growers raised only one hogshead a year. The $19 they earned could buy adequate, balanced food for an adult for an entire year, or pay at least eight months' rent for a modest house, and Hercules earned considerable money from his other jobs as well. By 1810, he was dealing in substantial sums, apparently borrowing to take advantage of opportunities that arose and then paying back the loans rapidly—which he could only have done after reaping a good return on his investments.[84]

In the time leading up to 1809, Hercules and a white man named George Backus carried out a number of transactions; Backus ended up owing Hercules more than $70. The white man could not, or would not, pay. Hercules then did what countless white people in Prince Edward did when confronted by recalcitrant or impecunious debtors: having become officially free by then, he sued Backus. Hercules produced his debtor's signed bond as evidence, and the county authorities took his suit seriously, sending a deputy sheriff to serve a writ on the white man, who threatened the deputy physically. Backus had resided near Petersburg to the east during his early transactions with Hercules, but he ended up far to the west in Botetourt County; his transience may help explain why he was not tracked down once and for all and made to pay his obligation before Hercules died a couple of years later. The same disappointment befell more than a few white creditors of the period. (The Backus debt was eventually paid, with interest, to White's estate.)[85]

George Backus probably assumed he was dealing with a free Hercules during the months, probably even several years, in which he ran up his large debt to the black man. He even sold Hercules a gun—no mere fowling piece, but a good rifled musket worth $20. Some whites in Virginia worried about free blacks carrying firearms; a law prohibiting their doing so without a special license was passed in 1806.[86] But if either Backus or Hercules realized that, neither cared.

Indeed, one element is conspicuously absent from the history of Hercules during the time leading up to the founding of Israel Hill: there is little evidence, in an openly white supremacist society, that his color—he was of jet-black complexion[87]—markedly affected his economic or legal dealings with white individuals. The spirit that produced the antimanumission law of 1806 did not demoralize him or cause him to fetter his ambition. It did not prevent whites from hiring him, paying him at least what they paid whites who were similarly situated, or doing business with him. And when push came to shove, it did not dissuade Hercules from demanding that the courts vindicate him against a white man.

Hercules seems to have carried himself as a free man even before his formal emancipation—so much so that whites who knew him were not sure exactly when that moment of legal transition occurred. For half a dozen years before Israel Hill took shape in 1810–11, some people thought of him as "Randolphs Harculass" or "negro Herculass," while others called him "free Hercules"; he finally entered the official record of Prince Edward County as Hercules White.[88]

Syphax Brown, too, accumulated personal property and claimed his place among free people. He may have retired from "waiting on gentlemen." At any rate, he demonstrated his competence beyond the domestic sphere when he began keeping hogs; he may have run them partly on Judith Randolph's Buffalo tract. Two years before most of Syphax's peers went free, some of his hogs invaded the garden of James Bennett, a white man. Bennett shot the animals.[89] Bennett may have behaved so aggressively because the animals' owner was black, but that is not certain; similar incidents sometimes occurred between white people in the neighborhood.[90] But Brown *was* black. What happened next would say a great deal about whether former slaves in Prince Edward could defend their property and their right to live unmolested as free persons.

Syphax Brown conceded nothing to white supremacy. The law ensured that no black, or woman, or white man of few means would face a jury of his or her peers, for only white male freeholders could be impaneled; furthermore, no black person could testify in court against a white. Even so, a black shoemaker in Prince Edward County had sued a white man over a debt in 1806, undeterred by the white sentiment that produced the free Negro expulsion law that same year. The defendant turned out to have no property that the sheriff could attach.[91] Now, in 1809, Syphax Brown sued James Bennett, seeking double damages.

Both law and custom put the burden of protecting crops on the party who grew them. Throughout the pre–Civil War period, herds of hogs like Syphax Brown's ranged free all across the South, foraging on acorns and other morsels they found on the forest floor. The law did not demand that the stockowner fence his animals in, but rather required the farmer to fence them out. Bennett asserted that he *had* fenced his garden; even Brown admitted that much, but he insisted that the fencing had not been adequate, and that the white man should therefore compensate him for the hogs he had shot. The white jury agreed with Syphax Brown, requiring Bennett to pay him £4 (more than $13) in damages as well as Brown's legal costs in bringing the suit. The papers Brown filed do not say how many hogs he had lost; but £4 would buy four of the largest and best hogs in the county, and the same amount would cover six, eight, ten, or even a dozen hogs of middling size and quality.[92] Brown probably got back fair value for his loss—and he may have recovered some or all of the meat from the slain animals as well.

James Bennett would not be the last white man in Prince Edward to attack the body or the property of a free black. But an all-white county court and jury had refused to countenance his aggression against this free Afro-Virginian. Perhaps encouraged by Syphax Brown's success, and within days of the old man's legal victory, a young free black sued a white man for assaulting him. The deputy sheriff sent to summon the alleged assailant to court reported that the defendant did not live in Prince Edward, and in fact that his place of residence was unknown.[93] That outcome, though it disappointed the black complainant, Archer Homes, replicated many a case in which the complainant was white; if Homes's grievance found no satisfaction, he had at least followed the example of self-assertion that Syphax had set.

Brown had once again refuted the stereotype—accepted by many black and white Americans today—that being a "house Negro" typically turned one into a psychologically dependent sycophant. Syphax had been personally close to the Randolphs for decades; though now in his old age, he had turned not to his ex-mistress for protection or charity, but rather to the courts for redress. Judith Randolph surely learned that her husband's beloved former servant had successfully defended his rights. She never fully convinced herself that her soon-to-be-emancipated slaves would prosper in a white supremacist society, but the assertiveness and the successes of Hercules White and Syphax Brown, in both the economic and the legal arenas, relieved her from having to assume automatically that they would not hold their own.

Judith finally scheduled the manumission for Christmastime 1810; she doubtless counted on the moral support of at least a few like-minded neighbors. Creed Taylor, eminent attorney, teacher of law, and activist in Jefferson's Republican Party, belonged to the group who called each other by the French Revolutionary title "Citizen."[94] Dick Randolph had felt confident enough that Taylor would respect his dream of emancipation that he chose the lawyer as an alternate executor of his will. Judith's dear friend John Holt Rice, an eminent Presbyterian minister, shared Richard's view that slavery was morally indefensible. Years later, Rice would express his disappointment that ministers of the Gospel could not "produce that state of the public will, which will cause the people to move spontaneously to the eradication of this evil." Later still, Rice's widow Anne, another close friend of Judy's, would free a number of her own slaves while she was still in the prime of life.[95]

Judith concluded that she would not be able to support herself at Bizarre once her slaves were gone unless she accepted more help—and more control—from Jack Randolph than she wanted to. She moved ahead to free the blacks all the same, and she reluctantly prepared to leave her home of twenty years. "I am unable to express how much that conviction cost me," she wrote to St. George Tucker. "But I owed to the memory of the best of men, & most indulgent of husbands, to assume a willingness I could not feel, to fulfil the task his will had rendered necessary." In the end, she and Jack decided to rent out the Buffalo tract, south of the Appomattox, while Jack himself leased from Judy the Bizarre land north of the river.[96]

Judith blunted the moral force of her mass emancipation in several ways. Her brother-in-law had become attached to two personal servants from Richard's group; Judy felt she had no right to let Jack keep the pair, but she made no active objection when he decided he would hold on to them. In fact, Judy, too, would continue to enjoy the services of the two slaves, for by now she had decided, at least for the time being, to stay at Bizarre after all and live with Jack.

The plantation continued to operate by exploiting enslaved labor: Jack's own field hands would work the land. Beyond that, the legacy to Dick and Jack from their long dead father was now formally divided for the first time, and Jack announced he was retaining still other slaves who had anticipated their liberty for nearly a decade and a half. Judith worried that accepting her brother-in-law's decision might open her to charges of maladministering her late husband's estate. Rather than protest openly, however, Judy blithely told St. George Tucker that she felt "satisfied if [Jack] reaps the benefit from the servants I have trained, & the rising generation." Meanwhile, she planned to raise some money and "purchase the necessary [house] servants for myself" now that most of Richard's bondpeople were leaving.[97]

For all her shortcomings as a liberator, however, Judith Randolph did keep faith with the slaves who remained under her control after the division with Jack—or, as she tended to see the matter, she kept faith with her late husband. During the winter of 1810–11, she formally certified the emancipation of the Hercules White and Rose Johnston families to the authorities in Prince Edward County and liberated her other slaves as well. She engaged a neighboring planter, who also worked as a surveyor, to lay out 350 or 400 acres of land at the western end of her Buffalo tract and divide it into separate plots, some 25 acres and others 50, with one freed black family to settle on each.

The area apparently was forested and would have to be cleared. Acre for acre, though, the land Judith Randolph granted her ex-slaves was the most valuable in all Prince Edward County, according to the revenue commissioner. Conveniently, the area lay two miles from the settlement of Farmville, established on part of the Randolphs' Buffalo tract on the south bank of the Appomattox a dozen years earlier as a market town and tobacco-shipping river port. The land's high assessment meant higher taxes, too, but not because of any discrimination against blacks; the same rates had applied while the Randolphs still owned the tract, and besides, the land tax was not onerous in a polity thoroughly controlled by landowners.[98]

In other respects, too, Judith finally acquitted herself as Richard had counted on her to do—and without bitterness toward him over the loss his dream was now imposing on her.[99] There was indeed a "rising generation" of slaves who had been born since Richard wrote his will. Judy might have sought to keep them enslaved—and thus maneuver their parents into staying and working for her—on the grounds that the young blacks were not covered by an emancipation ordained before they existed. Logic like this would subvert another planter's emancipatory will in Prince Edward not many years later.

Judy also could have exploited the law of 1806 that sought to expel newly freed blacks. She might have held on to the slaves born since that year, or even the whole group, and claimed she was acting to save them from a wrenching exile or from prejudice and destitution closer to home. Then, too, Judith could have seized on a technicality in Richard's will: he had ordained that his bondpeople receive land "in case I emancipate the said Slaves." The fact was, he hadn't liberated anyone, and his widow very probably could have aborted the land grant without fear of an effective challenge. But Judith Randolph made no attempt to avoid freeing the slaves and parceling out land among them. The county court cooperated, registering blacks born up to the very eve of the manumission as having been "emancipated by the will of Richard Randolph."[100]

Judith applied no color test in her act of liberation. Hercules White, notwithstanding his surname, was of purely African ancestry, and most of the other people Randolph freed were "black" or "dark brown."[101] Judy may simply have attempted to apportion land according to "the merits of the parties," as Richard had wished.

Judith's behavior in 1810 and 1811 undermines the notion that planters dreamt of surrounding themselves with shuffling, fawning blacks who had no will of their own. Though she became a liberator, Judy Randolph the plantation mistress liked having servants and knew as well as any other daughter of the elite what made a good one. The qualities she sought lay far indeed from the childlike "Sambo" of legend; rather, she valued the very traits of personality that led blacks to want to live independently and to believe they could pull it off. "Those of the free Negroes whom I should wish to hire," she lamented after the emancipation, "prefer settling on the land devised to them by their Master."[102]

A decade earlier, in one of her peevish complaints to St. George Tucker about her slaves, Judy had insisted "that my continuance among them, was the effect of necessity, but never of choice." Now that the blacks had actually left, she missed them sorely. Part of that feeling, as usual, was selfish: finding herself without "a creature about me who ever handled any utensil but the hoe," she later complained, "compelled [me] to do the drudgery of [a servant] myself."[103]

Two years later, a period of calamities began for Judy. In the early spring of 1813, a spark from the chimney at Bizarre ignited the roof. Judith was away from the house attending church at the time; "the first view which I had on my return," she wrote, "was of the house in flames." Her "once comfortable & peaceful dwelling [was soon] a heap of ruins, a scene of total desolation." After the fire, Judith despaired, "the yard [was] . . . strewed with the burnt pages" of Richard's books—works that had molded an intellect capable of conceiving one of America's most fervent indictments of slavery.[104]

After the conflagration, Judith moved across the Appomattox River to a "small & every way uncomfortable house" in Farmville. Before long, her son St. George suffered a mental breakdown. He would spend the rest of his life under intermittent treatment for mental illness, his legal and financial affairs handled first by John Randolph and then by a succession of court-appointed administrators. In 1814, St. George's younger brother Tudor contracted tuberculosis. John Randolph sent the young man to England for medical care, but Tudor died late the following year. An increasingly religious Judith had come to describe death by then as an escape "from scenes of woe to the mansions of the blessed," where all would be reunited and happy.[105]

At the very time of Tudor's illness, John—a man capable of paranoid flights of imagination—concluded that Judith's sister Nancy had murdered his brother Richard all those years ago by poisoning him. Judy and Nancy had become alienated from one another long before John made his accusation, yet Judith was deeply troubled by Jack's "dark insinuations" and "strange enquiries." Judy fell ill during a visit to Richmond not long afterward. She made out a will and died a few days later, in March 1816, at the age of forty-three, three months shy of the twentieth anniversary of her husband's unexpected passing.[106]

In her last act before that escape, Judith wrote a will that reflected her personal complexity. Though she had become a great emancipator, Judy left behind five bondpeople of her own, two children and three adults who were probably personal servants.[107] After providing financially for her family, Judith also left a $2,000 bond, which she split between two parties. One thousand dollars went to her friends and fellow questioners of slavery, Reverend John Holt Rice and his wife, Anne S. Rice, who had cared for her in her final illness. Judith left the other $1,000 to one Elizabeth White, an underaged girl "whom I have taken under my protection, and for whom I think it my duty to make some provision suitable to her condition in life."

Elizabeth White's identity is one of the mysteries of Judith Randolph's last statement to the world. An adolescent of that name, presumably a white girl, chose a guardian two years after Judy died; that man had to give a very large bond to guarantee his performance as her protector, perhaps because his new ward brought Judith's $1,000 legacy with her. On the other hand, Hercules White, a man who had won Judith's favor and respect, had a granddaughter named Elizabeth (Eliza) through his son Dick White. That girl was about a year old when Judith died, and few children shared her specific "condition in life": she was the daughter, born in freedom, of a man who until five years before had been Judith Randolph's slave.

As a free person, the black Elizabeth White could inherit property—$1,000 in cash, for example—once she came of age, or Judith's estate could allocate money for her support in the meantime. Baby Eliza was living with her parents on Israel Hill when Judith died in 1816, but subsequent official lists of free blacks, which survive for each of the following nine years, include Dick and Sally White and their children except for Elizabeth. The child, who lived at least until 1832, must have been residing elsewhere, as she might have done if she were under Judith Randolph's now posthumous "protection." Moreover, Eliza's parents, Dick and Sally White, gave their next daughter, born not long after Judy Randolph's death, the name Judith—as they might well do in honor of a benefactor.[108]

The circumstances leave plenty of room for uncertainty. Judith herself took care to shroud herself in mystery: in her will, she left strict instructions to open her secretary and destroy all the letters she had received over the years; she asked John Holt Rice to do the same with the papers of her dead son Tudor. But Judith Randolph may have chosen in her dying moments to bestow one last benefit on a person to whose parents and grandparents she had earlier given the greatest gift a free human being could tender to an unfree one.

The fall of Richard's branch of the House of Randolph had been both as literal and as full of irresistible metaphor as Poe's fall of the House of Usher. Richard and one of his brothers had died in their young manhood; the third brother, John Randolph of Roanoke, would live and prosper for years to come, but would never—and apparently could never, for biological reasons—father children of his own. He would gradually become even more eccentric and obstreperous, and he would die insane.

Dick and Judy's two sons likewise had been lost—Tudor to death; St. George, who never married, to mental illness—and Judith herself had died in despair. The blackened ruins of Bizarre and the yard strewn with charred fragments of Richard Randolph's intellectual patrimony had foreshadowed both the future of Richard's own family and the fate—for the next half century, anyway—of his dream of universal emancipation.

Still, Judith Randolph had got around to freeing nearly a hundred souls, and she had enabled them to found a community of their own. They called their new home Israel Hill and sometimes referred to themselves as Israelites, thus linking their story to an ancient, epic liberation from bondage that has inspired African Americans from that time to this. The black Israelites had actively protested their enslavement and had resisted abuse for a generation or more. The talent and initiative that Hercules White, Syphax Brown, and others displayed helped their mistress find the resolve in a less than nurturing political climate to carry out her husband's wishes for those people's liberation.

Judith Randolph lacked her husband's fiery indignation over human bondage. She never weaned herself from the comforts that personal servants could provide; she never even tried to. She declined to make heavy sacrifices that might have shortened the captivity of her slaves, and that could have extended liberty to some who never did receive it.

Still, had Richard lived into middle age on a debt-ridden plantation, he might have joined in some of his wife's vacillations. With all her flaws, Judith remained true enough to her husband's declared principles and to her own better angels that she gave up a large part of the only world she had ever known, and the only one to which she could imagine belonging.

For the ex-slaves themselves, the Randolph legacy, like the Randolph record as a whole, was mixed. Freedom had been promised, then delayed for most of them by more than a dozen years. Yet freedom had finally come, in no small part through these black Virginians' own efforts—the courage and achievements of the first few who went free, and the protests and demands of those forced to wait for their liberation. And with that freedom came the promised land on which the black Israelites might build new lives.

❦

CHAPTER 3

The Promised Land

As Comfortable as the Best in Israel Hill

The story of Israel Hill began as a quest by ninety-some newly liberated people to make a place for themselves in one small corner of a gently rolling Piedmont Virginia landscape. Their county, Prince Edward, today has the shape of a slightly drooping satchel, its northern edge traced by a bow in the Appomattox River. The county stretches fifteen to twenty miles north to south, a little farther east to west. A narrow protuberance extended westward to the headwaters of the river until Prince Edward donated that thinly populated section to the new county of Appomattox in 1845. Israel Hill and the town of Farmville lie on the northern border of the county, on the south bank of the Appomattox, at the trough of the downward arc that the river forms. Several ridges fan out roughly south- and westward from that area into the county's interior; they rise as much as 170 feet above the streambeds, tributaries of the Appomattox, that separate them.

By far the broadest and lowest of the valleys that meet around Farmville is that of the Buffalo River (later called Buffalo Creek), "a rather flat or level stream" that may have broadened in its lower reaches to a width of forty or fifty feet. The Buffalo Valley separates Farmville from a low ridge that runs to the west; along that ridge, and on adjoining portions of the bottomland carved by the Appomattox and the Buffalo, some two miles outside town, Judith Randolph's surveyor in late 1810 or early 1811 laid out the tracts that became Israel Hill. Buffalo River skirts the foot of the Hill and in those days meandered perhaps another two miles before it emptied into the Appomattox. The tributary's sprawling floodplain lies only a few feet higher than the larger river, so the Buffalo flowed languidly much of the time. For many years after Israel Hill's founding, only a bridle path fording the stream connected the black settlement—and the neighboring plantations—directly to Farmville.[1]

Judith Randolph distributed 350 acres of land; why 50 acres of the 400

FARMVILLE, VA.   Buffalo Creek

The Buffalo River valley, looking upstream from near the Appomattox in the early twentieth century; Israel Hill lies just beyond the right-hand edge of the picture.   (LIBRARY OF VIRGINIA)

Richard had mentioned in his will were omitted remains one of Israel Hill's mysteries.[2] The area where bottomland abutted hillside had the most promise, and the White family got it. Hercules White's 50 acres were the most diverse in the new community. He was the one settler who received a substantial portion of the Buffalo streambank; the water formed the southern boundary of his roughly triangular plot. White's land, which ran nearly a third of a mile from north to south, rose eighty-odd feet above Buffalo River at the tract's highest point. But the slope was gradual and, once land was cleared, cultivation would be fairly easy anywhere except perhaps in the western corner of the plot. There, a bluff overlooking the stream offered an ideal area to leave in timber, as landowners in south-central Virginia typically did with portions of their farms and plantations.

Hercules White and his wife, Molly, had four sons who settled on Israel Hill. Tony, Hercules Junior, and Dick were in their twenties; they joined the elder Hercules on his new land fairly quickly. Sam White was twice the age of his brothers—he may have been the son of an earlier marriage—and he had already established a family. He and his wife, Susan (Sooky), brought ten or a dozen younger Whites to Israel Hill, ranging from infancy to nearly twenty years old. The last child or two in

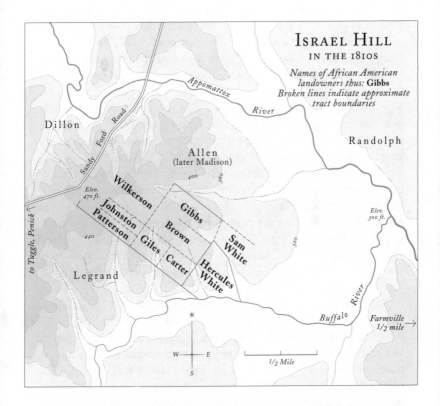

the group may have been grandchildren of Sam and Susan, and others would soon be born on the Hill.[3] Sam White's distinguished parentage, talents, and large family earned him fifty acres of his own. Sam's property began in the east where the Appomattox and Buffalo floodplains converged, on land that was low and mostly flat but not swampy; the tract shaded gradually uphill to father Hercules' place in the southwest.

The rest of the new black settlement formed a rectangle running nearly a mile northwest along the ridge and half a mile north to south. Seven black families received land in this area; four of those got twenty-five-acre plots on the southern slope of the ridge.

Immediately up from Hercules White's place, on steeper inclines, lived Tina Carter. Whites and blacks alike pronounced her given name "Teny"; in her mid-forties, she was mother and grandmother to a family even larger than Sam White's, numbering fifteen children and young adults at the time of their emancipation. Teny Carter may have been married to a slave, whose status as some white person's property would explain why no surviving list names him as a member of Teny's family.

The next plot to the west—a hilly tract much like Teny Carter's—went to Hampton Giles. Carter may have received twenty-five rather than fifty acres because she was a woman with no sons old enough to till the soil. Giles probably got one of the smaller plots because he and his wife, Phoebe—though he was at least twenty-six and she in her thirties—had only one child to feed, a young daughter. Hampton Giles, "a yellow man," stood out among a group that otherwise included mostly people of African features and a few described as brown.[4]

The westernmost corner of Israel Hill's southern tier was split laterally into two more twenty-five-acre plots, each of them long and relatively narrow. One of these plots went to Isham and Nancy Patterson; he was in his mid-fifties, she about ten years younger. They had six children ranging in age from infancy to about twenty. The elder sons, and perhaps Isham Patterson himself, knew how to run boats on the Appomattox; they and their former mistress probably calculated that the family could supplement its income in that way.[5]

Rose Johnston, about forty-five, received the second long, narrow tract, which lay a bit uphill from the Pattersons'. For the time being, however, she settled on Hercules White Sr.'s land, in a log house which her grown sons Jacob and George presumably built; Rose Johnston's daughter Rachel would marry into the White clan in 1814. Within a few years of Israel Hill's founding, Rose moved onto her own land; George married the daughter of a black Israelite neighbor, and both sons established families on their mother's plot.[6] Rose's husband did not settle in with the family because he was still enslaved. For both practical and moral reasons, masters—even those who sometimes split up families—routinely acknowledged the existence of unions such as Rose Johnston's. The law itself did not recognize marriages in which even one partner was a slave, but the ties between Rose Johnston and her husband must have been too strong or too well known to ignore. The county court clerk who registered Johnston as a free woman in 1811 departed from established practice to note that she was "married to Ceasar, slave of William Randolph of Cumberland."[7]

The three other Israelite families received fifty acres each, again west of the White family tracts. Those plots straddled the gently rounded crest of the ridge. Just above Rose Johnston settled William Wilkerson and his wife, Eve, sometimes called Edy; the pair, both in their later twenties, had five children. The Wilkersons seem to have taken longer to set up a farm than some of their black neighbors. They may have sojourned on someone else's land for the first few years, perhaps co-operating to clear another family's tract first in return for help later in preparing their own plot.[8]

Titus Gibbs's land stretched along the hillside between the Wilkersons' and Sam White's place below. Gibbs was about forty when he arrived on Israel Hill, his wife, Amy, nearly a decade younger. They brought five children ten years old and less, as well as an older daughter, Hannah—the young woman whom Rose Johnston's son George soon married.

Inevitably, Israel Hill was surrounded by the lands of white people, but one Israelite received a fifty-acre plot that lay in the very center of the new settlement, and he therefore had no immediate white neighbors. That man, paradoxically, was Syphax Brown, who had lived much of his life in white people's houses and sometimes slept in their very bedrooms. Brown may have moved from Farmville onto the Randolphs' Prince Edward lands—and kept his herd of ill-fated hogs there—even before he took possession of the tract on Israel Hill that Judith Randolph laid out for him. "Old Syphax" was literally old by now, around sixty by the most conservative reckoning, over eighty according to Hampton Giles's later testimony. He came with his spouse Betty, who apparently was his second wife,[9] and settled in a house built by his grown son, John. John Brown and his wife, Tilla (probably pronounced "Tilly"), soon joined the old man on his new land; they brought two teenaged children—one of them named Syphax, after his grandfather—and a two-year-old girl.

The way Judith Randolph assigned the Brown plot shows that the Randolph slaves, who had emphatically protested the delay in their emancipation, remained active participants in the act of liberation itself. According to one Israelite, Judith had first offered the Browns a twenty-five-acre plot in the southern tier of the planned settlement, but John Brown demurred; he asked instead for the fifty-acre tract between the lot Judy was proposing and the one taken by Hercules White. Perhaps because of Syphax's special status in the Randolph family, Judith granted John Brown's request, assigning the smaller and more steeply sloped lot to Hampton Giles.[10]

Judy Randolph freed a number of other slaves during the winter of 1810–11, but none of those received land. Some of the Randolphs' former slaves may have preferred life in town or city, or on an established plantation, to a rustic existence on the Hill. Belinda Giles probably was a sister or relative of Israelite Hampton Giles. But rather than move in with him, she ended up far away in Petersburg, the bustling port city at the falls of the Appomattox River, with its growing free black population and its economic opportunities. Not until around 1840 would she decide to return to Prince Edward County.[11]

Billy, Tom, and Zack Ellis, in their mid-teens when Richard Randolph died, already numbered among his most valuable slaves by then. The Ellises' prominence in the Randolph family stemmed not from brawn—Tom Ellis stood a mere five feet tall, and Billy only four inches higher—but rather from skill. Billy, whose personal magnetism John Randolph backhandedly acknowledged, worked as a carpenter and cooper, Tom as a shoemaker; Zack plied all three of those trades. The Ellises became neighbors of Israel Hill. Billy settled right away in Farmville, while Tom resided in both town and country at various times. Zack Ellis spent years on the Chambers plantation just south of Farmville and across Buffalo River from his fellow Randolph freedpeople, but his relationship with the Chambers estate differed greatly from that of slave to master. The Chambers place may have had first call on Zack Ellis's services, offering housing to keep him on retainer. But the administrator of the place (the owner was mentally incompetent) paid him in cash for each particular job he did there; from that one source, Ellis sometimes earned $15 or $20 annually—enough to buy nearly a year's supply of foodstuffs. He was free to sell his services to other parties as well, and to spend his earnings as he pleased. Similarly, Billy and Tom Ellis, who lived elsewhere, did occasional work on the Chambers place and bought goods there.[12]

Other ex-slaves of the Randolphs who received no land made a different choice, settling on the tracts of their fellow freedpeople on Israel Hill. Guy Howard, as an enslaved youth, had moved across the Appomattox with the family of Hercules White. He continued to live on the Whites' place after his emancipation; when Rose Johnston moved from the White tract to her own plot up the hill, Guy took over Johnston's old cabin with his wife, Pamelia (Mely), and their little son. Howard earned his living as a boatman, so he needed no acreage to cultivate; he did help Hercules White's family grow tobacco from time to time.[13]

Philip (Phil) White Sr. also settled on land granted to a fellow freedman. Phil seems to have been about the same age as Hercules White. Both men had been born in the deep colonial past—during the years around 1750—where family relationships among slaves are especially difficult to trace; but they were closely related, possibly brothers. Phil White, a carpenter, had remained one of the Randolphs' most valuable slaves even in his fifties. He was a decade older than that when he reached Israel Hill, however, and probably became too infirm to work much by 1814, for he received an exemption from taxes that year. He settled in, possibly on Titus Gibbs's land, with his wife, Fanny, and a child named Caty Carter, who may have been a daughter or granddaughter of Israelite Teny Carter.[14]

Phil White Jr.—a kinsman of the senior Phil, possibly his son—was about eighteen when Israel Hill began to take shape; he settled on the land of Sam White, who was twice his age. Phil Junior would eventually become a leading citizen of Israel Hill and a property owner in the town of Farmville. Although Judith Randolph apparently did not give either of the Phil Whites a tract of his own, some local white people considered them to be landowning Israelites. That impression may have arisen from the evident equality in ambition and status between them and their land-holding relative Sam.[15]

Hercules White wasted no time expanding on Israel Hill the freedom he had already used to such effect for several years. Having moved to that side of the river around the turn of the century, he conducted a flurry of building at the time the settlement was formally laid out. White bought door hinges in December 1810; he may have been in the latter stages of constructing a house. He went on to purchase some thirty pounds of nails from one store during the spring and summer of 1811, and possibly more from other vendors; he bought nails again the following spring. White may have been helping erect homes for his sons, who had not immediately settled on Israel Hill, or perhaps he was putting up out-buildings on his own tract.

Hercules had earned a good income for half a dozen years as a free man. Now, even as he spent money to build up his farmstead, he paid off his entire account at a local store up to that date—more than $20. During those first months on Israel Hill, White clothed his family mostly in thick, coarse Yorkshire cloth, or in osnaburg—the cheap and equally coarse cotton fabric from which garments for slaves and plain white folk were made. But as winter, and Christmas, approached in 1810 and again in 1811, White also bought smaller quantities of other textiles: red flannel in 1810 and "Stripted [striped?] Coating" a year later.

Some of the Whites would go on to join the pro-temperance Baptist Church, but they lived in a society where alcohol was the staple of local hospitality. Hercules apparently planned to entertain family and guests as their first Christmas–New Year season in freedom approached; he bought two gallons of whiskey toward the end of what seems to have been a satisfying first year on Israel Hill. Hercules White's mercantile account for that year contains two tantalizing details: crossed-out items recording the sale of writing paper and a quantity of "powder." There is good evidence that the Whites could not read or write in 1812, yet they did keep some abbreviated financial accounts and require debtors to sign IOUs over the years—literate white friends and associates did the writing for them—and they did keep one or more guns. These particular purchases of paper and powder were probably tallied on White's account in error. Yet to the white storekeeper who initially entered those lines, the idea of free Afro-Virginian Hercules White buying writing paper and gunpowder had not seemed far-fetched.[16]

Proslavery propagandists who wrote about Israel Hill years later stated that the Randolphs provided the newly freed Israelites "with means to build themselves houses, and with agricultural implements to till the soil."[17] These ideologues had a strong motive to exaggerate the advantages the pioneer black Israelites enjoyed: to do so rendered their tale of Israel Hill's supposed decline all the more shocking. In reality, Judy had complained several years earlier that she lacked the money even to keep her own home in repair; that house burned down only two years after the launching of Israel Hill. Then one of her sons lost his sanity and the other his life, and Judy herself died in 1816. Judith thus had little time or money to devote to Israel Hill. John Randolph, for his part, had worried before the emancipation that his brother's slaves might sue him for postponing their liberation. St. George Tucker may have reassured him on that point, however, for in the end, John does not seem to have offered the ex-bondpeople any substantial reparations or assistance.[18]

Hercules White, Syphax Brown, and perhaps others had accumulated assets of their own by 1810–11, and their new land abounded in wood from which families could build houses and fences. It is likely that Judith Randolph respected her husband's wish that she help the freedpeople establish themselves. She may have provided a few basic tools—axes, adzes, mauls, saws, hammers, and plows. Yet any material aid she and Jack gave the freedpeople amounted to very modest severance payments after years of unremunerated labor, nearly a decade and a half of it after Richard had called for them to go free.

Like Hercules and Molly White, the Gileses and eight other families of former Randolph slaves had already settled "on Rd. Randolphs Land" in Prince Edward County by the time the official free black list of 1811 was compiled, probably in the first quarter of that year. One or two, at least, had erected permanent homes by then: Hampton Giles, early settler though he was, later recalled that John Brown had nearly finished building his own house by the time Judith Randolph allotted the Gileses their tract of land.[19] That kind of speed, along with the limited means available to most of the emancipated families as well as other evidence, suggests two further things about the process of settlement: that at least some of the early houses on the Hill, like Rose Johnston's, were simple log houses, and that neighbors sometimes helped each other build. Not all Israelites lived permanently in log dwellings, however, and some may never have: when Phil White Jr. described a house he had built for a fellow resident of Israel Hill in the latter 1820s, he took care to state that it was a "Log House." He presumably would not have needed to make such a notation if the settlement had consisted entirely of log buildings.[20]

Hercules White's relatively heavy use of nails also suggests that at least some of the homes on Israel Hill amounted to more than rude log houses. Hampton Giles told the county court proudly in the early 1830s that he had built "a dwelling house . . . as good and as comfortable as almost the best in Isreal Hill."[21] He could hardly expect a panel of white planters to take that claim seriously if his and the "best" houses of the settlement by that time were simple log structures.

Although no detailed description of the Hill's best dwellings has survived, they may well have been frame houses, with at least two rooms on the ground floor and another room or two upstairs, similar to those of some white small farmers (or "yeomen") in the area. At least two or three of the Israelites had extensive experience in carpentry, and they could hew logs from trees they felled and saw them into boards—a common way of procuring lumber in old Prince Edward.[22] That the best-off black Israelites—over time, Sam White and Phil White Jr. emerged with that distinction—lived this well and possibly a good deal better becomes apparent when one considers the kind of house Isaac Gibbs could afford as a young boatman in the late 1820s.

Acting as builder of Gibbs's "Log House," Phil White Jr. did not construct a one-room cabin with a dirt floor, but rather a dwelling of a story and a half, with "coarse [floors] up stars & down" made of boards that Gibbs seems to have hewn himself. The house was small, sixteen feet by fourteen; homes of at least half again that area were common among people of middling means at the time. Still, the minimum size required for houses on town lots in the area around the turn of the nineteenth century was sixteen feet square.[23] Then too, Gibbs had acquired what today's market would call a "starter home." Isaac Gibbs was a second son, only twenty-five years old, and apparently still single; he could add on to

A SPRING SCENE NEAR RICHMOND, VIRGINIA.—[DRAWN BY W. L. SHEPPARD.]

Log houses inhabited by newly settled free Afro-Virginians, and later by those less affluent than Sam or Phil White, may have looked like this one.

(LIBRARY OF VIRGINIA)

or replace his house later. The Whites, the Hampton Giles family, and Isaac Gibbs's own parents, Titus and Amy, certainly lived in more spacious and comfortable dwellings, and some of the other Israelites probably did, too.

Every family on Israel Hill built multiple structures on its land. Even Guy Howard—the non-farming boatman who lived on Sam White's tract and would later be written off by Sam as "worthless"—eventually put up a number of "necessary houses" in addition to the cabin he and Mely lived in. The elder Hercules White, who possessed both fifty acres and ambitions that far exceeded Guy Howard's, naturally developed his tract much more extensively than the boatman ever did.[24]

Phil White Jr. supposedly held no land of his own, but he built, among other structures, a stable for his two horses and his gig (a two-wheeled

The more imposing houses on Israel Hill during its early years may have resembled this prosperous yeoman farmer's house, shown in a twentieth-century photograph. (LIBRARY OF VIRGINIA)

carriage). Sam White's house may have been a good deal larger than that of the average yeoman farmer, and his land must have encompassed more dwellings than his own and the Johnston-Howard cabin, for his household included some sixteen people during the early years, nearly a third of whom were adults.[25]

At the time of Israel Hill's founding, "it was the custom of the neighbours [in Prince Edward County] to assist each other in such matters" as raising barns; slaveholders, of course, provided this aid by lending the services of their bondmen. Among the people of Israel Hill, considerable evidence points to hands-on cooperation in the early years. The Johnstons lived on other Israelites' land before moving to their own tracts, and the Wilkersons may have done the same; Phil White Sr. did not merely occupy space on Titus Gibbs's land, but also attended official inspections of Gibbs's property lines, at least once in Gibbs's stead.[26] Residents of the Hill may sometimes have exchanged one good turn informally for another, but Phil White Jr.'s cabin building for Isaac Gibbs suggests that Israelites often received payment in cash or in kind for the services they rendered to their neighbors.

In simple fact, Israelites almost had to join forces at times. Proslavery writers would later suggest that the Randolphs had selected as settlers for the Hill those among their slaves who were singularly well equipped to wrest a living from the soil—but that was true, if at all, only in terms of intellect and character. The Hercules White group incorporated a substantial number of adult males, but the majority of the other settler families included only one man each who was old enough to do heavy work during the first few years; three families had two adult males apiece.

Phil White Sr. was elderly by 1811, Hercules White Sr. probably sixty or older. Kit Strong Sr. may have had a weak constitution; he worked as a weaver, a trade generally plied by women, children, or handicapped males. Teny Carter, who had the most young mouths to feed, had no resident husband and no son older than twelve when she took possession of her land.[27] Even if black Israelite women participated in the heavy labor of building the settlement, most of the families would have had difficulty establishing homesteads without some pooling of effort, a practice that was common throughout rural America.

One particular form of assistance among Israelites played an important role in the initial building of Israel Hill. By the end of his life, Hercules White Sr. owned not only the land he had received under Richard Randolph's will and the structures he had built on it but also other assets—livestock, crops, tools, household furnishings, and debts owed him by other men—worth between $400 and $500.[28] Many white yeoman farmers would have been delighted to bequeath such a legacy to their families. During the crucial months when the Israelites were settling on their tracts, White provided loans, living space, goods, or services to the liberated people who were moving onto his own land, and perhaps to others besides.

Three of White's adult sons ran up debts to him ranging from $33 to $53. These were large sums—enough, for example, to rent a house, a garden, and a field to till for a year or two elsewhere in the county, or to build a modest house. One or both of the Phil Whites, Hercules' kinsmen, owed him a total of $37 at his death in 1812, while the Johnstons and the Howards owed $8 and $12, respectively.[29] Hercules may have extended other credits that had been paid off and thus went unrecorded. Those who turned to White in this way seem to have undertaken their obligations in good faith: in an era when many people took years to pay their bills, White's black Israelite debtors returned in cash nearly a third of what they owed White's estate within a year or so of his death. Hercules furnished funds, housing, or space to live on to no fewer than six or seven of sixteen families on Israel Hill. He left behind other debtors who were not Israelites and indeed not black. White neighbors owed Hercules nearly $100 in 1812, more than a third of the total due him; one of those whites was the largest debtor on the list.[30]

Establishing even a small farm cost money, but above all it required prodigious amounts of work. A farmer not only had to build a home and outbuildings but also to clear fields and enclose them with fences made of timber from felled trees; otherwise he would find himself "much plagu'd to preserve his crop from being Injur'd by Cattle" and other roaming livestock. At least some of the black Israelites prepared their farms quickly, however; by the second year after settlement, Titus Gibbs had established a "plantation"—a cultivated area—substantial enough that whites took notice of it.[31]

Like other yeoman farmers, the black residents of Israel Hill set up farms that provided both subsistence and at least a modest amount of cash. The most common source of money was tobacco: Hercules White left a hogshead and a half of the crop—a ton or so—at his death. Some local planters raised large numbers of cattle for meat, milk, and leather, and even sold their surplus beef for profit; some herded sheep as well. By contrast, small farmers might keep a cow or two to meet their family's needs. As usual, White stood out, with his two cows, three heifers, and three steers; by 1815, there were more than twenty head of cattle on Israel Hill, with Sam White and Hampton Giles owning four each.[32] Like other farmers and planters, the Israelites also raised hogs—Hercules probably used much of the bushel of salt he bought late in the winter of 1812 to preserve freshly killed pork. A few plantation owners in Prince Edward grew enough cotton that they could market the occasional modest surplus. More typical were those other planters and yeomen who raised small amounts of cotton or flax, from which they made clothing. Hercules White himself owned a flax wheel and a cotton wheel.[33]

Grains, unlike cotton, had long played a vital part in Prince Edward's agriculture. Corn was a staple in the diet of both people and livestock, on Israel Hill and off. The county's farmers and planters frequently sold part of their crop to neighbors or to nearby millers, who ground the corn and marketed the meal, much of it to local buyers. Residents of the area also produced oats—Judith Randolph and some of her peers made sizable crops—and they had been growing wheat for at least a generation when the former Randolph slaves settled on Israel Hill.[34]

By the turn of the nineteenth century, at least a few plantations in and around Prince Edward harvested five hundred or even a thousand bushels of wheat a year.[35] The Randolphs and other substantial producers sold much of their wheat harvest, preferring to feed their slaves mainly on the less valuable corn meal. Millers sold some of the flour they produced to consumers from the neighborhood, but also sent part of their product to Petersburg by boat, or to Richmond on carts, wagons, or batteaux plying the James River.[36] Wheat could be grown on a small farm, but the families of Israel Hill do not seem to have planted much if any of that crop. Records at Allen & Fowler's mill for the few years preceding the Hill's settlement do show Hercules White bringing five bushels, which he may well have grown himself, to the mill for "manufactoring." But during the same two-and-a-half-year period he purchased flour seven times in large amounts, and bought bran on three other occasions. He left a supply of corn at his death, but apparently no wheat.[37]

It seems that White—whom no one ever accused of lacking drive, energy, or versatility—decided early on that it was more economical for him to earn money by growing tobacco and plying crafts, and then to buy flour at the store, than it was to raise wheat for sale or grinding. He chose literally to earn his bread rather than to grow it. The other Israelites, contemplating their tiny plots of ground—even a farm two and a half to five times as large as theirs was considered "a small tract of land" in Prince Edward[38]—probably made the same decision. Corn was a more versatile crop for the owner of a few acres: it could be cooked and eaten, fed to livestock, or ground into meal, and any surplus sold to one of the local mills.

Hercules White clearly earned much of his income from sources other than farming. His cart, his yoke of steers, and his five horses equipped him to haul wood and other cargo, as he had done earlier. The presence of that many draft animals on a small plot of land suggests also that White, who had earned money plowing before 1811, was supplementing his income by tilling land for others or having his sons do so. In addition, Hercules may have continued to market his skills as a carpenter and cooper; when he died, he left behind carpentry tools along with his farming implements.[39]

Guy and Mely Howard displayed their own brand of flexibility—a quality typical of free blacks. Unlike the White clan, the Howards made no pretense of being farmers; the spot they inhabited on Sam White's land measured little more than an acre. But even they grew food for themselves and augmented the income from Guy's boating by tending "truck pa[t]ches" on which they could grow vegetables for sale.[40]

The Israelites understood that once they had cleared "plantations" on their new plots, the forested areas that remained were a source of "valuable timber" that should be exploited—but at a sustainable rate. Nearly two decades after settlement, the wooded areas of the Hill would still be providing residents with construction materials, fencing, and income. Isaac Gibbs, second son of Titus and Amy, by then in his mid-twenties, cut and prepared logs for the home he wanted on his parents' land. He paid Phil White Jr. for building the house partly by cutting wood shingles for the older man and by "halling [hauling] poles for [White's] stable." Isham Patterson took care during the twenty years he lived on the Hill to preserve ample woodland, even though he had only twenty-five acres at his disposal. When he left land to each of his children in 1832, Patterson tried to make sure that each received some forested ground.[41]

Hercules White thus operated much as his black neighbors did, but on a larger scale and with particular success. Israelite Hampton Giles later recalled that Hercules had been "a great favourite with his former marster & mistress, as well as [with] the slaves emancipated" after him.[42] An enslaved person could easily arouse suspicion or resentment among peers by trying too hard to earn a master's approval. That Hercules drew the approbation of both testifies as vividly to his character as his more concrete accomplishments do. Yet Israel Hill never became a tightly organized unit centering on a charismatic leader, partly, perhaps, because the most plausible candidate for that status died less than two years after the founding of the settlement.

At the same time, the Israelites were united by a shared past, a common legal status, and a future that, inevitably, they would in some measure experience together. The most intimate of the relationships that developed within the community were the marriages linking founding families. Rose Johnston first settled near Sam White's property line; if Johnston's daughter Rachel and Phil White Jr., who moved onto Sam's land, were not already keeping company at that time, they began doing so then. The couple had a son in 1812 and took out a formal marriage bond in 1814, when their second son was on the way or newly arrived. Phil and Rachel went on to have at least four more children, three of whom proceeded to wed within the Hill by the mid-1840s—into the Sam White, Gibbs, and Howard families.[43] Another of Rose Johnston's children, her son George, married Titus Gibbs's daughter Hannah, and that couple's son grew up to marry a granddaughter of Sam White.[44] One of Sam's sons married Hampton Giles's daughter in 1822, though the groom, Sam White Jr., died not long thereafter. And still another granddaughter of Sam's married Sam Strong, who had grown up on the White farm and by then was becoming an entrepreneur in the league of Phil White Jr. and of Sam White himself.[45]

Not everyone on Israel Hill married within the community, of course. Sam White's much younger brothers Dick and Hercules Junior each chose wives whose parents had not belonged to the Randolphs—women, in fact, who had been born free even before Richard Randolph wrote his will.[46] Nevertheless, trying to follow the intertwined lineages of Israel Hill induces the same feeling of vertigo that one gets when studying the genealogy of the white Randolph family itself. Indeed, the ancestry and marriages of individuals such as Priscilla White White, granddaughter of Sam and daughter-in-law of Phil Junior, read strikingly like those of Judith Randolph Randolph.

Both Judith and Priscilla, each in her turn, lived in a social milieu in which her own distant cousins constituted a sizable fraction of the potential husbands. A good many of the wealthy, well-educated men of central Virginia who could hope to court Judith Randolph belonged to her own tribe. Similarly, a number of the free Afro-Virginian men of landowning families in Prince Edward County and vicinity, who had the best chance to win Priscilla White's hand, were members of *her* clan or of the wider group of people whom Judy Randolph had emancipated.

Another, much more abundant source of potential spouses for free blacks did exist in the slave population, and some turned there for love and companionship. But that path was fraught with uncertainty, even danger. Rose Johnston's husband, Caesar, though he resided in the general area, could not live with her. Israelite Teny Carter may have been one of the two Randolph slaves by that name who had wed men belonging to St. George Tucker after the two households merged in the 1770s. If so, her husband apparently stayed with Tucker, far away from Prince Edward County and from Teny.[47]

Tony White had reason to envy his brothers Dick and Hercules, who married free women, and his brother Sam, whose wife probably received her freedom from the Randolphs along with him. Tony eventually managed to purchase Milly, his enslaved wife—but not before the couple's five enslaved children had been divided among three different masters. One of those slaveholders then took the three young Whites he owned, including a boy named after his grandfather Hercules, to Missouri. It is hard to imagine a more bitter irony: the first Hercules White moved from slavery to a life in freedom on land of his own in his native state, only to have another Hercules, his grandson, end up in bondage a thousand miles from home and parents.[48] The same sort of tragedy might engulf any free black man who married an enslaved woman.

Records from Prince Edward and the rest of the Old South list many a free African American mother without a husband. One of the ablest historians of the period has suggested that some black women decided against marriage because of the onerous legal and economic restrictions that accompanied matrimony for white and black women alike. But the marriage of a free black person to a slave, like any other union involving an enslaved party, generated no official record; county lists of *free* blacks omit enslaved spouses by definition but include children of free women, who shared their mothers' status. We will never know how many free African Americans who appear from the record to have been single people were nothing of the kind, but Rose Johnston and Tony White raise a red flag. So does Rose's younger neighbor, Michael Patterson; his marriage to a woman who was apparently enslaved would enter the record only when the Freedmen's Bureau recorded such unions after the Civil War.[49]

Johnston, Teny Carter, and others of the older generation had taken slave spouses while they were still in bondage themselves. The younger Israelites had their freedom; the desire to enjoy that liberty fully and pass it on to future generations pushed them to marry fellow free blacks. But the Israelites' habit of intermarriage had still another source.

Many American slaves married people from plantations other than their own. Yet such unions could lead to heartbreak when one spouse's owner moved to some distant place, or when a slaveowner's bankruptcy or death led to the sale of his or her bondpeople. Perhaps in part as a hedge against such perils, a sort of endogamy—a tendency for slaves owned by the same master to marry—evidently became established among the Randolph slaves in the years preceding their emancipation. The marriages of Phil and Fanny White, Isham and Nancy Patterson, Hercules and Molly White, John and Tilla Brown, and Sam and Susan White all seem to have united couples from within the ranks of Randolph slaves while Richard still lived—though the Randolphs may occasionally have made an "outside" marriage into an "inside" one by purchasing the spouse of a favored slave from another owner. Such endogamy must have seemed even more attractive to the Randolph bondpeople after Richard left his emancipatory will in 1796: finding a spouse among the group destined for liberty could well mean that freedom, when Judith Randolph finally granted it, would embrace one's entire family. Hampton and Phoebe Giles, Guy and Mely Howard, and Titus and Amy Gibbs married within the Randolph fold during the years after Richard called for their emancipation, and they settled on Israel Hill at the first opportunity; each couple already had one or more children by then.[50]

Most marriages among the landowning founders of Israel Hill lasted a lifetime, and their households—except those of Rose Johnston, Teny Carter, and Tony White—consisted of two parents in residence with their children.[51] Sons and daughters generally remained in the house until adulthood, and more than a few then made homes of their own on their parents' land. On the other hand, several children who had been born to one landowning Israelite family of the founding generation went to live with another; they usually made the move during adolescence, perhaps to work for the host family or to learn a trade from them.[52]

The black Israelites lived in a compact settlement bound together by a web of relationships, but they also took their place among a larger local population of free Afro-Virginians. One wonders whether Richard Randolph, when he conceived his own experiment in black freedom, realized that a free black quest for self-determination and dignity was already well under way in Prince Edward County.

The extensive black Bartlett clan, free at least since the turn of the century and probably longer, lived only two miles or so from Israel Hill; a number of Israelite and Bartlett men worked as boatmen in the river trade that operated out of the Bartletts' hometown of Farmville. Joe Bartlett married a former Randolph slave, Polly Brandum, and came to live with her at Sam White's on Israel Hill before he settled among his own extended family in town.[53]

Some of the Afro-Virginians whom the Israelites joined in freedom in 1811 had never been slaves at all. Milly Homes's white grandmother had borne a daughter, Temperance, by a black man, probably during the 1730s. The law at that time required that "Tempy" and children of like parentage be bound out as indentured servants until age thirty-one; Milly was born during her mother's period of servitude, in 1757, and she, too, served her mother's master. Milly's father, like her grandfather, was evidently black, for she was classified variously as black and mulatto; she may have had some American Indian ancestry as well. The white man who had charge of Milly Homes apparently brought her from the Tidewater region into Prince Edward County by the time of the Revolution. There she became mother and grandmother to a large clan of free Afro-Virginians who valued family tradition: Milly named her first child Tempy, after her mother, and at least one girl in the generation after that received the name Milly.[54] The elder Milly Homes would manage to buy a small tract of land during Israel Hill's early days.

Other free blacks in Prince Edward may have been slaves at some time; their remote history is difficult to trace. But some had clearly been free for at least a generation, and a few had even had purchased land, by the time the former Randolph slaves settled on Israel Hill. Jethro Forgason Sr. bought a hundred acres in the western part of the county in 1786, only five years after the American victory at Yorktown; the Forgason men worked as farmers and carpenters. Their neighbors included a landed white Ferguson family; although it is not clear whether the two clans were connected by blood, Jethro Forgason and family were probably of mixed racial ancestry.[55]

In western Prince Edward, free mulattoes John and Charles Evans, who may have been brothers, bought sizable tracts of land—nearly 120 acres each—in 1794, two years before Richard Randolph died. Charles sold his land back to the original white owner a few years later for the same price he had paid for it; but John Evans's land stayed in the family for a quarter century before his heirs disposed of it at a handsome profit. The Evans family would remain prominent among Prince Edward's free Afro-Virginians well beyond the era of slavery. They became closely connected, sometimes through marriage, with their fellow early landowners, the Forgasons, and with the Bartlett clan. The black Israelites seem to have acquired their own link with these Evanses in the person of Jane Evans, an elderly woman who moved into Titus Gibbs's household on Israel Hill not long after Gibbs settled there.[56]

The Evanses had bought their land from a white planter, who held on to the remainder of his acreage. The Forgasons had done exactly the same thing, and the white seller in their case expanded his plantation in another direction on the same day he conveyed a hundred acres to Jethro Forgason.[57] These whites were not fleeing the neighborhood but rather accepting free blacks—and black landowners at that—as neighbors. Those transactions set a precedent that may have helped prepare some white people to accept the advent of Israel Hill.

Also in the western part of the county lived Absalom Fears, a white man who farmed without slaves on two hundred acres of land by the last years of the eighteenth century. In 1795, he gave his consent for his daughter Elizabeth to marry James Dungey, a man of similar economic standing, or at least with clear prospects of attaining it. A marriage bond was duly entered, and the pair settled down some three years later on two hundred acres that Dungey purchased next to his new father-in-law's home. As James and Elizabeth established a productive farmstead and began rearing a family, relations with Elizabeth's father remained good: the couple named one of their sons after the older man.[58]

The Dungeys' story would arouse no particular interest, except that

Absalom Fears and his daughter Elizabeth were white, and James Dungey black—or more precisely, mulatto. Interracialism became a tradition in the Fears-Dungey family. James and Elizabeth Dungey's son Absalom himself would take a white woman as his partner in the late 1820s, and one of the free black Forgasons came with his sons to live for a time on the plantation of the white Fearses. At least one household of Fearses and Dungeys would contain people of both races as late as 1850.[59]

The Dungeys' duly solemnized interracial marriage stands out as unusual even in a society that saw close black-white contact of many kinds. Yet James Dungey never faced an issue, including those raised by his lifetime union with a white woman, that other free blacks in the county would not confront at some time or other. A community of free Afro-Virginians was taking shape in Prince Edward County during the early 1800s, and the Israelites now emerged as a conspicuous part of it. All members of that community faced a common challenge: dealing with their white neighbors, and with the institutions that governed free blacks' lives without giving them a vote.

NEIGHBORS

Two thirds of white households in the Old South owned no slaves; Prince Edward County itself, however, was largely a society of masters and bondpeople. That did not mean that most white families in the county were rich. No more than a tenth of the county's white citizens in 1810 belonged to the "planter class," often defined to include households owning more than twenty slaves; only half a dozen people held fifty slaves or more. One sixth of Prince Edward's white families owned between ten and twenty bondpeople; one third held between three and ten slaves, and another sixth of white households kept only one or two. Farmers of modest means were numerous, and landless whites not rare; a quarter of the free households in the county included no bondpeople at all when Israel Hill was settled.[60]

The diversity of county society ensured that the black Israelites would interact with all sorts of people; that, in turn, may have magnified the effect that they and other free blacks had on the local society and on white people's consciousness. Yet in their own immediate neighborhood, the pioneers of Israel Hill found themselves surrounded not merely by whites but by some of the county's leading families. The plantation bordering the southern tier of the settlement belonged to a branch of the Legrand family. The Dillons lived across the northwestern boundary;

they owned the continuation of the ridge at whose head Israel Hill lay, as well as part of the Appomattox River valley below. Archer Allen's plantation occupied some six hundred acres between Israel Hill and the Appomattox to the north and northeast. Due east of the Hill lay the land that remained in the hands of the Randolphs after Judith granted the Israelites their portion.

At the time the black Israelites first occupied their small tracts, the Legrand, Dillon, and Allen plantations each worked between thirty-four and thirty-eight slaves. That put those families in the top 2 percent among Prince Edward slaveholders, an elite that also included several other whites who lived but short distances from Israel Hill. At least three of the Hill's four next-door neighbors owned additional land in other counties.[61] These white neighbors' wealth ensured that they wielded political and social influence. The year in which Israel Hill began to take shape was Archer Allen's sixteenth as a justice of the county court, Prince Edward's governing body; he also served as county sheriff at the time. Edward Dillon, an intellectual who had joined Allen on the county court in 1805, knew of the black Israelites' venture not only from living nearby, but also through his close friendship with John Randolph.[62]

Rather than fall into the orbit of such powerful, well-off people, however, Hercules White set a precedent for amicably businesslike relations between Israelites and white planters. When White died in 1812, he owed petty sums to one of the Allens and to Baker Legrand; another claim or two from whites, including one for about $100, came in much later. Meanwhile, other men, both black and white, owed *him* sizable amounts. Hercules, like many other propertied persons, left no will; the county court followed standard procedure, appointing two citizens of substance to lay off the portion of White's earthly goods to which his widow, Molly, was entitled by law. The court probably selected Baker Legrand and a member of the Allen family for the task because, as White's neighbors, they had some knowledge of his situation, yet had not been so closely involved with him as to create a blatant conflict of interest.[63]

Free blacks who, unlike the Israelites, had no land of their own typically resided on farms or plantations of whites and often worked for those same people. Groups of half a dozen or more blacks had formed at a couple of spots in Prince Edward. Most others found themselves scattered family by family or individual by individual. Many Afro-Virginian women spun, sewed, knitted, wove, or washed clothes; some men worked as waiters, while others plied various crafts. Free blacks of both sexes did farm work in fields owned by whites.[64] Even Hercules White sustained himself partly by working for white clients, of course. Several Randolph slaves and freedpeople earned money on the nearby Chambers plantation over the years, and some of the newly transplanted Israelites probably took on at least occasional jobs for the planters they had settled next to. Yet a family's freedom and their land, from the moment they felled trees and built a house on it, gave them a new level of self-determination—and they exercised it in a variety of realms, beginning with decisions they made as parents.

One of the clearest ways to honor a patron, and to seek his or her continued support, is to name one's child after that person; newly freed blacks even had the option of calling *themselves* after their liberator by adopting his family name. Yet not one of the emancipated families took the surname Randolph. Instead, they all used family names of their own that some, perhaps many, had embraced before their manumission. Among approximately eighty children born to blacks of the Randolph group between 1800 and 1820, a few—but only a few—bore given names of the group's white benefactors. Dick White had a daughter called Judith, born shortly after Judy Randolph died. The parents of Judith Gibbs, Dick Patterson, and Randolph Brandum may have christened them after their liberators, though the naming of one or more of those three may have been coincidental.[65]

The Israelites and other free Afro-Virginians did have to deal with the white authorities who ran Prince Edward County, many of whom, unlike Archer Allen and Edward Dillon, were not their near neighbors. Like white men of few means, and like all white women, free blacks lacked the right to vote or serve on juries; the requirement that a voter own fifty acres of land or the equivalent disfranchised at least half the state's adult white males until a very modest lowering of the bar in 1830 and a more sweeping reform in 1851. The prerogative of holding public office belonged exclusively to Prince Edward's leading men, for not a single county officeholder was elected by the people until 1851. The county court—the local legislative, executive, and judicial power all concentrated in one body—included roughly a score of men. Only a quarter to a third of these justices, and sometimes even fewer, showed up for a typical session. When vacancies arose on the body, the remaining members chose successors and sent the names on to the governor.

In addition to the disabilities they shared with plain white folk and with white females, free blacks could not testify in court against white defendants. They were also barred from militia and patrol duty—a convenient exclusion, but a badge of inferior citizenship. Free black men did possess an important right that married white women ordinarily did not: to own and dispose of property in their own right. Yet even ownership of land and substantial personal property could not alter a black man's color, which he shared with the enslaved masses—and which ensured that free Afro-Virginians experienced life differently than did whites who were relegated to the margins by economics or gender.

The Israelites had been liberated into a world in which not all free Afro-Virginians had recognized surnames; revenue commissioners listed some freed blacks simply as Rhody, London, Aron, Free Harry, or Free Clory—or even with cumbersome appellations such as "John a free Negroe Call'd free John."[66] The very law that called for free blacks to register with the county court marked them as inferior in status and at least vaguely suspect, even though neither Afro-Virginians nor white officials paid much attention to the requirement in most periods. During and just after the War of 1812, free blacks were saddled with a special annual head tax of $1.50 to $2.50; unlike white delinquents, they might be hired out by the sheriff to work off their obligations if they failed to pay these or other taxes. When a crackdown on tax delinquents of both races took place in 1815, the Prince Edward County Court warned fifteen free blacks that they would be hired out if they did not pay. Six or seven of the men on the list lived on Israel Hill, including brothers Tony White and Hercules White Jr., as well as Jacob Johnston, Rose's son. Half a dozen others were younger men from non-Israelite landowning families, though many of these lived away from their parents' farms.[67] Most of the free black men on the list promptly complied after they received the warning; another paid at the last minute, and two could not be found or otherwise fell through the cracks.

One man, however—the son and namesake of landowner Jethro Forgason—did find himself hired out to a white man for four weeks as a tax delinquent.[68] This proved to be the sole hiring out of a free black man even in a year of heightened tax vigilance, and the law permitting such measures eventually became a virtual dead letter in Prince Edward County. Still, a month's unfree labor is a long time for the person required to do it, and even the theoretical possibility of being hired out, like the special head tax itself, signaled lawmakers' callousness toward the free black populace.

Early in 1816, several members of the county court decided to fire a shot across the black Israelites' bow. Someone, probably a deputy sheriff, took a careful census of the Hill, listing all 114 residents by name and age and grouping them into households. A session of the court, at which four members were sitting, then used that list to draw up one of the most remarkable orders ever issued in old Prince Edward. More than seventy young people—all the residents of Israel Hill younger than twenty-one—were to be bound out as apprentices by the overseers of the poor, a committee of prominent men charged with aiding (and controlling) impoverished citizens.

Perhaps free blacks' slowness in paying the discriminatory head tax had irritated some officials. Or perhaps this was the moment when some people blamed the black Israelites for a rash of thefts from white-owned properties. Syphax Brown, Hercules White, James Dungey, and others had already discovered that white hostility was far from universal; the court order may have come as an attempt by intolerant whites to enshrine their own views as county policy, or as a symbolic gesture by four county justices to placate such people. The justices themselves must have known that hiring out so many youngsters would be impossible. Indeed, the order produced no apparent results. Lists of Prince Edward's free blacks over the next several years show the Hill's children and youth still in residence, apart from a very few individuals who may have died. Nine inhabitants of the Hill did register with the court three months after the hiring-out order, perhaps as a concession to unfriendly elements in the white community. (A second order, issued more than a decade later, to bind out twenty-four children from Israelite families came during a year that also saw the number of slave patrollers double; yet that order, like the one in 1816, seems to have been ignored.)[69]

Eight years after the settlement of the Hill, a white individual went so far as to question outright the free status of a black Israelite: one William Randolph challenged the credentials of Essex White Jr., a boatman. Randolph may have been exploiting the handiest threat available against White after some kind of scrape between the two of them. The court did issue a summons requiring White to answer Randolph's complaint, but an almost unique marginal notation in the county court's order book tells what happened next: the summons to Essex White was "filed with dead papers—never acted on."[70] Why the document ended up pigeonholed is unknown. White may have done something to pacify William Randolph, or Randolph may have backed off, satisfied that he had made his point simply by threatening White. At least as likely, county authorities considered Essex White's entitlement to his liberty through the Randolph manumission so clear that to move against him seemed both an injustice and a waste of effort.

Indeed, during these very years of friction over taxes and the threat-

A list of free negroes on Israel hill

	Names	Ages		Names	ages
1	Saml White	45	30	Christopher Strong	30
2	Susen White	43	31	Polly Strong	25
3	Jane "	23	32	Mariah "	10
4	Esser "	25	33	Stella "	8
5	Thamer "	20	34	Saml "	6
6	Nancy "	18	35	Wm .	1
7	Ellin "	16			
8	Hercules "	12	36	Hercules White	26
9	John "	10	37	Susen White	18
10	Hampton "	8	38	Harret "	2
11	Amy "	6	39	Molly "	70
12	Anny "	5	40	Tony "	30
13	Ampy Branden	36			
14	Susan White	9	41	Jefry Howard	28
15	Sally "	5	42	Amelia Howard	26
16	Phy "	1	43	Beverly "	6
17	Esther "		44	Virgen "	3
18	Phelip White	23			
19	Rachel White	20	45	John Brown	42
20	Caeser "	3	46	Tella Brown	41
21	Curtis "	1	47	Syfax "	20
22	Polly Branden	25	48	Rose "	23
23	Henry "	12	49	Lucy "	8
					2

Four justices of the county court consulted a list of black Israelites in 1816 (detail shown here) and ordered that all residents under twenty-one be bound out as apprentices. The order was never put into effect.

ened hiring out of Israelite children, the system of local government, undemocratic though it was in many ways, made some room for free blacks to participate in proceedings that affected their lives and livelihoods. Oddly, one of the most tradition-laden of county functions brought white and free black landowners face-to-face on a strikingly informal basis. "Processionings" had been a feature of rural English and Anglo-American society for ages. Five times during Israel Hill's first three decades or so, the county court commissioned a pair of citizens in each neighborhood to "procession." These men spent up to ten days walking every property line in their small district, confirmed where one person's land ended and another's began, ensured that the boundaries remained well marked, and recorded their own movements in writing.

The processioners were white men, many of them relatively prominent. But the work of "chopping" through underbrush until one's "shins [were] bruised" brought processioners, great landowners, and smallholders together, for a while at least, under circumstances that discouraged pretentiousness on the part of the better-off.[71] Citizens were not required to accompany the processioners in the nineteenth century, but monitoring the operation in person subtly asserted a person's rights and status as a landowner. Blacks including James Dungey and various Israelites did just that, participating regularly in the processioning of boundaries among their own lands as well as those lines they shared with white neighbors.[72]

A processioning tended to become a small social gathering in which immediate neighbors and a pair of processioners who came from the same area of the county exchanged news, gossip, humorous observations—and quite possibly, given the prevalence of drinking at nearly every other kind of encounter, some liquid refreshment.[73] Processionings occurred much less frequently than many other kinds of interaction between black and white; but few institutions brought people of both races together in a setting where the markers of social standing were as muted as they became when people hacked their way together through the brambles.

Another rural issue that brought government into contact with every citizen was the question of how to make social and economic activity easier. Prince Edward County's people lived scattered over hundreds of square miles of countryside, a landscape punctuated mainly by a few tiny villages at various crossroads and by an assortment of ordinaries (taverns), mills, and country stores. The physical obstacles to travel remained significant in the first decades of the nineteenth century, in the county generally and in the neighborhood that included Israel Hill in particular.

A country road ran more or less directly from a point near the Hill to the county seat, the crossroads then known as Prince Edward Court House and today called Worsham, which lies seven miles to the south. Another led northward across the Appomattox into rural Cumberland County and westward into the hills of the upper Appomattox Valley. Only the old bridle path connected the Israelites' neighborhood directly to Farmville, which became the county's economic hub. To carry any substantial load to or from Farmville's stores, tobacco warehouses, and river wharf required taking a circuitous route southwestward through the

Legrand place to the nearest bridge over Buffalo River, well upstream from the Hill. The Israelites' neighbor William L. Legrand complained as late as 1839 that "the people from this way travels almost a west course to get to Farmville which is east of us." That trebled the distance they had to cover—and every extra mile counted on roads that were often obstructed by deep mud, fallen trees or limbs, or privately owned fencing running across the right-of-way.[74]

In principle, travelers could ford Buffalo River, the natural obstacle that lay between Farmville and the vicinity of Israel Hill. But one ford on the Buffalo near Legrand's was "myry" with quicksand, and in times of high water or ice, fording often became impracticable even where the creek bottom was firmer; in that era of cold Virginia winters, Judith Randolph once noted, ice as thick as three inches could form overnight on ponds in the Appomattox Valley.[75] Raging "freshets" or floods often damaged or even washed away the bridges that did exist in Prince Edward.

Leading citizens of the area dreamt of connecting the Buffalo, and thus the Appomattox, with a tributary of the Roanoke (Staunton) River to the south. Such a canal could have made the Hill, with its resident population of black boatmen, into a way station on a waterway serving a vast sweep of Southside Virginia and northeastern North Carolina. But the Buffalo ran "very crooked" for a half-mile below the Hill; further meanderings, a dam, and a constantly replenished supply of fallen trees obstructed the way upstream. The canal boosters proposed to clear and straighten the little river, but the Appomattox-Roanoke canal plan followed many other navigation schemes of the time into oblivion.[76] Overland travel would remain the only way for most people to reach the Appomattox River, a crucial lifeline to the outside world.

Citizens of Prince Edward wanted and needed to travel to places other than Farmville. People in each neighborhood took their corn and wheat to the local mill for grinding and carried home corn meal and flour. The mercantile stores offered supplies and became meeting places for folk of every social group from planter to slave. The sitting of the county court each month attracted crowds from great distances: people of every class and both races packed the otherwise sparsely populated village of Prince Edward Court House for several days to conduct political, legal, and commercial business—and, just as important, to gossip with friends, gamble, and drink.

All these encounters depended on roads, and the county court expended considerable effort responding to petitions for new roadways. It sent commissioners to investigate those requests, and it pressed the many "surveyors of the road" to do their duty on existing thoroughfares. A surveyor was a landowner whom the court assigned to care for a given stretch of road: to fill potholes, ensure adequate drainage, lay down "causeways" made of logs in chronically muddy areas, remove fallen trees and other obstructions, intervene if a landowner ran a fence across a road, and keep signboards posted and legible. These surveyors performed their duties by assembling work parties that incorporated their own slaves and those of nearby masters for a few days each year; the county paid the surveyors by the day.[77]

The county court's function as sponsor and overseer of the public roads led to some of its earliest contacts with the people of Israel Hill. In 1813, two years after the settlement was founded, a pair of white men named Morton petitioned the county to authorize a road that would connect a mill they operated on the Appomattox River with the Sandy Ford road, which ran just northwest of Israel Hill. Following standard procedure, the court delegated several landowners who lived in the area to identify a route for such a road, and to determine how much a new right-of-way would benefit the public and damage the interests of those whose lands lay in its path.

The route the commissioners chose would begin at the Sandy Ford road, then run east through much of Israel Hill's northern tier before turning north toward the Appomattox. The road would take some land from each of the Israelites' immediate white neighbors; but, as the examiners noted, only small corners of the Legrand, Dillon, Allen, and Randolph lands would be affected. An entirely new road would have to be opened through Israel Hill, however, across the land of Titus Gibbs.[78] The commissioners confirmed the "great public utility" of opening the road that the mill owners had asked for, but noted that Gibbs would be seriously affected: the road would "run through near the middle of his land, & through his plantation"—that is, through the part of his property that he had cleared and cultivated.

A governing authority that wanted to harass a newly freed black smallholder could have embraced this proposed road as a way of doing so. Even a more benign county court and its appointees might be expected to subordinate Titus Gibbs's interests to those of white planters and mill owners. But the examiners were doing something quite different: to describe in vivid terms the damage Gibbs would suffer would justify monetary compensation to the black man. To recommend the awarding of reparations, in fact, was a central function of road commissions. The road, if opened with the then standard width of thirty feet, would take perhaps an acre and a half from Gibbs. That amount of land meant something to a man who owned only fifty acres, especially since part of the roadway would come out of Gibbs's productive ground. Yet the road would not deal him a devastating blow. Indeed, Gibbs and his fellow Israelites might also benefit from the new road, for it would offer them easier access to the Mortons' mill, as well as to the Sandy Ford road and thence to Cumberland County and western Prince Edward.

The law said that those who would lose land to a new road should receive an opportunity to show, if they cared to, why the way should not be opened. The court had already accepted newly freed blacks as litigants and vindicated their right to be secure in their property; the justices now summoned Titus Gibbs, along with Judith Randolph and three wealthy neighbors, to present their views. Whether any of those invited to speak actually appeared, or what they said if they did, went unrecorded. It may well be that Titus Gibbs at some point offered his opinion directly, if informally, to at least one of the commissioners, John Tuggle, a near neighbor who had many dealings with the Israelites over the years. In any event, for one reason or another, the county court declined to authorize the new road.[79]

Another Afro-Virginian of Prince Edward County stated his wishes about a road just three years after Gibbs's brush with the issue. James Dungey and his interracial family had improved their land markedly. Within three years of buying the place, the couple sold twenty-five acres for more than three times the rate per acre they had paid for it. Before long, their remaining land was valued at one third more per acre than the long-established farm of James's white father-in-law, Absalom Fears.[80]

The Dungeys' white neighbors had long since grown accustomed to the couple's union. White officials referred to Elizabeth as "Mrs. Dungey"; her marriage to a man of color had not cost her that everyday honorific. The authorities even found ways to fit the biracial Dungey family into an official framework that identified each person according to his or her race and each family by its head. As long as James Dungey lived, the revenue commissioner could enter him and his children on the annual list of Prince Edward's free Negro residents, omitting his white wife altogether. After James's death, the commissioner adopted the formula, "Elizabeth Dunge's Family," followed by her children's names, thus giving family hierarchy its due while using the possessive form to avoid directly enumerating a white person on a list of blacks.[81] The discreet apostrophe-*s* restored tidiness where categories had been blurred by events. The treatment of the Dungeys on the annual lists reflected a racial order that, by the early 1800s, recognized only two groups. People still sometimes used the term "mulatto" descriptively, and some very light-skinned biracial or multiracial people gained acceptance as whites. But society now placed individuals in one classification or the other, white or Negro; people of mixed race had the same legal status as those of black complexion.

By 1816, James Dungey wanted a more convenient way to travel to and from his home. So he did what a white landholder would do: he petitioned the county court to reroute the existing road in his neighborhood so that it would swing by his house. The court appointed commissioners to visit the site, and then ordered the road to be altered as Dungey had requested. As it often did, the court directed the petitioner himself to prepare the new roadway; thereafter, the road would be maintained like other country routes, by a court-appointed "surveyor" working a gang of slaves and paid by the county.[82] The court often granted requests to alter roadways, but it also proved ready to turn them down, so it is noteworthy that a public body in a Black Belt county of slaveholding Virginia in the 1810s would fulfill the desires of an ambitious man of color who lived with a white wife.

James Dungey used the county court to assert himself in other ways, too. At one point, he sold a ton of tobacco—a substantial crop by yeoman farmer standards—to a white woman, who may then have consolidated Dungey's crop with her own for marketing. The two made an oral agreement, as many did in those days. Then, according to Dungey, the white woman failed to pay him—that also happened often, no matter what the race of the parties—so he sued her, though he soon died and the suit abated.[83]

Dungey paid his taxes about as conscientiously as the typical white Prince Edward freeholder, meeting his land tax obligation some four years out of every five. He had a positive reason to do so: both his lawsuit and his road request show that he saw his county's governing body as an institution that would serve him. He bequeathed that attitude to his children. Several years after Dungey's death in 1818 or 1819, his family turned to the county court to divide his landed estate among them in a precise and official way—and the court duly sent a surveyor out to do just that. Still later, one of Dungey's sons, together with two white neighbors, sought compensation when the county proposed to divert a road through the men's lands.[84]

Another issue arose out of the need to improve transportation within the county: How was the large group of free blacks on Israel Hill to be treated when it came to road maintenance? They lacked slaves whom they could lend to the county for occasional road service; slaveless whites seem to have been omitted customarily from any role as laborers in road "surveying." But the Israelites were black, like the bondmen who worked on the roads. Would the county therefore call on the men of the Hill to work the highway? The answer was yes. The name of "Herculass" (White Sr.) had appeared on a list of hands to work on the road in 1807, and on another a little more than two years later. At about the same time, James Dungey became one of a number of men—all the others on the list were white—whom the court directed to supply hands for repairs on a certain roadway.[85]

In 1819, the county court ordered Charles Fore, a neighbor of the Israelites, to repair a section of the Sandy Ford road. As usual, the order named those whites from among whose slaves Fore was to conscript his road crew. But this particular document instructed Fore also to enlist "the free male labouring tithes at Israel Hill"—"tithes" being people old enough to count for purposes of taxation.[86] The term "labouring" by itself said little about the court's view of the Israelites; officials in early-nineteenth-century Virginia often applied the word "labourer" to white men, too, even to some who owned farms. But on the back of the court order, someone entered the names of five Israelite "Male Tythes." Whether this list simply named *prospective* suppliers of labor—all five men lived on the end of Israel Hill nearest the road that needed repair—or whether an official tallied afterward the names of people whom Fore had actually drafted to work, we cannot know.

Three of the five men were the only adult males in their respective households, and were under forty; if any Israelites actually repaired the road under Charles Fore, these were prime candidates. Isham Patterson, on the other hand, was sixty-three. Fore may have given him and Titus Gibbs, who was nearing fifty, the same prerogative that white slaveholders automatically received when called upon for road workers: to choose which of their hands would join the road detail for a few days. The great difference, of course, was that these black men's "hands" were not slaves but rather family members: Patterson had two sons in their twenties, and Gibbs had two in their latter teens.[87]

The incident crystallized lingering ambiguities among white people about the exact place that free blacks were to occupy in local society. For some whites, including certain members of the county court, it apparently came as second nature to see a large concentration of able-bodied free black men as a source of labor for a road detail. On the other hand, the county court already had a history of treating free blacks such as Syphax Brown and James Dungey much as it did other free men. And Charles Fore, the local road surveyor, himself was no enemy of free blacks.

At the time the county court ordered him to arrange the road detail in 1819, Fore, a prosperous blacksmith, farmer, and entrepreneur, had a free black apprentice, Peter Forgason. Fore had treated the young man considerately: though Forgason had been bound to Fore till age twenty-one, Fore in fact allowed him to work where he pleased well before he reached that age. Later, to close the books on Peter Forgason's apprenticeship in an official and positive way, Fore would certify in writing that Forgason had served the full term of his apprenticeship "faithfuly."[88] Given the Israelites' knowledge of Fore's personality and character, one wonders whether they complained to him about this order commanding them to do something from which the system exempted other free men. After all, these Afro-Virginians and their parents had a tradition, extending back more than three decades, of protesting injustice. Whatever the Israelites may have said or thought about the matter, however, the county continued over the years to call on men of the Hill and on other free blacks to supply labor on road crews.[89]

Even as Charles Fore's road detail evinced the weight of custom, another small sign that free blacks were altering white consciousness appeared—again, oddly enough, in the usually dry annals of highway maintenance. The county court defined a given "surveyor's" area of responsibility by citing a landmark at each end of his stretch of road. By 1817, one of these landmarks was the fork in the Farmville–Court House road just beyond the home of free black shoemaker and cooper Ben Short, who in 1811 had bought the plot of land he lived and plied his trades on. The county formally designated the white citizen in charge of repairs along that stretch as "the Surveyor from Benja. Short's to Watkins's." This by no means made Short the legal or social equal of the white Watkins. But it did mean that Short counted for something—that he and his shop existed as prominent, recognized fixtures on white people's mental maps of their county. Ben Short's place was not the first free black site to take its place in Prince Edward's geographic vocabulary; in fact, Israel Hill itself can probably claim that distinction. Neither would Short's house and shop be the last establishment owned by a free Afro-Virginian that made its way into the atlas of Prince Edward County governance: as late as 1864, a certain spot near the county's western border would still be known to authorities and the public as "Dungey's fork."

Ben Short, the Israelites, and other free blacks had begun to make their mark, both literally and figuratively.[90]

During the same early years when the people of Israel Hill faced the occasional attempt to circumscribe their liberty, free Afro-Virginians continued to make their presence felt in the way James Dungey and Syphax Brown did: by resorting to, or defending themselves within, the local courts. There, black plaintiffs and defendants alike obtained results that made them feel more secure as free people.

Brown's example may have encouraged black Israelite Phoebe Giles to go to the county court only a year after the Hill's founding. She did not confront a white person, however, but rather sued a fellow resident of Israel Hill, Sam White's wife, Sooky, for slander. Suits for that offense were not rare in early-nineteenth-century Prince Edward County, but women almost never filed them. The specific transgression that Phoebe Giles alleged likewise has no parallel in the county court's annals: the fortyish Sooky White had supposedly said, in the hearing of others, that Giles, who was a few years younger than she, had "tryed . . . to give [her] poison in a cabbage."[91]

That was an inflammatory accusation. For generations, some white Virginians had believed, as the colonial legislature put it in 1748, that "many persons [had] been murdered" by Afro-Virginian poisoners.[92] There may have been some whites among the people who heard Sooky White's words—or perhaps Phoebe Giles feared that white people would encounter the rumor that she was a poisoner through the long-standing black-white grapevine. Thoughtful people would realize that a black woman who had just won her freedom and established a new homeplace had every reason not to jeopardize everything by harming whites. Yet antimanumission laws and petitions, especially since Gabriel's attempted slave revolt in 1800, showed that some Southern whites feared free blacks as well as slaves. The settlement on Israel Hill remained a new implant in a society that had not yet proved how deep its tolerance ran.

Phoebe Giles had to calculate how she could best defend her character before the entire community, black and white alike. Then, too, Phoebe may simply have been so angry at Sooky White that she sought the most emphatic way she could think of to strike back at her accuser without resorting to violence. So Giles turned for vindication to the elite white males on the county court—but in a pragmatic rather than a servile way; that panel, after all, was the one public tribunal available to her. Indeed, by seeking justice in exactly the same way the wealthiest white planter did, Phoebe laid claim to a legitimate place in free society, just as Syphax

Brown had done three years earlier. After she had made her point by filing the lawsuit, tempers cooled, as often happened among white litigants. Phoebe Giles's suit was dismissed after fifteen months, probably
with her acquiescence; Sam and Sooky White's son went on to marry
Giles's daughter a decade later.[93]

Sometimes during those first few years, Israelites or their free black
friends became involved with county authorities through no choice of
their own. Not long after Phoebe Giles's lawsuit, Rose Johnston's family
faced a challenge that required the Israelites' white neighbors to signal
yet again what sort of future Israel Hill could expect. Masters constantly
worried that slaves were stealing from them. They knew that some of
their fellow whites avidly purchased those stolen goods, and some reflexively assumed that free blacks would be even quicker to buy stolen articles from slaves. That is just what someone accused Jacob Johnston,
Rose's son, of doing in May 1813: buying stolen corn from a bondman.

A fine—the usual punishment for knowingly buying stolen goods—
could hit the Johnston family fairly hard; the damage that a conviction
might do to the reputation of a new settlement of free blacks might prove
even worse. The Randolphs had considered the Johnstons especially
meritorious, and Rose's marriage had been solid enough to win official
notice despite her husband's enslaved status. If the son of such a family
would traffic in stolen goods, whites might well wonder, then what were
the rest of the Israelites up to?[94] Moreover, the charge against Jacob
Johnston alleged that he had bought the corn from a slave of Israel Hill's
well-to-do white neighbor, Baker Legrand; the corn—if any had indeed
been stolen—may well have come from the Legrand place. To incur the
anger of this influential man would have created practical problems: the
Israelites had to travel through Legrand's plantation to get to the nearest
bridge over Buffalo River leading toward Farmville.

The sheriff expended little energy making a case against Johnston;
ordered in August 1813 to summon the young man to court, a deputy
reported three months later that he had "not [had] time" to serve the
papers on the black Israelite. As typically happened with white defendants, more months passed before Johnston actually stood trial. He did
not spend the intervening time in jail—that would have been a severe
blow to his mother—nor was he required to post bail. A trial did finally
take place in May 1814, attended by a jury of men who, all being white
and owners of considerably more property than the Johnstons, were far
from being the defendant's peers. The record does not tell who accused
Jacob Johnston or what witnesses said at his trial. Two white next-door

neighbors of Israel Hill testified; perhaps one of them had lodged the initial accusation. Yet those men's families had orderly relations with the Israelites: the father of one witness and the brother of the second had known and done business with Hercules White Sr. The court may have called these men to testify simply because they lived near Israel Hill and thus had more opportunity than most people to observe what went on there.[95]

The jurors deadlocked and asked to adjourn until the next day; when they reconvened, they found Jacob Johnston not guilty. That outcome was not unusual—for *white* defendants. Prosecutors had difficulty winning convictions for a crime in which the only two eyewitnesses were typically unavailable: the law forbade the enslaved seller of illicit goods to testify against whites, and the white buyer could not be compelled to incriminate himself. But this defendant, Johnston, was black: the Commonwealth's attorney could have called Jack, the slave who allegedly sold the stolen corn, to the witness stand, but he apparently did not do so. The prosecutor and his successors in Prince Edward County would hardly ever use slave testimony against free blacks in times to come, except in some instances of black-on-black crime; in fact, authorities would seldom have occasion to try free blacks on criminal charges in the first place.[96]

Whether by design or not, whoever brought the case against Jacob Johnston had signaled the black Israelites that they had better not join slaves in questionable enterprises. But the men and women of Israel Hill had also witnessed yet another instance in which a former Randolph slave's status as a free man, more than his color or previous condition, governed his treatment by the legal system.

A trial held one day before Jacob Johnston's case went to the jury conveyed the same reassuring message. The defendants, boatmen Joe and Henry Bartlett, belonged to the large and growing free black clan in Farmville that specialized in that occupation. The Bartletts, unlike Jacob Johnston, stood trial in 1814 much as slaves would have—before a panel of county justices, with no jury present—perhaps because their alleged crime was deemed more serious than Johnston's. Rather than simply receive stolen goods, the Bartletts themselves had allegedly taken $5 worth of farm implements from a white man's premises in the company of "sundry slaves."

Yet the court acquitted both Bartletts. They probably received justice at least in part because of the good reputation that their family and the black Israelites' other predecessors in freedom had earned. It was already nearly impossible by 1814 to put together a judicial panel in Prince Edward County without incorporating men who knew and had friendly dealings with free blacks. The court in the Bartlett trial included at least two justices, John Purnall and Charles Woodson, who had close and deepening relationships with some of the county's more impressive free Afro-Virginians. Milly Homes and her extended family lived on Purnall's plantation, traded with him, and had bought land of their own in the neighborhood by the time the Bartletts were tried. A free black carpenter lived on Justice Woodson's place; when the man died shortly after the Bartlett trial, Woodson would become guardian of his children. One of Woodson's slaves was married to the industrious Betty Dwin, who had purchased her own freedom, bought one and possibly two or three of her enslaved sons, and acquired furnishings including several suits of "best Sunday Clothes."[97]

Neither John Purnall nor Charles Woodson, nor most of their peers, questioned the basic legitimacy of the slaveholding regime. Yet those men, and perhaps other justices, were more prepared by 1814 to recognize the Bartletts' innocence because those white notables had learned through experience that free Afro-Virginians could be upright, hardworking, law-abiding people. The Israelites—whose ranks Joe Bartlett would soon join—had been emancipated into a society that, from the black point of view, was ruled by despots. But despotic power entitles a ruler to choose justice over cruelty if he wishes. An unjust system was again showing signs that it could deal justly with free black defendants, even when the potentially inflammatory charge of criminally consorting with slaves was thrown onto the table.

Other early experiences of free blacks in local courts involved the same sorts of issues that entangled whites. Both groups lived in the shadow of economic hardship and occasional disaster. Everyone felt compelled to grow tobacco, yet it was commonplace for a third of the tobacco the county produced to fail state inspection at the river warehouses. Prices for the crop fluctuated, sometimes radically: one man in Prince Edward, forced to sell tobacco from the harvest of 1823 as low as $1.50 per hundredweight, then watched in frustration as prices rose back to $10.00 within seven or eight months. Among those who had little to begin with, economic distress sometimes reached extreme proportions: carcasses of distempered cattle had to be buried four feet deep in the early years of the nineteenth century, and their hides "so cut or mangled that no one might be tempted to take them up and skin them" and thus risk spreading the disease.[98]

The rural economy of Prince Edward County, and of Virginia in general, was a cash-poor system, chronically battered by vagaries of the national and international markets. Residents conducted most transactions on credit through store accounts and IOUs, or through the barter of goods or services. Men hired to harvest wheat typically received 1 bushel of that crop per day in payment; a white brickmason collected 250 bushels of wheat for his work in the construction of two houses.[99] A certain plantation owner in the years around 1830 paid his account at the blacksmith's shop with 105 pounds of pork, and bought a hat with half a barrel of corn; he gradually paid most of his tab at a second blacksmith's with wheat, oats, and some sugar, and then settled the balance of $1.34 in beans, as if paying cash were out of the question.[100]

Everyone was a debtor, and almost everyone at least sometimes a creditor. People therefore tended to show patience when a poor crop or other ill fortune caused a person to miss the due date on an obligation. Notes of indebtedness became a kind of currency passed from hand to hand, with each successive party endorsing a given IOU over to the next. Even in relatively prosperous times, this kind of "house that Jack built" situation could easily produce a string of lawsuits if someone in the chain of debt defaulted.

Then came the national economic Panic of 1819, in which the house of cards composed of interlocking debts largely collapsed. For a decade after 1819, citizens of Prince Edward County fought a grim battle with the aftershocks of the economic crisis. Lawsuits to recover debts and forfeitures of property to satisfy court judgments, never rare in Prince Edward, became epidemic.[101] The panic and its reverberations caught Israel Hill at an early and potentially sensitive time in the settlement's development. Yet merchants who filed rafts of suits over delinquent accounts neither singled out indebted free blacks for pursuit nor wrote off their obligations en masse. Nor is there any evidence that store owners or others used extralegal methods to dun free blacks who owed them money. Rather, the merchants treated the black customer as just another name on their long lists of delinquent accounts.

In 1820 and 1821, a family from Israel Hill found itself among a great many parties sued by a particular local merchant. Israelite landowner Isham Patterson and his son-in-law Edmund Clarke had signed a bond of debt for $56 to the man in 1819, perhaps to cover a cumulation of small purchases over time. They had since paid $15 toward the debt, but the merchant, as the holder of numerous unpaid accounts, was facing pressures of his own; so he sued Patterson and Clarke, among others, for the money they still owed him.[102] The black defendants lost the suit; they did owe the money, after all. Yet they engaged a lawyer who mounted a vigorous and sophisticated defense. And the pair did not lack friends; bail bonds required a "security," or cosigner, and county justice Samuel V. Allen signed as security for the two black men. For Allen, involvement with free blacks was nothing unusual; he had been a party in tendering a deed of trust that helped shoemaker-cooper Ben Short to buy land in 1811.[103]

Indeed, it seems that belonging to a family of free black strivers could help a man make friends—and friends mattered when economic troubles turned into legal difficulties. Dick White, son of Hercules Senior, together with another free black man named Miller Smith, signed a note of debt for $63 to a white man in Cumberland County. The creditor passed the IOU on to a third party, who sued White and Smith for the money in 1820. This, too, was an uncomplicated case, which the defendants lost.

But Dick White and Miller Smith experienced the affair quite differently. White, who lived on the land passed down to him by his father Hercules on Israel Hill and worked as a farmer and boatman, posted bail with two white men of substance as his cosigners, and he mounted an energetic legal defense. Both men who gave bond for Dick White probably knew him partly in his capacity as a batteauman; one of the pair regularly sent significant amounts of his own tobacco downriver to Petersburg, while the other owned a mercantile company that constantly shipped goods up and down the Appomattox. Meanwhile, Miller Smith, with no one to give security for his bail bond pending trial of the suit, went to jail for a time. Barely twenty years old, Smith was a decade younger than Dick White. Only after the lawsuit concluded does he seem to have found the kind of job, as a servant at Hampden-Sydney College, that might have attracted some white patron who would help him out of a tight spot.

Dick White's influential white acquaintances, by contrast, were not his patrons, nor he their servant. Those men did not pay off Dick White's debt or get it forgiven—few people, white or black, could expect that kind of deus ex machina. What White's friends did was to cosign a bond guaranteeing that he would come before the county court at the appointed time; whites in Prince Edward did that for each other frequently. Dick White was an industrious man of nearly thirty with a wife and children, who lived with equally well-established brothers on land owned by his family. The two white men who gave security for him did so not because he "belonged" to them in any sense, but rather because they knew he would show up in court and pay any judgment required of him—and, as the one solvent defendant in the case, White had to do just that in the end.[104]

Another of the few lawsuits filed against a black Israelite during the settlement's first twenty years showed not only that a free Afro-Virginian could prevail in court but also that a degree of prosperity could lead that man to embrace certain norms of the slaveholding community. By the dawn of the 1830s, Hampton Giles had the resources to hire occasional help, so he contracted with a white man to have carpentry done by that man's slave. By one estimate, the bondman did $60 worth of work on Giles's place; that amount, if accurate, would have covered a respectable dwelling or several outbuildings. The white slaveowner ultimately sued Hampton Giles, saying that the latter had not paid him for the bondman's work. The court dismissed the suit against Giles and in fact required the white plaintiff to pay damages and costs to the black man. As if to acknowledge the standing that Giles and his neighbors had achieved in county life, a document filed in court referred explicitly to Giles's place of residence as "Isrell Hill," taking for granted that people would be familiar with the settlement that went by that name.[105]

The use of slave workers did not take deep root on the Hill; the occasional purchase of a spouse or relative probably accounts for some if not all of the few enslaved individuals who lived there over the decades. Yet one does wonder about the 1830s and 1840s, when Sam White regularly kept a slave or two on his property, and when for a time he and Phil White each owned or hired two bondpeople.[106] These, too, may have been relatives—but perhaps not. Israel on the Appomattox, after all, was a community, not a utopian commune. Like their white neighbors, Israelites sought to make money, and they paid serious attention to IOUs, property lines, individual prerogatives, and businesslike arrangements.

When founding Israelite Isham Patterson drafted a will providing for his heirs to farm his land and support his widow, he called on his eldest son and son-in-law to settle on specific "terms" that they could "mutually agree upon" rather than enter haphazardly into their partnership.[107] One might attribute that formalism to Patterson's attorney rather than to the black man himself, except that so many other free Afro-Virginians behaved the same way.

Rose Johnston's daughter Rachel had married well; her husband, Phil White Jr., by then had become a prosperous, devoutly religious man. Yet Rose made sure in the depression year of 1838 to leave five of her twenty-five acres to her daughter *and her daughter's heirs,* foreclosing any possibility that her son-in-law might dispose of Johnston land according to his own lights. Like the Dungey family, the four surviving sons of Hercules White Sr. went to the county court in 1825 to have the land he left behind officially surveyed and divided among them "by metes and bounds," with the results entered in the official record; even Judy Randolph apparently had never bothered to do the latter when she parceled out the land on Israel Hill.[108]

Accordingly, free blacks proved ready to sue not only white people but also defendants of their own race. Phoebe Giles's action against Sooky White had concerned reputation, but most lawsuits filed by free blacks, like those of whites, revolved around money and property. The symbiosis between Phil White Jr. and Isaac Gibbs in the 1820s, in which each man provided a variety of goods and services to the other, had always been businesslike rather than altruistic, much like Hercules White's financial dealings with his black Israelite neighbors in the early days. For several years, Gibbs conscientiously made payments in cash and in kind for the construction of his house, and Phil White waited patiently. But when Gibbs had trouble coming up with the last $15, Phil did what countless white Prince Edward men and women did when neighbors or even family members owed them money: he sued.[109]

During the same period, the county court became an arena in which Israel Hill's only serious, long-lasting feud played itself out. The antipathy between the two parties, Hampton Giles and John Brown, extended back at least to the founding of the Hill in 1810–11. Giles said that Brown, son of the Randolph's esteemed valet Syphax, had prevailed on Judith to give his family a fifty-acre tract adjoining Hercules White's land; Giles had then received the smaller, less attractive plot farther up the Hill that Brown would have got otherwise.

In 1818, the dislike between the two men erupted into open conflict, and Hampton Giles filed suit against John Brown for assault and battery. Giles soon withdrew the action, perhaps after mediation by other black Israelites.[110] But the fall of 1825 brought another alleged attack by John Brown—this time, according to Giles's complaint, on "a certain man the property of" Giles. In reality, the victim in this incident was probably a slave whose labor Giles had hired; he did not actually own any bondpeople.[111] Hampton Giles himself felt physically threatened by John Brown, and the law offered a remedy. A person could ask a county justice to require an antagonist to sign a peace bond; by doing so, the signer guaranteed his own good behavior on pain of forfeiting a sizable amount of

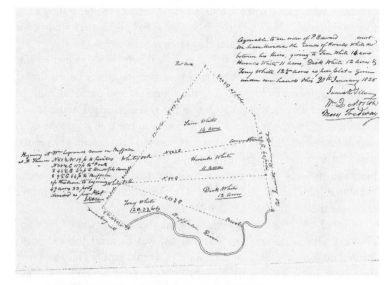

Black Israelites believed good fences made good neighbors. The four surviving sons of Hercules White Sr. asked the county court in 1825 to survey their late father's land and to divide it officially among them.

(*White v. White,* COUNTY COURT, JUNE 1825, ARCHIVES
RESEARCH SERVICES, LIBRARY OF VIRGINIA)

money. The county court summoned John Brown to appear before it in October 1825, presumably on Giles's complaint. For the time being, the court postponed further action.[112]

That delay proved costly to Hampton Giles: the following March, he came before a county grand jury and told it that Brown had recently assaulted him. Though only five feet three and nearing sixty at the time, John Brown must have had a volatile temper and much physical vigor; the grand jury "presented" (indicted) him for using a club to beat Giles, who was a dozen or more years younger and nearly six inches taller. The Commonwealth's attorney summoned two or three Israelites as witnesses. A jury convicted John Brown of assault and fined him $10, and the court required him to pay nearly that much again in costs.[113]

In the meantime, Giles had also got around to filing a civil suit against Brown for that alleged beating of Giles's hired worker the previous fall. What happened next showed that John Brown would not wait idly for another defeat. In early November 1826, as Giles's lawsuit against Brown made its way through the system, Giles and a prospective witness on his behalf, Israelite Guy Howard, found themselves accused of stealing a hog from a white planter. The two black men faced a summary trial before justices of the county court later that same month.

Hampton Giles was not a stupid man. It is impossible to picture him stealing a hog—from a longtime county justice and newly sworn sheriff, no less—and thereby jeopardizing the economic and personal gains he had achieved as a free person. One of the three principal witnesses, all Israelites, whom the prosecution summoned to the trial was none other than John Brown.[114] Brown thus stood poised to help destroy the reputation of the two key figures in Hampton Giles's pending lawsuit against him, and perhaps to bring about their incarceration. Indeed, it seems likely that John Brown had launched the prosecution by accusing his old enemy of theft.

A panel of five county justices heard the case against Giles and Howard. One of those men, Asa Dupuy, was General John Purnall's favored nephew and had conducted much of that family's business with its landowning free black neighbor Milly Homes and her family. Colonel Charles Woodson had served as guardian of the free black Epperson children, executed Betty Dwin's will, and seen to the emancipation of Dwin's son. A third justice, Samuel Carter, was the longtime administrator of the late Hercules White Sr.'s estate.[115] Justice Samuel V. Allen had issued the original warrant against Giles and Howard. Yet he had helped secure a deed of trust for free black landowner Ben Short years earlier, and he had played a similar role for former Randolph slave Billy Ellis only three years before the trial of Giles and Howard.[116] Given their fund of positive experience with free Afro-Virginians, these justices were perhaps even less inclined than the average tribunal in Prince Edward to find black defendants guilty without convincing evidence.

The court summoned a couple of slaves and half a dozen prominent whites to give testimony at the trial. These witnesses' words outweighed anything John Brown had to say; the court found Hampton Giles and Guy Howard not guilty.[117] Then, just a month after the court disposed of the hogstealing charge once and for all, Hampton Giles's suit against John Brown in the beating of Giles's hired slave went to a Prince Edward jury. Again, Giles prevailed. The jury required Brown to pay him some $30 in damages and costs.[118]

The rift between Brown and Giles was clearly unbridgeable. What had not happened on Israel Hill is no less striking, however. A feud as intense as this one, in a small neighborhood where everyone has known both antagonists for years, may force individuals to align themselves with one contending party or another, splitting the community in two. Yet neither this conflict nor other, less dramatic ones had riven Israel Hill into fixed, antagonistic camps. Sam White's experiences, for example, could have alienated him from Hampton Giles. The two men's wives had tangled in the poisoned-cabbage affair shortly after Israel Hill's settlement. Guy and Mely Howard were in Hampton Giles's corner at the moment, and Sam White had never liked that pair. White's daughter Jane had recently separated from her spouse, and the estranged husband had gone to live with Hampton Giles.[119]

Yet for all that, Sam White never became an enemy of the Gileses: Hampton's daughter had married Sam's son, and Sam's grandson Oby had moved in with the Giles family. Neither the Whites nor most other Israelites had fallen into the trap of choosing sides. Instead, over the years, they responded to each situation as it arose. Phil White Sr. even helped John Brown post bond at one point during his conflict with Giles; Brown had not ended up ostracized by the community he had helped to found. John Brown's father, Syphax, reputedly a centenarian, still lived with him, and that alone probably lent him some continued legitimacy.

To show forbearance toward John Brown remained a challenge, however, for he was determined to have revenge for his various defeats. Early in 1828, only a year after the hogstealing trial and Hampton Giles's civil suit ended, Brown took Giles back to the county court. Giles had no valid claim to the acreage he occupied on Israel Hill, Brown now alleged. Giles knew that the land rightfully belonged to the Brown family, he continued; therefore Giles was hastily "cutting down and carrying [from the tract] almost all of the valuable timber" and selling it to others before the court could make him hand it over to Brown. When John Brown, through his lawyer, called Giles "irresponsible" and asked the court to prevent him from "committing farther waste" on the disputed land, he was couching his plea in established legal formulae.[120] Yet the words "waste" and "irresponsible" were more than mere boilerplate terms. An elemental bitterness between two plain men bleeds through the overlay of jargon; the legal filings in *Brown v. Giles* embody a deeply felt argument over the stewardship of resources.

An ethic of hard work and frugality pervaded Prince Edward society, white and free black alike. Judith Randolph had toiled at spinning wheels and looms alongside her sister Nancy and her female slaves, and had ensured that her son St. George learned lathing as well as academic subjects so that he might grow up to "earn an honest subsistence." In later years, too, being "industrious and econamical" enhanced a man's reputation in Southside Virginia.[121] Accusations of wastefulness could imperil one's good name and become, as in John Brown's lawsuit, a weapon in disputes between one citizen and another. John Brown eventually permitted his suit to languish and die. But in the short term, he evoked from Hampton Giles a response so impassioned that even its transmission through Giles's white lawyer scarcely dilutes the original fire. Giles's formal answer came in a medley of tones: umbrage, scorn, sarcasm, and wounded but unbowed pride. At one point, the reply even resorts to a double exclamation point, making it perhaps unique among legal documents of the time and place.

Brown, Giles alleged, was claiming the Giles land only because Brown himself "had most shamefully cut down, sold, used & destroyed almost every stick of timber on the land given him [by Judith Randolph], and by bad cultivation nearly distroyed [the] soil." Giles maintained that he himself, far from wasting resources, had "been more careful of his timber than almost any one of the Isrealites"; he insisted that he had "sold none except when he was compeled to clear for timber to inclose his little plantation, and get land to cultivate."[122]

When he favorably compared his use of trees with that of his black neighbors, Giles was not casting aspersions on any of them, other than John Brown; to do that would render meaningless his claim of having been more careful than they. The families whose practices are documented at all—the Pattersons, Gibbses, and Whites, who together owned half of Israel Hill's total acreage—were still making prudent use of their timber after twenty years of sustainable harvesting of the kind their white neighbors practiced.[123] In his address to the court, then, Hampton Giles claimed his place in the ranks of sober farmers both black and white.

Hampton Giles's lawyer probably exaggerated the damage John Brown had done to his own land. Nevertheless, Brown, though the son of an impressive father, had apparently not become one of Israel Hill's success stories up to 1828. In fact, whether to escape financial problems or for some other reason, Brown had gone so far as to have his wife declare him dead in 1824. For two years running, the revenue commissioner's annual lists of free blacks reflected Brown's supposed demise. His "resurrection" had taken place not long before he crossed swords with Giles in late 1825 and 1826.[124]

When Hampton Giles said that John Brown had exploited his land "most shamefully," he was making a statement about his own worldview and about Brown's character. Giles expressed to the court his pride in having built one of the best homes and farms on Israel Hill and in having achieved a certain prosperity. "Let the sheriff of your county speak," Giles exhorted the court, "and you will then see" that he was a financially responsible taxpayer.

No attorney with an ounce of tactical sense would invent such bold language and put it in the mouth of a black client. The tone Giles used toward the white justices was his own; it exuded assertiveness and self-confidence rather than the exaggerated deference that the slaveholding system is supposed to have instilled in blacks. Hampton Giles considered himself a significant enough person that the sheriff would know him and his character. Like most other black Israelites, he had taken good care of his land—out of economic calculation, but also for a deeper reason: he believed literally that it was not merely unwise but also "shameful" to exploit land and timber heedlessly until they were exhausted.

Hampton Giles took it for granted that the county justices subscribed to the same ethics he did; he had lived under the austere, dollar-stretching regimen that Judy Randolph, a member of that elite, imposed at Bizarre. Yet he and other Afro-Virginians were showing every day that hard work and prudence were not white inventions. Free blacks shared those values and built livelihoods, and lives, around them.

To Inclose His Little Plantation: The Free Black Drive for Independence

Israelites and other free black landowners might share some basic assumptions with their propertied white neighbors, yet those Afro-Virginians never lost sight of their membership in a distinct people. White society with its exclusionary ideology reinforced that separateness, of course, but free blacks did not allow others to define their identity for them. Rather, they used their skills—and their small land-holdings, if they could acquire any—to bolster their autonomy. In doing so, they built a firmer base from which they could conduct their many interactions with white people.

Free Afro-Virginians who had no land strove to get some, but the days in which blacks—or, more precisely, mulattoes—in Prince Edward had managed to buy sizable tracts were all but over by the time the Hill was cleared. The Forgasons, the Evanses, and the Dungeys still held their farms of 100 to nearly 200 acres, but Sam White, the largest landholder on Israel Hill, owned only 64 acres even after he inherited part of the tract that had belonged to his father, Hercules. Most pieces of land bought by Afro-Virginians in Prince Edward after 1800 were smaller than that, even though some whites proved more than ready to sell to blacks. By the 1820s or so, investing in Farmville real estate seems to have looked more promising than buying a small farm, and free blacks who accumulated money more often than not put it to work that way or by purchasing and using capital equipment such as batteaux. Yet ownership even of small rural tracts still held powerful significance, both practical and symbolic, for free blacks. Economic life in the South centered on acquisition of land and slaves, and the typical Southerner of either race yearned for economic and personal autonomy. For free blacks, especially the many who had once been the property of other people, the word "independence" carried special meanings—freedom from white ownership of one's person, to be sure, but also from white control and supervision.[125]

Isham Smith, a blacksmith whose trade may have provided his surname, became a landowner in 1802. He had done well at his trade: from just one of his white clients in the 1790s, Smith earned enough in two years to cover his land purchase early in the new century. Smith's tract, in an area of substantial farms and plantations ten miles west of the courthouse, comprised one acre. It amounted to a mere "spott of land," as the deed called it; tracts that small were uncommon outside the town lots in Farmville and a few other villages. Smith's single acre was expensive, though; it must have contained a blacksmith shop out of which Smith was already working.[126]

Milly and Nathan Homes each managed to buy a few acres of land by 1820 after years of struggle; it would take Nathan another nine years to purchase a second little tract of about ten acres.[127] Neither Isham Smith nor the Homeses had any reason to think they would earn more money after acquiring land; on the contrary, such a purchase required an economic sacrifice. Moreover, they had lived peacefully on land owned by whites who behaved decently toward them—people, indeed, who in selling to them showed a willingness to have them as freeholding neighbors.

Buying land did bring some practical benefits. Slaves raised gardens of their own on tiny patches of earth, so free blacks knew they could grow a goodly fraction of their food on a small plot and produce a little "truck"—produce for sale—besides. They could also raise chickens and free-range hogs, and perhaps keep a cow. But landholding brought another benefit as well: the space to be more fully one's own man or woman. During the 1810s, when Milly Homes bought her land, she and her second daughter, Lucy, seem to have been saving money to buy two family members out of slavery. Yet even that goal did not induce them to sell off their little tract. They did not reside at all times on the ground they owned, but it always lay nearby to repair to if life on a white man's plantation became unpleasant. The land made the Homeses freer people, in their own minds and in the eyes of others.[128] Millions of white Americans, too, strove to acquire land. But the black drive for independence had about it a unique racial dimension. Among Afro-Virginians, the longing to own a spot of earth was the advanced expression of a dream of liberty that had arisen out of slavery itself.

The first step toward independence was simply to cease being a slave. The Israelites had received their liberty through the benevolent act of a master who abhorred slavery and a mistress who did her duty; yet even their road to freedom had been a hard and frustrating one, stretching over a span of many years. Slaves of other enlightened masters often had to serve well into adulthood before their manumissions took effect. Still other Afro-Virginians laboriously accumulated enough money on their own time to purchase their freedom.[129]

Most blacks who won their liberty had little hope of buying even the minimal amount of land that the Homeses and Isham Smith purchased, much less of acquiring larger tracts in a compact, all-black community like Israel Hill. But even free blacks who accepted one-year arrangements to live and work on the premises of white people did not typically find themselves with "little to set them apart from bond slaves," as one historian suggests.[130] Many, in fact, took care not to become tied down to any one white family. Moving from one place to another from year to year became common early on; many free black workers did not stay with any single employer for more than two or three years. The waxing and waning of white people's fortunes produced some of this mobility among those they employed. But Afro-Virginians had their own reasons to move about and choose their employers, as countless freedpeople would demonstrate once the Civil War brought freedom to all. Even bondman Jack Chaffin of Prince Edward, who thought enough of his master to adopt the white man's family name, elected to move to another person's land once he purchased his freedom early in the century.[131]

Then again, a white boss might force a free black worker to move elsewhere. But Thomas Bowman showed that even a landless Afro-Virginian could boldly assert his rights before his employer and the county court. Bowman was working on John B. Childress's farm in 1821, where he had something that was denied to slaves—a written labor contract. Bowman was to receive $50, ample food, and presumably housing, for his services during the year. If the black man should "abscond him self at any time," he would forfeit his entire annual wage; but should Childress "at any time drive . . . Bowman from his Employ," the contract obliged the white man to pay Bowman for the portion of the year he had worked. The contract afforded the white employer more protection than it did to his black hireling. But the document did entitle Bowman to his pay for all the time he served, and it is noteworthy that an Afro-Virginian could expect, perhaps demand, a written contract from his white employer in the first place. Moreover, Thomas Bowman's annual pay equaled or even exceeded that of some white men who hired out their labor on an annual basis.[132]

Childress and Bowman did lock horns at some point during the year, and Childress sent the black man packing, without paying him. So Bowman sued his white ex-employer. Childress defended himself vigorously, calling four white witnesses in his own defense. Yet a jury of twelve white men found for Bowman, awarding him $40 and forcing Childress to pay his former employee the $15 Bowman had spent in bringing the suit. Thomas Bowman, who in his work contract had what no slave possessed, had now done what no slave could do: he had resorted to the legal system to demand satisfaction from a white wrongdoer. Indeed, the amount he had won was greater than what many white overseers gained when they sued their employers for driving them away in the middle of a contract year. Moreover, Bowman apparently had options, and he chose his new employer well. Rather than move on after a year or two, as so many free blacks did, he was still working for the same man when the records break off four years later.[133]

Even when buying land was out of the question, a resourceful Afro-Virginian might fulfill his or her desire for independence, and for an additional boon—a life lived among other free blacks. Edmund Young, a short, black-skinned man born about 1783, was nothing if not imaginative, and he could assert himself as vigorously as Thomas Bowman later would. As the black Israelites were settling their new land, Young brought suit against a white man who he said had assaulted him; Young subpoenaed a second white man to testify on his behalf. The county court heard Young's suit on the very day that Israelite Jacob Johnston was acquitted of buying stolen corn. Although the jury gave Edmund Young only a token award, which often happened in suits for assault when juries considered both parties to be at fault, he had served notice that he would not passively accept abuse.[134]

Young appears in the records of Prince Edward, living alone, during the years when Hercules White Sr. was establishing himself as a free man. In fact, Young and White both worked at Allen & Fowler's mill. Young apparently even lived there for a while in 1805, the same time that White was performing various services and doing business at the mill.[135] Young wanted a place of his own, but he lacked the money or the opportunity to buy. He hit on a clever solution: he knew that a tract of eight hundred acres, to which no one had claimed title for many years, lay about six miles southwest of Prince Edward Court House. Young saw an opportunity: if he settled on part of that effectively ownerless land, it was quite possible that no one would challenge him. He proceeded to establish a farm and raise his family there.[136]

Other free blacks accepted the idea of settling on someone else's land, but preferred that the owner of that land also be black. Shoemaker and cooper Ben Short, whose house became a landmark on the Court House road, ultimately furnished that opportunity to nearly two dozen fellow Afro-Virginians. Short took on two free black boys as apprentices early in the century. He entered the ranks of landowners at the same time the black Israelites did when he bought the twenty-five acres surrounding the house he already lived in. Walthall Holcombe, Short's longtime landlord who sold him the tract, may have been friendly enough, but the white man extended the black buyer no charity: Short paid $7.60 per acre—a handsome price, but not exorbitant, given the tract's felicitous location from a tradesman's point of view. The land had considerable frontage on the main road—indeed, included land on both sides of it—near the northern terminus at Farmville. Short also got the right to use a spring that apparently remained part of Holcombe's property.[137]

The transaction with Holcombe testified to the frugality Short had practiced for years, and to the credibility he had built up among his white neighbors. The typical buyer of land, white or black, deferred payment on the bulk of the purchase price. But the deed of trust Short signed and a loan he took out covered only 40 percent of the cost of the tract; he may have paid the rest out of his savings and current earnings.[138]

The tract Ben Short had bought now became a magnet for others who shared the black drive for independence. Patty Bartlett had many connections with Short; for one thing, she was kin to—probably the mother of—Short's apprentice, Joe Bartlett. Patty saw an opportunity when Ben Short bought his little freehold. Within three years, she purchased one acre of his newly acquired twenty-five acres: a wedge of property about a hundred yards long and eighty wide at the broad end, with some road frontage of its own.[139]

Few acts could better exemplify the black drive for autonomy than Bartlett's little acquisition. Like his white former landlord Walthall Holcombe, Ben Short neither gouged Patty nor extended her any charity: Bartlett gave him $8 for the one acre, about 5 percent more than Short himself had paid. Bartlett could not expect to make much income from her tiny sliver of ground—unlike, say, Isham Smith, who had a blacksmith shop on his single acre. But she could do three other things: grow her own garden; feel herself mistress in her own house, however small the patch of ground it sat on; and provide a taste of independence to others. These things she proceeded to do, not instantly, but over the coming decade.

In 1821, apparently after several years' absence from the county, Patty Bartlett moved back onto the little place she had bought from Ben Short, and she brought five other Bartletts with her—all women and girls, possibly her own daughters and granddaughters. Two years later, Patty's kinsman, boatman Henry Bartlett, came with his wife and child to join the group. The following year, yet another boatman moved with his wife onto that single acre, which, after several additional births, was already home to nearly a dozen Bartletts. In the meantime, a couple of other free blacks had resided, possibly as renters, on the land left behind by Ben Short, who died in 1818.[140]

Short's modest purchase of land during Israel Hill's founding year had by now—a decade and a half later—afforded a new dimension of freedom not only to him but to at least twenty-three other Afro-Virginians. Many of these residents presumably either paid rent to the Shorts or the Bartletts, or otherwise contributed to the maintenance of the respective tracts, just as Patty Bartlett had paid Ben Short full market value for her one acre. The residents of the Short-Bartlett properties enjoyed the benefits of living in a cohesive Afro-Virginian mini-community, with all that may have meant socially and culturally. But they could have found these satisfactions on any of a number of plantations in Prince Edward where other free blacks lived, and where a bigger African American cultural fraternity existed in the slave quarters. Moving to Patty Bartlett's little patch of land did not even exempt one from the need to turn to whites for gainful work. There was but one plausible reason for free blacks to settle on the land of a Ben Short or a Patty Bartlett rather than somewhere else. That reason was the satisfaction of being responsible, in at least one important realm of life, to another black Virginian rather than to a white.

Short defended his own independence until his last days. As early as

1817, he knew that his health was failing; he must provide for his wife, Sylvia, and his son. He had one ready way to raise money: by selling his acreage. But Ben Short was unwilling to die on another man's land, or to require his wife to live out her life in such a place. His solution was to sell most of his tract—for a bit more per acre than he had paid for it—but to keep an acre or two on the north side of the road on which his house stood. Short also brought a free black woman into the household, perhaps to help his wife during his final illness and after his death.

Short's provision for his wife had to begin on the most basic level, for Sylvia Short was a slave—his slave. He had bought her from her previous master some time before; the law of 1806 requiring newly freed blacks to emigrate from Virginia must have persuaded him to keep her technically his property. But now he was dying, and the behavior of whites in Prince Edward during the dozen years since 1806 had been reassuring all in all. Short seems to have reckoned that no one would try to expel Sylvia if he emancipated her. He ordained that his wife go free, and that she have the use of his house and land for her lifetime as other free widows did.[141]

In the meantime, Israel Hill, too, attracted landless free blacks. The Israelites had made room from the beginning for former Randolph bondpeople, such as the two Phil Whites and Guy and Mely Howard, to whom Judith did not assign tracts. Boatman and shoemaker Ampy Brandum possessed the means to make a living and evinced no interest in farming, yet he, too, chose to live on Sam White's tract for a while during the Hill's early period. So did Polly Brandum, perhaps Ampy's sister, who brought her three children with her. Kit Strong, the weaver, and his wife—at least one and probably both of whom had been Randolph slaves—settled at Sam White's, too. Strong, who apparently lost his wife about 1819, moved away, returned, and left again. For him and a few others, the Hill may have offered a haven when fortunes waned in Farmville or elsewhere.[142]

When an Israelite married someone from outside the Hill, the option of rearing a family on ground owned by free Afro-Virginians proved attractive. That brides would join young Israelite husbands in those men's home community comes as no surprise; Jacob Johnston and George Patterson both married and established households in the settlement toward the end of its first decade. But the material and psychological pull of the Hill could also operate when Israelite women married men from the outside. Joe Bartlett came to Israel Hill in 1819 by marrying Polly Brandum, a tenant or guest on Sam White's land. Bartlett soon decided to take his wife and stepchildren and join his fellow boatmen and kinspeople in Farmville. But when outsider Edmund Clarke married Hannah, daughter of Israelite landowner Isham Patterson, and the couple began having children, Clarke and family moved onto the Hill to stay.[143]

Israel Hill also became home to free blacks who had no obvious ties of blood or marriage to the Randolph group. Robert Eldridge, nearly fifty, settled on and helped till John Brown's land. Eldridge, perhaps newly married, brought his wife to live with him there in 1817, and the pair stayed put.[144] Others dwelt on the Hill for periods ranging from one to a few years. Three or four boatmen, one of them with his wife and stepson, and a couple of younger women with their children, resided on various Israel Hill farmsteads during the settlement's first dozen years or so.[145]

In that period, eight of the nine freeholds on the Hill took in at least one resident who was not a member of the owner's immediate family; six tracts became home to more than one such person. Although Sam White and his wife, Susan, had thirteen to fifteen children and grandchildren living with them at any given time, they received at least twenty-nine other people for varying periods of time during the settlement's first decade. Hannah and Edmund Clarke spent five years at Sam's even though Hannah's father, Israelite Isham Patterson, maintained cordial ties with the pair. White's land became so attractive—whether owing to its advantageous location, or to White's personality and organizational skills, or to favorable financial terms he may have offered tenants—that Kit Strong's children remained there even after their father left.[146]

Some persons' relatively brief sojourns on the Hill remind us again that the tendency of free blacks to seek independence from whites and togetherness with one another was just that, a tendency rather than an iron law of behavior. Ampy Brandum left Sam White's tract and moved onto a white man's land by 1818; he contradicted the normal pattern among free blacks by staying there for years. Jack Baker was emancipated by his master and mistress at about the time the Israelites became free; he settled at one point on the land of the biracial Dungey family. Yet within a year or so, whether for economic reasons or personal ones, Baker moved to an adjoining plantation owned by a white man.[147]

Still, the drive to enhance one's independence remained widespread among the Israelites and other free blacks, partly because the negation of black freedom surrounded them and continued to touch the lives of many all too intimately. Ben Short had managed to liberate his enslaved wife; other free blacks, like Betty Dwin and Tony White, died leaving a husband, wife, or children in bondage. Still others, like Rose Johnston, lived apart from their enslaved spouses. Marriages that can be firmly documented among the second generation on Israel Hill show a continued preference for choosing a lifetime spouse; it seems likely, then, that some, and possibly most, of the women of the second generation for whom the records reveal children but no husbands were in fact married to slaves.

To see vividly what it could mean to be wedded—literally—to slavery, the Israelite pioneers could look also to the white family that lived next door. Archer Allen, whose plantation lay between Israel Hill and the Appomattox River, died just as the new community was founded. Archer's ambitious son, William A. Allen, former deputy sheriff and county tax collector, by then kept twenty-one slaves on a spread some four miles upriver from Israel Hill as the crow flies.[148] Allen was a close friend and associate of Colonel Charles Woodson, the county justice, and he shared Woodson's transracial eye for talent and industry. Betty Dwin and her grown son eventually moved onto Allen's plantation; Allen witnessed Dwin's last testament, and he hired the labor of her son-and-slave, Harry. It was to William Allen that Woodson apprenticed one of the free black Epperson youngsters who had been left in his charge. In 1822, Allen would serve as foreman of the jury that awarded substantial damages to the discharged free black hired man Thomas Bowman.[149]

Years before that trial, Allen himself had hired a free black man named Phil Bowman, who may well have been Thomas Bowman's brother, to run his grist mill. During the period just before Israel Hill's founding, official documents casually recognized the important part Bowman had come to play in running William Allen's operations. The county's annual tax rolls sometimes listed a man with his son or another family member—or, rarely, a master with his apprentice; William A. Allen and Phil Bowman were the only biracial pair listed in all of Prince Edward County in the years around 1810. Once the two appear as "Allen William a. & P.B.," as if Bowman were so well known that anyone would know who "P.B." at Allen's mill was.[150]

When it came to slaves, however, William Allen was all business. He bought and sold blacks, and hired them out; he made sure he received the money that was coming to him, even if he had to sue his own brother to get it. In language more explicit than most planters used, Allen required his overseer to keep his slaves "in Strict subjection having a regard to humanity."[151]

Phil Bowman acquired a special stake in William Allen's enterprises when he married Priscy, one of Allen's slaves. Then, in the latter 1810s,

Allen began to suffer financial reverses; by 1819, he landed in serious trouble as the national economic crisis flooded Prince Edward's county court with suits for bad debts. Allen's friends and associates, and even his family, started calling in their loans to him. Awash in lawsuits, William Allen sold his prized plantation on the Appomattox to a brother in 1821 and had much of his personal property auctioned off. He would still be struggling to recover nearly a decade after the Panic of 1819.[152]

For Phil Bowman, who had long since left Allen's employ, a planter's crisis threatened to become a black family's disaster. From 1819 to 1823, William Allen surrendered some ten slaves to secure payment of various court judgments against him. It is not clear whether all ten were actually sold by the sheriff, or whether Allen met some of his obligations by other means. But at least one human being did end up on the sheriff's auction block: Phil Bowman's wife, Priscy.[153] Another man from the neighborhood might buy her, leaving the Bowmans no worse off than before—or a slave trader might enter the high bid and take Priscy a thousand miles away.

Before Phil Bowman attended the sale of his wife, he spoke with Robert Venable Jr., son of a man for whom Bowman had worked as a miller years earlier and to whose employ he had now returned. The two men made an agreement: the younger Venable would lend Bowman the money he needed to bid for Priscy, and the black man, if he managed to purchase her, would gradually pay the money back out of his earnings as the Venables' miller.[154] The record does not tell whether Bowman faced spirited competition at the sheriff's auction, or whether the other potential bidders allowed him to buy his own wife at a moderate price. Either way, the plan he had made with Venable succeeded, and the black couple were reunited.

This happy ending to the Bowmans' story does not temper the magnitude of the tragedy that might have occurred, and it should not obscure the way this near catastrophe came about. The planter whose personal misfortune nearly led to the Bowmans' separation was, by the standards of the world he inhabited, a decent man. William Allen had allowed the Bowmans, indeed encouraged them, to live together. The regret Allen felt over the fate of the bondpeople he lost during his economic crisis seems genuine, if expressed too tepidly for modern tastes: he found it "very disagreeable" to have to sell one Venus and her family, as "she [had] been faithful" in his service, and he hoped he could at least persuade his enlightened friend, Colonel Woodson, to buy her.[155]

To compound the irony, William Allen became a party to the scatter-

THE CONDITION OF THE ABOVE OBLIGATION IS SUCH, That whereas *John Tuggle & Wm Penick assignees of Martin Pearce* ha*th* sued out of the *county* Court of *Prince Edward* a writ of *Fieri Facias* against the goods and chattels of the above bound *Wm A. Allen & Edward Booker* _____ upon a Judgment obtained in said Court; which writ, with the legal costs attending the same, amounts to the sum of *One hundred & forty five pounds, three shillings & two pence* _____ and directed to the Sheriff of *Prince Edward* And _____ *James Foster* _____ a deputy for *Edmund Lockett* _____ Sheriff of the said County of *Prince Edward* by virtue of the said writ, hath taken the following property, belonging to the said *Wm A. Allen* _____ to satisfy the same, to wit: *Four negroes Prissy, Monroe, Jennet & Jourdan*

William A. Allen's financial failure and John Tuggle's lawsuit against him put Priscy, the enslaved wife of free black miller Phil Bowman, on the auction block.

(DELIVERY BOND, *Tuggle and Penick v. Allen*, COUNTY COURT, AUGUST 1822, ARCHIVES RESEARCH SERVICES, LIBRARY OF VIRGINIA)

ing of innocent bondpeople through the actions of equally upstanding men who had been his friends. Those whose lawsuits helped seal Allen's fate and that of his slaves ultimately included Woodson himself, as well as three white neighbors of Israel Hill whose relations with the black Israelites had been at least civil, and in one case downright cordial.[156]

None of those men had anything against Phil and Priscy Bowman or evinced hatred of blacks as a race. At least two of Allen's creditors sat on a county court that had shown itself capable of treating assertive free Afro-Virginians fairly. As so often happened, though, African Americans found themselves knocked about not only by overtly hostile white individuals but also by the troubles of whites and by conflicts among whites that had nothing to do with them—and this because all lived in a system molded by white people largely to exploit blacks. Phil Bowman no doubt appreciated Venable's help, and he could accept that assistance with his head held high. After all, he had earned the white man's esteem by dint of his character and his skilled work, and he would pay back the amount it had taken to ransom Priscy. Still, having seen his domestic life placed in grave danger by the slaveholding system, Bowman, though free, had had to turn to a slaveholder for redemption.

In such a system, the drive for independence remained powerful even among those blacks who had already achieved some success in life. The drive expressed itself variously in different situations. Slaves aspired to freedom. Landless free blacks exercised their liberty to move about, or sought a home with propertied blacks, or struggled to buy land of their own. Those who already possessed land strove to advance their fortunes, and they often accommodated the aspirations of their fellows.

But independence did not imply withdrawal. Paradoxically, to defend and enhance their independence, free blacks had to assert their rights within the white-run institutions under which they lived—and they had to take part in the local economy. Slavery had produced skilled black workers, some of whom, on and off Israel Hill, now lived in freedom and sought to ply their trades among whites who worked at the same occupations. Amid the fabric of interactions that had always connected the two races, no strands stood out more prominently than those of work and trade. Hampton Giles might, as he put it, "inclose his little plantation" with timber fencing, but he could not and would not wall it off from the outside world.

CHAPTER 4

Work

SWEATING LIKE A HARVEST FIELD HAND

Hercules White Sr.'s eclectic life as a worker fitted him perfectly for the society he lived in. The typical resident of Prince Edward—whether white or black, slave or free—was a jack, if not of all trades, then at least of two and sometimes of more. A number of active planters also practiced occupations such as medicine, law, and land surveying; farmers worked as blacksmiths and carpenters. At the same time, some craftsmen used the proceeds of their labor to *become* farmers or planters. Many men, both white and black, actively worked at two or more skilled trades—at different times, or even simultaneously. Women, too, including some from well-off households, worked to earn money, often at more than one craft.

Hercules White's sons displayed something of their father's versatility. Tony and Hercules Junior continued to ply the coopering trade, even though young Hercules devoted the majority of his time to farming; elder brother Sam White or members of his household did the same. Sam and Hercules received payments for hogsheads and a whiskey barrel from white neighbor John Tuggle and others at least as late as 1830.[1] Tony White made coopering his primary occupation for some three years in the early 1820s, yet he also worked as a boatman and tilled the family's land during Israel Hill's first decade and a half. Outside the Hill, cooper-shoemaker Ben Short and miller Phil Bowman, who had also worked as a farmer and boatman, showed the same kind of flexibility.[2]

Plantations in Prince Edward had always valued enslaved craftspeople, who labored for their own masters and performed work that their owners undertook for others; such slaves could also bring in handsome amounts when hired out.[3] As exploitative as slavery obviously was, not all the fruits of bondpeople's labor went to their masters. Accounts throughout the period from Israel Hill's founding to the Civil War—whether of mercantile stores, plantations, or estates of deceased persons—record countless transactions in which payments for goods or services went to parties such as "negro Dilcy," "Franky (a negro)," "servant Solomon," or "Baldwin's Moses."[4] Bondpeople both male and female received payment, usually in modest amounts, for cotton, tar, hay, horse collars, chickens, and other items. One Virginia farmer paid his bondpeople more than $100 in 1835 for furnishing produce ranging from cucumbers to walnuts, as well as for trapping hares and making products that included "shoes for neighbouring slaves" and persimmon beer—a prodigious output from a group of only seven slaves, most of whose time was not their own.[5]

The Penick plantation near Israel Hill regularly paid its slaves for corn they had grown, or for tobacco; other local planters routinely drew up detailed "statements of negroes' corn."[6] In the years around 1850, an enslaved shoemaker named Abram enlisted someone's help to present white customers with formal bills. A few whites even paid interest to slaves when payments to the blacks were delayed, though the amounts naturally were small. Some parties—though by no means all—seem to have paid slaves below-market rates. On the other hand, one slaveowner compensated a bondman named Abraham in 1839 by setting up a separate store account for him, through which Abraham purchased $10 worth of merchandise, including an umbrella, a bonnet, fabrics, and provisions.[7]

Amid this commerce between whites and slaves—so matter-of-fact and so orderly—similar traffic between whites and free blacks seemed perfectly normal. Free blacks who resided on white persons' property did business not only with their landlords or employers but with other whites, too; those who had land of their own or lived in Farmville, especially those who practiced skilled occupations, also traded frequently with white people.[8] Here, then, was one realm in which free black life did somewhat resemble that of slaves—not because daily economic activity ground free Afro-Virginians down to the level of bondpeople, but rather because slaves participated more fully in the economy than their status as chattels suggests.

Even so, free status made a great difference in an Afro-Virginian's economic life. For one thing, free blacks purchased the labor of white people's slaves on occasion, as Israelite Hampton Giles did. In 1824, free black Sam Short hired Queen, an enslaved woman of about twenty-seven, from the Chambers plantation near Israel Hill for the entire year. In the following decade, Sam White at one point hired a slave named Harry.[9]

Most individual payments to free Afro-Virginians for goods or services recorded around the time of Israel Hill's settlement were as modest as the sums that slaves often received, from 30-odd cents to a few dollars. But a free black could earn many more such payments during the course of a year than could a slave, who had only limited free time. When a certain free Phil—not one of the Whites of Israel Hill—died about 1814, one white man owed him nearly $140.[10]

Many free Afro-Virginians, rather than settle into a paternalistic relationship with any one white person, sold their skilled labor or the fruits of their crafts to clients far and wide. All three of the Ellises did jobs at the Chambers place, but only one lived there most of the time; Billy Ellis bought a town lot of his own in 1819. The Homeses performed work or supplied goods for many whites other than their neighbors and sometime employers, the Purnall-Dupuys. The Dupuys did deliver to the elderly Milly Homes some of the corn meal that she had purchased from them, but the tenor of the Homes-Dupuy mill transactions of the 1820s was businesslike rather than charitable or indulgent on the whites' part.[11]

With such independence came burdens: masters provided regular medical attention to their slaves, but even free blacks who lived on white people's farms or plantations do not seem to have received doctors' services very often. Phil White Jr., Billy Ellis, Joe Bartlett, and probably additional free persons arranged and paid for doctors' visits on their own; others likely had less access to medical care than slaves did.[12]

The institution of bondage could still affect the working lives of free black craftspeople in ways their white counterparts never had to deal with. When cooper Tony White spent the years from 1822 to 1824 living at a white person's place, he was not the first early settler on Israel Hill who had left—but he was the first landowner to do so. The woman onto whose premises White moved lived in the northeastern corner of the county; she may well have owned his wife Milly, whom he had not yet managed to buy out of bondage.[13]

The pioneering historian of slavery, Ulrich B. Phillips, wrote in 1918 that rural free blacks "found a niche . . . much on a level with the slaves but as free as might be from the pressure of systematic competition." In fact, many skilled free blacks in Prince Edward not only did better for themselves than Phillips thought; they achieved this by holding their own among whites who plied the same trades.[14] White and free black craftsmen faced a common challenge: to survive in an economy where many slaves practiced the very occupations that they themselves did. It is difficult to compare directly what a customer would pay for a given job done, say, by a slave blacksmith with the fee that a white smith would earn. Yankees and disaffected white Southerners of the time believed, plausibly enough, that the availability of the slave inevitably depressed the earnings of the free man. Clearly, however, white blacksmiths and carpenters and shoemakers did continue to work, and some of them prospered.

White craftsmen showed little ability to unite around their whiteness, their class identity, or anything else. Some of Prince Edward's carpenters did try in the 1810s to agree on a unified schedule of prices. But when a prominent citizen complained that he had been overcharged by a carpenter he had hired, at least seven other white practitioners of that trade weighed in on the issue with an array of opinions, some of them supporting the customer over their fellow craftsman. The original carpenter had no desire to submit to arbitration by a delegation of his peers, each of whom, he said, would claim he could have done the job more cheaply than the others. That, he added, "was the way with workmen."[15] If it occurred to this beleaguered craftsman to blame black workers, slave or free, for the surplus of carpenters hungry for work, he did not say so. Skilled "mechanics" in Prince Edward County never coalesced to exclude free blacks from their crafts, any more than they did for any other purpose. The abundance of skilled workmen chasing a limited number of jobs could have allowed employers to draw a color line in hiring, had they wished to. But the absence of a discernible guild impulse among white craftsmen offered employers a much more attractive option: they could choose whatever tradesperson they believed would do the best job on the best terms—regardless of race, as it often turned out.

Josiah Cheadle's plantation lay in the western part of the county, just inside the partition line that would be drawn when Appomattox County was formed in 1845. Cheadle and his siblings owned additional land in Campbell County near Lynchburg; he frequently sold tobacco in that city and in Petersburg. Josiah left behind a disorderly but detailed ledger recording his economic dealings with whites and free blacks of his neighborhood.[16]

Near the Cheadles lived the free black Forgason family. Jethro Forgason Sr. owned a hundred acres of land, yet Charles Forgason, probably Jethro's brother, and Jethro's own six sons earned money at carpentry as well. House carpenters by definition moved from one job to the next; in 1819, all the Forgasons were residing on white people's property when the revenue commissioner drew up his annual list. Jethro sold off his land between 1820 and 1823; he may have fallen victim to the economic depression. Four years later, he received $20 in support from the county's overseers of the poor while under the care of a white neighbor—a form of aid that connoted economic need but not personal disgrace.[17]

Fortune had buffeted the Forgasons, but they retained their independent spirit. Amid all their peregrinations, the men of the family showed a preference for living alongside one another in groups of two, three, or more, and a reluctance to tie themselves down permanently to particular whites. No Forgason male spent more than three of the nine years from 1817 to 1825 with any one employer.[18]

None of the Forgasons settled on Josiah Cheadle's land, at least not through 1825, but various men of the family worked for him at both agriculture and carpentry. In the early spring of 1835, for example, Cheadle hired Charles Forgason to build a tobacco house. The planter recorded in writing the terms of the two men's agreement, just as he often did when he engaged a white craftsman.[19] Although Forgason was black and almost certainly nonliterate, he and planter Cheadle arrived at terms that a white carpenter would readily have agreed to. Tobacco houses varied considerably in size; building one could cost as much as $40 or as little as $7. In the early 1820s, Cheadle himself had apparently given three white men about $23 for building a tobacco house. He agreed to pay Charles Forgason $26.[20]

Under his contract with the planter, Forgason was to "find himself," which in the parlance of the time meant that he had to secure the materials to build the tobacco house. "Finding" for such a structure was often reckoned at one quarter to one third the overall cost of the job, so Forgason's net pay probably amounted to about $18 or $20. That was a substantial amount: Cheadle had recently given a white employee $35 and a modest house to live in as payment for serving nearly a full year, far more time than Forgason would work; another of the planter's white employees got only $14 minus provisions for nearly six months' labor.[21]

In other particulars, too, Charles Forgason struck a respectable deal. When an employer in Prince Edward hired a carpenter of either color, he might merely promise to pay, on completion of the job, "so much money as [the craftsman] therefor reasonably deserved to have."[22] Forgason expected better, and he got it: the agreement with Cheadle not only set the black carpenter's fee up front but established further terms to which Cheadle attached specific numbers. Craftsmen and free laborers in the area typically received foodstuffs and other goods from the employer, who deducted the costs from the worker's pay when the two of them settled accounts at the end of the job.[23] Cheadle undertook to furnish Charles Forgason with provisions "at the neighborhood price," a potential hedge in the employer's favor. But then, perhaps at Forgason's insistence, the planter went on to specify exact figures for corn, wheat, and bacon, the only three commodities Forgason would receive. Those prices were indeed the going rates at the time.

The Forgason family had decades of experience at farming, and their agrarian skills, too, interested Josiah Cheadle. The most lucrative kind of hired farm labor was harvesting wheat and other grains. Charles Forgason had supplemented his income at least as early as 1805 by reaping on a local plantation; one of Hercules White Sr.'s sons harvested grain in the same period, and Israelite Ampy Brandum cut hay in 1824, when shoemaking was his regular occupation.[24] Hands employed in the harvest ordinarily worked a twelve-hour day. Workers cut wheat or oats in Prince Edward by hand, not by machine, throughout the slave era and beyond, and it was hard labor. The job had to be done quickly, under a hot summer sun, after the grain ripened but before bad weather could intervene and damage the crop; every rural Southerner knew well the meaning of the popular expression "sweating like a harvest field hand."[25]

This requirement for haste led planters to hire additional help for "cutting." By definition, the work was available only a small number of days each year, but it commanded a high wage: $1 a day, or the equivalent paid in the crop being harvested, namely, a bushel a day for most of the period up to the Civil War. That easily beat the 50 cents that employers often paid for both white and hired slave labor, and even the 75 cents many skilled craftsmen earned in a day.[26]

Charles Forgason and other carpenter-farmers of his clan had begun cutting grain for Cheadle long before Charles built Cheadle's tobacco house. Charles himself and four of Jethro Forgason Sr.'s sons put in twenty-odd man-days in Cheadle's harvest of 1822, mostly in wheat; men of the family continued to harvest on the same plantation from time to time well into the 1830s. John Forgason, who may have been Jethro's grandson, would spend eight days cutting for Cheadle as late as 1845.[27]

White men had taken extra work as harvesters in Prince Edward at least as far back as the late eighteenth century, and in theory, planters could have tried to hire free black cutters for less pay than they gave whites. But in fact, the $1-a-day rate had long prevailed for white, free black, and enslaved workers alike—though in the case of bondmen, much if not all of the daily wage doubtless went to the slaves' owners. Black and white cutters not only did the same work for the same pay, but in some and probably many cases, they did it together.[28] Charles Forgason and another free black man reaping on the Flournoy estate in 1805, for instance, had been joined in the middle of their four days there by a slave and a white man. Years later, on Cheadle's land, Forgason, his relatives, and a free black neighbor again worked at the same tasks and wages as white men did, apparently side by side with them.[29] After all, white cutters routinely labored alongside their employers' slaves; working next to free blacks can hardly have felt much different. The racial etiquette that reinforced the caste system did not fade out completely even at harvest time: in his ledger, Josiah Cheadle never applied the title "Mr." to a free black, while he did attach that title to two white cutters on a single occasion. At other times, however, Cheadle referred to white harvesters only with a surname, or designated all free cutters of both races uniformly with first and last names.[30]

White men who cut grain for Cheadle toiled in the company of one black (or mulatto) man who had lived for years with a white wife. Stephen Forgason and his spouse were presented by a grand jury in 1828 for committing "fornication"—though the interracial character of the union was the real issue in the eyes of those who brought the charge. The prosecutor barely pursued the case and ultimately declined to follow it through; the federal census of 1830 still found Stephen Forgason living with a white woman in her thirties—presumably his wife, Susan Selbe—and with an aged white woman as well, perhaps Susan's mother. Stephen Forgason's domestic arrangements seem to have mattered even less to Josiah Cheadle than they did to the local prosecutor; Forgason's relationship with Susan did not cause the kind of friction with Cheadle's white hirelings that would have dissuaded the planter from keeping the free Afro-Virginian on the job. Forgason continued to cut grain for Cheadle from the early 1820s at least through the mid-1830s.[31]

Cheadle showed no inclination to favor his white workers. Ever the sharp trader, he readily bought wheat from a fellow white man for a mere 80 cents a bushel when he could drive such a bargain. After the harvest of 1822, the planter paid Charles Forgason in cash and Jesse Forgason partly so, while one of Cheadle's young white neighbors had to settle for an IOU that he could redeem only at Christmas. Strikingly, many planters and farmers allotted only half as much for feeding black temporary workers—at least those who were enslaved—as they did for whites. Yet even on one local plantation that recorded such discrimination in allocations for day workers' board, wages themselves were determined according to performance rather than race.[32]

Cheadle, like other planters, kept running accounts with workers and neighbors both black and white. The hirelings bought provisions from him, and he often issued payment to workers or craftsmen in the form of bacon, corn, salt, sugar, wheat, or shoe leather. White men, free blacks, and slaves exchanged "orders" that could be cashed or spent at Cheadle's place.[33] A white skin by itself afforded no advantage in this local commerce. Charles Forgason at one time got corn from Cheadle at as little as 60 cents a bushel. All in all, Cheadle and others in his position seem to have charged whatever the market would bear, no matter whom they were trading with.[34]

In Shadrach Forgason's account with Cheadle for 1834, however, the planter seems to have shortchanged the black man by $1.00. Then, in the lengthy tally for 1835, Cheadle made errors in both directions, but at one point arrived at a running total $9.00 in excess of what Forgason actually owed him, a discrepancy of nearly 50 percent.[35] However that second error arose—Cheadle kept chaotic records—the planter did correct the bottom line, entering a final figure of $21.08 in thick strokes of his pen on top of the earlier overcharge. Either Cheadle caught and rectified his own mistake, or Forgason challenged the erroneous figure and had the planter recalculate. Meanwhile, smaller overcharges in Cheadle's accounts with white men went uncorrected, and the planter had no qualms about buying hanks of silk from a merchant for the standard price yet selling one to an unlettered white employee at a 100 percent markup.[36]

Planters applied the term "hireling" itself cross-racially: a slave hired out for the year was a hireling, but so was a man of any color, other than an overseer, who worked for wages on a plantation, even if he earned the enviable $1 a day for harvesting. White cutters who toiled with blacks were not necessarily rootless, marginal characters, however, any more than their free black fellow reapers were. A number of Cheadle's white harvesters bore surnames—Faris, Hughes, Cason—shared by neighbors with whom the planter had extensive and respectful dealings over many years, and who in at least two instances owned land. One white man who, along with a member of the Forgason family, received pay from Cheadle for cutting grain in 1834 seems to have been a blacksmith with whom Cheadle dealt regularly—a man who earned substantial income from his regular trade during the balance of the year.[37]

Fuqua Cason lived across the Appomattox River in Buckingham County and spent a full sixteen days cutting wheat for Cheadle in 1822 and 1823; in the former year, he seems to have worked with two of the

Forgasons. Fuqua was then in his teens or very early twenties; he shared his pay with his mother, who was probably Sally Cason, owner of at least four slaves.[38] Fuqua could plausibly hope to rise higher with age and hard work—and fear falling lower should luck not break his way; he could improve his fortunes at least slightly by sharing the high-paying work at Cheadle's with men the same color as his mother's slaves. Cutters both black and white proved flexible and adaptable. Reaper and carpenter Charles Forgason also hauled tobacco and fodder to Farmville for Chea-dle; Sill Faris, a white man who cut wheat for the planter in 1834, made at least seventeen pairs of shoes for him the following year, and another white cutter repaired a cart for Cheadle in 1840.[39]

Josiah Cheadle was no altruist—he and men like him never parted casually with a dollar or a prerogative. When a white employee damaged a spade, Cheadle docked him a day's pay to repair the tool. If one of the white smiths Cheadle used failed to carry out his exact instructions, he required that the man do the work over. Again and again, Cheadle wran-gled in court with white neighbors over land and resources, with his overseers over their compensation, with a blacksmith and a ditcher over their fees, and with a nearby tenant farmer who Cheadle said had beaten him with a stick.[40]

The planter handled his slaves with equal calculation, treating them as kindly or as harshly as he believed he needed to in order to extract the results he desired. Cheadle took care to provide "Brandy for the negroes when wet of [a] storm." But he also ordered leg irons and handcuffs from the blacksmith—and doubtless had them redone if the workmanship fell short of his high standards. The one category of human beings with whom Cheadle never had a recorded conflict was free blacks, unless Shadrach Forgason did indeed challenge the figures in the planter's ledger—and Cheadle conceded that point.[41]

Josiah Cheadle's experience with the Bryant family in 1832 and 1833 shows what he was up against when he dealt with some of his resident white employees. Jack Bryant stopped working and then simply "went home." Alec Bryant soon began missing nearly one day's work out of every eight on average. Their kinsman William Bryant broke one con-tract with Cheadle, and later lit out twice for extended, unauthorized sojourns in Farmville. Yet the planter took him back each time and ulti-mately even raised his pay, perhaps in hopes of securing better behavior; William Bryant then "worked 2 days & quit." During his last month on the job, William took at least a third of his wages in whiskey—nearly three gallons of the stuff in a mere two weeks; he may have been too inebriated by the end of April to realize that Cheadle, in a small act of revenge, had doubled the price of the liquor he issued to Bryant.[42]

The contrasts between William Bryant and Charles Forgason can hardly have been lost on Josiah Cheadle and others in the area. Unlike a slave—and unlike Bryant, it seems—Forgason did not live with or get his daily bread directly from the white planter; he planned the tobacco house, selected and prepared the materials for its construction, and worked at his own speed, probably without reporting day by day to anyone. Forgason, though black in a society whose rulers were white, had won the extra measure of freedom that skill and reliability could command.

William Bryant, too, though not well-off, had substantial room to assert his independence—because he was white, perhaps, but also because he, too, at first appeared to possess qualities that Josiah Cheadle valued. Yet the white Bryants, in stark contrast to the black Forgasons, did not carry themselves in a way that garnered respect; William in particular asserted his freedom in ways that harmed his own interests and alienated others. A planter like Josiah Cheadle had to be a businessman as well, finding what worked and getting it at a good price. White solidarity would not reform a William Bryant, nor would it mend a cart or build a tobacco house properly.

Booker T. Washington's prediction that African Americans would earn the respect of whites by doing outstanding work may in fact have proved truer for free blacks in old Virginia—two or three generations before Washington broached the idea—than it ever would again. Ironically, whites could afford to recognize free black individuals as skillful, upstanding, productive members of society in part because most of their fellow Afro-Virginians remained enslaved. That fact insulated free black achievement from any suspicion that it posed a threat to white supremacy.

Again and again throughout the South's racial history, professed ideology gave way to white people's practical wants. Even during the darkest days of Jim Crow segregation in the latter nineteenth and early twentieth centuries, for example, the widespread racist belief that blacks were unclean would not prevent whites from employing African Americans to prepare their food.[43] Josiah Cheadle was no philosopher, and certainly no friend of emancipation. He simply knew from experience that neither blacks nor whites held a monopoly on laziness or dissipation—or on virtue.

Color still mattered in the world of work: neither Cheadle nor anyone else in Prince Edward seems ever to have hired a black overseer, and the entire system rested on racial slavery. But it was clear to all—even to the ideologues when they made practical, day-to-day decisions—that there were reliable and unreliable, skilled and unskilled, bright and dim people among both races, and that life abounded with situations in which it made more sense to apply that insight than to impose a simple racial test. Through their behavior as workers and as men and women, many free Afro-Virginians reinforced that conclusion and took full advantage of its consequences.

CRAFT, MYSTERY, AND OCCUPATION

Over the decades, dozens of young free blacks in Prince Edward County worked neither under renewable annual contracts with whites nor at odd jobs such as building corn houses, hauling cargo, and cutting wheat. An apprenticeship stationed a boy or girl with a particular employer, usually a white person, for a period of years. Free children and adolescents both white and black were "bound out" as apprentices either by the children's parents, or by the county overseers of the poor in concert with the county court. An apprentice lived with a master, worked for him or her, and submitted to the master's control until age twenty-one—or, in the case of girls, until eighteen. In return, the master signed an indenture: a contract promising, in an ancient phrase, to teach the apprentice the "craft, mystery, and occupation" of carpentry, tailoring, sewing, or some other trade.

Slave labor was moderately priced in old Virginia. At the time Israel Hill was taking shape and Forgason men were clearing $1 a day as occasional harvesters, the labor of a good hired-out slave sawyer fetched as little as a third of that figure; the services of an enslaved carpenter with minimal qualifications ranged from just a bit more than that up to about 50 cents a day.[44] Even with slave help so attractive, though, white craftspeople had good reasons to take on apprentices. The system gave the apprentice an incentive to work hard that it denied to most slaves—the possibility of becoming a self-sustaining, even prosperous adult craftsperson. The master or mistress profited from the apprentice's ambition for years on end; he or she wielded nearly the same degree of control over the youngster as a parent would over a child, and usually furnished in return only room, board, simple clothing, and a single cash payment of as little as $12 at the very end of the apprentice's term. By contrast, the annual cost of hiring a typical slave boy from his owner in the 1830s, over and above room, board, and clothing, could rise from $8 to $80 during seven years of his growing up.[45]

Nineteenth-century apprenticeship differed markedly from slavery. No one in that era was born into apprenticeship, and the institution included youngsters of both races. An apprentice's term was finite, and he or she could not be bought or sold. Yet to be bound out quite literally subjected a person to a form of servitude, sometimes from such an early age that the child had no real memory of any other way of life. One woman in Prince Edward at the turn of the century liberated a female slave and her three daughters, but specified that the girls be bound out until age twenty-one; the county assigned the children to three separate masters.[46] Of some four dozen indentures of free blacks contracted by the overseers of the poor from 1799 on and filed in county archives, over half and perhaps two thirds bound out children under age ten; eight or nine blacks were five years old or less when indentured. Only two contracts for black apprentices younger than ten cite the death of both parents as the reason for such early placement; in a few cases, the authorities did at least put small children together with elder siblings. The overseers apprenticed whites, too, before they turned ten—and as early as age three or four in a couple of instances—but black children were much more likely to be placed at tender ages.[47]

Whatever the potential drawbacks, parents of both races and different classes actively sought apprenticeships through which their sons could learn some "mechanical business." A prominent attorney in Prince Edward in 1787 wanted to supplement his sons' "liberal Education" with apprenticeships. On the latter, he explained, "will probably depend whether they shall become acquainted with the habits of morality, Industry & good Manners."[48] A far less affluent white woman, Bidy Godsey, implored the county court in 1810 to "come up & doo something with my Children for they are Suffering & I donte know what to doo with them." The court soon bound out her two sons. Free black John Dungey, son and heir of James and Elizabeth, fell between those two economic extremes. Should his two minor sons not assist his widow adequately, Dungey decreed in a will probated the week after the Civil War began, then his executor should "bind one or both of them out"—but only to a "good humane and industrious mechanic."[49]

Females of both races indentured by the overseers of the poor faced shakier prospects for economic advancement than boys did. The typical apprentice girl learned spinning, weaving, sewing, knitting, or some combination of these. Authorities bound out thirteen-year-old Jenny Massey in 1805 simply to learn "the necessary qualifications of a Girl of her rank"—namely, that of a poor, white, female orphan—and they placed other white and black girls, but not boys, in the same situation.[50] Such a girl might grow up to earn a decent living at traditional women's crafts, but some masters probably took on female apprentices through the overseers of the poor intending to use them at least in part as personal servants or menials.

The standard indenture required masters to teach their charges reading, writing, and simple arithmetic; that proviso disappeared from blacks' contracts early in the nineteenth century. Even before then, most black apprentices entered adulthood nonliterate; those who dictated wills could only make a cross or an X at the bottom. Neither law nor good intentions could have conferred literacy on nearly a score of children, white as well as black, bound out to masters or mistresses who themselves signed the indentures with an X.[51]

Even so, some masters and overseers of the poor took considerable care to help black apprentices succeed, especially in the years after 1830— paradoxically, a period in which laws discriminating against free blacks became harsher. More whites than blacks received $20 in "freedom dues" awarded on completion of their terms of service, rather than the standard $12, but a few indentures promised young black men four to six times the traditional sum. A bricklaying contractor offered $75 to each of two blacks after tendering only $12 to a white apprentice, probably his own relative, though the master's bankruptcy later terminated those apprenticeships prematurely. At least one contract awarded not only freedom dues to a black lad but also annual payments of $8 to his mother during his term. Prosperous shoemaker Booker Jackson, himself a free Afro-Virginian, offered the most generous freedom dues on record: $100 to a poor black boy bound to him in 1840.[52]

One overseer of the poor was delegated in 1851 to place two adolescent boys, apparently free blacks. He found a black master who would teach one lad blacksmithing and a white saddler who would accept the other boy. Free black John Homes was bound out at sixteen to learn blacksmithing from the most highly skilled white smith in the county and was promised $50 when he came of age.[53] A special commissioner toward the end of the 1840s found an apprenticeship with a prosperous cabinet-maker for a slave boy who was to go free when he grew up. When that man's health deteriorated to the point where he "could not teach an apprentice his trade," the commissioner saw that the boy moved on to the county's foremost carpenter-contractor; "no man," the commissioner believed, "could be . . . more faithful, and attentive to the instruction, comfort and kind treatment of the boy." That a master's ill health could abort an apprenticeship shows that there remained an expectation, at least when the apprentice was male, that the master himself would actually instruct the child rather than use him as a mere drudge.[54]

The overseers almost never bound out children of Israel Hill, despite the court's threats to do so in 1816 and 1829; most youngsters from there seem to have entered their parents' occupations or taken jobs in Farmville's growing tobacco industry. The free black Homes clan, by contrast, accounted for nearly one third of the indentures of free Afro-Virginians that authorities filed. Contracts for some of those children noted that their mothers could not maintain them. Yet three Homeses did come up with money to buy small tracts of rural land or the freedom of a relative, and Milly Homes became one of the few non-Israelite blacks of Prince Edward who drafted a will. Her grandson Nathan and others of his generation used the skills their apprenticeships had furnished them, or plied other trades, well enough to earn a living; one man, Joe Homes, even became a small-scale entrepreneur. The large number of Homes apprenticeships, then, did not arise from a culture of poverty that gripped the family. Rather, the Homeses seem to have concluded that apprenticeships arranged through county authorities offered a real chance at self-sufficiency and even upward mobility. Particularly desirable apprenticeships awarded between 1835 and 1840 to three Homes boys seemed to bear out that idea; so did the ability of various Homeses, beginning in the 1850s, to purchase more than half a dozen lots in Farmville.[55]

General John Purnall and another overseer of the poor who bound out some of the Homeses lived next door to that free black family. Purnall and his nephews dealt frequently with the Homeses on other matters; that these two officials decided the future of Homes children without hearing their black neighbors' views seems unlikely. Jacob Homes got an apprenticeship in 1818 to learn shoemaking from the very man who had sold Milly Homes her first patch of land six years earlier; Milly may well have had a hand in the placement of this boy, the one grandchild she would mention by name in her will. Similar personal relationships linked the free black Forgason and Bartlett clans with white officials and masters who set up apprenticeships for some children of those families.[56] It can be difficult in cases like these to decide where consultation between neighbors ends and free black dependence on the goodwill of paternalistic whites begins. But sometimes the families of indentured young blacks clearly displayed not deference, but rather a determination to defend their children's well-being.

James (Jim) League Sr. was a poor, nonliterate white veteran of the

Revolutionary War and a neighbor of the Cheadles in western Prince Edward. His daughter Martha, "rheumatick and infirm" by the late 1810s, lived with him, as did three of her mixed-race children. Three other mulatto League girls occasionally lived in the household; either Martha League had had a series of black lovers, or she had a de facto husband who was probably a slave.[57] The overseers of the poor had bound out two young white Leagues as apprentices early in the century. Then, in 1827, the year after old Jim League died, the county court ordered that two of his mulatto grandchildren, Branch and Judith League, be apprenticed. Their mother Martha, too, had apparently died by then. Patty League, Martha's sister, helped place young Branch with a man named Baldwin, where the boy would learn to be a "farmer and planter."[58]

Patty League suffered from penury and illness throughout those years of the late 1820s. The overseers of the poor sent the sickly white woman small donations of doctor's fees, food, and supplies, some of it through a free black woman to whom Patty had turned in her sickness.[59] Patty League had little to hope for in 1829, it seems, except that her mulatto nephew might live better than she had—and she decided one year into young Branch's apprenticeship that his situation with Baldwin was unacceptable. The county court could, and sometimes did, rescind the assignment of an apprentice when a parent or guardian complained. Patty League did exactly that, and the justices sent Branch back to her. By 1833, the court placed him in a new, much better apprenticeship to learn carpentry.[60]

Most people take it for granted that the worst enemies of blacks have generally been poor white Southerners—"white trash," as many are pleased to call them. Like the stereotypical rednecks of a later era, the Leagues were ignorant, their behavior sometimes rough-and-tumble; they carried on a running feud with at least one white neighbor over matters that had nothing to do with their cross-racial way of life.[61] Yet they defy our certainties about color bias among people of their class. James League Sr. stood by Martha and her mulatto children, and Patty stood by sister Martha and little Branch. Ultimately, Patty League, though she lived in a male-dominated, white supremacist world and depended on the authorities for material support, asserted her control over the welfare of her apprenticed brown nephew against a well-to-do white master—and she prevailed.

The men who ran the county, for their part, might feel real sympathy for the "deserving" poor, but they offered only modest aid to those people; they administered a system of apprenticeship that provided at least as great a benefit to masters as to their charges. In short, the elite did nothing for the disadvantaged that might change the social order in any way. Yet within that order, there was room for a Patty League to have her say—and for free Afro-Virginians to do the same.

Washington Lewis, a free black apprentice, grew up to challenge his white master. That man—Littleberry Royall, a bricklayer—lived near the Purnall-Dupuy lands and had many dealings both with those wealthy whites and with their black neighbors, the Homeses.[62] Royall took on apprentices and employees of each race over the years, and he exploited them all with a perfect lack of discrimination. Washington Lewis stayed on as Royall's employee after his indenture expired in the mid-1820s, but soon complained before the county court that Royall had stopped paying him. Royall countered that Lewis had quit working. The case languished after two juries failed to reach a verdict; the two men may have reached a compromise in the end. Meanwhile, two white apprentices complained to the court that Royall had abused them, too. Each of them, with a parent or guardian, asked to be freed from the bricklayer's control; in one case, the court complied.[63]

By 1833, Littleberry Royall seems to have gotten fed up with assertive poor people. He asked the court to order an unusual countywide sweep to compile lists of children "whose parents [were] incapable of supporting them & bringing them up in honest courses." Royall made no reference to race, nor did the justices and overseers of the poor infer any: only one person seems to have bothered to turn in a list, and some if not all the children on it were white.[64] Littleberry Royall and county officials alike tended to divide the free population into poor and non-poor just about as readily as they did into black and white. They differed in that some men of power, rather than smoke out potential troublemakers, made a reasonable effort to address cases of individual need and merit, black or white.

Washington Lewis was one of many black artisans who worked with whites both during their apprenticeships and in their adult careers. Indeed, a striking feature of the labor system in Prince Edward and vicinity—apart from slavery's failure, despite all odds, to destroy the work ethic entirely—was the way it brought skilled black and white workers together. No occupations situated black and white men shoulder to shoulder more consistently than the construction trades.

The term "carpentry" covered a formidable range of jobs. Carpenters constructed buildings ranging from impressive mansions down to log cabins, and from plantation kitchens to chicken coops. They put up "palings" (picket fences), built and repaired bridges, and dismantled and moved sizable structures from one place to another. At least in the early decades of the century, carpenters often hewed and sawed the lumber for their jobs, or had their own sawyers do it. They cut wooden shingles for sale to others and for use in their own work; sometimes they dried shingles and weatherboard siding in kilns.[65] They built coffins for the dead, and some of them—such as the Whites of Israel Hill—worked also as coopers, making barrels and hogsheads.

An ambitious master carpenter might employ a small nucleus of regular workers whom he could supplement with others—black or white, free or slave—as needed. The majority of workers on any sizable construction crew, however, would be enslaved blacks. White master carpenters often did hands-on work with black men they employed, especially if the crew was a smaller one. At one job for General John Purnall in 1813, white carpenter James Thackston "superintended the whole business and worked himself occationally" alongside several slave workers; two other Thackston men also joined the crew for part of the job. In other instances, two Thackstons "and two [or more] negroe fellows done some work" together for various clients.[66]

Some carpenters worked in biracial threesomes or pairs, as John Woodson, a white carpenter, did with his black "man Mat." By contrast, John Thackston fielded a crew of a dozen men in the early 1840s. His rosters included one slave of Thackston's own; a number of bondmen hired from other whites, usually for a year at a time; and one free man, Oby Carter, who was probably black and possibly a member of the Carter family from Israel Hill. Even in a larger group like John Thackston's, contact between white boss and black workers could be close, sometimes more so than the workmen might have preferred. One witness reported that Thackston "would frequently be in a drunken frolick, and . . . [his partner] and two [black] hands had to leave their carpenters business and take care of him."[67]

On one major construction job in Prince Edward that may typify many others, the segregation that prevailed did not divide workers mainly by race or condition, but rather separated the crews of different bosses. Carpenter-contractor Reuben Perry's men built a large two-story house for the president of Hampden-Sydney College in 1827–28; the smaller crew of another builder, James B. Ely, put up palings around the lot. Perry's group clearly included men of both races, and Ely's probably did, too. Perry jealously asserted his role as "undertaker" for the project, reportedly proclaiming at one point "that he Mr. Perry was master of the house." Accordingly, Ely's workmen left at the end of each day and lodged in a house offsite. Perry's own hands often stayed in a log dwelling; on nights when some of them worked late for overtime pay, those men "had their beds & slept in one of the rooms" of the house they were building at Hampden-Sydney. Thus the workers within each contractor's crew slept together, perhaps with little regard to race, even as the two *groups* bunked separately. Often during working hours, even the nonracial barrier between the two outfits crumbled; when it rained, Perry's men invited Ely's to "dress palings" in the protected basement.[68]

Accounts of the construction job at Hampden-Sydney mentioned the separation of the two crews because the house burned down before it was finished, and people were arguing over whose workers had caused the fire. That members of a biracial crew might lodge together, or that hired slaves could earn wages for overtime work, or that one group of workers would feel empathy toward another, struck no one as remarkable.

Distinctions of race did still count: the great majority of black construction workers were enslaved, and bosses, outside some family outfits like Charles Forgason's, were white. By the 1830s, when black men such as Sam and Phil White might have considered using their accumulated capital to go into the construction business, white contractors already dominated the local scene. The county government reflexively turned to white undertakers and suppliers, a few of whom actually sat on the county court. Such contractors often developed close relationships with blacks through their businesses, however. Henry S. Guthrey, a carpenter, became an important builder and county justice. He took on a number of apprentices; some of those were black, two of them Richardsons. Guthrey's ties with the Richardson clan lasted for many years; he would sell a small piece of his land to two members of the family in the 1850s.[69]

Guthrey also became friendly with Robert A. Franklin, a free black fellow carpenter. In the mid-1840s, Guthrey seems to have lent Franklin money that the black man needed as he prepared to buy his daughter out of slavery. Franklin lived in Guthrey's household for a time, and the white contractor eventually lent him money to develop his own tract of land.[70] Some years afterward, in 1860, on Guthrey's complaint, a white housepainter was charged with "breaking in and maliciously shooting into" Bob Franklin's house. Guthrey's testimony proved crucial at trial, since the law barred Franklin himself from testifying against a white defendant. Guthrey may well have been visiting Franklin at the time of the shooting and witnessed the crime, for a jury convicted the accused man and required him to pay $15 in fine and costs.[71] Guthrey never became a blind or quixotic defender of free blacks: he lodged two complaints against a free Afro-Virginian—a Richardson, no less—who had moved north and then returned contrary to law as the Union teetered on the brink of disaster in 1859–60.[72] Guthrey's friendliness toward other free Afro-Virginians had grown out of his direct experience with those black individuals on the county's construction sites.

Those workplaces drew on another trade, bricklaying and masonry, which resembled carpentry in a number of ways. Several contractors, all of them white, became prominent, and they employed free blacks as well as slaves whom they hired or owned. White and black workers collaborated closely on the job. Employers accepted apprentices, and some free black youngsters took that route into lifelong occupations.

Black and white brickmasons did what their name implies and a great deal besides. They built fireplaces and chimneys for residences and for separate kitchens; they "underpinned" (built foundations for) houses, and they constructed the occasional brick building. Brickmasons also plastered the interiors of houses, often if not always over laths that they themselves had put up, and then they whitewashed the walls.[73] These men typically used bricks made from Prince Edward County clay— available on the Chambers plantation near Israel Hill among other places—which were fired in local kilns. The making of bricks may have become something of an Afro-Virginian specialty, and a steppingstone toward more exacting work. Washington Lewis, the young free black apprentice who took brickmason Littleberry Royall to court in the 1820s, was listed first as a brickmaker and later as a bricklayer.[74]

Black and white bricklayers often toiled together. White brickmason James Whitice, for example, used a crew consisting of his own brother "& other hands" in the late 1820s; the brother was considered a "hand" among the rest, most of whom would have been hired slaves. Two free black Homes boys received attractive apprenticeships as brickmasons. One of them, and a younger kinsman, were working locally as bricklayers at the outbreak of the Civil War, and at least four other free Afro-Virginian brickmasons operated in Prince Edward County at about the same time.[75]

Black Israelites, too, became involved in brickmasonry. In 1842, Phil White Jr. hauled two loads of brick for Sam Strong. Strong, who had grown up at Sam White's place and married into the older man's family, by then had become an entrepreneur in various fields. He probably engaged Phil White's carting service because he had contracted to build a wall, a foundation, or even a brick building for a client.[76]

Free Afro-Virginian bricklayers could make fairly good money. At the King family's tavern and tannery near Prince Edward Court House, one of the Homeses earned $7 in 1848 for putting up a chimney—probably for a kitchen. Even a difficult white employer like Littleberry Royall offered Washington Lewis, fresh out of his apprenticeship, $11 or $12 a month, the approximate prevailing wage in skilled construction work. The mobility demanded of construction crews may explain why most free black bricklayers resided in Prince Edward only for limited periods.[77]

Competing with contractors who made heavy use of slave labor may have reduced the income of the ordinary free black or white tradesman. He himself might have to seek employment from such undertakers and fall back occasionally on agricultural labor or other jobs outside his craft. Free black carpenter Peter Forgason did precisely this in the early 1820s, when he worked in Josiah Cheadle's harvests while living with a white man who contracted for jobs in carpentry and in hewing and sawing.[78] Those black craftsmen who owned land could at least devote slack times to farm work on their own ground.

Yet even as undertakers in construction such as Reuben Perry, Henry Guthrey, and Littleberry Royall rose in the world—and sometimes fell— there remained a place for the small-scale, independent craftsman, white or black. The independent carpenter or other artisan could take the small jobs; there the economies of scale that flowed from a contractor's large force of hired slave labor would not apply. The contractor also had to bill at rates that would not only remunerate his workers (or his workers' owners), but also reward himself, and this boss's markup, too, may have given the independent craftsman a little room to compete for work. Finally, the independent artisan could try to do work so superior that the demand for it would never dry up.

Former Randolph slave Billy Ellis worked as a carpenter in Farmville for many years; he lived until about 1857 and, though he probably no longer worked regularly by then, was still listed as a cooper at the age of ninety-one. In his more active years, Ellis made at least part of his living by doing an abundance of small and varied jobs. By 1819, he had done well enough to purchase a town lot and, together with his son, a batteau. For the Chambers estate, a regular client of his, he made wheat cradles (harvesting tools) and coffins and mended a plow in the years around 1830; at least once he even got a small payment for mending shoes.[79] Like the Whites of Israel Hill, Billy Ellis dealt at times in substantial sums of money and made sure that others paid him what they owed. In 1824, two white men signed a note to Ellis for $100, due at the end of that year.

When the two did not pay, Ellis sued them within ten months, a short time by the standards of the era. The whites were required to give bail; they confessed the debt and apparently paid it.[80]

Small-scale white carpenters, like black ones, remained part of the scene in Prince Edward throughout the period up to the Civil War. They did the same kinds of jobs free black independents did: repairing or erecting gates, palings, or doors, making and installing shingles, erecting outbuildings, "Puting 8 bares [bars] in one winder frame," and the like.[81] One small-time white carpenter, Samuel Willard, billed his work at 50 cents a day—the same rate that free blacks and the masters of hired-out slaves generally got. Willard resembled free black craftsmen, and entrepreneurs such as the Whites of Israel Hill, in another way, too: he had someone else prepare the accounts he submitted to his customers and then signed them with his X. Willard did jobs on the King family properties in Kingsville in the same years that a Homes laid bricks and a Dwin made repairs there. Whether or not Willard worked side by side with those free Afro-Virginians apparently depended entirely on the King family's concrete needs at a given moment.[82]

Most Afro-Virginian construction workers remained enslaved, with few opportunities to make their own decisions and virtually no prospect of advancement in life. Among free people, too, race could still color one's outlook on the world, though sometimes in subtle, even unspoken ways. Two independent white carpenters, Thompson Baker and Charles Cody, made many mistakes when they began their career together not long before Israel Hill was founded. They nailed shingles and boards of green wood onto a stable they were building without first boring nail holes, and they made the eaves too short to protect the structure adequately. The two white men also refused to provide the troughs that were dug inside stables of the period. Challenged on the point, Baker—who manifestly had very little on which to base delusions of grandeur—nevertheless turned up his nose and "asked if it was a carpenters business to dig [troughs]." In the end, the pair simply abandoned the unfinished job.[83]

Billy Ellis did much better work than Baker and Cody, and he viewed his craft differently. Among many other jobs, Ellis built coffins, as other carpenters of both races did. He often turned out cheaper models than the $2.00 to $3.00 coffins frequently used for slaves and paupers, but he was not unique in that: the prosperous white carpenter Charles Fore once built a slave's coffin for a mere $1.00.[84] Ellis did build more elaborate coffins for clients who wanted them. When black Israelite Phil

White Sr. died in 1830, his family buried him in style in a coffin that Ellis made for $6.50. On another occasion, Ellis received $5.50 for building a slave's coffin and digging her grave. The digging was worth $1.00 or so—thus the black carpenter earned a tidy $4.00 or more for the coffin itself.[85]

Billy Ellis's digging of that grave contrasted sharply with Thompson Baker and Charles Cody's haughty refusal to dig troughs in the stable they shoddily threw together. In Prince Edward's system of haphazard employment, many white men, probably including some white carpenters, wielded pick and shovel at least on occasion; a kinswoman of Baker all but laughed in his face when he told her he had been too proud to prepare troughs. Yet slavery bred in some whites the kind of pretensions that Baker and Cody evinced. Even after that pair abandoned their work half-finished, they arrogantly refused to admit they had done anything wrong on the failed project.[86]

Billy Ellis, a former member of the elite among Randolph slaves, was a free person and a skilled craftsman with a loyal clientele. Yet he carried himself differently than Baker and Cody did. His experience as a slave and his efforts to expand his freedom had immunized him against naive illusions. Ellis did not dig graves regularly, but when he got the chance to build a coffin and prepare a grave to place it in, he did so, and enjoyed an excellent payday for an honest job well done.

Baker and Cody surely had noticed that most moving of dirt was indeed done by slaves; ditchdigging stands to this day as the ultimate metaphor for hellish, dead-end menial work. Planters used ditches and fences to stake out the boundaries of their property and to keep livestock out of places it did not belong; people in south-central Virginia considered these amenities necessary "to enable [a landowner] to make a crop" or to render a tract of land salable. Gutters lined major roadways, at least during the later antebellum period, and ditches drained the town of Farmville.[87]

"Ditchers" who undertook big jobs in fact supervised crews of slaves. Those workers straightened and cleared streams, widened creeks to reduce damage from "freshets," built and mended dikes along streambanks. Sometimes they even diverted watercourses; in 1828, Josiah Cheadle ordered a canal some nine hundred yards long and twenty feet wide to irrigate his plantation with creek water. Diggers built canals up to a mile or more in length to power grist mills. They dredged tributaries of the Appomattox and Roanoke Rivers; that allowed millers to boat flour down to those major watercourses and prevented water from backing up to the point where the bottoms of millwheels "waded" in the stream and ceased to turn properly.[88] Given these massive and constant demands for ditching and other digging, it is no wonder that bondmen did the great bulk of it; the backbreaking labor of "cutting a ditch" seems to have been one of those pursuits that earned slaves extra whiskey rations. Yet there was more to ditching than massive capital improvement projects. Ditchers also, at least occasionally, walled natural springs, dug or repaired wells, and even dug icehouses and graves; some specialized in well-digging.[89]

Some men who worked at ditching in the 1810s were free, and at least a few were white. As late as the 1850s, Archer Rennals, a nonliterate white man, was making his living as a ditcher, and J. W. Murphy, probably an Irishman, earned good money—$1 a day—cutting ditches on the Cheadle place. Whites who held few or no slaves routinely dug and ditched on their own property.[90] Decent wages help explain why at least seven free black men of Prince Edward worked at ditching in the 1820s, and why others of their race did so in the following decades. One who dug a ditch for Josiah Cheadle early in 1828 agreed to terms that the planter set out in writing. He was to receive $30 for what appears to have been four months' work or less; Cheadle deducted the cost of a spade.[91]

For free Afro-Virginian Thomas Bowman, ditching did not imply humility or degradation; he was working at that occupation in 1822 when he successfully sued the previous employer who had discharged him. Ditcher Ben Davis married a granddaughter of Milly Homes and thus joined a black family which, though not well-off, did own land. Moses Hill could boast the most impressive achievement by a free black ditcher in Prince Edward County: in 1820, he purchased 160 acres from a white party who offered him comfortable terms.[92] One wonders whether Hill employed a crew of workers or earned all his money through his own toil.

Hill had been born to an emancipated mother and had come from neighboring Amelia County. He and his wife, Sarah, apparently lived on their land only a short time—a year or so—before moving on to Nottoway, another adjacent county. Yet their tract in the southeastern corner of Prince Edward was the largest purchased by a free black in the county between 1800 and the Civil War, and the couple held it for more than a dozen years. The Hills bestowed middle names on their children beginning in the 1810s, before the habit of doing so had spread widely beyond some of the county's elite white families—another display, perhaps, of the pride and self-confidence that could rest comfortably on the shoulders of an Afro-Virginian ditcher.[93]

The mill canals that ditchers dug took their place in a landscape altered also by millponds that backed up behind dams as high as twenty feet. The county sustained mills of various sizes, which mainly ground corn and wheat; many ginned small amounts of cotton on the side, and sawmills operated both independently and as adjuncts to grist mills.[94] The occupation of millwright—erecting and repairing mills—was a crucial one; blacks in Prince Edward seem not to have practiced it, at least not at the master level. By contrast, many of the highly skilled men who operated the mills once they had been constructed were African Americans. One citizen remarked around 1840 that a neighbor had hired "a white man miller" lest his hearers automatically assume the new man was black.[95]

Masters and employers held black millers in high esteem. By 1800, Billy Bones (or Bowens), a slave, earned a reputation with his master as "an honest and upright man . . . who deserves his freedom," and his owner accordingly emancipated him. Richard Shepherd, a white man who long ran one of the more productive mills in the county, declared a generation later that a certain slave miller working there was "as good as" Shepherd himself at the trade. Free black men, too, worked as millers; they included Dennis Evans, who belonged to a clan of former landowners, and Phil Bowman, devoted husband of the slave Priscy. As late as the Civil War years, free blacks would man one or two of the county's mills.[96]

The miller's high status flowed from the sweeping responsibilities he took on. Besides running complicated machinery, a head miller had custody of other people's valuable property—not only the mill and its appurtenances but also his clients' produce awaiting processing or delivery. The typical mill also had a body of land attached to it, which might run forty to fifty acres or even more. The miller supervised this land and the one or several slaves assigned by the planter–mill owner to grow crops and raise swine on it. Not surprisingly, some millers lived in the mills they operated.[97]

Working at a large mill might put a man under the control of a white boss. The slave or free black who ran a mill himself, by contrast, dealt often with whites, but also enjoyed freedom from close supervision. At the same time, he might have contact with even more of his enslaved brethren than the average free Afro-Virginian did, for planters often assigned slaves to take corn, wheat, or cotton to the mill, or to pick up meal, flour, or ginned fiber there.

The miller of either race had to be both decisive and personable. Customers often arranged purchases with the proprietor of the mill, who then gave the client a handwritten order to take to the miller. The owner knew only approximately what commodities were on hand at any particular moment, and inevitably he would send some orders to the miller that the latter could not fill; the miller then had to break the news to the client. Other customers showed up at the mill without a note from the owner, asking to purchase goods or demanding meal or flour they claimed to have paid for.[98] Here the miller had to make a decision, based on his own best judgment, to hand over the goods or not. A black miller might handle such a moment easily enough when he was dealing with a customer's slave rather than with the client himself. But he sometimes had to disappoint or turn down white customers. That Phil Bowman and other blacks spent their adult lifetimes handling just such situations points both to a measure of flexibility in general race relations and to a diplomatic sophistication that allowed a black miller to keep white clients contented even as he guarded his employer's interests.

Men like Phil Bowman achieved all this without becoming literate. To keep track of who brought how much grain to the mill, who picked up or took delivery of how much flour and meal, who had left how many empty bags on the premises, how many barrels were needed from the cooper and how many already made—all without writing—was no small feat. Yet men of both races accomplished it: the white miller Richard Shepherd ran a large facility for years without knowing how to read, write, or figure. "Not being able to read and write," an ex-slave from Prince Edward recalled, black people "were compelled to resort to the next best thing within reach, memory . . . the means by which their mathematical problems were solved, their accounts kept."[99]

Richard Shepherd and Phil Bowman must have plied their trade much as Thomas Hardy's fictional character Michael Henchard, the mayor of Casterbridge, did. Though marginally literate, Henchard "used to reckon his sacks by chalk strokes all in a row like garden-palings, measure his ricks by stretching with his arms, weigh his trusses by a lift, [and] judge his hay by a 'chaw.' " Bowman and his peers probably learned to recognize their employers' signatures, and perhaps also the shapes of the numbers and of crucial words such as "corn," "wheat," and "cotton"; but those tricks by themselves would carry a man only so far. The black millers would have understood the ironic words of the Breton peasant in later years who recalled, "If we had been stupid . . . we would have starved to death. So we were condemned to using our minds in order to have some chance of staying alive."[100]

In some respects, a certain paternalistic coziness shaped Phil Bowman's relationship with his employers. He continued to work for the same white family for more than two decades.[101] The Venables provided the miller with what amounted to subsidized housing: a home and lot at $12 a year. Rather than pay Bowman's wages in cash, the Venables kept a running account of debits and credits; many years passed before the state of that account was calculated. In the end, when the dying Bowman feared that formally liberating his wife might lead to her expulsion from the state, he instead bequeathed her to someone he thought he could trust to care for her—one of the Venable men. Bowman also left his large positive balance in the employers' account book, ultimately some $270, to be used for his widow's upkeep.

Yet Phil Bowman's life differed sharply from that of a slave miller—and not only because he received wages and was free to leave after he paid back his wife's purchase price. His rate of pay was not dictated by the Venables but rather "agreed on from time to time" by the two parties. White overseers and other employees of planters typically received much of their remuneration in the form of housing and supplies recorded in a long-running account, as Bowman did. After the black miller's death in 1842, his employer said—truthfully, it seems—that Bowman had received interest on the surplus that built up in his account over the years. As only a free man could do, he left a will to provide for his widow.[102] Phil Bowman's status as a free person, along with his talent and tenacity, had enabled him to save his wife from the auction block. He suffered because of slavery, but he was no slave.

Afro-Virginian shoemakers were more numerous than black millers, and some of the free men among them developed wide-ranging and friendly relations with white people both plain and exalted. Thirty-five shoemakers appear on extant free black lists from the first quarter of the nineteenth century, and other free men probably worked at the trade part time; black shoemakers continued to play a noticeable role in Prince Edward's economy up to the Civil War. Shoemaking ran in some free Afro-Virginian families, especially the Evanses and the Homeses. Tom Ellis, the former Randolph slave, made shoes, as did Ampy Brandum, an early settler on Israel Hill and sometime boatman.[103]

The county's mercantile stores sold footwear that came from outside the area, but most people wore shoes that local craftsmen had made, often from leather produced by one of the nearby tanyards. Ben Short, a master craftsman, turned out boots and shoes for well-to-do planters. Carpenter Zack Ellis became one of many free blacks who made or mended shoes as a second occupation.[104] White men continued to make shoes, and so did many slaves. Certain enslaved workers produced fine shoes, while less skilled bondmen made coarse "Negro shoes" for other slaves, or leather horse collars at 25 cents apiece; some earned money by working on their own time.[105] Shoemakers typically charged 25 to 30 cents or so plus materials for each pair of "Negro shoes" they made. Shoes for white slaveowners, interestingly, could be had for about the same price, though Ben Short and others could sometimes make $1.50 beyond the cost of the leather for a pair of "fine" shoes.[106] That high-end trade may explain how some free black shoemakers happened to win the friendly attention of prominent white men in the community.

John Moss, a mulatto shoemaker and sometime farmer, was one of the very few free Afro-Virginians of his time in Prince Edward who could sign his own name—and quite possibly write other things besides. Moss became sufficiently prosperous, and was seen as a good enough credit risk, to run up a bill of more than $140 at a local store as of 1808; but by then he had suffered reverses, and the mercantile company sued him for the bulk of that amount. In 1815, Moss came close to becoming a rarity—a free black man actually hired out by the sheriff to work off an overdue tax bill for the year—but then he came up with the required payment at the last minute. In the meantime, Moss was suing a white man of middling rank for assault and battery, but like more than a few other plaintiffs of both races, he allowed the suit to lapse without supplying details of his allegation.[107]

At some point before the late 1820s, John Moss settled down with a white common-law wife. Such unions, though far from typical, were by no means unheard of, either. Moss, sometime wheat cutter Stephen Forgason, and their wives constitute two of five interracial couples mentioned in county records during the ten years following 1828, and there may have been others whom the county court never took notice of. Some whites did actively object to interracial cohabitation and marriage; the name of John Moss's wife, Nancy Bell, entered the record because four whites complained to the grand jury in 1828 about that pair, about Stephen Forgason and his wife, and about Absalom Dungey, who, like his father, had taken a white spouse. The days when a white landowner's daughter such as Dungey's mother could ceremoniously and officially marry a mulatto were over. Yet shoemaker John Moss and the others do not seem to have offended most whites overmuch. The sheriff's office took its time delivering summonses, and the Commonwealth's attorney ultimately dropped charges against all six defendants. In 1830, at age fifty-five or older, John Moss, like Stephen Forgason, still headed an interracial household.[108]

Neither his financial scrapes in earlier years nor his choice of a white wife had severed shoemaker Moss's connections with influential white men. When another literate free mulatto accused Moss of having passed him a counterfeit coin in 1831, Moss spent more than a week in jail. But then three prominent merchants and planters, one of them a county court justice, consigned his bail bond; Colonel Charles Woodson, Asa Dupuy, and three other justices later acquitted Moss of using counterfeit money.[109]

John Moss's fellow shoemaker Ben Short likewise earned sufficient income and a good enough reputation that whites extended him credit on a large scale even before he bought his land in 1811. When he was working at Allen & Fowler's mill with Hercules White, Short signed a note to a white citizen for $200. The white man proved a patient creditor, allowing Short to pay him back over a period of a dozen years or so. The loan catches the eye in yet another way: the black shoemaker signed his name on the original note of indebtedness. Short wrote laboriously, in large block letters, some capital and others lowercase, inscribing each character boldly with a pen over a faint initial attempt. Those wispy original letters apparently represent a dry run by the black man himself, for they themselves are crude, and the lowercase H in Short's surname was initially entered upside down. Perhaps Ben Short had more or less memorized the written shape of his name; or perhaps he asked someone else to print it on a separate sheet and then copied it onto the IOU. Either way, in a mere eight letters one sees the reflection of a free black man's pride. The document would have been legally binding had Ben Short merely scrawled an X, as other nonliterate people of both races routinely did. But against the odds, the black shoemaker was determined to sign the note as a man among men.[110]

In the last months of Short's life, his social circle included white men even as he kept his grounding in the Afro-Virginian community. Short had been coopering again in the 1810s, but at some point he began buying rather than making his own barrel staves, and he moved back into shoemaking in 1817.[111] Declining health seems to have limited the strenuous work he could do. During his final illness the following year, Short received visits from at least two white friends. These were not paternalistic planters calling out of noblesse oblige, but simple yeomen; one of

The land of free black shoemaker Ben Short became a focal point of the free
black drive to live independently. Short, deprived of education but determined
to sign this bond as a man among men, laboriously traced the letters of his
name.

(BOND TO A. COCKE, FILED IN COUNTY COURT, JANUARY–MARCH 1820,
ARCHIVES RESEARCH SERVICES, LIBRARY OF VIRGINIA)

them owned four slaves age twelve or older, the other none. Ben Short
discussed his impending death with them. He wanted his wife, Sylvia,
technically his slave, to go free and continue living on his remaining spot
of land with his son by a previous marriage; Ben wished for those two
heirs to share the possessions he would leave behind. Short asked Sharp
Spencer, one of his two white visitors, to draft a will incorporating those
wishes—but Spencer did not have time to do so that day, and Short died
before another opportunity arose. Short's two white friends kept faith
with him, however: they passed his wishes along to the county court,
which recognized them as a legally binding will.[112]

Rather than follow the law of 1806 requiring newly manumitted
blacks to leave Virginia within a year, all concerned honored Short's
desire that Sylvia go free and enjoy his land and goods in life estate.
Those goods included a cow and calf, a horse, a wagon, one set of
cooper's tools and another of shoemaker's equipment, farm and house-

hold implements, and a modest but respectable amount of furniture and kitchen utensils. Ben Short also left a gun, of which the deputy sheriff who compiled an inventory took the same notice as he did of Short's butter churn and looking glass, but not a bit more.[113] Sylvia Short did indeed remain on her late husband's small tract of land, at least until 1822, three years beyond the point when the law should have expelled her. As far as Prince Edward's officialdom was concerned, the little tract on the Court House–Farmville Road had become "her land." Whether Sylvia then died or moved elsewhere is unknown, but the land remained occupied by Susannah Short, who may have been Ben's daughter, until 1825 and perhaps longer.[114]

Ben Short's white neighbors do not deserve awards for practicing simple decency; but in a system where indecent things happened to black people every day, the respect shoemaker-cooper Ben Short commanded from whites merits notice. So, at the same time, do Short's continuing close ties to the slave community. Not only did he select a bride from that milieu; Short also chose a slave as the physician who would attend him in his last illness. This doctor, a man named Matt, rendered extensive service, and Ben Short valued it greatly; one of the same white men who had sworn to Short's dying wishes validated Dr. Matt's bill of $10. That white neighbor testified to his "Certain knoledge" of Matt's ministrations, suggesting that he and the enslaved doctor had at times attended Short's deathbed together.[115]

In shoemaking as in carpentry, an ambitious white man could become prosperous largely by relying on the work of skilled blacks both free and enslaved. As Judith Randolph finally began planning the liberation of her bondpeople, John Foster inherited a small amount of land, a horse, and a slave named Sy, "a good Shoe maker." Foster may well have learned that trade himself—indeed, learned it from Sy. During the following decade, Foster took on additional black workers, including at least two free black apprentices bound out by county authorities, and he built a thriving shoemaking business.[116]

Foster invariably wrote his name as a series of baroque, cursive capitals, and his prominence in the community came to match his flamboyant signature. He became a militia officer, county coroner, deputy sheriff, and secretary to Prince Edward's overseers of the poor. He could be hard-nosed when he dealt with enslaved blacks. One time he masterminded a successful effort to sell the slave of a deceased relative who had commanded that none of her bondpeople even be hired out, much less sold.[117] Foster viewed free blacks differently. He did hire one black apprentice shoemaker out to his brother for some three years—an act that was questionable at best under the terms of the lad's indenture. Yet Foster also released both of his free black charges, a Homes and a Richardson, before age twenty-one to work for themselves in the trade they had learned from him. In 1825, he served as foreman of a jury that awarded damages to black Israelite Polly Patterson when she sued a white man for assault.[118]

John Foster's success did not prevent Booker Jackson, a free black shoemaker, from establishing himself as a well-known, successful figure in Farmville in the early 1830s. Jackson had grown up in Charlotte County, which borders Prince Edward on the southwest. He bought two pieces of land in town, one of them on Main Street, and set up shop. The large and loyal clientele that Jackson won, including the Israelites' white neighbors, the Tuggles and the Penicks, showed that Prince Edward still had room for a free Afro-Virginian craftsman and entrepreneur who answered to no white employer.[119]

No black man achieved the same prominence in smithing that Booker Jackson did in shoemaking. Isham Smith, active as a blacksmith in the county at least since the 1790s, had served as a sort of founding father for free blacks in the trade. Though he moved to Charlotte County by 1814 and sold his one-acre "spott of land" in 1821, Smith seems to have kept some clients in Prince Edward into the 1830s.[120] During Israel Hill's early years, free black Peter Forgason, a generation younger than Isham Smith, completed his apprenticeship in blacksmithing with the Israelites' one-time road crew supervisor, Charles Fore. Forgason was the first of at least five black lads whom the overseers of the poor bound out to learn the smith's trade. A son and a son-in-law of the biracial Dungeys took their places among a dozen and probably more free black smiths who practiced their craft in the county at one time or another between the 1810s and the Civil War.[121] Some of these men surely worked as employees of white men, but Charles Henry Diuguid was doing business in "his black-smiths shop" in 1844, even if the establishment did stand on someone else's land.[122] Alexander Cousins, whom the overseers of the poor considered qualified to accept an apprentice, probably at least rented a shop.

Plantations with enslaved blacksmiths competed with free practitioners of both races; smiths' work done by the slaves on one plantation brought in so much money that collecting fees for their work became one of the overseer's regular duties in the late 1810s. General John Purnall's plantation had a combination smithy and wheelwright shop, and Purnall left behind three slave blacksmiths when he died in 1824. Some years later, one of the Tuggles, those neighbors and close acquaintances of the black Israelites, pooled funds with another white man to hire a slave smith.[123]

Facing such competition, free smiths, whites included, often struggled to support themselves. Josiah Cheadle alone used the services of six different white smiths between 1822 and 1835 rather than favor any of them consistently with his business. One of those men, Daniel Y. Jenkins, had to supplement the income from his craft by hauling rails, crops, and oats; by 1831, he declared himself insolvent.[124] Henry Y. Jenkins—Daniel's kinsman, perhaps his brother—inherited some land but little else. Yet with unusual skill and a good deal of black help, he became Farmville's most prominent blacksmith and a leading citizen. He took on an apprentice from the free black Homes family and doubtless employed slave workers in his shop, even as he continued to do exacting physical work himself.[125]

Modest but sometimes useful inherited assets, special talents, ambition, luck, membership in the favored race, and access to the skills of free and enslaved black men brought prosperity to Henry Jenkins, Henry Guthrey, and John Foster. Their material success exceeded anything that Afro-Virginian practitioners of their particular crafts were able to bring off. Even so, many free black men managed to earn money, and some made a good living, at smithing, carpentry, and shoemaking after learning skills from those entrepreneurial white craftsmen or from fellow blacks.

Afro-Virginian women played crucial roles in Prince Edward County's world of work. Besides taking care of household chores in and around the slave quarters, bondwomen labored in almost every phase of local agriculture, with the possible exception of harvesting wheat and oats. Indeed, women worked so hard in the fields that one overseer in 1840 apparently ranked an enslaved woman as "the best negro slave labourer" in his gang. Even a bondwoman with special household skills such as cooking might well be required to spend part of her time toiling in the crops.[126] Many free black women likewise divided their time between house and field. A number of such women resided on the land of white persons, presumably those for whom they worked.[127] Those who lived on ground that their families owned or controlled included, at various times, women of the Dungey, Short, Forgason, and Homes families, as well as the many who dwelt on Israel Hill and in the household of squatter Edmund Young.

The revenue commissioner for upper Prince Edward County—which included Farmville and Israel Hill—misleadingly labeled almost every free black woman there as doing either farming or "house work." Commissioners for the lower district of Prince Edward and for neighboring Charlotte County recognized that there were indeed some free black women who labored mainly as housewives or cleaned white people's homes. But they noted that most worked as spinners, washers, weavers, cooks, "waiters," or nurses (whether to children or otherwise). In upper Prince Edward, the catchall phrase "house work" clearly encompassed those same occupations.[128] Individuals who earned money by spinning, weaving, knitting, and sewing included some women of landowning black families. Almost every founding household on Israel Hill—including the upwardly mobile families of Phil White Jr. and Sam White—had one or more members explicitly recorded as doing "house work" at some point during the well-documented years from 1817 through 1825.[129]

On the other hand, female Israelites and their husbands may well have *preferred* not to sell those women's products and labor to outsiders. The years 1818 and 1821 were peak times for such women's activity on the Hill, and even then the majority of Israelite households apparently did little "house work" for pay. From 1822 through 1825, only one Israel Hill family was ever recorded as doing such work, and then only for one year.[130] The second generation of Israelites seem to have been even less likely than their parents to rely on income from spinning, weaving, sewing, and the like.[131] The landowning Dungeys and the households of Charles and Jethro Forgason Sr. evinced the same preference; the latter were listed as doing "house work" only occasionally between 1819 and 1825, and then only in years when they did not reside on their own land. The enumerator did list three free black female landowners as doing *only* "house work" in some years, but the husbands of all three were dead, enslaved, or absent for some other reason, and all three held very little land—one to nine acres.[132]

Black Israelites such as the Whites engaged actively with white people in Farmville's economic life. Some may have continued at least occasionally to sell produce to white neighbors or to perform specific, temporary jobs on nearby plantations.[133] Yet landowning offered new options to Afro-Virginians during the Hill's first decade and a half. Even landless free Afro-Virginians were not nearly as helpless as we sometimes believe, but the Israelites and other blacks who did own land took a further long step into independence when they elected not to hire on as agricultural workers or, as it appears, to sell the fruits of women's crafts to whites. By contrast, black women from non-landowning families—even those whose husbands plied good trades such as shoemaking, boating, carpentering, and ditching—often contributed to their families' support through "house work"; nine women with relatively well-situated spouses did so in 1821. The nearly thirty-five other landless free black "house workers" in that year were either single, or married to slaves and probably living on the farms or plantations of their husbands' owners.[134]

Free blacks who resided on whites' farms or plantations—especially those who lacked free spouses—might well find themselves living among slaves. Free Afro-Virginian Betsy Lyle remarked that she lived on William F. Scott's plantation in the 1850s "as sort of a hire[;] I sew for his negroes and weave." Sometimes she also helped slaves with their assigned tasks or took a turn in the kitchen when the enslaved cook was absent.[135] Lyle's situation differed greatly from that of a bondwoman; for one thing, she could leave her situation if she wanted to. Still, landed free blacks sought to differentiate their lives from those of slaves more emphatically than Betsy Lyle managed to do.

Black women who did sell their skills and the products of their crafts had more than a little white company. In some instances, a white woman who said she had been "doing sewing" may have meant that she "superintended" her female slaves, who did the real work. In other cases, however—and not only when free black apprentices worked under white mistresses—females of the two races labored together. Sometimes they lived under the same roof. In such a situation, close personal ties could develop. The employer of Orange Johnston, a young free black woman, wrote a short, simple will leaving her a "small dutch Oven, pot rack & pot Hooks."[136]

White farm wives and their daughters, like free blacks, often had to combine their own housekeeping with work for pay. In the one quarter of Prince Edward's households that contained no slaves during Israel Hill's early years, women worked especially hard, and small-scale slaveowning couples spent much of their time performing physical labor alongside their bondpeople. A white woman of moderate means who found herself widowed or otherwise separated from her husband might win some sympathy, but people fully expected her to "labour" in order to maintain herself and any children. "The duties of a house keeper," even a well-educated woman of a slaveholding family, often included a certain amount of physical work performed in concert with slaves. Catherine ("Miss Kitty") Martin left an estate of more than $3,000 when she died in 1848. Yet her brother-in-law felt compelled to cite the severe bronchitis and tuberculosis she had suffered from to justify the fact that "she could only keep house by giving instructions to the negroes."[137]

The wife of a prosperous cabinetmaker and county court justice supplemented the family income in the 1840s by working as a seamstress; a woman who merited the title "Mrs." in Josiah Cheadle's private account book appears there as a weaver. Other white women of respectable backgrounds lived in their employers' homes, earning their keep by sewing or weaving.[138] One white husband reportedly made his daughter cut a piece of cloth out of the loom in their house and "carry it and put it in the creek, because he said she should not work for people." But that man was a chronically abusive husband and father whose own wife, in fact, had worked as a live-in seamstress and weaver. That beleaguered woman's history as a hands-on worker did not prevent an employer from remembering her as "a genuine . . . pious and truly estimable lady."[139] In the end, then, women from landowning free black families had their own grounds, possibly rooted in their memories of slavery, for preferring to sew, spin, weave, or knit for their own families, but not for outsiders. Wanting to live like white women did not, and could not, figure among those reasons.

One vital and highly skilled women's occupation—midwifery—included white, free black, and slave practitioners from before Israel Hill's founding until the end of slavery in 1865; its potential clientele included every woman in the county, whatever her race or status. Well into the nineteenth century, people often referred to a midwife as a "granny," though she need not be elderly. Midwives do generally seem to have been middle-aged or older, probably because the job required years of observation and training.[140]

Midwives' fees remained stable for the entire period from 1800 to the Civil War at either $2 or $3 per delivery. Neither the race of the midwife nor that of the patient determined which of the two rates applied. The Chambers estate near Israel Hill often paid $2 to white midwives supervising slave births, even as it sometimes paid free black "Granny Patty" $3 for the same service. The overseers of the poor likewise once paid "Negro Hannah" the higher fee in the 1850s for delivering a pauper's baby, while the same officials gave free black midwife Betsy Hill and a white counterpart only $2 per birth. The versatile free Afro-Virginian Milly Homes sometimes received $3 when she delivered enslaved women's babies.[141]

Masters had a vital interest in maintaining the health of enslaved mothers and children. One family in the early 1820s paid the same $3 to white midwives supervising slave births as they did to the woman who attended their own mother in a difficult labor that she did not survive. By contrast, when poor white women gave birth at the county's expense, officials were loath to pay a midwife more than $2.[142] If race did not govern a midwife's remuneration, her social status could make a difference. Enslaved practitioners usually attended other slave women, and they (or their masters) received the lower of the two standard sums. White midwives whose standing rated the honorific "Mrs." in their clients' account books were more likely to receive $3; other white women, like free blacks, might be paid at either level.[143] Free midwives represented almost the entire social scale. The wife of George King, one of the county's foremost entrepreneurs, worked as a midwife; yet so did Elizabeth Hargrove, a white woman who could only sign receipts with an X, and Rachel Cole, "a [free] colloured woman [who] cannot write."[144]

Free black women such as Rachel Cole served prominently among the ranks of Prince Edward's midwives during various periods. At least two of them had close ties to Israel Hill. The Betty Brown who earned "granny fees" on the neighboring Chambers plantation in 1802 and 1803 was likely the same Betty who had become the second wife of Syphax Brown. Midwife Patty Morton lived in Farmville; Essex White of the Israel Hill group resided at her place for a time.[145] "Free Liddy" or "Granny Lydd," another black midwife who served the Chambers plantation early in the century, once earned the remarkable sum of $7 for attending a slave woman at what clearly was a terribly complicated birth. Milly Homes worked as a midwife at least as early as 1801, and she continued delivering babies after she became a landowner. Betsy Hill, whom the overseers of the poor called in to deliver paupers' children in the 1850s, was the wife of Booker Hill, a free black ditcher who himself got county work repairing a well during the same period.[146] Midwives both black and white—like a number of physicians—conducted their medical activities as a part-time pursuit; officials reported that women like Betty Brown mainly did washing, farming, or "house work."

It remains unclear whether middling and well-to-do white women ever hired black midwives to deliver their own children, nor do we know who attended Israel Hill's expectant mothers. Phil White Jr. at times used the services of a physician; male doctors may have supervised some births on Israel Hill, as they sometimes did elsewhere in the county. Some Israelites may have turned to free black or enslaved midwives, or to the white Fore and Tuggle families in their neighborhood, which between them boasted three practitioners.[147]

Midwives retained the confidence of a community that had access to a number of physicians, including a couple who boasted regional or even national reputations. Early in the 1820s, a dispute over the substantial property of Josiah Chambers, Israel Hill's mentally incompetent white neighbor, turned partly on whether his wife had engaged in adultery and borne a mulatto baby. Creed Taylor—Richard and Judith Randolph's old Jacobin friend, and by now one of Virginia's most prominent jurists—ordered an inquest to determine the child's race. Taylor chose three physicians from Chambers's vicinity and directed them to "take with them three of the most approved midwives of the same neighbourhood, and with their assistance, examine the child." Two midwives showed up to examine the baby, but the other appointees either failed to appear or "declined having anything to do with the examination."[148] It is not clear whether the doctors stayed away out of resentment over the high esteem midwives still enjoyed in the eyes of elite figures such as Creed Taylor.

Physicians and midwives did collaborate at times, but a woman specialist could prove remarkably assertive in the face of a medical doctor's supposed expertise. At about the same time the Chambers case was heating up, Dr. Edward M. W. Durphey became involved in a legal dispute over his ministrations to a slave and her newborn baby, both of whom died within days of the birth. Durphey's favorite remedies included bleedings, "pukes," and "purges" induced with "mercurial pills." White midwife Betsy Woodson, who had been attending the slave mother, accused the doctor of malpractice; she presented her opinion not in folksy argot, but in professional language. Durphey, Woodson recalled, had proclaimed at the critical moment that the patient "had a good pulse," but she had checked and found no pulse at all. She offered the court her considered opinion that the slave mother "died with inflamation, and [that] had the regular and proper course been taken, both the woman & child might have been saved." Fearing that the midwife's compelling deposition would convince an all-male jury of his peers, Durphey instructed his lawyer to throw in the towel.[149]

One wonders whether a black midwife ever challenged a white physician as forcefully as Betsy Woodson did. Perhaps black specialists asserted themselves more subtly; race did impose a certain social etiquette. Yet every pregnant woman entrusted to an Afro-Virginian midwife embodied white people's recognition of a fact that the county's working life reinforced every day: that an African American, just as readily as a white, could master skills that richly deserved the ancient title "craft and mystery."

To Run the Road with a Waggon
or the River with a Boat

Several occupations allowed black men to travel regularly within the county or even far beyond. Like most other realms of work, carting, wagoning, and coach driving regularly brought black and white, free and slave, together. Every construction job and many businesses required carting or wagoning of materials. Hercules White Sr. had hauled hoop poles and wood for white clients during his transition into freedom; Isaac Gibbs did similar work for Phil White Jr. in the 1820s, and Phil in turn hauled bricks for fellow free black Sam Strong. In local parlance, "hauling" often meant using a wagon or dray drawn by a team, sometimes of oxen or steers but typically of horses, rather than the smaller, two-wheeled cart.[150]

Planters often had their slaves "roll" hogsheads of tobacco to Farmville. They would lay one (or sometimes two) of the huge barrel-like containers on its side, run an axle through the center, and insert the two ends into a rig that allowed the hogshead to be towed; the overall effect was a bit like a much larger version of the manually operated, cylindrical metal rollers that people today use to pack down soil on a lawn or pathway. Slaves then yoked the rig to draft animals, which pulled it to its destination; other bondmen might brake the cargo on downhill slopes using a tether attached to the rig from behind. Planters also used enslaved wagoners to transport goods. In the 1840s, for example, a pair of merchants in Farmville were engaged in "running waggons," which they used largely for trading locally in large quantities of wood.[151]

In the 1830s and 1840s Josiah Cheadle, probably using a slave wagoner, hauled thousands of pounds of nails and other merchandise to country stores in his neighborhood from Curdsville in neighboring Buckingham County, site of a wharf on the Willis River, a navigable tributary of the James. Others used wagoners to carry their produce directly north or west to James River ports.[152] The Israelites' neighbor Charles Fore and others went so far as to send raw crops or even wheat flour the entire distance to Richmond by wagon—perhaps when low water or a shortage of room on batteaux made the extra expense of overland transport unavoidable.[153]

The wagoners who traveled to the capital city brought back finished products to be sold by stores in Prince Edward—herring by the barrel, whiskey sometimes by the hogshead, plates, gunpowder, dry goods, and more.[154] Henry Clay Bruce spent part of his childhood as a slave in Prince Edward County during the 1840s, on a plantation next to the great public road that extended from Richmond to the mountains and thence to the states of the West and South. Bruce remembered great covered wagons, each carrying seven to ten thousand pounds of cargo, traveling up and down that road in "squads" of four or five, each wagon drawn by a six-horse team. The enslaved wagoner, accompanied by a "water boy" and mounted on one of the horses in the team, had sole charge of the vehicle he drove. These wagons formed a "grand and impressive picture"; Bruce recalled seeing as many as twenty of them pass his home in a single day. The bondpeople who lived along the great road regarded the enslaved wagoner as "simply an uncrowned king." When wagons would stop for the night at one of the camping grounds that lined the way, blacks from the vicinity "flocked around to get a glimpse of this great man"—and, no doubt, to hear news and tales of faraway places.

It is easy to see why the enslaved wagoner won such acclaim. He bore the responsibility of carrying both produce and orders for merchandise to Richmond, seeing that those orders were filled there, and then dispensing along the way back west the goods he had assembled in the city; his job required physical strength, mental sharpness, technical skill, initiative, flexibility, and the ability to organize. The functions reserved to the white owner of the wagon and team were few: he would "come along about once a month paying and collecting bills." At times, slave wagoners may even have collected money themselves and brought it back to the wagon owner.[155]

The black wagoner dealt with white clients every day; they depended on his professional competence and, to some extent, even on his goodwill, yet his encounters with them were brief. Wagons sometimes completed the round trip from Farmville to Richmond in a week, but Bruce wrote that a month or considerably more might pass between the time a wagoner took an order from a given merchant and the day he returned to make delivery.[156] The black teamster spent the great bulk of his hours on the road without any supervision at all. He often found himself in the company of other black men who enjoyed similar day-to-day freedom, and he took his supper surrounded by admiring people of his own race.

Many wagoners were not slaves, however, and men of both races often drove wagons less grand than the ones H. C. Bruce remembered, including some drawn by two-horse rigs. A number of white men drove carts and wagons, and free Afro-Virginians took up the occupation, too. Some

The wagoner's job required physical strength, mental sharpness, technical skill, initiative, and flexibility. Benjamin Henry Latrobe painted this scene of black wagoners under a rainbow. (MARYLAND HISTORICAL SOCIETY, BALTIMORE)

free black and white teamsters drove wagons only occasionally, while other men made wagon driving a long-term occupation.[157] Peter Valentine, who married Sam White's daughter Jane (Jenny) and lived for a time with her and her children at Sam's place, worked as a wagon driver. One of Jethro Forgason Sr.'s sons, Peter, also served as a wagoner in 1819, and his kinsman Charles Forgason transported tobacco, apparently to Farmville, for Josiah Cheadle a decade later.[158]

Surviving documents portray white wagoners working under terms that may well have applied to free blacks as well. Some drivers earned a commission of a quarter to a third of the profits they generated; others got a monthly salary perhaps as high as $15, or received a combination of the two forms of payment. A wagoner might have some liberty to haul cargo on the side for clients other than his employer. Sometimes he could even become virtually a free agent—a "partner in the waggon." Wagoners often collected payments from clients, and some, at least, could spend part of the money due the owner as long as they paid it back on arrival.[159]

On the other hand, the responsibilities of wagon driving could weigh heavily on a man. The wagoner was largely responsible for loading up and "load[ing] down"; he had to see to the repair of any equipment that broke. If a horse sickened, he could be accused of "treating [it] Barbarously." If the animal died, the wagon owner might expect the driver to skin it and bring the hide home to prove that he had not simply sold the horse and pocketed the proceeds. A nonliterate wagoner, regardless of race, had to rely on his employer to keep accounts fairly; a driver might find on receiving a reckoning from the wagon's owner that he had "earn't a good deal, but [that] the expenses was so great that there was but little neet money made."[160] That a wagoner could be required to produce the skin of a dead horse typifies another burden that practitioners of that trade bore: as a class, they had a reputation for coarse and even shady behavior. A wagoner could easily acquire goods illicitly and avoid detection by selling them far from their place of origin. In 1838, a planter-businessman described a period of economic hardship in which "the waggoners, one of them told me, have to steal from each other. This is better than stealing from more honest people," the man added.[161]

Wagoning did not simply employ men of both races; it also brought black and white workers together. Some relationships were completely conventional: among potential witnesses to a suspicious fire in Farmville on Christmas 1828 were "a white man with a waggon" and "a negro boy with him at the time." The lad was probably the driver's water boy.[162]

But the rough-and-tumble world of wagoning produced other sorts of relationships, in which white and black—within the confines of that milieu—interacted on a basis of near equality. In 1846, two white wagoners, one accompanied by his father, happened to meet on the road to Richmond. They traveled to the capital together and returned by way of Prince Edward County, where they argued over a debt and parted. The father-son team, Isaac and Elijah Kirk, after spending the night in Farmville, headed southward and soon noticed the wagon of their erstwhile traveling companion, Samuel Davis, at the house of David (Davy) Bartlett, a free black boatman who lived on the Court House road about a mile outside of town. Davis may well have spent the night at the black man's place; now the younger Kirk decided that he, too, would get breakfast at Bartlett's house. Soon Davis and Kirk were fighting in Davy Bartlett's yard, the former armed with a knife, the latter with a wagoner's whip.

The social mix at Bartlett's that morning was even more complicated than that of a black host entertaining white guests: at least one black wagoner and a prominent white man were also present. According to one version of the confrontation, Elijah Kirk had "exchange[d] whips with

[the] negro waggoner to get a better whip to strike Davis." The white man on hand at Bartlett's when the fight took place was a well-to-do innkeeper who bore the Dickensian name of Thomas T. Totty. He lived near Davy Bartlett and had a wide variety of economic dealings both with free blacks such as Phil White and with various slaves.[163] The free black Bartlett, rather like the white tavern keeper Totty, may regularly have offered accommodations to travelers as a sideline to his principal work on the river—or perhaps he simply extended hospitality to friends, including whites. Either way, no one found it unusual for men both black and white, well-off and humble, free and enslaved, to spend time at a free black man's house, and for some of them—at least among the peripatetic and racially mixed brotherhood of wagoners—to eat or sleep there.

A few free black wagoners developed close relationships with propertied, even prominent, white people. One Afro-Virginian *became* a free man through such a personal connection. Alexander Patteson lived in the western panhandle of Prince Edward, near the place that would later be known to history as Appomattox Court House; he owned and ran the Richmond-to-Lynchburg stagecoach line for a quarter century until his death in 1836, and he kept a tavern. He used at least one of his own slaves, Charles, as a "wagoner [coachman] for the stage." At his death, Patteson emancipated Charles, who received permission from the county court to remain in Prince Edward even though his late master's will had provided money to send him to a free state.[164]

Free black wagoner John Cluff became a landowner by teaming up with a woman and her daughter who may well have been white. The record of their dealings leaves motives unspoken. Cluff already owned sixty acres in Hanover County, northwest of Richmond; Rebecca Hancock and her mother, Mary, like Cluff, were sometimes listed as living in Hanover, at other times in Prince Edward County. The Hancocks provided money for Cluff to buy twenty-five acres on the wagon road in Prince Edward in 1821, a highway that Cluff must have driven on regularly. The black wagoner deeded the land to Rebecca Hancock two years later, stating that this had been his and the Hancocks' intention from the outset. Meanwhile, though, Cluff, who had his own team of six horses, lived on the twenty-five acres for a time.[165] Whatever Cluff and the Hancocks were up to, the latter were not the only white women who readily did serious business with free blacks. John Cluff had found a willing seller of land in Mary Keeling, a white woman who was disposing of her late husband's estate in 1820 and 1821. It was she who, a short time earlier, had conveyed a tract of 160 acres to Moses Hill, the free black ditcher.

She sold the tract cheap and allowed Hill an unusually long period, four years, before payment would come due.[166]

Free black John Deneufville, a sometime coach driver, joined the ranks of landowners, held his property until his death, and made at least one friend in high places. Deneufville had been manumitted in New Kent County, east of Richmond, by a master who may also have been his father or grandfather. He worked at times as a hostler in taverns after coming to Prince Edward, and he managed in 1824 to buy a slave who almost certainly was his wife. He purchased a half-acre lot for $150 in 1833 in a section newly annexed to Farmville that attracted prosperous buyers. Four years later Deneufville added a house worth $250, and soon he had improved the property up to a value of $800.[167] By the 1830s, John Deneufville became friendly with Clement C. (Clem) Read, who belonged to one of Prince Edward County's founding families and served on both the county court and the governing board of Farmville. The prosperous Read later became a director of a bank and of the Upper Appomattox Company, which supervised and promoted river navigation. He helped found a school and an insurance company in Farmville and became an important tobacco processor.[168]

Clement Read also came to be a trusted associate of several black Israelites. When Phil White Jr. built a log house for Isaac Gibbs, Gibbs paid White in part through Clem Read, who passed the sum on to Phil; when White finally sued Gibbs for the balance, Read gave bond guaranteeing that Gibbs would appear in court. Eventually Read would witness the will in which Israelite Tony White desperately tried to provide for his wife and their enslaved children.[169]

It was Clem Read to whom John Deneufville turned when he suffered his untimely last illness in 1839. The dying black man not only selected Read as executor of his will but left all his property, money, and debts "to my friend Mr. Clement C. Read." He called on the white man to "let my family have any amount of money that may be necessary at such times as he may judge discret and proper for their comfort." Deneufville's Farmville property indeed remained in Read's hands for the next fifteen years; at some point during that period, the late coachman's family seems to have left the area.[170] John Deneufville left behind personal possessions, too, including ample furniture, a silver watch, and a looking glass.[171] One can only guess why he placed everything in Clement Read's hands— including the welfare of a spouse who, unlike Phil Bowman's wife, was already free and could legally inherit property. The dying man may have considered his wife incapable of handling the family's finances, or believed that asking her to do so would impose a hardship. In the end, Tony White would draw the same conclusion about the wife he had liberated.

Deneufville's request that Read step in can be read as a deferential appeal to a patron, especially since he referred to Read twice with the title "Mr.," an unusual practice in wills. Yet nothing in the black man's rise from waiter and coachman to lot owner points to any particular dependence on others, black or white. Moreover, Deneufville called Read his "friend" three different times in the will—and for that matter omitted the "Mr." on one of those occasions. Read was white, well-off, and influential, and that surely colored his dealings with the black coachman. But the normal course of life and business had connected Clem Read with various free people of color; "friend" may have described his relationship with John Deneufville as accurately as any other word could have.

The black coachman died young, but he had advanced to the point where he could ordain that his survivors receive "any amount of money . . . necessary" to ensure their "comfort." Many white men would have envied that achievement. John Deneufville and John Cluff had not been satisfied merely to enjoy the freedom that the road afforded to all wagoners and coach drivers, black and white; they had used their freedom to build families and livelihoods, and had made friends far beyond the circle of their fellow workers.

The roads that for decades stood as the picturesque emblem of life in Prince Edward and neighboring counties, however, were not the ones that Cluff and Deneufville traveled, but rather roads of water. On the rivers of central Virginia, black men became even more prominent than in wagoning.

Residents of northern and western Prince Edward County made much use of the James River system, which allowed them to ship to and from Richmond. Citizens sometimes carried their cargo through adjacent counties to Bent Creek or Cartersville on the banks of the James itself. Other shippers traveled a shorter distance beyond the Appomattox to wharves on the Willis River at Curdsville in southeastern Buckingham or at Ca Ira, a hamlet in southern Cumberland. The name Ca Ira commemorated a great anthem of the French Revolution and recalled the political enthusiasms of Richard Randolph, Creed Taylor, and others.[172]

The Appomattox River, however, took center stage in the commerce and the mind of Prince Edward County. Years before Israel Hill existed, and well into the nineteenth century, farmers and planters who had access to the Appomattox used enslaved crews or engaged free black and white boatmen to transport their wheat to mills and their tobacco to warehouses in the area that became the town of Farmville. Boats also made round trips to Petersburg, in contrast to the system on the New and Shenandoah Rivers to the west; natural obstacles on those rivers impelled boatmen to sell their vessels as scrap lumber after the downriver voyage rather than attempt to return upstream.[173]

Between 1795 and 1807, money from investors in the Upper Appomattox Company and the toil of slave laborers improved the river from Petersburg westward to Planterstown, a village in Buckingham County some twenty miles upstream from Farmville. In shallow stretches, the company built jetties and wing dams, each shaped like a letter V with its bottom missing and pointing downstream. These concentrated the river's current into sluices in which the water was normally deep enough to float a batteau. Some locks that allowed boats to pass around mill dams on the Appomattox dated back to the 1760s, and in the years around 1800, several short canals with locks were built for the same purpose. In the 1830s, the Upper Appomattox Company tried to overcome the inadequacies of the sluice system by building a number of additional dams and locks; shippers paid tolls to help maintain the network.[174]

The Upper Appomattox Canal ran to Petersburg from a point on the river five miles upstream; that waterway, too, was completed in 1807. Like other rivers in eastern Virginia, the Appomattox falls rapidly over a distance of a few miles as it moves from the rolling Piedmont region into the coastal plain or Tidewater. The canal provided a way around the falls of the river. It flowed parallel to the south bank of the Appomattox, descending gradually eastward into Petersburg. As boats approached the city, they went through a series of four locks and passed through a monumental stone aqueduct arcing across Indian Town (Rohoic) Creek, a tributary of the Appomattox. The canal ended at a large turning basin in Petersburg proper, where workers unloaded cargo into sheds; the overflow from the basin drained down a steep slope back into the river sixty feet below, and ultimately powered several mills and factories. Goods unloaded from batteaux in Petersburg could be shipped elsewhere by wagon or dray, or moved a short distance overland and reloaded onto deepwater vessels, which departed Petersburg below the fall line en route to the lower James, the Chesapeake Bay, and beyond.[175]

The batteaux that traveled between Farmville and Petersburg were distinctive craft up to sixty feet long, only six feet or so in width, and little more than two feet deep. After the river improvements of the early

In shallow stretches of the Appomattox River, sluices—shown here as twentieth-century remains—concentrated the river's current to allow the passage of batteaux. (MELVIN PATRICK ELY)

nineteenth century, each boat could carry 8 or 10 hogsheads of tobacco, or 250 to 300 bushels of wheat, or more than 65 barrels of flour. A tobacco hogshead weighed anywhere from around 1,100 pounds up to almost a ton, and thus the total load of a single boat typically ranged between 5 and 7 tons. The remarkable design of the batteau, featuring a nearly flat bottom, meant that two feet of water, or even twenty inches, could float a fully loaded vessel. The cargo on board might loom as high as six feet above the surface of the water, and boatmen often protected it with "tent cloths" of canvas or oilcloth draped over bowed poles in the style of a covered wagon.[176]

Each Appomattox River batteau had a crew of three. The captain or "headman" stood at the stern of the boat and guided the craft with a steering oar some sixteen feet long mounted on a forked iron swivel.[177] A plank walkway just inside each gunwale ran nearly the full length of the batteau. Along each of these walks, a boatman paced up and down throughout the upstream voyage. From the bow of the boat, he would plunge his pole, angled toward the stern, into the riverbottom. Bracing his end of the pole against a pad on his shoulder, the boatman would

The Upper Appomattox Canal skirted the falls of the river above Petersburg; its locks allowed batteaux to ascend and descend.

The batteaux on which this twentieth-century replica is modeled could float five to seven tons of cargo in waters as shallow as twenty inches.

then walk toward the rear of the boat. Of course it was the boat, and not the man, that actually moved as a result; each pace the boatmen took drove the batteau forward.

The physics of the moving batteau enabled those two men to propel their formidable load upstream the hundred miles between Petersburg and Farmville: the great mass of the boat and its cargo meant that, although the batteau moved slowly, each long push gave the craft considerable momentum, which sustained the vessel's forward progress while the boatmen walked back to the bow to begin their next push. A white boatman from the late nineteenth century recalled with a touch of exaggeration that "[you] hadn't lost no momentum at all when you walked back to get another holt."[178] The boatman's pine pole had an iron tip that engaged the riverbottom. The poles were strong and durable; someone found a sizable wooden remnant of one embedded in a cracked rock more than a hundred years after its user lost it there. The crew did not have to pole the boat on the downstream portion of a voyage—apart, perhaps, from some occasional help to the helmsman as he traversed shallow spots or obstructions.[179]

A black or white "headman" stood at the stern of the batteau and guided the craft with a steering oar some sixteen feet long, mounted on a forked swivel.

(JOHN EXLEY IN TROUT, *Appomattox River Seay Stories*, p. vii)

Two situations required boatmen to use methods other than poling or moving with the current. A towpath lined the five-mile approach to Petersburg on the Upper Appomattox Canal. Here the boatmen could attach their poles at right angles to the batteau, one fore and the other aft; the men then walked along the path, each pushing his pole to move the batteau. Some of the sluices upriver were bounded on one side by a "hauling wall," onto which the boatmen could disembark and tow the batteau through the sluice rather than try to overcome the rushing water by poling.[180]

When Appomattox boatmen returned from Petersburg, they carried a great variety of cargo: bushels of coal, sacks of salt, barrels of herrings, containers of lime, hogsheads of shells (probably used in the making of mortar), and all manner of finished products to be sold in the mercantile stores of Prince Edward and other upriver counties. Prince Edward had a couple of "traders in oysters"—for a time, the free black squatter

Edmund Young was one of them—and their wares, too, surely arrived on batteaux. There was a lively local commercial traffic in firewood boated along the river, presumably serving town dwellers who could not cut their own.[181]

It appears that most batteaux were built someplace other than Prince Edward, perhaps in Petersburg. But the maintenance of boats, about forty of which operated out of Farmville by the mid-1830s, provided work for local craftspeople of both races. The shop of blacksmith Henry Jenkins made or repaired spikes, hooks, and chains for batteaux, as well as "boat nails" and "boat forks." Around 1820, repairing a batteau and sawing timber for boat poles brought income—appropriately enough—to John Boatwright, a near neighbor of Israel Hill for whom free black carpenter Peter Forgason worked.[182]

The boatman's calling, like so many others, brought slaves, white men, and free blacks together. Plantations including the Chambers place near Israel Hill offered slave batteaumen, including headmen, for hire.[183] White headmen—some of whom owned their batteaux in whole or in part—boated wheat to the Union Mills a few miles downriver from Farmville in the early 1800s and carried flour and tobacco to Petersburg year in and year out. They sometimes, perhaps often, used white crews. White and slave boatmen and headmen did exactly the same work, and in some records of boating it is difficult to distinguish one race from the other; Josiah Cheadle, for instance, often recorded only first names for headmen of boats he used, some of whom were slaves, others apparently white men.[184]

Some free blacks worked as batteaumen from the first years of the century, if not earlier. Their numbers were small at first, and some worked on the river only intermittently.[185] From about 1820 on, however, only farm work and shoemaking employed anything like as many free black men in Prince Edward County as boating did. In the mid-1820s, at least thirteen to fifteen free Afro-Virginian boatmen lived in the county, all in the area of Farmville and Israel Hill; nearly that many more may have resided just across the river in Cumberland County. Perhaps one of every six or seven batteaumen working out of Farmville was a free black, and those men became a formidable presence within the free Afro-Virginian community. In 1824, active batteaumen and their households amounted to as much as a quarter of Prince Edward County's free black population.[186]

Residents of Israel Hill took on a high profile among free black batteaumen: authorities counted somewhere between eight and twelve

Israelites working on the river in 1824, an especially active year. Another notable group among free black boatmen were men of Farmville's Bartlett clan. Five Bartletts worked the river during the 1820s, along with a sixth man who lived on Patty Bartlett's single acre; this group with their households numbered thirty people by the middle of the decade. At least two Bartletts rented houses or bought them outright. A few other free boatmen—five to eight of them in the mid-1820s—lived in Farmville or on white people's land outside of town; some of the latter may have been married to enslaved women.[187]

Even though white men continued to navigate the Appomattox, locals and outsiders alike came to think of boating as an occupation conducted by blacks, and especially by Israelites. Early in the twentieth century, one white man who had owned a batteau in Farmville during the antebellum heyday of river commerce wrote a brief but vivid reminiscence of the boatmen; he stated flatly but innacurately that "they hailed mostly from 'Isreal Hill.' "[188]

Several free black men, both on the Hill and off, gained prominence when they managed to go into the boating business for themselves. Phil White Jr. and Dick White each owned a batteau by 1820, and Davy Bartlett bought a fully equipped boat for $60 in 1824. Such men sometimes did substantial business with each other, as when John White sold a boat to Joe Bartlett in the 1830s. By 1850, and perhaps earlier, black men owned one third of Farmville's forty-one batteaux, and they carried nearly 40 percent of the freight that came into and out of the town by water. Three of the top five boat owners were Afro-Virginians.[189]

Even an all-black crew might spend hours or days at a time with whites, for men who did not mind the lack of creature comforts rode as passengers on batteaux. In 1842, for instance, two white men traveled most of the way from Petersburg to Farmville, largely and perhaps entirely on boats captained by free blacks. Such journeys clearly happened often; this one entered the record only because the county court then had to consider whether one of the white passengers, who had "talked a great deal of nonsense" on the boat, should be committed to an asylum.[190]

White captains almost certainly voyaged at times with crews consisting of slaves they owned or hired, or of free blacks they employed. Shippers did not keep lists of crews, so it is impossible to answer a second question—whether a white man and a black sometimes poled across from one another on the same batteau. But sudden demands of clients or of weather, and fluctuations in the availability of boatmen, probably led boat owners or headmen sometimes to assemble a crew catch-as-catch-can in this society where biracial work was the norm. The small size of the batteau and the length of its voyages guaranteed intense contact among its little crew. But a boatman by no means mixed only with the other two men on his own vessel. Boats sometimes, perhaps often, set forth down the Appomattox in groups. On January 31, 1821, Venable & Company of Farmville shipped nine hogsheads of tobacco to Petersburg. But rather than send all nine on the same batteau, the company divided the cargo evenly among boats captained by Jacob Johnston and George Patterson of Israel Hill and by another free black man, James Ellison.[191] Apparently two of these boats, if not all three, had been waiting to round out a full load; that accomplished, the batteaux were ready to leave simultaneously and travel together.

A year and a half earlier, black and white men running batteaux had had an eventful group voyage. On August 5, 1819, six boats bound for Petersburg arrived at Stony Point Mills, where a dam spanned the Appomattox. They had likely left Farmville only a few hours earlier; Stony Point is sixteen miles or so downstream. Phil White Jr. and Grief C. Weaver, a white man, each owned and ran a single boat; the other four vessels belonged to white individuals or companies and were headed by free black Davy Bartlett and by three slave captains. The condition of the canal at Stony Point at first did not allow the boatmen to pass the dam; after a delay, they did manage to get through the obstruction.

It is possible that the boats had arrived randomly at different times of the day on August 5, piling up at Stony Point Mills because of the blockage there. But nearly three weeks later, the very same group of six boats with their white, free black, and slave captains arrived at Stony Point Mills again on the way back to Farmville—all of them on August 25. There they encountered the very same problem that had hindered them on the voyage down. The boats' proprietors asked the county court to levy fines against the mill owners, and the court complied.[192]

Various questions attend the journey of these eighteen boatmen—one to three of whom were white, if one assumes the black captains headed black crews. What the men may have talked about as they traveled, whether they camped or lodged together each night, ate meals together, made the riverbanks echo with song—all these are things one would like to know but cannot. One thing is certain, however: the twenty-day, 170-mile voyage from Stony Point to Petersburg and back afforded plenty of opportunities for the six batteaux to scatter, yet all reached the obstructed canal on the very same day. At a bare minimum, the crews must have been within sight and earshot of each other at a number of points along the way. More likely, they stayed together on purpose. The voyage of these six batteaux probably is unusual only in that the boatmen's complaints against the mill owners brought it into the official record.

The working batteauman faced challenges and hazards that equaled and sometimes surpassed those that long-distance wagoners contended with. The captain or headman of a boat was an important person: shippers and those who received shipments listed each boat they dealt with not only by its owner's name but also by that of its headman, whether the latter was white or black, free or slave. Allen & Fowler's mill was probably typical in requiring headmen to sign or make their mark on detailed cargo manifests; that mark represented the captain's promise to deliver the goods intact. Headmen also carried letters and documents conveying crucial information between shippers and tobacco factors or merchants in the city. Captains who actually owned the boats they commanded received large sums of money on delivering a shipment. It is not clear how often hired headmen were entrusted with substantial amounts of cash, but they did control several hundred dollars' worth of cargo at almost any given moment.[193]

A hogshead of tobacco or other produce could suffer "ducking" during loading onto the batteau or sustain damage from rain or river water during transportation downstream. When a batteau headman acknowledged responsibility for his cargo, damage caused by "the dangers of the river" was supposedly "excepted." In reality, the headman himself might have to make good on a loss: twenty-five-year-old Israelite Isaac Gibbs, boating for a Farmville mercantile store in 1828 and 1829, was docked $3.33 for "Damage on a Load [of] flour."[194]

"The dangers of the river" were many and varied. The depth of the Appomattox varied from season to season and even from week to week. "1838 was a very dry year & boating business was very backward," recalled a longtime resident. "In 39 and 40 the navigation of the River was good," he added, but those years also ushered in floods of longer duration than he had known in his twenty years living on the Appomattox.[195] Flooding powerful enough to wash away bridges and change the course of streams could disrupt boatmen's lives. The elements demolished a white man's moored batteau near the mouth of the Buffalo River just as the black Israelites were settling nearby. Floodwaters downriver in 1826 washed away the massive aqueduct through which the Upper Appomattox Canal ran near Petersburg; the structure had to be replaced.

The Appomattox Company eventually offered boatmen some protection by excavating "laybys"—wide spots in the short canals that traversed mill dams, in which batteaux could seek shelter during violent weather.[196]

In cold months, ice impeded boat traffic; then, when the ice started to break up, it might jam, checking the river's flow and causing flooding upstream. When the obstruction finally gave way, the sudden drop in the water level could maroon batteaux on the stream's floodplain. The river's frequent periods of low water, though not deadly, interrupted commerce more often than floods or ice did. Even after the improvements to the river basin that were completed in 1807, a fully loaded boat often had to "wait for a swell" of water before it could proceed downriver.[197]

A booster in 1836 could call the Appomattox "a fine stream, narrow but very deep," and claim that "the navigation of the river . . . is good at all seasons of the year," but locals complained that boat traffic remained "precarious, uncertain, and inadequate." The company's further work on the river in the mid-1830s did not solve the problem. A Farmvillian sent a loaded batteau to Petersburg in the summer of 1849; the boat "was stranded on the shoals some where near the middle of the voyage, no mails or wires could reach it, and it remained on a sand bank for a month, only heard from after a heavy rain raised the river and it came safely to port." The crude safety valve in central Virginia's transport system remained one that no one had designed: the same rains that turned roads into ribbons of deep mud also filled the Appomattox and made boating feasible, while the droughts that stalled river boating at least enabled wagoners to use the roadways.[198]

Delays harmed both proprietors of batteaux and their crews, for neither group was typically paid for its time. Rather, boat owners received fees determined by the amount of cargo carried, whether or not river flows halted their progress, and boatmen often were paid by the voyage; Phil White Jr. paid Isaac Gibbs $4.50 per round trip in 1828. In some cases batteaumen received a share of the voyage's proceeds; employers may also have provided a fixed amount of food to sustain the crew during a journey.[199] One recorded trip from Farmville to Petersburg and back lasted three and a half weeks before the improvements of the 1830s, and boats on average could move a little more quickly afterward, or at least more consistently. Two weeks or a month of low water thus could cost a boatman a substantial fraction of his yearly income; one midsummer voyage in 1820 took three weeks and a day *one way*. Irresponsible mill dam owners like those at Stony Point contributed to such delays.[200]

Low water and sandbanks posed an obstacle to navigation on the Appomattox River. (MELVIN PATRICK ELY)

In spite of the hardships—indeed, partly because of them—George W. Bagby echoed other white observers when he recollected that "the Negro bateauman gloried in his calling. The job was truly a man's job, demanding skill, courage and strength to a high degree." Bagby, a Virginian writer and humorist, was dead earnest in his homage to the black boatmen—so much so that he, like others, overstated their role, writing that "each bateau was managed by three strong slaves." Either the James River boating that Bagby recalled differed from the Appomattox navigation, or he shared the tendency to overlook the mingling of black and white, bond and free, that took place on the water.[201]

Memoirists of later years also forgot that the boating fraternity before the Civil War had had a mixed image in the public mind. Some batteau-men, including members of the Israelite White family, became known as men of good character. Other men of the river gained reputations as shady operators, much as wagoners did. One family in Farmville expected a shipment of four packages in 1852, but two never arrived. "The boatmen said they fell over in the river and was lost," the woman of the house complained; "there is no telling whether its true or not I reckon."[202]

Boatmen often received part of their pay in the form of liquor. One boat owner early in the century complained that his white headman "was such a drun[k]ard that he could not depend on him to do his business." But that did not stop the same owner from issuing his boatmen, also white, a quart of rum per trip—and these were short runs, entirely within Prince Edward County. Then as now, heavy drinking often contributed to antisocial behavior. William B. Fox, a white boatman from Petersburg, "got into a frolic," lost his money, signed on as a hand on a batteau in Farmville, but decided that stealing a horse worth more than $125 offered better prospects for a quick financial recovery. While in custody before his sentencing to five years' imprisonment, the irrepressible Fox broke a window out of the county jail.[203]

Some scrapes along the riverfront involved antagonists of different races, but confrontations between river people of the same color seem to have been more common. One slave killed another with a stick during a confrontation on a batteau owned by a white man in Prince Edward in 1813. Free black boatman Branch Epperson complained to his white employer in 1831 that a slave batteauman who worked with him had stolen his "pocket Book" containing his money and free papers. Boatman Dancy Brown, one of the free black people who had moved onto Patty Bartlett's acre of land, did file suit against a white man for assault in 1826, but let the action lapse; the details of the incident were never written down.[204]

Grief Weaver, the white boat owner and headman, lived just outside Farmville. He amassed a formidable record of violent conflict in which he displayed a perverse lack of racial bias. He faced criminal charges or civil suits between 1819 and 1826 for physically attacking at least two white men, one free black man, and one free black woman, most if not all of them connected to the shipping and boating sector. Weaver had a row with Phil White a year or so before they voyaged down the river and found the way obstructed. The black man sued the white for assault, but the two then made their peace. White consented to have his suit dismissed around the time of the two men's interrupted boat trip. Later, Weaver's career in Farmville ended when he received a two-year prison sentence for stealing money from a fellow white man.[205]

Authorities in Prince Edward County never accused any black boatman of assaulting a white person. The widely recognized character of certain free black rivermen kept them out of "frolics" and fights. So, more broadly, did the Afro-Virginian batteauman's knowledge that some whites saw him and his fellows, at least in the abstract, as a potential challenge to the slave regime. The black boatman traveled hundreds of miles, often with no white supervision at all. He used a vehicle that could hold—and conceal—large amounts of valuable property. He visited the city, where he could blend in with a large, poorly policed black populace, hear all sorts of ideas bruited about, and, if he was a slave, perhaps even take flight on foot or on a seagoing vessel.

It was no coincidence that Southern states and slaveholding polities elsewhere in the Americas passed law after law aiming to neutralize the dangers they thought arose from blacks involved in transport. Masters, for their part, tried to ensure that only reliable slaves assumed these roles; on hiring out one bondman he did not trust, the administrator of General John Purnall's estate made the hirer pledge that the "said negroe is not to run the road with a waggon nor the river with a boat." The Virginia General Assembly in 1836 introduced penalties for batteau headmen on the Appomattox or Roanoke Rivers who harbored slaves on their boats without a master's authorization; at least in theory, a black captain, free or slave, might suffer thirty-nine lashes for the offense.[206]

Such anxieties expressed themselves more in state legislation than in actual local enforcement. Even so, white people's suspicions occasionally led to trouble for black folk in Prince Edward. Two slaves named Thomas and Major faced charges in 1828 that they had stolen a hogshead of tobacco weighing more than 1,500 pounds from Farmville Warehouse on the Appomattox waterfront; the two may well have been boatmen or wagoners, for no one who lacked access to some conveyance could be suspected of stealing such a massive object. County justices discharged the two in a matter of minutes when they appeared for trial, without even hearing testimony.[207] Ten years later, similar suspicions moved someone to level accusations against a pair of free blacks. Kit Strong Jr., born on Israel Hill during the settlement's first years and by then nearing age twenty, faced a charge that he and another Afro-Virginian named Dick Clark had stolen a hogshead of tobacco worth $50 from Randolph's

Warehouse; one or both of the pair were apparently working as batteau-men at the time.[208]

Five justices, trying the case without a jury, acquitted the free black pair. Two years afterward, however, the two men faced a suit filed by two attorneys for the daunting sum of $60—probably the fee for the black men's legal defense in the tobacco-theft trial. The lawyers showed patience even after they took steps to get the money. They suspended their lawsuit at one point because "one of the [black defendants was] sick & the other down the river"; they had Kit Strong discharged from jail when he could not post bail, and they came to terms with Strong and Clark before the suit went much further.[209]

At the very time those men's story unfolded, free Afro-Virginian boat-man Randolph Brandum discovered that a brush with the law could cost even more than $60. Brandum had been raised largely on Israel Hill; he, his mother, and his siblings had lived for several years at Sam White's, and his dealings with Hill people continued into adulthood.[210] Brandum had followed Phil White, his own stepfather Joe Bartlett, and the other Bartlett men into boating. He did well for himself, buying a batteau before 1835 while still in his twenties; he hired the labor of other black boatmen, some of whom were slaves. Brandum conducted several large transactions with white mercantile companies and entrepreneurs; one of the latter shared with him the cost of hiring a slave for the year 1836, perhaps in return for a percentage of any profits Brandum might make during that period.[211]

Two years later, in Petersburg at the end of a downriver voyage, Brandum found himself accused of "employing & harboring" an enslaved boatman without the owner's permission. Brandum insisted the worker had "assured him that he . . . was a free man." In reality, Randolph Brandum had probably behaved as white men sometimes did, and as his fellow free black Joe Homes had done once not long before—eager to hire help at economical rates, employers did not always ask to see a black man's certificate of freedom. A local court in Petersburg fined Brandum for his offense.[212] Then, on Brandum's return to Farmville, a white man named Goodman claimed that the enslaved boatman had been under hire to him. As Randolph Brandum later told the story, Goodman and a couple of other whites hauled Brandum before the sheriff of Cumberland County; that official threatened to prosecute him a second time unless he paid Goodman for the labor the white man had supposedly lost. In order to avoid going to jail, Brandum said, he had made his mark on an IOU for $50.

Goodman then sued Brandum for that sum in Prince Edward County Court. The black man still had support in his hometown: an important white merchant who was also a friend of Sam and Phil White gave bail for him. Brandum defended himself vigorously—which cost him still more money. He subpoenaed the Cumberland sheriff and two other men, who presumably had witnessed the alleged shakedown on the other side of the Appomattox. Brandum contended in essence that the chief law enforcement officer of Cumberland had menaced him with double jeopardy even though he had not knowingly committed any crime in the first place, and that his IOU to Goodman therefore had no force.[213] The county court in Prince Edward saw the matter differently; it concluded that Brandum's promise to pay for the wayward slave's time was binding.

Randolph Brandum's setbacks reminded him of an important fact. The world of the waterman—fluid both literally and figuratively—removed a free black man from whites' field of vision for long stretches. Yet for that very reason, black activity on the river brought out the vigilant, repressive impulses of some white people. The treatment Brandum said he had received in Cumberland was not reserved exclusively for free blacks. White men, too, sometimes accused authorities of imprisoning them falsely, and whites suspected of misdeeds occasionally faced extralegal pressures. Even so, it seems likely that the men who made Brandum sign the $50 note felt freer to lean on him because of his color. Brandum, for his part, had kept alive the free black tradition of defending one's rights vigorously in Prince Edward's courts. In this instance, he had lodged serious accusations against a group of white men including a county sheriff, and required those men to come to his home county and give testimony.

Boating appealed to enterprising black men partly because the owner of a single batteau could prosper, even while big operators like Henry Guthrey and John Foster grabbed ever larger shares of other trades. In the early years of the century, a would-be shipper might simply contract with a boat owner to haul a load or two of cargo; the owner would then assemble a crew. Mercantile businesses became more directly involved in boating as time passed. By the 1820s, it was "the pride of many merchants here to own a boat," one Farmville businessman recalled years later. Yet the merchants also continued to hire batteaux operated by Phil White, Davy Bartlett, Grief Weaver, and other independents, either ad hoc or on a kind of retainer under which the shipper had the right of first refusal for a boat captain's services.[214]

The demand for boating remained generally high. Planters had tobacco and wheat to ship, and merchants in Prince Edward had to stock their stores, even in hard times. Yet for an entrepreneur to purchase a fleet of boats and keep free or enslaved crews on long-term hire might waste money during slow periods, while scrambling to man those boats voyage by voyage might just as readily squander time and nervous energy. A prudent merchant bought at most three boats and left the rest of the trade in the hands of independent black and white men who could be called on when there was cargo to ship and water to float it on. The independents themselves would provide crews, and often boats; they would bear the losses of slack business, dry seasons, floods, and the various other "dangers of the river." That arrangement also insulated mercantile firms from liability when a client's goods suffered damage. One company successfully fended off a claim from the Israelites' next-door neighbor William L. Legrand for a $200 "loss . . . (by Ducking)," denying that it was a common carrier at all. Rather, the company asserted, it made arrangements with independent boat owners as a friendly gesture toward some of its customers.[215]

William A. Seay, a white entrepreneur, did try to turn boating into a big business. It is unclear how many batteaux he owned at his peak, but he made payments to some two dozen free blacks, many of them boatmen from Israel Hill and Farmville, in 1820–22. Seay's finances collapsed in 1822, when he lost at least two batteaux and much other property. He never really recovered, and died twenty years later with virtually no net worth.[216] Meanwhile, Grief Weaver, perhaps the most forceful and ambitious of working white boat owners, suffered financial reverses of his own and then went to prison for theft. His and Seay's demise combined with the overall logic of the boating business to ensure that independent owners never became mere cogs in someone else's machine. The free blacks among them gained two things they valued: a livelihood, and a real measure of the freedom of choice and movement that Afro-Virginians in general treasured so.

The experience of Isaac Gibbs in 1828–29 illustrates the working life of those free boatmen who did not own batteaux. Gibbs boated for Phil White Jr., making two trips in August and September 1828. Then, in the following months, he made a series of voyages for N. E. Venable & Company; the latter did not record the number of journeys, but there must have been quite a few, for Gibbs received more than $60. In the meantime, Gibbs's sometime employer Phil White presumably continued to run his batteau under his own headship or that of a hired captain.

Of the total amount Isaac Gibbs earned from Venable's, he took $27 or $28 in the form of goods from the store. Gibbs probably spent more time working on the river that year than he did farming; he bought not only wheat and bran but also corn meal and bacon, which he could have raised on Israel Hill had he had the time. Beyond these staples, Gibbs got other basic items at Venable's store: women's shoes, calico and other cloth, buttons, coffee, sugar, soap, and "6 pounds very old Lard." Gibbs bought liquor only twice in a year's time, in stark contrast to certain other boatmen; he made his one large purchase of spirits at Venable's—a gallon—for Christmas week, as was the custom. Isaac Gibbs probably boated for employers other than Venable and Phil White, and his work history suggests that he also made money at odd jobs between voyages. He almost surely bought at other stores, too, for unlike many other workingmen, Gibbs took nearly as much of his pay from Venable in cash as he did in goods. He also had Venable pay some $12 directly to his creditors—primarily to Phil White, who had built Gibbs's new house.[217]

During his brief period of heavy investment in boating in the early 1820s, the white William Seay compensated his free black batteaumen largely through goods that they charged to his accounts at Venable's and other stores, and through cash payments those stores dispensed and added to Seay's tab. Various black Israelites received sugar and other staple foods, considerable quantities of clothing, buttons, shoes, and the like, as well as knives, brandy, and whiskey. Isham Patterson's son George, a captain on several voyages for Seay, got a good blanket in the winter of 1821 and a gallon of whiskey the following summer; he may have used a fair portion of the liquor to compensate his two-man crew. Jacob Johnston got a sack of salt valued at $4.50 in August 1821; the Rose Johnston household may have been planning to slaughter hogs that winter.[218]

Boatmen and other free Afro-Virginians who took their pay at stores occupied a different place in the merchants' minds than slaves did. Notations of cash and merchandise issued to free blacks on Seay's account always included their names—occasionally a given name only, but ordinarily the surname as well—while those to bondpeople were often recorded simply as having gone to a "Negro." Sam White, who received two gallons of brandy on Seay's account for Christmas week 1820, joined some of the big names in Prince Edward's economy as one of Seay's major trading partners.[219] Boating meant both less and more to the Israelites and to other free black batteaumen than these store accounts suggest. It signified less in that not all Appomattox boatmen, and perhaps only a minority of them, made their living solely from the river. A number of Israelites who boated for Seay, including a couple of headmen, appear also—and sometimes only—as farmers on official free black lists of the early 1820s. Jacob Johnston, who captained a boat for Seay, never shows up on the lists as a batteauman; he clearly earned only part of his livelihood through boating.[220]

But running boats also stood for more than income, important though that was: it offered great mental and spiritual benefits, too. For many of those who worked the Appomattox, boating provided a good way of life. The time a black batteau crew spent on the water gave those men, at a bare minimum, something that black carpenter Charles Forgason possessed when he built the tobacco house for Josiah Cheadle—the freedom to plan, pace, and carry out their work largely as they saw fit.

Some carpenters, shoemakers, and other skilled workers came to spend less of their time operating as truly independent craftsmen and more time working under major contractors or entrepreneurs. By contrast, the black batteauman, like the wagoner and the midwife, usually did his job unsupervised by whites (free black boatmen, it seems, did not often work under white headmen). Court-ordered apprenticeships, another form of subordination with all its benefits and drawbacks, likewise made little headway on the river. The overseers of the poor rarely placed boys of either race with boat captains; free black batteaumen apparently learned the business from fathers, brothers, or friends.

Just as holding land eased the pressure on Israel Hill's women to earn money by plying domestic crafts, it helped smooth over the ups and downs of boating. The Israelites would never lack food, and they could grow some tobacco, corn, or other produce to earn money; meanwhile, they could work at boating whenever they wished and their services were in demand. Indeed, their residency on the Hill seems to have led some men to boat less intensively than they might have done otherwise. The Israelites' additional option—performing odd jobs ranging from hauling to coopering, for whites and for other blacks—provided added economic insurance without entailing clientage or subservience.

Not least among the nonmonetary benefits of boating was the privilege of traveling considerable distances and frequently spending time in Petersburg. That small but lively city had perhaps six thousand residents when Israel Hill was settled; its population more than trebled by 1860.[221] Petersburg was a center of Afro-Virginian life and culture, a place to purchase special items that could not be had at home, and an attraction that most black folk of Prince Edward rarely if ever got to see. Yet despite the

One benefit of river boating was the opportunity to spend time in Petersburg,
a center of commerce and of Afro-Virginian life and culture.

temptations such a life must have presented to both white and black
men, the Afro-Virginian boatmen of Prince Edward County as a group
enjoyed yet another benefit—a much better reputation than some of
their white peers possessed.

White boatman William Fox gained notice for his "frolics," horse
theft, and destruction of county property while in jail, and Grief Weaver
for violent confrontations with all and sundry, drunken revels, and his
eventual incarceration as a felon. Certain free black boatmen, too, suffered blemishes on their record. Kit Strong Jr. and Dick Clark won quick
exoneration when someone accused them of theft, but William Lilly,
who may have worked on batteaux, was convicted in 1823 of stealing a
pair of shoes and three pairs of gloves, apparently from a white man, and
he received twenty-five lashes.[222]

Three years after the conflict over Randolph Brandum's alleged use of
another man's slave without permission, Brandum was accused of stabbing a slave in the arm. The prosecutor quickly dropped the charges,
however, and the boatman continued to get along well with most whites.
In 1850, for instance, a justice of the peace near Petersburg went to considerable trouble to help Brandum replace his worn-out free papers.
Brandum, fortyish and standing nearly six feet tall, cut an imposing figure. He had not complied for years with the law requiring him to renew
his registration; still, the justice found him "honest and inoffensive, and
willing to work when any offers." Unable to decipher the information on

ON BOARD THE "GOVERNOR DUDLEY"

In Petersburg, boatmen encountered a colorful assortment of characters both white and black.   (LIBRARY OF VIRGINIA)

Brandum's old certificate, the official wrote back to the clerk of Prince Edward County, asking in particular whether the black man had been born before or after the death of "Richard Randolph[,] brother to Congress Jack."

Randolph Brandum had left Prince Edward County at least eighteen months earlier—yet Prince Edward's county clerk Branch Worsham proved as eager to help the black boatman as his fellow official from Petersburg had been. The JP in that city had painstakingly copied out the surviving shreds of Brandum's old registration, and now Worsham consulted his court records, picked up a pencil, carefully filled in the blanks, and sent the text back to Petersburg; he added a promise to renew Brandum's registration officially if the boatman appeared before Prince Edward's county court that fall. To spare Brandum any risk of legal unpleasantness in the future, Worsham made sure to include in the new free papers a notation that the black boatman had been emancipated by Richard Randolph's will "prior to the year 1806"—even though Brandum had been born only in 1808 or so, well after the law calling for the expulsion of newly freed blacks had passed.[223]

The remarkable goodwill that Randolph Brandum typically elicited was shared by more than a few other black boatmen of Prince Edward; in

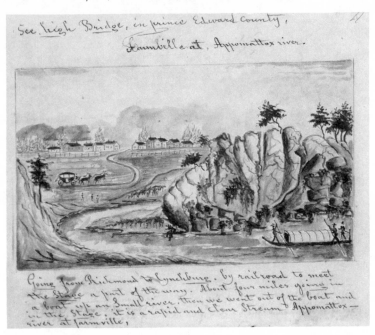

See Nigh Bridge, in prince Edward County,
Farmville at, Appomattox river.

Going from Richmond to Lynchburg, by railroad to meet
the Stage a part of the way. About four miles going in
a boat up an Small river, then we went out of the boat and
in the Stage; it is a rapid and clear Stream Appomattox—
river at farmville,

One traveler who rode upriver toward Farmville painted a unique picture of an
Appomattox batteau, complete with tent cloths.

(ABBY ALDRICH ROCKEFELLER FOLK ART MUSEUM, WILLIAMSBURG, VA)

fact, his own reputation probably benefited from his association with them. A white former boat owner decades later remembered fondly the batteau headmen of " 'Isreal Hill[,]' which was prolific in that day of many good free negroes." Phil and John White, Phil's son Curtis, and others, he added, had been "much respected for their ability as officers and [their] integrity . . . these were all colored men, but very much respected and trusted by all classes of citizens here." Today, such views sound patronizing; the very phrase "colored men but" lends a bad odor to the intended compliment. It would be easy to assume that when white folk in Prince Edward called the Whites and other free black boatmen "good free negroes," they really meant that those men were unthreatening—that, in the words of the justice of the peace who assisted Randolph Brandum, they were "inoffensive"—and perhaps even that they lacked pride and assertiveness.

Observant Baptists like Phil and Curtis White probably did seem safe to whites. But equating religious conviction, self-discipline, and decorous behavior with passivity or subservience is shallow and unfair; after all, the slave rebel leader Nat Turner was a Baptist lay preacher of dignified mien. Moreover, these Israelites did serious business with powerful white men, and they resisted aggression—financial, legal, or physical—on the relatively rare occasions they confronted it. Most striking of all, though these men might not swagger—the religion of those who became Baptists preached against that—they carried themselves with dignity and expected to be treated accordingly. The same memoirist who spoke of "good negroes" emphasized this very quality when he recalled the figure of the black headman, whom he called, with nostalgia rather than irony or condescension, the "captain" or "commodore" of the batteau.

The unnamed white old-timer reprised, and amplified, George Bagby's recollection of black boatmen performing a job "demanding skill, courage and strength": he vividly recalled "those old commanders, long since out of commission and passed away . . . , as proud of their command as many of the great captains of steamers of present day."[224] The black batteaumen did have much to take pride in. In what other setting in America before the Civil War did white people routinely and in earnest call black men "captains" or "headmen" just as they did those men's white counterparts?

As challenging as the boatmen's work could be, they took pleasure in it, too. It is easy for an observer who has never poled a boat a hundred miles against the current in all temperatures and weathers to romanticize life on the Appomattox. Yet to suppose that the river was nothing more than a mundane workplace for the boatmen would deny those men their due as perceptive people with an acute aesthetic sense. The Appomattox, when it behaved itself, was "a rapid and clear Stream." It contained abundant fish that the boatmen could catch along their way. The river presented a face that varied from one mile to the next as the stream alternated between calm stretches and sparkling, sonorous riffles, punctuated by several dozen locks, mill dams, and sluices. The river currents, one white boatman remembered, produced "most any beautiful shaped rock you want to look at"; sometimes the water's flow rotated smaller stones within a depression in a large one, gradually boring a hole and yielding a picturesque formation in the shape of a pot or a doughnut.[225]

The Appomattox passed through rolling hills and broad floodplains between Farmville and Petersburg. Considerably more cleared land lined the Appomattox in those days of intensive bottomland cultivation than in later periods; a boatman could often see farm and plantation fields beyond majestic trees that lined the riverbank along much of the stream's length.[226] Those fields, and the various mills and river hamlets along the stream, presented the humanity of the region in all its variety and provided numerous opportunities to interact with others—encounters that offset periods of quiet and solitude.

Beyond its sensual and social delights, the Appomattox River provided a superb venue in which to pursue the dream that so many other black Virginians, both free and enslaved, shared—that of independence. Different free blacks followed the dream in different ways, as their circumstances allowed: by moving from employer to employer, and by seeking out those who did not patronize their employees or hem them in; by mastering skilled trades; by practicing more than one occupation; by acquiring land; or by renting quarters in town or on the land of other free blacks.

The Appomattox River presented a face that varied from one mile to the next; calm stretches, as in this scene, alternated with sparkling, sonorous riffles.

(LIBRARY OF VIRGINIA)

Independence meant taking on a productive role within the broad, interracial economy while establishing a spot of one's own, figuratively or literally: a trade or business in which a person could labor at least part of the time without supervision by others; a little farm that a family could work according to their own lights, secure in the knowledge that they would never go hungry; the walkways or the helm of a batteau as voyagers cruised the Appomattox River and breathed some of the freest air available to any black man in the South. The boatmen of Israel Hill attained not only the last of these boons, but in fact all of them. That they dealt often with white coworkers, neighbors, and clients was unavoidable; given the firm foundation that underlay these black men's independence, and the fluidity of relations between free people of the two races, the interdependence need not be particularly troubling either.

The critical boundaries for the original, biblical Israelites, first between slavery and freedom, and later between wilderness and Promised Land, had been waterways—the Red Sea and the River Jordan. For the 250 years before Israel Hill's founding, the great passage of Africans across another, wider body of water had meant the opposite of liberty and land of one's own. Now, in America, yet another watercourse—the Ohio River—became a borderline between slavery and freedom that blacks suffered and even died trying to reach.

Rivers have long served as a metaphor for freedom in American life. This was true for Huckleberry Finn and, in a more elemental way, for Huck's companion, the fugitive slave Jim. The river might flow through a slaveholders' empire only to end at a slaveowning metropolis. Yet it might lead also to a vessel that would carry a fugitive to liberty on the seas and in lands beyond them—hence the laws aimed at controlling both slaves' access to waterways and the behavior of mariners and captains who might welcome their presence.

Even for enslaved people who could not bear to leave their families forever, and who knew the odds against a successful escape, the river could become, if not a route to liberty, then a place of temporary freedom. "To run the road with a waggon [or] the river with a boat" afforded a respite from day-to-day exactions and watchful eyes, for blacks still in slavery's grasp, and even for those who had left slavery behind.

One wonders whether some of the Afro-Virginian boatmen of the early nineteenth century had learned their job from grandfathers, or even fathers, who had worked as watermen in riverine societies of West Africa. Even if none received such a legacy, the realities of life in slaveholding America would have sufficed to embed the river deep in African American consciousness. It is surely more than coincidence that black men gravitated to boating in any number of New World slave societies.

Yet a fixation on water was no black monopoly. When officials in upper Prince Edward County described a person's homeplace for the record during the early years of the nineteenth century, they defined it by its distance and direction from the courthouse, the name of someone whose property it abutted, and the watercourse that skirted or traversed the parcel. If a landowner did not live on a named stream, there was surely a branch or gully that ran into one; such a tract typically entered the books as being situated "on waters of Buffaloe," or of whatever other creek or river absorbed the rainwater that fell onto that land.

For men and women of both races in Prince Edward, the river—*any* nearby river or stream—helped fix a location in one's mind. For the black batteaumen of Farmville, and especially those of Israel Hill, the river did even more to define a man's place in the world: it embodied labor, livelihood, and hardship, as well as dignity, public recognition, pride, and liberty. When one of those men announced—as Randolph Brandum, a son of Israel Hill, once did—that he was "a boatman . . . upon the waters of Appomattox,"[227] he was claiming a great deal, and he could expect others, both black and white, to know just what.

CHAPTER 5

Challenges

NAT TURNER

I n August 1831, Nat Turner, a slave and Baptist lay preacher in Southampton County in southeastern Virginia, led a group of his fellow bondmen from house to house, killing white inhabitants and marching toward the county seat. At least fifty-five whites lay dead before the revolt was suppressed. Panicked and vengeful whites killed scores of blacks, most of them unconnected to Turner and slain in cold blood, others actual rebels who died in the field or on the gallows.

In the aftermath of the slaughter, white Virginians engaged in an urgent debate about the future of slavery, but in the end made no basic change in the institution. Meanwhile, the Turner revolt put to the test another, smaller system—the life that free blacks, slaves, and whites lived together in majority-black Prince Edward County—and raised questions about the place Israel Hill would occupy within that local society.

Prince Edward belonged to an overwhelmingly rural South in which, we are told, white males grew up riding horses and shooting game, fathers sent their sons to military schools, and men kept their martial skills honed by participating in the state militia. No wonder, then, that whites quashed Turner's insurrection inside of two days. Prince Edward's own militiamen had served in the Revolutionary War, especially during Cornwallis's invasion of Virginia in 1781, and some local men bore arms again during the War of 1812.[1] But the county's largest purchase from the Venable mercantile store in the wartime year of 1814—a "Bugle Horn," along with "Ribbon & Silk for Colours"—hints at the real priorities of militia life.[2] Prince Edward's 63rd Regiment, like many others across the South in most periods, had more to do with show, conviviality, and social prestige than with military substance.

During the first years of Israel Hill, the regiment became an arena for infighting over who would receive officers' commissions; disappointed parties complained directly to the governor.[3] The county's male population contained a formidable collection of militia captains, majors, and colonels who retained their military titles until death. In many instances, however, the social prestige that attended such an appellation bore no real relationship to the martial experience of the man who sported it.

During the period between Israel Hill's founding and the Nat Turner rebellion, battalion militia musters took place annually. The experience of a couple of free black women in the 1810s gives an idea of the form those drills took. In the spring of 1813, the grand jury presented free Afro-Virginian Susannah Short—probably Ben Short's daughter by a deceased first wife—for selling liquor illegally; the same panel charged four other people, all white, with that misdemeanor or with having sworn profane oaths. All the alleged offenses had taken place at the same location on a single day: William Lindsey's old field on May 15. Lindsey's field was the drill ground for militiamen from Prince Edward during their annual battalion muster, and it was almost surely that gathering that produced the charges against Susannah Short and her fellow defendants.

Short and the other two accused vendors of liquor knew a good marketing opportunity when they saw one: the militia muster brought a large number of men together for a period of hours. The allegations of swearing—which in those days amounted to a charge of disorderly conduct—suggest that men imbibed the illegal spirits sold at Lindsey's field largely on the spot, and to considerable effect.[4]

The tradition of carousing at militia drills outlasted any effect that prosecutions of revelers or their suppliers might have had; Lindsey's old field, Clarke's muster ground, and the muster ground of Captains Madison and Penick produced other charges of liquor selling and cursing during the 1810s. Susannah (Sooky) Moss, daughter of free black shoemaker John Moss, faced charges of selling unlicensed liquor "to be drank where sold" at the battalion muster ground on two occasions, Saturdays exactly one year apart, in 1818 and 1819, and thus probably during militia "drills." In the latter year, Moss was one of at least two people charged as vendors of spirits at the muster ground.[5]

As news of the Nat Turner revolt spread in August 1831, large groups of whites in various parts of the state massed in private homes and prepared for Armageddon—and not wholly without reason: it quickly became clear that the militia was far from ready to put down a widespread rebellion, had one come. Militia officers in county after county gathered their men but "found themselves totally destitute of arms and ammunition," a condition that had gone unnoticed or aroused no concern through years of supposed drills. The government in Richmond did its best to allocate the few available firearms, to stop reprisals against innocent blacks (too late, in many instances), and "to quiet the publick mind."[6]

Leaders in Prince Edward and neighboring counties proved less alarmist than those in some other parts of Virginia—even though militia commanders in Prince Edward, Cumberland, Charlotte, and Buckingham found themselves as "destitute" of weapons as units in other localities were. Colonel Asa Dupuy of Prince Edward ventured the not unreasonable "opinion . . . that there should be arms in the hands of at least a part of the militia" there. "We have no public arms of any discription," he explained to the governor, "and as to fowling pieces (as inefficient as they are)," he estimated that he could assemble enough to equip a quarter of his men at best. The governor did in fact send some guns to Prince Edward and Cumberland.[7]

Within a few weeks of the revolt, militia leaders in the area were sending reassuring reports to Richmond. The commander in Cumberland told the governor in mid-September that there was "no cause for any apprehension in this quarter, [other] than . . . the great number of slaves among us," and the colonel from Charlotte County sent in a similar assessment two and a half weeks later. Asa Dupuy turned out to be one of the least excitable of militia commanders: in Prince Edward, he reported, "the slaves appear to be as quiet and orderly as I have ever seen them."[8] Leading men in Prince Edward disagreed among themselves about what their slaves might be up to, however. Colonel Charles Woodson told Dupuy that he had detected "suspicious" activity among his own bondpeople even before the revolt; Woodson had "since [become] convinced they were apprized of what was about to take place."[9] Farmville lies nearly a hundred miles from the site of the revolt; that a man as generally level-headed as Woodson could believe what he was telling Dupuy shows how deeply Turner's rebellion had affected the psyche of many white people.

Black boatmen made frequent trips to Petersburg—a city relatively close to Nat Turner's home area—yet Woodson apparently did not suggest that conspiratorial information had come to local slaves through those men. Colonel Dupuy passed on another troubling report about Israel Hill, however. It came from Major John Rice, who, like Woodson and Dupuy, served on the county court and in the militia. "In and contiguous to Farmville," Dupuy informed the governor, "there are several hundred blacks, a number of [whom are] free, and live about a mile from that place, and many of them engaged as labourers in ware-houses, Factories, and as boatmen plying between there and Petersburg." "Recently there appears to be much larger collections of negroes in Farmville than usual," Rice had told Dupuy, "with apparent dispositions to remain in bodies about the streets." The supposed tendency of blacks to congregate, Dupuy noted, "may proceed from accidental causes rather than design, but it has attracted attention, and it is thought expedient to keep an eye upon them."[10]

Dupuy was probably right when he said that a goodly fraction of the black people who appeared on the streets of Farmville in the wake of the revolt were free; whites presumably curtailed the movement of their slaves during those days of fear. Indeed, this was one of the many situations over the years that showed how much the adjective "free" in the phrase "free Negro" actually meant. Folk from Israel Hill in particular could easily have stayed at their own homes two miles away until the Turner alarm died down. Instead, it seems that free black residents of Farmville and Israel Hill, accustomed over the years to a high degree of personal liberty, spontaneously did the same thing whites were doing: they gathered with friends and discussed the extraordinary news from Southampton County and the rumors from so many other places.[11]

Colonel Asa Dupuy found little cause for concern in that. Like his uncle John Purnall before him, Dupuy had lived for years among the extended free black Homes family. When he contemplated free Afro-Virginians, he thought mainly of them, and they set off no alarm bells in his mind. Major John Rice, by contrast, lived in Farmville, near those concentrations of "several hundred blacks, a number of them free." One could easily conclude from Rice's conduct that he was one of the more vigilant law and order men among Prince Edward's elite, especially in matters involving free or enslaved blacks. Three months before the Turner rebellion, Rice had joined several others in complaining to the grand jury that Baxter Keirnan, a white resident of Farmville, had allowed unlawful assemblages of slaves on his lot and sold liquor to the blacks.[12]

Yet Rice was a more complicated character than that: he had a long-standing relationship with the Gibbs family of Israel Hill. Precisely in the period between 1829 and late 1831, John Rice was following, at Isaac Gibbs's invitation, the various financial transactions involving Gibbs and Phil White; Rice may even have transmitted a payment from one black man to the other. A decade later, the major would witness the will of Titus Gibbs, Isaac's father. Rice may simply have been one of the many men across Virginia who saw in the Turner panic an opportunity to enhance their own prestige. A number of worthies seized the moment to pursue officers' commissions. One man from Nat Turner's very neighborhood busied himself—once the rebellion had safely ended—organizing a cavalry company that he predicted would "hereafter *be renowned in story*" and designing special uniforms with "gilt bullet buttons."[13]

Whatever his motives in casting suspicion on blacks in and around Farmville, Rice avoided branding himself as a panicmonger. Even the phlegmatic Asa Dupuy retained enough confidence in the major not only to quote his warning to the governor but also to order that any weapons arriving from Richmond be placed under Rice's control. Dupuy, however, saw it as his job to "quiet the minds of the people." Though he sought weaponry for both an existing cavalry company and a new volunteer unit that Rice proposed to raise, Dupuy also instructed his subordinates "to make as little shew & parade as possible."[14] A massive military demonstration, besides being difficult to pull off with so few guns, would alarm whites and was not needed to overawe a black population from whom the colonel detected no threat. Dupuy's efforts to maintain calm apparently succeeded. County officials took no sudden action, nor does the record hint at any substantial unofficial activity against blacks. But at its regularly scheduled sitting in mid-September, the county court did revoke all licenses allowing free blacks to keep guns, and it ordered the constables of the county's two districts to collect "any arms found with any such free person" and hold them until the court issued further instructions.

The justices may have been responding to spontaneous pressure from white citizens. But the content of the resolution and the way it was adopted and carried out suggest instead that Asa Dupuy and men like him were working methodically to reassure white citizens that all bases had been covered; this, indeed, had been the principal reason the colonel had requested guns from Richmond. The court issued its order to confiscate blacks' firearms as part of a full day's agenda in which a raft of mundane issues were disposed of in perfectly banal fashion. The justices' very next action after the vote to confiscate guns was to order a routine accounting of John Tuggle's administration of the late Phil White Sr.'s estate.[15]

At least one county justice did see the issue of black-owned weapons as a serious one. He asked Major Rice to apply the court's confiscation order immediately in the area around Farmville; that particular JP believed "there [was] some reason to apprehend" that any arms free blacks owned might "be secreted or removed" before the formal court order had time to reach the constable and be carried out.[16] The justice obviously assumed that black people followed the county court's deliberations, and that they would not give up their firearms if they could help it. The JP also understood that others in authority felt no particular urgency about collecting free blacks' weapons. The court had been slow to adopt the confiscation measure; there is no indication in court papers that the constable of Prince Edward's lower district ever bothered to carry out the order. The constable of the upper district, which included Farmville and Israel Hill and thus the bulk of the county's free black population, moved languidly and without much apparent conviction. Four weeks after the court ordered him to collect guns, the constable, pleading illness in his family, reported that he had searched "six or eight" free blacks' houses and found no weapons. He added that he had inquired and had "heard of very few [blacks] in my district who had arms." Those people, he said, "as far as I can learn have been promptly disarmed by the citizens of my district, acting sometimes under special orders, & some times from a sence of public duty."[17]

That last statement turned out to mean that John Rice had attempted to carry out the "special order" he had received from the zealous county justice. The order authorized Rice to "take with [him] such force as [he might] find necessary" to collect weapons from free blacks, but the report Rice filed in mid-October leaves the impression that he had not thought any force called for. He reported most weapons as having been "rec[eive]d" rather than seized; only one was recorded as "Taken" from its owner.

Rice said he had located ten guns in all—a rifle belonging to his close acquaintance Isaac Gibbs, and nine shotguns, whose owners included Isaac's father, Titus, one young man each from the Israelite Carter and Wilkerson families, and the three living White family heads, Sam, Phil, and Tony. Rice also managed to collect "1 Old Sword, Broken & about two feet long," that had belonged to an "unknown" black person. Fully half the guns Rice reported on were out of order and unusable. Two—those of Sam and Phil White—were in the shop for repair at the time of the confiscation. The puny results of Major Rice's sweep leave us wondering whether some free blacks indeed "secreted or removed" their weapons before he began his canvass.[18]

One wonders, too, whether the three shotguns that lacked firing mechanisms had been intentionally disabled by black owners who hoped that the authorities would therefore not bother to collect them, or would return them quickly. Phil White Jr. in particular was in no hurry to bow to the court's order. Only after he reported, or Rice discovered, that he had a shotgun in the repair shop did it turn out that White owned a second gun, which was then confiscated. Sam White said that his own shotgun was being fixed in Petersburg; that weapon may have gone uncollected in Major Rice's roundup.

John Rice's report on the confiscation of guns reveals a couple of other remarkable facts. First, not one of the weapons that blacks gave up was in Rice's possession when the major made his report, and it is not certain that any of them had even passed through his hands. Phil White's second shotgun was "Taken by Mr. Fore"—presumably Charles Fore, the blacksmith who lived not far from Israel Hill. All but one of the other weapons not in the shop for repairs had been "left in C. C. Reads store" in Farmville. Black Israelites regularly traded at and through Clem Read's store. Just ten days after Major Rice filed his report on guns surrendered by Isaac Gibbs and others, Read would give bail for Gibbs in Phil White's lawsuit to collect money Gibbs owed him. Read also knew Israelite boatmen through his business, which shipped goods by batteau up and down the Appomattox. He would later play a role in Phil White's business dealings, witness Tony White's will, and care for the family of free black lot owner John Deneufville, a man who called Read his "friend."[19]

Why should the few guns that free blacks admitted to owning have ended up precisely in the hands of a man like Read? The gun owners themselves may have turned in weapons to this friendly neighbor in order to ease white minds in a time of stress and to lessen the chances of serious repression; they may have hoped to get the guns back from Clem Read once things calmed down. Or perhaps John Rice himself did collect the weapons, but then entrusted them to Read knowing that the Israelites would see the merchant as an honest broker. That Rice may have taken free black sentiment into account after Nat Turner's revolt seems incredible—unless the major's principal goal indeed was to enhance his prestige as a military figure rather than to neutralize a real danger.

Major Rice's report offers a second revelation: up until 1831, free blacks had been owning guns with the full knowledge and cooperation not just of those officials who issued licenses but of local whites generally. Phil White had placed one of his weapons with a local white craftsman for repairs. At the time of the confiscation order, the shotgun belonging to Nathan Wilkerson of Israel Hill was already in the hands of his white neighbor Amplias Tuggle, to whom Wilkerson had routinely lent the weapon. The neighborly interracial traffic in firearms seems to have moved in both directions: a third gun, though given up by James Bartlett of the free black boating clan in Farmville, turned out to belong to a white woman, who presumably had lent her gun to the black man.[20]

Nevertheless, the Nat Turner sensation clouded the atmosphere that had permitted a casual neighborliness between whites and free blacks in Prince Edward County during most periods. The response of John Rice in his role as militia officer, and then that of the county court—whether they acted on their own concerns or in response to those of white citizens—reinforced an essential fact: as successful as free Afro-Virginians had been in defending their interests over the years, they remained a minority, subject in time of crisis to suspicion and to special measures. Indeed, that message may have had a greater impact in 1831 precisely *because of* the successes various free blacks had achieved. This combination of tangible progress and vulnerability was one that blacks who fell victim to race riots in American cities during the first decades of the twentieth century would come to understand well. So would Japanese Americans during World War II, and Jews in many European societies at different times in history. Moreover, whatever repression did come would be decided on exclusively by the white population, or by its leading elements; though free blacks may have influenced the form and scope of the gun surrender, they had no means to prevent it.

At the same time, the reaction to Nat Turner in Prince Edward County turned out to be self-limiting. The number of patrollers trebled to nearly a hundred in the year of the revolt, and many of those riders claimed to have served long hours; but vigilance waned the following year, and only thirty men patrolled in 1833–34. Neither white authorities nor, so far as we know, white individuals in Prince Edward attacked or incarcerated free blacks in 1831. In fact, the county court arrived at an exquisite way of maintaining its image of itself as a tribunal offering justice to all. In March 1832, the court finally ordered the constable of the upper district to advertise and auction off the weapons free blacks had given up—and then to "pay the proceeds over to the [black] persons to whom the guns belong." The court must have been pleased with itself: by its own lights, it had treated free black people fairly and signaled them that in spite of everything they remained free members of society. It had vindicated property rights even while it assuaged the worries of some whites about public safety. It had even dealt generously with the constable, whom it ordered to deduct 5 percent of the proceeds from the gun sale as a commission for himself.[21]

In the meantime, the rising and then ebbing tide of repression made itself felt here and there in the lives of both white and enslaved individuals in Prince Edward. At least two slaves were arrested in September on charges of "plotting rebellion & murder of free white people." One of them, named Flem, went before a tribunal that included Asa Dupuy. The court deferred Flem's trial for nine days, perhaps to let passions cool, and then acquitted the defendant after hearing testimony from slaves. Another bondman charged with "conspiracy" was exonerated after a trial in which the court summoned witnesses from as far away as adjacent Nottoway County. Records concerning the county jail note that one slave "suspected of insurrection . . . [had been] placed there a few days for safe keeping."[22]

Two white men in Prince Edward found themselves accused during the Nat Turner panic in September 1831 of having allowed unlawful assemblages of blacks on their property. Interestingly, transplanted New Yorker Otis Williams was charged with having allowed fifteen free blacks—not slaves—to assemble at his house in September; the record offers no details of the event. William Beach faced charges of having permitted more than eighty slaves to come together "& remain" on his plantation. If a gathering of that size did take place shortly after Turner's revolt, it must indeed have worried Beach's neighbors. But again cooler heads prevailed. The charge against Beach was dismissed, and Williams was acquitted.[23]

By early 1832 at the latest, then, Prince Edward County's day-by-day race relations had largely returned to normal. The alarm one man raised that summer of a murderous slave plot led only to the acquittal of the supposed ringleader.[24] The fall and winter of 1831 did bring a modest flurry of free black registrations. Perhaps Major Rice asked to see free papers as he inquired about weapons, and discovered that some blacks lacked them. Of the twenty-five people who enrolled between September and January, however, two thirds were women—not the group that whites concerned about potential rebellion would have worried about most. When one free black man went to court in September and applied to have his lost free papers replaced, Nat Turner was still at large, but the county court obliged the applicant with no fuss or delay.

Subsequent years would bring similar moderate bursts of registrations—nineteen in September 1834, eighteen in October of the following year. Yet most of those registered *en bloc* in 1834 were slaves who had just won a lawsuit demanding their freedom—a jury verdict unlikely to issue from a white society that remained hunkered down after the events of 1831. Then too, a similar-sized bloc of registrants had enrolled in 1829, two years before the Turner rebellion.[25]

In the weeks after the county court voted to confiscate black persons' firearms, it continued to interact with a number of those Afro-Virginians in the most normal ways imaginable. The very same court session that rescinded gun licenses dealt with Phil White Sr.'s estate account and with an issue involving the division of his assets among his heirs. The following month, as John Rice reported the results of his search for weapons, the court considered and acted on yet another motion in the legal battle between John Brown and Hampton Giles over their competing land claims on Israel Hill. In January 1832, before the county court had even decided what to do with the guns Major Rice had located, the justices granted the request of the late Dick White's children to have a permanent (white) guardian appointed, and Guy Howard's wife, Pamelia, sued Sam White for the right to maintain her residence on a corner of his land.[26]

In bad times as in good, of course, everyday life goes on. But Prince Edward's free blacks showed a striking readiness in the period after Nat Turner's rebellion to conduct business before the authorities who governed them much as they had earlier. The fact that they had done just that for years helps explain why most county justices and other whites, most of the time, tended to see individual people with real personal and financial lives, and not some anonymous, threatening abstraction, when they glanced up at Israel Hill.

Even so, the gun confiscation of 1831 was not the first official act of its kind. In November 1826, long before anyone outside Southampton County ever heard of Nat Turner, the Prince Edward County Court had revoked gun licenses held by free blacks and given them a month to sell off their weapons. The justices did not record their reasons, but they did act while Guy Howard and Hampton Giles were facing trial for supposedly stealing a hog from a white man. The charges against the two Israelites and the court's gun order both point to a body of suspicion that some of the county's white citizens harbored at the time. Yet the court, an even-tempered group as usual, found Giles and Howard not guilty literally moments after it revoked free blacks' gun permits.[27]

In that same season, some whites had tended to see the county's free black populace more as a prop for levity than as an object of dread. Only four months after the gun order of 1826, an anonymous wag got an idea for a prank. He submitted to a newspaper in Richmond an account of a political meeting that supporters of Andrew Jackson had supposedly conducted in Prince Edward. The writer reported that the gathering had taken place at "Israel Hill"; the names of the participants he listed were in fact those of free black residents of the county. "Mr. Christopher Strong" had ostensibly presided over the meeting, with "Mr. William Ellis" serving as its secretary; other "gentlemen" participating in the fictive gathering included Joseph Bartlett, Samuel White, Hercules White, and John Moss.

Apart from those names, the report read in every detail like dozens of genuine political notices that appeared constantly in the press. Its author did not aim to ridicule Jacksonians; two men at a pro-Jackson dinner in Prince Edward some three weeks later proposed toasts to the unnamed writer of the piece. The challenge for the author of these "Israel Hill Resolutions" had been different: to write a report so legitimate-sounding that an urban newspaper would publish it, yet to include in it a twist that white people back in Prince Edward County would find diverting. The prank reminds one of a modern high-schooler who submits to the youth page of his city's newspaper a set of senior-class superlatives in which he has inserted improbable or even fictional students' names as best-looking, most popular, and most likely to succeed.

The author may have wished partly to deprecate individual blacks; he reserved the title "Doctor" for Burwell (Burrell) Moss, who had lost an ear to an ax-wielding free black woman a few years earlier. The deeper source of amusement for white folk back home in Prince Edward, however, lay in what they would have seen as an absurd juxtaposition—political pronouncements couched in elevated language, supposedly issuing from the mouths of people whose race and status denied them all access to education and political activity.[28] The element most conspicuously absent from the "Resolutions" prank was anxiety over a supposed threat from free blacks. Not surprisingly, then, the revocation of free blacks' gun permits that the court had adopted a short time before did not stick: as early as March 1827, Sam White applied for and received from the county court a license to keep a gun and ammunition, with no apparent argument.[29] The events after the Turner revolt in 1831 would show that White was far from alone among free blacks in acquiring a gun after—or keeping one in spite of—the order of 1826.

One day during the period between the court's two orders revoking free blacks' gun licenses, Prince Edward's county clerk received a slip of paper listing the militia officers elected that year. On the back of the slip, written in pencil, appear the words: "Call Phill White."[30] The clerk and others fairly frequently jotted down reminders, calculations, or doodles on the backs of official papers, and there is no reason to think that the notation about White had anything to do with the militia election. More likely, the clerk or someone else at the courthouse needed to consult Phil White Jr. about his late father's estate or one of the other matters that brought the ambitious black man to the county court fairly regularly. Whatever its origins, the cryptic sentence scribbled on a list of officers symbolizes a continuing reality of life in Prince Edward: the county's generally casual security arrangements, epitomized by a grandiose but nearly toothless county militia, went hand in hand with local officials' habit of dealing matter-of-factly with their free black neighbors.

EDMUND YOUNG AND FREE BLACK RESISTANCE

A drama surrounding the free Afro-Virginian Edmund Young reached a climax of its own during the year of the Turner rebellion. Other free blacks achieved more worldly success and won far more esteem from white people than Young did. Yet he managed to enhance and defend his liberty in ways less spectacular but more effective than anything Major John Rice feared, or said he feared, after Nat Turner's revolt.

Young, the former coworker of Hercules White Sr. and sometime vendor of oysters, had moved onto the derelict tract he called home at about the same time the former Randolph slaves were settling on Israel Hill.[31] The ground Young chose occupied an odd place in Prince Edward's mind and on its maps. A Scottish-owned mercantile firm had acquired a couple of tracts in Prince Edward, including this property on the road from the county seat to Charlotte Court House. The company's local representative had returned to Britain at the time of the Revolutionary War. Legal complications had ever after prevented the selling of the land, which entered a kind of limbo: people recalled that it belonged to "some British subject" and called it "the British land," but taxes on the tract went unpaid for decades, and nature gradually obliterated the visible markers around its perimeter.[32]

Edmund Young had chosen the perfect place to settle at no cost to himself: the legal owners of the British land, long since dead, would never show up to claim it, and no one in America had the right to sell the tract out from under him. Because Young did not hold formal title, he would not even have to pay taxes on the land he now lived on. The legal phrase "quiet and peaceable possession" described Young's new situation aptly. There was plenty of space for him to meet his own needs without getting in anyone else's way; he built his house fairly deep within the eight-hundred-acre parcel, half a mile in from the road.[33] He must have cleared some of the acreage or restored old fields, for in most years the county listed him as earning his living by farming. Still, Young did not live in isolation; he developed various relationships both with whites and with other blacks. He and his family were not even alone on the British land; John Perrin, a white man, also squatted on the tract at about the same time. As the only adult male in a slaveless household of seven or eight, Perrin probably had no chance to buy land of his own. Young, like other blacks both bond and free, also had regular, friendly contact with the extended white Colley family, who lived nearby. Edmund Colley would testify on Young's behalf when a conflict did eventually arise over ownership of the British land.[34]

Edmund Young's home ground became a magnet for other free Afro-Virginians, in much the same way, and during the same years, that Israel Hill and the Ben Short–Patty Bartlett tract did. Many of those who joined Young were related to him or to his common-law wife, Betsy, a member of the Forgason clan of carpenters and farmers. Betsy's own children, perhaps fathered by an enslaved husband now dead or removed from the area, were serving as apprentices during the years around 1810. Her son Dick worked with free black shoemaker Ben Short, another son with the white blacksmith Charles Fore. But her two daughters stood to benefit far less from the gender-bound apprenticeships that the overseers of the poor had found for them. Betsy's union with Edmund Young enabled those two girls to return to their mother over the next few years; they lived with her and with stepfather Young on the British tract until they were ready to venture out for themselves. Other members of both Young's and Betsy Forgason's families joined the household at various times: a couple of these likely were Edmund's daughters by an earlier marriage. Edmund Young and Betsy Forgason may also have produced a child or two of their own.[35]

For a while around 1818, a free black woman named Nancy Hamilton came with her daughters to join the Youngs on the British land. After their stay there, the Hamiltons settled on Israel Hill. Nancy Hamilton married Syphax Brown II, grandson of the former Randolph valet and son of the contentious John Brown. Nearly a quarter century later, black Israelite Titus Gibbs would leave his entire estate to one Nancy Hamilton, probably the daughter of the original Nancy; the younger woman may have nursed Gibbs in his old age or even become the widower's de facto second wife.[36]

Edmund Young's amicable relations with white neighbors did not arise from any passivity on his part. Having earlier sued a white man for assault, he proved ready to protect "his" land and his expanded household whenever a threat arose. That happened for the first time in the fall of 1819. The two British tracts in Prince Edward were "escheated to the Commonwealth" on the grounds that their owners had died without heirs. That meant that Justice Charles Woodson was appointed to take control of the acreage and sell or lease it for the benefit of the state. Woodson filed a lawsuit to expel Edmund Young.

Woodson's lawsuit did mention Young's white fellow squatter, John Perrin, but not as a formal defendant. Racial bias on Woodson's part seems an obvious explanation—except that Woodson had a history of friendly relations with the free black Eppersons and Dwins, and he always operated "by the book" in his interactions with white and black alike, whether that brought grief or relief to the person he was dealing with. In fact, a verdict against Edmund Young would strip Perrin, too, of any right to the land; in good time, the authorities would show that they were determined to remove the white man as well as Young.[37] Woodson may have targeted Young because he had settled on the British land first. Or perhaps the colonel assumed he had a better chance of winning before an all-white jury if the defendant of record were black. If Colonel Woodson believed that, however, he underestimated both Edmund Young's perseverance and the legal system's readiness to hear a free black man out.

Woodson called three white witnesses. A jury found that Young did hold possession of the British tract "against [Woodson's] consent," that he had already squatted on the land for more than three years, and that Woodson as escheator ought therefore to recover all eight hundred acres.[38] To the average person, that sounds like a perfectly logical verdict, if perhaps a lamentable one. But in fact it proved that the jury, and the justices who presided at the trial, either did not know the law or chose not to apply it. The law had long permitted—and today still permits—a party to gain permanent use or even outright possession of another's property by squatting on it and meeting certain conditions. Occupying a piece of land openly, visibly, continuously for a period of years prescribed by law, and *without the owner's permission* creates a legal right to permanent use of the property through "adverse possession." Edmund Young's occupancy of the British land without permission had certainly been open, visible, and continuous; his relationships with others in the community, both black and white, were numerous and varied, and the county's own free black lists had recorded him as living on the British tract year in, year out. The jury recognized all that, yet rendered a verdict exactly opposing the one its own findings required.

The list of jurymen in the trial may help explain that outcome. Three jurors, one of them the panel's foreman, had signed an official inquest only two years earlier stating that the British land ought to revert to the Commonwealth.[39] The official who drew up the jury list may have stacked the deck against Edmund Young intentionally. On the other hand, jurors and commissioners were always chosen from among those propertied white males who were more or less willing to serve; in a rural county with a limited supply of such men, it was common for the membership of any two panels to overlap simply by luck of the draw. Either way, however, men who had sworn in writing that the British land had no owner and should belong to the state must not have been eager to contradict themselves now.

Edmund Young had lost a round, but he was no quitter, and he had hired a competent lawyer. Young may even have known and counted on the principle of adverse possession before he ever settled on the British land. His attorney appealed to a justice of Virginia's General Court, a court of appeals; only two days later, that jurist stayed the county court's judgment against Young and sent the case to the circuit court, a tribunal superior to the county court and presided over by a single judge trained in the law. The following April, the circuit court for Prince Edward County confirmed Edmund Young's right to his home. The circuit judge ordered escheator Woodson to pay all Young's costs both for the appeal and for fighting the original suit in the county court.[40]

Once again, the system—this time after a legally indefensible outcome in the county court—had come through for a free Afro-Virginian. Both the appellate court justice who ordered a retrial and the circuit court that conducted the proceeding knew explicitly from suit documents that Edmund Young was black. Furthermore, he was a squatter facing a challenge from one of Prince Edward's foremost citizens: a county court justice acting as an agent of the county and state governments. Yet Young had the law on his side, and the law worked as it was supposed to. He and his extended family remained in their home. So, thanks to a black man's stalwart self-defense, did the white Perrin family.[41]

Half a dozen years passed before certain powerful white people in Prince Edward again cast longing eyes at the land on which Young lived. In the mid-1820s, the Commonwealth of Virginia called on each county to set up a poorhouse in which inmates who were able would be put to useful work. Prince Edward's county court chose as the site of its new poorhouse a portion of the British tract. The justices did not revive the legally discredited idea of expelling Edmund Young, however. Beginning in the fall of 1826, some 400 yards from Young's home, builders began erecting a complex that was supposed to encompass half a dozen structures, including a residence for the steward, or superintendent, and his family. In July 1827, just as the poorhouse was about to open, the new steward's house, still unoccupied, burned down, and Edmund Young was immediately charged with having torched it.[42]

Thomas Rice, who accused Young of arson, himself lived near the British tract. He had served on the jury that attempted to expel Young in 1819, and had then seen the higher courts make mincemeat of that verdict.[43] Rice may have hoped to accomplish through a conviction of Young for arson what he, his fellow jurors, and Charles Woodson had failed to achieve eight years earlier. Or perhaps Rice had jumped to a sincere though hasty conclusion—that Edmund Young saw the building of the poorhouse complex near his home as an imposition, and that Young thus had a strong motive to thwart the project by burning down the building without which the facility could not open.

Young may well have spent the month between his arrest and trial in jail; the county justices had not found the situation so pressing that a special meeting should hear the case. At trial, prosecution and defense subpoenaed nearly a score of witnesses. Young's wife, Betsy Forgason, and the couple's grown children were called and presumably offered alibi evidence. Young's lawyer summoned at least one member of the neighboring white Colley family, and one slave whom Young's fellow squatter John Perrin had acquired not long before. Some of the prosecution's witnesses, too, may actually have aided Young's cause—for the county court found the black man not guilty.

On the one hand, any rejoicing Edmund Young indulged in after his acquittal must have been muted. He had got no more than his due as an innocent defendant, he had spent time in jail, and the highly effective defense his lawyer provided had cost him dearly: seven months after Young's acquittal, the attorney would sue his ex-client for a $100 fee. On the other hand, attorney and client proceeded to settle their accounts informally, and the same lawyer would represent Edmund Young in another case a few years later.[44] Moreover, Young had discovered that he still had friends both black and white after a lifetime of self-assertion, and he had won a crucial legal triumph.

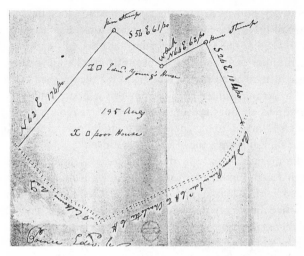

The county built its poorhouse not far from free black Edmund Young's home, as marked on this plat. Officials tried to expel the black man, but were rebuffed by local and appellate courts.

(*Justices of Prince Edward v. Young*, CIRCUIT COURT, SEPTEMBER 1833, ARCHIVES RESEARCH SERVICES, LIBRARY OF VIRGINIA)

Young's life now returned to normal, his relations with various white neighbors seemingly not affected by the recent struggle. He continued to buy corn meal from the Dupuy brothers' mill; the Dupuys remained willing to put purchases on Young's tab, and when they did impose limits on extensions of credit, they did it almost apologetically.[45] But Young's defense of his home, even after two signal victories separated by eight years, was not over yet. The county had the burnt-down steward's house replaced, and the poorhouse went into operation. Inmates were required to sustain the institution by farming its lands, and within a year, by mid-1828, the overseers of the poor began to chafe over the continued presence of squatters on the tract. "If we had full possession of the premises," the president of the board told the county court, "the Poor house institution, would nearly support itself. What is the reason we cannot obtain possession, of that which we have purchased and paid for?" he demanded.[46]

In the summer of 1830, the overseers of the poor ordered their president to "take the necessary steps to remove Edmund Young . . . from the possession he now holds" on the poorhouse tract. The county justices proceeded to sue Young for ownership of the land. Escheator Woodson had conveyed another parcel of the British land to a local buyer, and that man now filed a similar suit against the white squatter, John Perrin.[47] It is not clear whether these suits were aimed at physically expelling Young and Perrin from their houses. The plaintiffs may have hoped simply to establish their right to plant crops wherever they wished on the two tracts. The action against Perrin did produce at least a temporary defeat for the white man. But the county in the end made some sort of arrangement with Edmund Young and agreed to drop its suit against him; the law, after all, still favored the black homesteader.

In the meantime, though, this most recent conflict went through phases that were anything but amicable. Edmund Young and Betsy Forgason had lived as de facto man and wife for some fifteen years, perhaps longer, when the county court sued him over the land. Yet a deputy sheriff who served papers at Young's house entered an unusual notation stating that he had presented the documents to Young's "nominal wife" and told "said woman" what they meant.[48] The deputy may simply have been taking care to document his action precisely, but one suspects he was expressing his jaundiced personal opinion of Edmund Young's domestic arrangements.

Then, in the spring of 1831, while the case between the county and Edmund Young ground on, Young accused five white men of having assaulted his nearly grown stepson, Jordan Forgason. Young sued the group, adding that they had held the youth "in duress & falsly imprison[ed]" him for two days. One of the alleged assailants was a tavern keeper who would one day face charges of having shot at a white fellow citizen—just the sort of character one could imagine doing what Edmund Young and Jordan Forgason now accused him of.[49] The identity of one of the other men Young charged, Reverend Joseph Goode, raises eyebrows.

This minister of the gospel, it turns out, had a particular bone to pick with Edmund Young and family. Goode had been hired as the original steward of the new poorhouse, for which he was to receive generous compensation—an annual salary of $250, along with all the provisions he and his family might consume and the use of a handsome new four-room house with five fireplaces and a full cellar. Then, back in 1827, just as the house had been finished and made ready for the Goode family to move into, it burned down, Edmund Young was blamed, and the Goodes had to wait an extra half-year for their living quarters.[50] Young's acquittal for arson probably counted for little with preacher Goode, and the bad blood between the two men had clearly continued as they lived on the same tract of land.

The suit for assault that Edmund Young and his stepson filed against Goode and the others played out in a manner that was common enough in Prince Edward even when adversaries belonged to the same race. The court continued the case month after month, waiting for a written complaint or "declaration" from Young and Forgason. When, after nearly a year, none came, the suit was dismissed. Perhaps someone had intimidated the blacks into letting the matter die—but Edmund Young had stood up to many other pressures over the previous two decades and was resisting the county court's lawsuit even then. Or perhaps Young's goal in filing the action had not been to win actual damages, a chancy proposition in lawsuits for assault. Instead, he may have intended mainly to serve notice on his enemies that he would not be cowed—and on county officials that they had better come to terms with him.

That seems to be what happened in the end. The settlement that the county justices arrived at with Edmund Young may have left him in his home; that he and various members of his family remained in the neighborhood is certain. By 1838, two of Young's sons had found wives who settled down with them there. Those young men had inherited their father's determination to go his own way: Ned and Billy Young chose white spouses, a pair of women (perhaps sisters) from the extensive and economically diverse Bigger clan, whose lands lay near the Young homestead.

Like their father, Ned and Billy neither sought gratuitous confrontations with whites nor backed down when challenged. A grand jury presented them and their wives in 1838 for "living together and committing fornication." Many whites, however, apparently saw no need to act against the four. At least one of the two mixed-race couples already had a year-old child before any citizen even bothered to bring charges. When a deputy sheriff finally went out to arrest Ned Young and Parthena Bigger in 1839, he wrote on the back of the warrant that the two had been "found But The door shut and could not be caught." Then the deputy altered that notation to read simply, though falsely, that the suspects were "not found." The deputy's tinkering with the warrant allowed him to justify his failure to apprehend the couple—but without suggesting that they had evaded him or resisted arrest, which could have got them into deeper trouble.[51]

Something besides the mere fact of their cross-racial unions seems to have led to the filing of charges against Ned and Billy Young. Newton Cunningham and David F. Womack, who complained about Billy and his wife before the grand jury, were hardly the sort to stare aghast at marriages uniting white and black. Both men had long been civil, even congenial, near neighbors of the free black Dungeys, Mosses, Forgasons, and Goffs—the first three of whom were themselves biracial families.[52]

The two white men, both of whom would soon become county justices, had a particularly close relationship with John and James Dungey Jr., who were free mulatto sons and brothers-in-law of white women. Womack would eventually witness John Dungey's will; in that document, Dungey named Cunningham his executor and gave him broad discretion to look out for the interests of his surviving family. Cunningham would advance food, and ultimately a coffin, for the wife of the less prosperous James Dungey Jr. Newton Cunningham's father and brother had constructed the poorhouse complex on the British land, including the steward's house that Edmund Young had been accused of burning down. Perhaps hard feelings toward the Youngs lingered from that incident.[53]

Nothing that white witnesses said seems to have carried much weight against the Youngs and their wives, for the prosecutor himself moved to have the case against all four dismissed, and the two couples continued to live together. Some people remained unhappy with the Youngs' and Biggers' way of life, however; the two pairs were presented again, this time in the circuit court two years after the earlier incident, for "living together unlawfully as man & wife."[54] Authorities did not carry forward this second challenge to the interracial households. On the eve of the Civil War, Billy Young would still be living with Elizabeth Bigger and a couple of their children, on land belonging to Betsy's white relatives; she was now sixty years old and Billy forty-eight. And in 1851, a group of "bright yellow" Bigger children—apparently those born to the second couple, Ned Young and Parthena Bigger—registered at the courthouse. The youngest was only six years old at that time, which suggests that the biracial pair had stayed together for at least seven years after charges were first brought against them.[55]

Edmund Young's sons inherited his talent for gauging how far a man could go without setting himself up for an irreparable fall. By the time they faced charges in 1838, Ned and Billy Young must have noticed that many whites in Prince Edward, though not all, tolerated stable interracial marriages. None of the three biracial couples charged ten years earlier had been convicted. Martha League and at least a couple of others bore children by black men, apparently without incurring punishment. Prosecutions of white couples for fornication or adultery occurred about as often as those of biracial pairs; courts and juries seemed considerably more perturbed by the former than by the latter. One white couple were convicted in 1821 of "living in adultery" and assessed a substantial penalty. Another white man and woman would be fined the remarkable sums of $150 and $100, respectively, "for Lewdly & lasciviously associating & cohabiting together" in 1851.[56]

The story of Edmund Young and his family encompasses a broad range of free black experience in Prince Edward County. No other free Afro-Virginian group faced nearly as many challenges from whites as the Youngs did. Yet their saga also displays the ability of resourceful free black people to protect themselves, and the readiness of more than a few whites, both influential and simple people, to behave temperately and sometimes even sympathetically. Each struggle the Youngs went through is known to us either because whites who had differences with them pursued those quarrels in court rather than through lawless attacks, or because Edmund Young proved perfectly ready to complain in court about the few who confronted him outside the law.

The whites who governed Prince Edward caused Edmund Young far more trouble than an honest man ought to have to endure, yet they also determined that theirs was and would remain, for free people both white and black, a society of laws. Throughout it all, Young kept his white friends, with never a whiff of truckling subservience. Ranging from fellow squatter John Perrin through the modestly situated Colley family and up to the well-off and influential Dupuys, those whites continued to deal with Young as just what he was—not a paragon, perhaps, but still a neighbor whom one treated as such and perhaps even defended in the face of injustice. Against that backdrop, and in part because of it, Edmund Young managed to resist every force that threatened to bring him down. He began with little except his own ambition, found land to settle on, stayed there for nearly two decades and probably longer, reunited one black family, reared another, gave shelter to a third, and made a living.

Major John Rice had been right to suspect, in the wake of the slave revolt of 1831, that free Afro-Virginians would struggle to expand their liberties. In those days of fear, though, he overlooked something that free blacks had made clear long before: however much the particulars of their lives might differ from Edmund Young's, their strivings and their acts of resistance would follow his model rather than Nat Turner's.

IDLENESS, POVERTY, AND DISSIPATION: THE BIRTH OF A PROSLAVERY MYTH

The aftermath of Nat Turner's rebellion reminded free Afro-Virginians, and especially black Israelites, that even some white people who dealt with them routinely as individuals sometimes viewed them collectively as an "issue." The bogus "Israel Hill Resolutions" back in 1827 illustrated the same duality.

Had the names of free black individuals mentioned in that newspaper piece not been familiar to white citizens of Prince Edward County and vicinity, few readers would have got the joke. Yet the Resolutions also showed that "Israel Hill" had become a shorthand phrase that one could use—with approval, amusement, or disdain—to stand for the county's entire free Afro-Virginian population, in something like the way people today employ the name "Hollywood" to refer to the American film industry as a whole. It made little difference to the author or his readers that not all the persons whose names appeared in the Resolutions actually lived on the Hill, or that most free blacks in the county did not. For certain other whites, Israel Hill offered fodder not for sophomoric pranks but rather for proslavery propaganda. The story of Israel Hill's supposed failure as an experiment in black freedom would reach a national public and even outlive the era of slavery. That narrative first took shape practically within sight of the Hill some four years after Nat Turner's revolt.

Edmund Ruffin of Virginia, one of America's foremost agricultural reformers and defenders of Southern society, began the process. Having heard about Israel Hill, Ruffin published an appeal for information about the settlement in an early issue of his important journal, the *Farmers' Register*. One of the Israelites' white neighbors, Colonel James Madison—a planter, merchant, tobacco manufacturer, and distant relative of the former president of the United States—wrote a reply to Ruffin; it appeared in the *Register* in 1836.[57] Madison's history of Israel Hill ran only about a third of a printed page, but its vehemence and the importance editor Ruffin attached to it made up for its brevity.

Madison actually had a good word to say for the original settlers of Israel Hill—or more precisely, for the system of bondage that he thought had molded them. "As long as the habits of industry, which they had acquired while slaves, lasted," Madison wrote, the emancipated Israelites had "continued to increase in numbers, and lived in some degree of comfort." But the next chapter of the story, according to the colonel, showed what would happen whenever African Americans were permitted to grow to adulthood without white supervision. As the elder generation of Israelites aged or died off, Madison asserted, "a new race, raised in idleness and vice, sprang up." The "idleness, poverty, and dissipation" of this new cohort had "render[ed] them wretched in the extreme, as well as a great pest, and heavy tax upon the neighborhood in which they live."

Edmund Ruffin urged his readers to grasp the global significance of Israel Hill's supposed decline. The Randolphs' experiment, he declared, had been "a fair and decisive . . . trial of the effects of negro emancipation, made under the most favorable circumstances"; the Randolph family, he insisted, had freed only blacks who were "trained to labor," and had "abundantly provided [them] with fixed farming capital." Ruffin added that the free blacks had squandered even the opportunity to prosper from river boating, which he said they preferred over other occupations "because it is the nearest to idleness." For Ruffin and Madison, the case was closed. Africans and African Americans were born to be slaves; freedom would bring nothing but disaster to them and trouble to the white people among whom they lived.

Edmund Ruffin's prominence ensured that Colonel Madison's report on the Israel Hill "experiment" would receive serious attention. The *Lynchburg Virginian* reprinted Madison's letter in July of the same year, adding an endorsement as emphatic as Ruffin's had been.[58] Other, more distant newspapers apparently did the same, for within weeks the Madison thesis stirred emotions at least as far away as the Princeton Theological Seminary, whose Committee on Africans and Colonization quoted Madison's letter in a written report. Soon the journal of the American Colonization Society, which promoted the resettlement of free African Americans in Liberia, reprinted Madison's article from the *Farmers' Register*. Colonizationists constantly battled against the belief of Madison and his kind that Africans could not long survive in freedom—for if that were true, black colonization and self-government in Africa would surely fail. The colonizationists publicized Madison's diatribe partly to expose the prejudices free blacks would have to contend with if they remained in the United States. They also wanted to make clear that this jaundiced epitaph for Israel Hill had not flowed from the pen of former President James Madison, an influential promoter of the Liberian project who had died that summer.[59]

Although Colonel Madison was the first published writer to single out Israel Hill as a proslavery exhibit, much of what he said about black freedom had been stated before. Some of the key words he used came from writings and from talk that had circulated in Virginia and elsewhere for half a century by the time his letter appeared. In 1796, St. George Tucker, Richard Randolph's stepfather, had proposed gradual emancipation of the entire slave population, yet he worried that generations of bondage had left blacks unprepared to cope with freedom in the short term. If liberated blacks were colonized in some isolated corner of the United States without at least temporary white supervision, Tucker wrote, they might become "hordes of vagabonds, robbers and murderers." Alternatively, Tucker feared that ex-slaves left to fend for themselves among white Americans could become "a numerous, starving, and enraged banditti," posing a threat to "the innocent descendants of their former oppressors." Nearly two decades after Tucker wrote, Thomas Jefferson still quietly professed interest in the idea of gradual emancipation, but he did nothing whatever to promote such a plan; he predicted that freed blacks, if not expatriated, would become "pests," their "idleness" inclining them to theft.[60]

These characterizations were offered up by the likes of Tucker and Jefferson before a large free black population even existed. By contrast, Colonel Madison wrote from a county in which, by 1836, one free person in ten was black.[61] He himself had had considerable personal contact with free Afro-Virginians. Yet his published statement about that group constituted not a detailed narration of his own observations and experiences, but rather the recitation of a litany composed before his time, reiterated for years after his death, and repeated in other contexts about other African American communities well into our own era. Moreover, though Madison and like-minded men echoed certain statements of St. George Tucker, they rejected out of hand one of Tucker's central premises—that differences between the races stemmed mostly from decades of oppression rather than from inborn disparities.

Madison and his contemporaries had ready access to the working vocabulary on which the antiblack litany drew. Thomas Roderick Dew, professor of history, metaphysics, and political law at the College of William and Mary and later president of that institution, became one of the foremost intellectual defenders of Southern society. Four years before Madison's piece about Israel Hill appeared, Dew had published a work in which he envisioned Virginia evolving slowly into a free-labor society. Yet he defended slavery in the interim as a morally sound system that benefited both masters and slaves. Dew called free blacks "the most worthless and indolent" of people, "the very *drones* and *pests* of society."[62]

The term "pests," employed years earlier by Jefferson, had become an axiomatic characterization of free blacks—so much so that Colonel Madison reflexively called the Israelites, twice within three sentences, "a very great pest." Madison also echoed other themes of the earlier writers, sometimes using their very formulae. Reprising Jefferson, Madison used the words "idle" or "idleness" three times in two sentences, and decried a lack of "industry" among the Israelites a few lines later; lest any reader miss the point, Edmund Ruffin used the word "idleness" yet again in his editor's note. St. George Tucker's "starving" free blacks likewise reared their heads among Madison's black Israelites, in whose case "dissipation" had purportedly helped "to diminish their numbers."

Here Colonel Madison introduced yet another theme that would pervade writings about Israel Hill, and about blacks in general, for decades to come. The Israelites' dissolute habits, he said, made it "impossible that the females can rear their families of children—and the consequence is, that they prostitute themselves, [acquire venereal diseases,] and consequently have few children." On those youngsters, Madison added, "time, profligacy and disease" then took a further toll. (The colonel did not explain how infertile women could produce "families of [neglected] children.") By the end of the nineteenth century, racial theorists would confidently make similar assertions about the entire black South: inherent racial character flaws, they said, would cause the African American population to wane and ultimately die out.[63]

Madison's own volley against Israel Hill responded in part to the lengthy debate after Nat Turner's revolt over the legitimacy and viability of slavery in Virginia. The institution had survived that crisis intact. Yet some whites had shown themselves ready to consider ending slavery gradually; others continued to emancipate bondpeople privately despite laws discouraging the practice. Colonel Madison sought to warn fellow white Southerners, especially Virginians, against misplaced humanitarianism by depicting the supposedly disastrous effects of setting blacks free. Madison also wanted to strike back at the abolitionist movement that had begun to spread in parts of the North. The Lynchburg newspaper saw the colonel's piece as a direct retort to "the pseudo-philanthropists of the nation," "afflicted" with a "mental malady and pious phrenzy."

Edmund Ruffin, too, considered a good offense the best defense against abolitionism. A year before running Madison's letter, his *Farmers' Register* had reprinted an article from a newspaper in Cincinnati that chronicled the alleged failure of two settlements of manumitted blacks in southern Ohio. The article trotted out the well-worn themes that earlier opponents of black freedom had used, and that Madison would borrow the following year. The Ohio communities had been set up, readers learned, as an "experiment . . . to test the merits of the negro race, under the most favorable circumstances." But the venture had supposedly produced, aside from a few virtuous households, nothing but "exhausted and worn out" plots of land inhabited by "excessively lazy and stupid" people "too listless even to fiddle and dance."[64] Reports like that one, and notices in Northern papers of Madison's piece on Israel Hill, would not convert any abolitionists. Nevertheless, their authors might hope to influence the many white Americans in the North who did not press for immediate abolition, yet who wondered about the morality of slavery. The Lynchburg paper assured those waverers that freedom "would prove a curse of the sorest character to the very people" they wished to help.

The abolitionist critique stung white Southerners because it attacked them on the very moral ground they claimed to inhabit. Slaveholders believed they had been among the principal authors of the democratic American creed and exemplars of Christian morality, and now they found themselves accused of flouting those very values. Some responded by insisting that the slaveholding regime protected its laborers while the unbridled capitalist system of the North chewed workers up and spat them out. As long as the Randolphs had still owned the future Israelites, wrote the *Lynchburg Virginian,* those black folk had been "industrious . . . contented laborers" enjoying "comforts and benefits to which *free laborers* elsewhere are strangers." The blacks' emancipation had divorced them from those boons.[65]

The thoughts of George Wilson McPhail, who studied for three years at Hampden-Sydney College in Prince Edward County, capture the intellectual dilemma that some white sons of slaveholding Virginia wrestled with. The year before Colonel Madison wrote, McPhail had departed for Yale College to complete his studies. He found New Haven "truly beautiful," its inhabitants pious and moral, and "the scholarship much higher" at Yale than at Hampden-Sydney. Yet his stay there required him to suffer the company of "frozen yankees," whom he found "phlegmatic and distant." New England society was riven by political "animosities" and saturated with female reform societies of every description, he added disdainfully.

The Northerners, McPhail complained, "seem determined to set our negroes free at all hazards, and raise them to a level with the white population and if possible a little above it." But he found the Yankees hypocritical: "If the Virginia people would collect together, the inhabitants of 'Israel hill,' and various other free negro settlements in the state, and sent them all to New England," he wrote, "we should never hear any more of abolition after that, for the yankees would dread it five time [sic] as much as the people of the South. They talk here of amelioring *our* coloured population, when they treat those they have among them with supreme contempt and indignity."[66]

McPhail expressed his sentiments in a private letter. That allowed him to concede obliquely what Madison and Ruffin could not even hint at in public: Yankee society possessed spiritual credentials that lent weight to its critique of slavery. That discomfiting fact prompted some in the South to reply to antislavery agitation not with haughty dismissal, but rather with strident claims to Southern moral superiority, and with assertions like McPhail's that the New Englanders did not practice what they preached. Those retorts were bound up with a further proposition: the African American character was deficient, and the Israel Hill experiment had proved that through its supposed failure. That Madison, Ruffin, and McPhail concentrated their fire on that little community shows that the Hill by the 1830s had already taken on symbolic importance out of proportion to its size. Some people had even come to assume, mistakenly, that Prince Edward, mainly owing to the Israelites' presence, had the largest free black population of any county in Virginia.[67]

It is easy in the twenty-first century to dismiss out of hand the statements about Israel Hill and about black character that poured from the pens of Madison, Ruffin, and their like. To call such men racists and propagandists is not to engage in mere name-calling but to practice simple truth-in-labeling. Still, those men's assertions about Israel Hill cry out to be evaluated in light of the documentary record, and they arouse our curiosity about the man who set the ball rolling, Colonel James Madison of Prince Edward.

Madison's depiction of Israel Hill was demonstrably false in almost every particular; much of what he said sprang not from mere ignorance but rather from an active desire to mislead. Madison had every reason to know that his statement about Israel Hill's population waning "without emigration" from the colony was untrue, for example; he himself had become in effect one of the main promoters of emigration from the Hill. By the year in which he wrote, Farmville already had five "factories" in which workers processed tobacco leaves by hand. Madison, licensed as a tobacco manufacturer since 1823, had been one of the pioneers of the industry. Those facilities employed some 250 people; most of their workers were black, some of them young Israelites and other free people who now resided in town.[68]

When Madison wrote that Israelite families were not reproducing themselves, he said nothing of the many children and grandchildren of Teny Carter and Sam White; White at least had become prominent enough by then that Madison must have known about his big extended family. Other black Israelites may indeed have shown a lower rate of natural increase than slaves did—but masters encouraged the women they owned to bear many children, while free people might try to tailor their family size to their own desires and to the resources available.

There was a further reason Israel Hill's population grew more slowly—rising from the original 90 or so to about 150 residents by 1850—than it would have in a society without slavery. Some people who would gladly have lived with their Israelite families—for example, Tony White's five children and Rose Johnston's husband—were the property of white people and had no such option. Moreover, the desire to purchase family members created a drain on some black Israelites' budgets that Madison and Ruffin never talked about. By 1830, a few years before Madison wrote, Tony White had bought his wife; in the same year, Sam White and at least two other free blacks in the county—an Epperson and a Homes—held a total of four slaves, some of whom were probably related to their nominal masters and mistresses. Two Bartletts and two Homeses, and a few other free blacks as well, had bought individual bondpeople at one time or another, probably for the same reason.[69]

Colonel Madison never explained how "good" Negroes, imbued for life by the benevolent Randolphs with "habits of industry," came to rear their children "in idleness and vice." He got one thing more or less right when he spoke of a generational shift, however: the dozen years preceding his letter to the *Farmers' Register* had indeed seen the deaths of founding settlers who had grown up as slaves of the Randolph family.

William Wilkerson, who lived on the crest of the Hill, apparently died about 1824; the life of Teny Carter may have ended about 1826. Of the four sons of Hercules White Sr. who owned tracts on the Hill, boatman Dick died in April 1826, and farmer Hercules Junior late in 1832. In the meantime, Phil White Sr. and Isham Patterson died in 1830 and 1831, respectively. As the ranks of the elder generation thinned, the first cohort of persons who had actually been born on Israel Hill reached adulthood in the early 1830s. These included Sam White's older grandchildren, Phil White Jr.'s son Curtis, two daughters of Dick White, and a few members of the Carter, Gibbs, and Howard families.[70]

There is no evidence that the passing of nearly half the original land-holders of Israel Hill—counting Hercules White Sr.'s four sons as members of that group—produced the wholesale disruption and loss of morale that Colonel Madison alleged. Some things changed, but many Israelites carried forward the way of life their parents and grandparents had established.

Hercules White Jr., like many propertied residents of the county, left no will; we have little information on what his estate consisted of beyond his land and the house he would have lived in there. The same is true of Teny Carter and William Wilkerson. All three, however, left descendants who would still be living on Israel Hill as the Civil War approached.[71]

Dick White was found dead on Titus Gibbs's land in Israel Hill's northern tier. A coroner's jury took considerable care to investigate, calling eight witnesses, and found that White had died of natural causes. He was not buried at public expense, which indicates that his survivors made fitting arrangements on their own. The inventory of his possessions included what one might expect of a boatman: there were simple domestic furnishings and tools, but no farming implements. Dick White did leave behind a sow and a shotgun, both of which suggest he had supplied his family with a portion of its meat ration over the years.[72]

Dick's children, all daughters, may ultimately have followed husbands to other places of residence. But first, in 1832, lacking both a male provider and a family tradition of farming, the girls successfully petitioned the county court to have a wealthy white man, Thomas A. Morton, named as their guardian. The sisters may have lost their mother by then; the guardianship could also have had something to do with the large cash legacy that Dick's daughter Eliza may have received a decade and a half earlier in the will of Judith Randolph, of which perhaps some funds were left. How the young women's relationship with Morton had come about, the records do not say. The girls probably joined their new guardian at his residence in Cumberland. Hercules White Jr., too, had mostly daughters, who apparently married and moved off the Hill with their spouses; but his one son, Washington White, would still be boating and farming the family plot in the late 1850s.[73]

The dying Isham Patterson tried to accommodate all his children on his 25-acre tract, leaving part of his land to each. He called on his daughter Hannah and her husband, Edmund Clarke, to live with his widow in the house he left behind. The Clarkes apparently did that, and a couple of their sons were still farming there at the end of the 1850s. Certain other Patterson children may have moved off the family land, but not all; some Pattersons would still (or again) be in residence as the twentieth century dawned. Colonel Madison should have known a good deal about the methodical transition from one generation to the next within this particular free black family, for he himself, with his nephew, witnessed the signing of Isham Patterson's will.[74]

Madison's accusations in 1836 that the Israelites had by then sunk into poverty and crime—like the story of the generational shift—had some fragmentary basis in fact but were radically misleading. One free black woman, Sally White, who probably had connections to Israel Hill, had indeed died a pauper's death in 1829. She was found dead on the old Randolph tract between Farmville and Israel Hill, of natural causes, according to the coroner's inquest. Who she was remains uncertain. Dick White's widow bore the name Sally, but one wonders whether her brother-in-law, Sam White, would have allowed her to be buried at public expense by the coroner, as happened to this woman.[75]

Israelite or not, the unfortunate Sally did not represent the Hill community's general economic situation. In the late 1820s, after all, Hampton Giles had expressed pride in his farm and its appointments during his wrangle with John Brown before the county court. Of course, Giles had no better claim to objectivity than Madison did, but he would have been laughed out of court had he tried to turn a Madisonian sow's ear into a silk purse. Other Israelites—the Phil and Sam White families, at a minimum—were even better off economically than Hampton Giles.

Phil White Sr., who died six years before Madison wrote, had held no land of his own on the Hill, yet he left implements for building, weaving, spinning, and farming—in about that order of importance—as well as a gun. His possessions fetched nearly $150.00, not counting the $6.50 he had left behind in his "pocket book." White's legacy easily covered his few debts to white and black alike, as well as some legal fees and a commission to white neighbor John Tuggle for administering the estate; that left nearly $100.00 for White's heirs. They used part of that money to pay Billy Ellis for the fancy coffin Phil Senior was buried in.[76]

In fact, Madison chose a strange moment to depict Israel Hill as impoverished and declining. As early as 1822, one of the Phil Whites, probably the younger, had purchased a six-acre lot in Hampden, near Prince Edward Court House; he resold the parcel only three years later at a profit of 120 percent. Sam White, Phil White Jr., and John White—

probably Sam's son, who by then lived in Farmville—purchased thirteen lots and part lots in that town in the 1830s, seven of them before Madison chronicled the Israelites' supposed poverty. They also sold parts of their new holdings, in one case at a 500 percent markup after Phil White quickly improved his new property. The year before Madison wrote, Sam White paid taxes on two slaves and six horses, Phil White on two slaves, three horses, and a gig. There is no way to tell whether those four bond-people were family members or actual chattel slaves of the Whites. Either way, Sam and Phil could hardly have acquired them had the pair not prospered on Israel Hill.[77]

The Whites were not alone: their fellow Afro-Virginians John Deneufville and Booker Jackson were developing their own lots during the first half of the decade. Colonel Madison surely knew about the ventures of these various black men. A heavy investor in Farmville real estate himself, he bought a lot diagonally across the street from those of Jackson and Deneufville, and he helped preside over some of the lot sales at which the Whites made their purchases.[78]

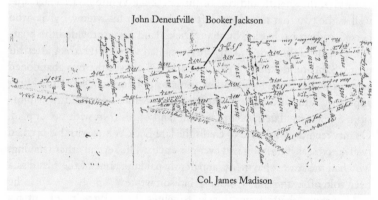

Colonel James Madison derided Israel Hill as a failed experiment in black freedom. Yet he did business with free blacks, and in the early 1830s he bought a lot across the street from free Afro-Virginians Booker Jackson and John Deneufville.

(*Watkins v. Venable's heirs*, COUNTY COURT, JUNE–JULY 1835,
ARCHIVES RESEARCH SERVICES, LIBRARY OF VIRGINIA)

On the other hand, some black Israelites in the years before Madison wrote did fail to pay the annual tax on their little parcels of land. They had plenty of company. In any given year, taxes went unpaid on a number of landholdings in Prince Edward; a review conducted in 1815 showed that no fewer than 650 citizens had failed to pay in anywhere from one to most of the preceding twenty-six years.[79] The county court had the power to sell off land belonging to persons of any color who did not pay up. That happened relatively rarely, but some people actually did have to watch their tax-delinquent land sold out from under them. Many other tax bills, typically for small amounts, went unpaid simply because the landowner had died or moved away from the county.[80]

In the late 1820s, some of the properties on Israel Hill began appearing sporadically on the annual list of unpaid land taxes—the roll for 1827 listed half a dozen Hill tracts. The sums owed were trivial, yet there is no evidence that extreme poverty, such as Madison alleged, had caused the failure to pay. Isham Patterson may have been distracted by failing health in the late 1820s. Heirs of Teny Carter, Dick White, and Hercules White Sr. were slow to begin paying taxes on newly inherited or recently divided land. But Titus Gibbs, who had years of life ahead of him, also failed to pay the land tax in 1831, as did William Wilkerson's heirs. The Johnstons' two missed years likewise have no obvious explanation.[81]

In 1832, the sheriff sold two of the late Dick White's twelve acres, as well as the two that Ben Short left as a home for his widow, Sylvia, who herself had probably died by then. Dick's land never provided the boatman's main livelihood, and his survivors had vacated the tract after his death. Sam and the other Whites clearly did not see the two abandoned acres as worth paying even a few cents to hold on to. The white buyer apparently did nothing with the two acres before he moved to Mississippi a few years later, leaving behind land of his own with tax unpaid. County records continued to credit the late Dick White with his original twelve acres, as if nothing had ever gone awry. The several other Israelites who had missed tax payments apparently paid up; none of their land had been sold off at the time Colonel Madison wrote.[82]

Madison's charge that black Israelites had degenerated into a wretched state of health is difficult to weigh systematically. But the economic activity of the Whites and others and the physical exertions of Israel Hill's boatmen exceed what one would expect of people prostrated by ill health; Israelite women did continue to bear children, contrary to Madison's lurid assertions about disease-induced infertility. Phil White Jr. and sometime Israelite Joe Bartlett received and paid for professional medical care; they appear in the doctor's ledger during a period not long before Colonel Madison shared his thoughts with the world.[83]

As a member of the Prince Edward County Court, Madison was well situated to know the record of the black Israelites when it came to crime. Authorities in the county rarely if ever brought charges for prostitution against anyone, white or black, so the evidence on that score is inconclusive; grand juries seem never to have accused a free black woman of a morals offense, apart from the few presentments of non-Israelite females for liquor-selling early in the century. Madison would have had a difficult time finding signs of criminality of any kind among free Afro-Virginian men in the annals of the court he sat on. The feud between Hampton Giles and John Brown had continued for a long while, and according to Giles, came to blows on three occasions. Yet that conflict, and a fight in 1825 between the wives of Tony and Hercules White Jr.,[84] constitute the entire recorded history of violent behavior involving black Israelites from the founding of their settlement until the time Madison condemned them a quarter century later. In the same period, a jury had acquitted Jacob Johnston of buying stolen goods from a slave in 1813, and the county court had found Titus Gibbs and Hampton Giles not guilty of hogstealing in 1826.

Many contemporary white citizens of Prince Edward quietly acknowledged the good citizenship of Israelites and other free blacks. When the newspaper memoirist writing as "Rip Van Winkle" in 1906 reminisced about black Israelites of "ability . . . and integrity," he prominently included Curtis and John White. Curtis belonged to the second generation, born into freedom, that Madison had singled out for contempt, and John had been liberated as a child. The voluminous records of the pre–Civil War decades show that "Rip's" memory was accurate. Israel Hill had aroused some doubts and even worries among whites on occasion, but all in all, its residents had won a recognized place in the life of the county, and even a measure of respect.

It is important to evaluate the Madison-Ruffin story against the facts and to note the political work that its authors wanted it to do. Just as illuminating, though, is the public and professional life of Colonel James Madison, the man who first applied the Jefferson-Tucker-Dew litany of anxiety to the Israel Hill "experiment."

Madison ranked as one of the most prominent and influential citizens of Prince Edward County during Israel Hill's first quarter century. He achieved his colonel's commission in the local militia, then retired but used the title for the remaining two decades of his life. At one time or another, Madison filled most of the influential positions the area had to offer. A justice on the county court for many years, he served from 1824 on the board of trustees that governed Farmville; he became the board's president during the 1830s, when the trustees expanded the town markedly. Madison was serving in the Virginia House of Delegates at the time he wrote to Edmund Ruffin about Israel Hill. He began his years of political activity as a Jeffersonian Republican, worked for Andrew Jackson's reelection as president in 1832, and remained prominent among Jacksonians in Virginia's southern Piedmont.[85]

Madison's political orientation by itself does not explain his willingness to denounce Israel Hill publicly. The colonel's comrades in the local Democratic Party did include John Rice, who supervised the confiscation of free blacks' guns after the Nat Turner revolt. And moral reservations about slavery—usually of the colonizationist variety—were loosely associated with Whiggery in antebellum Virginia. Nevertheless, both parties in the South defended their constituents' right to hold slaves, and both condemned abolitionism. More significant still, whites who dealt congenially with the Israelites and with other free blacks included both Whigs and Democrats.

Newton Cunningham, county justice and friend of the free black Dungeys, worked actively for the Democratic Party in the 1840s and 1850s and would campaign for the "Southern rights" Democratic candidate for president, John C. Breckenridge, in the fateful election of 1860. Henry S. Guthrey, the building contractor who offered "comfort and kind treatment" to his various free black apprentices and helped Robert A. Franklin buy his daughter's freedom, matched Cunningham's record in the Democratic Party in almost every detail. County clerk Branch Worsham, who rendered friendly service to free blacks, was another longtime Democratic activist.[86]

Clement C. Read—associate of the Whites of Israel Hill and friend of free black landowner John Deneufville—lent active support to the Democrats, at least in the 1840s. Democratic voters in 1840, an election from which polling records survive, included the black Israelites' neighbors and trading partners John and Amplias Tuggle, as well as Granville Nunnally, who took in two orphaned Homes boys as apprentices on good terms and helped Sam and Phil White establish the Farmville Baptist Church in 1836.[87]

Whigs seem to have been less assertive in Prince Edward County than Democrats, but Whig voters in 1840 included Josiah Cheadle, who often employed the free black Forgasons, as well as Benjamin M. and John N. Robertson. Ben was a founding member of Farmville Baptist, and both Robertsons frequently cooperated with the Whites and other free Afro-Virginians in land and boating transactions. Another Whig voter, boat owner and merchant Merit Steger, gave bail for Randolph Brandum during the dispute over Brandum's use of a runaway slave on his batteau, and he did the same for two of the Whites in more mundane lawsuits over financial matters.

Asa Dupuy, cool head during the Nat Turner crisis and friendly neighbor of Edmund Young and the free black Homeses, was a Jacksonian Democrat in the latter 1820s but became a Whig by the following decade; his habits in dealing with blacks proved less changeable than his politics.[88] Clearly, the way James Madison and other white citizens of Prince Edward treated or talked about Afro-Virginians had little to do with partisan orientation.

Colonel Madison's prominence in civic and political life owed much to the important role he played in economic affairs. He purchased a batteau by 1820 and served as a superintendent of the Upper Appomattox Company. He owned a tavern in Farmville and became a partner in a couple of mercantile stores there. Madison held more than thirty-five slaves in Prince Edward in 1830, and owned over sixteen hundred acres of land in three parcels by 1836.[89]

The colonel's involvement in tobacco processing and in mercantile commerce did not dictate his position on Israel Hill any more than his party affiliation did. Merit Steger, Ben Robertson, and Clem Read all followed an economic path similar to Madison's while maintaining close ties to black Israelites.[90] Then, too, the colonel had to look no farther than his own family to witness businesslike, even friendly relations with free blacks—which, by the way, could not have arisen if those Afro-Virginians had been idle, vicious, and impoverished. Just as James Madison was publishing his piece about Israel Hill, his nephew James M. Jackson cosigned with Phil White when the black man purchased a town lot. James would go on to conduct transactions worth hundreds of dollars with two free black boating entrepreneurs, John White and Randolph Brandum.[91]

The tobacco business did create certain pressures on Madison, and those stresses intensified during the years just preceding the colonel's diatribe against the Israelites. Tobacco "manufacturing" in Farmville took place in an aggregation of buildings near the Appomattox River. The crop was processed essentially by hand—"manufacturing" in the original,

Latinate sense of the word. Madison and his peers staffed their facilities largely by hiring bondpeople from masters on an extended, usually annual, basis; the less numerous free black employees received their own earnings directly. Manufacturers sent both raw leaf and the processed tobacco from their works to Petersburg on batteaux, many of which, like the factories themselves, were manned by free or enslaved blacks.

A tobacco facility might operate as a "stemmery," in which moderately skilled workers separated stems from large, coarse leaves of tobacco, rendered the latter into "strips," and finally "prized" or pressed the strips and stems into hogsheads to be shipped on for further processing. A "factory," the dominant type of plant in Farmville, required highly skilled workers to carry out a more extensive series of operations on tobacco that was either of inferior quality or of "superior texture & fineness of grain." Those processes included stemming, twisting or making rolls, and prizing the end product into kegs or boxes. Portions of the work in both facilities required strength as well as skill; the press for prizing "manufactured" tobacco was two feet wide and five feet tall, while that in a stemmery could be twice as wide and as much as seven feet high.[92]

The average manufacturing facility employed between forty and sixty people. A stemmery could operate with as few as a dozen or fifteen, though at times it might take on up to twice that many. In later years, and probably in the 1830s, too, the industry employed women workers as well as men. According to one source from the period, Farmville's five tobacco factories gave work to nearly a third of the town's eight hundred men, women, and children by the time Madison wrote about Israel Hill.[93] Factory owners faced a shortage of adequately skilled labor. "It is always very difficult to procure hands" in Farmville, Colonel Madison lamented. "Stemming and twisting tobacco . . . is the greatest part of the labour and the most difficult to have well done," another manufacturer remarked in 1837, and "the hands got about Farmville generally are not as good as those about Richmond and Petersb[ur]g."[94]

Madison did not specifically mention factory workers in his published attack on Israel Hill. Still, it may have galled the colonel to realize that his profits depended partly on the scarce, skilled labor of free Afro-Virginians, that those black workers' wages were increasing as a result—and that, unlike the hire of slaves, the money he had to pay them was going straight into free blacks' own pockets.

Madison's relations with individual free and enslaved blacks varied. Early in the 1830s, he controlled more than a hundred slaves: the three dozen he himself owned, and some seventy-five belonging to the mentally incompetent Josiah Chambers, whose plantation Madison administered. He hired out about two thirds of the Chambers bondpeople. Madison routinely paid slaves for goods and services they produced on their own time, as many of his peers did. Indeed, he behaved more considerately than the average master in some ways. He recorded both the given names and surnames of some slaves he owned or controlled. In at least one document, he listed many of his slaves in groups consisting of mothers and their children, each family on a separate line, a nicety many did not observe in written records.[95] In his day-to-day life, Madison seems to have liked Afro-Virginians perfectly well as long as they remained in bondage.

Madison's record as a member of the county court is more ambiguous. On two occasions during the mid-1820s, he issued warrants against free or enslaved blacks accused of stealing, only to see his fellow justices declare those warrants defective and release the defendants. That may never have happened twice to any other member of the court.[96] Perhaps Madison's peers stepped in to curb an excessive readiness on his part to accuse blacks of criminal behavior. Only a few years earlier, however, Madison had joined the husband of free black Sally Stonum in giving bail for her when she was charged with having assaulted a fellow free black; the nature of Madison's relationship with the Stonums remains a mystery. The colonel had also signed a petition in 1825 asking the state legislature to permit Billy Brown, a free black man, to remain in the county. Brown, known as "College Billy" for his work as a servant at Hampden-Sydney, had purchased his liberty years earlier with the help of a white man.[97]

The colonel knew, or knew about, free Afro-Virginians other than those who worked for him and the two who owned property across the street from his own. Many enslaved and free blacks had accounts at the store in which Madison was a partner, and they were especially frequent customers. When the store went out of business in 1837, two free blacks—the very same two who dealt in large sums with Madison's nephew—would owe nearly $400 in what were considered "Bad & Doubtfull debts"; other blacks owed much smaller amounts that were thought uncollectable.[98] These growing debts may already have influenced Madison's opinion of free blacks by the time he wrote his attack on Israel Hill in 1836—except that prominent whites appeared on his bad debt list, too. In fact, at the very time Madison wrote his piece, he was collaborating financially with free Afro-Virginian Randolph Brandum—the pair hired a slave from a white man for the year 1836. Brandum probably used the slave on his batteau. Madison seems to have committed himself to contribute part or all of the bondman's $125 hire as an investment on which he would have expected a return.[99]

At the end of the hire, however, neither Brandum nor Madison paid up, and the pair faced a lawsuit as the national economic crisis of 1837 rocked both of them. This unpleasant final chapter to Madison and Brandum's collaboration unfolded too late to influence the colonel's piece in the *Farmers' Register*. The real significance of the story lies elsewhere: Madison was investing a large sum of money in the operations of a second-generation black Israelite even as he proclaimed to the world that that very generation had become worthless, even criminal, for want of white supervision.[100]

Madison had other contacts with the former Randolph slaves. During the year before his letter appeared in Ruffin's *Register*, the colonel bought the old Allen plantation, which lay at the foot of Israel Hill, and moved his residence there. Given that Madison now lived literally within sight of the black community of which he was writing so bitterly, it is striking that his piece contained not a single word of physical description. There was still no road directly connecting Madison's new home to Farmville—only the old bridle path. Simply to get back and forth between his plantation and the town, Madison now either had to ford the Appomattox and approach Farmville from Cumberland County, or ford Buffalo River, or travel south—directly past if not through Israel Hill—to Legrand's bridge across the Buffalo and thence east to Farmville.[101] Had physical conditions on the Hill offered Madison any evidence to bolster his story of the settlement's decline and fall, one assumes he would have hastened to use it.

Madison had a mercurial relationship with one former slave of the Randolphs. Zack Ellis lived for years on the Chambers plantation not far from Israel Hill, an enterprise that the colonel supervised; the black man did shoemaking work for Madison and other clients. Ellis had a daughter named Ginny, a slave who either belonged to Madison or was otherwise under his control. Friction developed between Zack Ellis and the colonel over Ginny Ellis's right to visit her father. In 1832, Zack filed a suit in the circuit court complaining that Madison had entered his house and assaulted him. The colonel, angrily looking for the missing Ginny, had apparently found her at her father's place and taken his fury out on Zack Ellis. Madison produced in court a pass scrawled above his own forged signature. Ginny Ellis must have carried the document to cover

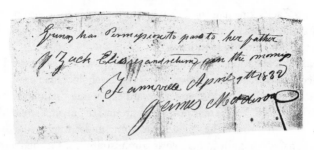

A forged pass supposedly permitted the enslaved Ginny Ellis to visit her father, Zack Ellis, a free man. A stormy confrontation between Ellis and Colonel James Madison, nemesis of Israel Hill, ensued.

(*Ellis v. Madison,* CIRCUIT COURT, SEPTEMBER 1838,
ARCHIVES RESEARCH SERVICES, LIBRARY OF VIRGINIA)

her visit to her father's house, and that doubtless aggravated the Ellises' offense in the colonel's mind.

Zack Ellis and James Madison each complained that the other had criminally blurred the line separating freedom and slavery. In Madison's view, Ginny, abetted by her free father, had presumed to move about when and where she chose, as though she, too, were a free woman. Meanwhile, Zack protested that Madison had barged into his home and beaten or whipped him as though he were still a slave. Madison seems to have defended himself against Ellis's lawsuit not by denying that he had attacked the black man but rather by pointing to the forged pass to justify his outrage; he did not subpoena a single witness. Zack Ellis summoned seven or eight white men, including one who would soon join the Whites of Israel Hill in founding Farmville Baptist Church; bizarrely, the law permitted Ellis to sue Madison but not to testify against him in court. The apparent fact of Madison's aggression must have warred in the jurors' minds with a lack of eyewitness testimony from the men Ellis brought to the stand, and with the flouting of slave discipline embodied in the phony pass. In 1833 and 1834, three successive juries failed to reach a verdict. In the end, Ellis and Madison reached a settlement under which the colonel paid $10 toward the black man's costs in bringing the suit.[102]

Even after Madison published his critique of Israel Hill, however, he continued to deal correctly with certain free blacks. He occasionally hired carpenter and cooper Billy Ellis, as he had done for years, even though

Billy was Zack's kinsman (probably his brother). Madison also recorded at least one payment in 1838 to one "J Johnson," who may have been Israelite Rose Johnston's son Jacob.[103]

Madison's behavior toward blacks, in short, was less categorical than the piece he wrote for the *Farmers' Register*. Slaveholder ideology and the debate over human bondage go far toward explaining the tone and content of his screed. Yet there is no getting around the mental stress Madison faced at the time. The colonel had come under fire personally and professionally, especially in his role as administrator for the mentally disabled Josiah Chambers. In the 1830s, some of Josiah's relatives accused Madison of putting Chambers's slaves to his own use rather than hiring them out for the benefit of the estate. They also alleged that he had permitted "a woman of infamous character" who claimed to be Chambers's wife to support herself at the plantation's expense.[104] That second allegation led to the attempted inquest by a panel of doctors and midwives into the racial identity of Patsy Chambers's child.

Madison's critics were in full cry by the time he wrote about Israel Hill, and he saw his prestige and power begin to wane further after the piece appeared. That very year, 1836, he petitioned the county court to authorize a road, featuring a seventy-five-foot-long bridge over Buffalo River, that would run between Farmville and his new plantation abutting Israel Hill. Even though the norms of the day would have required Madison to pay for the road at least partly by himself, his fellow members of the county court turned him down, perhaps sensing that the beleaguered colonel might have trouble financing such a project.[105] As a county justice himself, Madison may have noticed that the refusal put him in the same category as one of those black Israelites he had just disparaged. Tony White had asked approval for a road between his land and the "bridle way" to Farmville half a dozen years earlier. Why White wanted a road leading to a path on which no wagon or cart could run remains a mystery; the county court looked into his proposal but did not approve it. White could console himself by recalling that even road requests from men of wealth and power were sometimes rejected. Madison, by contrast, now had another reason to worry that his very claim to be such a man stood in peril.[106]

The year after Madison published his piece and saw his road petition denied, the community learned, as the phrase of the time put it, that he was "greatly embarrassed in his pecuniary affairs." He "failed & became notoriously insolvent": two volumes of Plutarch's *Lives* were the sole property he had left for the deputy sheriff to seize. Madison died during the winter of 1840–41 before he could carry out his plan to apply the classic remedy of failed Virginians—a move to another state.[107]

The travails of the early and mid-1830s that would end in Madison's ruin may help explain the dyspeptic tone of his article for Edmund Ruffin. But the colonel's tangled business affairs also reveal specific aspects of his character that shaped his denunciation of the black Israelites. As a member of Farmville's board of trustees, Madison pushed hard to expand the town in the years after 1830. The trustees laid out and sold lots on the Chambers lands that he himself administered; most of the proceeds should have gone to the Chambers estate. Madison's associates and a court of law later concluded that he had diverted much of the estate's income into a futile attempt to repair his own personal finances. At his death, Madison left an unpaid balance due to Chambers that approached $40,000.[108]

Madison's habit of shoring himself up by unethical means may have led him to accuse others of dishonesty and immorality. Even as he gathered his thoughts about Israel Hill, he was charging that one of his competitors in the tobacco industry had bested him in business by using false weights. The man sued Madison for slander.[109] The black Israelites offered a second convenient target for Madison's moralistic rage—and one perhaps less likely to try to make him pay for his verbal attacks.

But the targeting of Israel Hill may have had other deep sources. Even before the Chambers manipulations, Madison had used his official posts to increase his personal wealth. In 1833, he bought two lots from Farmville's board of trustees, the governing body on which he himself served. He paid $460; a mere three days later, he sold the bulk of his new acquisition for $800. Then he took in another $150 by selling the remainder of his new real estate to the local Methodist congregation. Madison, the insider, had doubled his money almost instantly. The buyer who paid $800 came from Charlotte County and may not have realized he was being gouged. The other Farmville trustees posed no obstacle. The board was a cozy nest to which a few elite men basically elected each other; the dozen or so votes cast for trustees in 1835 constituted a high tide of democratic participation in town affairs.[110]

Other officeholders in Prince Edward County profited from decisions of bodies on which they served. But they generally did so by selling goods or services to the county; non-officeholders got county work, too, and watchdogs like Colonel Charles Woodson tried to make sure citizens got value for their money. Madison's property deal in 1833 appears to be one of the gamiest cases of profiteering that the county's records have to offer—until the much bigger scandal broke over his role in selling the Chambers lots a few years later. Against that background, James Madison's condemnation of the black Israelites, twice within a single paragraph, as a "heavy tax upon the community," takes on new meaning. Madison would not have got as far as he did in life had he lacked energy and ability. Yet he made thousands of dollars through what today would be called insider trading, sweetheart deals, and—ultimately—embezzlement. One wonders whether the colonel projected his own sense of guilt onto free blacks when he accused them of subsisting on the resources of more honest citizens.

When Madison pounded away at the black Israelites' alleged idleness, he was echoing a sentiment expressed by many privileged men of his time—and not only when they spoke about free blacks. Established Virginians could muster some sympathy for "worthy" folk who suffered economic setbacks, but the "undeserving poor" of both races drew the contempt of the better-off. Benjamin Watkins Leigh—a proslavery political figure and lawyer who represented both Judith Randolph and Colonel Madison—defended the traditional idea that only those white men who owned property should be allowed to vote. That requirement, he argued, eliminated from civil life only the "veriest paupers and drones in the community, whom all agree upon excluding."[111] "Drones," of course, was one of the very epithets that Thomas Dew hurled at free blacks.

Just as Leigh believed that many idle folk were not black, other whites recognized that most free blacks were not idle. The official tally of free blacks for Cumberland County in 1851 listed 224 Afro-Virginians age twelve and over, but described only 15 as "idle"; a mere 3 of those were adult males.[112] Yet James Madison and Edmund Ruffin applied the term "idle" in a specifically racial way and gave it a unique definition. Ruffin accused black boatmen of choosing their occupation "because it is the nearest to idleness." More candid white Southerners readily acknowledged, and batteau owner Madison well knew through his business, that boating required brawn, skill, brains, and sometimes even courage. What seems to have offended Ruffin about boating was that free blacks chose that occupation for themselves and conducted their work beyond the supervision of whites, proudly and sometimes quite profitably.

Madison and Ruffin's anti–free black vitriol may have had additional roots in their frustration with Virginians of their own race. Ruffin's journal served as a weapon in its editor's crusade to reform agriculture in Virginia: to replace soil-depleting tobacco monoculture and old-fashioned forms of crop rotation with modern methods, especially replenishment of the soil by planting grasses and applying manures. The famous agrarian reformer had his apostles in Prince Edward, including both Madison and Colonel Woodson. Nevertheless, Ruffin became bitterly exasperated by the refusal of many planters to pay attention to his ideas or to apply them competently; one observer lamented in the mid-1830s that Prince Edward County's own "very good" soil had been "exhausted" because local planters exploited it "without any regard to system." A disillusioned Ruffin closed down the *Farmers' Register* in the early 1840s after less than a decade of publication.[113]

Any devotee of efficient, systematic methods in south-central Virginia confronted many examples of the opposite. One farmer, rather than clear his cropland fully, girdled a number of large trees in order to kill them— not an unusual technique in itself. But then, for ten years running, the man simply planted around the trees and the dead limbs they gradually shed; by the time he tired of the bother around 1820 and decided to sell the trees for timber, they were rotten on the outside and too brittle on the inside to be used.[114] The anecdote represents countless other manifestations of laxity—from building houses without lips on the windows or stables without adequate eaves to letting slaves wander almost at will and trade privately—that drove progressive planters like Ruffin and Charles Woodson to despair. By contrast, those black Israelites who cleared cropland and built houses in short order in 1811 had nothing to be embarrassed about.

Madison and Ruffin deprecated free blacks on transparent racist grounds. But they attributed to Israel Hill many of the very failings they saw among fellow whites: ignorance, improvidence, and lack of initiative; later writers who elaborated on Madison's critique would specifically condemn the Israelites' alleged failure to grow wheat or plant apple orchards. Ruffin and Madison could not recruit white planters to progressive agriculture by hurling invective at them. No such constraints, however, prevented an evangelist of progressive farming from displacing onto free blacks the dismay and anger he felt toward his own backward white brethren. In antebellum Virginia, as perhaps in America today, much of what whites found to criticize in blacks was what in fact they deplored about themselves and each other.

Displaced anxieties also help explain the white disparagers' comments about the supposed failure of Israel Hill's population to grow. Progressives of Ruffin's sort deplored unenlightened farming techniques in part because they robbed Virginia of its rightful power and prestige in the

American Union. The Old Dominion had ranked as the largest and most powerful state at the time of the Revolutionary War and for a generation afterward. Since then, Northern states had overtaken Virginia; by the thousands, the Commonwealth's sons and daughters left its exhausted lands, and its great days seemed to have passed.

Thomas Jefferson is supposed to have predicted once that Virginia would have 2.27 million residents in 1835. By the time Colonel Madison savaged the black Israelites, leading Virginians lamented that the actual figure had fallen a full million shy of that mark.[115] In the most obvious psychological projection of all, Madison imputed to Israel Hill the very demographic stagnation that he and his class saw besetting the state of Virginia as a whole. As if to avoid any inconvenient resonance between the two cases, the colonel "explained" the supposed trend on Israel Hill by invoking the stereotype of sexual promiscuity among blacks.

Many white Virginians looked at the rapid demographic and economic advance of the Northern states with both awe and humiliation. They wanted to replicate the Yankee's success even as they scorned the Yankee himself and disavowed any wish to become like him. Attacks on Israel Hill and on free blacks in general allowed some people to give vent to that tension while disguising its source. Southern apologists from the obscure Yale student George McPhail to the celebrated agronomist Edmund Ruffin could mask their anxieties still further by throwing the Yankee's abysmal treatment of free blacks in his face, even as they themselves declared African Americans unfit for freedom.

As keenly as Madison and Ruffin wished to argue back at Yankee critics, however, they knew that their readers were mostly Southern planters like themselves, and that even among that public they had some convincing to do on the subject of race. Madison was old enough to remember that six years had passed after Gabriel's attempted revolt in 1800 before white Virginians mustered a majority to adopt a law calling for the expulsion, not of all free blacks, but rather of those liberated in the future. Within a few years, they had empowered county courts to grant exemptions from that requirement. Madison and Ruffin well knew that many whites of their own day took a live-and-let-live attitude toward free Afro-Virginians. The Madison-Ruffin propaganda line of 1836 did not represent a triumphant consensus among Virginia whites, but rather aimed to whip up an attitude of militancy on the free black issue that the hard-liners rightly feared was lacking.

For every published sally such as Madison's, and for every anti–free black law or pronouncement emanating from Southern legislatures, there came a petition from white citizens to exempt some "honest[,] unoffending[,] industrious man" of color from those very impositions.[116] And for every such formal petition, a hundred civilized interactions between whites and free blacks took place, not because whites actively sought to defy racial orthodoxy, but because applying that orthodoxy strictly in the real world would have been unpleasant, inconvenient, uncharitable—and unlikely to accomplish anything valuable enough to offset the trouble involved.

Madison and Ruffin thus had their work cut out for them. Their own day-to-day interactions with actual black human beings showed that they lived in a far more complex Southern society than the demands of propaganda let them admit. Madison's decision to collaborate financially with boatman Randolph Brandum contradicted everything the colonel said he believed about freeborn Israelites. Even Edmund Ruffin, who conducted his business and his experiments with the help of a trusted, talented slave assistant, knew that a person got through life with greater ease if he or she judged people as individuals and recognized the affinities that might arise across the color line.

Racial views like Madison's played an important part in the life and thought of the Old South; few whites bothered to argue publicly against those opinions, or even thought of doing so. But modern observers have paid more attention to what some of the most vocal white Southerners said they wanted life to be than to what daily life for free black individuals and their white neighbors actually was. The whites who broadcast their views most widely—men such as Madison and, paradoxically, both Northern abolitionists and Southern advocates of African colonization for American blacks—left us a web of myth that has misled many who attempt to read the historical record.

In fact, Israel Hill itself became the subject of two vivid myths. The first of these was a local variant of the oft-repeated myth of free black degeneracy, which alleged that the black race, if set free and left to its own devices, would revert to the savagery that whites believed was rampant in Africa itself. Colonel Madison inherited that myth from earlier, more important writers. But he became the first to apply it to Israel Hill in a public forum, just when the more general myth of degeneracy was taking on new importance as a retort to antislavery agitation in the North. The myth of free black degeneracy had a simple moral: that slavery was the only proper condition for blacks in America.

Another view that won the allegiance of some influential Virginians, the African colonizationist credo, echoed a key tenet of the myth of degeneracy—that free blacks lived in degraded circumstances. Abolitionists condemned the colonizationist program, with some justice, as a scheme to remove already liberated blacks while keeping millions of their brethren in chains. Yet many of those who proposed to resettle free blacks in Africa acted partly out of genuine humanitarian conviction: they were certain that the darker race would remain enslaved or immiserated in a state of near bondage as long as it remained in America. The more enlightened colonizationists based their grim prognosis not mainly on any supposition of innate black inferiority but on the permanent, implacable prejudice of the dominant race. "Despised and suspected by the white man, & envied by the slave," colonizationists proclaimed, "the free negro wanders a miserable outcast. . . . [D]eprived of the ordinary motives to virtuous actions, [free blacks] pervert the shadow of liberty which they enjoy, into purposes of crime, and self abasement."[117] These colonizationists might not blame free blacks for their supposed degradation, but degradation it was all the same, and many of the words they used to describe it could have flowed from Colonel Madison's pen.

Promoters of black colonization had trouble interpreting the Israel Hill experiment to suit their beliefs. To agree with Madison that the Israelites lived in squalor would bolster the case for resettling them and other free blacks in Africa, but it would also imply that ex-slaves were unfit to govern themselves in Liberia. The alternative strategy—to refute Madison's piece and proclaim Israel Hill a success—would contradict the American Colonization Society's insistence that free blacks could never thrive in the United States. In the end, the society reprinted Madison's piece in its journal without any editorial interpretation, allowing each subscriber to apply some colonizationist gloss of his or her own devising to the Israel Hill experiment.

Overall, however, the colonizationists' line that free blacks lived miserable lives proved a hardy one. After all, there was an element of truth in it: free African Americans did face racial discrimination of various kinds, and more than a few of them lived in poverty. The very trumpeting of the myth of degeneracy by proslavery hawks such as Prince Edward's James Madison seemed to confirm that white Americans would never allow blacks to share the American continent with them in freedom and dignity. To publicize free black misery won converts to colonizationism in another way, too: it gave whites who wanted to feel decent and Christian a way to conceive the whitening of America as an act of kindness toward the blacks who would depart for Africa. Meanwhile, many abolitionists called for racial justice *within* the borders of the United States. They wished to reform a society in which they, like their opponents the colonizationists, said free blacks were currently degraded at every turn.

A mountain of antebellum commentary thus sustains in our own day the view that free African Americans in the South lived as virtual slaves. Colonizationists, abolitionists, and proslavery propagandists despised each other. But just as Zionists, socialists, Bolsheviks, and anti-Semites in Eastern Europe during the early decades of the twentieth century all said—each for their own reasons—that Jews in that region lived in ignorance, superstition, and squalor, all three of these American groups agreed—each offering its own explanation—that free Southern blacks led wretched lives.[118] The web of anti–free black and antimanumission laws passed in the nineteenth century seem to clinch the case. Small wonder that the basic image of the free black as pariah, which strangely linked these antagonistic movements, remains widely accepted in our own time.

A second racial myth circulated in antebellum Prince Edward—one that, like Madison's myth of degeneracy, revolved specifically around Israel Hill. This story told of a rash of thefts from neighboring plantations; searches for stolen goods in homes on the Hill, however, turned up nothing and led whites to exonerate the Israelites completely. "The good conduct, including the honesty," of Israel Hill's people had become "so evident that they won the entire good will of the white community," a local scholar would write in 1934 after talking to county old-timers. In an "unbroken tradition" that lived on for a century after the events that spawned it, whites ranked the Israelites and their descendants "among the best negro citizens in the County."[119]

Many social myths have some basis in fact. People may have embroidered this "myth of the upstanding Israelite" in the retelling, and they certainly adapted it to speak to their own times, but the story does seem to have originated sometime before the Civil War among people who personally remembered the drama it recounted. Just as real was the "good conduct" of black Israelites, which included their concrete achievements and their wisdom—knowing when, how, and how far to assert themselves, and when to be circumspect.

Both the tale of the upstanding Israelite and the story Colonel Madison publicized deserve the label "myth" because both met certain deep needs of those who told and retold them: each helped its white adherents justify themselves and their society. Most white Virginians believed in white supremacy, regarded slavery as the proper situation for most blacks in the United States, and accepted or even advocated the principle of legal discrimination against free African Americans. Yet many of those same whites dealt amicably with free black individuals from one day to the next and benefited economically and emotionally from those interactions. This incongruity between white racial ideology and daily experience created a certain mental tension, which one's myth of choice helped to resolve.

The solution that Colonel Madison offered seems at first glance simple and crude. The myth of free black degeneracy told whites: Slavery and white supremacy are the only rational, moral system, because those black individuals whom freedom would not ruin are the rarest of rare exceptions. Even after slavery ended, the myth of degeneracy would justify in many white Southerners' minds both the world their ancestors had built and their own latter-day oppression of blacks. Yet Madison offered a small qualification to his otherwise sweeping indictment: he exempted the old settlers of the Hill from condemnation because they had supposedly learned civilized ways from their masters. Years later, other proslavery writers would repeat that idea, singling out Sam White as a model citizen.[120] This first-generation loophole, and later the Sam White proviso, allowed whites who believed as Madison did to say: We are decent, Christian people; we adamantly defend slavery, but not out of blind, hardhearted prejudice—for we recognize the surprising exception, the Sam White, when we see him.

The myth of the upstanding Israelite had even subtler functions. For decades, it crystallized with great power, and in turn helped to shape, white perceptions of race, slavery, and black freedom in Prince Edward County. The myth never questioned the white posse's decision to search for stolen property on Israel Hill. Rather, its first message was: Whatever good things we are about to say about the black Israelites, we are not sappy sentimentalists; we are properly vigilant; our white supremacist outlook is valid and prudent as a general worldview. On the other hand, the myth of the upstanding Israelite went on to say, we are fair-minded and self-controlled. Facts are facts; our investigation revealed that the Israelites (and not merely those reared in bondage) were trustworthy, so we not only called off our search but tendered those people a permanent designation as good Negroes.

For the keener minds of white Prince Edward, a third message of the myth came as a corollary to the second. It stated: We do have indiscriminate Negrophobes in our community who jump to accuse blacks when something goes amiss. But cooler, fairer heads reliably prevail; they did prevail in the investigation of Israel Hill, and even the hotter heads were persuadable by clear evidence of the Israelites' innocence. This third message was an especially elegant one: it gave the "better sort" of citizens a chance to compliment both the free blacks of Israel Hill and the rougher element among their fellow whites, even as they asserted their own superiority to both groups by the very act of passing judgment on them. A final message of the myth of the upstanding Israelite was as simple as the latter one was subtle. To declare that the residents of Israel Hill had passed a reliable test of character eased the anxiety, expressed overtly in the days after Nat Turner's revolt, that some white people in Farmville felt about that concentration of free Afro-Virginians living up on the Hill.

Many whites in Prince Edward seem to have found the myth of the upstanding Israelite more congenial than that of free black degeneracy. It conceded a good deal more to the blacks of Israel Hill—and by implication to other "good Negroes" in the county—yet endorsed caution when it came to dealing with free blacks as a category. In short, it reconciled the reigning white supremacist worldview propounded baldly by Colonel Madison with the complicated and often civil daily practice of race relations in Prince Edward. In doing so, the myth reinforced the satisfying lessons that sensitive whites must have drawn from courtroom acquittals of slaves and free blacks, faithful execution of emancipatory wills, orderly financial transactions between whites and free Afro-Virginians, and the oft-proclaimed social preference that bondpeople receive "humane" treatment. Whites in and around Prince Edward County could retain the benefits of slavery and white supremacy and still consider themselves just and decent; all they had to do was to overlook the quotidian horrors inherent in human bondage.

And that they did, for the need to be so comforted, to reassure oneself of one's own decency in the face of a disapproving world, has been an underappreciated but utterly basic one among Southern whites then and later. Many white Southerners never fully succeeded in persuading themselves of their own virtue—not in the antebellum years, and not in more recent times either. Yet their strenuous effort to think well of themselves did lead them to ameliorate somewhat the conditions under which blacks lived, even as it made deeper change seem morally unnecessary.

Two racial myths ensured that Israel Hill, conspicuous from the day it was founded, remained at the heart of life in antebellum Prince Edward County, even amid endlessly rich interactions among non-Israelite free blacks, whites, and slaves. Proslavery propagandists made sure that one of those myths—that of degeneracy—worked its way outward to the rest of the South. In the 1850s, expanded versions of the same myth would reach the whole country, and they would be repeated for decades to come.

In the regional and national arenas, the true story of the Hill, and of free blacks generally, could not compete with the mythology, for an intricate narrative of white ambivalence and black accomplishment did not promote the platform of any organized interest. Richard Randolph seems to have hoped that the community later known as Israel Hill would be held up as an example well beyond the banks of Appomattox and Buffalo. His wish came true—though not in the way he would have liked.

✺

CHAPTER 6

Law and Order

BOISTEROUS PASSIONS AND PANELESS WINDOWS

Critics of slavery as different as Thomas Jefferson and Frederick Douglass agreed that the institution could be sustained only through violence. Jefferson decried human bondage as an "unremitting despotism" that inevitably called forth "boisterous passions." Douglass averred that those passions could turn an angel into a devil. Ultimately, masters and overseers controlled enslaved blacks with physical force or threats of force; law and custom empowered whites to punish even as they denied slaves the right to resist. What hope was there, under such a system, that white Southerners would respond fairly when slaves or those bondpeople's free black brothers and sisters did defend themselves, or when they stood accused of crimes against whites?

In theory, the law did provide some curbs on violence against bondpeople. Prince Edward's county coroners performed some sixty inquests between 1800 and the Civil War, nearly half of them on slaves. Some violent or unexplained deaths of enslaved blacks doubtless went unreported. But when the coroner did become aware of such an event, he and a special jury appointed for the purpose might investigate with dogged thoroughness; through their reports, for example, we learn of a possible preference for using switches on slaves even in a county where more than a few men owned cowhide whips. The coroner's juries were not shy about noting signs of beatings on the bodies of slaves—but they proved reluctant to attribute the death of a bondperson to that cause.

The very few prosecutions against whites for murdering slaves came early in the nineteenth century, around the time Israel Hill was settled. The Commonwealth's attorney pursued two of three cases during those years with particular energy; in one instance, the coroner's jury issued an explicit accusation of homicide, and sixteen whites were called to testify at trial. Yet the prohibition of slave testimony against white defendants helped ensure that none of the prosecutions yielded a conviction.[1] Those meager results hardly encouraged people to bring charges in the future. At the same time, the tenacious efforts of some whites to pursue people who killed slaves may have discouraged such crimes in the years that followed.

The master's property interest in his slaves usually kept the use of violence against them within certain limits, and many slaveholders disapproved of what they called—without really defining the term—"barbarity" toward bondpeople. Yet everyone assumed that those who controlled slaves would have to use physical punishments at least occasionally, and most people were reluctant to tell others how they should handle their affairs.

One diligent inquest into the death of a slave named Robin at the end of the 1850s offhandedly exposed the prevalence of whippings on the plantations of Prince Edward County. The jurors all agreed that "the slave [had] been flogged" on more than one occasion "& paddled severely" on the buttocks, yet they doubted that those beatings had caused the man's death. "I have seen negroes as badly whipped before, who are still living," one juror explained. Another examiner agreed, saying, "I have seen a great many negroes worse whipped than I thought Robin had been."[2]

At the same time, masters readily pressed charges when some other white person assaulted a slave of theirs. Occasionally such a complaint led to a trial with vivid incriminating testimony, but punishment was rare. In one instance, a white man who had wounded a slave with a knife did receive a two-year sentence—but the jury announced that it considered that "too great a punishment for the offence, the law allowing no smaller punishment."[3]

At least once, a slave may have suffered violence at the hands of a free black. The arrest of boatman Randolph Brandum for cutting a slave with a pocketknife came shortly before Christmas 1841, after a Sunday gathering at the house of a free black woman. The witness list suggests that the guests included slaves, free blacks, and at least one white man, a non-slaveholder. Brandum seems to have spent several weeks, including Christmastime, in jail awaiting trial. The wounding had probably occurred during a fight and caused only a moderate wound, for the prosecution dropped the case, and Randolph Brandum went free—just as white men who hurt slaves usually did.[4]

In some cases, slaves used violence against white people—yet cooler heads in Prince Edward could prevail over alarmists even then. In a few instances, whites even endorsed the right of a slave to defend himself against an assault by a white person. Such expressions hardly rendered the system fair, but the white attitudes that underlay them may have encouraged free Afro-Virginians to lodge complaints against white assailants, as squatter Edmund Young did twice.

A divided court acquitted Dudley, a bondman, of stabbing a white man in 1821. A slave named Stepney went on trial in 1829, accused of having "assault[ed] and beat[en] . . . a free white man" with the intention of killing him; but after hearing four white witnesses, a panel of five county justices acquitted the black defendant. Four years later, a slave called Lindsey was similarly acquitted of stabbing one white man and beating another with intent to murder. In all three instances, white men who got into struggles—or indeed picked fights—with slaves must have encountered more resistance than they had bargained for; then they ran to the authorities with accusations of attempted murder.[5] County justices would never have exonerated a slave who actually had tried to kill an innocent white man, but neither would they gratify a defeated aggressor merely because he sported a white skin.

One white serial offender against people of both races was charged in 1842 with having attempted to rape an enslaved girl and assaulted a "negro fellow . . . for [his] attempt to rescue the said girl." The legal codes of the Old South recognized no such phenomenon as the rape of an enslaved woman by a white man, and countless such rapes indeed went unprosecuted. Yet here a grand jury *did* recognize the existence of such an offense and acknowledged a male slave's right to defend a woman against it. As happened all too often, however, the case against the white aggressor was dismissed, possibly because the only witnesses happened to be black.[6]

Perhaps the most remarkable endorsements of a slave's right to defend himself came in 1825 at the trial of Tom, an enslaved man who had killed his overseer, Richard Foster, in the presence of many witnesses by plunging the blade of a hoe six inches into the white man's brain. This should have been the quintessential open-and-shut case. Yet witness after witness—some half a dozen whites and a similar number of slaves—extenuated, even justified, the bondman's deed. The plantation mistress—the sister of the slain overseer, no less—testified that Foster had been the aggressor, and that Tom, under violent attack, had inflicted only one blow with the hoe rather than the two alleged in his presentment, which would have aggravated the offense. Another white witness, probably a brother of the mistress and the dead man, confirmed her account of the incident. After the fight, Foster's survivors testified, Tom had instantly expressed his regret and his hope that the blow had not been fatal. The dead man's sister noted that Foster had been drinking on the day of his mortal wounding but was sober by the time he attacked Tom; a drunkard by habit, he was nevertheless fully responsible for his aggression against the slave.

The court allowed, and Tom's lawyer encouraged, enslaved witnesses to describe both Foster's habitual pugnacity toward Tom and the manly pride that the black defendant melded with the self-restraint expected of people in bondage. A slave related that Foster had once threatened to "blow [Tom's] brains out." "Blow away," Tom had replied. "I have done nothing." The mistress testified that the fatal confrontation had begun when overseer Foster insulted Tom by calling him a liar over a trivial matter. She also recalled Tom trying to protect her crops against her drunken brother's negligence. Two slave witnesses and one white testified that the overseer had uttered menacing words about his sister's husband, who had taken the helm of the family plantation and kept Foster on as a mere employee. However tense relations among the Fosters may have been, it is remarkable that Tom won the understanding of the family of the man he had slain. The court nevertheless condemned him to hang; the regime would not exonerate a black man who had cloven the skull of his overseer in two.[7]

Slaves and free blacks alike could take pride in themselves, as Tom had, and they might even garner some white sympathy if they resisted aggression. Yet Tom's case shows yet again how different the lot of the slave was from that of the free Afro-Virginian. The latter did not stand at the mercy of an overseer or master, and he or she could file suit against a white attacker (though white witnesses would be needed to prevail in court). A slave had either to swallow indignation and accept physical abuse or lash out in an act of self-defense that put his or her own life in jeopardy. The open-mindedness of some whites could not save a bondperson who did what Tom had done, but it might make a difference in cases where the injury to the white party was less extreme, or where the rigidities of slavery did not apply—namely, in confrontations between whites and free blacks.

Naturally, in most cases where slaves physically attacked whites, no member of the dominant race extenuated the act in any way. Still, courts developed the habit of listening to the facts and distinguishing carefully between culpability, qualified guilt, and innocence. In September 1810, a slave named Will choked his master to death while a compatriot held the white man's legs immobile. The court condemned both defendants, but acquitted a third slave who had been present at the killing; a fourth enslaved suspect was cleared of suspicion before trial.[8]

In another case, county justices sentenced two bondmen to death after they murdered a pair of slave traders who were transporting them through Prince Edward in 1834, but the panel acquitted a third suspect who had been present at the scene. The prosecutor filed no charges against other slaves who had run away with the murderers but pleaded that they had done so under duress. In 1848, two slaves ambushed a local planter and beat him to death; their protracted battle with the white man left him "very much mangled." The court sentenced the pair to hang, but moved to commute the death sentence of a third slave, even though the condemned men said he had masterminded the crime.[9]

White officials proved capable of such judiciousness because violent resistance by slaves remained uncommon. Whites in and around Prince Edward County generally looked at the struggle with their bondpeople as one for good order and productivity rather than for survival against an implacable foe. In such an environment, there was little tendency to look upon free blacks as "incorrigible subversives": courts could consider free Afro-Virginians, and often even slaves, as individuals, not as members of an inherently threatening mass.

Slaves who ran away typify the problem of order that whites perceived—and illustrate its limits. Josiah Cheadle recorded a number of escapes, including four by a persistent bondman named Miles. Asa Dupuy reported in 1821 that an escaped carpenter-wheelwright had announced his intention to get to Ohio or some other free state. Other slaves sought a prolonged but not permanent absence; some hoped to win better treatment by demonstrating that they could withhold their labor. One Phoebe stayed away "[a] good part of the year" in 1829, and may well have returned voluntarily; she had left her children in the care of friends or family in the meantime.[10] Slave escapes generally aroused irritation, not fear, among white people. In fact, absconding served as a kind of safety valve: the runaway evaded violence against him- or herself, but flight also prevented violence *by* that slave against the master or overseer. Escapees damaged the master's interests without confronting him head-to-head.

By contrast, some whites did worry that slaves might poison them; the county court convicted one female slave of trying to poison a white woman in 1852 despite local doctors' testimony that the substance under suspicion could produce no more harm than cooked cabbage.[11] Fortunately for free and enslaved blacks, however, many white people remained level-headed on the subject. Prince Edward County saw few actual trials of slaves for poisoning, and even then, more often than not, the defendant had allegedly poisoned another slave; acquittals outnumbered convictions. Even the occasional "reputed poisoner" might go unpunished if good evidence against him was lacking. A bondman named George faced charges of having plotted to poison his own mistress in 1797, and then, sixteen years later, for conspiring to kill a married couple, to whom he may have been hired out. He won acquittal in both cases; in his first trial, Judy Randolph's friend, the great attorney Creed Taylor, was assigned to represent him.[12]

Fires of unknown origin occurred fairly often, and some whites found it easy to blame disgruntled slaves. Arson, like poisoning, was difficult to detect, much less to prove; unusually large numbers of witnesses were called in the occasional trials of slaves for arson, no doubt because most could provide no definitive information. Courts regularly dismissed charges or acquitted enslaved defendants after effective presentations by their defense attorneys. White people, too, sometimes fell under suspicion of having committed arson, or even of having poisoned others. In Prince Edward County during the fifty years before the Civil War, Edmund Young was the only free Afro-Virginian charged with setting a fire, and the court acquitted him.[13]

Whites regarded stealing by slaves as a chronic problem—not surprising under a system in which enslaved people lived with few creature comforts near sometimes well-off members of the race that exploited them. More slaves faced trial for theft than for any other crime, and countless bondpeople suffered informal punishments from masters or overseers for the same offense. Whites who thought of slaves as natural thieves might hold the same opinion of free blacks—an inclination Colonel Madison played on when he alleged that the Israelites had degenerated into thievery. Even so, whites perceived stealing, like escaping, as a nuisance rather than a threat to their lives or well-being, and they handled it in ways that did not lead to wholesale repression.

Many landowners in Prince Edward County used padlocks to prevent theft. At least one woman accompanied her cook back and forth between home and outbuildings, keys in hand, in order to prevent slaves from taking provisions. The loot that slaves were supposed to have stolen from their own masters or from other whites ranged in value from a single knife valued at 25 cents up to a hogshead of tobacco and, in one case, watches and jewelry worth $1,000.[14] For convicted slave thieves, the prescribed penalties were severe, especially before the 1810s. Stealing bacon or the like, in the absence of any aggravating factors, earned thirty-nine lashes on the bare back, "well laid on" at the public whipping post.[15] Fearsome punishment attended a slave's second offense as a hogstealer around the time of Israel Hill's settlement: in addition to suffering thirty-nine lashes, a slave could have both his ears nailed to a pillory for two hours and then cut off, and be branded with a hot iron. A third offense brought a death sentence—which in practice was usually commuted to transportation outside the United States.

As with arson and poisoning, however, whites had a difficult time identifying slave suspects. Many bondpeople earned money, however modest the amounts; whites were not necessarily surprised to see slaves sporting pocket handkerchiefs or "cravats" purchased with their own income, at least at church on the Sabbath, or to find them consuming food and beverages beyond the standard plantation issue. Against such a backdrop, slaves who had come by such items illicitly did not necessarily stand out. More important, whites generally did not suffer crippling losses to theft. To arrest bondpeople in a scattershot manner or to convict them in error would impose a burden on masters, deputy sheriffs, county court justices, and innocent defendants alike. During the half century before the Civil War, a good many more slaves charged with stealing in Prince Edward County won acquittals or saw charges dismissed than were convicted.

Within the plantation or farm, of course, the slave might not encounter such favorable odds. Moreover, there were times when white anxiety increased. Vigilance mounted particularly in the days after the Nat Turner revolt; John Brown's raid at Harpers Ferry would trigger a similar response in 1859 and 1860. The Turner panic waned fairly quickly, however. Overall, judicial punishments for slaves convicted of stealing gradually became less harsh between 1800 and the eve of the Civil War. In 1823, a court found two slaves guilty of stealing goods from a store owned by the employer of free black miller Phil Bowman. The pair received the same penalty, whipping and burning on the hand, for having broken in and stolen on three separate occasions, that slaves had routinely suffered for a lone instance of simple theft not many years earlier. By 1856, a slave convicted of boring a hole through a store window and stealing $1,000 worth of watches and jewelry was whipped but not branded.[16]

One might speculate that the increasingly judicious attitude of the county justices would not carry over to prosecutions of free blacks, since no slaveholder's economic interest protected them against arbitrary treatment. But in fact the courts in Prince Edward weighed the guilt or innocence of free Afro-Virginians as discerningly as they did cases involving other defendants, and issued acquittals about as frequently. All in all, the courts' behavior reflected the mentality of a white population that remained watchful without descending into unreasoning fear. The overall absence of racial hysteria stemmed partly from a habit of seeing most black lawbreaking not as an attack on the slaveholding regime itself but as part of a more general problem of crime. Whites faced charges of stealing less often than slaves did, and acquittals and dismissals outnumbered convictions even more overwhelmingly for them than for enslaved defendants. Still, accusations against whites were no rarity, and those found guilty occasionally suffered penalties that, if less harsh than those sometimes meted out to bondmen, were both stringent and humiliating.

A white man convicted of petty larceny after stealing half a dozen glass tumblers in 1815 was sentenced to receive fourteen lashes. Another white man, Samuel H. Goins, was found guilty in 1831 of stealing 125 pounds of tobacco. When Goins tried to pin the crime on a black man, the court refused even to admit testimony on the subject; it sentenced Goins to serve forty days on a "low & coarse diet," in addition to the month he had already spent in jail, and to receive forty stripes, half at the beginning of his sentence and half on his release.[17] White boatman Grief Weaver, with his two-year sentence for stealing a companion's money, serves as an example of how seriously judges and jurors might regard theft, no matter who perpetrated it.

Whites rarely accused, much less convicted, free blacks of stealing. Two years before the Randolph emancipation, Charles Forgason found himself accused of stealing $7 from a white man's pocket, but a panel of county justices acquitted him.[18] One free Afro-Virginian was charged and found guilty, however: William Lilly, convicted in 1823 of stealing gloves and a pair of shoes, suffered a serious punishment. Nevertheless, unlike the white thief Samuel Goins, Lilly was not sentenced to serve time in jail, and unlike a slave, the free black man saw the court "remit" or forgo fourteen of the thirty-nine lashes that a jury recommended he get; that meant that Lilly received fifteen fewer stripes than Goins. The conviction seems to have tainted Lilly's reputation in some whites' minds, but not in others'. Accused again, just sixteen months after his earlier conviction, of having taken $37 worth of coins in the burglary of a silversmith's shop, Lilly was soon discharged from custody.[19]

One category of theft that again involved white, slave, and free black defendants was the stealing of livestock. A degree of racial specialization did emerge. Whites viewed "hogstealing," written as a single word, as the classic slave crime, perhaps because a hog could be quickly butchered, the pieces hidden away and then cooked and eaten discreetly. White men usually emerged as the prime suspects in horse thefts. People easily recognized individual horses, so stolen ones had to be taken far away for sale—a difficult proposition for a slave. For stealing livestock as for other thefts, acquittals and dismissals of bondmen were common, and occurred even in two cases where slaves were charged with multiple offenses. Some dismissals probably came after the defendant's owner agreed to make restitution and punish his bondman privately. In a number of instances, though, masters used every device in their power to fight charges lodged against their slaves.[20]

County justices who acquitted so many enslaved blacks of theft proved ready also to exonerate Israelites Hampton Giles and Guy Howard when they stood trial for hogstealing in 1826—another of those exceedingly rare instances in which free Afro-Virginians were accused of theft. Meanwhile, white men charged with stealing a horse or other animal faced more than a trivial danger of conviction; that could bring five or six years' imprisonment, for a good horse was one of the society's most valuable categories of personal property.[21]

A generation after the Giles-Howard trial, in November 1855, free black ditcher and well-digger Booker Hill received a vote of confidence in ironic circumstances when he was charged with having attempted to steal two hogs owned by a white man. A prominent local attorney gave security for Hill's bail bond. So did the constable who had been sent to make the arrest—scion of an old slaveholding family and, incidentally, father of a child by a free mulatto woman. The charge against Hill, listed for a time on the docket as a felony, was redefined as a misdemeanor, perhaps to exclude the possibility of a severe sentence, or simply to avoid making Hill wait for trial until the circuit judge sat in Prince Edward the following spring. The defense summoned a dozen witnesses, the prosecution none; Hill's witnesses included both slaves and prominent white citizens. One of the latter was a justice of the county court, another the wife of the very man whose hogs Hill had supposedly tried to steal. The court dismissed the charge, and Booker Hill won his county contract to repair a well only weeks later.[22]

Prince Edward's county court behaved just as deliberately when free Afro-Virginians themselves complained of theft. Someone stole a bay horse from Phil White Jr. of Israel Hill in July 1841. The charge against Jim Bradley, also a free black man and perhaps a transient from another county, came from the Israelites' white neighbor Amplias Tuggle, and the witnesses summoned, other than Phil White himself, were also white. Even so, Bradley's attorney and the county court afforded the defendant a careful trial, including a referral of the case to the circuit court, before the justices convicted him of grand larceny and sentenced him to five years, the same sentence meted out to white horse thieves.[23] Whites in Prince Edward yet again had taken seriously the property rights of one free black man—and also the legal rights of a second.

During the same decade, Martha Young, a teenaged free black, faced charges of stealing twice in less than two years. First, free Afro-Virginian Susannah Forgason accused Young of taking clothing and other goods. The county justice who issued the warrants in the case, a neighbor of Young and Forgason, quickly reduced the seriousness of the charge by striking the allegation that the defendant had broken into Forgason's house; the county court then discharged Martha Young from custody on a technicality. Less than a year and a half after the first case against her ended, Young was presented for stealing a bedspread and some calico from a store. She faced both white and free black potential witnesses, but again she went free on a technical point.[24]

Martha Young's story holds a unique place in the history of Prince Edward's Afro-Virginian community: no one else ever stood accused of two distinct criminal offenses, charged first by fellow blacks and then by whites. But Young's experience also shows that a free black accused of a crime could avoid conviction in the county without being a property owner or a close associate of influential white people. Young's father apparently had been a slave whose wife, Martha's mother, had managed to purchase him. Thereafter, county officials had recognized the mother, Esther Young, as a poor but deserving person and issued her aid.[25]

White *political* discourse about free blacks alleged not only that they stole but also that they lured their enslaved brethren into illicit activity. Whites in Prince Edward did not often cite specific instances of such conduct, however. The occasional complaint against a free black for unauthorized trading with a bondman or -woman won neither more nor less attention from the authorities than similar charges against whites did. When free black Mack Gregory was accused of buying chickens illicitly from a slave in 1853, his attorney made a game effort to get the presentment quashed, but Gregory ended up paying a $20 fine; white men sometimes paid the same amount for similar offenses.[26] Henry Mettauer, another free Afro-Virginian, seems to have traded fairly regularly, and openly, with slaves during the same period, usually without arousing concern among whites. Once, however, he faced a charge of having illegally bought chickens from a slave. The evidence in the case included a barely intelligible note purporting to convey a mistress's approval of the transaction. The justices presumably viewed the note as a forgery, for they convicted Mettauer, yet the court imposed only a $5 fine against the free black man. An attorney in the case shared the court's view that unauthorized commerce between slaves and free blacks posed no grave threat to public order; he distractedly doodled a sketch of three chickens on the papers documenting Mettauer's trial for buying stolen fowls.[27]

Allegations of active criminal partnerships between slaves and free blacks came before the county authorities even more rarely than charges of illicit trade between the groups. One free black man, Henry Homes, was accused along with a slave in 1845 of having stolen $75 worth of goods from a wagon one night as it passed through Prince Edward. But as in some other cases in the 1840s, the prosecutor himself asked the court to dismiss the charges on a technicality: the warrants against the two men had not described the goods that had been stolen from the wagon.[28] A Commonwealth's attorney would not likely have discontinued the prosecution so summarily had the white public been deeply troubled about criminal confederacies involving free and enslaved blacks.

The few alleged crimes or conflicts that involved free Afro-Virginians amounted to a trivial sideshow by comparison with the numerous instances in which whites accused members of their own race of trading illegally with slaves or of receiving stolen goods from them. Black-white trade occurred so often, and with so little regard for the written permission required by law, that it was difficult to prove that a white man who received stolen goods had done so knowingly. Prosecutors sometimes devoted considerable energy to prosecutions for that offense, usually to no avail.[29]

Colonel Charles Woodson used the pages of Edmund Ruffin's journal in 1834 to decry his fellow whites' eagerness to traffic with slaves. That commerce, Woodson insisted, made bondpeople too independent and thus not dedicated enough to their masters' interests; moreover, freelance trading kept slaves abroad at night, leaving them exhausted and unable to work efficiently.[30] Woodson's complaint mentioned free Afro-Virginians only in passing, yet he had put his finger on a feature of the environment that affected free blacks' lives in a crucial way: slaves, for all the oppression they suffered, moved about far more freely than most people assume today. Whites did not police free black residents as vigilantly as we think because they also monitored slaves less closely than we imagine.

Slaves on the move were supposed to possess—and patrols were supposed to demand—written passes issued by their masters. Yet trial testimony reveals that many enslaved people routinely visited others and went out on errands of their own at all hours of the night on all days of the week, often without asking permission of whites and unmolested by them. In one case from 1832, it turned out that a number of enslaved witnesses and the slave defendant had been out of their quarters at various times of night—and this was a weeknight, not a Saturday.[31] That scene was repeated countless times on other plantations. As Charles Woodson complained, slaves' comings and goings elicited neither surprise nor alarm from many whites—except, of course, in those unusual instances where an enslaved individual actually did something disturbing during his or her peregrinations. Too many whites benefited from trading with bondpeople, or from letting slaves circulate to earn money, which gave them a small stake in the economy and thus rendered them less likely to cause real trouble.

The illegal sale of intoxicating liquor in particular brought black and white together in various ways. Old Prince Edward belonged to a hard-drinking country in a hard-drinking century. Customs surrounding death illustrate the pervasiveness of imbibing. The estate of one well-to-do man in 1801 paid for "$3^{7}/_{8}$ Gallons brandy for the Company while sitting up with the Corps" at his wake. A few years later, the late Philip Wade's household supplied "Brandy at the funeral," and then liquidated the estate in more ways than one by dispensing some eleven gallons of that beverage during a three-day auction of Wade's property.[32] Decade in and decade out, the monthly court sessions at Prince Edward Court House, where men socialized and conducted much of the county's business, included several consecutive days of heavy drinking and all manner of misbehavior.

Liquor flowed copiously and openly to slaves as well. Bondpeople of the Chambers estate, as elsewhere, received spirits as compensation for rolling tobacco hogsheads, "measuring corn," rolling logs, and killing hogs. A carpenter who surely headed a mostly enslaved crew presented a bill that included a charge for "2 gallons of whiskey for raising the house." From the Penick place near Israel Hill to Josiah Cheadle's in the west, slaves received liquor when they worked in the annual harvest.[33] The Chambers plantation, like a number of others, dispensed liquor to slaves upon hiring them out at year's end—a time when bondpeople celebrated both the Christmas holiday and their brief reunion at the old homeplace between yearlong separations.[34]

Some whites did worry that slaves' access to spirits would promote disorder and crime, if not outright subversion. The law therefore attempted to forbid selling alcohol to a slave without the master's permission. As usual, those who worried most about bondpeople and liquor tended to be concerned about "the other person's slave"; complaints to the grand jury about whites selling alcohol were only rarely lodged by the owner of the enslaved purchaser. White merchants proved happy to sell spirits to the many slaves who had money in their pockets. Hillery G. Richardson would become the face of law and order in Prince Edward when he served as county sheriff in the 1850s. But he was also a store-keeper, convicted on at least three separate occasions during the four years before he took office of selling liquor to slaves without their masters' consent.[35] Many such charges were "nol-prossed" (not prosecuted) or dismissed, or resulted in acquittals. Richardson and other merchants apparently totted up the occasional fine as a cost of doing business.

Many saw the dispensing of liquor to slaves less as a threat to whites' security than as part of a universal problem of drunkenness and disorder. Clement Read was a well-known "temperance man"; that alone may explain his complaint to the grand jury in 1832 that a merchant in Farm-ville had sold spirits to a slave belonging to Read's wife.[36] People charged with illegal liquor selling to whites found themselves convicted at about the same rate as those who sold to slaves, and they often paid higher fines.

Temperance people, like drinkers, came in both colors; anti-tippling evangelical churches drew hundreds of whites, slaves, and free blacks, including Clem Read's associates, the Whites of Israel Hill. Meanwhile, free black vendors of illegal alcohol occasionally faced charges, but they tended to do their business in the same times and places, and with about the same clientele, as illicit white traffickers. No one seems to have regarded these black individuals as anything other than one small part of the general liquor problem that some citizens worried about, and no one ever accused a free black in the county of selling spirits to slaves.

Half a dozen times during the five decades before 1861, someone did bring charges against a free Afro-Virginian for unlicensed liquor selling, but prosecution of the accused proceeded without apparent regard to race. Whites found themselves charged along with free black Susannah Short after the revelry at the militia drill ground in 1813, for example. The white woman presented for vending liquor that day was not convicted, but the same jury that fined Short $30 treated her white male fellow defendant identically; other whites accused of selling unlicensed liquor during the period suffered the same fate. More than four years after Susannah Short's conviction, she and Hugh Ritchie, a white man convicted of swearing at the muster field, still had not paid their fines. "Any person acquainted with Short or Ritchie can have no doubt of their insolvency," a deputy sheriff explained to the court, and the justices waived the fines against both.[37]

Shortly thereafter, when Susannah (Sooky) Moss faced her own charges of selling illegal liquor in 1818 and 1819, she, too, received jury trials. In each instance, she was assessed the same $30 fine levied against a young white man for the same offense at about the same time. The court waived at least one of Sooky Moss's fines on grounds of insolvency, as it had for Susannah Short; whether Moss saw her second fine canceled as well is not clear.[38]

A generation later, free black trafficking in liquor still set off no special alarm bells in white minds. A jury did convict free Afro-Virginian Charles Henry Diuguid in 1846 of having sold "ardent spirits" at his blacksmith shop. A few years earlier, however, jurors had acquitted another free black man of a similar charge even as a white defendant paid $30 for the kindred offense of keeping a house of entertainment without a license. Since Diuguid purveyed his merchandise "to be drank where sold," his fellow blacks may sometimes have imbibed together with whites who went to Diuguid's to have smithing work done.[39]

White people often spent as much energy suppressing vice among members of their own race as they did attacking any problems they thought blacks might pose. Scores of presentments for gambling or for permitting gaming on one's premises span the entire period from the early nineteenth century to the Civil War; they far outnumber prosecutions of free and enslaved blacks and of whites who allegedly trafficked with slaves. Many gamblers behaved much more brazenly than blacks usually did, and thus drew much fire. One gaming session in 1837 lasted at least three days and featured vendors of liquor and of food for man and horse alike.[40] Free blacks were almost never arrested for gambling. It seems unlikely that white men who labored with blacks, sometimes ate and drank and slept with them, bought from them, and sold to them, hermetically excluded them from games of chance on racial grounds. But slaves and most free Afro-Virginians lacked the money to play at the high-stakes games that drew the most complaints. There a man could readily lose $40—nearly a year's pay for an agricultural hireling—within twenty-four hours.[41] Some blacks who did have that kind of money, Sam and Phil White, for instance, opposed gambling on religious grounds.

In a system where citizens often detect and punish crime outside the judicial system, however, official records may omit much of the picture. In the Old South, most punishment of slaves took place on the farm or plantation and went unchronicled. Even when a defendant ended up before a court in Prince Edward County, the first response to the alleged crime by citizens or lawmen had taken place days, or weeks, before county justices sat to consider the case.

The record in at least a few instances shows or strongly suggests that sheriff's deputies or posse members coerced a slave suspect into confessing, or a witness into implicating another person, and other such cases may not have been mentioned in writing. Fragments of evidence suggest that county justices and judges took a dim view of such confessions. Had coercion of suspects became commonplace, it would be difficult to explain how such a large fraction of defendants both black and white successfully defended their innocence in court.[42]

Slave patrols had ample opportunity to discipline bondpeople—and, at least in theory, free blacks—spontaneously and in ways that would not necessarily enter the record. A detailed description of one patrol's behavior on a certain evening in 1849 does survive. Late in the summer, a young enslaved woman hired by a Presbyterian clergyman, Dr. Benjamin H. Rice, decided to marry. Although the prospective bride did not belong to the Rices, a strong personal relationship had developed between her and the family, and Rice's daughters decided to give the young bondwoman a large, festive wedding at the family home. With Benjamin Rice's approval and that of the bride's owner, the Rice daughters consulted the bride-to-be and sent out written invitations to all the slaves in the neighborhood whom "she specified."

Thirty or forty bondmen and -women attended the wedding and the reception that followed. Between ten and eleven in the evening, the local slave patrol arrived and demanded passes from all the enslaved wedding guests; Benjamin Rice himself had not asked to see any. The patrol then "whipped so many of the slaves as had no written permission from their masters to be present" and sent home those who did have passes. A grand jury charged Rice himself with having permitted an unlawful assemblage.

The usually understated dissonance among whites over the treatment of slaves had burst into the open. Benjamin Rice insisted that "the slaves were guilty of no improper or disorderly conduct." He also defended himself by asserting that the wedding invitations, though issued "in the name of the negro girl" and addressed directly to her enslaved friends, must surely have been read to the recipients by their masters, who thereby gave tacit consent for their slaves to attend. Rice also pleaded ignorance of the law against allowing "assemblages" of slaves, noting that he had fairly recently returned from a stay of eighteen years outside Virginia, largely in the North. In reality, however, laws to curtail gatherings of blacks had existed for many years. The minister made a more plausible point when he asserted that he had done nothing unusual by holding the wedding celebration. "The conduct of my neighbours," he wrote, had given him the "impression" that the kind of event he had sponsored was not prohibited.

Rice, seeking his own exoneration, probably overstated the ordinariness of his actions. Yet his attorney well knew how many whites tolerated slaves' moving about without passes; he would never have approved his client's appeal to local custom had he not expected the court to find it credible. Indeed, the occasional white person had been charged earlier in the 1840s with having permitted unlawful gatherings of blacks, but convictions were rare. The charges against Rice, too, seem to have been dropped.[43]

Differences in white attitudes about the governance of slaves created room for bondpeople, free blacks, and sympathetic (or apathetic) whites to maneuver. But the same discrepancies also produced a degree of unpredictability that could become nerve-wracking.[44] These inconsistencies and tensions within white society could even get patrollers themselves into trouble. In 1851, less than two years after Benjamin Rice's slave wedding, a patrol apprehended "more than twenty" slaves, perhaps for moving about without passes. This time, however, the patrol encountered white resistance more formidable than the mannerly protests of Benjamin Rice. According to the patrollers themselves, they suffered an assault by five fellow white men, one of them a justice of the county court, who "rescued" the slaves from their custody. The patrolmen's complaint brought meager results: three of the accused rescuers of slaves saw their cases nol-prossed a year later, and the other two were acquitted by juries.[45]

White men in Prince Edward had not gone soft. The same grand jury that brought charges against the alleged rescuers also presented two citizens for allowing individual slaves "to go at large and trade as free men," and those prosecutions did lead to convictions and fines.[46] The party of "rescuers" probably had included, or acted on behalf of, the captured slaves' owners. Presumably, they aimed to veto by force an unjustified, overly aggressive, or simply inconvenient exercise of power by the patrollers. The men of the patrol then discovered they had little backing among propertied citizens of Prince Edward County—or at least from the prosecutor and two sets of jurors.

Patrols sometimes policed fellow whites. Patroller John Sears alienated citizens in the northwestern part of the county, including a member of the Wright family, by charging them with various offenses in the late 1820s and early 1830s. At Christmastime 1832, Sears and his patrol captured a slave who belonged to one of the Wrights; the white clan then formed a group and "rescued" the bondman by force. Charges filed against two of the rescuers were dismissed. The potential for such collisions accompanied the slave patrol to its latter days as an institution. As late as November 1860, with the crisis of the Union already under way, a grand jury charged a white man in Prince Edward with resisting and threatening a patrol.[47] Even so, the Rice wedding demonstrated what Afro-Southern folklore and reminiscences chronicle: the capacity of at least some patrollers for punitive, cruel behavior toward blacks. Patrollers did visit slave quarters, and they did demand passes from bondpeople, as they were commissioned to do. How often and how assiduously patrols did these things, or confronted free Afro-Virginians, is an open question, however.

Ostensibly, patrols were expected to police free blacks as well as slaves—yet patrollers could be forgiven for wondering what, exactly, that meant. Patrollers' written commissions charged them with apprehending "all slaves[,] free negroes or mulattoes assembled at any place whatever without a permit *from their master*[,] *mistress or overseer.*"[48] Clearly, legislators awkwardly wrote free blacks into a system of control that they had actually tailored to deal with enslaved people. Free blacks in Prince Edward certainly encountered patrollers at least occasionally. One patrol captain in the summer of 1808 took the trouble to list the places he and his men had visited; their rounds included two stops at General John Purnall's plantation. The store that Purnall operated was the accustomed assembly point for the neighborhood patrol then and afterward. Purnall had one or more free blacks living on his tract at least intermittently during that first decade of the century. One supposes that patrols continued to visit Purnall's in the 1810s, when free Afro-Virginian Milly Homes and then others of her family took up residence on or next to the plantation.[49]

Free blacks rarely ran afoul of the law, however, whether through the activities of patrols or otherwise. Neither patrollers nor militia nor white vigilantes seem to have broken up the suspicious assemblages of free blacks that Major John Rice thought he saw in Farmville's streets during the Nat Turner panic. If patrols did not accost free Afro-Virginians then, it is difficult to picture their doing so with any frequency in other, less nerve-shattering periods. Free blacks had good cause not to court trouble, and patrollers had reasons not to *make* trouble for free blacks gratuitously. Free Afro-Virginians, as owners of their own bodies and labor, of personal property, and sometimes of land, had much to lose by participating in crimes or creating disorder. Though disfranchised, they even had a certain positive stake in the system that enforced law and order; their victories as both plaintiffs and defendants in the local courts reminded them of that. By the same token, any patroller who might feel tempted to abuse free Afro-Virginians had reason to think twice. Free black residents of Prince Edward, after all, had shown themselves ready to resist abuse by filing suit against aggressors, and the courts had proved open to blacks' demands for relief.

Legend has it that patrols typically enlisted insecure "white trash" who abused blacks for the sheer sport of it.[50] Indeed, it is easy to imagine resentful white have-nots resolving to teach a lesson in racial etiquette to the august, permissive Dr. Benjamin H. Rice when he sponsored his slave wedding. Yet for Prince Edward County, at least, there are two good reasons to question the "white trash" model. For one thing, lower-class whites in general did not necessarily abuse blacks more readily than their social betters did. The planter class included people who strove to mitigate their slaves' lot, or even set them free—and also masters whose brutality became proverbial in the community. The same class ranged from the anti–free black polemicist Colonel Madison to men who attended church, and regularly did friendly business, with free Afro-Virginians such as the Whites of Israel Hill. Likewise, the simpler, more deprived white citizenry must have included some vicious Negrophobes, yet there were also plain white folk who associated with blacks on terms of friendliness and even intimacy. A few whites were even prepared to kill in defense of those relationships, as we shall see. Prince Edward County furnishes another, quite direct reason to question the "white trash" stereotype of brutal patrollers: the patrols that operated there included men of all social classes. A number of those delegated to monitor Israel Hill during its early years had close and amicable relations with the black inhabitants of the settlement.

It is true that wealthy planters made up only a small fraction of patrollers, as of white society as a whole, and that many men who rode on patrol came from modest origins. Skill with the pen correlated only imperfectly with social class, yet a number of patrol reports—such as the one from a captain who wrote that his group had "patter role all Night witch is [22 hours]"—suggest the humble background of more than a few men who served. Indeed, the captain who submitted that particular claim owned only one slave, a young boy.[51] At the same time, relatively prosperous farmers and craftsmen and even young men of the planter class also rode on patrol. As late as the 1850s, solid yeomen, planters, and county justices' sons still participated in patrols.[52] For much of the half century before the Civil War, the county organized patrols by precinct, or neighborhood, which ensured that patrollers monitored a limited landscape and population that were well known to them. Familiarity does not guarantee harmony. Still, during Israel Hill's formative decade, the patrols that rode in its neighborhood included men of substance—Penicks, Tuggles, Fores, an Allen, and a Legrand—at least some of whom clearly had smooth relations with the Israelites and other free blacks over the years.[53]

The regimen that the patrollers followed did not lend itself to thoroughgoing repression of blacks. Most patrols operated only occasionally. Patrol commissions during Israel Hill's first generation required excursions "at least as often as once a month." William Dodd's patrol stuck to that minimum in the spring of 1813, always making their lone monthly rounds between the 13th and the 17th; the infrequency and predictability of their outings hardly enhanced their deterrent role. Even in the previous year, when Dodd's patrol had been more active, its expeditions were few: three in May, none at all in July, and one or two in the other months through October.[54] James Gilliam Jr.'s patrol went out two or three times a month between May and August 1812. They spaced their excursions randomly, whether because of haphazard planning or a desire to keep the slaves guessing, but the group's activity mostly petered out after the beginning of September. One to three outings a month seem to have been the norm for patrols during Israel Hill's early years; a particular patrol that rode five times in December 1810 stands out as uncommonly diligent. Only toward the end of the antebellum period did patrol commissions order captains to take their men out more frequently—at least once a week.[55] By then, however, the number of patrollers had shrunk, perhaps because the county was relying more heavily on its five regular constables to maintain order.

Between 1810 and 1850, the number of individuals who rode on patrols in Prince Edward within a given year fluctuated radically, ranging from twenty-five or even fewer up to nearly a hundred. The latter is not a trivial number, but not a massive one, either, in a county measuring nearly twenty by thirty-five miles. The length of service that these men's captains claimed for them over the entire year ending in June 1815 ranged from 4 to 146 hours per individual, with the typical patroller serving only 30-odd hours in twelve months.[56] A patrol's rounds on a given date might last as little as 2 or 3 hours, but patrol captains typically filed returns claiming 10 to 12 or more hours of service on each excursion. In fact, many said they had served 18 to 24 hours per trip.[57] One could read the latter figures as evidence of extreme diligence. On the other hand, the county did compensate patrollers on an hourly basis, and thus provided a clear incentive to claim many hours of work: 24 hours of supposed service would yield a handsome payment of $1.50. That exceeded the daily rate paid to county road "surveyors," and trebled the daily sum that property-line processioners received during Israel Hill's early years for what was probably more difficult work.[58]

It seems self-evident that any patrollers who truly were abroad for eighteen, twenty, or twenty-four hours would have spent some of their time eating, napping, and conversing with the neighbors they encountered. Some, perhaps many, patrols assembled well before dark and served through the evening, so they surely had face-to-face contact with many of those whose property they policed.[59] One unusually detailed patrol return suggests that the men stayed, on average, some forty-five minutes at each farm or plantation they visited. Some patrols may have spent that entire time probing diligently for violations; perhaps many did. But if at least some of those visits did not include a round of drinks and a plug of tobacco, then patrolling stands as all but unique among interactions between man and man in Prince Edward County. Even one of the more conscientious patrols did not hesitate to visit a tract belonging to one of the group's own members—yet another welcome opportunity, presumably, for some rest, food, and drink.[60]

Patrollers' tolerance for discomfort had definite limits, and no-shows were not rare. A certain captain found himself the only member of his group to appear at the appointed place one October night in 1808 "on account of its being rainy." He tried again a week later, and this time only one other man showed up; the pair, "not having a sufficient Company, declined going."[61] Inclement weather probably depressed slaves' mobility, too, yet it is also clear that patrols in Prince Edward County did not necessarily keep themselves on a war footing.

Only a rash optimist would conclude that the slave patrols in Prince Edward were empty vessels. Patrols did function year in and year out; some, like that of John Sears, may have policed strictly much of the time, and most probably did so some of the time. Otherwise the confrontations with white "rescuers" of captive slaves would not have happened. Even spotty enforcement—especially if applied brutally on occasion, as at the Rice wedding—can have an effect out of proportion to the number of man-hours expended or of punishments actually administered. Still, the evidence offers little reason to believe that slave patrols made free blacks' lives miserable in Prince Edward.

White men of the county enforced the law by methods other than patrolling. Sheriff's deputies served papers for the courts; they and the county's few constables arrested suspects, or took custody of them from civilians who had apprehended them. Free Afro-Virginians had as much contact with these lawmen as other free people in the county did—but not more, and the transactions seem almost always to have been businesslike. Deputies readily noted disorderly or hostile acts by citizens they were sent to deal with, but they almost never reported a moment's difficulty with free blacks. Lawmen often proved less than tenacious in seeking out black defendants: more than one reported that he had "not found" a free black he was to summon, or had "not [had] time" to execute a warrant on such a person, even though the designee might be a well-known, longtime resident of the county and the papers had been issued weeks in advance.

Free blacks Cyrus Hill and Davy Smith did complain of false arrest or manhandling in the years around 1840, though details have not survived; the race of another complainant in the 1850s remains unclear. Even two such incidents command attention, and there may well have been others over the years that led to no formal action. Yet various white individuals lodged similar accusations against lawmen at one time or another; victory against the authorities in such a lawsuit proved unlikely regardless of the aggrieved party's color.[62] Hill and Smith, like free blacks who sued civilians for assault, at least did not hesitate to complain when affronted, which leads one to doubt that a pattern of widespread, unreported abuse lurks beneath the surface.

For better or worse, sheriffs and their deputies were not so much lawmen as they were placemen—citizens from middling or well-to-do families who profited from long- or short-term official appointments. For most of the era before the Civil War, the office of sheriff rotated approximately at two-year intervals among justices of the county court, who were planters, farmers, craftsmen-businessmen, or members of the professions. The sheriff received a salary along with a richer source of income: fees for specific duties he performed and portions of the funds he collected.[63] Together with their other duties, deputy sheriffs kept

records of tax delinquents and conducted "sheriff's sales" of goods forfeited by people who could not pay court-ordered judgments. These
deputies, like the sheriffs they served, were not necessarily chosen for any
particular aptitude as crime-stoppers. Rather, they joined together to
"farm the sheriffalty"—meaning, in the utterly frank language of the
time, that the deputy sheriffs split both the "labour" and the "profits"
attending the functions of the sheriff's office.

The deputies divided the county geographically, bargaining over who
would get the "most proffitable" districts; then each deputy went out and
"done the business" in his own bailiwick.[64] This system did not exclude
domineering physical specimens or hard-nosed enforcers, and all sorts of
people participated in the occasional posse, or acted as guards in or on
the way to the county jail. But the corps of men deputed to keep order in
Prince Edward and elsewhere in rural Virginia tended to take a less over-
weening, intimidating form than we may assume today.

Two other county officers whom free Afro-Virginians dealt with fairly
often were the commissioner of the revenue and the court clerk. The former compiled the annual county list of free blacks, and so was reasonably
familiar with that two thirds of the free Afro-Virginian population
whose names actually made it onto the rolls. The county clerk had some
power to simplify or complicate free blacks' lives, for it was he who drew
up replacements for missing "free papers," and who registered or reregistered as free people those Afro-Virginians who complied with the law
requiring them to enroll.

The clerkship brought in substantial fees and commissions, and the
redoubtable Branch J. Worsham held the post for nearly forty-five years,
through and a bit beyond the Civil War. That was something of a help to
free blacks, for, as boatman Randolph Brandum knew, Worsham sometimes smoothed the way for black individuals who needed his services.
County coroners had less contact with the average person. They investigated the deaths of free and enslaved blacks as vigorously as those of
whites—in small part, perhaps, because two of those coroners, Charles
Woodson and John Foster, had long and positive relationships with various free Afro-Virginians.

Many other whites had occasion to shape the fate of free black individuals in an official setting when they served on juries in trials of black
defendants or of civil cases involving blacks. Juries in Prince Edward, like
the county court itself, operated in ways that today seem uncomfortably
cozy. In a rural county with a modest white population, it was difficult to
assemble twelve propertied men (the law as of the 1840s required a petit

Prince Edward County's elite enjoyed earthly comforts but not fabulous wealth. Clover Hill was the home of Andrew Baker, who left a will emancipating a number of slaves and providing for their education. The place later belonged to Branch J. Worsham, the longtime county clerk who assisted free blacks in getting proper "free papers."

(HERBERT CLARENCE BRADSHAW, *History of Prince Edward County, Virginia* [RICHMOND: DIETZ PRESS, 1955], PLATE XXIX)

juror to own at least $300 worth of property)[65] without some of them knowing the accused or the litigants who stood before them. Defendants awaiting trial at the courthouse on a given day even served on the juries that heard each other's cases. Today's worries about the effects of pretrial publicity on jurors would have seemed utterly foreign in such a society. This system, which strikes modern folk as patently flawed, helps explain the fair treatment free blacks often received in court. Jurors tended to judge them as individuals whom they knew, not as appendages of that abstract, aggregate free black *category* against which legislators and editorialists aimed racist laws and rhetoric.

Free Afro-Virginian defendants did not always appear before juries. After 1832, the law required them to stand trial before the same "courts of oyer and terminer" that tried slaves. Most people referred to such a panel as a "called court," because in theory it was supposed to be called into special session within ten days of an arrest. The tribunal included only five county justices, chosen from among all those who sat on the county court. Those five men determined the defendant's innocence or guilt; in the latter case, they fixed a sentence, to be carried out immediately with no right of appeal—except in death sentences passed on slaves, which were sent on to the governor for review from the beginning of the nineteenth century until the Civil War.[66] A white person charged with a serious offense might also come before a called court, but in his case the tribunal, if it thought him guilty, would send the case on to the circuit court, where the defendant was entitled to a jury.

Every feature of the called courts except one—the requirement of unanimity for a conviction[67]—seems to prove that blacks both free and enslaved who went before them were denied due process. Yet even toward slaves, called courts behaved more deliberately than one might think. Occasionally a panel did designate an attorney for an enslaved defendant only when the latter actually appeared before the court, but a defense lawyer appointed minutes before trial might do an effective job and win a reduced charge or outright acquittal for a slave. Justices were also prepared to overlook the requirement that a called court sit within ten days of an alleged offense, deferring trial for a month rather than have a slave defendant appear without an attorney.[68] In fact, justices routinely waited to conduct trials until the next monthly session of the county court. That might leave a slave defendant—or even a free black or a white—sitting in jail for an extra couple of weeks awaiting trial, but it also bespeaks officials' general lack of desire to rush to judgment.

Called courts—so easy to write off as vehicles of drumhead justice—awarded substantial fees, typically $10 but sometimes, by the 1830s at least, as much as $25, to attorneys they appointed to defend slaves. The money came from the defendant's owner, as did expenses involved in bringing in defense witnesses and housing the slave defendant in jail. Although some have seen the provision of lawyers to slave defendants as a mere "legalistic" formality, these attorneys often enough put on vigorous, creative—and successful—defenses, actively exercising their right to summon white and black witnesses, whom the county then compelled to appear.[69] Free blacks, like whites, paid for their own counsel.

Called courts sometimes showed great patience, hearing many witnesses of both races.[70] The system is rightly damned for prohibiting a black person, whether free or enslaved, from testifying against a white aggressor. On the other hand, blacks could and often did take the stand to contradict the testimony of whites who had accused a black defendant. Those defense witnesses frequently carried the day. The law was grossly unfair, as slavery itself was. But in practice, the legal establishment did not work as arbitrarily as it threatened to; the frequent acquittals of black defendants, both slave and free, testify to that.

The system of slavery, exploitative as it was, built in one obvious incentive for trying slaves fairly: a defendant's master had an interest in preventing an unwarranted conviction of his slave, if only to avoid the inconvenience of losing that person's labor. The compensation that the Commonwealth awarded to masters of slaves who were executed or transported could seem a poor substitute for the continued services of a strong, talented—and innocent—bondman or -woman.

Beyond that, many slaveowners knew their slaves well and might have a personal interest in vindicating one who they believed had been wrongly accused. It is difficult to explain white people's exertions to protect Tom—who, having killed overseer Richard Foster, was sure to be transported or executed no matter what they said on his behalf—except by suggesting that they acted on principle. The same applies to a young slave named Anderson, charged in 1837 with the attempted rape of a fourteen-year-old white girl. Even after the court convicted Anderson and he was almost certainly lost to his master, his attorney went on fighting, preparing objections to the conviction on four technical grounds. The court overruled these, but the justices accompanied the slave's death sentence with a unanimous recommendation that the governor spare Anderson's life because he was only sixteen.[71] The point is not that the system was fair—no structure designed to defend human bondage could be that—but rather that within the system, white individuals often remembered the humanity even of persons whom they owned, bought, sold, and punished physically. In such an atmosphere, the courts' treatment of free Afro-Virginians begins to seem less surprising.

The experience of free black William Lilly showed that trials by called court rather than by jury did not necessarily constitute a denial of justice. When Lilly faced the charge of stealing gloves and shoes in 1823, he went through the entire multistep judicial process, including an examination of the charge against him by a grand jury and trial before a petit jury, only to find himself convicted and punished in the end. At the time, in fact, the justices who presided over Lilly's first trial referred to examination by a called court as a "right" that Lilly, perhaps misguidedly, had voluntarily chosen to "dispens[e] with." It was those justices of the county court who reduced Lilly's punishment—perhaps in deference to his status as a free person—from the full thirty-nine lashes that the twelve men good and true had thought he should receive. The next time Lilly faced a criminal accusation, he showed no interest in a jury trial—and sure enough, a called court seized on an arcane technicality to throw out the charge and release him.[72]

County justices' general readiness to give a fair hearing to free blacks had at least two sources beyond their personal knowledge of the individuals who appeared before them. Their grasp on power was secure; as lifetime appointees, they need not prove anything or pander to anyone. At the same time, though unelected, the county court possessed legitimacy in the eyes of the white male citizenry. Residents of the county demonstrated that when they finally got the right to elect local officials: voters returned eleven incumbents to the county court of 1852, which now consisted of twenty members. The nine new men joined the court mainly because deaths and retirements had thinned the panel's ranks in the seven years since the last appointments. The group installed in 1852 was reelected almost in toto in 1856.[73] The county court won this legitimacy in part because, even before the 1850s, it evinced just enough openness to avoid appearing as a rich man's clique. A working, albeit prosperous, craftsman like cabinetmaker George W. Clibourne, whose wife worked as a seamstress, could serve on the county court in the 1840s; so could a man such as Henry S. Guthrey, who had built a thriving business after working as a master carpenter.

Prince Edward's justices operated a century before the Italian Marxian thinker Antonio Gramsci advanced the idea of ruling-class "hegemony," but they seem to have understood intuitively that a governing elite strengthens its own position by giving ordinary people positive reasons to accept its claim to rule. An astute elite creates laws and norms of government that offer a significant degree of protection to citizens; people then seek redress of grievances within the existing social and political framework rather than through frontal challenges to the system itself. In Prince Edward County, members of the elite, including county justices, were subject to sanctions from the system that they themselves led. Less affluent people could and did successfully sue well-off men in court. Leading citizens faced presentments and sometimes fines for not "surveying," or maintaining, the stretches of county road assigned to them, for building fences that impinged on public roads, for failing to answer summonses to jury duty, and sometimes for more serious offenses.

Abner Nash III came from a family whose members had served in the state legislature, on the county court, and even in the governor's mansion of North Carolina; he himself would become a revenue commissioner for Prince Edward County. Yet Nash could be presented in 1811 for selling liquor illegally—the very misdemeanor alleged during that same decade against Susannah Short, Sooky Moss, and a man known only as Morton, all of whom were free blacks.[74] Setbacks on this scale did no profound damage to the leading citizens who suffered them, but they immunized the elite from charges that it stood above the law.

Would the white public have bristled at free black victories in court if it had had less respect for the county justices and circuit judges who presided over those trials? Perhaps not—but free Afro-Virginians in Prince Edward never had to find out. A self-assured body of men who knew many blacks personally and judged them as individuals handed down decisions; most whites seem to have considered those determinations authoritative, at least partly by dint of the character of the men and the nature of the institutions that rendered them. Jurors behaved about as fairly as the justices did, and there is little evidence that white men of more modest means in Prince Edward despised free blacks and were restrained only by their social betters. Still, another kind of elite could have created, or allowed others to create, a very different kind of life for the free black populace.

White Southerners' very defense of slavery may have deepened citizens' already considerable respect for their local and state courts, and bolstered the determination of those courts to follow the law as scrupulously as was possible in an inherently unequal system. Southern whites were as prone to inconsistency as anyone else; they alternately defended states' rights or called for federal mandates such as the Fugitive Slave Law of 1850, depending on which would advance slaveholders' prerogatives in a given situation. Yet they regularly demanded, especially during the thirty years before the Civil War, that Americans in other sections of the country tender to slavery the same respect that other fundamental social institutions merited. This insistence on the sanctity of established institutions may have enhanced white Southerners' regard for their courts and for the canons of justice under which those bodies operated. The same attitude could benefit free blacks in a more specific way: because slavery was based on "principles of right and justice," one statesman from South Carolina argued, white Southerners must not flout such principles by re-enslaving or otherwise degrading free blacks.[75]

Life's realities emerge much more accurately from the authorities' day-to-day behavior than from laws recorded in the statute books. The law, for instance, required free blacks to register with the local court in the county or city where they lived; rural Afro-Virginians, including those in Prince Edward and surrounding counties, were supposed to renew their registration every three years. If someone employed a black person who lacked "free papers"—a certified copy of his or her registration—both that employer and the black worker were subject to punishment. The mutilated condition of some old free papers that blacks turned in for one reason or another suggests that their owners had kept the documents on their persons day in, day out.[76] Indeed, some people held on to their own papers, or even those of the dead, for prodigious lengths of time. When Peter Patterson of Israel Hill re-registered in 1851, he handed in the papers issued to his long-deceased parents, Isham and Nancy, in 1811 at the time of the Randolph emancipation. Various black folk who lost their papers over the years took the trouble to get them replaced: James Mettauer and Israelite Donaldson Gibbs reported to the county court in 1850 and 1851 respectively that they had lost their registrations, and they applied successfully for new ones.[77]

From time to time, a black person in Prince Edward was challenged to show free papers, failed to produce them, and faced a formal charge under the statute. That happened to Israelite boatman Essex White Jr. in 1819, and again, three years later, to Edmund Clarke, son-in-law and heir of Isham Patterson, an original settler of Israel Hill. Over a six-month period beginning in December 1845, one punctilious constable brought charges against as many as half a dozen free blacks, apparently for lacking papers. None of those people seems to have been convicted or deprived of freedom, however. During the forty years before the Civil War, at least seven free blacks, including Edmund Clarke, were ordered to pay jailor's fees for the time during which their free status was under question. Whether that requirement, prescribed by law, was actually enforced is not clear: one black man on whom it was formally imposed received new free papers from the court before he served even one day in jail.[78]

The standard outcome when papers went missing was for the black person in question to present an excuse: people reported their free papers stolen, thrown into the fire by children, or otherwise "casually lost or destroyed." Then—some twenty times between 1830 and 1861—the court reregistered the applicant, in most cases apparently acting mainly on the word of the paperless Afro-Virginian and on his or her familiarity as a member of the community. A dozen additional people got lost papers replaced during the Civil War alone.[79]

Authorities may have enforced the registration law much as police at the turn of the twenty-first century issued traffic tickets for failing to wear a seatbelt only if they first stopped a driver for some other reason. During the flurry of cases in 1845–46, James Cabell became that rarest of exceptions to a general rule—a free black man arrested for gambling—and at that point apparently failed to come up with a valid registration. Some white authorities and employers took special care, as county clerk Branch Worsham did, to *prevent* punishment of paperless free blacks whom they knew personally and to help such people secure proper documentation. A couple of local white employers vouched for free blacks who lacked papers; former Israelite Otha Carter's supporter bolstered his endorsement by noting that Carter was "in possession" of the land abutting his own in Charlotte—perhaps as a renter.

When a constable in Farmville asked Micajah Walden for his registration in 1848, the free black man's employer wrote back to Walden's distant home county of Surry in southeastern Virginia to request a copy of the original free papers, which Walden said had been stolen. Black shoemaker Edward Hitchins, a former resident of Prince Edward, reported his registration stolen in western Virginia; a constable, a justice of the peace, and Hitchins's employer in the black man's new home all wrote letters back to Prince Edward on his behalf.[80] Had the registration law been a mere dead letter, none of these black men would have sought papers or asked a white man's assistance—however willingly that help was then granted. Then, too, there were those occasions when a number of free blacks registered within a short period; it is difficult to imagine why that would happen without some kind of pressure from whites. Perhaps the flurry of 1829 followed a crime scare such as the search for stolen goods on Israel Hill that gave rise to the myth of the upstanding Israelite; the registrations during the months after the Nat Turner rebellion seem easy to explain.[81]

Still another rush of registrations, the biggest of all, began at the end of 1850. After six months in which only one or two free blacks registered or renewed each month on average, the number for November 1850 leapt upward to seventeen. Thirteen more registered in December, and fully thirty-eight in January 1851. Nearly sixty additional Afro-Virginians enrolled over the following six months before the rate returned to its usual trickle.[82] Meanwhile, when a free black woman from neighboring Nottoway County applied to register in Prince Edward early in 1851, the county court denied her petition—an unusual step.[83] Oddly, that denial and the wave of registrations came not during the furious North-South debates of 1850, but rather after the famous Compromise of that year gave white Southerners a temporary sense of victory and inaugurated a relatively calm interlude in national life.

The occasional wave of enrollments ironically reminds us how casually the county's officials and citizens took the free black registration law most of the time. Had people observed the law with any consistency, after all, no flurries of activity would have been possible; registrations and renewals would have proceeded month after month, year after year, at a fairly steady rate. Moreover, many of those free blacks who registered or renewed, in 1850–51 or at any other time, had gone a long time without having done so previously. Those who had waited "only" six, eight, or ten years between registrations instead of the legally prescribed three look downright conscientious compared with the many others in the wave of 1850–51 who had not renewed for fifteen or twenty years. The latter included black Israelite Peter Patterson and soon-to-be landowner Robert Franklin. Others had gone undocumented even longer, including Israelites Sooky White, who waited twenty-six years, and Jacob Johnston, who had not renewed since Judy Randolph emancipated him forty years earlier.[84]

The historian who writes that "a free Negro who failed to register was fined five dollars and could be sold into servitude in default of payment" is in fact quoting the text of the law rather than describing its application; there is no record that a fine was ever assessed against anyone in Prince Edward for failing to register or for waiting years to enroll or renew. Such a history suggests that whites rarely checked blacks' free papers, or that when free Afro-Virginians were asked to produce documents, even radically out-of-date registrations were accepted as valid.[85]

One of the aims of the registration law was to monitor Afro-Virginians' movements from one locality to another. A second statute, adopted in 1801, empowered local authorities to apprehend any free black who might "intrude" from another county and to treat that person as a vagrant if he or she had no honest employment.[86] A rural county in Piedmont Virginia did have one advantage when it came to keeping track of who entered its borders: to a great extent, residents of the county knew each other through all sorts of interactions—commerce, attendance at court days, worship at church and camp meetings, and group vices such as tippling and gambling. In old Prince Edward, living "only a few miles" from a fellow citizen meant, by definition, being "well acquainted" with him or her. Next to the name of one white man on the list of tax delinquents for 1825, a deputy sheriff elaborated on the man's insolvency simply by writing, "every body knows"—and probably nearly everyone did know what had befallen the unfortunate fellow.

By 1810, Prince Edward's population, at 12,400, was already nearly as large as it would ever be; most citizens all the way up to the Civil War would have repeated one resident's claim in 1814 to "Bein acquainted

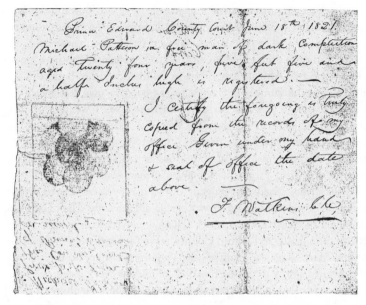

Michael Patterson of Israel Hill renewed his free papers half a dozen times over the years. By contrast, his neighbor, Jacob Johnston, went four decades without bothering to renew his registration.

(ARCHIVES RESEARCH SERVICES, LIBRARY OF VIRGINIA)

With the disposition of Every Man in the . . . pursincks."[87] At the same time, though, Americans in both the North and the South were famously mobile during the nineteenth century. Free black transiency and whites' responses to it partook of a more general counterpoint between neighborly familiarity and social flux. A steady parade of people passed through Prince Edward County—"pedlars," hog drovers, beggars, slave traders and their human merchandise. White families and individuals, some with their slaves, moved into the county from eastern Virginia, while others left for the West. Shortly after the death of the local congressman in 1834, the author of a guidebook to Virginia found it noteworthy that the late politician lay buried in the same family-owned soil as his father and grandfather. "Seldom does it occur in this country," the writer remarked, "that the same family resides at the same place for so long a time" as three generations.[88] All this movement of people made it impossible to monitor free blacks as diligently as the law suggested, even if citizens and officials had wanted to.

Free Afro-Virginians moved into and out of Prince Edward, as whites did. The county's annual lists of free black residents—a supposed means to keep track of that population—in fact reveal how many people the white authorities managed to overlook. The federal census counted around 470 free African Americans in Prince Edward in both 1830 and 1860[89]—yet the number of names on the county's own free black lists hovered between 300 and 350, and sometimes even fewer, both during the 1820s and on the eve of the Civil War. The system of monitoring that sounds so formidable when described in the statute books bears only a tenuous relationship to local authorities' actual success in keeping up with the free Afro-Virginians who lived in their midst.

Blacks who joined the general westward movement shared certain experiences and emotions with whites who did the same. Mary Forgason, daughter of free black carpenter Charles, moved with a man of the Richardson family to Bedford County, far to the southwest, in the 1830s. When Mary Forgason finally received a letter from her brother Joshua, she dictated a brief reply that revealed her distress over the family's separation. "This [letter from you] shows that you think anything of me[,] never has rote a letter to [me] if I was dead or live," she said. "I thank you brother Joshua[;] I am yet a living . . . an also wishing to see you a gane."[90]

At least once, free black and white individuals directly shared the migrant experience. In 1814, the family of Samuel Booker, owner of a dozen or more slaves, set out by wagon from their home in Prince Edward County for a new life in Kentucky. With the Bookers went a free black woman, Tyler Evans, and her own family; the Evanses and a group of their fellow slaves had won their freedom in a lawsuit. The black mother and children had never belonged to the Bookers, nor were they working for them—the two families had simply chosen to make the long journey "in Company with" each other. The black Evanses traveled with their own cart and horses.

The Evanses and the Bookers had something else in common: a prominent white man named William Bouldin back in Prince Edward claimed that both owed him money. Bouldin took off "pursuing" the free blacks a few days after they and the Bookers left for Kentucky; he hoped to bring the black Evanses back and have the oldest three work off their supposed debt. Bouldin finally caught up with the biracial party in the mountains of western Virginia—but the Evanses, quick to assert their prerogatives as free people, "refused to come back with him." The white Bookers showed no sympathy at all for Bouldin and lent him no aid;

instead, they continued forward on the month-long journey with their black companions.

The two families had left Prince Edward to pursue a shared dream of self-improvement in the West. Perhaps the newly emancipated Evanses were motivated also by Virginia's oft-ignored requirement that people like them leave the Commonwealth within a year of manumission. But neither they nor their white fellow travelers thought anything of breaking Kentucky's statute of 1807 that supposedly prohibited free blacks from entering that state. The white Kentuckians whom the group of emigrants encountered proved equally cavalier about the statute: the black youth Anthony Evans immediately found a job with a shoe- and bootmaker, and two of his younger brothers took day work to help their mother support the family. The Evanses built their new life in the same locality in which their white traveling partners, the Bookers, had settled.[91]

Another sort of geographic mobility among free blacks—*into* Prince Edward County—should have set off alarm bells if white Virginians had felt as nervous about migratory blacks as some believe. Certain free Afro-Virginians were downright peripatetic: by age thirty, the shoemaker Ed Hitchins, an immigrant from Lunenburg County, had moved on from Prince Edward to the area of Charlottesville and back again before taking a job at White Sulphur Springs in present-day West Virginia; by the time of the Civil War, he would return to Prince Edward one more time.[92]

Probably more typical than people like Hitchins who moved again and again were those free blacks who came to Prince Edward from other places in Virginia and settled indefinitely. A review of old free papers turned in by their owners and of other documents filed among court records readily turns up sixty people—out of about five hundred registrations, including renewals—who clearly came from other counties and cities during the fifty years before the Civil War. The actual figure is much higher. For one thing, court records identify only a few free blacks as having come from nearby Appomattox River counties. Yet scattered documents suggest that batteaumen, their families, and others often moved among these counties without bothering to change their registrations, and that whites very seldom made an issue of it. Moreover, some immigrants, like county natives, probably registered only if special circumstances required them to. According to the federal census of 1850, more than one in six free Afro-Virginians in Prince Edward had been born outside the county.[93]

The years after 1851 did see a slowdown in registrations of black newcomers. It is impossible to tell, however, whether that happened because fewer free blacks were actually entering the county, or because whites—after the spasm of registrations in 1851—once again relaxed their vigilance, allowing black immigrants to come in without necessarily reporting to the county court.

One would expect whites in Prince Edward who read newspapers and other organs of opinion to have been particularly concerned about blacks moving in from Virginia's cities. White urbanites in the South often called for tighter controls on free African Americans. Together with the enslaved populace, free blacks in the bigger towns formed a growing, anonymous mass of people among whom, many whites thought, subversive ideas threatened to take hold. Prince Edward's white folk, however, evinced little fear that free blacks would bring troublesome "city notions" into their midst. On the contrary, at least 40 percent of the free blacks whom the court registered on the strength of out-of-county free papers came from the cities of Richmond, Petersburg, and Lynchburg, and mainly from the first two of those towns. It was exceedingly rare for one of these newly arrived black urbanites to arouse the kind of suspicion that led to trouble. An exception occurred in 1850, when a white merchant in Farmville did suspect a free black newcomer from Petersburg of stealing a pair of pants from his store, but the court dismissed the case.[94]

Local whites apparently made little effort to differentiate among categories of free black potential immigrants. Some newcomers did menial labor, while others brought skilled trades to Prince Edward. At least four immigrants became—or already were—prosperous enough to buy land: shoemaker Booker Jackson from Charlotte County, ditcher Moses Hill from Amelia, carpenter Robert A. Franklin from Cumberland, and coachman John Deneufville from New Kent County east of Richmond.[95] Overall, most whites in Prince Edward, ordinary citizens and officials alike, paid little heed to calls from the General Assembly to record and restrict the movement of free blacks.

This attitude typified other counties, too. In 1821, for example, the legislature attempted to require local overseers of the poor to compile monthly reports on free blacks within their jurisdiction. The overseers in Lancaster County in the Tidewater protested the imposition, and the same apparently occurred in other localities. The requirement seems quickly to have become a nullity. Whites as a rule believed they had more important things to do with their time than to sleuth after their free black neighbors—even when some of those people were new and unfamiliar.[96] Yet paradoxically, representatives of these same less than vigilant citizens went to Richmond and passed laws that sounded—and to the extent anyone enforced them indeed were—repressive.

The paradox is less difficult to resolve when one considers the relationship between politics, law, and actual behavior in any society. The white citizen's habit of placing the abstract free black "problem" in a mental realm separate from the one inhabited by his or her own Afro-Virginian acquaintances—a pattern common in ethnically diverse societies—explains a great deal. That disconnect allowed hundreds of white Virginians (though apparently not in Prince Edward) to sign petitions calling on the legislature to fund the mass resettlement of free blacks outside the state, while other hundreds—indeed, some of the same individuals—endorsed formal pleas that particular free Afro-Virginians be permitted to remain.

The difference between social attitudes toward categories of people and the treatment of actual human beings emerged in a new and even more striking way as the Civil War approached. In state after Southern state, legislators proposed measures to enslave or expel free blacks, and that suddenly presented the South's white citizens with a basic, practical social choice. To the surprise of the expulsionists, their efforts evoked "a surge of popular opposition," based partly on the white public's "horror" at the "injustice and inhumanity" of such measures.[97]

In earlier, more placid times, the politics of the free black question had usually unfolded according to a familiar pattern that politicians understood but rarely if ever put into words. Many white citizens probably accepted the abstract proposition that free blacks formed a potentially disturbing element; even skeptics had no strong motive to crusade *against* that generalization. Thus, a legislator gained little by opposing laws that defined free blacks as a public nuisance—blacks themselves, of course, had no votes to withhold from him—while he might keep some hardline constituents happy by supporting those measures. At the same time, the lawmaker could be fairly sure that, on the ground, such measures would not affect most free blacks catastrophically, and thus would not upset whites who were ready to live and let live. Indeed, as the historian Luther P. Jackson discovered, "oftentimes the very legislators who quickly voted for some measure hostile to the free Negroes as a class were the very first to come to the rescue of some free Negro in the home community who was about to become a victim of the law of 1806."[98]

Then, too, however comfortable relations between whites and free Afro-Virginians might be in one's own home area, one never knew what "somebody else's" free blacks in some other corner of the state might be up to, or even what some bad apple back home might do. Whites must have found it reassuring to have the means for monitoring and repression available, "just in case," especially since they also had the luxury of letting the bothersome task of enforcement lapse during normal times, which is to say most of the time.

An incident in 1826 neatly illustrates the mentality of many white people in this slaveholding, majority-black county. Someone burglarized Ebenezer Frothingham's store; a court convicted one enslaved suspect and exonerated another. Some testimony at trial addressed the question of whether the crime had involved breaking and entering—an aggravating factor. Frothingham testified that he had nailed his store windows shut for security. But then he admitted to one defendant's lawyer that some of those windows in fact lacked glass panes; that meant that the defendant might have entered the store without breaking in.[99]

Frothingham's windows stand as an apt metaphor for the ambivalent attitudes about security that prevailed in white Prince Edward. Slaves—and, very rarely, free blacks—did commit crimes, and so did whites. Every now and again, a white citizen had a run-in with a slave, or even with a free Afro-Virginian. Frothingham himself came to blows with Phil White at about the same time the slave burglarized his store. People took measures to protect themselves, as Frothingham did when he kept his windows nailed shut even in the middle of the Southside Virginia summer. Yet any worries about theft that the storekeeper entertained did not seem urgent enough to make him replace the glass in his nailed-down windows. Indeed, he probably enjoyed the occasional breeze those paneless windows admitted to his store. Frothingham, like every other person then and now, struck a balance, logically inconsistent though it might appear at times, between comfort and security. Rarely did white folk in Prince Edward perceive enough of a threat from free or enslaved blacks to justify making themselves miserable through obsessive vigilance.

Free Afro-Virginians in particular benefited from that mentality. Even in the weeks following Nat Turner's rebellion, they did not find themselves beset by the kind of supercharged, security-driven atmosphere that could have made life a hell for them. A conspicuous, disfranchised minority, they still managed to carve out a reasonably secure place for themselves and to win recognition from most of their white neighbors as law-abiding people.

TO MAIM, DISFIGURE, DISABLE, AND KILL

By defending themselves against white men's aggression, Syphax Brown, Thomas Bowman, Edmund Young, Phil White, and other free blacks claimed membership in society and declared that they meant to enjoy the benefits of liberty. To deliver those messages early and repeatedly was crucial in nineteenth-century rural America, and particularly in the South, where violence between man and man—and sometimes between man and woman—was all too common. Slavery helped create a climate in which blows came to seem a normal part of human interaction, even among whites. For many men, moreover, no slight or insult—particularly one delivered in public—could be suffered in silence; the code of personal honor, they believed, required an aggrieved male to seek "satisfaction" from the individual who had shamed or injured him.

Andrew Jackson's Carolina mother is said to have instilled in the future Old Hickory a core principle: "the law affords no remedy that can satisfy the feelings of a true man."[100] In other words, by cravenly taking a complaint about another person's aggression before the sheriff or the county court, a man admitted that he deserved whatever injury or disrespect his antagonist had directed at him.

Blacks' lawsuits against white attackers challenge the idea that cowed free African Americans suffered abuse passively, or that they could ward off aggression only by appealing to the paternalistic impulses of white protectors.[101] Yet some say that free blacks inhabited much the same space in the white mind—as persons with no honor to defend—that slaves occupied. If that is true, and if Southern society, like Mrs. Jackson, actually marginalized the judicial process as a settler of disputes, then free blacks' very resort to the courts could be seen as an admission of weakness and of differentness from their white neighbors. In reality, the courts in Prince Edward served as crucial venues for conducting and resolving conflict throughout the county's history up to the Civil War. What they decided made a real difference to many hundreds of white litigants and defendants, as well as to free blacks both on Israel Hill and off.

As some historians have recognized, the dictates of honor faced considerable opposition in the Old South, above all from evangelical Christianity, which preached humility, forgiveness, and reconciliation. Just as important, though, "honor" itself often played out differently in Prince Edward County than Mrs. Jackson's dictum would seem to allow. Men did cherish their personal honor, yet many in all strata of society, including those who used fists or weapons to make their point on other occasions, chose to defend both their reputations and their concrete interests in courts of law, much as men in other parts of the United States did. In such a culture, blacks' legal victories could mean a great deal, and local court proceedings overall take on real significance as records of the county's life in all its sweep and essence.

Citizens of Prince Edward, both black and white, filed hundreds of lawsuits every year. A goodly percentage of these cases were settled before the county or circuit court actually heard them. Others were wholly amicable proceedings—filed, for example, by families who sought official help in dividing estates of the deceased. Prince Edward people also sued members of their own families under less friendly circumstances, as William A. Allen, owner of Priscy Bowman, did when his fortunes declined; the shoemaking entrepreneur John Foster billed a neighbor for expenses he incurred during "my attendance as a witness for you at suit vs your father."[102]

The overwhelming majority of lawsuits revolved around money. Many creditors gave debtors extra time to pay up or settled for a fraction of the amount owed. But if flexibility did not work, filing suit became the natural next step. Even a gentleman like Colonel Charles Woodson, enforcing a contract he had drawn up, was prepared "with pleasure" to use "all the phacilities possibly in my power" to ensure that the party he favored "could obtain any advantage" over an opponent. One plaintiff in the early 1830s did not hesitate to file a suit that forced the defendant to spend eighty-one days in jail.[103]

Then as now, people jokingly disparaged the legal profession—Josiah Cheadle gave the name "Lawyer" to one of his horses—and a prominent citizen of Prince Edward warned in 1849 against the tendency to "become too fond" of lawsuits.[104] But that very complaint amounted to an admission that the cause was lost: even the man who issued it disliked legal action not because it violated the code of honor but because he thought court suits wasted money, time, and goodwill.

One historian recognizes Southerners' litigiousness and says it was slavery that drove them to it; ownership of slaves was "worth taking relatives to court for." But Southerners—including free blacks and non-slaveholding whites—litigated over *every* kind of property, and over issues that had nothing to do with property, human or otherwise. Legal actions over money or slaves that might land an opponent in jail, break him financially, or bring out the ruthless side of worthies such as Colonel Woodson were the relatively dispassionate lawsuits. Beyond them lay scores of civil and criminal court actions generated by emotional confrontations; in theory, those conflicts should have led the aggrieved party to seek "satisfaction" without ever darkening the courthouse door.[105]

No offense is more closely linked to honor and its defense than slander—the deliberate injury of a person's reputation by words falsely uttered in the hearing of others. Many people in Prince Edward County did indeed react sharply to verbal insults, but a number of them defended their honor precisely in the courts that Mrs. Jackson denigrated rather than issue the kind of personal challenge that risked violence. In the 1850s, one man, though of modest means, spent hundreds of dollars in lawyers' fees to sue a wealthy neighbor for slander—yet he told his lawyers that he "did not desire [the other man's] money, but only vindication of his [own] character."[106] Few cases could better illustrate both the sense of personal honor that typified men of Prince Edward and the conviction that the law offered a "true man" appropriate means to defend that honor.

In 1822, rumors began to circulate that one Charles Woodson—a man much more modestly situated than the county justice of the same name—had murdered his sister-in-law and concealed her body near Holliday Creek, a headwater of the Appomattox River. Woodson, fulfilling the stereotype of the hot-blooded, honor-addicted Southern white man, "attempted to give . . . the cow hide" to one man he considered responsible for spreading the report, and he allegedly beat and kicked another in the mouth. But then Woodson put away his cowhide whip and pursued the alleged slanderers by filing lawsuits. His adversaries turned to the law and to legalisms with similar alacrity. One reported Woodson's assault on him to the grand jury. The second took refuge in a technicality: he protested to the court that he had never said anything direct about Woodson, but had merely suggested that "if the Holliday hills could speak they would tell where [Woodson's] wife's sister's bones lay."

For his own part, Woodson disclosed that he had sent his sister-in-law away, very much alive, because "she was in a pregnant state (and as I believed) by a Colored Man." Here Woodson offered a rare public glimpse of sexual relations between a white woman of the yeoman farmer class and a free Afro-Virginian male (the term "Colored Man" was rarely applied to a slave). He also gave an interesting twist to the notion of honor not only by filing suit, but by holding his own wife's sister up to disgrace. The jury accepted the one alleged slanderer's legalistic defense; Woodson's suit against the other man was dismissed.[107]

The nineteenth century up to 1861 saw at least two dozen slander suits filed in Prince Edward County. Although the frequency of such cases was highest in the 1810s and 1820s, new suits continued to reach the courts as late as the 1850s.[108] Sometimes a planter or a prosperous yeoman farmer sued for slander; members of the middling group in society—a miller, an overseer, a farmer—proved especially ready to defend their reputations in court. At least the occasional artisan or other plain man filed suit for slander against a person of standing. William Trent ascended to the county court bench in 1833 not long before that very court required him to pay more than $100 to an obscure citizen who had sued Trent for calling him a hogstealer.[109]

People who filed suit said that their slanderers had accused them of telling lies in court, stealing swine, sheep, tobacco, bacon, or money, burning down mills or houses, and committing adultery or other crimes. An accused slanderer at the beginning of the 1850s allegedly said that another man had once been "sent to the Penitentiary for stabbing a boy," and that "his mother & sisters [were] whores" in Petersburg.[110] If such accusations did not provoke a physical rather than a legal challenge, one wonders what sort of insult would have pushed its victim over the brink. All in all, free blacks' preference for suing rather than physically confronting white antagonists begins to seem as much an embrace of community norms as a concession to white supremacy.

It is one thing to say that some citizens of Prince Edward sought legal redress rather than extralegal "satisfaction" for personal affronts. It would be a mistake, however, to forget that such insults did have the power to evoke violent reactions. Slander suits are significant because county residents of widely varied backgrounds filed them, but they were not frequent. By contrast, citizens of all classes and both races filed scores of suits against those they accused of having attacked them physically; many others asked county justices to require peace bonds from neighbors who had allegedly done them physical harm or threatened to. Still other citizens triggered criminal prosecutions when they reported violent offenses to the authorities.

Some challenges to meet on the field of honor, and even the occasional actual duel, may never have made their way into court records and, clearly, many less ritualized fights never caught the authorities' attention. Still, the numerous violent incidents that did come before the courts illuminate those that did not. All sorts of men filed suit for assault, beginning at least as early as the close of the Revolutionary War. Whites of middling or upper rank who sued alleged assailants over the years included planters or planters' sons, well-situated yeomen, merchants, a constable, and a brick contractor. Less prominent citizens proved equally ready to sue others for assault. Some men took legal action against individuals of their own social level, others against manifest social inferiors; some sued folk who outranked them.[111]

Neighbors did not generally regard those who sued for assault as cowards. Merchant Peter Fore maintained a reputation as one of the most rough-and-tumble men in the county and repeatedly faced complaints from people who said he had attacked them, yet even he did not hesitate to take others to court when they supposedly assaulted *him*. In a number of suits—perhaps a quarter or more of all those filed—parties manifestly reached a settlement before trial, or seem to have done so. Merely by initiating legal action, some of those plaintiffs extracted monetary compensation from those who had injured them; others apparently settled for an apology, which validated their personal honor.[112]

Other Prince Edward men, rather than file civil suits, reported assaults on themselves to the grand jury. These people, too, included members of all social classes, and they spanned the entire period from Israel Hill's founding through the 1850s. In 1846, Josiah Cheadle confronted a tenant on an adjoining plantation who had supposedly broken the fence that separated the two tracts; Cheadle said that the neighbor had responded by striking him several times with a stick. Planter Cheadle certainly possessed as much self-regard as any man in Prince Edward, yet like many others he preferred to take his complaint through official channels; a grand jury presented Cheadle's neighbor for assault. Other men of standing pressed charges after an alleged attack; so, by contrast, did a schoolmaster who accused a militia colonel.[113]

Free black men could not testify against white offenders before a grand jury or a court. When Archer Homes was shot and wounded in 1854, apparently by a white man, the testimony of four other whites did not produce a criminal conviction, probably because none of the men was an eyewitness. Free blacks could file civil lawsuits, however, so they usually took that route when they wanted a white person punished for some aggressive act. Lawsuits may have worked about as well as pressing criminal charges; criminal trials produced more acquittals than convictions even when race was no factor. The white man who shot into free black Robert Franklin's house in 1860 was convicted and fined $5—more than a token amount, but not by much. (The culprit had "defaced" Franklin's home but not hurt any person, and perhaps had intended to do no more than that.)[114]

In one criminal case, the racial roles were reversed. In November 1838, a grand jury headed by the black Israelites' neighbor John Tuggle presented shoemaker Randolph Richards, "a man of colour," for "striking" Abner Willard, a white man; the same panel also charged a white citizen, Jeremiah Porter of Farmville, with an assault on a fellow white. Each attack had allegedly taken place in the victim's own house; the confrontation between Richards and Willard may thus have begun with an Afro-Virginian's routine visit to the home of a white person. In both instances, the supposed victim himself rather than some third party had complained to the grand jury; in other words, the white Abner Willard had answered the alleged blow from a free black man not by beating or whipping Richards or assembling a lynch mob, but rather by appealing to the authorities. Willard may in fact have got into a fight with Richards and then turned to official channels when he lost the battle.

The Commonwealth's attorney soon asked the court to dismiss the charge against Randolph Richards. Jeremiah Porter, the white defendant in the other case, was convicted and fined $3 plus costs.[115] Perhaps the prosecutor believed, or thought a jury would conclude, that Richards had been justified in dealing a blow to this particular white man, even under the latter's own roof. By contrast, the case against the white Jeremiah Porter must have looked fairly compelling. Lawmen and courts are *supposed* to exonerate the innocent and punish the guilty—but we tend not to expect such judiciousness from institutions dealing with racially charged cases in a society founded on racial injustice.

Many white men asked the court to require people who threatened them to post bond guaranteeing good behavior. Some based their complaints on acts of violence they said had already occurred, others on the suspicion that metaphoric bad blood might lead to actual spilled blood. It is difficult to say who contradicted Mrs. Jackson's idea of honor more: the many who sought physical protection through these peace bonds, or those men *against* whom peace bonds were requested by women, who should have been exempt from attack under almost any concept of honor.

The willingness of respectable white men to sue for assault, to pursue criminal penalties against aggressors, and to seek peace bonds from antagonists throws an entirely new light on those free blacks who sued whites for attacking them. Free Afro-Virginians' lawsuits no longer look like gestures of a helpless pariah caste excluded from more honorable and manly ways of seeking redress, or like appeals for paternalistic protection from the elite sitting on the county court. Rather, Edmund Young, shoe-maker John Moss, and other free blacks who turned to the courts defended their persons and their interests in much the same way that white men, including members of the upper crust, often did—except that the blacks concentrated their efforts in the civil rather than the criminal realm while whites pursued both.

One free black man apparently became a two-time victor in court. In 1839, Thomas Bowman—presumably the same one who had successfully sued an employer for assault and for lost wages as an agricultural worker nearly two decades earlier—filed suit against a second white man for assault. A jury awarded him $20, a sizable amount as such cases went.[116] If one were aware only of the two attacks on Bowman, he would seem to epitomize the defenseless free black victim of white aggression. But knowing how vigorously and tellingly he responded to that aggression gives Thomas Bowman to us as the man he really was and provides a dif-ferent view of the biracial community in which he lived. Not many white men in Prince Edward County asserted their prerogatives to greater effect.

Polly Patterson, who at about age twenty still lived with her aging parents Isham and Nancy on Israel Hill, filed suit against the white bat-teauman and boat owner Grief Weaver in 1822, alleging that he had com-mitted two assaults against her. Lawyers in such suits typically filed complaints in formulaic language that exaggerated the alleged offense: that the attacker had attempted "to maim, disfigure, disable, and kill" his victim, and that the latter's "life [had been] greatly despaired of," were two of those stock phrases. Patterson's declaration departed from the for-mulae; her lawyer seems to have transcribed something like her own explicit account of events. She complained that Weaver "seized . . . squeezed and pulled her about," struck her "about her face, breast, arms, legs" and elsewhere, threw her to the ground, struck her some more, and "tore [her] clothes." Had these been attempted rapes, Patterson—so ready to lodge concrete and detailed allegations—might well have said so. More likely, Weaver's assault on her resembled the fits of temper the boatman inflicted on his fellow males. The county court showed Polly Patterson considerable patience. She failed for some time to file a decla-ration, and her suit was therefore dismissed, but the court then allowed her to revive the action. She subpoenaed a well-to-do white man, who may have witnessed personally at least one of Weaver's attacks.

Grief Weaver's defense exposes the readiness of a white Southerner—

even a two-fisted, habitual roisterer—to behave in ways that contradicted the code of honor in order to protect his pocketbook from the prospect of an adverse verdict in court. Having beaten up a woman in the first place, Weaver did not deny his actions, but rather contended that he had done so to defend himself against *her* assault. He did not mention that his supposed attacker stood a mere four feet ten and a half inches tall. Because Polly Patterson was black, Weaver may have hoped that white jurors would not fault him for slapping her about, but the twelve men who considered the case disappointed him. A jury that included John Tuggle, two other sometime neighbors of Israel Hill, and county coroner and shoe entrepreneur John Foster awarded Patterson £2 ($6.67), along with more than twice that amount in court costs.[117]

Juries awarded damages that were greater—sometimes much greater —in certain other assault suits. Many awards fell between $5 and $50, but others ran higher, with a few well into three figures even before court costs were added in.[118] Yet most white plaintiffs fared considerably worse than Polly Patterson did. Some saw their suits dismissed; others either lost in court or received only token awards. The code of honor did exist, even if it often played out differently than we might expect; sometimes jurors seemed to be telling antagonists to settle their differences outside the courtroom. In the seven years before Edmund Young "won" a judgment of 1 cent in 1814, juries had made similar awards to at least four white plaintiffs, including a county constable and a prominent merchant.[119] Polly Patterson received approximately the same award as a number of white men who sued fellow whites for assault during the same period, including one plaintiff who won $7 from an individual he said had struck him "many blows" with a stick.[120]

A couple of twists attended the aftermath of the Weaver-Patterson case. Grief Weaver was slow to pay the fine and costs that he owed—he seems to have forfeited two feather beds to a sheriff's sale in place of the cash. And Polly Patterson's attorney, Samuel C. Anderson, who frequently and skillfully represented slaves and free blacks, took special steps to collect his fee. Anderson gave "directions" to the deputy sheriff that Weaver's payment of damages should go directly to him, the lawyer; "no arrangement that [Weaver] might make with [Polly Patterson] . . . would be good."[121] It was unusual to do business this way—or at least to spell out the arrangement to the deputy sheriff in writing. Ordinarily, it seems, attorneys waited for payment and then sued their erstwhile clients if they did not receive it. Samuel Anderson himself would do that a few years later after he successfully defended Hampton

Giles and Guy Howard against charges of hogstealing. But in the Patterson case, Anderson launched a preemptive strike, apparently doubting that Polly would pay him.

The lawyer's caution seems to have arisen from some specific circumstance of Patterson's situation rather than from the simple fact of her race. Some years later, Anderson would impose a comparable arrangement on another client who apparently was white. Polly Patterson's color may have made her white attorney feel freer to give, and a deputy to accept, "directions" about what should happen to the money she had won from Grief Weaver. But it appears just as accurate to say that Samuel Anderson decided on a case-by-case basis whom he was prepared to risk money on; in another instance, he did not hesitate to pledge his own funds to guarantee the appearance in court of free black ditcher Booker Hill.[122]

Thirty-three-year-old Polly Artis, one of the two other free black women in Prince Edward who sued white men for assault, complained of a person who had as many dealings with free and enslaved blacks as Grief Weaver did. Thomas Totty was a less volatile sort than Weaver: he faced charges several times not for beating people but for trading with slaves and allowing them to assemble on his property. Polly Artis did not follow up after filing her suit against him in 1835. The action was dismissed and then reinstated before Artis finally withdrew her complaint against Totty. Artis's record of having challenged a prominent white man did not bar her later in life from receiving aid from the county's overseers of the poor.[123]

Free black residents of Prince Edward other than Polly Patterson and Thomas Bowman who filed suits for assault either received token awards like Edmund Young's or did not press their causes to a conclusion. Shoemaker John Moss did not follow up his lawsuit against a white man in 1815, nor Phil White his against Grief Weaver a few years later, nor boatman Dancy Brown his in the following decade. Archer Homes sued the father of a teenaged white youth whom Homes accused of assault in 1817, but he did not see his lawsuit through, either.[124] Some parties—boat captains White and Weaver, for instance—may have reached a mutually satisfactory accommodation. But other suits filed by blacks were presumably thwarted because direct testimony against white defendants by these plaintiffs or by other Afro-Virginians was not admissible in court.

Phil White filed another action for assault in 1826, this time against Ebenezer Frothingham, the merchant. Though of New England birth, Frothingham seems to have absorbed the Southern habit of expressing displeasure by dealing blows; three years later, he would whip a boy for stealing wood from him. White—perhaps lacking white witnesses on his behalf—permitted his suit to be dismissed, even though he was then required to pay Frothingham the $4 the latter had spent on his defense up to that point.[125]

If many suits brought by free Afro-Virginians did not yield monetary awards, neither did most actions filed by whites. When one counts only awards of substantial damages, not 1-cent token judgments, as victories, and tallies as failures those suits filed but not carried through, then free blacks' rate of success in assault suits against whites emerges at one in every five or six, compared with white plaintiffs' one in three. These odds of winning, along with the possibility of forcing a defendant into a settlement without a formal courtroom triumph, proved sufficient to bring forward both white and black plaintiffs.

At least four free black men of Prince Edward besides Thomas Bowman sued whites for assault between 1830 and the outbreak of the Civil War. None of them won the success that Bowman achieved toward the middle of that period, but none evinced any fear of challenging authority, either. Zack Ellis's action against Colonel James Madison produced three hung juries and then a payment of $10 from Madison to the black plaintiff. Branch Roach, possibly a fairly new arrival in the county at the time, filed a suit against an alleged white assailant in 1840 but did not follow through. Roach may have been something of a magnet for trouble; a fellow free black man would wound him with a shotgun a dozen years later.[126]

When free blacks Cyrus Hill and Davy Smith filed their unsuccessful suits against men who were apparently deputized to enforce the law, they complained about individuals who generally maintained businesslike, even friendly, relations with free Afro-Virginians. Hill said in 1837 that he had been handcuffed and abused by Benjamin C. Peters, an English-born doctor and civic leader who carried out a number of business transactions with blacks. Davy Smith, who had married Sam White's granddaughter, complained in 1842 that John N. Robertson had "forcibly tied" and ill-treated him. Robertson had recently testified against the man who stole Phil White's horse, and he had earlier backed batteauman Joe Bartlett's purchase of a boat.[127] Race may not explain much about Robertson's collision with Davy Smith; the White clan itself would eventually have conflicts of its own with Smith's wife, their kinswoman and neighbor.

As in so many other areas of life, free blacks' experience with personal violence overlapped that of whites. A lawsuit filed by one black man against another illustrates how a great many of these cases must have originated, regardless of the antagonists' race. In 1844, James Jackson sued Booker Jackson, one of Farmville's two or three most prominent black residents, for assault and battery. The two Jacksons were probably not related, but James does seem to have worked as a shoemaker in town, as Booker did; perhaps theirs was a professional rivalry. The jury found for defendant Booker Jackson. James Jackson was granted a new trial of the case, but a few months later he made his X on a letter asking the court clerk to discontinue the suit, "as I consider myself the aggressor." The language in that note was not James Jackson's own, but the sentiment may well have been. There clearly had been a collision between the two Jacksons, which resembled dozens of other heated arguments that occurred in Prince Edward in any given year. James Jackson had not been a helpless victim, and may even have initiated the hostilities. Yet he felt free to pursue the conflict by other means—turning to the court— whether out of wounded pride or the sense that he might squeeze a sizable award out of the prosperous Booker Jackson. The two men had behaved "like whites"—or more accurately, like men of Prince Edward in general.[128]

Even though a man could report or sue an assailant without disgracing himself, many violent acts between free people in Prince Edward County produced neither lawsuits nor criminal prosecutions. The number of suits and criminal charges for assault—not including requests for peace bonds—reached a peak of eleven cases in 1811. At the opposite extreme, in nearly one quarter of the years between 1802 and 1860 there was only one charge or suit for assault, or none at all. In most other years, the number ranged between two and half a dozen. The main significance of suits and prosecutions lies in the variety of individuals, including men who possessed high status or physical robustness or both, who proved ready to initiate them.

Then, too, the scores of violent offenses that people did formally complain of paint a detailed and wide-ranging picture of violence in Prince Edward. There were shootings and stabbings, as well as whippings other than those inflicted by masters or overseers; people assaulted each other with rocks, sticks, and fists. These acts took place in homes, yards, fields, roads, and streets, and at least once on a boat. But the most common venues for physical confrontations were the county's taverns and stores, which served as community gathering places and dispensed intoxicating liquors. Occasionally, an assault caused death. A typical decade in the county would see a couple of murder trials, and some homicides went unsolved; on two separate occasions in 1841 alone, and in various other years, coroners' juries examining black or white corpses suspected murder but either could not say so with certainty or could identify no suspect.[129]

Most physical conflicts, whether spontaneous or premeditated, occurred between people who knew each other, often very well; some antagonists had been socializing congenially up to the moment of the flareup between them. Frequent economic turmoil in rural Virginia supplemented the free flow of liquor as a catalyst for assaults. The gnawing if statistically ill-founded anxiety about furtive, anonymous assailants that besets today's large cities did not plague the people who lived on Israel Hill and in the counties that surrounded it; the danger lay closer at hand, and wore a familiar face.

Enslaved people, especially men, constituted one source of violence in the Old South. Most who raised a hand in anger did so against other slaves, however. Bondpeople lived and worked at close quarters, and they confronted formidable pressures under a regime designed to prevent them from taking out their frustrations on whites. Moreover, blacks had no doubt that they possessed personal honor. Many slaves displayed a sensitivity to insult that equaled that of their masters, and they proved just as ready to defend that honor physically. Occasionally a member of the dominant race explicitly admitted as much; a newspaper in southwest Virginia reported a very formal—and deadly—duel between two slaves using rifles in 1823, finding in the display of "honor . . . an example which ought to make some gentlemen of high condition blush."[130]

Contrary to modern-day assumptions, masters sometimes permitted slaves to hunt with guns, but most enslaved Virginians had no regular access to firearms.[131] Many did own pocketknives, however, and any blunt instrument could become a weapon; thus when slaves in Prince Edward County did attack each other, over points of "honor" or otherwise, the results could be fatal. On a boat in 1813, Isham, a slave, confronted another bondman named Bob before a group of their peers over a demand for personal "satisfaction." Bob cut Isham, who then proceeded to kill Bob with a blow to the head, dealt from behind with a stick or spike as Bob jumped into the river. Isham was sentenced to hang. Eight years later, a slave named Isaac found himself "shamed" by two fellow bondpeople for stealing from a fellow slave and then lying about it; he demanded satisfaction through physical combat from one of those who impugned his honesty. The man Isaac challenged, after bearing a series of physical threats and curses from Isaac, killed him by a sudden blow with a rock. He was exonerated in a trial whose witness list included two free blacks.[132]

These affrays between slaves unfolded ignobly and ended with death blows being struck without giving one's opponent an even chance. Notions of "honor" regularly led to such outcomes in old Virginia, not just in altercations involving slaves but also in confrontations between whites or between free blacks.

The most astute observation that historians of Southern honor have offered, and the most often overlooked, is that ideas of honor in the first half of the nineteenth century had become clouded and confused. Both evangelicals and rationalists attacked the code of personal honor; even white men who considered themselves its devotees and exemplars found themselves puzzled about what, exactly, the code called upon a man to do. Many men of both races felt bound to vindicate their honor, but seized means of doing so that scarcely rose above the level of common mayhem.

Charles Edie and Ned Langhorne, students at Hampden-Sydney College in 1857, were best friends. One night, Langhorne heard that Edie was drunk and went to help him. Edie had disgraced himself after vowing to take the temperance pledge, and he now denied his obvious inebriation and cursed Langhorne roundly. Langhorne, for his part, "had been taught by his father ever since he was a child never to take an insult from any body," and he proposed to fight Edie if the latter did not take back his curses by morning. Challenger Langhorne, however, saw no hope of beating the larger, stronger Edie in a fair fight—so he tilted the odds the next day, extracting a concealed knife without warning and stabbing his friend to death in a college hallway. "I could not do otherwise as a gentleman," said the distraught, honor-driven, but risk-averse killer after his act.[133]

Defense of one's "honor" by underhanded, even ruthless means was not confined to slaves at one extreme and to pampered college gentlemen at the other. Four decades before Langhorne slew Edie, a man named John Swinney invited three drinking buddies to come home with him. An argument eventually broke out. Swinney suddenly drew a knife and cut the arm of Robert Wright, one of his guests. The wounded Wright told Swinney that "he would go home and if he lived till his arm got well he would fight him fist and skull or he would [ex]change a ball with him [at] any distance." Answering this appeal to the etiquette of honor, Swinney shouted to his already injured, unarmed friend, "Clear the way[,] I am ready now," and proceeded to shoot him dead at a distance of some sixteen feet.[134]

The outcomes of the Swinney and Langhorne cases evinced yet again the society's lack of agreement on the definition of honorable and dishonorable behavior. Some clearly thought the six-year sentence John Swinney received was too harsh, while others disagreed; the jurors at a new trial argued among themselves at great length before reducing the term to only two years, for involuntary manslaughter. After much moral anguish in the college community, followed by a contentious four-day trial, a jury acquitted Ned Langhorne.

Many in the Old South were puzzled about what, exactly, Southern "honor" required a man to do. An attorney's caricature of two cowardly duelists ridiculed a particular incident and perhaps satirized the code of personal honor itself.

(*Commonwealth v. Samuel Smith*, COUNTY COURT, AUGUST–OCTOBER 1851, ARCHIVES RESEARCH SERVICES, LIBRARY OF VIRGINIA)

All the while, however, certain demands of honor seemed crystal-clear to most people. One of those was the principle that a man who violated the liberty of a free black person forfeited his good name; paradoxically, that doctrine applied even as some whites bemoaned the presence of free Afro-Virginians in the aggregate. One local white man attempted to save himself from disgrace in 1841 by issuing a statement "To the Public": he strenuously denied "reports affecting his character & standing as a gentleman & a man of honor"—namely, rumors that he had "sold a free negro boy, as a slave."[135]

Prince Edward's few recorded acts of violence involving free Afro-Virginians resemble those between whites or between slaves, both in their banality and in the particular notions of honor that sometimes drove them. Some confrontations took place in racially mixed company.

In 1836, a grand jury presented a white man for having stabbed one Edmund W. Furgerson, who also was white. The alleged assault took place at the house of free black Jesse "Furgerson" (Forgason), carpenter-farmer and sometime harvester for Josiah Cheadle (both whites and blacks in the neighborhood bore variants of the Ferguson surname).[136] Eleven years later, Robert Rutledge, apparently a free Afro-Virginian, was charged with having attacked Douglas Evans, another free black, with the help of a poor white farmer called Worley; the court summoned a fourth man—also probably white—as a witness.[137]

The impulse to respond violently to personal slights spanned not only the boundary of color but also that of sex. Sally Stonum, a free black boatman's wife, lived in Farmville in the 1820s. One late October day at the beginning of that decade, Stonum and several other free Afro-Virginians found themselves in and around the house of Patty Morton, the noted black midwife. At one point Sally Stonum bragged that "her kin was so rich they could buy Mrs Cook"—a phrase that sounds cryptic today, but may have meant something like "so rich they could buy and sell everyone here." Stonum and her husband lived a modest life; the overseers of the poor would seek to bind out their son as an apprentice the following year. Accordingly, a free black carpenter named Burwell Moss challenged Sally's boast, suggesting that "if [her kinfolk] were so rich they ought to give her something," for "she stood in need." This sort of affront, issued in the presence of other people and suggesting that Sally Stonum was not merely a pauper but a liar or a fool as well, was the classic trigger for a defense of Southern honor, at least among males.

Sally Stonum responded to her public shaming by throwing a pole ax at Moss and lopping off most of his right ear. Moss proceeded to threaten Stonum ineffectually with a stick; then he complained to the authorities. Had a county justice or Commonwealth's attorney regarded the Stonum-Moss affray as unworthy of his attention, he could have halted the prosecution within hours of the incident. Instead, a panel of five justices sent the charge against Stonum on to the circuit court grand jury, as they would have done with any other serious offense. That second panel declined to put Sally on trial, and she was released. Perhaps the white grand jurors considered Burwell Moss's verbal affront provocative enough to justify a vehement response. Perhaps, in other words, they recognized that Sally Stonum possessed a measure of honor that she was entitled, even bound, to defend.[138]

One naturally wonders what would have happened if, under the same circumstances, Sally Stonum had severed a white man's ear. We have no direct answer; though free blacks in Prince Edward might sometimes defend themselves physically against whites, they did not attack them. Yet that fact in itself conveys a basic truth. Old Virginia, for all its racial surprises, was still a society in which color affected transactions among free people. A free black Virginian who thrashed an aggressive white person on the spot might end up bearing some blame for the confrontation; the courts, meanwhile, offered a more than trivial chance of gaining redress. Small wonder that free blacks typically chose the latter course. For this and other reasons, a white citizen remained much more likely to suffer injury at the hands of a drunken, overly touchy fellow white than from a black person, free or enslaved.

Criminal prosecutions or lawsuits alleging violent acts were uncommon but not unheard of on Israel Hill itself. In the five decades between the Hill's founding and the beginning of the Civil War, six such incidents took place, including the three generated by the Hampton Giles–John Brown feud. These conflicts never seem to have involved anyone from outside the Hill; even the witnesses were Israelites, apart from a physician who testified at one trial.

In 1825, Tony White said that his "servant" had been beaten by Susannah White, wife of his brother Hercules Junior; that probably meant Tony's wife, Milly, whom he had purchased out of true slavery. Records of his lawsuit provide no details about the altercation, but there may have been enough fault to go around: although Tony White did subpoena two younger black Israelite women, he then pursued the case sporadically at best. The county court eventually threw the suit out and required Tony to pay his brother $5 and another $4 for the costs of the defense.[139]

A stabbing that took place on Israel Hill at the end of July 1843 exposed other complexities of life in the little community. Sidney Howard, the twenty-six-year-old son of boatman Guy Howard and his wife, Mely, was arrested for attacking Sam Strong, who was several years older. The ties between the two men stretched back many years. Born just as his parents were freed by Judith Randolph, Strong had spent much if not all of his childhood on Israel Hill; in fact, he had been living at Sam White's at the time Sidney Howard was born there in 1816 or 1817. Strong, like his accused assailant's father, was a boatman. By the 1840s, he had become an entrepreneur as well, having already purchased and sold at least one batteau. Both antagonists had married into the White clan during the previous seven years: Sam Strong wed a granddaughter of Sam White, Sidney Howard a daughter of Phil White Jr. Of the more than half a dozen people summoned to testify at Howard's trial, every one was entwined in this warp and weft of kinship. Moreover, the Phil White family and Sam Strong had carried on a series of financial transactions over several years. In the two weeks before the alleged stabbing, the Whites had signed bonds of indebtedness to Strong totaling nearly $70, one of them drawn up just a day before the incident. Sidney Howard may have resented the power that Sam Strong might now wield over Howard's in-laws during those tension-filled, depression-ridden early 1840s.

Although a physical confrontation clearly had occurred, the warrant against Sidney Howard was quashed in short order, and he continued to live on Israel Hill for many years. Howard went free despite—or perhaps because of—victim Sam Strong's status as one of the up-and-coming free black entrepreneurs in Prince Edward County. Strong's standing in the black community gave him room to show forbearance, and he, Sam White, and Phil White all had an interest in calming the situation. Strong may not have wanted to press charges in the first place; the stabbing was reported not by him but by a member of his family. Strong had probably already moved to Farmville by the time the stabbing occurred. The unpleasantness with Sidney Howard and its quick resolution paradoxically demonstrate the ties that continued to link the residents of the Hill with the sons and daughters of the settlement who now lived in town. The extended community still managed, if not to avoid all problems, then at least to contain them.[140]

Less than a year and a half later, however, another ugly fight within Israel Hill came before the county justices. William Johnston allegedly stabbed Isaac Gibbs two nights before Christmas in 1844; he was arrested on Christmas Eve. The Johnston and Gibbs families had united through a marriage in the second generation: the fortyish Isaac Gibbs was the uncle of his accused assailant, who was about twenty-five. William Johnston's parents had remained close to the Gibbs family; William had a younger brother who was named after the very man he was now accused of stabbing.

The conflict between Johnston and Gibbs showed that close ties continued to bind Israel Hill's residents into the third generation, thirty-four years after the Randolph emancipation. The late Dick White's daughter Matilda reported the affray to the authorities; Syphax Brown II cosigned the bond that guaranteed Matilda's later appearance at trial. All the other potential witnesses were likewise children or grandchildren of Israel Hill's founding generation: a son of Teny Carter and grandsons of Titus Gibbs and Isham Patterson. Most, and possibly all, of these people continued to live on the Hill, and at least three of them would still be farming there as the Civil War approached. It seems that Isaac Gibbs's wound was not grave. He saw a doctor without delay, was prepared to testify when William Johnston stood trial less than a month later, and would live for years to come. The family ties between the two parties likely dampened Gibbs's ardor to see the younger man convicted; the wounding may have been one event in a scuffle, or even an act of self-defense, rather than a wanton attack. The charge might never have been formally lodged had the matter not come before county justice Clem Read, who had long been friendly with Isaac Gibbs.[141]

The several recorded fights on Israel Hill typified the county as a whole in that none was lethal and none involved a gun. Firearms were neither rare nor ubiquitous in Prince Edward County. Weapons did not come cheap—a shotgun sold for more than $20 by the 1830s. Christian churches taught that "persons carrying about them . . . Deadly weapons is unfit to be members of a Church of Christ." County authorities sometimes arrested men in the 1840s and 1850s for violating the law against "going armed with deadly or dangerous weapons without reasonable cause to fear violence to [one's] person, family, or property."[142] Those arrests, however, demonstrate that some men did carry weapons, including "revolving pistols," introduced in the 1830s, as well as dirks and Bowie knives. The scarcity of convictions among those accused suggests that public opinion tolerated the bearing of weapons as long as those involved did not menace others. The cold-blooded, almost point-blank slaying of Robert Wright by John Swinney in 1815 stands as an exception to the rules that even violent men usually followed, as does the sensational murder by shotgun of a white man by one of his own relatives in 1854–55 (it took the victim, shot two days before Christmas, several weeks to die).[143]

Free blacks, too, had firearms, as the events following the Nat Turner revolt showed. Hercules White Sr. owned a gun before Israel Hill was even settled. Ben Short left one behind at his death in 1818; Dick White left a shotgun at his demise eight years later, and Phil White Sr. a gun and powder gourd in 1830. Sometimes blacks sought a license to "keep and carry" firearms, as the law required of free Afro-Virginians. Samuel Short, Tony White, John Brown, Nathan Homes, and Sam White all did so in the 1820s. Others did not bother with that formality, however.[144] The state legislature passed a blanket prohibition against black ownership of guns after the Nat Turner rebellion. Yet free black households seem to have resumed owning firearms after the alarm over Turner subsided, and they did not feel they had to do so in secret: one gun was matter-of-factly recorded by a white acquaintance as part of a trade between Sam Strong and John White in 1845. The single recorded incident in which a free Afro-Virginian may have used a firearm against a human being was the alleged nonfatal shotgun assault on free black Branch Roach by one William Green in 1852, reported by the white contractor Henry Guthrey.[145]

White men, slaves, and the occasional free black attacked others with fists, sticks, and sometimes rocks or knives. One of the Bartletts was acquitted in 1851 of murdering a fellow free black with a heavy stick, probably on grounds of self-defense.[146] At the same time, white males in Prince Edward displayed some patterns that were rarely if ever recorded among free Afro-Virginians—in particular, certain kinds of dirty fighting, of which the shooting of John Swinney and the stabbing of Charles Edie at the college were only the most flagrant examples. Don Pedro Taylor, attorney, tavern owner, and sometime county jailor, attacked cabinetmaker George Clibourne with a stone in 1852 at the courthouse, even though the victim, just concluding his service on the county court, was in such chronic ill health that he could scarcely conduct business. This last incident was too much even by the relatively lenient standards of the time, and a jury imposed a fine of $500, easily one of the two or three heaviest penalties imposed in criminal cases up to the Civil War.[147]

Court records from the county also reveal an appreciable amount of violence against women and even children, and there were surely many incidents that women never reported. Such behavior exists in almost any population, yet county documents reveal strikingly little of it among Prince Edward's free blacks. Bricklayer William Homes became the exception who proved the rule as far as the official record tells us: his wife, Lucy, left him in 1857 and demanded that he give bond not to harm her after he threatened, according to her complaint, "to strike his dirk into her Heart."[148]

A number of white men, by contrast, abused their own spouses or other white women. Of some wives, we know only that they sought peace bonds from their husbands. Other proceedings record women's complaints of repeated beatings or of being "frequently driven . . . in the night time to [one's] neighbors for safety." One wife accused her husband of stabbing her. In 1853, a doctor found himself patching, stitching, and splinting a woman whose husband had cut and broken her leg with a stick and an ax and inflicted other wounds on her head and face.[149]

A generation earlier, James D. Harrison, a white man of Prince Edward, was sentenced to twenty-eight years for raping Harriet and

Caroline Harrison. There had been neither aggravating nor extenuating circumstances surrounding the crime, the district court noted—"except," it added laconically, "that the offence was committed on the daughter[s]" of the convicted man, one of whom was only eight years old.[150]

Another kind of violent behavior was recorded exclusively among white men: ganging up to attack an isolated victim or two. In 1832, a married couple sued a group of thirteen men for besetting them with hickory sticks, guns, fence rails, chairs, fire irons, and other implements, and causing the pregnant wife to miscarry. A jury awarded the victims $6.67 from one of the assailants—the same amount free black Polly Patterson had won from Grief Weaver.[151] This violent group may have been applying vigilante "justice" after some offense the aggrieved man or his wife had supposedly committed. That had certainly happened twenty years earlier when a white man named Stafford Gibbs received a potentially fatal two hundred lashes from a group of five men, one of whom had seen Gibbs abusing his wife. While supposedly punishing the ill-treatment of a woman, the whipping bee had become a sadistic competition in which two of the vigilantes averred that their own compatriots "ought to be whipped" for not having "worn out their whips" on the unfortunate Gibbs's back. Other individuals complained in the 1820s and 1830s of having been attacked by groups of three, four, seven, or even ten men. Verdicts against defendants were hard to come by—owing partly, perhaps, to a lack of corroborating witnesses.[152]

The one recorded group assault on a free Afro-Virginian was the attack Edmund Young said the poorhouse steward and others had committed against his stepson.[153] The underreporting of crime is an abiding social fact. Additional acts of collective aggression against free blacks may have taken place in Prince Edward County, leaving victims afraid to denounce attackers or convinced that it was not worth the trouble. No category of historical evidence can prove that vigilantes did *not* intimidate free blacks. Yet presumably people of color who readily sued white aggressors, including officers of the law and a prominent, intimidating person such as Grief Weaver, would not have suffered gang attacks without seeking redress in the same way Edmund Young did. Mob violence against blacks occurred in antebellum Northern cities, and sometimes in the South as well, especially during slave insurrection panics. But it seems possible, even likely, that Prince Edward County did not see any such events up to 1865.[154] The record reveals no acts of group aggression committed by free blacks, even against others of their own race.

One further category of violence—or more accurately, a species of violent person—seems likewise to have been a monopoly of the white race and the male sex. Certain men in Prince Edward again and again became involved in confrontations, many of them physical, with their fellow citizens. The word "bully" comes to mind, except that these men, contrary to the stereotype, sometimes did pick on others their own size. "Ruffian" might be a more accurate term, and its nineteenth-century flavor recommends it, too. These ruffians differed from one James D. Shepherd, whose long record of violence included the slaying of a relative and numerous attacks on white and enslaved people. Shepherd served five years in the penitentiary for murder, and later—in an exceedingly rare development—was sentenced to a year in jail and a fine of $438 for shooting and wounding a slave. He ended up committed to an asylum for the insane.[155] The conventional ruffian's emotional stability might leave something to be desired, but he stopped short of murder, and no one ever seems to have tried putting such men away in a mental hospital. Again unlike James Shepherd, the typical ruffian managed to stay out of the penitentiary. Indeed, a man with that kind of record could hold a recognized position in the community and sometimes even play a leading role.

Such a man was Hillery G. Richardson, who accumulated $150,000 in assets, including forty slaves, by the time he died in 1861. He was charged with stabbing a fellow citizen in 1845, though he went free on a technicality. Even during his term as county sheriff, Richardson was required to give bond to keep the peace toward a man he had fought with. Richardson's behavior observed no color line: he acquired a reputation as a "barbarous" master of slaves as well.[156]

Peter Fore owned a store, a tavern, and more than 450 acres of land. Between 1809 and 1821, Fore faced trial for two shootings and a stabbing; he was acquitted of each. Men formally accused him of assault on at least four other occasions. When two enslaved men arrived at Fore's place of business with a pass that he found technically deficient, Fore and a friend tied the pair up and hit one of them in the head with a broadsword. Fore recklessly charged that various white neighbors had stolen his fence rails and timber or burned down his mill. With his son and namesake—a chip off the old block who had recently been presented for disturbing a church service—Fore set dogs on a female slave who belonged to a white family with whom he carried on a running feud. Over the years Fore paid various judgments and fines for his exploits.[157]

An incident on the Fourth of July, 1817, typified Peter Fore's approach to life. Some forty yards from Fore's store stood that of a competitor named McDearmon. Fore had already assaulted one of the McDearmons in 1809 or 1810; he would later be arrested by, and escape from, another member of the same family who served as a constable. McDearmon's business was outdoing Fore's. The latter responded with a novel expression of the competitive entrepreneurial ethos. Fore stationed himself at his window with a gallon of liquor and two guns; he claimed he had another four weapons at the ready. Then he sent one shotgun blast through a window of the rival store and another into an entering customer, who luckily took only one piece of shot, in the face. Fore was acquitted by a jury that apparently felt reluctant to imprison a man who, in a drunken state, had wounded another only lightly.[158]

The attack on McDearmon's store showed how little Peter Fore cared about "fighting fair." Another man whom Fore attacked said his assailant had jumped from behind a tree and fired a shotgun. Yet Fore was usually anything but furtive: verbal threats typically preceded his sallies. Some of Fore's worst behavior occurred while he was drunk—as he himself once admitted to save himself from a slander suit.[159]

The salient facts about ruffians like Peter Fore and free blacks are two. First, the record does not reveal a single free Afro-Virginian who remotely qualifies as a ruffian. John Brown of Israel Hill did nurse a long feud with Hampton Giles and allegedly committed three attacks on members of Giles's household. But unlike Hillery Richardson or Peter Fore, Brown apparently tangled with only one family. A black habitual aggressor could have found victims among his own race—yet neither free blacks nor masters of slaves complained on the record of any such individual in half a century.

The second fact about the county's ruffians is that free blacks had to watch out for them as everyone else did, but that none of those serial attackers singled out free black people as targets. Peter Fore did not lack opportunities to get into scrapes with free Afro-Virginians: he not only ran a store with a biracial clientele, but also lived in western Prince Edward County not far from a cluster of free blacks, including the Jethro Forgason clan and James Dungey's family. In 1819–21, several free blacks lived at his place without any sign of disharmony.[160]

Like Peter Fore, Grief Weaver bore all the identifying marks of the ruffian and had his hand in several areas of the local economy. He owned one or more boats, bought eighty-odd acres of land on credit in 1821, and apparently opened a store by the latter 1820s.[161] In contrast with Fore, Weaver did attack two free blacks—or so Phil White and Polly Patterson plausibly asserted. But even he did not center his aggressive attentions on Afro-Virginians. He settled his differences with Phil White, boated alongside him, and joined him to press charges against the Stony Point Mills in 1819. Weaver's physical confrontations with other whites over the years outnumbered those with blacks by as much as two to one. Perhaps deservedly, Weaver paid a higher price for attacking black Israelite Polly Patterson than he did for tangling with these various white men; one criminal charge and one civil suit initiated against him by whites were dropped.[162] Weaver finally met his undoing when he received a visit from a drunken white acquaintance carrying $50 at the end of August 1832. The boatman plied his friend with more liquor and then stole his money. It was this crime that sent Grief Weaver to the penitentiary for two years—an outcome applauded, no doubt, by Polly Patterson, but also by various whites who had got on the wrong side of Weaver over the years.[163]

Whatever threat of violence the Israelites and other free blacks of Prince Edward County confronted over the decades thus resembled the dangers faced by all free citizens. The Afro-Virginians' membership in a disfranchised race and the law that prevented their testifying against whites posed a potential threat to their physical security, but that potential remained mostly unrealized. Perhaps the judicious actions of the county court and other authorities conveyed a warning to white citizens who otherwise might have committed aggression against free blacks. But the behavior of those authorities may simply have expressed the prevailing worldview—a sometimes messy version of live-and-let-live. That social mentality produced many civil relationships between white and free black people in a society whose fundamental assumptions about race seemed to dictate the opposite.

CHAPTER 7

Worldviews

KINDRED CULTURES

One night in the 1830s, Dr. William B. Smith of Cumberland County, riding through the lower end of Prince Edward to see a patient, heard a banjo playing. He stopped at the house of Samuel Poe, who, it turned out, had given his slaves permission to brew a barrel of persimmon beer and hold a dance. As Smith, Poe, and some other white men approached the door of a log house, they observed what the doctor called a "wild fantastic" scene.

A "banjor-man" sat in a chair on the beer barrel, his head adorned with "a long white cow-tail, queued with red ribbon" draped down his back, and his three-cornered hat "decorated with peacock feathers, a rose cockade, a bunch of ripe persimmons, and . . . three pods of red pepper as a top-knot." As the man played his instrument, two "athletic blacks" stood in front of him "clapping *Juber*"—each keeping time to the music with his right foot patting the floor, the heel stationary, and with his palms clapping "on the corresponding extremities." A fourth man used a drinking gourd to serve persimmon beer to the partygoers. Meanwhile, Dr. Smith related, two women baked bread from persimmon dough in the huge fireplace, and "a little squat wench" smiled and held a torch that lighted the room. The other slaves in the house danced to the music "in the merriest possible gaiety of heart," with "the most ludicrous twists, wry jerks, and flexile contortions of the body and limbs, that human imagination can divine."[1]

Smith depicted the performance of the slaves with condescension, "looking," as he said, "*down* in life, in order to explore the dark corners of nature" and appreciate "that God has placed us [whites] high in the scale of human beings." He also tacked on the obligatory political moral: the dance, he wrote, suggested "that Virginia slaves were the happiest of the human race," which in turn gave the lie to the "northern abolitionist, with his pocket filled with inflammatory documents." Yet amid the caricaturing and the racialist boilerplate, Smith offered some authentic details of the culture of Prince Edward County's slave community, from which the Israelites and the area's other free blacks sprang, and to which they remained closely connected through marriage, friendship, and daily work.

Some elements of the scene—the banjo music, the loose-limbed dances, and the intricate combination of clapping and foot-tapping—would have been familiar elsewhere in the South; they exemplify the way African Americans had created a vibrant folk culture that drew partly on African sensibilities. The banjo player's tricorn hat and rose cockade were European devices, but this enslaved man of Prince Edward had modified them strikingly with adornments of his own devising—the peacock feathers, persimmons, and red peppers—and with a cow-tail that may have been modeled on the traditional African fly whisk.[2]

Smith described the speech of the slaves, too, as distinctive. In another nod to conventions of the time, he called their talk at one point "a complete Babel jargon, a confusion of tongues!" But he went on to reproduce, often with reasonable accuracy, samples of African American speech comprehensible to almost any speaker of American English and full of imaginative, evocative turns of phrase. "Molly look like killdee," a party-goer said of one dancer, comparing her to the bird whose off-center skitters divert enemies from her nestlings; "she move like handsaw—see how she shake herself." A second onlooker noted that "when he grin, [Ben's] mouf and teeth like hen-ness [nest] full o' eggs"—another vivid and comprehensible simile, which in the white ear resonates with a racial stereotype but doubtless carried no sting when uttered among blacks. In fact, without realizing it, Smith was witnessing a popular African American pastime sometimes known as "marking"—a game in which participants compete to describe others' physical characteristics outlandishly, yet accurately; one authority compares the sport to the drawing of caricatured portraits among Europeans and white Americans.[3]

William Smith marshaled these anthropological details of the persimmon beer dance partly to support the idea that black slaves were an intriguing but eccentric and inferior "other." That message helps explain why Edmund Ruffin, popularizer of Colonel James Madison's ideas about Israel Hill, chose to publish Smith's impressions in his *Farmers' Register.* From Smith's time to our own, whites have cited, and often seized on, cultural distinctions between whites and blacks to justify slavery, segregation, and discrimination.

More than a century after Smith wrote, Walter White, head of the

National Association for the Advancement of Colored People, would list the racial markers that whites had exploited or invented in order to brand African Americans as inferior: "the skin, the odor, the dialect, the shuffle," and even the endearing "imbecile good nature" that white people ascribed to blacks as a race.[4] William Smith applied such markers to slaves of his own era, and the same stereotypes could be used to label free African Americans, too, as foreign, peculiar, and undeserving of the liberty they possessed. After all, manumission altered their legal status but not their color or their culture. At the same time, some of the cultural differences that white Southerners would later cite to justify racial segregation seemed less obvious and compelling before the Civil War. Afro-Southern culture did differ from that of whites—yet many points tied the two races together as well.

Elements of familiarity and empathy between black and white appear even through the chuckling, condescending veneer of Smith's propagandistic vignette. He quoted with meticulous care verses of three songs that the slaves had sung at the beer dance; he conveyed the language without gratuitous dialect spellings or caricaturing, and indicated that he had known at least one of the songs before he heard it at the party. Aside from the word *juba* (or *Juber,* as Smith rendered it), no words of African derivation, nor any other phrases that a white Southerner would not understand, appeared in the three songs or in the snatches of dialogue Smith reported.

Overall, the doctor may have believed he needed to exaggerate the exotic in order to attract readers' interest. In reality, he not only saw much in the slaves' culture that was familiar; he also found things to admire and even emulate. The music of the banjo "strikes the most delicate and refined ear with pleasing emotion," Smith wrote, and "produces a sound as it dies away, that borders on the sublime." Moreover, the doctor had long promoted the persimmon tree, which he touted as providing substitutes for foreign wines, molasses, sugar, tea, coffee, and beer; wise use of this native resource, he said, could save Virginia's economy "thousands [of dollars] annually." In effect, Smith used the pages of Ruffin's agricultural journal to hold up Samuel Poe's slaves, with their persimmon beer and persimmon bread, as people from whom whites could learn something.

Differences pervaded by commonalities—no phrase more aptly describes rural culture in Southside Virginia before the Civil War. Shared attributes and assumptions amid difference helped make possible the tolerant, sometimes friendly relations that linked whites and free blacks. One such common assumption was the belief of blacks and many whites that some African Americans possessed special expertise in chemistry or conjuring. Prince Edward County justice John Rice, the confiscator of free blacks' guns in 1831, took seriously the African and Afro-American belief that ingesting the hair or nails of an enemy could kill a person; he once issued an arrest warrant against a slave accused of poisoning another by that method.

Naturally, such ideas bred suspicion toward alleged slave conjurers and poisoners. But those fears were counterbalanced by the conviction of many in both races that certain slaves commanded healing arts that could usefully complement or even replace treatment by white physicians. Prince Edward people often used the services of "Negro doctors," at least on slaves, until the 1830s and probably later. One of those healers earned a handsome fee of $3 in 1808—more money than many white doctors got for a visit. The title "Doctor" stuck so tightly to some black practitioners that it became their given name. Some enslaved parents bestowed that name on a son, presumably either to honor a folk-physician forebear or to express a hope for the boy's future career.[5]

Neither the practice of folk doctoring nor belief and disbelief in it broke down strictly along racial lines. The white Ann Meador earned a $4 fee for curing cancer on a slave woman in 1824; Phil White Jr. and certain other free blacks, meanwhile, turned to a white physician. There is no way of knowing how frequently white patients themselves used the services of black doctors, though it surely happened sometimes. Clearly, however, no master would have subjected a valuable slave to the ministrations of someone he did not consider competent.

The free black shoemaker, cooper, and landowner Ben Short valued the services of the slave doctor Matt so highly that he brought the healer in from seven miles away and died owing him $10; at about the same time, Dr. William Smith, the man who described the persimmon beer dance, was collecting as little as $1 per visit. Whites, too, took Matt's skills seriously. Matt's master referred to the black man's activities as "administer[ing] medicine," and Ben Short's written account with Matt—presumably kept by the same master—applied the respectful term "Medical Services" to the bondman's work.[6]

In other realms, too, attachment to folk traditions in the face of modern inroads, far from marking blacks off as quaint or primitive, typified both races. Calendar dates and clock time, for example, had to compete with older ways of understanding time among white and black alike. Frederick Douglass and Booker T. Washington were the most famous of many ex-slaves who did not know exactly when they were born. But well into the nineteenth century, Prince Edward had numerous white citizens, including men of considerable standing, whose ignorance of their time of birth was even more complete. One white citizen said in 1816 that he was "not . . . more than 48 year" of age, while another could only observe that he was "45 or 50 years old." Of seven children born to a certain white veteran of the Revolutionary War, not one could state his or her birth date or age.[7]

People only occasionally used the clock to denote specific times of day, even when the lives or freedom of human beings hung on the timing of events. Slaves, free blacks, and whites alike often resorted to a system of sun time. Some of its elements are clear enough even today: people spoke of events happening "about 3 hours after night" or "an hour before day." Other formulae—"about day light down" and "next morning at an hour or two by sun"—may puzzle the modern reader; reckonings "by sun" applied to the afternoon as well as the morning. By the 1840s, many people had acquired clocks or watches, and the revenue commissioner counted more than eight hundred timepieces in Prince Edward County in the early 1850s. Still, sun time and clock time continued to coexist even as civil war loomed.[8]

Just as the old, approximate ways of keeping time were shared by whites and blacks, so to some extent was the march of clock time and calendar dating as the century advanced. Shoemaker Booker Jackson acquired both a watch and a clock. John Deneufville, the free black coachman and hostler, left a silver watch worth $18 when he died in 1839. Perhaps he had driven stagecoaches and become attentive to clock time then—not to mention considerations of status or aesthetics that may have led him and many white citizens to acquire timepieces. Free Afro-Virginian Milly Richardson apparently knew the exact birth dates of her five children; four of them were born early in the nineteenth century, when more than a few whites were still leaving birth data unrecorded. Rhoda Artis knew her child's date of birth in 1811, and Branch and John H. Cousins, though they were poor free black boys, gave precise birth dates when they were bound out as apprentices in 1852.[9]

Even literacy, though whites tried to monopolize it, never quite became their exclusive property. A Virginia law of 1831 made it illegal to assemble free blacks for instruction or to teach them for pay. Nonliteracy prevailed among free Afro-Virginians both before and after passage of the law, but as many as one in six free blacks in 1850 could do some reading and writing. Most white men in Prince Edward County by the early

1800s could probably write at least a few words. Many could do a good deal more than that, and book learning spread as the century wore on, mostly through small schools set up by individual citizens or groups of subscribers.[10] Nevertheless, more than a few whites throughout the antebellum period remained barely more literate than the disfranchised free blacks. In the late 1850s, deputy sheriffs trying to serve court papers might still have to "explain [the documents'] purports" to white women who apparently could not read. Poor white children in Virginia had access to schooling at county expense, yet attendance at county schools in Virginia remained notoriously spotty; many impoverished scholars received only a few weeks of instruction per year.[11]

Even some important white citizens lived out their lives only marginally literate and unable to compute. In the 1820s, militia Major James Ewing, a solid, slaveholding yeoman farmer, "[did] not understand calcula[tion] in figures." Captain John Stevens transacted substantial business, but he could not write well enough, "nor [had] he sufficient knowledge of language and word," to set a simple agreement down on paper. In such a society, Sam and Phil White's reliance on others to keep their written accounts did not brand them as inferior in the way it would have in a later era.[12]

None other than a schoolteacher "stepalated" (stipulated) conditions of employment; an important tobacco dealer in Petersburg submitted an "Abscratt [abstract] from the Book's" of his firm as evidence in a court case in 1833. Years earlier, a white man had designated his sons as the "holy and soly [whole and sole] Executors" of his will.[13] Such malapropisms are precisely the sort of dialogue that white entertainers would put in the mouths of black characters from the days of the minstrel show to those of *Amos 'n' Andy*—but these came from respectable, even prominent, white men. Whites of humbler station found themselves stretched almost beyond their limits when asked simply to confirm receipt of official papers. "Eye exnowledg the within," scrawled one, stumbling over a word that other whites rendered as "exnokleg" or even "actngle." Meanwhile, Henry Clay Bruce and his brother Blanche, growing up as slaves in Prince Edward, learned to read and write; their master's son "took great pride in teaching [Henry] his lessons of each day from his books." It turned out that other slaves of the same household could read, too; the master was pleased that they now had direct access to the Bible.[14] We will never know how many other slaves in the county acquired the literacy that eluded some whites, but there likely was at least a sprinkling of others.

Of the several dozen free Afro-Virginians in Prince Edward who had occasion to sign papers, most applied an X or a cross—as some white men and women did. But certain free blacks signed their own names, including John Moss, the farmer and shoemaker who lived with a white wife, and Lorenzo D. Scott, who accused Moss of passing a counterfeit coin. Signatures of brothers Curtis White and Philip White III appear to be authentic, and county records indicate that boatman-entrepreneur Sam Strong and perhaps his wife signed official documents. Some of these free black people may have been able to write considerably more than their names: Lorenzo Scott and Robert Franklin, the free black carpenter and landowner, pretty clearly could do so.[15]

The letter that free Afro-Virginians Samuel Richardson and Mary Forgason sent back to Buckingham County from southwest Virginia was apparently written by Richardson himself. The writing is laborious and contains a number of small errors, but it equals or surpasses a great many patrol reports and other prose documents that whites produced, especially those from the first few decades of the century. The Richardson letter survived only by happenstance; other documents written by free blacks may well have been discarded.[16] Old Virginia's laws did condemn most free and enslaved blacks to ignorance—yet the boundary between learning and nonliteracy did not separate free blacks from whites as conclusively as the law demanded.

The spoken language linked black and white more closely than literacy could. In America as in other societies, a person's speech goes far toward branding him or her by race, ethnicity, region, and class. Antebellum white minstrels in Northern cities caricatured black speech for comic effect, and eccentric characters spouting "black" dialect remained a staple of American entertainment and popular literature for more than a century thereafter. Differences in language reinforce the racial dividing line to this day. Yet in the slaveholding society of which Israel Hill was a part, speech patterns differentiated whites from blacks far less definitively than they would in later periods.

Many distinctive features of the modern spoken language of central and eastern Virginia had already appeared by the latter 1700s if not before.[17] Some of those speech patterns existed among whites before they encountered Africans or Afro-Americans—forms such as *waw* for *war*, the "double negative" (*he don't know nothin*), and *-in* for *-ing* (as when people wrote of wood *shavens* and *weadin* hoes). But the average person today labels certain other usages as "black." Most would instantly identify as African American any speech that includes forms such as *he go,*

I is, ribba (for *river*), *mens* and *feets, she done tell / told, he be goin.* The letter from Samuel Richardson and Mary Forgason, brief though it is, contains some ten examples of dialect features, including the verb forms "*has*
[*w*]*rote*" and "hope that you *is* well," along with the spellings *live* (*alive*),
an (*and*), and *no mo* (*no more*). In Virginia before the Civil War, however,
most of these supposedly black dialect features were common among
whites as well.

Many white citizens of Prince Edward had just enough schooling that
they ventured to put pen to paper, yet not so much as to master spelling
rules; that turns the documents they wrote into a mother lode of linguistic evidence. One citizen's remark about another individual's writing—
that the man's "words were spelt as he generally talks"—applied to more
than a few of the county's white residents. When, for instance, a woman
spells the surname Morecock as Mocock, we know that she pronounced
the word without an *r*-sound after the first vowel—and as linguistic
detectives we rejoice that, though the same lady bought a spelling book
at one point, she never mastered its contents.[18] Beyond their thousands of
phonetic spellings, old documents offer a second category of evidence. A
person indoctrinated to avoid some common dialect feature often mends
imagined errors, or "hypercorrects." Thus, if someone writes about hanging *curtings* in a window or frying *chicking* in the *kitching*—and whites in
Prince Edward did write such things many times—we can be sure that in
the spoken language the final *g* was often dropped in words like *playing*
and *laughing*, and that purists were unhappy about it.

As remained true in Virginia well into the twentieth century, whites
were about as likely as blacks to drop or absorb *r* after vowels. They wrote
boad for *board*, *potion* for *portion*, and *faulk* for *fork*; *father* and *farther* were
pronounced almost identically. Drawing on actual spellings found in
documents, one might imagine a white Virginian reporting that he had
found a house servant of *Cunnill Magrudah* washing *posimmons* on the
poach of the house. Some insecure white people sought to avoid "dropping" *r*'s in writing; that led them to produce hypercorrected spellings
such as *kin forks* for *kinfolks* and *Horse Pittle* for *hospital*.[19] It is always easy
to chuckle at such errors and to assume that they came from barely educated folk, but these forms appear in articulately worded documents
written by otherwise sophisticated people, some of whom held public
office.

White people of all classes regularly joined blacks in simplifying clusters of consonants; planter Josiah Cheadle often spelled the word "build"
without the final *d*. A man seeking to fulfill a *contrack* to hang *blines* in

windows might believe he had a *perfeck* right to *pos'pone* the work until the *fith* of the month; his impatient employer could either take legal action *agains* him or *deduck* money from his fee until the contractor *tole* his hired *hans* to begin work straightaway. Even some prominent whites pronounced words like *secatary* and *possesion* (meaning *procession*) in ways that later generations would stereotype as black speech.

Americans consider the dropping of unstressed prefixes—as in the song, "I Been Buked and I Been Scorned"—a hallmark of Afro-American English. But in old Virginia, whites, too, spoke of bridge *butments*, of *praising* (appraising) the estates of the dead, and of banknotes in "the *nomination* of fifty dollars."[20] White people said—and wrote—*gree* for *agree, bove* for *above, bout* for *about, banden* for *abandon, sleep* for *asleep,* and *leventh* for *eleventh.* Conversely, whites, like blacks, sometimes added an unstressed prefix where the standard language has none (*endurin* for *during*).

In many other ways, too, the sounds of white people's English in Prince Edward resembled those of black speech. Staves and trivets became *stabes* and *tribbets,* while wills *bequeved* property to fortunate heirs. Whites might pronounce the last name of a Mr. Stith as *Stiff*—just as the pronunciation of the given name *Othello* as *O-fella* took root in the Afro-Virginian community. The devoicing of certain consonants—*Gipson* for *Gibson, Cupit* for *Cupid*—which today are mostly confined to African American English, at least sometimes spanned the color line in old Prince Edward. White people, like blacks, might omit the final *s* in the possessive, yielding *Perkinson hoe, Mr Miller Iron, Mrs Woodson sister,* or *Col Charles Woodson place.*[21] In white speech, and probably among blacks as well, the vowel sounds were distributed differently than in standard English. *Pen* and *pin* sounded identical; local people wrote *chest, kettle,* and *pestle* as *chist, kittle,* and *pisel.* One man labeled a bill from carpenter Jesse Jennings as "Jasse Jinnings bell." An unstressed or secondary vowel that was long in standard English might become indistinct in Virginia speech: when white or black folk spoke of Israel Hill's Hercules White, they pronounced his given name *Herculus.* These same tendencies inclined people of both races to render *Negro* as *nigra,* a pronunciation that came to be seen by some as contemptuous a century later.[22]

A final unstressed *a* was generally pronounced *-ih* by white and black alike, with *subpeona* spelled *surpeny;* hence the pronunciation of black Israelite Tina Carter's first name as *Teny, Barbara* as *Barbary,* and so on. The pronunciation of *master* as *marster,* so familiar in "black" dialect as purveyed by nineteenth-century whites, did not belong to one race only;

both whites and blacks often used the "broad *a*" in words such as *master,* *bastard,* and even *Patrick.* Some, perhaps many, people of both colors rendered words like *boil, appoint,* and *annoyance* as *bile, appint,* and *annyance.*

Certain features did distinguish black English from white. Afro-Virginians used third-person verb forms such as *she go,* as well as the possessive *he* for *his;* they pronounced a *d* at the beginning of words such as *the* and *this,* yielding *de* and *dis.* No evidence from old Prince Edward shows white people using those forms, or saying *we done go/gone/went* and *he be sayin*—though the use of *done* and pronunciations such as *de, dis,* and *dat* did make inroads into white Virginia speech at some point.[23] These and other, subtler differences between black and white dialect would often have provided enough clues to identify a person's race if one heard him or her speaking in the dark, or in the next room; language *was* one marker of racial difference then, as now.

Nevertheless, whites used far more nonstandard verb forms than most do today. Stephen Foster had Old Black Joe say, "I'm a-comin," and whites in Prince Edward described their peers *a quarreling, a pecking,* and *a thinking;* the last phrase was uttered by a college student at Hampden-Sydney in 1857. A white person of any social class might talk about how he *done* the business at hand, how "the [medicinal] Springs *done* [him] no good," or how one white man *give* another person payment for some corn in the past or *had went* to visit relatives.[24] "I have three negroes that *is* . . . infirm . . . their names *is* Nead Harry and Judy," a certain white person declared. One leading citizen wrote to John Randolph in 1799 to discuss the rumor "that you *was* an advocate for the immediate emancipation of our slaves." A man might well propose to his neighbor that they proceed "as we *was* talking about." White people employed other verb forms, too, that blackface minstrels could easily have used in their shows ("David M. Doswell *have* paid me"; "I *believes*"; "I now *lives*"; "some people *trys*").[25]

What schoolteachers call double negatives were apparently common in white speech as well as black, for they sometimes made their way into writing, as in "I . . . *never* gave *no* account of her." Documents record people of both races using *them* where standard English has *those;* one trial revolved in part around the issue of whether one witness had spoken "*them* very words" to another.[26] One even finds the forms *patterrole* and *paterroller,* now supposed by many to have been quaint slave pronunciations, written just that way in many of the reports submitted by patrollers themselves, at least up to 1830.

Who, then, learned the language from whom—whites from blacks, or vice versa? When a white man in Prince Edward County in 1786 left a legacy to one heir "in douring hur natrel life," and called for the property afterward to be "equal divided between my daughter Sarah childrens,"[27] had he learned his English from Afro-Virginians? Some citizens of Prince Edward believed so. "Oft the pert youngling quits the mother's side / To mess with slaves, to follow as they guide," a local poet complained; "He learns their jargon, all their maxims learns." The poet bewailed the fate of "the kidnapped brood" from Africa, but his lament mainly concerned the effects that the slaves' "sinful deeds and vulgar ways" might have on the conversation and behavior of whites.[28]

In truth, many features of the local dialect derived from speech patterns in England; yet the sharing of "jargon" and "maxims" between black and white really did occur, and it did not stop at the end of childhood. Indeed, affinities between black and white could run far deeper than the striking similarities in language. Thomas Ford, a well-to-do farmer who lived on the border between southern Prince Edward and Charlotte Counties, had a close relationship with his sixteen slaves; he respected their private, domestic decisions—honoring the marriage of one of his bondwomen to a free black man, for example. Unlike most of his peers, he wrote his own will, in 1821, rather than have a lawyer draft it, and he could write just well enough to set down his thoughts semiphonetically.

"I Thomas Ford of the County of Charlott is sicke in body, bute in my perfeck sences," he began. "I firs reques my body to buried in a Cristan like manner, then I do appinte Robert Kelso" as executor of the will. That sentence and a half could have been uttered by a person of either race: *I . . . is, perfeck, firs, reques, appinte.* The remainder of the will overflows with dialect forms—*buve* for *above, whar* for *where, twelve munts cradit* for *twelve months credit, arisin* for *arising, thur names is* for *their names are, Sary* for *Sarah, onable* for *honorable.* Thomas Ford spoke much as his slaves did. They may have been the main day-to-day companions and conversation partners of the unmarried, childless farmer; he apparently did not even employ an overseer. Indeed, Ford's slaves were the principal subject of his will. He ordered that they all be emancipated and relocated in free territory with money raised by selling off the rest of his estate. There is no indication Ford was liberating children he had fathered with an enslaved woman. Almost all his bondpeople were of wholly African ancestry, and Ford gave the "blacks" the same benefits as the two "yellow" individuals in the record, who may have been man and wife.[29] Neither did Thomas Ford set his slaves free to spite his relatives; he bequeathed to the latter whatever should be left over "after all my buve requests is complid with . . . [and] after all the . . . [blacks'] exspences is paid." But that last clause is the key to the document. Again and again, Ford reiterated his absolute determination that his slaves be emancipated and comfortably resettled. That litany of liberation, rendered in good cross-racial Southside Virginia dialect, becomes eloquent through its sheer repetition and the patent intensity of feeling behind it.[30]

Speaking alike by no means guarantees harmony or mutual respect, as numberless broken families and civil wars attest. Many slaveholders talked much as their bondpeople did, but few joined Thomas Ford in emancipating any. Dr. Smith's account of the persimmon beer dance shows that people who wanted to define blacks as culturally exotic readily found ways to do so. Still, black speech resembled that of Southern whites too closely to serve within the Old South as the unmistakable badge of differentness and inferiority that it became in the mouths of blacked-up Yankee minstrels.

In our own time, many point to the names people acquired under slavery as emblems and even reinforcers of division and inequality between white and black. When enslaved people arrived in America, masters routinely imposed names that would separate them from their past and demonstrate their new owners' control over their fate. Some authorities go further than that, adding that masters favored "comic, animal-like names" that humiliated slaves and emphasized their degraded status. Slaveholders supposedly preferred diminutives (Tom and Sooky rather than Thomas and Susannah), eccentric monikers such as Christmas and Rastus, or ironic names of gods, heroes, orators, and statesmen from ancient Greece and Rome (Ajax, Caesar, Jupiter, Cato, Remus, Venus).[31]

Odd names became comic tags applied to blacks from the antebellum minstrels' Zip Coon through the Buckwheats, Alfalfas, Pompey Smashes, Stepin Fetchits, and Algonquin J. Calhouns of the first half of the twentieth century. Yet naming practices on Israel Hill, among other free Afro-Virginian families, and in the slave quarters of Prince Edward County tell a story that diverges sharply from what we think we know about cultural separation and racial oppression during the era of slavery.

At first glance, many black Israelites' names may seem belittling or ironic. After all, at least three of the most prominent original settlers—the two Hercules Whites and Syphax Brown, all born in slavery—carried names from classical literature and history.[32] (The original Syphax was a North African king who figured prominently in the Punic Wars between Rome and Carthage.) Similarly, any list of Israel Hill's people records many mature adults under what we would call nicknames rather than "full" given names. Members of the founding White family—Sam and Sooky, Dick and Sally, Phil and Fanny, Tony—stand out, as do other Israelite adults including Ampy and Polly Brandum, Kit Strong, Tilla (Tilly) Brown, and Teny Carter. Free Afro-Virginians who lived outside the Hill and appear in documents under "nicknames"—Billy, Tom, and Zack Ellis, Davy, Joe, and Patty Bartlett, Milly, Joe, Sam, Lucy, Fanny, and Mima Homes—had hundreds of counterparts on lists of slaves owned by local whites.

Naming practices among free and enslaved Afro-Virginians, however, tell a much more nuanced story than one of whites deprecating blacks. Whichever white person in the remote past gave the names Hercules and Syphax to newly arrived Africans may indeed have done it to amuse himself. But the black folk who carried those names, and their spouses and children, embraced the appellations, made them their own, and perpetuated them even after those families had gained their freedom. John Brown named his son after Brown's own father, Syphax; Hercules White Sr. passed his own name on to a son and a grandson. The same bequeathing of names happened among slaves, most of whom by the nineteenth century chose their own children's names just as they selected their own spouses.

Moreover, white record keepers proved ready to apply formal, "standard" given names to free Afro-Virginians. Israelites William Wilkerson and Hampton Giles regularly appear as such, rather than as Billy or Ampy, on the county's lists of free blacks, and Wilkerson's wife Eve shows up as Edy only two or three times. No one, not even his most devoted white adversaries, ever called Edmund Young Sr. "Ed" or "Ned"—though his son and namesake does appear under both names. Susannah Forgason apparently did not hesitate to correct a justice of the county court when he recorded her name as "Sukey" in a document she was filing; the official made the appropriate change.[33]

Sam White and all three Phil Whites occasionally appear in documents as Samuel or Philip, Davy Bartlett as David, the Ellises as William, Thomas, and Zacharias. That happened particularly in the wills of free blacks such as Mildred Homes, Anthony White, and Richard White, whom the record otherwise generally calls Milly, Tony, and Dick. When white lawyers and others mentioned blacks who were not their paying clients, they could have referred to them in whatever manner they chose—yet these functionaries, too, sometimes opted to apply formal names rather than "nicknames."[34] Often, it seems, whites wrote down whatever names free blacks specified. Other times, far from seeking to demean blacks with diminutives, white people who drew up documents gussied up informal given names that black parents had bestowed and that the recipients were perfectly happy with.

One mercantile store at which Phil White Jr. and his son Curtis had a running account in the 1840s may have hit on the usage that gave the elder White the honor he deserved without inflating his given name beyond what he himself desired. The company unself-consciously referred to him and addressed him in writing as "Mr. Phil White." (The store also seems to have applied the honorific "Mr." to free black carpenter and future landowner Robert A. Franklin.)[35]

Many of the "nicknames," diminutives, and classical names that blacks carried could not have struck whites in south-central Virginia as stamps of otherness or inferiority—for whites themselves followed similar naming customs. For example, only a small minority of slaves and free Afro-Virginians—fewer than 5 percent—bore those classical Greek or Roman names that modern observers often see as mocking. Meanwhile, whites, too, gave their children classical names, hardly surprising in an age and a region that revered classical architecture and literature. During the years when a Syphax and two men named Hercules were establishing themselves on Israel Hill, the propertied white citizenry of Prince Edward County included worthies such as Gaius Williard and several men named Augustus, two of whom served as county court justices. Black and white families respectively continued over the years to bestow the names Hercules and Augustus; one of the latter was leading a slave patrol in 1850.[36]

Few whites in Prince Edward County or anywhere else in America during the generation preceding the Civil War saw anything odd about the presence on the political scene of such luminaries as Cassius Marcellus Clay of Kentucky, Lucius Quintus Cassius Lamar of Mississippi, and Hannibal Hamlin of Maine. Caesar, Rose Johnston's enslaved husband, had white counterparts as famous as Caesar Rodney, signer of the Declaration of Independence, and as obscure as Caesar Smart of Prince Edward; the Johnstons proudly passed the name down to the third and fourth generations, and men on Israel Hill would still carry it forward as the twentieth century approached.[37]

Some classical names were indeed mostly confined to blacks, and particularly to slaves. Whites seldom bore names of classical gods or other mythical figures, while slave rolls of Prince Edward do include a small number of bondpeople named Apollo, Neptune, or Venus—and even a Virago and a Cupid (the last, as in mythology, a male). Yet again, however, the few who carried those names purged them of any sting they may once have borne. An enslaved Neptune in Prince Edward passed his name down to the next generation during Israel Hill's early years. Milly Homes's daughter Lucy, though untouched by any family history in slavery and not commemorating any relative who appears in the record, chose to name one of her own daughters Venus. At least one white citizen did share the name Romulus with Hercules White's son, and Achilles Puryear, a white man, named his own son after himself. But white parents generally preferred to give their boys names of Roman emperors or generals if they opted for classical appellations at all. Hercules White's given name does not appear among the county's white men.[38] Still, one has to wonder what the first master who bestowed the name Hercules on a newly arrived African was thinking; to name a man after a classical hero who possessed both superhuman strength and ingenuity seems an unlikely way to humiliate him.

The overwhelming majority of free and enslaved blacks bore names from the standard Anglo-American repertoire of the era—John, Margaret, Thomas, Susan, and the like, or the nicknames associated with them (Jack, Margie, Tom, Sooky). Many whites, too—some men and countless women—went through life being called by diminutive names even in the most formal situations. The prominent men of Prince Edward during the time between Richard Randolph's death and Israel Hill's early years included individuals whom official documents invariably call Dick Holland, Tommy Bigger, and Jack Vaughan—the last a physician, justice of the county court, and sometime sheriff. The use of such names by and for white males in formal documents did wane during the nineteenth century, but the same sorts of papers frequently applied informal names—Kitty, Betty Ann, Biddy, Polly, and the like—to mature white females. Defendants in a typical lawsuit over plantation land in the 1820s included white women called Lucy, Patsey, Betsey, Tabby, Betty, Salley, and Nancy.[39] One of the leading ladies of Farmville for many years was Patty Morton, who happened to share both her given name and her family name with Granny Patty Morton, the free black midwife. The name Sooky (Sukey)—the first syllable of which rhymed with "book," and which some now consider a quintessential slave name—appeared among both black Israelites and comfortably situated white women.

Popular entertainment and literature have habitually assigned eccentric given names to slaves and other black characters. But few bondmen in Prince Edward bore given names such as Christmas and Champion, and the latter, who was born as late as 1840, may well have received his name through the choice of his mother.[40]

In reality, whites held a near monopoly on the most bizarre given names. Hercules White Sr., Ben Short, and Edmund Young worked early in the century for white miller Lavender Fowler. Massanello Womack sold part of his land to the free black Evans family. Other white men with creative parents included citizens christened Linnaeus, Gulielmus, Lancelot, Pulaski, and Legrafton, as well as two brothers named Powhatan and Corsica Burton. Don Carlos Green, Don Carlos Clay, and county jailor Don Pedro Taylor played prominent roles in nineteenth-century county life. One white man was even called Dred, which Dred Scott and Harriet Beecher Stowe only later established as an emblematic black name. White women sported monikers including Saluda, Missania, Demarius, Blizzard, and Barshebea. Names such as Mourning and Pamelia—the full name of Israelite Mely Howard—were shared by white women and black.[41]

Conspicuously biblical names—as distinguished from common ones such as John, James, Peter, and Mary—were occasionally used by black and white, slave and free. A number of white and black Hezekiahs lived in the area. Shadrach, Meshach, and Abednego of the Babylonian fiery furnace were all represented in Prince Edward County; free Afro-Virginian Jethro Forgason—himself named after an Old Testament figure—had a son named Shadrach, while Meshach Boaz, a white man, happened to bear a biblical surname, too. Obscure names from the Bible such as Benajah and Micajah could apply to boys of either race. Unusual biblical names for women—Magdalen, Ketturah, Masurah—appeared among whites, not blacks. Families of both races used the biblical name Jemima, inextricably tied to the black mammy stereotype many decades later by a pancake syrup company.[42]

Some enslaved Afro-Virginian women carried the name America, and so did a few prominent whites, including the wife of Cary C. Allen, co-owner of the plantation that lay between Israel Hill and the Appomattox River. Several white women were named Missouri, while the mother of a slave girl born about 1840 called her Indiana.[43] One rare divergence in naming practices between whites and blacks involved the given name Africa, which a certain number of male and female slaves bore during the years between the Revolution and the Civil War. Prince Edward's free Afro-Virginian community included neither Africas nor Americas.

The practice of using famous family names as given names—in modern times a trademark of Virginia's white upper crust—had already begun in the eighteenth century, and blacks observed the custom about as frequently as whites. Bondmen named Harrison, Carter, Randolph, and Cary lived on the neighboring Allen place when Israel Hill took shape. Israelites born shortly before or after the Hill's settlement included Randolph Brandum, Archer Wilkerson, Archer Gibbs, and Beverly Howard.[44] A few other free blacks in Prince Edward during the first quarter of the nineteenth century bore prestigious surnames as given names: Branch Epperson, Archer Richardson, Beverly Mettauer. One might assume that black parents who chose these names revered or identified with the master class. Again, however, reality confounds so facile a conclusion. Free Afro-Virginians gave prestigious white family names to their children just often enough to refute the idea that they spurned any connection to whites, but not so frequently as to suggest that the elite white clans loomed large in free blacks' consciousness.

One area of naming in which white and black custom differed, at least as to timing, was the adoption of middle names. Some white parents began to bestow these on their children in the latter eighteenth century; middle names rarely appear among free blacks until after 1820.[45] That gap of one or two generations suggests that Afro-Virginians were not simply imitating white practices; so does their apparent readiness to use the full middle name while most whites signed with a mere initial.

Even if given names did not become labels setting the disadvantaged race apart, one might point to the supposed absence of family names among slaves as a marker distinguishing them from white people. Yet some blacks—perhaps many—adopted surnames long before their liberation. A less than complete reading of county court papers turns up between sixty and eighty slaves who bore family names that whites recognized. The slave surnames we can document represent a much larger phenomenon: almost every enslaved individual who appears in the record with a last name would have shared it with a number of family members. More than twenty slaves with family names appear in the records of the Purnall-Dupuy family alone, out of about a hundred all told. If that ratio, or anything approaching it, applies to plantations where masters kept less thorough records, then many hundreds of slaves in Prince Edward bore family names. Asa Dupuy stands out among white citizens of Prince Edward in recognizing slaves' surnames—he recorded those black family names he knew even when he administered someone else's estate. At least some of Dupuy's slaves apparently reciprocated the regard that he and his uncle John Purnall showed for them: the black children on Dupuy's place included one named Asa and another who bore the given name Purnall.[46]

Some slaves laid claim to their full names assertively and persistently;

even whites who doubted the legitimacy of family names for slaves did sometimes use them in writing, placing the surname in parentheses or after the notation "alias."[47] White people generally became more likely to recognize enslaved people's family names precisely during the period when white hostility toward free blacks, and toward slaves who behaved like free people, is supposed to have intensified: of the enslaved individuals mentioned with family names in Prince Edward documents, more than 90 percent entered the record between 1825 and 1860.

After some hesitancy or confusion in the late eighteenth century and the first few years of the nineteenth, most white people became fully accustomed to using free Afro-Virginians' surnames.[48] Only a few free blacks took on the family names of their white liberators. How most of the rest had acquired their surnames remains unknown, but some of them honored an enslaved parent or other ancestor by applying that person's first name to the entire emancipated family. The large free black Ampy and Cato clans of Cumberland County doubtless had done just that. Few bits of evidence more vividly illustrate the process by which classical names and diminutives such as Ampy, even if they had originally been foisted on slaves by disdainful whites, came to serve Afro-Virginians as emblems of pride and family tradition. The Ampys and the Catos of the Appomattox Valley had many counterparts elsewhere in North America and the British Caribbean who took family names such as Scipio, Horace, Caesar, and Syphax. These free African Americans did not share the view of modern observers who say such appellations carried the stench of slavery.

These particular surnames, unique to black families, remind us yet again that black folk did not absorb Euro-American cultural habits wholesale. Even that vast majority of African Americans who bore given names and surnames that resembled those of whites made their own choices, for their own reasons. Those decisions—like many features of black people's speech and their understandings of time and nature—did not necessarily label them as peculiar in the minds of their white neighbors, for a biracial, hybrid culture had evolved in the South long before Israel Hill came to be.

CALLOUSNESS AND CLOSENESS

The things blacks and whites in old Prince Edward often did similarly—seeking medical attention, measuring time, speaking, and naming their children—arose from the constant contact between races that the slaveholding system not only permitted but required. Ironically, old Virginia became an incubator for a kind of person-to-person intimacy that often eludes citizens of today's more democratic America. Manumitted Afro-Virginians had lived for years alongside whites in a bondage that combined callousness and closeness, and the society their freeborn children grew up in was likewise molded by that strange blend of forces.

The callousness never faded from view in Prince Edward, partly because the county lay on a main route slave traders used to transport their human merchandise from the slave markets of Richmond and Baltimore to the cotton states. Former bondman Henry Clay Bruce remembered seeing "many gangs of slaves driven over [the] old road" that ran by the plantation on which he spent his childhood. Such a party, he recalled, typically included as many as forty enslaved men handcuffed to either side of a long chain, women and children walking unmanacled, ailing slaves in wagons, the slave trader himself, and four or five white guards. "The road is thronged with droves of these wretches & the human car-case-butchers, who drive them on the *hoof* to market," John Randolph wrote as early as 1818. "One might almost fancy one's self on the road to Calibar or Bonny," slaving ports on the West African coast.[49]

In November 1842, a two-day sheriff's auction at Buckingham Court House, advertised in newspapers across the South, sold fully 120 slaves whom depression-plagued masters had lost as a result of court judgments. "The greater portion [of those sold were] boys and Girls from eight to seventeen Years of age," a local man recalled. In another typical case, in the 1830s, slaveholders in the area contracted with Alabamians who would convey slaves to the Gulf states and sell them. The Virginians provided the slaves' clothing and travel expenses, as well as coffins for any who died along the way; the transporter received a third of the profits from the eventual sale.[50] Putting monetary value on different categories of black human beings—"common" and "likely," men, women, boys, and girls—had long since become a skill that every leading businessman in the county was expected to possess. One man in Prince Edward received "a negro lad" of fourteen in lieu of interest on a sum he was owed; an enslaved woman and her small child changed hands as security for a loan.[51]

Slaveowners might defend themselves, accurately enough, by pointing out that they almost always provided for aged and infirm slaves. Often, however, whites showed less consideration to slaves at the beginning of life. Though many masters preferred to keep enslaved mothers and children together, in practice the exceptions were frequent. One sheriff's sale not only removed a three-year-old boy and his six-year-old sister from their mother and siblings, but then sold the two to separate buyers. At a similar auction of property left by the deceased would-be batteau mogul William Seay in 1845, the sheriff sold a four-year-old boy separately from Seay's other slaves.[52] Some masters shunted individual black children among white relatives, even though it might play havoc with black family connections. Even the desire to bring up a white youth responsibly could lead a white adult to separate a black child from his or her parents. One of the Legrands took in his schoolboy grandson as a part-time overseer and decided, as remuneration, "to buy him a little Negro" worth $200. The elder Legrand told a friend that "he had reather give [his grandson] a little negro than the money for he was young." Legrand wryly explained that he feared the youth "might spend the money [but] did not expect he would spend the Negro."[53]

Battered as bondpeople often were by whips and switches, by economic forces, and by the thoughtlessness of their owners, slavery at its core revolved around personal bonds between individual blacks and whites; so, to a lesser extent, did the lives of free African Americans. Many in our own time casually assume that white Southerners clever enough to keep several million inventive, assertive black people enslaved were not sufficiently astute to notice those people's diversity and the complexity of their personalities. They did notice. White people not only knew their own slaves well; they also knew *each other's* slaves by face and frequently by name. Whites often could recognize other people's "hands" when they looked into a field from the road at some distance, and they could distinguish within a combined group at labor between those of one master and those of another. Years after the fact, many could cite details about black individuals whom they had never owned or hired. Whites regularly talked about slaves as distinct individuals—complex, diverse human beings.[54]

Familiarity could arouse affection and sympathy. A "negro trader" offered one man an attractive price for a certain slave, but the man and his son "did not think [it] proper to sepparate . . . said negro from his neighbourhood and connexions." Other masters went to extraordinary lengths to prevent the loss of a particular, favorite slave when financial or legal tangles threatened a separation.[55] But familiarity, as the proverb reminds us, could also breed contempt, and the consequences could be dire when one human being owned another. Some masters reserved special treatment for those slaves they did not like: one dying slaveholder called for most of his bondpeople to be treated well, but singled out a slave named Sam who was to "be sold to the Highest bidder" along with "three Horses [named] Hello, Tenisee & Kentuckey."[56]

What this ruthless yet intimate system lacked was any strong impulse on the part of rural white Southerners to keep themselves physically separate from enslaved or free blacks. It would scarcely have occurred to anyone in the Southern countryside before Emancipation that white supremacy implied, or depended upon, the thoroughgoing brand of racial segregation for which the region became famous in a later age.

Casualness about black-white contact stemmed in part from a more general informality and fluidity that pervaded life in the county. Prince Edward had a white elite; but the erratic economy ensured that there was considerable mobility into—and out of—the upper crust, and no one attained fabulous wealth. Frustrated dreams of great riches can produce a grasping, tyrannical elite, but many people of substance in and around Prince Edward County retained a certain unpretentiousness. Gentlemen still chewed tobacco together—and if one found himself without it in another man's home, he might break off a piece of the host's "twist" without asking permission. Some of the county's leading white folk evinced a disarming lack of self-importance when they named their properties. The Legrands owned a farm called Mole Hill; the family of Clement Read acquired a plantation "known from time immemorial" as Hard Times, and they retained the name.[57]

The same sort of men found nothing unusual or offputting about attending, say, an estate auction along with white craftsmen and free blacks such as Edmund Young and Tom Ellis. Their wives might well have a black servant or two—women or boys—sleep in the same bedroom with them when the man of the house was away. Living quarters, including a house and lot in Farmville owned by Phil White, passed casually from black renters or owners to white.[58] Most sales of real estate by white people to blacks amounted to invitations—moneymaking ones, to be sure—for Afro-Virginians to live alongside whites; often the white seller him- or herself continued to live or do business on an adjacent or nearby lot, unperturbed at having brought in a black neighbor. By the 1850s there were one or several clusters of dwellings in Farmville in which most inhabitants were black, yet many people of the two races continued to live interspersed throughout the period.

In a region where, three generations later, blacks would not be permitted to try on a hat or garment before buying it, or to sit near whites on streetcars, or even to enter a restaurant, no white person in old Prince Edward thought twice about engaging in close physical contact with blacks. White shoemakers fitted slaves for shoes as a matter of course; one of them was able to describe the configuration of a slave defendant's foot in a criminal case that revolved around tracks the suspect had allegedly left in the dirt.[59]

Whites—and by no means only physicians—avidly applied medical treatments to the bodies of blacks. One white man talked in 1861 about taking in a slave girl who had temporarily run away and got a frostbitten foot; he reported that he "cured it—by steaming, bathing, and application of Roast Turnip & fish brine." The expectation that masters, overseers, and especially mistresses would personally attend sick or injured bondpeople was well-nigh absolute. Only a mistress who herself lay seriously ill could be excused from going to "the quarter" to see to the needs of ailing slaves.[60] A bondman named Armstead became sick in the late 1820s, and his elderly mistress routinely "picked" the boils that erupted on the black man's skin. She never felt repelled by the procedure until a doctor told her that Armstead was in the late stages of a venereal disease, commonly known then as "the foul disorder." "If she had known what was the nature of the boils," she told someone, "she would not have picked them, for nothing"—but neither the patient's race nor the presence of lesions on his body had put her off earlier.[61]

The ultimate intimacy between white and black, sexual intercourse, incensed some whites some of the time, but it happened often. Sex between masters and enslaved women went unpunished and thus usually unrecorded. Yet not all white males who had relationships with black women wielded power over their female partners, and not all such relations took place surreptitiously. A white man in Prince Edward named William Colley had no slaves but frequently associated with bondpeople owned by others in the 1840s. He gave cotton and flannel fabric, a cap, and a music box to an enslaved woman named Selina. Colley did not flaunt the relationship, but he evinced no shame over it, either; he pointed Selina out to his white housemate at a religious camp meeting as his "sweet heart." He ultimately knifed a male slave nearly to death, apparently for trying to come between him and his beloved.[62]

Sexual intimacy between white women and free or enslaved black men came in for heavier censure, of course, and thus happened less frequently—but more often than we may think.[63] As we have seen, when sexual contact between a black man and a white woman did occur, or people thought it had, the white community often reacted much less repressively than it would in later eras. That relative tolerance deeply affected the fortunes of a number of free Afro-Virginian families.

The complaints some whites made against women of their own color who bore mixed-race babies may leave the contrary impression—that "miscegenation" ranked among the very worst of crimes. Clear evidence of that seems to emerge in the protests that beset the wife of Josiah Chambers, the black Israelites' mentally incompetent white neighbor, when she bore an allegedly mulatto child, and in other husbands' petitions for divorce from wives who gave birth to brown babies. Yet the Chambers affair and other cases centered as much on the issue of marital infidelity as on that of cross-racial sex per se: of all the instances in which white women bore children not their husbands', virtually the only provable ones in an era without DNA testing were those in which the baby was brown. In the Chambers case, the allocation of Josiah's wealth depended on whether "the supposed wife be improperly there" in his home, and that issue, in turn, hung on whether she had borne a child by a man other than Chambers. Josiah's relatives had challenged the woman's standing even before the question of children arose, and the presence of a bastard child would give them the ammunition they needed to clinch their case, remove her from the premises, and go to the bank. For some white husbands, a wife's unfaithfulness with a black man may have stung more than her straying with a fellow white, but the desire not to support a wayward spouse and another man's child posed the paramount issue. Race was a forensic clue more than it was the root of the problem.[64]

For county officials, the sex that raised the greatest concern was the kind that produced impoverished bastard children and mothers whom the county would have to support. No couple in Prince Edward consisting of a free black man and a white woman during the half century before the Civil War ever seem to have faced allegations of casual fornication; in each of the well-documented liaisons, an intact pair were supporting any children they produced.[65] The county's economic challenge thus centered on white single mothers, from whose white lovers the authorities sought child support. That priority, and perhaps the prevalence of interracial contact in the society generally, help explain officials' lackadaisical response to the occasional, belated complaints about free black men and white women that did come in.

In one instance, differences among whites over the issue of cross-racial sex led to a catastrophic result. In mid-June 1826, the body of Nancy B. Morgan, a white woman, was found in some woods in northwestern Prince Edward County. Her jaw was broken, her skull fractured in at least three places, and her throat cut. Some physical evidence pointed to a slave named Solomon, whom Morgan had once accused of having "talked Saucy to her"; a called court found him guilty of the crime and sentenced him to hang. After his conviction, though, Solomon revealed that William Hill, a white man, had helped him slay Nancy Morgan—indeed, had planned the crime. It turned out that the black man and William Hill were close friends: Solomon visited Hill often and sometimes stayed the night. The white man had a daughter, Lavinia; the neighbors believed she was Solomon's lover. Hill hotly denied that his daughter was "too thick with negroes," but did not seek to spike the rumors by severing his ties with Solomon. Instead, he and his enslaved friend murdered Nancy Morgan to avenge her spreading gossip about Solomon and Lavinia.

Those who know something about race relations in later generations might expect William Hill's neighbors to have confronted him, and perhaps even to have got up a lynch mob to deal with Solomon, long before either man had a chance to plot retribution against Nancy Morgan. Yet even after both Solomon and William Hill were safely locked up, the most the white witnesses had to say was that Solomon had "seemed free and easy and took too many liberties," and that he and the whites in William Hill's household "seemed to be upon equal terms." Hill's neighbors did disapprove of those things, but no one had done anything about them, except for two who claimed they had stopped visiting the Hills because of Solomon's "intimacy" with the whites.

William Hill joined Solomon in the county jail. The two would spend more than a month there, shackled to the floor, while Hill stood trial and Solomon awaited his death by hanging. Solomon's race precluded his implicating Hill in court, so the authorities scrambled to find white witnesses. Fifty of them were summoned in the end; evidently none had any direct knowledge of the crime. Even so, a circuit court jury sentenced Hill to ten years' imprisonment for second-degree murder.

The whole bloody business captured a striking fact about honor, and about relations between blacks and whites in Prince Edward, that helped shape the existence of the Israelites and other free Afro-Virginians: *disparaging* another for his or her intimacy with blacks, like public shaming of any kind, could get a person injured or worse, but the intimate interracial contact itself most likely would not. In fact, it would have been all but impossible to draw up a list of fifty whites in Prince Edward, such as the roster of witnesses for William Hill's trial, without including people who were well acquainted with situations of black-white intimacy. In the Hill case, at least two potential witnesses themselves had a female family member or relative who had borne children by a black partner, and one witness had been prosecuted a few years earlier—unsuccessfully—for "Suffering Slaves and free Negroes of the Neighbourhood to visit [him] frequently." The internal contradictions of this society, in which some whites indulged in cross-racial contact of almost every kind while others set limits on such contact, had led in the end to the violent death of two human beings, Nancy and Solomon, and the incarceration of a third— but it had happened according to a very different script than would become familiar during the era of lynching decades later.[66]

Cross-racial intimacy in old Prince Edward encompassed still other complexities, among them the differences in skin color among "Negroes." Some, perhaps most, of the free black men in the county who had lasting relationships with white spouses were mulattoes. Color bias may tell only part of the story, however. At least one of those men, John Moss, could sign his name and perhaps read and write; in good years, he earned a healthy income. James Dungey's record as a landowning farmer suggests that he, too, had exhibited good economic prospects as a young man. Some mulatto men may have inherited literacy or material assets from white fathers. In any event, potential partners such as Dungey and Moss, though "colored" and disfranchised, may have had more to offer a woman than a nonliterate white suitor of few means. The post-Reconstruction belief that only "the vilest white persons" entered relationships with free blacks is a product of white supremacist wishful thinking, even though many liberals today would readily accept the corollary—that interracial unions were automatically branded as "disgraceful," and that they were often broken up by "privately organized bands of white persons supported by community sentiment."[67]

James Dungey's son Absalom, whose own mother was white and respectable, surely saw nothing odd about settling down with a white woman himself, and his parentage and complexion may have put his common-law wife at ease. In other pairings, however, at least shorter-term ones, white women did not confine their affections to free, light-skinned men; one woman bore a daughter whose reputed father was "as black a negro as [one] witness ever saw."[68] That girl, Betsy Lyle, grew up to have an interracial sexual relationship of her own. In 1850, Lyle, like many other unmarried women over the years, bore a baby and identified the father to the county overseers of the poor, who then sought child support from the man. Betsy apparently needed assistance urgently, for she had given birth in the county poorhouse. The man Lyle pointed to was William F. Scott, on whose plantation she would later work as a seamstress and weaver.

Scott replied to the county court that Betsy Lyle was half black and therefore could not legally testify against him. Indeed, Betsy looked mulatto enough that Scott called her before the court so that the justices might draw their own conclusions. Moreover, Betsy's neighbors knew— or believed they knew—exactly who her father was: a certain slave named Nelson. Yet Betsy Lyle had grown up in her white mother's home, and one witness reported "that at Church she usually sit with the family." People obviously had gossiped about Betsy's paternity, but no one, it seems, had ever questioned either her membership in the Lyle family circle or her right to associate with white people in public. Once the bastardy case came to court, however, the system's laws subverted the system itself: the legal bar against Betsy Lyle's testimony relieved William Scott of any responsibility for his child, and that left the county and Lyle herself holding the bag. Scott's behavior does reveal just how little a man might fear having it known that he had fathered a child by a free black woman.

Virginia—and the South as a whole—would one day become a society whose laws strove to define people out of the white race with the infamous "one-drop rule." But when Betsy Lyle had her baby, Virginia law still defined people *into* the white tribe: a person with more than three quarters white ancestry could qualify for membership. That criterion was not loose enough to include Betsy. Yet, had the bastardy case not arisen, little might ever have been made of her racial identity; the census taker still recorded her as white in 1850.[69] Ironically, Betsy Lyle suffered because she lived in a society whose customs tolerated and often encouraged close contact between white and black, but whose laws attempted to define two separate races of humanity and draw a border between them.

CLASHING VALUES

Forces more subtle than sexual attraction drew black and white people together in old Virginia. The simple need to wrest a living from the land, to carry on economic life in an orderly manner, and to advance one's fortunes if possible led to encounters of many kinds between whites and free blacks. The values that underlay the drive to work and accumulate wealth knew no color line; neither did the religious beliefs that, for more and more people in the nineteenth century, both complemented and transcended the desire to make money. Meanwhile, some Virginians befriended others of a different race for no obvious reason other than personal affinity.

All three interracial couples who faced prosecution in 1828, and then saw the charges dropped, lived in the western part of Prince Edward County, sixteen miles or so from the courthouse. The history of that area shows yet again that the ways whites and free blacks looked at and treated each other in the neighborhood of Israel Hill typified the customs of the county overall. The west was the locale in which the free black Forgason clan worked for Josiah Cheadle and others, and where shoemaker John Moss handled large sums of money. Jim League Sr.— the white Revolutionary War veteran who lived with his daughter Martha and her mixed-race children—resided in the same vicinity. In this end of the county, James Dungey and his white wife, Elizabeth, had openly married and reared their family.

After James Dungey died, his children continued to carry on business with their white neighbors; as in the old days, they attended processionings of the acreage they had inherited from their father. Land passed back and forth between the Dungeys and the white Gilliams; one day in 1850, men of the two families bought complementary sections of the same neighboring tract. The man they bought it from, Joel Elam, would serve as a county justice during the 1840s; at one point he joined John Dungey and a white neighbor to seek damages from the county when the court authorized a road through the area.[70] Another neighbor who ended up on the county court was Newton Cunningham, the man who assisted James Dungey Jr.'s wife during lean times, and whom John Dungey entrusted to carry out his will.

The white Selbe clan of western Prince Edward, who occupied a more modest place on the social scale, interacted with free blacks in a number of ways. One of its female members, Susan, became the wife of Stephen Forgason, son of Jethro, and Susan's mother apparently came to live with the couple. Sherwood and Anthony Selbe held little property and no slaves; at least one free black Forgason woman was living at Sherwood's place as late as the end of the 1850s, and Sherwood and Anthony once stood accused of entertaining slaves and free blacks too "frequently," but they easily got the charges thrown out.[71]

Not every transaction between black and white in the western end of the county went as smoothly as these. After all, the neighborhood at one moment also produced formal complaints, however ineffectual, against Stephen Forgason, Absalom Dungey, John Moss, and their white wives.

It would be easy to conclude, then, that whites in that area and elsewhere in the county divided into hard-line and permissive camps on matters of race. Some whites did find themselves pigeonholed. Otis Williams struck some people as imprudently casual in dealing with slaves, if not downright hostile to slavery. A Yankee from New York state, Williams moved to Prince Edward in the latter 1820s to manage the plantation of his wife's uncle; several free blacks joined his household.

New Englanders such as contractor James Ely and merchant Ebenezer Frothingham had taken to the slaveholding life without a hitch, but Otis Williams had his troubles fitting in, even though he provided an additional service to the community by teaching school. One neighbor later quoted the uncle who brought Williams to Virginia as complaining that he "had tried [Williams] with negroes and . . . he did not know what to do with them." Otis never quite shook his reputation: in 1842, someone caught an escaped bondman from Prince Edward in what is now West Virginia, and Williams was arrested—though not ultimately prosecuted—on suspicion that he had enticed the black man to flee and forged a pass for him to use.[72]

It would be too simple, however, to sort Prince Edward's white populace neatly into two phalanxes—easygoing Otis Williamses and hard-line folk such as those who accused him. Even David F. Womack, who witnessed John Dungey's will, and Newton Cunningham, longtime friend of that same interracial family, gave evidence before a grand jury about the de facto marriage of one of Edmund Young's sons to a white woman. Those men's comfort with most of their free black and interracial neighbors did not prevent them from making trouble for one they may not have liked. Meanwhile, the extensive dealings that gun-confiscating Major John Rice had with the Gibbs family of Israel Hill show that an apparent hard-liner might be less race-obsessed than he seems at first glance.[73]

Free black shoemaker Nathan Homes encountered both friendliness and treachery at the hands of whites; from one man, Homes experienced both. Nathan and his grandmother, the venerable Milly Homes, had each acquired land from General John Purnall by 1820. A white man named George W. Bell befriended Nathan Homes and began keeping the black man's accounts. Before the decade was out, Homes, now in his early thirties, bought an additional tract of about ten acres from another white neighbor, Josiah Sharp. Nathan paid Sharp off in installments and erected buildings on the land; the black man's friend George Bell, on Homes's behalf, carefully saved all the receipts from Homes's payments.

George Bell already owned several hundred acres of land and sixteen slaves, yet eventually he started brandishing the Sharp receipts and claiming that he, not Homes, had purchased Sharp's land. When Homes objected, Bell threatened to "cane" the black shoemaker. Bell also attempted to collect for his own use debts that other white men owed to Homes, insisting that the black man owed *him* that much money and more. A number of white men in Prince Edward then showed that they valued individual character above racial solidarity. Josiah Sharp, who had sold the land to Homes, defended the black man vigorously. Others likewise offered testimony damning Homes's faithless friend. Bell "told me N Homes belong to him," one white citizen deposed. "I told Mr Bell I had allways understood that Nathan was a Free Man." The justices of the court rejected Bell's claims on Homes's ten acres.[74]

Before the panel threw George Bell's case out, however, two of Prince Edward's overseers of the poor—perhaps egged on by Bell himself—menaced Nathan Homes in another way. They asserted that Homes already had "one or two . . . wives in the neighborhood" and had now brought in yet another, along with her children, from an adjacent county. The two officials wanted to expel these free black newcomers before they became public charges—a procedure that the board of overseers initiated from time to time against paupers of both races. But white solidarity and race prejudice, it turned out, did not extend to the forcible breakup of a free black family any more than they justified the fleecing of that family's head: Nathan Homes, his wife, and several children would still be together in Prince Edward as the Union slid toward dissolution more than two decades later. Nothing in county records, by the way, sustains the charge that Homes had any wives other than this one. In fact, his success in buying land suggests that the white witnesses in the conflict with George Bell had taken Homes's measure accurately: he was a solid, self-disciplined man, and that reputation helped vindicate him when certain hostile whites threatened his interests.[75]

By and large, white folk in Prince Edward County, like people in other societies, valued good neighbors and esteemed good behavior; most were repelled by personal dishonesty and viciousness, even as they accepted the exploitative institution of slavery. These Virginians' estimation of individuals did not jibe neatly with the racial theory on which the society rested. When whites noticed that industry and laziness, integrity and dissimulation, were distributed in much the same way among both whites and free blacks, values could at least partly override color as a social yardstick.

Men like John and Amplias Tuggle, brothers who lived just up the road from Israel Hill, had good reason to judge their neighbors largely as individuals rather than as members of a particular race. John Tuggle knew well the accomplishments of the Whites and other residents of the Hill: he had traded with them, witnessed documents and performed services for them in much the way that whites did for each other, and even administered Phil White Sr.'s estate. Moreover, the white populace of Israel Hill's neighborhood—to which the Tuggles were bound by an intricate web of genetic, marital, and financial ties—included at least one person whose behavior made that of a Sam or Phil White look even more exemplary.

The Penicks, relatives of the Tuggles, lived between Israel Hill and the Tuggle lands to the west. Young Jonathan Penick had enjoyed great advantages—good schooling and a handsome legacy left by Penick's father in 1819. John Tuggle helped administer the estate and even served as Jonathan's guardian as the boy neared the age of majority. But in the 1830s, Jonathan began deserting his wife, Judith, and their three children for up to six weeks at a stretch, spending his time in Richmond and Petersburg, "living in a state of dissipation and recklessness bordering on derangement." Every so often, without warning, someone would show up back in Prince Edward and present an IOU from Penick, until eventually between a dozen and twenty slaves had been sacrificed to the young man's gambling debts and other costs of his carousing. "The distress of his wife was extreme," reported Amplias Tuggle, who at one point tracked Jonathan Penick down at the circus in Richmond and made a fruitless, last-ditch appeal to the young man's better nature. Only by filing suit against Jonathan and one of his gambler-creditors did Judith, with the Tuggles' help, manage to save part of the family plantation.[76]

When the Tuggles worried about irresponsible, destructive behavior in their neighborhood, then, they thought not of the Afro-Virginians on nearby Israel Hill but rather of their own kinsman. Their lives would have been much simpler, and Judith Penick a great deal wealthier and happier, if the character of Sam or Phil White could have been transplanted into the wayward Jonathan.

Other whites in the vicinity of Israel Hill also tangled with fellow whites rather than with free blacks. The Israelites' next-door neighbor William L. Legrand became the area's resident curmudgeon. He bitterly protested against county road-building plans involving his land, and he griped about taxation. He cut off a long-recognized bridle path through his plantation, for years denying access to a route on which his white neighbor depended. Legrand also complained in 1839 that "some body is constantly taking my wood a long the road" running through his property; perhaps he should post a guard, Legrand added sarcastically. The black Israelites who lived just across the old man's property line could have made handy scapegoats for him: they frequently hauled things between Farmville and Israel Hill across Legrand's tract. Yet this imaginative collector of grievances did not allege that the Israelites were the culprits stealing his wood, nor had he pointed the finger at them years earlier when someone stole his sorrel horse (he accused a white man instead). With the possible exception of his testimony in Jacob Johnston's trial for purchasing stolen corn—testimony that may in fact have benefited Johnston—Legrand never suggested that his black neighbors were causing him any problems. His own father had traded with Sam White in the 1820s, and Legrand thus had every reason to know what sort of people the Israelites were.[77]

Legrand was not alone in that knowledge. In 1821, a grand jury presented Michael Patterson, the grown son of Israelites Isham and Nancy Patterson, for selling liquor without a license at a local mill. The same grand jury also charged a white man, Thomas Gregory, with having willfully disturbed a church service. Gregory's and Patterson's alleged offenses were roughly comparable in seriousness, though the customary fine for liquor selling was higher, and the two men's cases played out identically—up to a point. The county court summoned both defendants to answer the charges, and in each case a deputy sheriff reported back that the accused now resided across the Appomattox River in Buckingham County; new summonses for Patterson and Gregory were then issued to the sheriff of Buckingham.[78]

At this stage, the two cases diverged. Buckingham's sheriff reported, after nearly three months, that he had not had enough time to execute the paper on Michael Patterson. Eventually, the prosecuting attorney in Prince Edward moved that the case against the black youth be dismissed; never having set foot in a courtroom, Patterson was in the clear. Meanwhile, far from letting the white Thomas Gregory off the hook, a jury convicted him in absentia of disturbing religious worship and fined him $10. Even if Michael Patterson had indeed crossed the Appomattox—he did marry a woman from Buckingham a few years later—he would have been easy to find, and in far less than three months. The authorities in Prince Edward or Buckingham, or both, had let the summons sit on their desk until it was too late to execute it. In Patterson, the authorities knew well whom they were dealing with. If in fact he had sold liquor illicitly, that was the only blemish on his record. Though even Patterson did not renew his registration as often as the law required, he did so more frequently than any other free black on Israel Hill, and perhaps in the entire county; his slate would remain clean through a long life that lasted until after the Civil War.

Thomas Gregory, on the other hand, was just the kind of bad apple that no one suspected Michael Patterson of being. If the authorities did not know that at the outset, it became clear to them at one point while the prosecution for disturbing worship was pending: a white citizen charged that Gregory, now back in Prince Edward, at least temporarily, had "snaped a pistol" at him in an effort to shoot him. In theory, the allegation of an attempted shooting had no bearing on whether Thomas Gregory had disturbed worship months earlier. But he was building a reputation as an obnoxious, perhaps dangerous figure. Unlike Michael Patterson, Gregory was the type of person the men of power in Prince Edward believed should be taken down a few pegs. They convicted the absent defendant for the attempted shooting and added a fine of $100 to the smaller one on the original charge.[79] The system of neighbors judging neighbors had operated rationally once again, pursuing an aggressive white character while forgiving a slip by an inoffensive free black man.

The county's lawmen and ordinary citizens were prepared at times to personalize law enforcement in unsubtle ways, as when one member of a sheriff's posse gave a slave suspected of burglary "three cuts with a cow hide" on the way to jail in 1826.[80] Yet circumstances could outweigh color when county officials decided how to treat a free person. Deputy Sheriff James McDearmon bought land from the free black Evans family. But every time McDearmon thought he owned the tract free and clear, another free black man or woman came along claiming to be an heir of John Evans, the deceased owner of the land. Over a period of a dozen years, McDearmon pliantly paid off each group of black claimants, including three members of the boating Bartlett clan. He shelled out more than $8 per acre by the time he was done—a high and almost surely excessive rate by the standards of the era.[81] It never seems to have occurred to Deputy McDearmon to say a simple "begone" to any of the black Evanses or to raise a hand against them. And if the idea had crossed his mind, he had ample reason to doubt that the county court would vindicate him against the Afro-Virginians who approached him.

A generation later, in 1860, the census taker for Prince Edward expressed a hierarchy of values shared by many whites in the county, both officials and plain citizens. The enumerator noted the presence of two white households who "lived on only .5 acres of poor land in two small log cabins" and had "no employment but hunting." In fact, these people did have another occupation: the census taker noted with a combination of disgust and satisfaction that the group were a "nest of thieves driven off for Sheep stealing" earlier in the year. The same scribe made a tiny marginal note evincing mild surprise but no great agitation when he came across free black William (Billy) Young, son of the redoubtable Edmund Young, still living with his white wife, Betsy Bigger, alongside Betsy's white relatives after at least twenty years of marriage. Of them, the census taker had nothing more to say than simply, "Man & Wife."[82]

On the brink of the Union's demise, as throughout the previous decades, this white man and many others like him found "race-mixing" at most an irritant, while crimes like livestock rustling, regardless of the perpetrators' race, constituted a real threat warranting the banishment of those who indulged in them. Law-abiding citizens had basic values in common that spanned the color line—and they knew it. At the same time, solid citizens both white and black felt alienated from the wastrels, ruffians, and outright criminals of their own color.

Black Israelites Sam White and Guy Howard had known each other throughout the younger man's life. As a youth, Howard had moved across the Appomattox with the Hercules White family while all still belonged to Judith Randolph. What happened thereafter became a matter of dispute between Sam White and Guy Howard's wife, Pamelia (Mely), during the 1830s. Mely Howard claimed that Judith Randolph had granted land to Hercules White Sr. on the condition that he in turn donate an acre and a half to the Howards. Mely said she and her husband, the boatman, had then built themselves a house and outbuildings, laid out a garden, and grown vegetables for sale, but that now, years later, Sam White was trying to expel her. She sued to stop him.

Sam White contradicted Mely Howard's story on every point but the last—his desire to be rid of her. White said that his father, Hercules, had received his fifty acres unconditionally, had taken Mely Howard into his own home to work for his wife, had then "put [her] to live in the yard" in an outbuilding, and finally had permitted the Howards to move into the cabin Rose Johnston vacated on a corner of the White tract. Eventually, the Howards had indeed built a house of their own, Sam White added, but only after they asked him and his brothers for permission. White said that even now he would have allowed Mely to stay on his land, "but that the bad behaviour of the said Pamelia and the utter worthlessness of her

Husband Guy have put them out of the pale of protection from the honest and industrious." Some of the wording clearly came from White's attorney, but the sentiment was genuine. Sam White did not list the supposed transgressions of Guy and Mely Howard, but he was clearly accusing the couple of lacking, as he put it, both honesty and industry.[83]

The ambitious and energetic White did say, with obvious disdain, that the Howards had not bothered to replace their old cabin until it "had rotted down or nearly." He may also have been thinking about Guy Howard's arrest with Hampton Giles for allegedly stealing a hog half a dozen years earlier. Neither man had been convicted, but White may have blamed the boatman for putting the good name of Israel Hill and of Sam's friend Giles in jeopardy.

Sam White would help establish the Farmville Baptist Church in 1836, during the adjudication of Mely Howard's suit. The congregation had been crystallizing over a period of several years,[84] and White may have become an observant Christian even earlier that that. Whatever the Howards' specific transgressions had been, drunkenness, other misbehavior, or even mere sloth committed on his very own land were certain to offend a devout Baptist—even to the point of alienating him from lifelong acquaintances of his own color, whose son had married into the White clan.

All in all, White seems to have looked upon the Howards much as John Tuggle viewed his wastrel relative, Jonathan Penick. White, Tuggle, and others like them of both races united in their distaste for the drunkard, the layabout, and the scofflaw of any color. John Tuggle (either the elder or the younger) had reported liquor selling and other misbehavior by people of both races at the militia muster ground in 1813. Phil White and Reuben Seay, soon to become founding members of Farmville Baptist Church, both complained of attacks or threats from the white boatman and sometime criminal Grief Weaver. One white woman lamented in 1835 that "the sabbath is shamefully abused by many who call themselves christians[,] and some have been seen so drunk that they could not walk the street without assistance"; she was speaking mainly of fellow whites, not of free blacks or slaves.[85] Also like white people of similar beliefs and comparable economic standing, Sam White did not necessarily separate moral disapproval from class consciousness. He and Mely Howard may have had a common origin as Randolph slaves, but he linked his judgment of her morals with a reminder that she had been a mere servant living "in the yard" of the propertied White family.[86]

In his battle with Mely Howard, as in most things, Sam White got his way. The county court did delay any eviction during the five years it took Howard's case to move through the system, but it ultimately rejected Mely's claim to a corner of White's tract and ordered her to pay Sam's legal costs of more than $7. Sam White may have allowed the chastened Mely Howard to remain—on his own terms; at any rate, her two sons, one of them Phil White's son-in-law, would still live on Israel Hill with their families twenty years later.[87] The Baptist church imposed a stern morality, but it also preached reconciliation and forgiveness—boons that a victor can well afford to offer the vanquished.

The churches of Prince Edward County rigorously promoted moral standards that could unite white and black and alienate a person from others of his or her own race. The evangelical denominations, Methodists, Baptists, and Presbyterians, had supplanted Anglicanism/Episcopalianism in Prince Edward by the 1780s. The majority of citizens never joined a church, but many of society's casual assumptions and part of its working vocabulary were rooted in evangelical Christianity. A substantial fraction of the population did join churches; the demand for space in which to worship became urgent enough that a somewhat hesitant county court agreed in 1837 to open the courthouse for Sunday evening religious services "so far as [the court had] any right" to do so. Revivals and camp meetings at least from the early 1800s on attracted many, as did other sorts of religious gatherings. One man spoke in 1842 of regular Sunday evening prayer meetings led by two white men in his slave quarter. The Baptist congregation that Sam and Phil White helped to form met for several years in private homes before it erected a building of its own.[88]

Every congregation in Prince Edward was dominated by whites; between the 1830s and the 1850s, overcrowding and physical separation of worshipers by race left black members in some churches "either peeping wistfully in at the doors, huddling attentively together about the windows, or leaning against the walls of the house, and trying to catch as much of the sermon as they can." Even so, the Baptist churches in particular attracted hundreds of black congregants. Like free blacks, enslaved people generally decided for themselves where to worship; the Cumberland Presbyterian congregation itself owned slaves whom it hired out to earn income, but a number of those Presbyterian-owned Afro-Virginians actually chose to attend Sharon Baptist Church.[89]

Though more than a few Christians wavered in their commitment at times, no one of either race would, or could, join a church casually; the "personal experience of religion" was essential for evangelicals. No Baptist could receive baptism without first being inwardly "convicted" of his or her own depravity and then converted. Free black Archer Homes was not baptized until he was about thirty-two, and that was not unusual.[90] Black people, like whites, were received into church membership on the strength of their personal religious conversion or of a letter from their former congregation; if necessary, they faced admonition or expulsion, just as whites did. Each church apparently "received the experience" of some of its black members—that is, heard them relate, at meeting, their encounters with the Holy Spirit—as it did the testimony of whites.[91] The church, like the larger society, placed whites in control, and it ordinarily seated its members separately by color, but it also ratified and nurtured the moral affinities between godly people of both races.

Sharon Baptist Church kept lists of white and black members in separate sections of its minute book but maintained both rosters with care. When a visiting minister wrote a brief notice announcing the formal birth of the Farmville Baptist congregation, he spoke of the "21 white members" but not of the two blacks (and likewise of "brethren" but not of sisters). Yet when the clerk of Farmville Baptist sought a list of charter members from a longtime congregant in 1872, the latter made sure to record the names of two black Israelites, both dead by then, with the special phrase, "Sam & Phil White, <u>colored</u>, the first members."[92] The word "colored" was underscored—perhaps for fear that coming generations would not realize that the congregation, almost all of whose black members had withdrawn after the Civil War, had once included, and indeed had been founded by, members of both races.

The church exposed the equality of black and white not only in their spiritual gifts but also in their capacity for sin. A Baptist church like the one Sam and Phil White helped build appointed committees to investigate allegations of immoral behavior by its members, held church trials, and pressed the guilty to repent publicly; each congregation expelled numerous individuals who did not show sufficient penitence. Blacks found their own misdeeds revealed in church, but they also saw paraded before them the whole panoply of human weaknesses, crimes, and perversions indulged in by white people. In the Sharon Baptist congregation, out of which Sam and Phil White's church grew, the typical sins were drunkenness, nonattendance at church, and the discreetly worded catchall, "grossly immoral conduct." A single church building could be used amicably by two or three different denominations, yet communing with Methodists or associating with Campbellites could get a Baptist "admonished" by his or her congregation.

Sharon Baptist Church became a sort of mother congregation to the church
that black Israelites Sam and Phil White helped found in Farmville in 1836.
(Bradshaw, *History of Prince Edward County*, PLATE IX)

In the three decades or so before the Civil War, members were disciplined for playing backgammon, dancing, prevaricating, living in adultery, denying their wives the necessities of life, fighting, carrying knives, and bearing, then burying, an illegitimate child. The occasional report that an enslaved member's "general conduct was disorderly" may have meant that the bondperson was not submissive enough to his or her master; but overall, the church was the one institution in Southern life that applied essentially the same rules to whites and blacks alike.[93]

The evangelical impulse produced tensions between believers and skeptics. Some citizens worried that an unhealthy focus on spiritual matters could produce an emotional disorder known as "religious melancholy."[94] A surprising number of individuals physically attacked churches and churchgoers; just as black and white Christians defined sin and salvation similarly, so they stood together against the aggression of their profane fellow men.

Thomas Gregory, the white man who interfered with a religious service at the same time Michael Patterson allegedly sold illegal liquor, was far from alone in his offense. From before the turn of the nineteenth century until the 1850s, disrupting religious worship and damaging church buildings served as a kind of sport for some of the local men—one best accompanied, in the view of some, by assiduous drinking.[95] One man faced charges for defacing a church with a knife, another for disturbing worship at a meetinghouse and then beating the minister eight days later. Three other men allegedly threatened a congregation with a pistol and a drawn knife; a Hampden-Sydney student was said to have shot a gun near a Methodist Church at Prince Edward Court House before forcing open the doors and "breaking up an assemblage of ladies . . . collected for the purpose of singing." Not all those accused of these crimes were young blades. In 1844, William Verser, a colonel of militia, was presented "for contemptuously . . . disturbing a religious Congregation" and for "assaulting the [church's pastor] by shaking a stick over his head and using menacing Language."

Some men accused of such acts paid fines as high as $25; more escaped conviction.[96] But their behavior disturbed religious people of both colors—and the offenders, without exception, were white men. Yet again, being devout in antebellum Prince Edward County greatly complicated one of the chief tasks of racist thinking: to identify moral worth with color.

By the early 1840s, the spread of evangelical religion had brought more meetinghouses and ministers to the area than William Verser could shake a stick at. A generation earlier, John Randolph had written scornfully of "baptist preachings . . . in log cabins" attended by "the lowest order of freeholders."[97] Now, though the churches still attracted humble folk, they also included a number of citizens who played prominent roles in the economic and civic life of the county. The religious affinity that arose between such people and their black fellow evangelicals had practical effects on the quality of free Afro-Virginians' lives. Several white members of Farmville Baptist Church owned mercantile stores or tobacco factories; they constantly shipped cargo on batteaux, many of which were run or even owned by free blacks. Transactions between whites and blacks who had money would have occurred even without the influence of the church; Colonel James Madison's collaboration with Randolph Brandum proves that. Yet religious ties and economic dealings reinforced each other and bound these white and black Baptist entrepreneurs closely together.

In the early 1840s, former Israelite Sam Strong sued Phil White over a $40 debt. The man who gave bond for Phil's appearance in court, Benjamin M. Robertson, had organized the first Baptist Sunday school in

By the early 1840s, the spread of evangelical religion had brought more churches to Prince Edward and nearby counties, even as some local white men terrorized worshipers for sport.   (MELVIN PATRICK ELY)

town in 1835 and helped launch the Farmville Church; he also owned a tobacco factory. It must have seemed only natural to the white Robertson that he should sign a bond for his fellow charter congregant Phil White. Ben played a similarly helpful role in another suit against John and Phil White at about the same time, and a few years later he would testify against the free black man who stole Phil's horse.[98]

The feeling of trust that developed among black and white Baptist men of affairs radiated outward, drawing in those men's relatives and neighbors. During the early years of Farmville Baptist Church, Ben Robertson and free black John White of Farmville each bought a town lot from charter congregation member Reuben Seay. In the same period, John N. Robertson cosigned the IOU with which sometime Israelite Joe Bartlett purchased a batteau; John Robertson was a partner and relative of the Whites' friend, Baptist pioneer Ben Robertson. Joe Bartlett went broke in the Panic of 1837, and John Robertson, his guarantor, had to pay off Bartlett's IOU. The white man then gave Bartlett nearly six years' grace before trying to recover that money. Robertson's patience with Joe Bartlett may appear not merely friendly but downright paternalistic at first glance—except that white men often practiced similar indulgence toward one another, and Robertson ultimately did sue for his money rather than write off the loss.[99]

Some white men performed clerical or financial services for nonliterate but enterprising free Afro-Virginians, and here, too, religious ties came into play. Coach maker C. E. Chappell, yet another white charter member of Farmville Baptist, drew up bonds through which other men acknowledged the debts they owed to Sam and Phil White. The church tie may have encouraged Chappell to take on those tasks; there is good reason to doubt that he put on patronizing airs when he agreed to perform them. The literacy that Chappell possessed was too rudimentary to build undue pretensions on—his handwriting was a scrawl, his spelling eccentric, and his capitalizations whimsical even by the norms of the time. Moreover, Chappell did not hesitate to depict himself as Phil White's "agent." A typical document read: "I sighn [assign] the with in B[ond?] for valiew Rece[ived] . . . C E Chappell Agt." And an agent he indeed was in such transactions. He may have received fees or commissions from Phil White. The two men's shared religious commitment had probably brought them together, but if any element of charity shaped White and Chappell's business relationship, the benevolence may have flowed from the black man to the white. Chappell found himself in financial free fall after the crash of 1837, his property either sold off or tendered as security for his overwhelming debt; he just may have appreciated the bits of work that the Whites could give him here and there.[100]

Sam and Phil White probably realized that their religious ties to men like Ben Robertson, Reuben Seay, and C. E. Chappell brought certain practical benefits. But in their day the church was no easy or convenient means to achieve worldly ends; few would submit to its surveillance and its code of conduct in the absence of real conviction. As for the white Baptist businessmen, we might well ask whether an earlier openness toward free blacks had allowed them to join a new congregation whose first members were Afro-Virginians of substance, or whether sharing religious fellowship with the White family broadened their outlook. Surely both these things happened.

Common religious beliefs were not the only ideological ties that bound together people like the Whites of Israel Hill on the one hand and white citizens such as Chappell, Seay, and the Robertsons on the other. Those men shared an additional array of values, quite compatible for the most part with those of evangelical religion. In particular, many whites and free blacks evinced a drive for economic advancement and an entrepreneurial spirit whose power we easily underestimate amid popular moonlight-and-magnolia stereotypes of the Old South. Judith Randolph once wrote that her neighbor, General Peter Johnston, was as "ambitious . . . as any Yankee" in his desire for "profit" and public acclaim. But in fact, the economic ambitions that many associate with the North had long prevailed in Virginia. A New Jerseyan sojourning among wealthy Virginia planters shortly before the Revolution already noted that "he seems now to be best esteemed and most applauded who attends to his business, whatever it be, with the greatest diligence."[101]

We rightly think of slavery as having demeaned labor and undermined the work ethic. Yet remarkably, that ethic survived. Some masters demanded a great deal of themselves even as they squeezed as much as possible out of their slaves. One white family in Prince Edward became known to their neighbors in the 1840s as "a very Persevering People so much so that they take night as well as day to labour." Not surprisingly, their slaves had it even worse, giving "the appearance of broken down worn-out negroes . . . stinted for something to eat as well as drove hard."[102] One of the richest men in the county complained that some of his neighbors had "turned gentlemen and merchants," and that one of them in particular was of "no account, and a fox hunter." This curmudgeon reared his own nephew to be "right industrious" by working him for years "as one of the [plantation] hands without wages"; the same man divided his legacy in order not to "make a fool" of his son by pampering him.[103]

The old man need not have worried so about Prince Edward citizens' dedication to work. Throughout the era of slavery, neighbors continued to judge planters and farmers by whether they were "industrious and economical," "adding to [their] property," and being "careful in the sale of any thing [they] had for market . . . to get a good price."[104] The same values animated merchants, who themselves usually belonged to the planter class. A certain willingness to defer gratification (made easier, to be sure, by those comforts that slavery provided), a belief in long-term economic progress even when conditions went sour, litigiousness, a willingness to try innovative ways to make money—all these qualities existed abundantly in Prince Edward County. The town of Farmville arose as an embodiment of them. The town held in esteem those who could be "spoken of as [men] of capital"; only a mature man who had "his capital employed" in some active enterprise really qualified. People spoke dismissively of other, younger, more impecunious men who had never "made any thing."[105]

There was plenty of room in this little world for black-white economic cooperation, but not because Afro-Virginian workers became indispensable. By 1840, blacks made up a little more than 10 percent of Prince Edward County's free population; the county contained more than a dozen enslaved African Americans for every free black. Each one of those free Afro-Virginians followed an occupation—farming, shoemaking, smithing, boating, weaving-knitting-spinning-sewing, carpentering, coopering, tobacco stemming and manufacturing—that slaves, and in many cases whites as well, could and did perform.

Rural Virginia contained a surplus of slaves. Had the free black craftsmen and laborers suddenly vanished, Prince Edward's economy would have suffered some inconvenience but no serious harm; at worst, slaveholders could have taken up any slack by selling somewhat fewer bondpeople southward. Free blacks who were engaged in business or investment—Sam, Phil, and John White, Sam Strong, Booker Jackson, and a handful of others—would achieve much in the 1830s and afterward, but their absence would not have affected the overall life of the county any more than did the exodus of numerous white men who had filled similar roles in the economy. When white Virginians supported petitions of free black individuals to remain in the state, it made tactical sense to cite those people's economic contributions. But in fact, most whites in Prince Edward and elsewhere—even those who worried about the "free Negro question" in the abstract—saw their own free black neighbors as neither indispensable nor threatening.

At the same time, there was money to be made by and with free blacks. Afro-Virginians who managed to advance their fortunes did so in some of the same ways their white counterparts did, and apparently with many of the same motives and assumptions. Nonliterate though most free blacks were, a number of them preferred to formalize economic arrangements that could have been handled "off the books." They divided their inherited land by official surveys and presented bills for services rendered; they sued fellow blacks for unpaid debts and sometimes even demanded that a black defendant give bail pending his appearance to answer a lawsuit. Hampton Giles was not the only free Afro-Virginian who hired a slave from a white person and put him or her to work. Two white men leased a female slave from shoemaker Booker Jackson in 1841; although the black man apparently "sublet" the woman after hiring her himself from the Chambers estate, he also owned or otherwise controlled a couple of additional slaves during the same decade.[106] Because free blacks did these things, it would be easy to suggest that they were sucked into an individualistic, competitive, exploitative white American ethos. Yet affinities in economic outlook are of a piece with the religious and cultural sharing that characterized old Prince Edward. Sam and Phil White, Sam Strong, and Booker Jackson were no more ensnared involuntarily in the particular economic system that surrounded them than were the whites among whom they lived—and every bit as much so.

Free Afro-Virginians practiced no-nonsense economic behavior because it could pay off even for people whom the system disfranchised politically. An IOU from a black man of substance could be "spent" as if it were money: when batteau owner Ben White signed such a paper for $100 to an attorney, the lawyer used (or "assigned") the note to pay his own account at a local mercantile company, which readily accepted White's endorsed bond.[107] White people with money to lend or services to offer extended credit to numerous free black individuals, whom they reckoned to be at least as good a risk as many white potential debtors. Those who cosigned free blacks' notes of indebtedness made the same calculation.

The longing to gain and hold on to independence in a place of one's own, the struggle to get money and to make that home one's castle, belonged to a set of values that white and black, artisan, yeoman, and planter, could partake of in spite of everything that separated them. The dream remained unattainable for the enslaved, and for many poor free people of both colors; persons who did fulfill their own ambitions often did so by exploiting slave labor. Free African Americans, especially former slaves and relatives of bondpeople, had good reason to ponder their society's inequities more deeply than most whites did. But the existing economic system was the one they knew, and some of them navigated it as skillfully as batteaumen did the Appomattox River.

At the same time, the financial and even the moral reputation of the free black populace as a whole was colored by the modest circumstances in which many Afro-Virginians lived, and by the abject poverty that beset some in the group. One phenomenon in particular seems at first glance to dramatize black penury: the nonpayment of taxes by noticeable, and sometimes very large, numbers of free black men. Free people of both races were liable for taxes on any land they might own and on certain kinds of personal property. The landowners who dominated society kept the rates on land and lots very low; the real estate on Israel Hill had been assessed relatively high even before blacks acquired it, yet a landowner's tax liability there in most years was only 20 or 40 cents, depending on the size of the plot. The failure of some Israelites to pay the land tax in certain years, and the sheriff's theoretical auctioning off of a few disused acres in the early 1830s, would be repeated a couple of times in the decade that followed. But Israel Hill as a community would remain intact. Most free Afro-Virginians did not own land in the first place, so the tax had no relevance to them.

The personal property tax applied to slaves and horses every year, to carriages, watches, and clocks in many years, and occasionally to other categories of property. This levy, sometimes called the "revenue tax," offends us in that it put enslaved human beings in the same category as beasts and inanimate objects, but it did not impose a heavy burden on most free blacks. Few of them owned carriages; the tax bill on a horse normally came in at only 12 or 13 cents a year; and most free Afro-Virginians held no slaves, or perhaps one, usually a spouse.[108]

The records of the "county levy," a flat tax to fund county government operations, tell a different story. Each free adult male, whatever his race, had to pay the tax annually. The amount often fell between 30 and 65 cents; the latter sum amounted to more than a day's wages for many workers.[109] Most of those who failed to pay were white, but the *rate* of nonpayment was noticeably higher among free blacks. While about a tenth of the county's free population during the generation before the Civil War was black, Afro-Virginians constituted something like a fifth of the county's tax "insolvents." Neither white nor black tax delinquents were invariably poor; Phil White's son Curtis, for example, was not impoverished and was known as a model citizen, yet his name occasionally appears on lists of tax insolvents.[110] Some free blacks do seem to have paid their taxes regularly; Sam and Phil White Jr., for example, rarely appeared on the delinquent lists.

An additional tax and a special law branded free Afro-Virginians as second-class citizens. In the mid-1810s and again in the 1850s, the state imposed the annual "specific tax" exclusively on free blacks at a flat per-head rate, often $1 per man. That $1 represented two days' pay for many individuals, and even more for agricultural workers who labored on a yearly basis; some free black men responded to this tax and to other levies as they did to the government's impositions generally—simply by not complying.

According to law, black tax delinquents could be hired out by the county to work off any unpaid obligations. Few official documents from the Old South shock the modern reader more, or have done more to influence historians' understanding of free blacks' fate, than lists from places such as Prince Edward titled "Free Negroes and mulattoes For

Hire," or even, on some occasions, "A list of free Negroes to be sold for taxes."[111] The laws governing such hiring out were both outrageously exploitative and at least ostensibly self-limiting. Under the statutes, a sheriff might credit a black delinquent working off his tax debt with as little as 8 or 10 cents a day. The law, to the extent officials actually applied it, was a blatant and insulting abridgment of black freedom, yet it did not aim surreptitiously to re-enslave free blacks. The code also specified that any man forced to work beyond the number of days needed to meet his obligation could recover $1 from the sheriff or deputy who had hired him out for each day of overwork.[112] Thus whoever spoke of "selling" free Afro-Virginians for back taxes misapplied the term and made an unjust law sound even more so.

As with the registration requirement imposed on free blacks, the real effects of the hiring-out statute depended not on the letter of the law, but rather on its application year in and year out. For a few years during and just after the War of 1812, the state legislature levied the specific tax on free Afro-Virginians; the tax reached an onerous $2.50 at one point. Not coincidentally, 1815 was the year in which the county court threatened a number of black tax delinquents and actually hired Jethro Forgason Jr. out to work off his obligation. On at least three occasions in the 1820s and 1830s, the court issued orders to hire out men who owed various taxes; the record does not show whether the men paid up, worked off their tax debt as the court specified, or did neither.[113]

In the late 1830s and early 1840s, the specific tax on free black men was no longer being collected. Yet some lists of nonpayers in the annual county levy for that period included as many as twenty men who either lived on Israel Hill, most of them from the second generation, or resided in Farmville but had Israelite parents.[114] By the mid-forties, as many as eighty or a hundred free black men a year left one or more taxes unpaid; those numbers represented a majority—sometimes a substantial one—of the free black adult males in the county. In 1844, one official drew up a master "List of Free negroes to be hired for Taxes" of various kinds. Among the nearly seventy individuals he listed were members of every single founding family of Israel Hill, including Sam and Phil White themselves.[115]

On more than half a dozen occasions during that same decade, the county court adopted orders to hire out the dozens of black tax delinquents. Yet there was far less to this supposed crackdown than meets the eye. The 1840s instead turn out to have been a time of sustained, mostly

According to law, black tax delinquents could be hired out by the county—or "sold," as some people put it colloquially—to work off their unpaid obligations. But when free blacks resisted taxation without representation, few actually found themselves hired out by the sheriff.

successful passive resistance by many blacks against taxation without representation. In the county's upper district in 1842, eighteen black men did not pay the county levy by the due date. But one paid late, and the authorities wrote off eleven other delinquents as blind, dead, or not residing in the county, or as having drawn "no bid"—meaning that no one made an offer to the sheriff for the forced labor of those free blacks. That leaves six men from the district who may have been hired out. The comparable list for the same district in the following year, 1843, initially included fully thirty-six free blacks—and this time, all but three of them were marked "no bid" or "no inhabitant."[116]

It begins to seem, then, that the sheriff hired out only a minority, perhaps a very small one, of free black tax delinquents to work off their obligations. But even that is not necessarily so. For example, at least some free blacks not marked on the lists as deceased were in fact dead when their names appeared there. Thus the absence of the notation "no inhabitant," "dead," or "no bid" after a man's name does not mean the sheriff ever hired him out; forgetting to enter notations such as "no bid" on delinquent lists for the county levy was all too easy, for free blacks' names were randomly interspersed with those of whites.[117]

By the 1850s, the situation becomes crystal-clear. The free black specific tax had been reintroduced in 1850—its proceeds, humiliatingly, earmarked to finance the removal of free blacks from the state. Many Afro-Virginians proved no more eager to pay it than they were to respond to the county levy. In March 1852, the county court ordered the sheriff to hire out blacks who had failed to pay taxes in 1850 and 1851; the order listed the men by name. Someone then painstakingly noted which of those black men ultimately paid up—between a fifth and a quarter of the group. The same scribe transferred every single remaining name— there were several dozen of them—to a new list of men "for which no bid could be obtained."[118]

The fact that not a single bid came in almost surely indicates that the sheriff's supposed auction of free black men's labor had never taken place; the county's free Afro-Virginians and its officials had turned a state law into a dead letter. The same thing happened in other counties and towns across Virginia in the early 1850s: local functionaries reported that no bids had come in for the services of free blacks who declined to pay taxes. One sheriff who did claim he had tried to implement the law managed to hire out only one man. Two other exceptional sheriffs hired out a few black nontaxpayers—one twelfth and one quarter of the men on their delinquent lists, respectively. The state auditor, however, seems to have realized quickly that many sheriffs were not actually holding auctions of free black men's labor. The auditor's office candidly advised one sheriff to "go through all the forms of *trying to hire out*" even dead men and nonresidents in order to satisfy the letter of the law; those "forms" involved procuring a formal court order and posting a list of delinquents at the courthouse.[119]

Why did county officials expend so much energy drawing up these long lists of delinquents if they had no plans to round up and hire out the free blacks whose names appeared there? Doing so allowed them to document to Richmond their technical compliance with the law. Moreover, county officials did want free blacks (and whites) to pay their taxes, and did devote effort trying to collect; that explains the late payments received from some black individuals after delinquent lists were drawn up. Just as important, however, the sheriff and his deputies received the same amount in commission for each tax "insolvent" they listed as they did for a man who actually paid.[120]

A dollar or two in commissions, combined with a reasonable devotion to duty and some pressure from Richmond, could motivate a deputy sheriff to compose a list of a few dozen names—but actually to round up and auction off and keep track of the forced labor of so many men would have been spectacularly unrewarding for that deputy. Bidding out a hundred men a year, had it ever been attempted, would have become an undertaking of almost epic proportions. Free blacks understood how little desire the sheriff had to hire them out; many of them called the state's bluff by simply not paying taxes. In fact, the sheriffs showed little zeal for wrangling over unpaid revenues with men of modest means, white or black. Deputies frequently certified that delinquents of both races had no property at all that the county could seize to cover their obligations, though that cannot have been true. The county court also proved ready to issue tax exemptions to incapacitated free blacks.[121] In the end, Prince Edward County pretty much settled for receiving tax revenue "from each according to his ability"—and his willingness—to pay.

Local officials' habit of not hiring out tax delinquents affected free black residents of the county in two contradictory ways. On the one hand, to have enforced the hiring-out laws or collected the discriminatory head tax in those years it was levied would have been tyrannical and exploitative; nonenforcement provided some economic relief to many free blacks. On the other hand, the mere act of listing free blacks as subject to hiring out may have undermined the reputation for ambition and entrepreneurial spirit that some in the race had won. Even when the hirings out of free Afro-Virginians were fictitious, deputies copied the names of black nonpayers onto a list, which they were supposed to display on the courthouse door. This was no honor. Free blacks were damned if they paid and damned if they did not. To pay taxes that one had no say in imposing was to acquiesce in patent injustice, and the race-based specific tax of the 1810s and the 1850s was doubly odious. But to take advantage of the system's flexibility was to risk labeling oneself a pauper or a scofflaw or both. The effect may have been a little like that of slaves taking small amounts of masters' property, calculating that the white man would wink at the loss: a bondperson justifiably expropriated a fraction of the remuneration that slavery denied him or her, yet in doing so reinforced the master's belief in the slave's moral inferiority.[122]

The reluctance of many blacks to pay taxes in the 1840s may have arisen partly from the difficult economic times that free Afro-Virginians, like everyone else, faced during the years after 1837. White and free black people on the economy's sidelines experienced life's hardships in some of the same ways, and at times drew similar responses from the better-off. In particular, authorities who allotted public aid to the poor tended to classify people by their economic condition and their perceived character as much as by their race. The county's efforts to help the needy even brought blacks and whites together physically.

Before the county opened its poorhouse at the state's behest in 1827, it helped the poor either directly or by compensating better-off citizens who had spent their own funds to feed, care for, or bury poor people. Some of this aid went to free blacks.[123] One white man received $20 a year when he provided care to Jethro Forgason in the mid-1820s; the man also attended to four poor white women. During the same period, the overseers of the poor furnished food and supplies to free black Esther Young and her husband.[124] The board approved other aid to blacks over the years ranging from food to a wool hat; it provided coffins and burials for a number of free blacks—seven of them in the peak year of 1860. A few years before that, John White, the free black boatman and Farmville lot owner, had received compensation for a shroud and burial he provided, probably for a poor fellow black man. In some instances, blacks received aid in large amounts: one free black woman in 1856 got $30 for house rent, firewood, board, nursing, and finally a coffin; aged former Randolph slave Zack Ellis was awarded almost that much a few years later, and the county allotted $100 to the care of a single free black man during a period of illness and insanity in 1860.[125]

No particular stigma attached to poor people who received aid at their places of residence—pity, perhaps, but no opprobrium. More than a few female recipients of such assistance still merited the titles Miss and Mrs.; officials did not apply the honorifics to free black women (nor to all whites), but the white widow of free black James Dungey still qualified as "Mrs. Dungy" when the overseers awarded $11 for her medical care in 1829–30.[126]

Too few free blacks received public assistance to provide ammunition for the race's detractors. Blacks sometimes furnished aid to one another without any monetary support from the county. Occasionally, such arrangements became formalized, as when Edmund Young's son Ned became guardian of a girl named Patsey, perhaps a niece of his, with Edmund's backing in 1826.[127] Some blacks received money from the overseers of the poor not in the form of charity but as pay for work or goods they rendered to the board. A slave sold corn, fodder, and a day and a half's work to the overseers in 1828; several black midwives delivered babies for poor people at county expense. In 1858–60, more than twenty years after two overseers of the poor proposed in vain to expel Nathan Homes's family from the county, he earned good money making shoes to fill orders placed by that same county board.[128]

After 1827, the poorhouse concentrated in one place a category of poor people who by and large enjoyed little respect from their fellow citizens. Officials never applied honorific titles to inmates of the new institution. John Foster, shoemaking entrepreneur and longtime secretary of Prince Edward's overseers of the poor, wrote that the "worthy" impoverished would do without any aid at all rather than "consent & go to live at the poor or work house."[129]

The poorhouse's founding principles required it to sustain itself economically, or nearly so. Inmates would grow their own vegetables, and would produce corn and some tobacco to earn income for the institution. At first, the residents even had to make their own clothing out of a dollar's worth of materials provided to each of them annually. James McDearmon, who supervised the opening of the poorhouse, proclaimed that, for anyone not working up to his or her ability, "Bread and water [was] the Penalty!" Rules forbade drinking "ardent spirits" except on doctor's orders.[130]

The poorhouse averaged about fourteen inmates at any given time during its first year.[131] In the 1840s and 1850s, for which fuller records survive, the yearly population fluctuated between that level and as many as thirty-six residents, the average during the 1850s being somewhere in the twenties. The number of black inmates ranged between two and six. A few of these black residents were free people, but others were enslaved. Well-established norms called for masters to provide care for elderly and ailing bondpeople. Yet occasionally a master would cast an infirm slave adrift, sometimes on the pretense of "freeing" him or her; county authorities fought this practice, and a person guilty of it could face a substantial fine. Nevertheless, by the 1850s one or more enslaved blacks lived in the poorhouse in almost any particular year.[132]

Black and white residents of the institution worked under the same rules. Whites were as likely as blacks to be sent out to tend the fields, and blacks as likely as whites to spin and sew or to be excused from work owing to age or infirmity—blacks who came to the institution tended to be elderly or sick.[133] Inmates of the two races apparently spent much of their time side by side, and not only during working hours. If the poorhouse complex was completed according to the original plan, it consisted of the steward's pleasant frame house—the one Edmund Young was accused and acquitted of having burned down—as well as a series of hewn-log buildings: a smokehouse, a corn storage house, a stable, and three residences for inmates. The living quarters were small; each house in the plan measured sixteen feet square on the outside, and each was divided into two rooms downstairs and two up. Every room had two windows, a fireplace, and jointed plank floors; each downstairs room had its own door.[134]

That setup would have made it possible to segregate black and white sleeping quarters. Documents of the time say nothing about whether race affected room assignments, though they do reveal that black and white inmates dined together. The institution's "little code of bye laws" dictated that "one common table shall be kept for all to eat at, who are able to go to it." The president of the overseers may have painted too rosy a picture when he wrote that "the Paupers, with a few trevial exceptions [were] well satisfy'd" after nearly a year of operation—but there is no evidence that the policy of blacks and whites eating together caused any trouble. In fact, unsegregated facilities seem to have existed in some other county poorhouses in Virginia as well.[135]

The county continued to aid poor individuals who lived outside the poorhouse, and it provided certain specific accommodations for ailing whites and blacks. Space for new inmates rarely became available in the state's two mental hospitals; the insane whom the county boarded locally at considerable expense included two free black men. One was quartered in the county jail, the other apparently on a white citizen's premises.[136] In 1836 and 1837, the county spent more than $1,000 building a two-room smallpox hospital between Israel Hill and Farmville and treating four patients, one of them a free black man. In outbreaks over the next two decades, the county again covered treatment of victims both black and white. It paid to vaccinate some twenty women and children in 1854; a dozen of those people, including two children of Israelite Susan White, were free blacks.[137]

By that year, local authorities had long since abandoned the idealistic pretensions of the poorhouse movement. The institution had become, with only rare exceptions, a facility for destitute women and the children that some brought with them; some inmates declined to work, and the facility came nowhere near sustaining itself.[138] Now more than ever, officials and citizens saw the mostly white denizens of the poorhouse much as Colonel Madison had once viewed the county's free black population—as a mostly degenerate lot, a very few of whom surprised observers by demonstrating some industry and capacity for self-improvement. No surviving record deprecates the character of any black resident of the poorhouse; one free black inmate, Judith Forgason, even managed to recover from a mental "derangement" of some years and to work fairly regularly in 1854–55. Meanwhile, officials disparaged certain white inmates who allegedly proved "unmanageable" or "too lazy to work," or who "did nothing but [sit] & sleep."[139] As happened so often in Prince Edward, the behavior and demeanor of flesh-and-blood people were nibbling away at the society's racial preconceptions.

Shortly thereafter, however, the poorhouse became the setting for a sad final act in the life of one Afro-Virginian. Priscy Bowman's moment on the sheriff's auction block had been followed by years of stable existence with her husband, Phil, the miller. When he died, Priscy continued living at the Venables' place, her needs met by the fund he had left for her benefit. But then it turned out that Phil's mother, Fanny Bowman, was still alive—and Fanny saw an opportunity to contest her son's legacy of nearly $300. The mother-in-law filed suit against James Venable, brother of the man who had helped Phil buy his wife. Priscy had never been formally manumitted; she remained technically James Venable's slave. Fanny Bowman's lawyer argued that Priscy, being property herself, could not legally *inherit* property. Fanny, as a free woman of color and mother of the deceased Phil, claimed to be the sole heir to his small fortune.

As a strict matter of law, Fanny Bowman was probably right. But the circuit court in Prince Edward struggled to find some way it could honor the wishes of Phil Bowman and of his former employers, the Venables, who still supported Bowman's will energetically. James Venable had already drawn on Phil's accumulated assets to provide a mourning cloak and black silk bonnet for Priscy and to hire a slave woman to take care of her during an illness of two months. The court now appointed a commissioner to gauge Priscy Bowman's probable needs in the coming years; the panel's clear goal was to see those needs met somehow. The court's time-consuming investigation allowed Priscy to continue living off Phil's endowment for the time being—and then Fanny Bowman resolved the judge's dilemma by dying before her suit could be decided.[140]

Priscy Bowman lived on at the Venables' for another decade. By 1854, James Venable was applying to the overseers of the poor for help in taking care of her, and the board obliged him with money that year and the next.[141] Undoubtedly, the fund that Phil Bowman had left behind, generous though it was, had run out after all those years, and it was only prudent for Venable to request a subsidy. What Venable did next, though, puts him in a different moral light: he sent Priscy Bowman to live at the poorhouse in 1856. Years earlier, when Fanny Bowman had sued to win Phil's cash, morality and self-interest had both pushed James Venable in the same direction. By defeating Fanny's brazen money grab, he defended the will of his late black employee—and also avoided having to care for Priscy at his own expense; he had done good even as he had done well. Now, all those years later, he apparently followed his pocketbook and sent Priscy Bowman packing. Priscy died at the poorhouse a little more than two years later, in January 1859, still technically a slave as she had been all her life. At least she had been exempted from labor at the county facility owing to her age.[142]

The death of Priscy Bowman closed out a long life punctuated by unforeseen twists. Her biography exposes the ravages of slavery—the institution that put Priscy up for auction, gave an avaricious free black mother-in-law grounds to try to disinherit her, and ultimately, it seems, made James Venable feel entitled to jettison her. But Priscy's story also encompasses love that bore up under slavery's stresses, and empathy that crossed the racial divide; once upon a time, after all, the Venables had lent Phil Bowman the money to buy his wife. Priscy's narrative even features a court of law attempting to defend the fruits of black striving rather than observe the letter of the law.

Finally, the scene of Priscy Bowman's last months, the poorhouse, embodies the ambivalence toward poverty that pervaded this society of ambitious people and largely transcended color. That worldview combined a measure of goodwill toward the upright or "deserving" poor, white and black, with disdain for the "idle" of either race. Underlying it all was society's assumption that people of either color, unless struck down by ill-fortune, could and should be about the business of advancing themselves economically and morally.

THE WISDOM OF SOLOMON

The story of Phil and Priscy Bowman conveys two fateful truths about citizens, public officials, worldviews, and behavior in Prince Edward

County and in the rural Old South generally. First, it was mainly the county institutions that affected the daily lives of people in this localistic rural society; any history that concentrates chiefly on enactments by state legislatures and pronouncements in the urban press is sure to leave out much of the story. Second, for better or worse, most people of both races felt their way along day by day rather than behave according to any particular ideological prescription. Phil Bowman did that, and so did James Venable. So did Major John Rice, and even Colonel James Madison when he was not writing for publication.

In our modern society, the institutions that govern us often seem remote and impersonal. In the countryside of the Old South, the varied, sometimes befuddled individuals one dealt with face-to-face in a variety of ways included the very officials who could make or break a person's day—or alter his or her entire life. Shared moral standards, cultural norms, and economic dealings, along with the human empathy these helped produce, could smooth relations among black and white people.

But slavery, too, remained an entrenched part of the local and regional culture. From time to time, a jury—that institution designed to encompass a range of freeholding white male sentiment—found itself called on to weigh something fundamental: a particular black person's claim to freedom itself. When that happened, jurors could display both openness to the notion of liberty for black individuals and persistent skepticism, even hostility, toward that idea. The most dramatic display of broadmindedness by jurors in Prince Edward County came in 1814, when a panel in the superior court granted liberty to a group of about forty slaves of a single estate. Some of those bondpeople showed no physical signs of non-African ancestry, yet the group persuaded the court that they were descended in part from an American Indian woman who had been improperly enslaved in the remote colonial past. The Evans family, who hitched up their wagon and traveled to Kentucky with the white Bookers, were part of this newly emancipated group.[143]

The will of Thomas Baldwin, a local man whose death closely followed that of Richard Randolph, produced a more ambiguous result for an enslaved youth named Jacob. Possibly drawing on Methodist convictions, Baldwin had called for his half-dozen slaves to go free at age twenty-five. But when Jacob reached that age, he discovered that his name had been mistakenly omitted from the list of those destined for emancipation, drawn up as Baldwin lay dying. He secured the help of an able attorney and assembled white witnesses who supported his cause, including the lawyer who had drafted Baldwin's emancipatory will years earlier. Virginia law required that a court give permission before a slave could sue for his or her freedom. Prince Edward's justices readily did so and paid Jacob's costs in pursuing the case.[144]

Baldwin's survivors seem to have allowed Jacob to live essentially as a free man beginning at some early stage of the litigation; Jacob may have persisted in court mainly to ensure that no Baldwin heir would come out of the woodwork later and claim to own him. Yet in the courtroom, Jacob won only a series of hung juries—eight of them between 1824 and 1838.[145] Obviously, some white jurors found his cause morally valid and kept it alive from one retrial to the next, even if his emancipation had not followed the letter of the law. Other members of a whole succession of juries, however, may have believed that a verdict supporting Jacob would encourage other blacks to claim that their masters had intended to set them free.

The phonetically spelled will in which Thomas Ford freed his slaves and left money to resettle them in the North produced a legal drama of its own during the same years Jacob's case made its way through the system. When Thomas Ford died in 1830, his brother Hezekiah wanted Thomas's property for himself; Colonel Charles Woodson at one point accused the greedy brother of having concealed or destroyed Thomas's will. Once the testament was revealed, Hezekiah challenged its validity and persuaded the county court to put his brother's slaves at least temporarily under his own control. He immediately began making good money hiring them out to others.[146] At almost the same moment, though, Thomas Ford's slaves filed suit to defend their late master's wishes and their own right to be free. The bondpeople had no trouble finding lawyers who would press their case vigorously. Prince Edward's county court permitted them to do so, and a steady stream of subpoenas went out to witnesses whom the slaves wanted to call from places as distant as Lynchburg.[147]

There were no witnesses to the testament Thomas Ford had laboriously written out. And now the Nat Turner drama unfolded—a train of events that could have stiffened people's resolve to keep all slaves under firm white control. Yet the same Prince Edward County Court that would soon confiscate free blacks' weapons required two crucial white witnesses from Charlotte County to testify on the Ford slaves' behalf. Just days after Nat Turner himself was arrested, both those men swore that they knew Thomas Ford's handwriting well, and that the emancipatory will was authentic. The court accepted and recorded the document.[148] To make Hezekiah Ford actually set them free, the slaves pursued their lawsuit against him for false imprisonment. That case eventually came to trial in March 1834. Harry, a tiny man in his sixties, was the eldest of the enslaved group, and he became the lead plaintiff against Hezekiah. After the Turner revolt, Virginia's House of Delegates had expressed a wish—never backed up by coercive laws or substantial funding—that free Afro-Virginians emigrate. Harry and his fellow slaves now asked a jury of whites in Prince Edward to add them to the free black population that the General Assembly had hoped would conveniently vanish.[149]

The panel that heard Harry's plea included two men who clearly saw free and enslaved blacks as potential troublemakers and decried their fellow whites' laxity toward Afro-Virginians. One juror had complained immediately after the Nat Turner rebellion that ex-New Yorker Otis Williams had permitted an "unlawful assemblage of Free Negroes & mulattos" at his house; years after the Ford manumission suit, the formal complaint against Dr. Benjamin Rice for having sponsored a festive slave wedding would apparently come from the same man. Another juror had charged a neighbor a few years earlier with having allowed a slave to "go at large" and hire himself out.[150]

But other jurors brought different perspectives to the panel's deliberations. John Tuggle, who lived only about three miles west of Israel Hill, administered Phil White Sr.'s estate; Israelite Isham Patterson had named Tuggle to execute his will. Reuben Seay would soon become, along with Phil and Sam White, a charter member of Farmville Baptist Church; the congregation was already organizing at the time Seay heard Harry and company bid to join the Whites in freedom. Another Baptist juror, a minister, had sat as a justice on the called court that acquitted Edmund Young of arson at the new county poorhouse in 1827. One panelist apparently had done business with Hercules White Sr. The same man would be convicted a month after his jury service of trading with a slave without the master's consent.[151]

A couple of citizens on the panel had had free Afro-Virginian families living and working on their land, and the shoemaking entrepreneur John Foster employed free black apprentices. Juror Branch O. Scott had been a neighbor of the free black Homes family for years; as a county overseer of the poor, he would soon arrange an apprenticeship with a white blacksmith for Milly Homes's grandson.[152] Not many months after this jury deliberated the fate of Thomas Ford's bondpeople, Colonel Madison would declare free black poverty an axiom and use it to prove African Americans' supposed unfitness for freedom. But Branch Scott knew the

Homeses' industriousness. He and John Foster also understood full well that there was a system in place to prepare less fortunate young people, including free blacks, for productive roles in the economy: that system was apprenticeship, and Scott himself helped run it.

For jurors such as Tuggle, Seay, Foster, and Scott, the free Afro-Virginian population that Harry and the other Ford slaves now demanded to join was part of the natural order of things, not some looming, faceless menace. Yet if John Tuggle's friendship with free blacks led him to exert a moderating influence on the jury, he gained credibility because his peers knew him to be "solid" on questions of slavery and of law and order. Like some of the other jurors, he had ridden on slave patrols in his younger days, and he or his father had borne witness against Susannah Short when that free black woman sold liquor without a license some twenty years before. When Tuggle joined this particular jury, he owned or controlled as a trustee some thirty slaves, and he was steadily adding to their number.[153]

These twelve jurors found themselves unable to agree on a verdict in the case of Harry and company against Hezekiah Ford.[154] Biases like those of the two relative hard-liners may explain that outcome, for Thomas Ford's will freeing Harry and the other slaves had been declared genuine before the panel even deliberated. Still, if the jurors failed to unite around the proposition that a recognized will should be carried out, they also reached no consensus that the plaintiffs' race or station in life should condemn them to a life in slavery.

Harry and his fellow plaintiffs would have to make their case before a new jury in August 1834. Again, the jurors who served brought a mixed bag of impressions and biases to the case. Three jurors were repeaters from the first trial, including the two who were so inclined to complain of other whites' laxity toward free and enslaved blacks. To complicate matters, another panelist, entrepreneur George King, was the very man who had offended one of those hard-liners by letting a certain slave hire himself out.[155] As in the first trial, at least half the jurors had had significant direct experience with free blacks or with issues of black liberty. Absalom Dungey—mulatto son of a white mother and husband of a white wife—had given a deed of trust on his land to one of the jurors a few years earlier, and then quickly paid it off. At least one juror had employed a free black apprentice; a number had sat on earlier juries that heard Joe Homes's assault suit against Littleberry Royall, or Israelite John Brown's trial for assault against his neighbor Hampton Giles, or the plea of the slave Jacob to have his liberty recognized.[156]

As a deputy sheriff for many years, Samuel Allen would find himself instantly disqualified from jury duty today, yet in 1834 he could sit in the jury box even after serving papers on Hezekiah Ford in this very suit.[157] His official duties ensured that Allen knew Prince Edward's blacks, both enslaved and free, perhaps better than any other member of the panel. Allen had seized and sold many a slave at sheriff's auctions. He had played an official role in each stage of the feud between Hampton Giles and John Brown. He knew in detail Hercules White Sr.'s character as a man of substance and drive, having administered White's estate for some years.[158]

The Ford slaves' fate now lay in the hands of a panel that included at least two potentially unsympathetic men and a number of others whose real-life experience could have pushed them in various directions. The earlier acts in the legal drama had demonstrated two things. First, legality did matter. The county court had declared Thomas Ford's emancipatory will genuine. Then, in the first trial, at least one juror—and possibly as many as eleven—had concluded that that will must be carried out. But the hung jury had taught a second lesson: the future of Ford's twenty-one slaves would ultimately depend on whether a full dozen propertied white men of Prince Edward County (not five or six, or even eleven) could overcome their society's ideological bias against black freedom.

This second jury did not deadlock. Indeed, the twelve men reached a Solomonic decision. Those who use that term as a simple synonym for "wise" forget their Bible. King Solomon's actual decree in the dispute between two women, each of whom claimed the same child as her own, was in fact viciously absurd: to cut the child in two and give one half to each self-proclaimed mother. The wisdom of that barbaric verdict lay in the aftermath that the king anticipated: Solomon identified as the real mother the woman who spurned his compromise, offering to forgo her claim to the baby rather than see it butchered.

The verdict of the second Prince Edward jury resembled that of Solomon, minus the king's hidden purpose: the twelve declared that *freedom* was divisible—that that blessing was due to some of Ford's slaves but not to others. The jury decided that those slaves whom Thomas Ford had named individually in his will should indeed "recover their freedom" and the costs they had incurred in suing Hezekiah Ford. Since those people had rightfully been free since Thomas Ford's death and the proving of his will in 1830, the four children born to them since Ford's passing were therefore free as well. But what of the enslaved children born during the years after Ford wrote his will—and therefore not mentioned in that document—but before his death put his testament into effect? The jury declared that the seven children in that group who survived in 1834 were "not free persons, but slaves."[159]

Three Afro-Virginian women, awarded their long-promised freedom, now faced a bitter choice, as had the true mother who came before King Solomon. They could exercise their liberty by moving away from their erstwhile oppressor and thus from their children, or they could ask Hezekiah Ford to let them remain as free persons alongside their enslaved offspring. Slaveholders in Prince Edward knew as well as anyone that most black mothers, like white ones, would not willingly live apart from their sons and daughters.

The slaves had sued Hezekiah Ford not just for their freedom but for $12,000 in damages (which they eventually reduced to $5,000) for having kept them in captivity. Here, too, the jury was of more than one mind. Having recognized the freedom of two thirds of the plaintiffs, some jurors had wanted to award damages to those fourteen people—but others evidently dissented. The jury foreman started to enter the amount of a proposed award as he wrote out the verdict, but stopped in the midst of recording the dollar figure and scratched it out. Perhaps the hard-liners prevailed at the last moment. In the end, the monetary award to Harry and the other thirteen victorious blacks was a token 1 cent.[160]

There may be a less cynical explanation for the lack of compensation to the ex-slaves. Hezekiah Ford apparently had few means other than those he had taken over from his late brother. Thomas Ford himself had supposedly exhausted most of his assets other than the slaves themselves between the time he wrote his will and his death years afterward. One of the ex-slaves later recalled that there had been no money left to resettle the newly liberated people in a free state, as Thomas had called for so insistently. Prince Edward's officialdom—embarrassed, perhaps, at what Ford's former slaves had had to put up with—at least did not enforce the legal requirement that freed blacks leave the state within a year: the newly emancipated fourteen registered as free residents of the county.[161]

Had the decision regarding Harry and the other Ford slaves been the product of a single mind—of an individual judge—one could say it proves little more than that the law, as Dickens's Mr. Bumble had it, "is a ass—a idiot." But this verdict was hammered out by twelve men, whose differences are reflected both in the mixed decision itself and in the last-minute altering of the damage award. Men who held slaves, yet felt comfortable among free Afro-Virginians and had formed the habit of judging them as individuals, may well have compromised with others (perhaps only one man or two) who opposed black freedom on principle. The earlier jury had divided irreconcilably along similar lines, as the three alumni of that body who now sat on the second panel may have reminded their colleagues. Some jurors who voted to free Thomas Ford's slaves may have done so mainly to vindicate the absolute right of a slaveholder to dispose of his property as he saw fit—even if that meant emancipating black people. But for other members of the two panels, the specific seems to have altered the contours of the general: the day-to-day history of the black Israelites and of the other free Afro-Virginians who lived in the county sanded some of the sharp edges off the prevailing white supremacist worldview.[162]

White people in Prince Edward County lived amid tension between a fundamental idea, the supposed inferiority of blacks, and a concrete reality: that each race contained an infinite variety of people, and that affinities of culture, interest, and affection could cross racial lines. The outcomes of this tension varied endlessly. By 1840, they included Richard Randolph's bequest, the rise of Israel Hill, and Colonel Madison's attack on both; the actions of emancipators such as Thomas Ford and of people who tried to subvert their wishes; the successes and travails of Edmund Young and Phil Bowman; brotherhood and racial inequality at Sharon and Farmville Baptist Churches; the threat to auction off free black tax delinquents and the quiet decision not to carry out that threat. The contradiction between the governing racist ideal and the impulse to treat people as people crystallized in the contrast between Virginia's web of anti–free black laws and the actual practices of many white Virginians.

For most white Northerners in the 1830s (or in the 1930s, for that matter), race was mainly an idea, the black man an abstraction, though a deeply evocative one. That held true both for racists, who did their best to exclude and segregate a group they knew next to nothing about, and for many antislavery people as well. For white Southerners, too, black people constituted an idea. That idea encompassed the claim of white racial superiority, along with worries about disorder and resistance among blacks; it justified slavery; it produced antimanumission laws, special taxes, and disabilities imposed on free blacks. But for Southern whites, African Americans both slave and free were also, vividly and unavoidably, a set of individuals.

Paradoxically, the very loopholes, the myriad personal and institutional exceptions, that permeated the system of white domination reveal how entrenched that hegemony was. Had whites not felt secure in their control of society, they would not have behaved so flexibly. White Virginians never did relax, even slightly, the barriers in some areas—the vote, participation on juries, and militia service (though bending the last of these, as we shall see, became at least thinkable during the crisis of the Union in 1861).

Whites in Prince Edward County, and probably in much of Virginia, repeatedly showed that they could be just as fair to a black Virginian, especially a free one, as they chose to be. And at least toward free blacks, many chose to be fairer than we typically think, more often than we think. Those who indict whites in the slaveholding South for denying that blacks were human make a needlessly weak case, and an unhistorical one. The real shame of the Old South was that white people recognized the humanity of blacks in dozens of ways every day, yet kept them in bondage or second-class citizenship despite that knowledge.

Blacks, too, made choices. Such flexibility as white individuals and institutions showed came about in no small part because of black accomplishment and assertiveness, and the wisdom that told black folk what forms of self-assertion would or would not benefit them. The Randolph freedpeople chose the hardships of clearing farms for themselves over the secure niche as hired servants and craftspeople that their liberal former mistress, Judith Randolph, offered some of them. Ben Short, Patty Bartlett, the Homeses, and others preferred to possess their own plots of land, however small, rather than attach themselves to a white planter, however benevolent he might be.

All the while, black Virginians enjoyed the distinctive aspects of their own rich, sometimes exuberant culture, as Dr. Smith discovered at the persimmon beer dance. Yet simple practicality required frequent contact between blacks and whites, and beyond that there was much—religion, speech patterns, understandings of nature and the cosmos, and notions of how to get ahead—that drew white and black in the same direction. All this would remain true during the quarter century just preceding the Civil War, even as dramatic changes came to the economy and demography of Prince Edward County.

Kindred cultures and common beliefs could bring people together despite differences in color; clashing values could drive apart those who belonged to the same race. Whatever affected personal interactions also shaped the behavior of local institutions. And so it happened that a society predicated on racial subordination never became as ruthlessly discriminatory toward its free black members as it repeatedly proclaimed itself to be.

CHAPTER 8

Progress and Struggle

FOR RICHER, FOR POORER

Twenty-five years separated Colonel Madison's opening salvo against Israel Hill from the bombardment of Fort Sumter. That quarter century brought economic and social change to Prince Edward County: boom, depression, recovery, another recession, the coming of the railroad. Free Afro-Virginian men became prominent in local commerce, and a new cohort of black men and women bought lots of their own in the growing town of Farmville. During the latter years of the period, the impending crisis of the American Union kindled suspicions among whites about some of their free black neighbors, and led proslavery writers to parade the myth of Israel Hill's degeneracy before the entire nation. Yet local organs of government and of justice continued to hear and heed the voices of free blacks, and some whites still expressed moral qualms about owning human beings.

Technological innovations infiltrated many realms of life in Prince Edward, and especially in Farmville. Henry Y. Jenkins, the town's foremost blacksmith, produced more and more nuts and bolts along with old standbys such as nails, spikes, and chain links for batteaux; a foundry was built in Farmville not far from the Appomattox.[1] The use of machines, though spreading, was not integral to the definition of a "factory" in antebellum Farmville, as the tobacco industry proved. Facilities did not specialize in one phase of making a product, but rather incorporated several stages of production within their own walls. Farmville could boast a "boot and shoe factory" in the 1830s; a "Coach Factory" built its product in the traditional way, and a tailoring business in the town employed six men and one woman in 1850.[2]

By the mid-1830s, Farmville had a population of about eight hundred. A somewhat excitable observer called the place "one of the finest towns in proportion to its size and commerce in Virginia"; the same authority ranked the town as Virginia's fourth largest tobacco market, handling half a million dollars a year, and as the best in quality. Merchants in Farmville now purchased goods at wholesale from as far away as New York City; sometimes Colonel Madison even ordered "Negro Clothing" from there. The owner of the local coach factory felt ready by the 1850s to try selling vehicles from a New Haven company, while tobacco manufacturers in Farmville increasingly sold their products through "commission-merchants in the northern cities."[3]

Prince Edward and the surrounding counties were still predominantly agricultural. The area's industries largely processed its staple crops, tobacco and wheat, and business establishments could buy provisions fresh from local farms and plantations. Agriculture in central and eastern Virginia remained wedded to slavery; many masters still paid slaves for special tasks or for goods and services that the bondpeople produced on their own time.[4]

Meanwhile, as always, whites of Prince Edward sold slaves to the region that Virginians called "the South," or moved there with their bondpeople. Those locals who sought to market blacks in the Cotton Kingdom tried to accommodate "southern judgment and taste"—devoting "great attention," for example, to the "person, appearance and manners" of those marketed as body or house servants. To "pay Millener bills for 'fitting out' negro girls for sale" in New Orleans was considered a "usual" expense, as was up to $15 worth of new clothes per young woman. Slaves, male and female, could easily sell for between 20 and 50 percent more "in the South" than they would have in Virginia.[5]

Factory owners in Farmville relied heavily on black, mostly enslaved labor. The crucial tobacco industry even retained some of the artifacts and working vocabulary of plantation slavery. At the town's warehouses, where local growers' tobacco was inspected—there were two such houses in the 1830s—potential buyers of raw leaf were summoned to auctions by a black man blowing a horn of much the same type used on plantations to signal starting and quitting time. A building that housed African American "stemmers" and "twisters" who processed the tobacco was denoted "a negro quarter," just as on the plantation, and whites who supervised the work of black men and women in the factories were known as "overseers."[6] Factories employed a few additional white men in clerical or supervisory jobs. At least some of them, like plantation overseers, worked under annual contracts and received room and board from the owner. The proprietor might well live at or next to his factory; in one instance, black hands twisted tobacco regularly in the lower room of their employer's dwelling.[7]

Some factory owners shunted people back and forth between industrial and agricultural work. An overseer for a planter who also manufactured tobacco in town reported in the early 1840s that "sometimes the hand from the Mill & sometimes some hands from the Factory cultivated the crop."[8] Gradually, though, a recognizable category of "factory slaves" came into being. Masters worried that extended exposure to factory and town life could corrupt slaves. One man in 1833 "considered the temptation [to unruliness] greater in Farmvile," and remarked that he "would prefer hiring [out] negroes of my own in the country if I could have obtained as fair prices as in Farmvile and as good masters." But this was no longer possible, for even by that early date the hire paid for slaves "running the River, and working in Tobacco Factories . . . [was] much higher than for Farming purposes."[9]

Like industrialists of other eras, Farmville's manufacturers dreamt of holding down the costs of labor and raw materials by reducing competition among themselves—but they dreamt in vain. The addition of two new factories to the town in 1836–37 aggravated the scarcity of skilled black labor there—the $100 annual hire of "experienced labourers" rose by 25 to 50 percent during that single winter—and a similar trend affected the entire state of Virginia.[10] The rise in annual hires did not profit enslaved laborers directly, for the money went to the white people who owned them. Free workers, by contrast, received their own pay and therefore reaped the benefits of the tight labor market; a number of free blacks, especially younger folk from Israel Hill and elsewhere, gravitated to the factories of Farmville. Slavery prevented the rise of a working class in the modern sense, but the factories did foster a commonality of experience and a certain solidarity of feeling among free and enslaved black workers. More and more slaves lived at factories or in housing provided by employers in Farmville, far from the abodes of their own masters; free black fellow workers resided and socialized among them.[11] Some whites in Virginia's larger towns and in the cities worried that these new arrangements might breed disorder or awaken dreams of freedom among factory slaves.

One encounter among black workers in Farmville in 1858 illustrates the kinds of changes that factory life had helped to produce by then. John Morris Roberts of Lynchburg complained before a county justice in Prince Edward that a local free black man, Nathan (Nat) Artis, a factory worker and sometime boatman, had cut him with a knife. Roberts, who himself had worked in a factory, had been living among free and enslaved black laborers in Farmville; most people considered him a mulatto. Yet a lawman in Farmville had also noticed Roberts drinking with a white man. Roberts had shown to others of both races a court document from his home town certifying that he was not black; a state law of 1833 exempted certain people of racially mixed ancestry from the legal disabilities that applied to free Afro-Virginians.

The discord between Roberts and Artis had begun while they played cards with a group of men in the room of a slave named Joshua Mottley. Witnesses said the group had agreed "that if any white man came" Mottley should create a diversion—he was to "play the fiddle & make them believe [he] was playing for [his black friends'] amusement." Neither the men's gambling nor Nathan Artis's alleged attack on Roberts had posed a threat to any white person. Yet testimony at Artis's trial—at which he was acquitted—depicted a society of free blacks and slaves, some of them recent arrivals from larger cities as distant as Lynchburg, Danville, and Petersburg, living at close quarters and spending off-hours together on a particular "back Street" in Farmville. Those black men gambled illegally, devised methods to evade detection by the authorities, and viewed almost "any white man" as a potential enforcer.

The men appeared to share a culture: much of the testimony revolved around black men playing the fiddle for gatherings of their peers. They had shown themselves capable of violence, at least toward one another. One central figure in the Artis case, Joshua Mottley, was a slave whom everyone routinely referred to by a given name and surname, and who may well have been hiring himself out; another key player was a person of ambiguous racial identity. All in all, the scene painted at the Artis trial crystallized what some whites had long imagined when they contemplated urbanization and factory work under a system that relied on black labor.[12]

Even so, many leading people in Farmville maintained good relations with free Afro-Virginians throughout the quarter century that preceded the Civil War. Ben Robertson, for example, owned a tobacco factory—he had even been Colonel Madison's partner—yet he remained a friend of Israel Hill's White family.

Prosperity may have helped ease people's minds during the years leading up to 1837. Farmville went through two of its periodic boundary expansions between 1834 and 1836, and newly laid out lots sold briskly. The county court had built a modest-sized but visually imposing new home for itself early in the decade; the main chamber of the new courthouse boasted a fourteen-foot ceiling adorned with an Ionic lintel cor-

In Prince Edward County's new courthouse, built in 1832, free blacks continued to file lawsuits and defend themselves against civil actions and the occasional criminal prosecution.

(Bradshaw, *History of Prince Edward County*, PLATE IV)

nice, and the county justices ordered armchairs all the way from New
York City.[13]

At the same time, the boom years may have amplified social distinctions among people. The county justices elevated their own bench four
and a half feet above the floor of the new court chamber, and disparities
in class and status literally followed citizens to their graves. A person's
standing in life doubtless had always helped determine his or her final
resting place, just as it did the simplicity or ornateness of the coffin. But
by the 1840s at the latest, people recognized economic differences with
striking candor: an attorney, preparing to argue a case about trespassing
on Farmville's public burying ground, casually sketched a map of the
place showing distinct sections for "rich," "poor," and "negroes."[14] Even
more striking than the physical separation of the races is the reflexive
segregation of "poor" whites from the "rich" of their own color, with no
intermediate category mentioned at all.

The catchall label "negroes" in the cemetery sketch obscured another
fact of life in Prince Edward: the marked differences in resources and sta-

tus between free and enslaved blacks, and within the former group. Specific data on consumption in Prince Edward are far too fragmentary to permit anything like a methodical comparison, but some records hint at how much better some free blacks fared materially than they would have if they had remained in slavery.

Josiah Cheadle noted Shadrach Forgason's purchases of corn meal and flour for part of the year 1834. One of the few planter-overseer contracts that spells out slaves' rations comes from the plantation of the Israelites' sometime neighbor Merit B. Allen and covers the year 1845. Forgason consumed corn meal and wheat flour in equal amounts, whereas Allen's slaves probably received only the former. In three months, Forgason bought between six and seven bushels of the two grains; divided between him and his wife, that would have amounted to more than three times the per capita ration for Allen slaves. Forgason may have shared or saved some of those provisions—but his very ability to do so, not to mention his right to exercise the option, suggests that even this not particularly

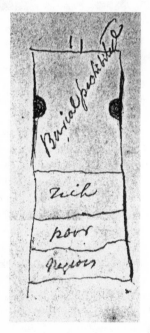

With striking candor, an attorney in the 1840s sketched a map of Farmville's cemetery showing distinct sections for "rich," "poor," and "negroes."

(*Commonwealth v. Moss*, COUNTY COURT, JUNE–AUGUST 1847, ARCHIVES RESEARCH SERVICES, LIBRARY OF VIRGINIA)

prosperous free Afro-Virginian lived a good bit more comfortably than his enslaved brother or sister.[15]

Better-off free blacks, naturally, had a still higher standard of living. A store account of Phil White Jr. for the period around 1840 shows that he bought cologne, an umbrella, silk handkerchiefs, many fabrics of various kinds including silk, a modest amount of imported cordial or liqueur—and on one occasion, 31 cents worth of whiskey. The rarity of the last two transactions suggests that the good Baptist White used the liquors for medicinal purposes or perhaps gave them as part payment to someone working for him, though the purchases at least open the possibility that he was a temperance man, not a teetotaler.[16]

Phil White seems to have possessed "the natural good taste, so remarkable in free negroes," that the English writer and traveler Harriet Martineau noticed during a visit to Alabama in 1834; yet his family, for all its prosperity, stayed friendly with a range of their neighbors on Israel Hill. In addition to the daughter who wed Guy and Mely Howard's son Sidney, two of Phil's children found spouses within the settlement between the mid-1830s and the mid-1840s.[17] Because Phil White himself had married Rose Johnston's daughter, each of these marriages united not two founding Israel Hill families but three.

For ambitious men such as Phil and Sam White, and for everyone else in Prince Edward County, the year 1837 began a long, agonizing period of economic chaos; the prosperous years just preceding that calamity came to seem almost like a parenthesis between recessions. Well into the 1840s, citizens of Prince Edward talked and wrote about "the hardness of the times" and the "grate falling off in business." "Every body seems to be pressed and failing in every direction," one local woman lamented in 1842. As late as the middle of the decade, a knowledgeable local man averred that the period since 1837 had seen "the heaviest pressure ever known in this Country."[18]

Mercantile stores, which ran extensive tabs for their customers, became casualties of the depression when clients could not pay up. Many people had used certain stores and trading companies in Farmville as substitutes for banks, depositing money there at interest; that left them vulnerable to the fortunes of those firms. Individuals saw their possessions attached by the sheriff when merchants and others, themselves desperate, sued for payment of debts. Justice John Rice of the post–Nat Turner gun confiscation joined those who declared themselves insolvent, and he headed for Missouri.[19] As usual, the white man's misfortune was the slave's disaster; scores of enslaved blacks were officially auctioned off

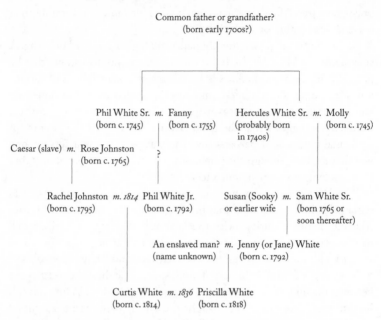

Intermarriage within Israel Hill was common enough that some couples, such as Curtis and Priscilla White, united three founding Israelite households.

to satisfy their masters' unmet obligations. Even those free Afro-Virginians who had participated only modestly in the expansion of the earlier 1830s found themselves pummeled by the hard times. Beverly Howard and Robert Giles of Israel Hill's younger generation had borrowed a total of $65 in 1835, possibly to buy a house or a batteau. By the mid-1840s, Howard and Giles's debts were added to the thousands of dollars that creditors had to write off as unrecoverable; Giles's father, Hampton, had already faced a suit over money he owed one of the local stores.[20]

The depression complicated nearly all economic relationships, yet long-standing ties between whites and free blacks generally held fast. As co-owner of a store, Merit Steger, the tobacco manufacturer, found himself in a financial pinch, and he sued to recover money that one free Afro-Virginian boatman owed him in 1838. Over the next couple of years, however, Steger also signed bail bonds for two free blacks, Sam White and Randolph Brandum, who themselves faced lawsuits.[21] Steger, perhaps hoping to buy low and sell high later, purchased two of Sam White's town lots in 1840—Sam may have sold because he needed cash to pay obligations of his own. Steger's gamble on Sam White's lots did not pan out, and he failed to pay White fully for them. After a few years of waiting, White proved for the thousandth time that litigation over money need have nothing to do with people's moral estimate of one another: he sued Steger for the balance due, but waived the requirement that the white man post bail. Steger was rapidly heading toward financial ruin; snowed under by lawsuits, he declared insolvency in 1843.[22]

The economy punished other free people of color more rudely than it seems to have done Sam White. Free blacks of modest means appear, along with a great many whites and some better-off Afro-Virginians, on local stores' lists of uncollectable debts from the depression years; most of those people owed moderate amounts. Blacks of substance naturally had more to lose. Randolph Brandum, who had owned his own boat and town lot and been creditworthy enough to borrow hundreds of dollars from whites, saw most of it vanish by 1839.[23]

Sam Strong, the boatman born just as Israel Hill was founded, had done business with Phil White and with the Israelites' white neighbor John Tuggle; the men's three-way trading had involved pine trees, backbones and heads of hogs, firewood, cabin logs, and the hauling of bricks. Like Brandum, Strong had become a boat owner. He sold a batteau and rigging to fellow free black John White not long before the depression struck. Strong had some financial trouble thereafter, but he turned out not to have peaked as early as his contemporary, Brandum. By 1850, Strong was running three batteaux, and he transported more freight than any white-owned concern in Farmville. Over the next few years, he would come into his own as an investor in real estate.[24]

John White himself, who like Strong lived in Farmville for much of his adult life, would be remembered decades later as one of the town's foremost boatmen. He transacted hundreds of dollars' worth of business in the 1840s, faced several lawsuits, at least two of them over large amounts, and saw one store list his large balance there as "Bad [or] Doubtfull" debt. Nevertheless, White apparently kept his good personal reputation and rehabilitated his creditworthiness in the mid-1840s. He faced some further setbacks at the end of the decade, yet his boating enterprise emerged in 1850 as the most lucrative in Farmville. When a now-forgotten issue prompted White to sue the Upper Appomattox Company in 1856, an all-white jury proved ready to award him nearly $250.[25]

Ben White, probably a relative of the Israelite White family, borrowed more than $100 in concert with a beleaguered white merchant in 1840, but whatever the pair hoped to accomplish did not come to pass. Ben recovered impressively. He joined John White and Sam Strong among the top five boat owners in Farmville by 1850 and took on a free black apprentice. Then he seems to have faced new reverses; he ended the decade working as a depot hand on the new South Side Railroad.[26] Meanwhile, David Bartlett's experience showed how the depression forced one person to press the next in ways that might not have happened otherwise. Bartlett had bought a batteau and rigging in 1824. The white seller proved patient: after fourteen years Bartlett still had not finished paying for the boat. But in 1838, as hard times set in, the creditor went to court to ask for the rest of his money.[27]

In the depression year of 1839, John Deneufville and Israelite Rose Johnston died, and Milly Homes followed them two years later as the hard times continued. Each of the three took care to distribute property to his or her heirs. Deneufville and Johnston left their real estate, and the former a fair amount of personal property as well. Milly Homes's legacy was more modest than Deneufville's—nine and a half acres of land near the Dupuy place, furniture, some personal possessions, and a black cow—but she made sure to take care of two surviving daughters and those of her grandchildren whose mothers were no longer alive. The two daughters proved as punctilious and formalistic as most residents of Prince Edward in staking their claim to private property: they immediately had a survey performed and a deed drawn up to divide their small parcel of inherited land into two separate tracts.[28]

The years of economic hardship evoked within the free black community the same range of cooperation and friction that they did among whites. Free Afro-Virginians still helped each other out by giving security or bail for defendants in suits over debts, as Randolph Brandum did for John White and White in turn did for one of the Bartletts.[29] At the same time, free blacks tried to collect money that their fellow Afro-Virginians owed them. As with white litigants, the process could become a game of musical chairs among financially distressed people. Sam Strong filed suit in the early 1840s to get back money that Phil and Curtis White owed him. Phil White, for his part, sued John White after years of waiting patiently for payment of rent on housing Phil owned. Meanwhile, John sued Joe Bartlett for the purchase price of a batteau.[30]

Phil White's financial career after 1837 resembles the course of many white men during those years, and it reveals a good deal about his character and personality. Having begun adult life as a boatman and farmer, White became a significant player in Farmville's economy before the depression hit. He had bought half a dozen lots by 1837, built houses on at least two of them, and resold three parcels at a profit. One part lot, on which White had built and rented out a house and a separate kitchen, fetched him a remarkable $1,500. Like virtually all investors, Phil White filed suits and saw others filed against him, often over what by his standards were modest amounts of money, or over technicalities having to do with title to property. When the white buyer of Phil's improved lot withheld $45 of the $1,500 purchase price, for example, White took legal action, and the two reached an accommodation.[31]

Farmville was built largely on the land of tortured souls—Richard and Judith Randolph—and of lunatics—St. George Randolph and Josiah Chambers. Sizable portions of those lands had been offered for sale by incompetents or worse: trustees and commissioners managed to leave ambiguous titles in the hands of dozens of purchasers, including Phil, Sam, and John White. The courts and the state legislature ultimately required some buyers who had not yet paid up to do so or surrender their lots; with money hard to come by in those depression years, Sam White gave up one of his parcels.[32] For Phil White, these complicated proceedings were an irritant. Some of them cost him attorneys' fees, and he may have had to produce back payments on earlier land purchases at a time when money was scarce.

One round of litigation had its origins in the misbehavior of Colonel Madison. When citizens bought new town lots laid out on the Chambers land that Madison administered, they signed bonds of indebtedness to cover the purchase price; the colonel then endorsed some of those notes over to his own creditors as if they were made out to him personally and not to the estate he was entrusted to shepherd. Phil White had purchased one lot, and Phil's white fellow church founder, Ben Robertson, had bought four. Colonel Madison used the bonds those two had signed to keep one of his biggest creditors at bay. When the transaction came to light after Madison's death, it sullied the reputation of the late colonel, not that of White or Robertson; "both those men"—so the legal documents referred to them—kept their lots.[33]

White people had long since come to see the White clan as regular participants in the town's economy. A man who wanted to buy a developed lot from Phil did not presume to summon him, but rather "went to him." It turned out that White had given that particular lot to his son and namesake. Philip III was only around twenty at the time, but he had grown up into an imposing brown man six feet tall, and he had inherited his father's assertiveness. When the white businessman offered $200 for the lot, Phil III's answer was firm: "he said his price was $400."[34]

The depression did take its toll on the elder Phil White as the lean years dragged on, however. The trustee of Judith Randolph's son, after waiting for some years, had to sue Phil to get $50 in rent on some land near Israel Hill—which suggests, by the way, that White was still earning part of his living by farming. Phil faced, and may have settled, two other lawsuits, one of them from a white laborer who sought payment for work and materials.[35]

White enlisted neighbor John Tuggle to sell two lots for him in 1842; in that recession year, he got only half of what he had contracted to pay for the parcels a few years earlier. Even so, Phil White remained ambitious, pouring some of his resources into the $100 building that he and his wife, Rachel, erected shortly afterward on the five acres she had inherited from her mother on Israel Hill.[36] Then the store where Phil bought food and fabric—as well as the cologne, liqueur, umbrella, and silk handkerchiefs of better times—asked him to settle his account. He could not; the merchants won a judgment against him in 1844, yet seem to have waited another five years before having it carried out. Ultimately, though, in 1849, Phil White took the oath of an insolvent debtor in regard to this particular suit; that required him to surrender part of his property to the sheriff to cover the debt to the store. He turned over one of his Farmville lots.[37] In losing only the one tract, Phil fared far better than many white defaulters.

Phil White came through the troubles of the latter 1840s with his pride intact. He attended an auction of town lots in 1850 or so, and when his old parcel came on the block, he was heard to announce "that he had a deed for that Lot[,] that he had bought it & paid for it," even if he had since lost it. But now a complication arose: although the lot White had meant to give up for sale was an undeveloped one worth perhaps $50, Phil did not specify that on the document he furnished the sheriff. The purchaser, a white merchant named Hilliard who had many dealings with free blacks, seized on the ambiguity to claim that he had bought another of Phil's lots, on which stood a weatherboarded, shingled log house; that parcel was worth $200 and could bring in $35 a year in rent. When Hilliard and a partner took over the developed lot and rented the house out to two free blacks, Phil White decided that he would have it back.

White earned the money to pay off the store account that had precipitated his troubles, and he sued Hilliard for the return of the lot and house. The circuit court judge responded with active sympathy. After finding that the facts favored White but that his filing in the case was technically flawed, the judge invited Phil to submit a new document, advised his attorney what it should contain, and then decreed that the developed lot should be returned to the black man. The decree said nothing about White's recovering five or six years' rent for the place, which would have totaled between $120 and $150—but he had stood up for his rights just as Syphax Brown, Edmund Young, and others had done years earlier, and he had seen a court vindicate him. Phil would soon sell the lot to another free Afro-Virginian, a woman of the Short family.[38] He was back in the game, if on a smaller scale than during the 1830s.

The depression proved far less harsh for Booker Jackson, the free black shoe- and bootmaker, who had already purchased one full lot and part of another. Jackson catered to the quality trade, which must have helped him weather the hard times; a single finely made pair of boots could bring in $5 to $8. Individual households and companies alike became Jackson's regular clients. His literacy and ability to handle written numbers gave him an additional advantage that most black entrepreneurs lacked. Jackson bought a house and lot in the depression year of 1840 for the impressive sum of $1,500, and would acquire another lot in 1855. By that time he employed half a dozen workers and produced as many as 1,400 pairs of boots and shoes a year—an aggregate product worth twice that of his neighbor, Farmville's most esteemed and prosperous white blacksmith, Henry Jenkins.[39]

Not all of Jackson's customers could pay their bills during the depression; on two occasions he sued whites for unpaid balances between $20 and $30. In one instance, the black shoemaker sued a writ out of the county court that forced a white debtor either to pay what he owed or surrender his horse to be auctioned off by the sheriff. In general, Jackson was probably no more ruthless than other creditors, yet he took this particular action on a debt that was only two years old.[40] As the area gradually pulled out of the economic depression, Booker Jackson continued to prosper, selling his wares and repair services to numerous white families in the county during the 1850s. He had married a woman from Petersburg about 1839, and their two sons eventually learned their father's occupation and joined his business. Jackson would be remembered by the white memoirist who wrote of old Farmville in the local newspaper in 1906. After singing the praises of Henry Jenkins, the white smith, the writer recalled Jackson as "another worthy citizen of the town . . . [an] honored colored man who was as highly respected by all the citizens of Farmville at that time as any man here, was faithful and upright in his profession, [making] fine boots and shoes."[41]

Two incidents in the 1840s confirm how thoroughly integrated into the local economy and society Booker Jackson became. In 1843, he sued two white men who had failed to pay him for a slave woman named Sooky whom they had hired from him. Sooky belonged to the estate of Josiah Chambers; Jackson seems to have hired her labor for a year and then "sublet" her to those other men. Later, in 1848, the county court ordered Farmville to be divided into four districts from which hands could be called up for work on the roads. The commissioners selected "Booker Jackson corner" as the point from which the two boundary lines of one quadrant would radiate.[42] As with Ben Short more than thirty years earlier, a free black man's home or shop had come to seem permanent and prominent enough to serve as a geographic landmark.

It would be easy to suspect that Booker Jackson was what later generations would call a "white man's Negro"—except that he did sue white men for money they owed him, and he won the esteem of fellow blacks. Israelite Tony White, seeking to provide for his shattered family, needed someone reliable to carry out his will, mitigate the damage slavery had wrought, and try to sell his land if necessary, even though White had no written deed to convey. To carry out those complicated tasks, Tony White chose his "friends Booker Jackson and John Jackson," Booker's half brother.[43] Free blacks in Prince Edward almost never named others of their caste as executors. White's confidence in the Jacksons must have been both profound and justified by manifest ability on their part.

By the time Tony White wrote his will in 1848, Prince Edward County was making its way out from under the financial rubble of 1837. The county felt able in 1850 to modernize the six miles of road from Farmville to Prince Edward Court House in order to handle "the large amount of Tonage & travel passing" between the two places. The local government found an even bigger sum in the 1850s to build a county clerk's office on the courthouse square.[44]

After the Commonwealth of Virginia introduced popular election of local officials in 1851, the county court remained an assemblage of planters, bank directors, trustees of Hampden-Sydney and other educational institutions, boosters of internal improvements, tobacco merchants and manufacturers, and at least one partner in Farmville's foundry.[45] The twenty justices seated in 1852 included at least five men whose involvement with free blacks had been extensive and mostly amicable. Contractor Henry Guthrey was there—and still getting a hefty share of county construction work; he served alongside the Dungeys' associates from western Prince Edward, Newton Cunningham and David F. Womack. So did Clement Read, who also became president of a local bank, and Joel W. Womack; the latter had witnessed Tony White's will, knew the Israelites almost as well as Read did, and had recently been accused of "rescuing" slaves from a patrol.[46]

As in earlier years, a goodly part of the county's revived commerce moved through the hands of white men who had long records of dealing civilly with free Afro-Virginians. Israelites had transacted business through Clem Read's store, and Read had temporarily held free blacks' weapons in 1831; he still operated his tobacco factory and employed young Israelites and other blacks in the 1850s. Ben Robertson of Farmville Baptist Church served as inspector of tobacco at Farmville warehouse and, at least for a time, owned a part interest in the facility; this was probably the warehouse in which a son and grandson of Phil White would find employment by 1860–61.[47]

The 1850s brought economic change for free blacks—but in some realms, less than one might think. The number of free Afro-Virginian women listed as doing "domestic" work in Prince Edward County went as high as a hundred on the official county list of 1860. That situation might seem to foreshadow the post–Civil War era, in which countless black women would have little choice but to perform domestic work in white people's homes. Yet the same list records only half a dozen women doing domestic labor *at* some white person's place; that seems to suggest that the others were keeping their own houses. Indeed, the same tally counts as "domestic" certain women who almost surely did not work for whites as maids: the prosperous Booker Jackson's wife, Phil White's spouse, Rachel (sixty-seven years old by then), and seventy-five-year-old Milly Homes II. The federal census of 1860 shows that some of the women whom the county revenue commissioner listed as "domestic" were farming, and others "work[ing] about house"—which clearly means in their own homes. Fewer than twenty free blacks, five of them men, were working as servants of any sort. For the time being, it seems, most white people who had black women cleaning or cooking still used enslaved workers.[48]

Laundering clothes did become an important occupation among free black women by the latter 1850s. Some apparently earned most of their income from washing, while many others laundered clothes part of the time. A few free black women were still classified as seamstresses; some women who spent the bulk of their time keeping their own houses may have supplemented their income by selling the products of their domestic crafts as in former years. Betsy Hill continued her career as a midwife through the decade.[49]

The county lists for 1860 and 1861 show between forty and fifty free Afro-Virginians, including at least twenty Israelites or their children, working in Farmville's tobacco factories, at the foundry, and in the warehouse where Curtis White and his son Hercules were employed; the actual number was twice that large and encompassed a third of the county's working free black population if not more. One in three of those industrial workers was a woman, and some were children or adolescents.[50]

Mostly-black neighborhoods in town had expanded. In 1860, the federal census taker noted that one group of seventy-five free blacks "live principally on one street in Farmville in rented houses"; a slight majority of the adults on that street were factory workers. The Randolph experiment still loomed large in the enumerator's mind: he assumed, wrongly, that not merely some but "many" of the Afro-Virginians in this particular neighborhood were "the descendants of the Israel Hill Negroes."

The revenue commissioner had still listed as many as twenty-five "farmers" and "planters" on Israel Hill as late as 1857, half of them forty years old or younger. But the number of men in that age group who were tallied as farmers fell drastically over the next few years, even before the war diverted manpower from normal pursuits. The 1860 census classified only three Israelite men as farmers, and four as farm laborers; on the Hill, working one's own "patch" of land had become largely a woman's job by then. Some twenty men and women from the community were earning their living as day laborers. Other Israelites had simply left the settlement, heading either to Farmville, as the census taker thought, or to other places. The Hill's population dropped from some 150 in 1850 to 118 ten years later.[51]

Just as striking, land tax delinquencies had multiplied among free blacks during the 1840s. Some Israelites paid the land tax part of the time; Sam White did so regularly. Yet in most years of that decade, most real estate on the Hill was delinquent. When the sheriff recovered back taxes by selling various lands from all over the county in 1845, he auctioned off parts of five tracts on the Hill; all the affected plots except Dick White's old place, it appears, were still inhabited. The fifty-acre Brown and Wilkerson tracts lost thirteen and eight acres, respectively. County officials had long since forgotten the sheriff's supposed sale of two acres from Dick White's little plot a dozen years earlier; they now sold an acre from the same parcel. The Patterson tract lost seven of its twenty-five acres and the Carter plot fully seventeen. In another county-wide sale of delinquent land in 1850, all twenty of the acres George and Jacob Johnston had inherited from their mother, Rose, were sold off; only the five Johnston acres that Rose had bequeathed to her daughter, Phil White's wife, Rachel, remained in the hands of a black owner.[52]

Why would people living on Israel Hill permit portions of their family lands to be sold? The economic depression did linger well into the 1840s, but Israelites did not allow these sheriff's sales to proceed simply because they were impoverished. Trivial sums, often far less than $1, would have sufficed to prevent the sales. For the Carter family, collecting 5 cents or so per year from each adult in the group would have done the trick.

Founding Israelite families had no intention of abandoning the Hill; members of each would still be living there during the years around 1860.[53] But for those people who allowed part of their land to be taken, Israel Hill seems long since to have become a homeplace where they could grow some produce for subsistence or to earn a little cash, and where they could keep chickens and perhaps a couple of hogs, even as they earned much of their income by other means. Forty-two acres, or eighteen, or even eight—the amounts left to those Israelite families who lost land, other than the Johnstons—offered enough space to accomplish these things. White neighbors seem to have noticed that the importance of farming on the Hill had waned: though the federal census gathered statistics on farms in 1850 and 1860, including some as small as a dozen acres, the enumerator did not include any of the tracts on Israel Hill in the tally.[54]

No evidence suggests that the whites who bought delinquent land on the Hill actually did anything to exploit it or to interfere with its black former owners. Even Jacob Johnston, who supposedly had lost all his land, would be living on Israel Hill with his wife and other members of the Johnston family as the Union dissolved. The census taker in 1860 still wrote that the black-owned real estate on Israel Hill "consists of 350 acres,"[55] the amount of the original grant from Judith Randolph. The sheriff's sales of land had made about as much difference as the law allowing free blacks to be hired out to make good on other delinquent taxes. The Israelites still lived on their land and ran their own affairs, and they still fed themselves partly by farming—but *only* partly.

Longtime county official John Foster had written at the end of the 1820s that industrious people of limited means could "make out very well from their own exertions on their little farms," with little or no public assistance.[56] That remained largely true in the 1850s, at least for those willing to diversify—and free Afro-Virginians were nothing if not versatile. Donaldson Gibbs, Titus's grandson and by now Phil White's son-in-law, received one payment of more than $30 in 1855, possibly by furnishing either work or produce. Several years earlier, the trustee who handled the Penick plantation paid someone named Patterson $2 for fixing a clock. Perhaps this was one of the Pattersons of nearby Israel Hill; if so, he had added yet another skill to the list of those proffered by Israelites over the years.[57] When the census taker of 1860 recorded many individuals on Israel Hill as "work[ing their] patch" or "work[ing] on [their] farm," the picture he painted was accurate, but far from complete.

The number of free Afro-Virginians in Prince Edward recorded as living at some white person's place became very small by the latter 1850s.[58] Some craftspeople, factory workers, and boatmen lived on black-owned lands, and many others in Farmville. The county's enumerator probably failed to identify some instances where blacks still lived on white people's farms and plantations. Clearly, though, the black drive for independence and the rise of Farmville as a manufacturing center had together reconfigured free black demography in the county.

The three most entrepreneurial Whites—John, Phil, and Sam—did not repeat in the 1850s the accumulation of property they had achieved two decades earlier. John gave up his last parcel to Phil, who ended up owning one lot, in addition to his place on Israel Hill, as the decade concluded.[59] Yet other black men and women in Farmville now became owners of real estate in numbers never before seen. Free blacks evinced a tendency to keep real property, once acquired, within the race, and even to "buy back" lots given up to white buyers by other blacks in earlier years. Boatman and former Israelite Sam Strong became one of two Afro-Virginians who recovered such a parcel from a white owner in the 1850s; he did so during a string of purchases that brought him nearly $900 worth of land in and next to Farmville. Strong resold one of his new lots to a female member of the free black Homes family in 1859, and a man from the Bartlett clan of boatmen bought part of another lot from Strong's estate not long thereafter. Sam Strong left enough property behind when he died in 1860 that the court required his white executor to post a $2,000 bond before taking on that role.[60]

Free black persons other than Strong acquired at least ten lots and part lots in Farmville during the 1850s and another three or four during the Civil War. Almost all this real estate came from white sellers, so the relative weight of free African Americans among lot owners grew noticeably. The black-owned tracts were located in various sections of town. Black carpenter Robert A. Franklin became one of three Afro-Virginians who bought land outside Farmville; by 1860, he developed his three-acre tract near Hampden-Sydney College, purchased for only $63, up to a value of $800.[61]

How did they do it? The stronger economy of the early and mid-1850s made it more likely that diligent work would pay off—until another recession in 1857 interrupted the good times. A couple of blacks bought lots from Henry Guthrey and Newton Cunningham, men who had long dealt comfortably with people of color; Guthrey lent Bob Franklin a large sum to improve his three acres. But Afro-Virginians who bought real estate apparently managed to do so without receiving special concessions or discounts. Most, perhaps all, made offers and entertained counteroffers from whites who "named their price," just as happened in the opposite direction when a white man sought to buy a lot from Philip White III.

Benjamin C. Peters, a prominent white citizen, sold two lots to free blacks in 1854 and 1863, and at least three more after the Civil War; he had more dealings than most whites with men and women of the other race. But he did not run his life as though he were a benevolent society. He was the man who bought a lot from Phil White in 1835, then withheld the last few dollars of the purchase price, prompting White to sue him. Peters sold to free Afro-Virginian Robert Franklin the daughter whom Franklin wanted to liberate, but whether he acted as a helpful intermediary or made a healthy profit we do not know. Free black Booker Hill accused Peters in 1837 of assaulting and handcuffing him. Whether or not that charge had merit, Peters comes across as a man who had no qualms about making deals with blacks, but who also knew how to drive a hard bargain.

Most Afro-Virginians who bought town lots in the 1850s and 1860s seem to have saved money painstakingly out of the proceeds of their work over a period of years. Many children of the extended Homes family had been born into households that lacked an adult male, whether because their fathers were enslaved or for other reasons; the overseers of the poor had bound out numerous Homes children as apprentices. Yet Milly and Nathan Homes had managed to buy small patches of land by 1820, and other members of the clan eventually followed their example, purchasing at least seven lots and part lots between 1853 and 1863. Perhaps in the end three generations of steady effort simply paid off. The prominence of women in the leadership of the family yielded its own legacy: all but one of these new Homes lots were purchased by females.[62]

The Evans family ran a close second to the Homeses in the purchase of land and lots. Theirs, too, reads as a tale of resilience—a comeback by a free black clan that had owned land in the distant past but given it up early in the century. Again, the money to finance a re-entry into the ranks of landowners appears to have come, quite simply, from years of work. Eliza Evans, who bought a town lot in 1850 when she was in her late thirties, earned the $150 purchase price largely by sewing and washing clothes. Dennis Evans purchased fourteen acres of rural land for a bargain price at about the same time, after he had passed age sixty; his various jobs as a carpenter included repairing the lot on which the county clerk's office sat.[63]

Many believe that white Southerners, prompted by agitation of the slavery issue on the federal level in the 1850s, tried to reduce free blacks to near slavery. Indeed, some of the more repressive legislation touching on free people of color emerged during that period. But historians have also documented the continued, and sometimes accelerating, spread of real estate ownership among free blacks across the Upper South during the very same decade.[64] The North-South conflict did generate new pressures and stresses. Yet it seems unlikely that the Strongs, the Homeses, the Evanses, and other free blacks who branched out economically during those years believed they were experiencing the nadir of their lives.

As in earlier times, whites and free Afro-Virginians in the 1850s could readily find themselves rubbing shoulders at estate sales, public events, or places of business. Meanwhile, the county government offered occasional odd jobs to free blacks—Booker Hill earned the relatively large sum of $15 when he repaired a well, and he accumulated a modicum of personal and real property by 1860—but the lucrative county contracts still went to white companies. The private sector offered some opportunities to earn good money. Independent black carpenter Thornton Evans was paid $8 a week in the late 1840s and in the 1850s; during a twelve-year period, he took in some $500 from one of his white clients, and he doubtless had additional customers.[65]

Some free blacks and whites still entered into apprenticeships through the overseers of the poor and the county court, and at least a few actively sought them. Henry Cousins of neighboring Amelia County asked Prince Edward's court in 1858 to bind out his seven or more children to merchant James V. Musgrove; the latter would teach the youngsters hotel work and, Cousins said, would "do all by the children that I will desire as he has already done much towards their support." During the generation leading up to the Civil War, several bindings out provided a generous lump-sum payment to an apprentice completing his term. An unsatisfied parent still could request rescission of an apprenticeship, and some did so successfully.[66]

Other aspects of day-to-day life distinguished even well-off free blacks from their white counterparts in ways more subtle than the special head tax or denial of the vote and jury service. Whites gave security for free blacks' notes of indebtedness and witnessed and executed their wills. White men signed bail bonds to guarantee black defendants' appearance in court in civil suits and in the rare criminal prosecutions. Blacks did all these things for each other, too. But free Afro-Virginians, no matter how much property they might own or how actively they might transact business across racial lines, do not seem to have filled the same roles for whites. That few propertied free blacks could read and write would seem to explain why they seldom if ever formally witnessed documents; perhaps the habit of not turning to them for that purpose carried over into the giving of bail or security. But white women, no matter how well educated, likewise almost never secured loans, witnessed wills, or gave bail.[67] White males, probably without giving the matter much thought, simply did not see people other than themselves as candidates to perform these functions.

The economic activity of free Afro-Virginians in the 1850s took shape as the contours of life and work in the county shifted yet again. The most portentous single development was the building of two railway lines. The Richmond & Danville cut across the southeastern corner of the county.[68] The South Side Railroad ran roughly parallel to the Appomattox River and thus traversed the entire width of Prince Edward's northern tier, apart from one section of track that swung into Cumberland County. Depots went up in Farmville, at Prospect farther west, and in other locations. In future decades, the South Side would become a component of the Atlantic, Mississippi, & Ohio, and then of the Norfolk & Western.

When the South Side Railroad came to Farmville and Israel Hill in 1851, it immediately and directly affected dozens of Prince Edward's residents on whose land it needed to lay track. The route led across both Israel Hill and the land that free black James Dungey had left to his children in the western part of the county. That the South Side cut through both those places raises suspicion in the mind of anyone who watched interstate highway construction devastate African American neighborhoods in the second half of the twentieth century. Yet the railroad spared few if any white landowners by traversing those two small spots on the map. The company took little land from Afro-Virginians and did not discriminate in any obvious way between white and black when it paid for what it did take. A few whites received compensation of some $20 per acre or even more, perhaps because they sacrificed buildings or other valuable features or because their land bordered on the growing town of Farmville. But the Tuggles, Israel Hill's prominent white neighbors, got $5—well within the Israelites' range and far below the $8 an acre that the Whites and Gibbses were paid. The latter two families did as well per acre as the neighboring Allen plantation, while the Dungeys' compensation matched or exceeded that given to their white neighbor, county justice Joel Elam.

The railroad's physical effect on free blacks' lands varied. Afro-Virginians gave up as little as Becky Dungey's one seventh of an acre and as much as her brother John's 3.9 acres. The loss of an acre or two from a tract as small as those on Israel Hill was significant, but apparently not devastating. No record tells whether any buildings had to be demolished or cultivated land sacrificed, but the different levels of compensation tendered suggest that such things did happen. The roadway averaged a roomy 125 feet wide where it ran across Sam White's land, 88 to 99 feet elsewhere on Israel Hill, and only 80 feet where it crossed the Dungeys' acreage. By contrast, on white-owned tracts between Israel Hill and Farmville, the railroad took a swath averaging nearly 150 feet wide.[69]

After the tracks were finished, trains passed through the county only a couple of times a day, but their noise and speed impressed all who beheld them. Freight trains averaging eighteen cars ran at fifteen miles per hour. Three-car passenger trains went twenty-five miles an hour or more—eight or ten times as fast as a person could walk. A freight train could travel from Farmville to Petersburg in about seven and a half hours, as compared with the days that a batteau or a wagon required.[70]

County officials proved perfectly ready to prosecute the railroad company for obstructing roads or failing to maintain a grade crossing, and juries in Prince Edward did not hesitate to impose fines.[71] Yet these modest reminders of who was boss in no way negated the effect that the railroad's magnetic field had on commercial habits, the social structure of the community, the lay of the land, and even perceptions of time and space. Petitions to open new roads came from groups of citizens who sought quicker and easier access to the depots at Prospect and at Pamplin on the county's western border, or to the station at Meherrin on the

Richmond & Danville, "the point of access to our market." The railway stations now competed with country stores and the village of Prince Edward Court House as centers of social life. Citizens banded together to request that polling places be moved to or near railway depots; petitioners in northeastern Prince Edward won the day by asserting that voting would be more convenient at Rice station now that the depot had become "a place of public resort."[72]

The railroad inevitably reduced the demand for shipping by batteau. In a supreme irony, the black boatmen of Israel Hill and Farmville not only witnessed the eclipse of their occupation but were enlisted to contribute actively to its decline. One former batteauman from the Hill later told of hauling stone upstream, which was then used to build piers for bridges on both the Richmond & Danville and the South Side railway lines. Some forty batteaux worked out of Farmville in 1850, perhaps as many as had ever plied the river from there; but later that decade the young batteauman found himself laboring variously at farming, tobacco processing, and railroad work. At least half a dozen men of Israelite families were still listed as boatmen in 1860 and 1861, and the Civil War would prove even more disruptive than the railroad—but trains had already sent the batteau on its way toward obsolescence.[73]

Like the river that it was replacing as an avenue of commerce, the railroad beguiled the senses. Enslaved blacks had always found sources of amusement and companionship in their off-hours, and the coming of the railroad added to their options. One slave who lived near Prospect "was in the habit of going to the Depot every night at the time the cars were passing"—half past midnight; he was surely not alone among black and white county residents in his love of watching the trains go by. That there was a good chance of finding a black depot hand awake at any given hour, perhaps sitting comfortably before an outdoor fire with no supervisor anywhere about, only enhanced the young man's experience.[74]

The railways, like every other enterprise of any size, hired "hands" from among the slave population; the South Side line also employed at least half a dozen free blacks in the years just before and during the Civil War. These included Ben White, then in his fifties; he and one free black youth were listed without elaboration as "depot workers." The other free and enslaved black railway employees were in their twenties; they seem to have maintained the facilities, fueled and watered trains, and the like.[75]

The railroad also introduced free blacks, slaves, and whites to a new ethnic group, the Irish. Prince Edward County had seen people of foreign origin before—a few European immigrants had settled there over

Ironically, the black boatmen of Israel Hill and Farmville contributed to the
rise of the railroad and the decline of their own occupation: they hauled stone
upstream, which was then used to build piers for the Appomattox High
Bridge, an engineering marvel of its day.   (LIBRARY OF VIRGINIA)

the decades—but outsiders remained something of a curiosity. One local
man in the early 1850s recalled a business transaction as having taken
place "in the year the Jew Goodcup left Farmville."[76] The county court
had implausibly blamed an outbreak of smallpox in 1829 on "Sundry
Indians [who had supposedly] passed through" bearing the disease, and a
fragmentary note from the same period refers to "poor Irish Behoys"—a
caricatured Irish dialect pronunciation of the word "boys."[77] That such
stereotypes could exist in a county that had seen its last Indian many
years earlier and had yet to receive any significant influx of Irish people
hints that locals were primed to take notice when the real Irish immigration began.

Now the railroad, in Prince Edward as in much of the rest of the
United States, brought in a largely Irish workforce to lay track. Novel
words entered the local vocabulary, particularly the term "shanty" or
"shantee," which referred to the shacks the company built along the railway line to house its laborers. Soon black railroad workers were also living in shanties and toiling alongside Irishmen, and members of the two
groups were visiting each other's little dwellings.[78]

The mixing of the two races spilled over from the railroad into other endeavors such as the construction of a new Appomattox River bridge at Farmville. The crew of stonemasons that built the abutments included half a dozen hired slaves, a man listed simply as "Tom, Irishman," and several other whites, at least two of whom were probably Irish. The men made good money, $1 a day, though the slaves' pay, of course, was not their own.[79] Irishmen, like free blacks, became prominent for a few years on official lists of tax delinquents in the early 1850s.[80] That poor, transient workers would seldom pay comes as no surprise, but the Irishmen's tax delinquencies may have aggravated a reputation that was suffering on other grounds.

The American stereotype of the Irishman was of a rowdy habitual drunkard, ready to fight at the drop of a hat and wedded to an unenlightened, even menacing Roman Catholic Church. Railroad workers seem to have kept away from native whites a good part of the time, rarely if ever clashing with locals of either color. Occasionally, a fight among Irishmen or the sale of illegal liquor by one of them did catch the authorities' attention, however. In the most sensational incident, a certain John Sullivan allegedly cut and broke the leg of his wife and beat her with a stick.[81] Another time, one railroad builder shot another in the neck with a pistol. The circuit court eventually acquitted the shooter, probably on grounds of self-defense. But his trial before the county court revealed a great deal about local prejudices.

Records of testimony from Prince Edward only rarely record witnesses' dialect, and then in a straightforward, almost incidental way. But the transcriber in this particular proceeding, not content to use stereotyped Irish dialect spellings, actually underscored them: one witness, for example, described the assailant's pistol as having had "a sight to it like a goon and with a thrigger under nathe." The defense attorney ended his cross-examination of the prosecution witnesses by eliciting from them the statements, "I am a Catholic," or, "I am an Irishman."[82] That presumably undermined their credibility and downgraded the shooting to an affair among Irish "Behoys" involved in a typical donnybrook.

The real lesson of Prince Edward's encounter with the Irish in a time of economic flux may be that the unfamiliar created the greatest discomfort in the minds of some—perhaps many—local whites. Afro-Virginians were anything but unfamiliar. That simple fact helps explain the many instances of civility and mutual regard between free black and white that punctuated life in Prince Edward County through boom times and hard times alike.

BLACK FREEDOM AND THE CRISIS OF THE UNION

People in Prince Edward County in the 1840s and 1850s did not know they were living in "the antebellum period." They spent most of their time thinking about everyday concerns: economics, family life, relations with neighbors. Yet America's annexation of Texas and its declaration of war against Mexico in 1846 did spark controversy over slavery. Northern critics of the Mexican War branded it from the outset as a thinly veiled scheme to conquer new lands into which slavery could expand.

The war was barely two months old when it figured in the trial of a slave named Cephas in Prince Edward, who stood accused of "conspir[ing] to raise insurrection." Other slaves testified that Cephas, during a worship service at Buffalo Meeting House that June, had sat on a log outside the church and asked other blacks what they thought of "the subject of having a free country." Cephas speculated that the Mexican War might somehow change the status of slaves. He argued with another bondman about the number of white Americans already killed in Mexico. Cephas, according to testimony, insisted that twenty thousand had died, and that the figure of a mere sixty, which the other man quoted, "was a lie told only to deceive the slaves." He supposedly added that "he intended to raise an army & kill all the white people as they came out of the church."

What the slaves actually said that day is difficult to know. The court must not have believed the part about Cephas proposing to assemble a slave army; two white witnesses called his guilt into question, and the court acquitted him.[83] As usual in Prince Edward, cooler heads had prevailed in the end. But Cephas's trial did prove several things.

First, some whites believed that slaves took a personal interest in national issues such as war casualty figures; one white man passing the slaves outside the church had asked, apparently without sarcasm, "if they were talking pol[itics]." Moreover, those who thought slaves cared about current affairs were right. One enslaved witness even quoted Cephas as having said that if people "had known that [President James K.] Polk was so great a rascal they would not have voted for him." Some people felt insecure precisely because slaves did follow the news. Since colonial times, thoughtful persons had credited blacks with "the wonderful art of communicating information" across "hundreds of miles" about events that might bring them freedom. Justice Joel Elam, a normally level-headed man who had good relations with the cluster of free blacks in western Prince Edward, issued the warrants in Cephas's case. Other white men allegedly "took [one of Cephas's enslaved friends] & put his head under the fence through the rails & gave him one or two licks" to get him to talk against Cephas.

Concerned whites may have had their worries confirmed when a couple of enslaved witnesses at trial showed an insouciant readiness to expose their real feelings to the court. One slave testified that, far from rebuking Cephas that day outside the church, he had merely said, "hush boy[,] white folks hear you." Another bondman told the court "that he liked . . . very much" Cephas's idea of having a free country.[84] Proslavery propagandists might insist that slaves were contented, but many ordinary Southern whites understood that bondpeople dreamt of liberty.

The years between the Mexican War and the breakup of the Union brought other outbursts of nervousness among whites in Prince Edward; there were the five or six arrests of free blacks in 1845 and 1846, apparently for lacking free papers, for example. Even so, most prosecutions for permitting slaves to go at large, allowing them to gather, selling them liquor, or trading with them without their masters' permission differed little from those in earlier years. Many such charges came amid much broader campaigns against gambling and other breaches of public order, in which most of the defendants were white.

There were a few noteworthy exceptions. Mary Jane Franklin began seeking formal permission to remain in Virginia shortly after her father, the future landowner Robert Franklin, bought and liberated her in the fall of 1846. The following year, despite her father's solid reputation, the county court turned down her application to stay. The law required that three quarters of the court's members in attendance vote positively, and the record of the proceedings hints that the vote fell only slightly short of that figure.[85] County officials may not have worried much about Mary Franklin as an individual. No one actually forced her to leave the state; she married one of the Bartlett men and bore two children. But the county court had considered her application during the months just after Congressman David Wilmot of Pennsylvania had proposed to exclude slavery from western territories surrendered by Mexico. The bitterness that the Wilmot Proviso aroused in the white South may have tipped the scale in the county court, costing a newly emancipated black woman a crucial vote or two on a matter that might otherwise have aroused no controversy.

Four years later, two other free Afro-Virginians found their lives complicated by national politics. In late April and early May 1850, a grand jury in Prince Edward Circuit Court handed down a staggering seventy-three charges against three dozen individuals, almost all of them white. Most of the presentments involved gambling or permitting gaming; other charges included fighting, stealing, and selling liquor illegally to slaves. A presentment against free black Jesse Woodson differed from all the others. Woodson, manumitted in 1847 by his mistress's will and now in his twenties, stood accused of having remained in Virginia for more than a year after his liberation. Three months later, a county grand jury lodged a similar charge against another free Afro-Virginian, Isaac Coles.[86] That anyone should single Woodson out seems surprising at first glance. He had learned the highly skilled trade of cabinetmaking from Farmville's foremost white practitioner, who then kept him on as an employee. The black man's emancipation had become final under the supervision of Tarlton Woodson, whose father, Colonel Charles Woodson, had himself carried out an emancipatory will in the past; the county court had duly registered Jesse Woodson as a free man. Rather than simply ignore the law requiring him to leave the state, Jesse had even petitioned the General Assembly for permission to remain.[87]

Unfortunately for Jesse Woodson, however, a stormy debate over the expansion or restriction of slavery in the western territories raged during the early months of 1850; fistfights broke out between Northerners and Southerners in the halls of Congress. The case of Isaac Coles may explain how that controversy created trouble both for him and for Jesse Woodson. Less than a year after his presentment, Coles would purchase the freedom of his wife, a slave in Prince Edward County; by that time he was living in Pennsylvania. Coles himself had obtained his liberty in the county in 1847, likely through self-purchase; he may have traveled to that Northern state to set up a home, then come back south in 1850 to negotiate his wife's freedom.[88] Such a stay in Pennsylvania—a fount of antislavery ideas—may very well have triggered the presentment against Coles, which aimed to ensure his permanent departure. One wonders whether a similar sojourn in the North had clouded Jesse Woodson's reputation, too.

If the political stresses of 1850 led whites to make trouble for free blacks other than Woodson and Coles, they took their time about it and approached the issue fairly narrowly; apparently the only unusual development beyond those two cases was the flurry of black registrations that came late in 1850 and in 1851. Perhaps a tacit formula crystallized in the minds of some white people: expulsion for the rare well-traveled free black who might become a vector for subversive Yankee notions; orderly registration of undocumented Afro-Virginians who lacked any such taint. The court and the prosecutor would vacillate in cases involving a couple of other manumittees between 1850 and 1859. As for Jesse Woodson and Isaac Coles themselves, deputy sheriffs sent to serve papers on the men reported that neither resided in Prince Edward any longer. Coles clearly had settled in the North. Woodson may have done the same despite his popularity among whites in his neighborhood, who had drawn up a petition asking that he be allowed to stay on.[89]

National events had no discernible impact on the administration of justice in another case involving a free Afro-Virginian. When one Patsy Bartlett stood accused of having sold liquor without a license in the spring of 1850, a jury acquitted her; she may well have been a daughter, granddaughter, or niece of Patty Bartlett, who had owned one acre of land near Farmville years earlier.[90] Meanwhile, nearly two thirds of the white men accused of gambling or permitting gambling during the great crisis of 1850 were convicted and fined, as was one white citizen charged with assault. Local authorities had proved they could create considerable difficulty for a man like Jesse Woodson. Still, in the years from 1845 to the Civil War, those officials would spend far more time and money prosecuting white gamblers than seeking to expel free Afro-Virginians.[91] Authorities reacted calmly even on the one occasion when a free black was accused of helping a slave to escape. In the fall of 1855, someone suspected Henry Homes of having helped a white man procure free papers for an absconding slave. Unimpressed county authorities "mislaid" the warrants against Homes; at trial some months later, the county court acquitted him.[92]

Legislators in various states did pass new laws discriminating against free blacks during the 1850s. Those enactments have persuaded many that, by the last antebellum decade, "the free Negro was receiving practically no consideration in the South"—that "the trend toward degrading [him] to a lower status had become evident even in the apparently benevolent slaveholding states" such as Virginia.[93] In 1856, the state's General Assembly adopted, among other measures, a now famous law that gave free blacks the option of becoming slaves. Today, people regard that enactment as a sign of Afro-Virginians' deteriorating position, but the actual history of the statute suggests that such laws signified little. The state's self-enslavement law may not even qualify as a concession to white popular sentiment, for it seems to have won little attention at the time. One out-of-state newspaper editor asked his readers: "Do many, even of the Virginia people, know" that such a law exists?

The new statute permitted voluntary self-enslavement to a master of one's choice; there apparently had been a few black petitioners for that dubious privilege, and the General Assembly had framed a bill to cover such cases. Rather than encourage blacks to opt for bondage, however, the law set up a series of procedural obstacles, and it provided that any children already born to a female applicant would remain free. Proslavery ideologues might declare slavery a positive good, but the legislators recognized that liberty for most blacks was a boon not to be tampered with lightly. The editor who wrote about the self-enslavement statute in 1857 defended the Southern system as a benevolent regime superior to "free negroism," yet even he labeled the law a "curious" artifact—a bizarre quirk of the legislative process.[94]

Three free black men in Prince Edward County actually did apply to the circuit court in 1858 for assignment to masters, however. These would-be slaves may have been offering a lifelong commitment in return for desirable conditions agreed to by their prospective owners. The court made each applicant and his white sponsor jump through the various procedural hoops that the law required, but the parties followed the matter through. The affair remained an anomaly in Prince Edward as elsewhere; it appears that fewer than two dozen free blacks enslaved themselves in the entire state of Virginia between 1856 and 1861.[95]

Three untimely deaths in the 1850s show how matter-of-factly free blacks could still interact with whites—and not only with businessmen but with simple folk as well. One night in November 1853, the two daughters of Micajah (Mike) Walden, a free black man who ran his own batteau out of Farmville, perished in their bed during a house fire. In that era, as in earlier times, the county coroner investigated deaths of blacks as exhaustively as he did those of whites.[96] This time, he collected testimony revealing that Walden and his wife had behaved irresponsibly—and also that their lives were thoroughly intertwined with those of white people. Both parents were drinkers, and each had spent the entire night of the fire away from home; Walden himself had passed the time imbibing and sleeping at a white man's shanty. The Waldens had shared the house with white men, too, each party occupying a different end of the building. The white tenants knew the Waldens' habits in detail, including which room their children usually slept in and when Walden and his wife quarreled. A white and a black man together had approached the burning house, but no one managed to save the girls.[97]

Death also came in the 1850s to John Coakley, a white shoemaker. He had plied his trade around Farmville at least since the 1830s, when he did work for the Chambers and Penick families near Israel Hill. Free Afro-Virginian Theophilus Scott, himself a shoemaker and former apprentice to Booker Jackson, came home one Tuesday evening in December 1858 to find John Coakley waiting for him. The two men do not seem to have lived together, but neither Scott nor two free black women who were present expressed any surprise that the white man proceeded to stay at the black's house for four days and nights. Coakley, nearly seventy years old, had been drinking and looked ill. He gave Theo Scott half a dollar to buy more whiskey and handed smaller amounts to the two women; he may have been paying them for care they gave him, or perhaps simply ordering more liquid groceries. At one point, the wobbly white man tried to get out of bed; Theo Scott "took hold of" Coakley and laid him on the floor. The ailing guest "died in [Scott's] arms" on Saturday. John Coakley's pathetic death and his burial at county expense contrast tellingly with the success and popularity of his black fellow shoemaker, Booker Jackson. Coakley's white skin had neither prompted him to avoid the company of blacks nor enabled him to match the achievements of some of them.[98]

Apart from the trial and acquittal of Cephas for plotting insurrection during the Mexican War, the national debate over slavery had astoundingly little effect on the way authorities in Prince Edward County dealt with slaves accused of crimes during the 1850s. Officials and county justices behaved prudently even when bondmen stood accused of having sexually attacked white women. In September 1858, Sarah Gregory of northwestern Prince Edward accused a neighbor's seventeen-year-old slave, Jim, of having entered her house at night and attempted to rape her while her husband was out. Her spouse took the accusation as seriously as one might expect, cutting Jim severely with a knife at one point when the black man appeared in court.

But Gregory may have had a reason beyond the obvious one for striking out at Jim: frustration over other whites' refusal to rush to judgment. When Sarah Gregory came to Jim's master to lodge her complaint, he had postponed locking the suspect up until after he, the slaveowner, ate the midday meal that was about to be served. The overseer who summoned Jim in from the field took care to have the black youth wait in the shade of a tree, and then left him there for a time without supervision. Later that day, when Sarah Gregory's husband moved toward Jim with a large switch, even Sarah's mother found herself holding her son-in-law back and "hollering to the boy to run." The justice of the peace who first questioned Jim did so calmly and asked for the names of alibi witnesses, and the county court delayed Jim's trial to allow his counsel to prepare a case.

Jim's lawyer mounted a skilled and unrelenting defense. Sarah Gregory said she had recognized Jim's face in her pitch-dark bedroom when lightning flashed during a thunderstorm; the defense attorney showed that the Gregorys' bed stood fully eighteen feet from the single small window in their bedroom. The lawyer cast doubt on Sarah's claim that she could recognize Jim's voice. He also drew out testimony from white and black witnesses about the timing of the storm and Jim's movements that night, raising questions as to whether he could have been at Sarah Gregory's house when she said he was. As usual, no one evinced surprise over a slave's nocturnal wanderings. Jim's master testified that he had "raised" the young man and had never found him "vicious in any way" or "guilty of any fault, except occasional negligence in driving up the cows." That last touch neatly established Jim's character as both virtuous and a bit ineffectual; both traits cast doubt on Sarah Gregory's portrait of him as a brutal attacker.

None of this was enough to avoid a conviction. The prosecution demolished one of Jim's enslaved alibi witnesses, and the other alibi testimony was less than ironclad. Still, in a free society devoid of racial bias, a court might have found enough reasonable doubt to acquit Jim—not because Sarah Gregory had not suffered an assault, but because it was questionable that Jim had committed it. A court in such a society would at least have convicted Gregory's husband of attacking Jim with a knife. But old Virginia, for all its surprising flexibility, could not be counted on either to acquit Jim or to punish his assailant when a "respectable" white victim of violent crime adamantly insisted that she could identify her black attacker. The court sentenced Jim to transportation outside the United States. Bizarrely, the justices may have decided to remove Jim rather than acquit him partly in the well-founded belief that, if Jim stayed in Prince Edward County, Sarah Gregory's husband would kill him.[99]

Another rape case four years earlier shows that an accusation against a slave could lead to a different sort of outcome. Mary J. Tatum, a thirty-six-year-old white wife and mother, frequently visited her elderly aunt,

Mary Meadows, on the plantation where Meadows lived and worked for William F. Scott. Scott was the man who had impregnated Betsy Lyle, then thwarted her identification of him as the father by disclosing her mixed-race parentage; now Lyle lived in a house in Scott's yard, weaving cloth and sewing clothing for his slaves. In January 1854, Mary Tatum announced that one of Scott's bondmen had threatened her with a stick and raped her along a path just after she ended one of her visits at Scott's. A twenty-year-old slave named George was arrested, identified by Tatum as her assailant, and tried in a proceeding that lasted some four days, one of the longest in the annals of Prince Edward County. George's defense attorney energetically pursued a fourfold strategy: to call the content of Mary Tatum's testimony into question; to establish an alibi for George; to substantiate his good character—and to impeach that of the white supposed victim.

Mary Tatum had at first named two suspects other than George, and she gave conflicting testimony on how she had identified him as the culprit in the end. Her dress and person had shown few if any signs of struggle after the alleged rape. An enslaved charcoal burner working near the site of the supposed attack testified that he and his companions had heard no "halloo" from Tatum. Scott's overseer, and especially Mary Meadows and Betsy Lyle, established that George had been ill on the day in question; the two women said he had not left their presence all afternoon except once for a few minutes to relieve himself.

The white Meadows and the racially ambiguous Lyle were able to offer such a strong alibi because white and black spent so much time together on the Scott plantation, as at other places in Prince Edward. Betsy Lyle testified matter-of-factly that she associated largely with the slaves, but also that she often worked in the house with the white Mary Meadows and sometimes "laugh[ed] and talk[ed]" with the overseer. Meadows said she had "raised" George, and that she regularly associated with him and the other slaves. She had taken her pipe into the kitchen where George lay sick and smoked, talked with him, and nagged him to take better care of himself for the entire period during which her niece said George had raped her. The overseer testified that he, too, had nursed George.

A number of whites, including George's master and the overseer, told the court that he was "an humble obedient and honest boy." Mary Meadows added that he was "the best one I ever had about me," and told how horrified she had been when a posse of white men, still drunk from a day at the monthly county court, rode up to take George away. Mary Tatum's character, by contrast, ended the trial in tatters—less because of any specific deed she had done than because of the kind of white people she represented. Witness after witness noted that Tatum "forever & eternally stroll[ed] over the country," alone or with her children, seeking handouts. When Tatum did labor, her aunt Mary Meadows said, she would "trade and deal" with Scott's slaves, receiving payment in the form of food from "the negroes for whom she worked." Neighbors portrayed Tatum's husband, a former schoolmaster, as a deadbeat, "suffering rather from laziness than infirmity."

Witnesses did not savage the Tatums simply for being poor or of plain stock, however. The prosecutor hinted at Betsy Lyle's racial background and had her state that she had once lived in the county poorhouse—but she was a modest, industrious woman, and the court apparently found her credible. Mary Meadows, too, was a woman of low estate. Both Mary Tatum's and Mary Meadows's testimony—unlike that of the half-black Betsy Lyle—was recorded partly in rustic dialect. Yet the trial record shows that George's defense lawyer elicited starkly contrasting images of niece and aunt.

Tatum's *daresn't* (doesn't dare), *throwed,* and *without my Aunt knowed* subtly sharpened the picture of her as ignorant, abrasive, and defensive. Mary Meadows soon followed with the mention of her homey pipe, the phrase "middling early," the recounting of her motherly ministrations to George, and her tale of having "talked a heap to him about sich things" as his health. Where Tatum's commonness worked, or was turned, against her, both the defense lawyer and others depicted Mary Meadows as a hardworking, salt-of-the-earth old lady full of folk wisdom and mother-wit; one white male witness proclaimed his "very great respect for her."

Witnesses even compared favorably the wanderings and activities of William Scott's slaves with those of the white alleged victim. Scott issued overnight passes that did not even specify a destination; "I don't know any thing about the negroes at night," Mary Meadows testified, as if surprised that anyone would care where they went or why. With Scott's blessing, George and other bondpeople trapped partridges, cooped and picked them, and sold them to whites. The work ethic that even slavery could not kill was alive and well, and it still crossed the barrier of race—a fact that now worked to the disadvantage of the allegedly shiftless Mary Tatum.

The county court did not merely spare George's life; it acquitted him of raping Mary Tatum.[100] The readiness of a court in slaveholding Virginia to reach such a verdict, especially in the 1850s, surprises us, but the justice of George's acquittal seems clear. Two witnesses, one of them the aunt of his accuser, confirmed his alibi. The case leaves an aftertaste, though, of the right outcome emerging partly for less than noble reasons. To defend against a rape charge partly by damning the alleged victim's character, and by faulting her for going about on her own, discomfits us—less, perhaps, because it reveals warts in antebellum Southern society, of which there were so many, than because it reminds us of some of the flaws in our own.

George's remarkable trial probably confirmed slaveowners' belief in the justice of their social system. But private emancipations of bondpeople carried a different message. The person who freed even one slave cast doubt on the idea that bondage was a positive good; to liberate a sizable group would concede a good deal to the antislavery critique of the South. Even so, the 1850s brought new manumissions and court decisions upholding them in Prince Edward and neighboring counties. A few people continued to liberate blacks almost up to the moment that the vice president of the new Southern Confederacy declared "the great truth . . . that slavery—subordination to the superior race—is [the Negro's] natural and normal condition."[101]

We tend to exaggerate the waning of moral doubt about slavery in the nineteenth-century Upper South because we miss two essential points: the Revolutionary generation was less liberal than many used to believe, and the later decades less uniformly reactionary than we think.[102] Two potential sources of moral unease about slavery persisted until the Civil War: natural rights philosophy and evangelical Christian morality. Both had their roots in that famous Revolutionary generation.

Richard Randolph represented a pure version of the former worldview; his neighbor, contemporary, and fellow emancipator Thomas Baldwin, on the other hand, probably derived his "conscientious scruples on the subject of slavery" from the evangelical Christian ethos. A person could easily base his or her qualms about slavery on both those foundation stones. Judith Randolph's contemporary Andrew Baker surely liberated his slaves in part because of his Presbyterian faith, yet he also wrote of his wish that they enjoy "that freedom to which they are entitled by nature."[103]

The law of 1806 requiring newly freed people to leave the state did have a chilling effect on some would-be emancipators who did not want to put their former slaves at risk of being expelled. One frustrated master in Prince Edward had sought in 1824 to protect a favored elderly slave from deportation by directing that she not be formally manumitted, but rather treated "in the manner of a free person so far as the laws of the country will permit such a state of things."[104] Other slaveowners, however, simply ignored the law of 1806 and expected others to do the same. One man left a will that freed five "old and faithful negroes," four of them women; he clearly meant for them to remain within the state, for he enjoined his children to provide for their comfort in recognition of their service to the family. The churches in the South had gradually abandoned their official antislavery stance, yet in the middle of the 1820s, the pastor at Hampden-Sydney College could still publish an article—albeit an unsigned one—in a Richmond paper, in which he called slaveholding not a regrettable necessity but rather "the *great original sin . . .* at *all times* and in *all situations,* a *violation of the* [golden] *rule.*"[105]

Neither the Nat Turner revolt nor worries about the rise of abolitionism in the North dissuaded Alexander Patteson, the stage line operator, from writing a will in 1836 that liberated his slaves; his experience with some already free blacks who lived at his place over the years may have encouraged him to do so. After emancipating his coachman almost immediately, Patteson ordered that the rest of his bondpeople be hired out to "humane masters" for ten years and then manumitted and resettled in free territory using $500 from his estate.[106]

In 1841, saddlers Richard and William Chappell purchased a mulatto slave named Emaline for the express purpose of setting her free. She became one of the few liberated blacks who clearly went through the legally prescribed process of applying to remain in the county; at the time, that involved posting a statement of her intentions on the courthouse door for two months. Emaline's former owner supported her application by certifying that she was "honest and upright." "As she possesses unusual refinements for one in her situation," he added, "I am well persuaded that she will not associate with the generality of coloured persons bond or free." Decades of county history suggest that few whites would have objected to contact between Emaline and other blacks, but her ex-owner still assumed that some of his more hard-line peers might want assurances on that score. The county court unanimously approved Emaline's application. One might suspect that this "unusually refined," "bright mulatto" woman went free because of a relationship of love or blood to her liberators, who were kinsmen and business partners of Phil White's "agent," C. E. Chappell. In any event, William Chappell went on in 1849 to sign a deed that allowed another young slave, saddler Henry Chappell, to purchase his own freedom.[107]

In 1840, two white saddlers purchased Emaline, a slave, for the specific purpose of setting her free. She became one of the few liberated blacks who posted a statement, as required by law, of her intention to remain in Prince Edward County. (ARCHIVES RESEARCH SERVICES, LIBRARY OF VIRGINIA)

Two years after Emaline's emancipation, the circuit court began to oversee an unusually generous manumission and to defend its black beneficiaries. David Ellington left a will in which he freed his adult slave Nelson, and provided that an enslaved boy named Henry be exempted from work until 1853 and then emancipated. Remarkably, all of Ellington's nine hundred acres, eight of his slaves, and much of the rest of his property were to fall immediately under the control of Nelson and Henry and remain so for as long as either should live. David Ellington left no wife or children, but his sisters, nephews, and nieces reminded Nelson, if he did not already know, that the law required him to leave Virginia within a year. Nelson agreed to sell those people his 50 percent life estate in Ellington's property for $800, and he moved to Indiana.

Nelson might have got more money had he not been under pressure to leave—yet this was a small fortune for a newly emancipated man. Then, too, some of Ellington's holdings were nearly decrepit, and Nelson was selling a lifetime half-interest in the property, not full ownership with the right to bequeath to heirs. But what would happen to the boy Henry now that Nelson, his erstwhile guardian, had departed? Ellington's relatives went to the circuit court and claimed Henry as their slave until 1853, the year he was to become legally free. They also asked to take over the entire Ellington estate, camouflaging their greed with a promise to put aside some money for Henry to have when he finally got his liberty. Ellington's executor stood up for the black heirs. With the court's help, he made sure that Ellington's foot-dragging white survivors paid the $800 they had promised to the now absent Nelson. The court provided an annual allowance to maintain young Henry.

The court also appointed a commissioner who sought an opportunity for Henry to learn a profitable craft; though exempted from work by Ellington's will, young Henry said he "prefer[red] to do so rather than be idle." A full seven years passed, however, before the commissioner finally lined up two attractive apprenticeships in succession. The white official complained in the interim that the boy was "shabbily dressed, & had every appearance of having been treated as ordinary laborers on the farm."

The year of Henry's liberation, 1853, arrived during a decade in which Southern white hostility to black freedom supposedly reached new heights. Yet the court did not simply declare Henry free. It also required the white heirs to pay the costs of all the intervening litigation, and it awarded the young black man more than $1,200—$800 that he chose to accept for his lifetime half-interest in the Ellington property, plus interest accrued over the years. When the executor of one heir delayed paying Henry, the young black man went to the circuit court to demand his due. That apparently was enough to shake the payment loose. The victorious Henry, bearing the surname of his old master and benefactor, told the county court he planned to leave Virginia, yet he still lived at Prince Edward Court House in 1857.[108]

Another pair of court decisions, this time by a jury and by the supreme court of Virginia, granted liberty to a group of slaves only two years before Virginia left the Union and went to war to preserve its social order. The black plaintiffs had belonged to the very Randolph family that had enabled its ex-slaves to launch the experiment on Israel Hill. For decades after Judith Randolph's death, her estate had continued to function under a series of executors. Thirteen slaves belonging to that estate filed suit in Nottoway County, just east of Prince Edward, in 1858, demanding that the estate's administrator give them their freedom.[109] One of those slaves, named Aaron, had labored for Judith; so had another named Jinsey, now dead, whose dozen children and grandchildren joined Aaron as plaintiffs. Perhaps Aaron and Jinsey were the two slaves of Richard Randolph whom Judith had let John Randolph have at the time she emancipated ninety others in 1810.[110] Whether by this route or another, Aaron and Jinsey had in fact lived for years with Jack.

John Randolph died in 1833, leaving a will that emancipated his slaves and provided for their relocation in free territory. After much litigation, that will was finally carried out a decade later, but Aaron and Jinsey remained in the hands of Judy's estate administrator. Still more years passed—and then Aaron and his fellow plaintiffs brought their suit. They did not claim that Aaron and Jinsey had been covered by Richard Randolph's will. Instead, they insisted that those two had been the legal property of John Randolph and therefore had been liberated by *his* last testament.

The blacks faced a formidable opponent in Hunter H. Marshall, administrator of Judith Randolph's estate. Marshall was a politician who, before the slaves' lawsuit ran its course, would be elected judge of the judicial circuit that encompassed Prince Edward, Cumberland, and several other counties (the slaves filed suit in Nottoway, which was not part of Marshall's circuit).[111] Marshall insisted that Aaron and Jinsey had belonged to Judith Randolph and had come into John Randolph's household only because Jack had administered Judy's estate. Since Jack had not owned the pair, his emancipatory will did not apply to them, and Judith's will had not freed any of the few slaves she held in her own right. Thus, Marshall argued, Aaron and the descendants of Jinsey should remain enslaved and under his control.

Marshall got considerable help from the judge in the case. An inventory of Judith Randolph's property had been taken at her death in 1816, but the names of Aaron and Jinsey were nowhere to be found in that document. That simple fact seemed to confirm that the two had not legally belonged to Judith's estate—yet the judge would not allow the slaves to show the inventory to the jury. The document somehow made its way to the jurors anyway after they retired to consider their verdict, and that single paper overcame both Hunter Marshall's prominence and his well-planned case. The jury declared the enslaved plaintiffs free. When Marshall appealed to Virginia's supreme court, that body set aside the verdict for the slaves and called for a new trial, largely because the jury had received Judith Randolph's inventory improperly. But the high court also insisted that, on retrial, Aaron and his fellow plaintiffs be allowed to present that all-important document. Records of the new trial have not survived, but the right to exhibit the inventory probably strengthened a case that had already persuaded one jury.[112]

The suit of Aaron and company illustrates anew how strange life in the American South could be. Here, a group of African Americans sought their freedom by insisting that they had been the property of a famous defender of Southern rights, John Randolph. Twelve local whites, most if not all of them slaveholders, endorsed those people's right to liberty not long before the Union broke apart, at a time when white Southerners had supposedly formed a solid phalanx to repudiate "free negroism." Indeed, the jury vindicated the blacks against one of the most powerful men in that part of Virginia. The county court in Cumberland, where Marshall was apparently working the slaves at the time, followed up by ordering that the thirteen be taken out of Marshall's control pending a new trial.[113]

It is easy to question the importance of court cases in which white juries in Black Belt Virginia sustained bondpeople's claims to freedom. Such suits were few in number, and not all who claimed their liberty succeeded; the slaves born during the "wrong" years on Thomas Ford's place found that out. Even Aaron and the descendants of Jinsey had to wait years to prevail. Jinsey herself did not live to see that day. Still, in 1857, the Supreme Court of the United States—a panel dominated by Southerners—had opined in its *Dred Scott* decision that slaves (and perhaps free blacks) historically (and perhaps still) had no rights that a white man was bound to respect. Two years later, the supreme court of Virginia, in Aaron's suit against Hunter Marshall, declared that blacks—even slaves—*did* have certain important rights, including in some instances the right to claim their freedom.

The same tumultuous decade of the 1850s brought not just confirmations of long ago manumissions but new acts of emancipation by individuals in and around Prince Edward County. One master in Nottoway County set a bondman free on the very day in November 1859 on which John Brown, the would-be leader of a war to liberate slaves, was sentenced to hang.[114]

The national political climate did make a difference—not by destroying the emancipationist impulse, but rather by impelling some of those who wanted to liberate blacks to provide in advance for their transfer out of the state. The idea of sending emancipated blacks to free territory held by the United States was an old one by the time Jack Randolph adopted it. Andrew Baker had raised that possibility for his slaves at the turn of the century. Andrew Porter of Prince Edward left a will in 1821 allowing two of his bondpeople either to accept freedom and $30 each to fund their relocation in a free state, or to stay in Virginia under masters of their choice; he had concluded that the law offered no third alternative.[115] But sending ex-slaves to free territory carried its own dangers. Hostile whites in Ohio prevented John Randolph's former slaves in the 1840s from settling on the lands they were to have received there. As the twentieth century ended, some descendants of those emancipated people would still be seeking compensation for the land they had been deprived of.[116]

The idea of freeing one's slaves for resettlement in Liberia, West Africa, seemed more promising to some whites of conscience. A major impediment to colonization lay among blacks themselves, most of whom did not want to leave their homes for a distant continent almost none of them knew. Meanwhile, white Virginians, including some who railed against black freedom in the abstract, displayed a "paradoxical regard for free blacks' 'vested rights' " and an unwillingness to force their black neighbors to leave. After the Nat Turner revolt, county courts conducted informal surveys of black opinion and reported back to Richmond that most Afro-Virginians had no desire to go to Liberia; official support for colonization remained tepid, spotty, and noncoercive.[117]

Abolitionists accused colonizationists of advocating not the emancipation of slaves but the sloughing off of America's existing free black populace. The oft-repeated desire to "remove from our country a [free black] population . . . degraded in their intellect and morals"—though partly a device to win support from the general white public—has damned the colonizationists in the eyes of history.[118] Yet colonizationist leaders in Virginia—Chief Justice John Marshall served as president of the society in Richmond for a time—also made claims for black capacities that put them well ahead of most white opinion north or south. Freedom and self-government in Africa were already having "the same influence" on blacks as "with other men," they insisted, "elevat[ing] & giv[ing] to the human nature its true dignity." In Africa, Virginia colonizationists added, former slaves could become "respectable members of the social compact, ornaments to science and the arts." Advocates of colonization repeatedly exerted themselves to secure the "health and comfort" of black colonists in Liberia, and they were careful to frame the idea of resettlement as depending on the active consent of free blacks.[119]

The conflict over slavery after 1846 changed the colonization movement as it did so much else. By the 1850s, the Virginia branch of the

American Colonization Society felt impelled both by politics and by conviction to trumpet its supposed role as a bulwark "against the mischievous and reckless enterprises of Abolitionists." It disavowed any intention to influence masters other than those "spontaneously liberating their slave[s]." Privately, however, individual colonizationists lamented the hardening of proslavery opinion in their neighborhoods, and they complained that white Virginians had taken to proclaiming bondage a positive good (a doctrine that historians used to say had dominated Southern white opinion since the 1830s).[120]

Prince Edward County still had colonizationists in the 1850s who put humanitarian principles into practice. Anne S. Rice was the widow of the distinguished Presbyterian intellectual and critic of slavery John Holt Rice; Judith Randolph had died in the Rices' house. Anne Rice was also the granddaughter of a Revolutionary War veteran. Her aunt, Patty Morton, had left a will forbidding public auctioning of her slaves or the separation of families, and commanded her executor, when selling her bondpeople, "to consult rather the comfort of the negroes than the price they bring."[121] Anne Rice owned a library that contained many religious works; she also kept a biography of the British abolitionist William Wilberforce, which may have helped inspire her to go much further than her aunt had: after sending one family and several other bondpeople to Liberia in the years around 1850, Rice proceeded in 1853 to free five adult slaves and seven children. Those people may have constituted a single extended family; they, too, apparently settled in Liberia.[122]

Like several other emancipators in Prince Edward, John Watson knew firsthand that blacks could function as free people. Ampy Brandum, the former Randolph slave and sometime boatman, lived on Watson's plantation for years. When Watson died in 1855, truculent Southern defenses of slavery punctuated a bitter North-South debate. Yet Watson left a will emancipating his sixty-seven slaves; he allocated money to transport them to Liberia and to provide "for their comfort after reaching [that country]." Although Watson's white heirs challenged the will, a jury upheld it. Watson's executors spent some $9,000 conveying the freedpeople to Africa and bestowing new clothes and $60 in gold on each of them.[123]

Virginia humanitarians in the era of slavery disappoint Americans living after the civil rights movement, much as they attracted the scorn of abolitionists in their own day. Even sincere, principled emancipators such as John Watson often liberated slaves only in their wills—having their cake in this life and eating it in the next—or after those bondpeople should serve an additional period of years. Others freed certain individuals but kept others in bondage, even though both Christian antislavery and natural rights philosophy saw freedom as a right that all were born with, not a privilege that an individual had to earn.

Calls by non-emancipators to keep their slaves' families together or to sell them only to "humane" buyers, besides being unenforceable, implicitly recognized that the slaveholding system was immutable, perhaps even valid in principle, and that society would not rein in masters who chose to behave inhumanely. Even many whites who regretted the suffering of slaves in a general way could imagine no alternative to keeping them in the bondage "to which our policy compels us to confine them."[124] Catherine Baker had confronted the dilemma long before the 1850s. She found herself pulled in one direction by the humane principles she had shared with her emancipator-husband Andrew, and the opposite way by an unsympathetic legal code and a pack of greedy relatives. Not long after the founding of Israel Hill, Baker settled on a novel solution. She ordained that most of her slaves be sold at her death in two groups, keeping mothers and children together. But each group was to have "the liberty of choosing their master"—and then the slaves themselves, not Catherine's nieces, were to receive the very money they were sold for. Baker also left her knit bedspreads "to my negros equily." The county court rebuffed a challenge to the will from Catherine Baker's heirs.[125]

Proslavery hawks, unreflective, unrepentant slaveholders, and ameliorators differed from one another, yet they all accepted the main ideological pretensions of slaveholder society. The ameliorators did so by persuading themselves that the slaveowner who practiced Christian stewardship justified his or her mastery. The local James River Association of Baptists in 1844 condemned the buying and selling of slaves for profit, but in doing so suggested that masters who did not profiteer had nothing to apologize for. Those whites who showed the greatest openness toward free blacks were themselves slaveholders. The Israelites' friend Clement Read actually served as an expert witness on the valuation of bondpeople in the internal slave trade.[126] By contrast, the relatively few whites who practiced or even contemplated manumission questioned at least some of the system's claims. Some ameliorators, too, might have opted for manumission, except that the expulsion law and other measures made it seem futile or even inhumane to go that far. Slavery remained more firmly in place than ever in the South of the late

1850s—yet certainty about the morality of human bondage and about free black degeneracy never became as absolute or as universal as the Colonel Madisons and Edmund Ruffins wished.

Aggressive defenders of slavery thus faced a dual challenge in the 1850s. They sought to repel the antislavery onslaught emanating from elements in the North, but they also had to discredit the liberal ideas of some of their own white Southern neighbors. In 1858, an article from Farmville's newspaper, the *Journal*, made the rounds; it deprecated not only John Watson's decision to liberate and resettle his slaves but the entire colonizationist enterprise as well. Entitled "Liberia a Swindle," the piece reported that two ex-Watson slaves had returned from that country, denounced conditions in the colony and the treatment they had received from the Colonization Society, and voluntarily re-enslaved themselves in Prince Edward County.[127] The three free black men who did ask to become slaves in that year may represent an element of truth around which the *Journal* built its story.

For similar reasons, proslavery ideologues during the 1850s revived the old tale of Israel Hill's supposed degeneracy. A much more detailed, purportedly updated, and even grimmer version of the story appeared in newspapers as far north as New York City in the mid-1850s.[128] An unnamed writer for a Baltimore paper said he had visited Prince Edward County, and like Colonel Madison and Edmund Ruffin before him, he depicted Israel Hill as a failed test of blacks' capacity to live in freedom. The Randolphs' ex-slaves, nurtured by lifelong association with "intelligent whites," had received partially cleared land, tools, and building materials, this writer averred. They had even found themselves "surrounded by kindly disposed neighbors, who gave them employment at harvest, and at many other times during the year; who ministered to their wants in sickness, and who gave them advice in matters of business." With such unparalleled assets, the Baltimore reporter insisted, the Hill should have "become rich [and] populous," with "every inch of the soil productive."

According to Colonel Madison, the rot had set in on Israel Hill only as the first generation began to die out; the Baltimore writer now asserted that the Israelites had degenerated "*from the day of their liberation*" (the italics are his own). Israel Hill in 1854, he said, consisted of a "few miserable huts," their doors surrounded by weeds, crabgrass, and briers, inhabited by "diseased, depraved, miserable people." "The men are drunkards, the women prostitutes, the children scrofulous and syphilitic.

Almost all steal," he added, the few exceptions being those who had grown to adulthood under the supervision of white masters.

The Hill's population, the writer said, had declined by a quarter to a third between 1850 and 1854 alone owing to "the indolence and improvidence characteristic of [the black] race." Landowners on the Hill had "wantonly destroyed their woodlands" and "exhausted their soil by unsystematic and improper [cultivation]."

That last charge raised to new levels agronomist Edmund Ruffin's displaced anger over backward agricultural practices in Virginia generally—and Ruffin himself took up the issue of Israel Hill again at about the same time the Baltimore article appeared. On a visit to Prince Edward, Ruffin asked a prominent local citizen, Francis N. Watkins, to research Richard Randolph's "experiment" anew and to send him the results. Watkins produced a letter—the longest treatise yet about Israel Hill—which was eventually published in *DeBow's Review,* one of the South's most influential periodicals and a voice of Southern nationalism, in April 1858.[129]

Watkins seems actually to have taken the time to investigate the origins of Israel Hill in the county court's order books and wills, and in conversations with a few old-timers; he devoted the first half of his piece to a reasonably accurate and detailed history of the Randolph manumission itself. But from there on, he largely contented himself with generalizations, most of them adopted from the Baltimore article. Watkins did restore the Israelites' "very kind friend" Judith Randolph to her rightfully prominent role in the story (the Baltimore writer had omitted any mention of her). But he said Judy had given her ex-slaves "much profitable employment on the Bizarre farm," when in fact she had lamented the blacks' unwillingness to work for her as free people, and had quickly stopped farming Bizarre herself.

Watkins added a new detail to an old theme, praising by name "a venerable patriarch of the [Israelite] tribe," Sam White—a figure "as highly respected for tried and well sustained character as any man." Those superlatives gave Watkins a yardstick to measure how far the other Israelites had supposedly degenerated from the good stock that had first settled on the Hill. To Watkins, the moral of the story was clear: "When two races attempt to occupy the same territory, the weaker must give way to the stronger and more enlightened, (as the Indian race for example,) or occupy to their superiors the relation of slaves."

Watkins and the Baltimore writer adopted the working vocabulary not only of Madison and Ruffin but of the earlier thinkers those men had borrowed from. The writer from Baltimore damned the black Israelites as "a pest to their neighbors," echoing Jefferson. He characterized them as thieves, recalling St. George Tucker's fear of free black "banditti." He charged the Israelites with "indolence," reprising Thomas Dew, and idleness, repeating virtually everyone. Francis Watkins, too, picked up the ancient refrain of "idleness" and of "dishonest" and "dissolute" behavior. The Baltimore reporter even asserted that the Israelites had been protected from "competition with white labor—the bane of the African who settles in the free States." Watkins repeated that thesis verbatim, and the eminent historian U. B. Phillips would say the same thing about free blacks in general more than six decades later.[130] That notion would have amazed entrepreneurs such as Sam Strong and the Whites, as well as Prince Edward's free black carpenters, shoemakers, boatmen, and midwives—all of whom made their living in occupations pursued also by white people.

The Baltimore writer and Francis Watkins both wanted to reassure white Southerners of slavery's moral validity, so they did their best not to sound mean-spirited. They paid homage to Richard Randolph's "extraordinary goodness of character" and his "well-intended benevolence," criticizing only his "impolitic and unwise philanthropy." Far from gloating now, white Virginians were "saddened" by Israel Hill's fate, the reporter from Baltimore claimed. Watkins found the whole story "melancholy." In living out "the relation of master and servant, established by God himself," Watkins intoned, "we shall accomplish far more for our slaves and for humanity, than impious and fiendish abolitionism or sickly sentimentality."

Watkins not only lived in Prince Edward but had purchased, at least in theory, part of Israel Hill's Wilkerson tract in the sheriff's sale of 1845. He had also observed intimately some of the Israelites' achievements. The county court had named him in 1835 to audit the estate of the formidable Hercules White Sr. Afterward, as the court-appointed examiner of the late Colonel Madison's accounts, Watkins had investigated minutely the sale of new town lots in 1836. Phil White had bought one of those, but Watkins studiously omitted that embarrassing fact from his article.[131] Instead, Watkins conveniently based his story largely on what he called "the unwritten, but well-known, 'annals of the parish.'" It must have taken a comparable effort to ignore the additional purchases of lots, erection of buildings, and investment in business ventures that the Whites, the Gibbses, and other free blacks on and off the Hill had brought off since the 1820s. Yet the Baltimore writer denied that the Israelites possessed any drive for "progress" or "improvement." And when Watkins said he "doubt[ed] if one family or individual among [the Israelites] have materially added to their fortunes" since the founding of the settlement, he can only have been writing for an audience outside Prince Edward County that he knew had no access to the facts.

It is impossible to determine whom F. N. Watkins was thinking of when he asserted that at least one Israelite had died "from suffering and absolute want and poverty." People on the Hill apparently asked for, and certainly received, almost nothing in the way of aid from the county's overseers of the poor; the county paid for between two and four burials of Israelites over a half century. Meanwhile, scores of other residents of Prince Edward, most of them white, did receive aid or go to the poorhouse. Again without citing names or dates, the Baltimore writer told of "two [Israelite] sisters, one of whom makes a midnight foray into the corn patch of the other, and pulls the entire crop up by the roots." He also mentioned "a sickly poor creature placed under the charge of a drunken women [sic] who goes to town to buy whiskey, leaving her charge to die of sheer neglect." "Reports of broils and battles are common" on Israel Hill, he insisted; "scarcely a day passes without some of the adjacent [white] farmers being called in to interfere."

The reporter claimed to have witnessed one such incident himself: "But yesterday, two of the Israelitish women came to the house where the writer to [sic] this article is sojourning, to lodge a complaint against a fugitive slave who was harbored in the Hill, and who had suddenly rushed upon them, threatening to cut off their heads with a scythe blade which he held in his uplifted hand." Here it all was: anomie among blacks; a runaway slave, succored by certain free Negroes and wielding a deadly weapon; the utter dependency of blacks upon whites to furnish a semblance of order. That the anecdote plucks every string in the lyre of white anxiety and white supremacy does not prove that it was false—but a proslavery writer, concocting a story to support his case, could scarcely have done better.

In the real world, the report of free blacks aiding an escaped slave would doubtless have triggered action by the authorities. A violent attack by that fugitive on a pair of free women might have led to criminal charges. A free person's death by neglect should certainly have generated an inquest by Prince Edward's doggedly conscientious coroner, who examined so many other deceased blacks. In fact, the commentator from Baltimore wrote that disorders on Israel Hill "not unfrequently" led to intervention by county authorities. The county court records, then, should provide at least the occasional hint of any widespread free black criminality and of "broils and battles" involving people of the Hill. Yet the charges filed against Sidney Howard and William Johnston for stabbing fellow Israelites in the mid-1840s—serious incidents, to be sure—stand alone in the county's annals during the quarter century before the Baltimore reporter wrote.[132]

Francis Watkins enthusiastically took up the old theme of demographic stagnation. He maintained that a physically and socially healthy Israel Hill should have increased its population by 230 percent since 1810; he even had the temerity to call the Hill a "rotten borough."[133] That term denoted a locality in nineteenth-century Britain that had lost most of its inhabitants yet retained representation in Parliament. But Israel Hill was just the opposite: the community had grown after 1811, only to see its population of landowners and others permanently *denied* any voice in government. Had three hundred free blacks resided on the Hill's limited acreage by the 1850s, moreover, the same proslavery writers who now harped on the community's supposed failure to grow would probably have written the place off as a teeming, Malthusian warren.

The commentators of the 1850s had much more to say about Israel Hill's agriculture than Madison or even Ruffin, the agronomist, had ventured. The Baltimorean indicted the Israelites for supposedly growing only "Indian corn and tobacco, with a few potatoes and peas. . . . The idea of planting an orchard, a vegetable or flower garden," he continued, "seems never to have entered their heads." "Wheat they never grow," he added dismissively.

The people of the Hill probably did still grow vegetables; even non-landowners Guy and Mely Howard had done that much. Yet the Israelites' very economic diversification since the 1830s gave the propagandists an opening to criticize them for not concentrating enough on their farms. It had long made as much sense for the people of the Hill to purchase flour as to produce wheat. But for scientific agriculturists in Virginia, wheat culture and crop rotation epitomized progressive farming, and reliance on tobacco was the antithesis of good practice.

In the 1850s as in Colonel Madison's time, the myth of free black degeneracy reflected the ambivalence some proslavery ideologues felt toward the North: they envied the Yankee's achievements even as they flayed him for condemning slavery and embracing a catalogue of radical "isms." In the 1830s, critics of Israel Hill had taken the scorn they felt radiating toward them from the Northeast and redirected it at free blacks. During the contentious decade that preceded the Civil War, Francis Watkins and his contemporaries still wrote about Israel Hill much as Yankees wrote about Dixie.

The Baltimore reporter, an economic progressive from the Upper South like Madison, Ruffin, and Watkins, described the place he said Israel Hill should have become but supposedly had not: "a handsome village, surrounded with orchards and gardens, and sheltered by luxuriant shade trees . . . [filled with] the sound of the hammer, the saw, the plane, the church-going bell, the evidences of thrift, of industry, and of good morals." The classic image of a New England town—but in this instance the Baltimorean was depicting, without admitting it, not an Israel Hill that never was, but rather a prosperous, progressive rural South that he feared his fellow white people were failing to create.

These new obituaries for the Israelite "experiment" became lurid exhibits in the deepening contest over slavery during the 1850s. That struggle took on new dimensions some eighteen months after Francis Watkins's article appeared: in October 1859, abolitionist John Brown and a small party of men briefly captured the federal arsenal at Harpers Ferry, Virginia. That event, and the admiration Brown ultimately won among many in the North, convinced slaveholders that they were under siege. On November 21, five weeks after the raid, a grand jury in Prince Edward County presented three free blacks and two whites on charges that clearly displayed whites' worries about race and security. The blacks all faced charges of not having left the state within a year of their manumissions. One of those presentments seems particularly callous: the status of the defendant, Betsy Minnis, may have come to light as she arranged for the county to bury her child at public expense.[134] The difference that the John Brown affair made emerges clearly from the facts of the other two cases.

For a dozen years after her manumission in 1846, white officials had denied Mary Franklin formal permission to remain in residence. But they did so only in sporadic and halfhearted fashion. When a grand jury presented her for remaining in the state in 1856, the prosecutor quickly dropped the charge. Back in 1851, Franklin had told the court she intended to leave Virginia, and the rhythm of her brushes with authority thereafter suggests that she just may have moved north and then returned, perhaps more than once. Such exposure to dangerous Yankee ideas would explain local officials' cold shoulder—toward Mary Franklin as toward the free Afro-Virginian emigrant to Pennsylvania, Isaac Coles, before her. The very same session of the court that again rebuffed

Franklin in 1856 authorized another, perhaps less cosmopolitan free black man to remain in residence. Ultimately, John Brown's raid seems to have prompted officials, after years of empty gestures, to ensure once and for all that Mary Franklin depart and stay away. She did so by the winter of 1859–60, though her father, Robert, went on living and working in Prince Edward, his registration renewed as a matter of course by the county court.[135]

Another free black, Julius Richardson, definitely spent time in the North, and that sealed his fate in the wake of John Brown's attack. Richardson, like Mary Franklin, had a checkered history with county authorities. In the spring of 1856, grand jurors had expressed their growing anxiety about undocumented free blacks. Richardson, Franklin, and one other Afro-Virginian were presented for lacking free papers or remaining in the state without permission, and the grand jury recommended that the court appoint an officer to ferret out the "many" blacks around Farmville who supposedly lacked free papers. No one took up that suggestion, but county justices, who traditionally had paid little attention to free black migration, did turn down a black man from another county who asked permission to move into Prince Edward that summer; the court would act similarly in two other instances over the next two and a half years.

Julius Richardson himself quickly got off the hook, however; he persuaded the court that he had simply lost his free papers. But he found himself presented again, along with Betsy Minnis and Mary Franklin, in November 1859. Building contractor Henry Guthrey, a man generally friendly to free blacks, filed the complaint; Guthrey's persistence in the Richardson case suggests how markedly Brown's attack at Harpers Ferry had affected white attitudes. The charge against Richardson for remaining in the state did not stick—after all, he had registered with the county court only three years earlier. So Guthrey lodged a new accusation that cut to the heart of the matter: he charged that the black man had spent more than a year in Ohio and then returned without obtaining permission. Deputies did not actually take Richardson into custody until a few days before he was to be tried on the new presentment, and the case was then dismissed. The late arrest and the dropping of the charge may well have come as part of an agreement under which the defendant would leave Virginia permanently and take any abolitionist ideas with him.[136]

The same grand jury that presented free blacks Minnis, Franklin, and Richardson turned an equally suspicious eye on two white citizens. The panel presented Susan and Stephen Colley for "unlawfully associating with the slaves [of a certain mistress] & playing at cards with them" on their owner's premises. For whites and slaves to while away time together was a tradition in Prince Edward; now, after John Brown's brief, failed crusade, some white citizens objected to a simple interracial card game. A deputy sheriff reported the Colleys "no inhabitants" of the county, and the court then dismissed the charge against them.[137]

Even after John Brown, however, white Prince Edward did not fall into wholesale panic. Some continued to parrot the proslavery myth of Israel Hill—but as a tale reflexively, almost complacently, passed from one generation to the next rather than a call to vigilance. In the margins of the federal census tables for 1860, the county's enumerator almost clinically described Israel Hill as "quite an interesting . . . experiment" that "would appear to demonstrate that the 'free negro' is only nominally free in a free White community." In a couple of equally nonchalant sentences, the official repeated the old argument: the Israelites' history proved that emancipated blacks, even those freed under the most favorable circumstances, would inevitably succumb to "degeneracy, & degradation." Yet he suggested no peril to public order, focusing instead on the Hill's alleged economic and demographic stagnation.[138] Unlike Colonel Madison, F. N. Watkins, and others, the census taker was not writing for the public and could expect to score no propaganda points. His rendering of the story suggests both the tale's abiding currency among some local people and the disinclination of most—John Brown or no—to see Israel Hill as a threat to their own interests.

As late as 1859 and 1860, courts in and around Prince Edward still gave black defendants fairer hearings by far than would generally be the case from the latter nineteenth century to the 1960s. Next door in Nottoway County in June 1859, before John Brown's attack, a white woman accused her slave Peter of attempting to murder her. A fresh two-by-four-inch gash on her head might have made an open-and-shut case for a later, post-Reconstruction generation. But the slave's attorney summoned two white men as defense witnesses; a called court delayed judgment until that pair could be brought in to testify, and then it acquitted Peter. The wound had obviously been inflicted. Peter may have pleaded self-defense, or asserted that he was being blamed for an attack committed by someone else. In any event, the court accepted the evidence in the slave's favor over the sworn word of his mistress.[139]

A year later, after the John Brown crisis, as the nation moved toward the presidential election that would break it apart, a called court in the same county acquitted an enslaved woman accused of burning down her mistress's house; the same period saw a "nest" of whites in Prince Edward "driven off for Sheep stealing." A slave defendant, in short, could still get a fair trial, even as white livestock rustlers might find themselves rooted out summarily.[140] Then, just after Lincoln's election, a jury convicted and fined a white man for having shot into the house of free black Robert Franklin. The attack on Franklin, like the accusation of arson against the slave woman in Nottoway, may have arisen out of the frantic political atmosphere of 1860—but local authorities were having no part of vigilantism against an innocent free black man. Prince Edward's authorities had made a related point that summer when they sentenced the unbalanced James D. Shepherd to a jail term for shooting and wounding a slave.[141]

Throughout the sectional debates from 1850 to 1860, a Southern ideologue could prove to be a relatively liberal master of slaves, as Colonel Madison had been a generation earlier. During the gathering crisis of the Union, some of the most generous payments to enslaved people for extra work came from none other than Francis N. Watkins, who at the very same time was embroidering and helping to popularize the myth of Israel Hill's decline and fall: Watkins paid bondpeople fully $190 for corn in 1856 and early 1857. Watkins also engaged the services of free blacks, belying the low estimate of the group that he offered to his reading public.[142]

The deeper rhythms of existence in Prince Edward continued as always, bringing an end between 1858 and 1861 to the lives of five free Afro-Virginians whose stories had played out in a variety of ways. The biography of Matilda White contains more than its share of mystery. She drowned in the Buffalo River at the foot of Israel Hill in May 1858. Someone, presumably neighbors of hers, moved the body to her house on the Hill, where a coroner's jury concluded that she had fallen into the stream accidentally. Founding Israelite Dick White had had a daughter named Matilda, who would have been about forty in 1858; it was probably she who drowned. Many years earlier, Matilda and her sisters had taken one of the biggest slaveholders in the area as their guardian after the loss of one or both parents. Yet by the late 1850s, the authorities stated that Matilda White had no assets to cover the expenses of her coroner's inquest and burial. In the end, it seems, she had fallen into the sort of penury that proslavery men ascribed to all the black Israelites. The county justice on the scene was willing to have the county shoulder the costs attending Matilda's death rather than burden her relatives. Still, one wonders why her uncle Sam or her kinsman Phil, or even someone from her white former guardian's family, did not provide the $11 required to usher Matilda into the grave.[143]

Zack Ellis, a former Randolph slave though not an Israelite, died around the same time as Matilda White; he, too, was buried at the expense of the overseers of the poor. Residing for years on the Chambers place near Farmville, Ellis had made a steady living as a carpenter and shoemaker, and had tangled with Colonel Madison when Zack's enslaved daughter paid him an unauthorized visit. The Ellises were long-lived; Zack and Billy both reached or passed the age of eighty. A lengthy illness, or simply an old age more prolonged than his savings would cover, may have left Zack in need after a lifetime of solvency. The overseers of the poor found him morally deserving. They allotted him more than $23 in aid at his residence during the last months of his life—one of the most generous awards to any individual that year—and then they paid for his coffin.[144]

Hampton Giles, one of the founding settlers of Israel Hill, died in 1859. He had apparently outlived by many years both his first wife, Phoebe—accused by Sooky White so long ago of having poisoned a cabbage—and his neighbor and nemesis, John Brown. Hampton Giles still had children from his first marriage living on Israel Hill, now grown and established, with families of their own. Thus Giles took special care at the end of his life to provide for his second wife, Sooky, who was half his age, and for the children she had borne. Giles had expressed great pride in his farm, and regularly paid taxes on it; he now left it for his widow's use. The couple's three sons were to divide the plot at Sooky's death or remarriage, and Giles directed them to accommodate their two sisters at home until the girls came of age or married.[145]

John Dungey and Sam Strong departed life within a brief span of time in 1860 and 1861. Dungey, son of the interracial spouses James and Elizabeth, had become a prosperous yeoman farmer by 1850, his 140-acre farm worth $500. He grew wheat, oats, corn, tobacco, and even cotton—thirty bales of it in a single year—and he raised a few sheep and cattle as well as swine. Dungey tried as methodically as Hampton Giles had to provide for his family. He drafted and redrafted his last testament early in the 1850s, seeking both to protect his widow and children against various contingencies and to exhort the young ones to "industry"—that generations-old slogan of so many Prince Edward families white and black. But then the depression of 1857 intervened. By the time John Dungey died, at the very outbreak of the Civil War, events had forced him to sell part of his land and use the rest, along with most of his movable property, to secure debts; only three and a half barrels of corn worth $14 remained free and clear.[146]

Entrepreneur Sam Strong, in sharp contrast, died at the end of a decade in which he had reached the top of his form. He had come back from the trials of the earlier depression years to buy and sell town lots and land. In his will of 1860, Strong left an intriguing, unexplained legacy of $100 to James Daniel White, a young factory worker who likely belonged to the White clan of Israel Hill. Strong bequeathed the rest of his property to his wife, Fanny, and his stepdaughter, leaving them among the most comfortably situated blacks in Farmville.[147]

Ten years earlier, Tony White of Israel Hill had tried as valiantly as Strong, Dungey, and Hampton Giles to provide for his surviving family. Yet those very efforts, and his relatives' acquisitiveness, led to conflict within the White clan toward the end of the 1850s. Not long before he died at the beginning of that decade, Tony had given up the idea of leaving money to his enslaved and scattered children. He added a codicil to his will calling for one Susan Smith to move in with his wife, the former slave Milly. When Milly died, White decreed, the house and the twelve acres on which it stood should go to Susan, not for her lifetime only but "to her and her heirs forever."[148]

Susan (Sooky) Smith sometimes went by her maiden name, Susan White; she probably was Sam White's granddaughter, so she would have known Tony and his wife all her life. Tony may have decided to leave his homeplace to Sooky in return for the thing he wanted most—good care for his widow after he was gone. Sooky seems to have lost or parted from her husband not long before Tony White wrote his will; a secure situation and the prospect of inheriting a house and a piece of land must have looked attractive to her.[149]

Milly White survived her husband by some half a dozen years. She had agreed with Tony's decision that, on her own demise, the twelve-acre tract should pass to Sooky Smith. But half a dozen members of the White family went to the circuit court early in 1858 and demanded that they, and not Smith, receive Tony's house and land. Their legal strategy repeated the one that miller Phil Bowman's mother had used years earlier against Phil's technically enslaved widow, Priscy. The Whites' lawyer asserted that Milly White had been a slave—Tony may never have drawn up a formal deed of emancipation—and that under the law she therefore had been unable either to inherit or to bequeath land. The attorney added that Tony's original will had likewise been invalid because it named as heirs "certain persons supposed to be his children but who were and are slaves and [not] capable of holding land." According to the Whites' lawsuit, that left Tony's brothers and their survivors as the sole legal heirs to his property.

What impelled Tony White's family to challenge Sooky Smith, apparently their own relative, over a mere twelve acres? Perhaps the Whites disliked or disapproved of Smith personally. In any case, Tony White's little piece of land had its attractions. Unlike other parcels on the Hill, Tony's fronted on Buffalo River; it therefore consisted partly of much-valued bottomland. Most of the Whites who sued Sooky Smith owned very small tracts. Sam, with sixty-four acres, was a grandee compared with his brothers' heirs; Dick and Hercules Junior had each left a mere eleven or twelve acres, which their children then had to share two or three ways. To such people, twelve additional acres of good land, even if divided up, might come in handy.

The Whites may have brought the suit not to evict Sooky Smith from the land, but rather to induce her to let them share in the use of it. Only eight months after filing the action, Sam White dropped out of it, and the others soon followed; they may already have received what they wanted from Smith. Sam had not come as far as he had, nor weathered the post-1837 depression, without knowing when to push and when to fall back and settle for half a loaf. Sooky Smith remained on the Hill, possibly in the house that Tony and Milly White had left her.[150] As in times past, tensions on Israel Hill gave way to reconciliation, or at least to a modus vivendi.

For a number of free Afro-Virginians in Prince Edward County, the years of national tension before the Civil War brought relative prosperity, progress, and even, in some cases, the fulfillment of dreams. Another tiny moment in the life of the White clan reveals a free black man advancing himself yet one step further as white neighbors look on with interest, but without alarm. In February 1860, the Union of American states looked more fragile than ever. But for a young free black woman of eighteen named Harriet Smith, the tyranny of personal concerns wielded its usual iron hand. Her identity is not clear; she may even have been a daughter of the very same Sooky Smith whom the Whites had sued over Tony White's legacy. In any case, Harriet wanted a legal guardian, and the person she chose was Israelite Philip White III. The law required White and a cosigner to execute a bond guaranteeing Phil's performance as guardian to Harriet.

Whichever white man filled out the bond took it for granted that free

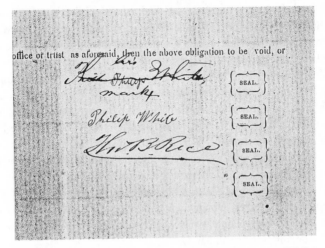

A white official prepared a document to accommodate the mark of Philip White III. The free black man surprised those present by writing out a graceful signature, first in the space provided for his mark, then in a roomier spot.
(GUARDIAN'S BOND FOR HARRIET SMITH, COUNTY COURT, FEBRUARY 1860, ARCHIVES RESEARCH SERVICES, LIBRARY OF VIRGINIA)

blacks did not know how to sign their names. So, at the bottom of the document, he wrote, "Phill White, his mark," in the accustomed configuration—the four words distributed left and right, up and down, so as to enclose a small blank area that would accommodate an illiterate man's X. White, then in his late thirties, took pen in hand and—to the surprise of at least one white person in attendance—neatly wrote the name "Philip" in the blank spot before discovering that he had no room left for his surname. He then decided, or the justice of the peace invited him, to start over at a different place on the bond where he would have enough space to write his full name. As the white cosigner looked on, the officiating justice, perhaps a bit embarrassed, marked through the superfluous words bidding White to make "his mark." White's name may have been the only thing he knew how to write; perhaps he had tried to sign inside the little box of words because he could not read what they said. But the penmanship of Philip White III is neat, fine-lined, and elaborate, like the typical signatures of literate men, so he may well have been able to read the phrase "his mark" perfectly well.[151]

Philip White had always been a self-confident person: he had not hesitated to turn down a white man's bid on a lot in Farmville when he thought the offer too low. But like most men, White did not sign legal documents every day. He saw that someone in charge of the process had designated a spot for him to write his mark, and he figured he had better do as the man said. It just so happened that Phil White's "mark" was a full, legible, even graceful signature. For neither the first nor the last time, a free Afro-Virginian had accomplished something unexpected—something that the existing system had done nothing to equip him for, and that the professed ideology of white society all but ruled out as a possibility. Signing the guardian's bond, though important to Harriet Smith, was a trivial act; the entire event lasted perhaps five or ten minutes. Yet Philip White's signature, and his possible literacy, constitute one more chapter in a remarkable story that had taken on new dimensions during the 1850s, even as sectional tensions deepened and new laws and pronouncements against free blacks multiplied.

The third Phil White had witnessed the economic and social rise of his once-enslaved father, the older man's wrenching setbacks of the 1840s, his gritty recovery, and the successes of other free blacks who followed the elder Phil's example. White had listened as the railroad's clatter drowned out the rippling of water parted by his family's batteaux, and looked on as steam engines shunted a proud tradition to the margins. He knew that fluidity and change had been and remained integral parts of a society, the Old South, that popular stereotypes of our own day picture as static. Now, on a winter day in 1860, one white and one black Virginian left the bond-signing and walked out into an American society that was embarking, against its will, upon a revolution. The glare from that explosion would blind future generations to the richness, variety, and surprising transformations that had already pervaded those Southerners' lives for so long.

CHAPTER 9

Appomattox and the New Birth of Freedom

E ven as the 1860s dawned, most white Virginians hoped to avoid open conflict with the North. Ties to friends, relatives, and trading partners in the free states remained strong; Prince Edward's Saylor family, with branches in New York, Pennsylvania, Ohio, Indiana, North Carolina, and Illinois, was not alone in its geographic sweep. Several of the county's stalwart citizens, including builder James B. Ely, storekeeper Ebenezer Frothingham, Asa Dupuy's wife, and Colonel Charles Woodson's mother, had been transplanted New Englanders or New Yorkers. When Virginians spoke of "the South" during the 1850s, as often as not they meant the Cotton Belt—a discrete region with which they had some major interests and assumptions in common, yet from which they still felt separate in important ways.[1]

Among Virginia's voters in the presidential election of 1860, Southern Democrat John C. Breckenridge ended in a virtual tie with Constitutional Unionist John Bell, who advocated compromise between North and South; about a tenth of the state's ballots went to the "national" or Northern Democratic candidate, Stephen A. Douglas. Prince Edward County supported Breckenridge a little more strongly than did the state as a whole, yet Unionist Bell came in a close second. Bell's vote in the county combined with that of the Illinoisian Douglas to constitute a slight majority against the extreme "Southern rights" position.[2] Nevertheless, the state and the county began to prepare for the worst within weeks of Abraham Lincoln's election to the presidency. In mid-January 1861, Prince Edward's county court issued bonds to finance the purchase of arms and ammunition. Three months later, "citizens of the County . . . assembled in the court room in large numbers"—undoubtedly to hear news and exchange views about the Confederate capture of Fort Sumter that had taken place the day before.[3]

Within days of Sumter's fall, as Virginia moved to secede from the Union, at least a few militia units in the south-central part of the state pronounced themselves ready for war. Yet the county court had already voted down a proposal to create a "special police force" in February, and worries about domestic unrest, as after John Brown's raid, deepened only modestly after war broke out. Five weeks after Fort Sumter, four of seven presentments that Prince Edward's grand jury issued did involve blacks. The panel lodged an unusual charge against two white men, alleging that they had received stolen equipment from two free blacks—not slaves; but the cases against the two defendants were soon dismissed, and the free black men were never even charged. The other two presentments accused a white man of having allowed slaves to trade as free people, a garden-variety accusation if ever there was one.[4]

Meanwhile, officials in Prince Edward were finding it difficult to sell the $100 war bonds they had issued, and many militia officers around the state issued desperate pleas for weapons, unwittingly echoing their predecessors' alarms during the Nat Turner panic. The Old Dominion Rifles reported that they lacked, of all things, rifles; an artillery unit near Richmond requested six field pieces, but conceded that they would "take muskets . . . if we cant get [the big guns]." As late as mid-June 1861, the governor complained that the state's appropriation to the military contingent fund had been a mere $2,800, and he discreetly appealed to the governor of North Carolina to "furnish Virginia ten thousand stand of arms."[5]

Individual citizens of the Commonwealth broached the issue of how free and enslaved blacks might contribute to the war effort. Daniel Flournoy of Buckingham County suggested that "for every five or ten thousand men Virginia has in the field she should have one thousand negro men" to do everything from cooking and hauling water to building forts and driving teams. Flournoy also became perhaps the first person in the South to assert that slaves could "even fight if needed." The clerk of Brunswick county court, who volunteered the services of five slaves, reported that those men had "expressed to [him] a willingness & readiness to do any thing for the protection of our Homes."[6] At least some whites felt as certain of free blacks' talents and loyalty to Virginia as Flournoy and his counterpart in Brunswick did about the allegiance of slaves. The *Richmond Dispatch* proclaimed that "the free colored population . . . are ready and willing to do anything that they be called upon to do in the present emergency. This is the proper spirit," the paper went on. "Let them act up to it, and they will be fully protected and provided for."[7]

James R. Branch, a white resident of Petersburg, sent word to the governor that "one hundred (100) free negroes[,] the pick of the place, good & true men[,] will offer their Services to the State & ask me to command them." Whether Branch believed he would end up leading uniformed black troops or mere work details must remain an intriguing question. In any case, Branch was eager to command black men if it brought him a captain's commission. More than that, he took it for granted that he could tout his free black potential recruits as "the pick of the place" and be taken seriously at the state Capitol. Branch's stance, like the behavior of countless white men before him, directly contradicted the portrayal of free African Americans in proslavery propaganda as sluggards and criminals. The secretary of the Commonwealth did the same when he unhesitatingly repeated the phrase, "Picked free negroes good and true," in his brief summary of Branch's telegram.[8]

If some free Afro-Virginians did volunteer to serve the Southern cause, they may have been motivated partly by the desire to repel invaders or by fear for the safety of their homes in wartime. They surely wished to avoid the suspicion of their white neighbors; they may have hoped to have some say over the conditions of any service they might give rather than wait passively until the state assigned them to duties of its own choosing. Proposals far less benign than James Branch's were already being floated: on the very day he telegraphed his offer of free black recruits to Richmond, a minister and several other men who lived not far from his hometown of Petersburg proposed to "press [thousands of] free men of color into the service of the state." With perfect candor, they explained that "the Country would feel & be more safe" if free blacks were placed under military control.[9] On July 1, 1861, the state convention of Virginia did create a framework to draft free black workers. The ordinance "authorized" county courts and city governments to compile a roster of "all able bodied free negroes" aged eighteen to fifty; when any commanding officer asked a county to supply free black labor, a panel of three local justices would consult its list and determine whom to send.

The notion that blacks might actually bear arms for "the cause" had gained no traction: all black men drafted would be detailed "for labor in erecting batteries [and] entrenchments" or to fill other, similarly menial roles. The system did include some safeguards for the free blacks it would affect. The three-justice boards were supposed to take men's "condition and circumstances" into account when they selected individuals for service. The men so chosen would receive the same pay, rations, quarters, and medical care that went to "other labor of a similar character." The drafters of the ordinance may have been thinking of the terms that would apply to hired slaves, except that free blacks would receive their own pay. Under the law, free men supposedly could not be "detained, at any one time," to work for more than sixty days without their consent.

The conscription ordinance discriminated blatantly against free blacks; the Confederacy would not introduce a general draft for white men until 1862. At the same time, the lawmakers determined that the punishment for a free Afro-Virginian who refused to respond to a call-up would be identical to the penalty exacted against a white militiaman who failed to obey a summons; free black military workers would be governed under the articles of war that applied to soldiers. Some Israelites and other free blacks were ordered to report for duty soon after the new law was adopted—by November 1861, three Whites, two Carters, and a Gibbs had already been released from a tour of duty building fortifications in Isle of Wight County in the Tidewater. For some, the mustering out may only have signaled a respite before they were drafted again.[10]

As in peacetime, gaps arose between what the law required and what actually happened in the field. At least some among the Virginia and Confederate authorities did seek to provide decently for free black workers, but they had to contend with bureaucratic inertia tinged, presumably, by race bias. Even before the conscription scheme took effect or wartime stresses created chaos, General John Bankhead Magruder had to remind his headquarters that many of his free black workers "have families, who must starve if they are not paid, and to all [of them] I promised prompt payment."[11]

While some free Afro-Virginians labored for the Confederacy, others aided the Union war effort. Some served as spies or "agents." A Union officer on the Virginia Peninsula assured his superiors in 1862 that "many free negroes can be found who could be fully trusted with the transmission of messages in cipher." One ardent Massachusetts cavalry officer considered his volunteer free black guide "true as steel," and "found the colored people almost always to be so." He added that the intelligence they provided "was invariably correct and often of the highest importance." A Confederate general near Richmond in 1862 noted with alarm the "dangerous" phenomenon of free blacks lending their services as "good river pilots" to the Yankees.[12]

Meanwhile, white officials in many counties—having been "authorized" but not required to enroll free black prospective laborers—proved no more eager to draw up lists of black potential draftees than they had been to hire out free black tax delinquents in earlier years. In February 1862, a new state ordinance *required* the laggard county courts to enroll their free black men, and this time to submit the lists to the state's chief military officer. Any sheriff or constable who failed to produce free black workers when the army called for them under the act faced a fine of as much as $100.[13] The new law built in a further incentive for white officials to provide free black conscripts: every free draftee a county produced meant that one slave fewer would be called up for duty, and that reduced discontent among slaveholders. The new framework included one other fateful change. By 1862, everyone expected a long, arduous conflict; free blacks could now be required to give six months' service rather than sixty days.

Prince Edward's officials had enrolled ninety-six free black men even before the second conscription act required them to do so. By early 1862, at least twenty-six men were actually serving in the army, and others may have gone uncounted; Israel Hill alone had supplied eight men by then, if not more. Later that year, the army requisitioned thirty men from Cumberland County to serve as attendants at Farmville's Confederate hospital, a huge facility of between twelve and fifteen hundred beds located partly in tobacco warehouses and factories. In March 1863, the chief of the Engineer Bureau in Richmond asked General Robert E. Lee to call up more than a thousand free black laborers from twenty-four counties and cities; Prince Edward alone was to furnish over fifty.[14]

Even Prince Edward's annual free black lists, with their haphazard data on people's ages, reveal that some free Afro-Virginians who fell outside the prescribed age group nevertheless entered the service. One member of Farmville's Bartlett clan supposedly worked in the army at age sixty-one, another at fifty-five. At the other extreme, John Giles and Tom Johnston of Israel Hill joined up or were called at fifteen, and one lad who may have been a member of the Israelite Wilkerson family appears as an army worker at thirteen. Free black women, too, worked for the army; at least a couple served in the Confederate hospital, one of them as a nurse. Some of these people whose age or sex should have exempted them from service may have turned out for the army voluntarily, perhaps to earn steady if modest pay, room, and board.[15]

In 1863 and 1864, the number of free blacks noted on Prince Edward's annual lists as performing army service dipped to around sixteen—but the enumerator probably included only those who actually resided in the county at the time. The military had stationed others in faraway parts of the state. One Israelite farmer who worked for the Army, Bob Webber, may have been away from home performing his duties when his twelve-year-old daughter accused an enslaved man of raping her early in 1863 (county justices acquitted the suspect). The experience of another Israelite, William H. White, in his twenties at the outbreak of war, offers a more typical example of how the conflict disrupted free black life. White was the young batteauman who had helped his father transport stone upriver to build the High Bridge of the South Side Railroad; he had gone on to work in tobacco factories, for the railroad company itself, and at farming. When the Civil War came, White recalled years later, he "was taken [by the army] to work" on a waterside battery in the Tidewater. White was apparently released from duty after a while, for he spent an interval blacksmithing in Richmond. Then the army conscripted him again and sent him to work, probably at a forge or foundry, in the Allegheny Mountains until the end of the war.[16] By that time, William H. White had involuntarily seen two or three times as much of the world as even his fellow boatmen had done on their voyages before the conflict.

While men such as White traveled the state under the auspices of the army, life on Prince Edward's home front remained as complex as ever, partly because of the conflict, and partly in spite of it. Local whites, regardless of their prewar politics or habits, saw the war effort as an attempt to defend Virginia from invaders—indeed, from aggressors who threatened to undermine slavery and thus the entire social order. Naturally, then, white people who had maintained long, friendly, and profitable relationships with free blacks played prominent roles in that effort. When the county court again issued war bonds in June 1861, for example, Clem Read and Newton Cunningham served on local committees that the court appointed to allocate proceeds to equip soldiers and aid their families.[17]

The Confederacy was fighting to defend itself as a separate republic in which the right of masters to own and control slaves would remain safe from any challenge. Only three months into the war, a shocking event forced whites in Prince Edward to contemplate the moral issues that attended absolute control over other human beings. On the second Saturday in July 1861, in an oat field half a mile outside Farmville, a slave named William, in his late thirties, attacked his owner, Hillery G. Richardson, with a scythe blade attached to a wheat cradle. The black man virtually obliterated Richardson's left knee joint. The grievously injured Richardson contended in an affidavit that his other slaves had

The Confederate Army conscripted free Afro-Virginian men to serve in laboring units, often far from home. Black workers did much of the digging of fortifications and of graves (shown here) for Union and Confederate armies alike.

(LIBRARY OF CONGRESS, PRINTS AND PHOTOGRAPHS
DIVISION, LC–USZC4–1820)

complained of William's failure to work as he should, and that he, Richardson, had then disciplined the man mildly. As Richardson moved away from his bondman, he said, William had "cut me down in the twinkling of an eye." Richardson added that William had swung his blade at a fellow slave who tried to intervene, and that four or five other bondmen had then "knocked [William] down with some rocks."[18]

The assault on Richardson would instantly have registered as one of the most dramatic by a slave on a master in the county's history, even if Richardson had not been a former sheriff and the wealthiest man in Prince Edward. Yet as word of the attack spread on Saturday evening and Sunday, the black and white public began to focus on rumors that William "had been very badly whipped" before he wounded his master.[19] White citizens began appearing at the jail asking to see William's back; the eminent Dr. John Peter Mettauer examined the prisoner, partly, he said, because of "what I heard on the street." To one citizen who looked at William, it appeared as though the black man had been "cruelly whipped." Mettauer found that "the skin [on William's back] seemed to be removed in places as wide as my finger" by blows from a large stick, and that half the skin had been beaten off on one side of the slave's back. Another physician agreed, adding that both of the bondman's eyes were injured, and that William was missing some teeth.[20]

In the meantime, Hillery Richardson, whose apparent readiness to inflict agony on slaves was now the talk of the town, refused to allow doctors to dress his wound properly because "he dreaded the pain." After two weeks, the ex-sheriff began to decline, and he died after a third week of suffering. William now went on trial not for assault, but rather for the murder of one of the county's most prominent slaveholders. No one denied that William had committed the attack—yet at his four-day trial, an indefatigable defense attorney produced many witnesses both black and white who all but justified the bondman's fatal deed. Mettauer and another physician undermined the charge of murder, testifying that the wound need not have killed Richardson except for the already "diseased state of his system" and his refusal to accept proper medical treatment. Benjamin C. Peters, the doctor whose dealings with free blacks had been so many and varied, reported that the abused William had been as badly off medically after the wounding as his master Richardson had been. Peters recalled having said at the time, "I would as soon take [Richardson's] chance to live as [William's]."

A torrent of testimony suggested that William's master had provoked the attack. The very constable who had taken William into custody testified to Richardson's reputation as a man who was "very cruel . . . very barbarous to some of his slaves." William's fellow bondmen took the stand and added gruesome details. Over the years, Richardson had beaten William repeatedly on the bare back with sticks and switches, each whipping lasting fifteen to twenty minutes; he had held the bondman down during beatings by placing his foot on William's head. After one such assault, the master had washed his slave's wounds in salt water. On more than one occasion, Richardson had pulled sound teeth out of William's mouth as a punishment, forcing a fellow slave to restrain the victim during the procedure.[21]

William had run away three weeks before he cut Richardson, testimony at his trial showed. The man who captured him had shot him in several places, yet Richardson had kept the bondman shackled with an eight-pound chain around his ankles ever since; the chain was exhibited and weighed in court. Richardson had also chained William to the ground every night while he slept. William's eyesight had been so impaired by his master's blows, including one dealt with a stick, that the black man could not see to whet his own blade. Yet Richardson had twice broken sticks over William's head on the morning of the wounding, then threatened to kill the shackled slave for not keeping up with the other harvesters.

Enslaved witnesses, whose testimony the court heard at great length, added that William's sufferings had been merely an extreme manifestation of Richardson's general practice. "He whipt all of us," said one. "Master was in the habit of catching us by the fingers & bending them back," remarked another; "his object was to hurt us." In the face of such testimony, the prosecuting attorney was reduced at one point to showing that Richardson had not singled William out, having also "threaten[ed] to kill other of his hands, when he was mad with them."[22] Two white witnesses did say that, after the cutting, William admitted he had intended to kill Richardson. Yet the enslaved defendant came out of the testimony sounding not only long-suffering but at times almost noble. Even the lone slave who spoke unsympathetically about William recalled his saying that morning, "I intend to cut my row like a man[, but] I cant see to cut my row like I would wish to cut it."[23]

The relentless depiction of Hillery Richardson as a sadist recalled the trial in 1825 of the slave Tom, whose killing of the overseer Richard Foster the dead man's own brother and sister tried to extenuate. In both trials, all concerned seem to have assumed that a slave could not kill his master or overseer and escape punishment; in each case, the defense attorney and his witnesses aimed instead to save the defendant from execution. In William's case, the court returned a conviction for second- rather than first-degree murder and spared his life, sentencing him to be transported outside the Confederate States.[24]

The systematic public denunciation of Hillery Richardson prefigured a trend that would soon develop within the Confederacy. Reformers, many of them ministers, argued that secession from the Union had shifted the South's moral terrain. Slaveholders no longer needed to defend themselves from abolitionists by denying slavery's abuses; now that Southern whites had their own republic, they could afford to, and they must, rid the system of its worst cruelties.[25]

The conviction of William—even though the charge was reduced— reminds us for the thousandth time that slavery as a system was irredeemable. Hillery Richardson had had his share of run-ins with whites;

many jumped at the chance to condemn him now that he was no longer on the scene to intimidate them.[26] Yet neither his personal enemies nor those who disapproved of his treatment of slaves had challenged Richardson's well-known brutality years earlier, when it might have counted. The logic of treating people as property continued to exist in tension with the impulse toward human empathy. The contradictions between the two did not diminish with the coming of the Civil War; if anything, some people gave voice to them more openly than before.

The concerns of war itself naturally seized citizens' attention as Virginia became the most fought over state in the conflict. Until the last days of the war, the military action took place far from Prince Edward, but refugees from the fighting poured into the county as early as 1862. Farmers and planters in much of the state struggled to produce tobacco as their cash crop and, at the same time, to grow food for the civilian population, the massive Army of Northern Virginia, and the swollen population of Richmond, now the Confederate capital.[27] With goods scarce and paper money being printed at prodigious rates, prices rose disastrously. Prince Edward residents of both races struggled to get by. In the fall of 1864, $20—once nearly half the price of an Appomattox River batteau—would buy only a single bedsheet; seven hogs were worth fully $1,000, and a coffin that formerly went for perhaps $5 now cost $200. Clement Read, friendly associate of so many free blacks, still struggled to distribute food and clothing to impoverished families of Confederate soldiers. The term "soldiers" was applied literally; none of this aid went to families of free black conscripts and wage workers.[28]

Confederate defeats at Vicksburg and Gettysburg in the summer of 1863 eroded whites' morale. So did periodic worries that Union forces would try to disrupt rail traffic by attacking Farmville or the High Bridge, which crossed the Appomattox and its sprawling floodplain in northeastern Prince Edward. At half a mile long and almost 130 feet above the water, that span was one of the most impressive in the world at the time, and it did present an inviting target.[29]

Enthusiasm for the Confederate war effort waned in some quarters, and willingness to sacrifice for the cause proved less than universal. Nearly eighty masters in Cumberland were told to produce one or two bondmen each to work on local fortifications in September 1863. More than one slaveholder in ten failed to deliver on the first notice, and a couple ignored even a second summons. Some white citizens began to suspect others of harboring "disloyal sentiments"; in the first months of 1864, twenty-seven men in and around Farmville felt it necessary to draw up a declaration defending a peer's credentials as "a faithfull citizen of the Southern Confederacy." Another man had already faced a formal charge of having permitted a hundred slaves owned by others to gather on his property a few weeks after Lincoln issued the Emancipation Proclamation.[30]

Few whites in the area, it seems, suspected their free black neighbors of sedition. One might even suppose that champions of slavery, having drawn a national border between themselves and their Yankee critics, would have had little further use for the old tale of Israel Hill's supposed decline and fall. Yet that myth had always had a second function—to ease moral doubt about slavery among white Virginians themselves. The uproar after Hillery Richardson's violent death showed that secession had not put those ethical concerns to rest.

The Virginia essayist and humorist George W. Bagby offered a picture of the decline and fall myth in its wartime form. Bagby had his narrator speak in 1862 of the "grand experiment at emancipation made some forty or fifty years ago by Dick Randolph." The narrator, like Bagby's antebellum predecessors, announced the settlement's supposed failure, noted the Israelites' alleged improvidence and fondness for strong drink, and predicted that the people of the Hill would "doubtless die out in the course of a few years and disappear." But Bagby also devoted half a page to "old Uncle Sam White," the purported exception to Israel Hill's overall degeneracy. By now the free black "patriarch" sounded almost superhuman, yet unthreatening: "a more honest, upright man, a more truly pious and devoted Christian," Bagby's narrator averred, "cannot be found in this whole Confederacy."

Bagby described Sam White's disposition (cheerful), his laugh (resonant enough to be heard half a mile off), his pastimes (walking along the railroad track and greeting friends, though he was "more than one hundred years of age"), and his hospitality (unfailingly setting out a decanter of wine for any visitor, white or black). It is not clear whether personal acquaintance, or hearsay augmented by literary license, produced these details about Sam White. The writer had indeed spent his childhood in Buckingham and Cumberland Counties and attended school in Prince Edward, and he maintained ties to those places. Whatever its sources, Bagby's story of Israel Hill in wartime jettisoned some of the shrillness that had permeated the prewar versions. Yet it still carried the same moral—most blacks would degenerate without white tutelage—that Colonel James Madison had pressed a full generation earlier.[31]

No such nuances leavened white opinion of another group of blacks—those who enlisted in the Union armies from 1863 on. Most of those African American soldiers had recently liberated themselves from slavery through flight or been freed by Yankee advances. No Union soldiers of either race appeared in Prince Edward until three days before Lee's surrender, yet Confederate warriors from the county sometimes encountered black Union troops in the field.

One soldier from Farmville remembered fraternizing with his white Yankee counterparts when the two groups found themselves in neighboring trenches between Richmond and Petersburg during the winter of 1864–65. The men cut firewood together from a stand of trees in no-man's-land and "got to know each other by name," the opposing pickets "not firing at each other at all." But when black troops arrived in the Yankee works, the Prince Edward man recalled, "the killing of everything in sight began again. . . . There was no rest for the negro."

The Confederate veteran proudly recalled the day he joined a fellow sharpshooter to slay in a single instant two of the three black soldiers in an emplacement two hundred yards distant. "The other gentleman in that pit," the marksman recalled snidely, "did not show himself again during that day. . . . I suppose he thought two dead niggers in one pit would do for one day." Hunting season ended and goodwill was restored once white Yankees reappeared opposite the Confederate lines, calling, "Hello, Johnnie, don't shoot! There are no negroes on this side, this morning." The opposing but now racially homogeneous troops again "chatted . . . , swapped tobacco for coffee, exchanged [news]papers, and had a good time generally."[32]

The contradictory tendencies of the Old South had only intensified during the Civil War. White men of Prince Edward could fathom, even justify, a bondman's lethal resistance to the cruelty of a Hillery Richardson; yet a mere three years later, men from the same locality took pleasure in slaying black strangers who fought to end bondage itself. The consolation for enslaved African Americans came with the Northern victory in 1865 and the ensuing general Emancipation. As it happened, the last great scenes of the Civil War played out within a short distance of Farmville and Israel Hill, as Robert E. Lee raced westward from Petersburg to try to save his army from Ulysses S. Grant's onslaught.

On April 6, 1865, at Saylor's Creek on Prince Edward's eastern border with Amelia County, Union forces captured several thousand troops from Lee's crumbling army. Near Farmville, Yankee cavalry took more

On April 6, 1865, at Saylor's Creek on the border between Prince Edward and Amelia Counties, Union forces captured several thousand soldiers from Robert E. Lee's crumbling army.

In the closing days of the Civil War, Union and Confederate forces tried to deprive each other of the use of the Appomattox High Bridge near Farmville. The Southerners burned four spans of the structure, and Union engineers restored them.

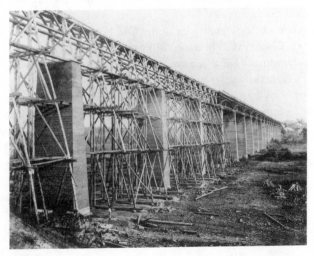

than three hundred of the Confederates' black teamsters into custody. Union and Confederate forces tried to deprive each other of the use of the High Bridge; the Southerners burned four spans of the structure on April 7. That same morning, Lee passed through Farmville, where he met with the Confederate secretary of war and other officials.[33] The general then moved north across the Appomattox to meet the main body of his army in Cumberland County.

Union troops attacked Confederate forces in Farmville during the day of the 7th. The Southerners withdrew northward under Yankee artillery and rifle fire, burning the bridge into Cumberland, and formed a line of battle on the hills near the remnants of Bizarre, Richard and Judith Randolph's house. From there, the Confederates fired artillery toward the pursuing Union troops at Farmville and repelled them for the moment. Some townspeople fled and others lay low that day as the sound of rifles and cannon echoed through the streets and resonated across the valley of the Buffalo River to Israel Hill.[34]

The Federals lost fifty-eight dead and nearly ten times that many wounded, missing, and captured in the fighting at Farmville—but Lee's army was on the run. Many civilians in Prince Edward had caught their first glimpse of the blue-coated African American soldiers whom some whites despised so. Those black men figured prominently among the troops under Union General Edward Ord, who pursued Confederate units to the outskirts of Farmville and then moved west to bottle Lee up at Appomattox Court House.[35] Grant arrived in Farmville within hours of Lee's departure, and from there, on April 7 and 8, he corresponded with the Southern commander over the possible surrender of the Army of Northern Virginia. Thousands of Federal troops passed through the town on their way west; a couple of Federal Army units garrisoned the town in turn. Within a few days, Union doctors would begin to work with Confederate surgeons tending those Southern wounded at the Farmville Hospital who were not fit to be moved.[36]

Although the Union Army seized horses, cattle, sheep, hogs, and bacon near the town on April 7, Yankee officers in Farmville also supplied "guards of protection [to] those [local civilians] who applied for them." Grant's general policy during these days was to hold destruction and theft of private property to a minimum; before long, the Union commander in Farmville would send for cavalry to stop Yankee stragglers from plundering.[37]

Meanwhile, Lee found his army hemmed in thirty-odd miles west of Farmville at Appomattox Court House, a village that had been part of

Prince Edward County until two decades earlier. On Palm Sunday, April 9, the Confederate general capitulated to Grant. Church bells rang out across the county to announce the momentous event. Those peals brought dejection and apprehension to many whites—ironically at a glorious time of year when apple and peach trees had reached full bloom.[38] Yet Lee's stubborn resistance had concealed a profound readiness in much of the South for the conflict to cease. Nearly three months before Appomattox, one local man had written from the front that each Yankee victory was "hailed with universal Joy all through the army[;] the soldiers think every success of the federals & every defeat of confederate arms shortens the time of this most unholy war."[39] For more white folk than may have cared to admit it, the struggle's end brought not only dread but also relief.

No one recorded responses of free Afro-Virginians to Lee's surrender. Sam White, the grand old man of Prince Edward's free blacks, did not live to see the new world rung in, having died as a reputed centenarian perhaps a year or so before war visited his neighborhood. For enslaved residents of the area, the news from Appomattox caused rejoicing—and for some, a bit of confusion in the face of a new and uncertain future. "Never was no time like [it] befo' or since," recalled a house slave named Fannie Berry, who lived in Pamplin, a village on the boundary between Prince Edward and Appomattox Counties. Her fellow slaves, she remembered, were "shoutin' an' clappin' hands an' singin'! Chillun runnin' all over de place beatin' tins an' yellin'. Ev'ybody happy." A new boldness seized some blacks, including a group of "smart alec boys" who shouted at Berry's mistress, "Ain't got to slave no mo'. We's free! We's free!" Yet Berry herself, happy though she was at the news from Appomattox, decided to turn down the offer of a paying job from another white woman and returned to her former owners.[40]

For whites and blacks, Northerners and Southerners, "Appomattox" now became a watchword. The Appomattox River had long bestowed livelihood and identity on Israel Hill and the counties that lined its banks. The river had also lent its name to a rural crossroads where two generals met, and thence to the realm of American myth. Forevermore, the word "Appomattox" would evoke both the tragedy of a war among Americans and the stanching of the rivers of blood which that struggle had spilled. Appomattox had long afforded a special kind of freedom to scores of batteaumen and other blacks on Israel Hill and in Farmville. For 4 million Afro-Southerners, and for those who wished them well, it now embodied the hope that the moment of redemption, so long striven for, had finally, truly arrived. Yet a great question remained to be answered. Would the freedom that Appomattox offered the 4 million be like the liberty it had granted to the boatmen of Farmville and Israel Hill: real and invigorating, yet also circumscribed? Or did Appomattox herald the birth of a new, all-embracing kind of freedom based on ideals and strivings like those of Richard Randolph and Hercules White nearly three generations earlier?

War's end did change the lives of local Afro-Virginians in profound ways. After his stints as a laborer for the Confederate Army, William H. White returned to Israel Hill little more than a week after Lee's surrender in April 1865. But he stayed only a few days before he moved permanently back to Richmond—without a cent, he later recalled. There he would erect telegraph poles for the Richmond & Danville Railroad, work at the city's renowned Tredegar Iron Works, get a few months' book learning, and take up storekeeping in Jackson Ward, Richmond's principal African American neighborhood. By 1895, William White would own five houses; Richmond's black weekly newspaper, the *Planet,* commended him as a prosperous businessman, "a model Christian gentleman," and "an example worthy of imitation [by] the learned."[41] White had become another Israel Hill success story, but the Civil War had helped ensure that he did it far from his native community.

Back in Prince Edward, "Negroes commenced working on wages" within ten days of Lee's surrender. On at least one plantation, their pay was set according to "the custom in the Neighbourho[od]"—which apparently meant the rate earned by free agricultural hirelings before Emancipation. By summer, the Freedmen's Bureau in the county regularly provided rations to nearly two thousand destitute or ailing black people. That number tapered off to double digits, along with a hundred or so hospital patients, by the following spring. A great benefit from the Union victory was the opportunity to reunify black families and gain legal recognition for them. Even before Congress launched Radical Reconstruction in 1867, Virginia's postwar legislature granted official status to former slaves' de facto marriages and legitimized the children those unions had produced.[42] In Prince Edward County, the Freedmen's Bureau registered some 750 wedded pairs and their minor children. In some of those families, one or even both partners had been free before the war. One who signed up was Michael Patterson, an original settler of Israel Hill, charged in his youth with selling liquor, married since 1826

The Confederate Army drafted former batteauman William H. White into
labor detachments and stationed him far from Israel Hill. After the Civil War,
White became a successful small businessman in Richmond.

(*Richmond Planet,* JANUARY 26, 1895)

and now age seventy-eight. The same registration process permitted
nearly 90 black fathers, separated from their wives by death or by the
vicissitudes of slavery, to claim paternity of almost 170 children.[43]

The Bureau also selected Farmville as the site of a hospital for freedpeople. The schools for blacks that the Bureau opened in the town from
the close of the war up to 1869 were among the best and most numerous
in the state. They attracted large numbers of pupils and boasted a staff
that included a few black teachers along with the whites. The superintendent of a freedpeople's school in Farmville wrote in November 1865
that "the colored people [were] anxious to learn and interested in their
school"; soon freedpeople, poor though they were, were contributing part
of the money for their children's instruction. Officers in the Freedmen's
Bureau reported late in 1865 that "there is no open hostility or opposition
to this movement [for black schools] by the white people of the county,"
and even "some interest . . . in the enterprise" on their part, in contrast to
Buckingham just across the Appomattox. A benevolent society in Pennsylvania set up one school for blacks in Farmville that enrolled up to four
hundred pupils; at times as many as one in ten came from families that
had been free before the war.[44]

Three years after the end of the Civil War, Freedmen's Bureau agents
reported some wavering in white goodwill toward black schooling in

Prince Edward, but still no active hostility. As late as 1869, at least one local white woman, Miss S. W. Hubard, was teaching in a black school in Farmville. "For a Southern lady brought up in affluence . . . to be called 'School Mom' and to be known as 'Teaching Niggers,'" wrote one admiring Federal officer, "was a test that not one in a hundred could stand."[45] That official may have overstated his case, for Hubard's work had not left her friendless. She apparently lived in the home of Howell Warren, who had served as a popularly elected county justice in the 1850s; he would become active in Conservative (Democratic) Party politics under the new state constitution of 1870.[46] Warren had had a brief encounter with black literacy a decade before Miss Hubard's residency when he presided over the bond-signing at which Philip White III had written out his name rather than scratch an X.

The missionary and Freedmen's Bureau schools seem to have declined rapidly in 1869–70; the Bureau ended its activity in the latter year. For decades to come, the Commonwealth's new public school system would struggle along. Virginia remained an impoverished state, and many who did have money and power considered education an unwarranted luxury for most children, black or white. In the new public system's first year, only one in five white children and one in eight blacks were actually attending school in Prince Edward on any given day during the relatively short academic session.[47]

Emancipation and Reconstruction brought remarkable changes in the way Prince Edward County and the Commonwealth of Virginia were governed. Years after the war, some white citizens would complain that they had "had no liberty or freedom of action until the last blue coat of our conquerors had disappeared from among us." In reality, Union general George Meade had sought less than two weeks after Lee's surrender to vest civil authority in the incumbent mayor of Farmville—only to discover that the town's form of government did not include any such office.[48] Gestures like Meade's did not long mollify those white people in Southside Virginia who viewed the Radical Republicans in Washington as "imps of hell in human shape." Military defeat and Emancipation were followed in 1867 by a third epochal event: the political empowerment of black men. As a majority-black county, Prince Edward from then on tended to support the Republican Party of Lincoln and Grant; Afro-Virginians and the occasional non-native of Virginia or "carpetbagger" won some local offices. One man complained that tendering blacks the "rite to vote" had made them "impudent." "I am a friend to the Negroe as long as he will keep himself in his proper place," the disgruntled citizen continued. "They may have their rights, but to take them in my house and eat & sleep with them, is a dose I can not swallow."[49]

In fact, Afro-Virginians evinced little desire to eat and sleep with their former owners, and black votes did not prevent the native white minority from playing a role in the county's affairs. Francis N. Watkins, the most prominent local disparager of Israel Hill in the 1850s, served as the sole judge of the newly constituted county court throughout the 1870s. Seizing several opportunities to appoint fellow Conservatives to vacated local offices, Watkins found himself wielding more power than he ever had in pre-Emancipation times.[50] As in much of the South, whites played a disproportionate role in leading the Republican Party. Their advantages in education and experience, their hunger for personal political advancement, and the party's desire to attract at least some white voters ensured that. Prince Edward nevertheless produced a few of the most notable black political leaders in Southside Virginia.

James W. D. Bland became a leading light of the Virginia Senate, who worked both with fellow Republicans and with Conservatives. He seemed destined for even greater influence when part of the state Capitol building collapsed in 1870, killing him along with many others; his widow married into the White family and settled on Israel Hill. Tazewell Branch, who represented the county in the state House of Delegates for several years in the mid-1870s, by then had become an important leader among local Republicans. Branch alienated some in his own party when, like Bland, he sought opportunities to cooperate with local white Conservatives, but he kept his black following. Bland was born free, his mother having been purchased out of bondage a short time before his birth; Branch spent his childhood in slavery. Both had learned to read and write before the Civil War, either from whites or from literate fellow slaves. No one from Israel Hill took a leading role in politics after the war, but William Dennis Evans, who came from a long prewar line of free Afro-Virginians, won election to the Farmville town council and the House of Delegates. Two of Evans's clan had been pioneer free black landowners, holding over two hundred acres around the turn of the nineteenth century.[51]

Samuel P. Bolling, a black businessman in Farmville, was elected to the Cumberland board of supervisors in the 1880s and then represented that county and Buckingham in the House of Delegates. Having bought his own freedom before the war, Bolling eventually purchased part of the plantation he had once worked on as a bondman, hired his former master as an employee, invested heavily in Farmville real estate, and established a thriving brickyard that employed fifteen young men. Bolling, who lived until 1900, did not purchase his standing in the community by truckling to the desires of conservative whites. In the brickmaking trade, he "repeatedly [drove] white competitors out of business," and he embraced the radical, biracial Readjuster Party, which briefly dominated Virginia politics in the early 1880s.[52]

Some of the leading native whites in Prince Edward became accustomed to, if not happy about, the participation of Afro-Virginians in politics. A black politician might win praise as a person "who thinks for himself . . . though mistaken in many of [his] opinions"—or, to the extent he became less radical, he might be deemed a "wholesome influence on his race." A local modus vivendi reserved the office of the deputy sheriff/jailor for a black occupant, and that arrangement continued until about 1891. Meanwhile, Republicans in the county sometimes fought bitterly among themselves; dissidents even ran a successful joint ticket with the Conservatives in Farmville in 1875.[53]

At other moments, Conservatives moved to seize power rather than share it or try to win it through free and fair elections. Once in the early 1870s, during a Republican celebration of Emancipation Day in the streets of Farmville, Conservatives stationed sharpshooters "in second story windows near the corner of Main and Third Streets . . . with instructions to shoot white Republicans who were participating in the celebration." The shooters supposedly planned to spare black revelers. The slaughter never took place, partly because Judge Francis Watkins, pressed by a local minister and others, intervened. Apparently conservative in temperament as in politics, Watkins is said to have warned the targeted white Republicans not to join the parade.[54] As one Conservative elected official later recalled, men of his party (they eventually renamed themselves Democrats) sometimes stuffed ballot boxes or rigged the counting of votes. A well-documented instance in which Democrats physically barred a Republican observer from a polling place was probably not unique. Such methods helped ensure that, by the early 1890s, white Democrats dominated politics in Prince Edward County.[55]

One postwar change proved much longer lasting than anything that happened in the political arena: black Southerners formed separate religious congregations by 1867. Founding churches for themselves allowed Afro-Virginians to govern their own religious life, elect pastors from among their own race, and worship in the style they preferred. Some whites regretted the separation, partly owing to personal attachments they felt to their black fellow Christians; some may also have felt uneasy watching blacks attain the autonomy they savored. The black exodus radically changed the atmosphere in the congregations they left behind: the venerable Sharon Baptist Church, which had more than 600 members in 1864, diminished to only 137 in 1871 after the departure of its black membership.[56]

Some men who had been free before the war assumed prominent roles in the new black churches. The prosperous Booker Jackson became a trustee of the black Methodist congregation, which purchased a lot in town in 1868. African Americans from the Farmville Baptist Church and elsewhere also formed their own church in the center of town. The founding of that congregation, known as First Baptist, imposed a moment of truth on the White family of Israel Hill. While Caesar White—presumably Phil White Jr.'s late-middle-aged son—served as a trustee of the new church, Caesar's brother, boatman Curtis White, remained in the predominantly white Farmville Baptist congregation.[57]

Religious connections between black and white did not dissolve overnight. One local white pastor, Richard McIlwaine, a Presbyterian, wrote sympathetically if a bit paternalistically many years later about black citizens who "not infrequently . . . called on me . . . to marry them, preach funeral sermons, etc." during the postwar years; they usually could afford to pay no fee in those straitened times, he recalled. McIlwaine united his "house girl" in marriage with state senator James Bland, whom the minister remembered as "a very intelligent negro, coal black, unusually gifted as a speaker." McIlwaine also claimed to have preached a memorial sermon for the daughter of a black Israelite, whose name he did not mention, even though a black minister had earlier delivered a sermon for the same family.[58]

Curtis White was not the only black individual who remained in the "white" Baptist and Methodist congregations; some stayed on for a period of years, a few permanently. White was buried from Farmville Baptist. So was another native of Israel Hill, Nannie Carter, a member of original settler Teny Carter's household and probably the older woman's granddaughter. White people knew her as "Aunt Nannie."[59] Since whites typically applied the sobriquets "Uncle" and "Aunt" to older blacks as a paternalistic token of affection, one could speculate that Nannie Carter stayed at Farmville Baptist because she was a "white people's Negro," and that the same applies to others who remained in the white-dominated congregations. Yet to write off a Curtis White as out of step with his people would be presumptuous. White was staying, after all, in a congregation that his father had helped to found; he probably saw no reason to conclude that his family's church now belonged to someone else. Then, too, some of Curtis White's fellow congregants had been business associates of his father, and he himself now dealt with those same men outside of church. Still, his path was one that few other black folk trod. Times were different now, and even Curtis's own children apparently did not remain behind with him.

Curtis White may also have looked askance at the birth pangs that the new black Baptist congregation suffered. The group called as its first pastor one John W. White, who came from outside Prince Edward and was not related to the Whites of Israel Hill and Farmville. Within a year of Pastor White's arrival, he and his new wife, Jemima, separated, and he sued her for divorce. Witnesses supporting him suggested that Mrs. White had threatened to kill her husband, engaged in adultery, and had to be removed physically from the church doorway when she disturbed a meeting there. As divorces tend to do, the case degenerated into a trotting out of alleged villainies on both sides. One witness even asserted that a church trustee had paid him $5 to say falsely that he had had sexual relations with Jemima White. The case took a particularly discomfiting turn when witnesses testified that the "nearly white" Jemima had expressed disgust at her husband's dark complexion; that "John was a great big Black Nigger & she did not know what made her marry him" supposedly ranked among her milder utterances.

Whether or not Jemima White had said such things, her husband's witnesses expected others to believe she had. That assumption suggests a genuine undercurrent of color antagonism within the black community. Then as later, such tensions tied into class differences; Jemima's detractors depicted her as a haughty woman who disdained life in provincial Farmville in favor of the bright lights of Richmond. The witnesses in the divorce suit deprecated not blackness, but rather the supposed prejudice of light-skinned people *against* blackness. A very dark complexion posed no bar to leadership among local Afro-Virginians, and may even have counted as an asset. After all, voters had sent the "coal black" James Bland to the state Senate, and Farmville's black Baptists had called the literate and relatively cosmopolitan John W. White to become their pastor; he went on several years later to win election to Farmville's town council on the Radical Republican ticket. The prominence that dark-skinned members of Israel Hill's White family had won before the war may have set a precedent for those developments.

In the short term, however, the calamity of the Whites' marriage shook the black Baptist congregation deeply. Some members thought Mr. White—to whom the court denied a divorce—should relinquish his pulpit, though a majority stood by him. The affair also aired much dirty linen before the white community. As it happened, Jemima White's attorney would soon become a leader of the local Conservative Party and go on to serve as governor of Virginia.[60]

The several years that spanned the Civil War and Reconstruction also brought the passing of three prominent members of a single Israelite family. Phil White Jr., father of Curtis and Caesar, apparently died during or shortly after the war at about seventy, as had Sam White at a much more advanced age. One of the Israelite Gibbses—his family still close to the Phil Whites after half a century—reported the death of Philip White III in 1866.[61]

Another kind of transition unfolded in the economic sphere. Free blacks other than the Whites and Sam Strong had made their presence felt in the Farmville real estate market during the 1850s, and that process continued apace during the Civil War and afterward. Some postwar buyers were newly liberated people, but a disproportionate number of lot purchasers apparently had been free before general Emancipation. The liberty that some blacks enjoyed under the slaveholding regime, though circumscribed, had afforded a substantial head start to those who possessed it. Some black citizens bought and sold multiple lots. William D. Evans, the state legislator, did so, and brickmaker-politician Samuel Bolling ranked among Farmville's most active investors in real estate. Where black Israelites had predominated among black lot owners a generation earlier, members of other old free black families now stepped in. A few of these buyers were women; Clementine Bartlett's economic rise seems particularly impressive in that she had worked for years as a clothes washer.[62]

Black people's economic achievements did not prevent a white man in 1875 from publishing yet another rendition of Israel Hill's supposed decline and fall. "Some two or three miles west of Farmville," wrote a reporter for the *Richmond Whig* newspaper, "the traveler on the Atlantic, Mississippi and Ohio railroad will see a few huts, on exhausted lands, occupied by a few descendants of the tribe of this modern Israel." The Civil War by then had put the issue of slavery to rest forever—yet this writer still felt duty-bound to proclaim the "failure [of Israel Hill] as an emancipation experiment." The *Whig*'s reporter might have seen more of the settlement had he not ridden through on a train. A number of houses on the Hill apparently were not visible from the tracks: some stood beyond swaths of woods, and the railway cut so deeply through the crest of the Hill that one could see nothing but steep, man-made slopes along much of its path through the settlement. One complex that did lie in plain view of the railroad was no mere string of huts, but rather a large house and a series of outbuildings—probably the farm built by Sam White. The writer naturally neglected to note how badly white-owned property in the county had declined in appearance during and after the war. The ex-slave Henry Clay Bruce, on returning there for a visit and meandering through now-overgrown countryside, said he could scarcely find many of the roads and farms he had known in childhood.[63] But to the white supremacist, none of this mattered. The decline and fall had long since taken on a life of its own, removed from time and tide— leaving the probing reader to wonder how anything could be left of Israel on the Appomattox after forty years of rapid movement toward certain, even imminent, extinction.

The future civil rights crusader W. E. B. Du Bois, then a young social scientist, spent the summer of 1897 studying the black communities of Farmville and Israel Hill. He found that black property ownership had continued to expand during the years since Reconstruction. Administration of a building loan association in the town was "largely conducted by the whites," Du Bois noted, but the institution had both black and white shareholders and had "greatly facilitated the buying of property by Negroes. Ex-masters and white friends," he added, "also [had] often helped" blacks buy land, lots, and houses. He remarked, however, that other whites had cheated freedpeople in real estate transactions. About one third of Farmville's land and lot owners in 1897 were black, though the total valuation of white property in both town and county remained eight or ten times that of blacks.[64]

Du Bois described a "large, pleasantly situated" five-room public school for black youngsters in Farmville, but he found the quality of the faculty uneven. The annual school session ran six months at most. Only half the district's Afro-Virginian children were enrolled, just half of those attended the full term, and most boys dropped out by age fifteen to go to work. A number of better-off black families sent their children away for schooling. That slightly more than half the town's blacks from ten to twenty years old could read and write represented both the race's great progress since Emancipation and the limits of that progress.[65]

Du Bois found Afro-Virginian craftspeople and common workers in situations that seemed novel to him, but which in fact resembled practices that had existed before the war. The local woodworking factory paid

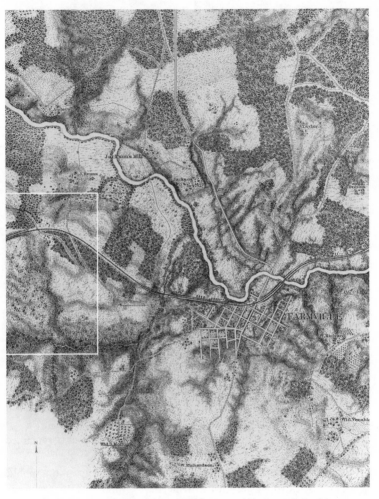

A white reporter who scorned Israel Hill in 1875 would have seen little of the place from the train; a number of houses on the Hill apparently were hidden by woods and by steep slopes flanking the track, which cut deeply through the crest of the Hill (at the left-hand edge of this map). One area that did lie in plain view contained no mere string of huts but a complex of buildings, probably those built by Sam White.

black and white workers the same wages, just as planter Josiah Cheadle and others had done so long ago. Carpenters, painters, and masons of both races were "often seen working side by side on the same jobs, and [got] on without apparent friction," although Du Bois noticed some racial discrimination in their wages. The new era had brought at least one innovation: black contractors "often" hired white craftsmen by 1897. At the same time, blacks in their twenties and thirties were finding better-paying factory jobs in the cities than they could get locally, and emigration was depleting their age cohort noticeably.[66]

The several score blacks who still worked as domestic servants in and around Farmville were "coming to regard the work as a relic of slavery and as degrading"; many resorted to it only as a temporary expedient. That trend recalled the apparent preference of free Afro-Virginian women before the war to maintain their own houses and earn money through farming, domestic crafts, or laundering rather than by working in white people's homes.[67]

The rise of a sizable, prosperous black middle class in Farmville caught Du Bois's eye at the end of the century. He reckoned that only 1 black family in 9 was poor; more than 100 of the town's 262 Afro-Virginian families were "comfortable" or "well-to-do." Du Bois singled out the black business owner as "a [significant] new figure among Negroes." He did not know of the entrepreneurship practiced long before the Civil War by free black men such as Booker Jackson, Ben Short, and those Whites, Strongs, and Bartletts who had owned and operated their own batteaux. In the late nineteenth century as in the old days, whites accepted, and some actively encouraged, black economic advancement. Du Bois found that some enterprising freedpeople had been helped into business by former masters or members of ex-masters' families.[68] Black grocers, restaurateurs, barbers, blacksmiths, shoemakers, building contractors, and others, along with the owners of a steam laundry and a new hotel, were much more numerous now, and in several cases wealthier, than their forerunners before the Civil War. Their attainments, and those of black educators and ministers, had made an impression on local whites. "The economic importance of the black population of Farmville," Du Bois wrote, "has brought many white men to say 'mister' to the preacher and teacher and to raise their hats to their wives."[69]

Life in Prince Edward County in the late nineteenth century had its ugly aspects, the most extreme of which was the lynching of a young black man accused of raping a white woman in the 1880s. In the fullness of time, Du Bois noted, white opinion had "generally conceded" the murdered man's innocence, but that presumably came as small consolation to the black community. Afro-Virginian citizens of Farmville by the 1890s lived largely in identifiably black neighborhoods—a trend that had begun to gel by the 1850s if not earlier. Du Bois said that three small areas merited the title of "slums." Yet close contact between the races still existed, and not only at the store and in the workplace. Du Bois in 1897 found two instances where black men had married white women and settled near Farmville—unions that remained "undisturbed, despite the law."[70]

Patterns on Israel Hill in the late 1890s resembled those in black Farmville, except that twenty-two of the settlement's twenty-five families owned their homes, and the other three rented from black landlords. The Hill's limited physical area and the temptation of better jobs in Farmville or in bigger cities kept the community's population in the low three digits, where it had stood historically. Descendants of the original settlers had brought in spouses from Prince Edward and neighboring counties, and many still farmed their plots of land. Some held only a few acres after tracts were divided among heirs, and Du Bois observed that "the small, impoverished farms" by themselves did not provide an adequate living. Yet pursuing farming "as a side occupation" while earning money in other occupations enabled a family to "live prosperously." Hercules White's old formula still worked. The Hill's four carpenters and masons in 1897 were "in a flourishing condition, with neat, new frame houses and decent-looking farms." Israelite factory workers and those with grown children earning money did "next best"; "the rest . . . have a hard time scratching sustenance from the earth," Du Bois reported.

Three of Israel Hill's families lived in three-room frame houses, and six in dwellings of four rooms or more; the other sixteen families resided in one- or two-room log houses. The little community at century's end thus offered "two pictures in strange juxtaposition—one of discouragement, stagnation, and retrogression, the other of enterprise and quiet comfort."[71] That kind of economic stratification had begun to emerge on the Hill as early as the 1820s and 1830s, though the young sociologist had no way of knowing it.

Du Bois studied black Farmville and Israel Hill during a period that historians today consider the nadir of black existence in the American South after Emancipation. The codification and expansion of racial segregation, the rise of lynching, the virtual elimination of black voting, and the spread of pseudoscientific racist doctrine in respectable circles had accelerated all across the South during the 1890s; white Virginians would convene to disfranchise their state's black citizens only three years or so after Du Bois's article appeared in print. Yet as realistic as he prided himself on being, Du Bois depicted the latter part of that decade as a time of progress and promise for the Afro-Virginians of Farmville and Israel Hill. "Instead of the complete economic dependence of blacks upon whites, we see growing a nicely adjusted economic interdependence of the two races, which promises much in the way of mutual forbearance and understanding," he wrote. "A peculiar hopefulness" reigned among Farmville's black folk. "No one of them doubts in the least but that one day black people will have all rights they are now striving for, and that the Negro will be recognized among the earth's great peoples."[72]

That optimism owed much to a lively community life among blacks, which Du Bois located largely in churches and in fraternal and sororal organizations.[73] Israel Hill retained its share of social vigor beyond the turn of the century and on into the 1910s and 1920s. Pearl Walker Hartwill, a public school teacher born in 1913, lived most of her life in the little community. She recalled a warm and lively group life on Israel Hill. "Everybody knew everybody; everybody took time to visit," she remarked in 1989. "Sunday was a great day"; "the whole crowd" of latter-day Israelites, people of all ages, would eat a big dinner at a different family's house every week. Christmastime also brought much visiting back and forth among neighbors.[74]

Israel Hill had its own one-room public school until 1926. Ms. Hartwill reported that all black families sent their children to school by then—a marked improvement over the period of Du Bois's visit a generation earlier. Though the seventh and eighth grades were offered in Farmville, there was no true black secondary school in Prince Edward County, and many African American families lacked the money to send their children away to high school.[75] Nevertheless, there were no one-room houses left on the Hill by the 1920s, and the largest homes had some eight rooms, Ms. Hartwill recalled. Elizabeth Hill Watkins, another career schoolteacher born on the edge of Israel Hill in 1908, remembered that "some [families in the settlement] were a little better off than others," but neither woman recollected anything like the degree of social stratification that Du Bois had described.

The formula for economic advancement remained what it had always been: a combination of farming and working at remunerative occupations. Pearl Hartwill's father laid rails and later worked as a brakeman for the railroad. Elizabeth Watkins's father worked as a kind of "second

Pearl Walker Hartwill, born in 1913, lived in her family home on Israel Hill for much of the twentieth century. (MELVIN PATRICK ELY)

boss" in a tobacco factory; her mother took in washing. The "small, impoverished farms" that Du Bois described were in fact relatively productive for their size, both women said. Israelites still grew tobacco "for a little bit of money,"[76] as well as corn, other produce, and even wheat for home consumption. Ms. Hartwill's family would thresh their wheat themselves, have it ground at one of the nearby mills, and use it to make their own bread. The twentieth-century Israelites also raised hogs and kept cows.

Relations with whites ranged from correct to downright friendly, both women remembered. Elizabeth Watkins's family once received for dinner a white family from Michigan who had moved to a spot near Farmville. Pearl Hartwill spoke of another white family, originally from the Dakotas, who lived a short distance up the Hill and "did a lot of visiting. . . . They used to come talk to my mother and sit . . . and eat." Neither Northern roots nor such fraternization with blacks seem to have cost that family its standing among fellow whites; one son ended up on the local police force.

Native white people, by contrast, did not sit at table with black Israelites. But Charlie and Annie Dowdy—whites who owned a large farm nearby—sometimes hired adolescent boys from Israel Hill to work in their tobacco fields. Elizabeth Hill Watkins remembered the Dowdys as "real friendly people." The white Singleton family lived on the edge of the Hill and, like a number of black Israelites, routinely drew water from the well owned by Ms. Watkins's family. The Singletons "were friendly with my mother," Ms. Watkins noted, and besides, everyone benefited from the watering arrangement: "looked like the more the water was drawn . . . the purer it was." Many years later, after public schools were desegregated, Pearl Hartwill found herself teaching with a white neighbor she had known in her youth. In a social system that remained patently unjust through at least two thirds of the twentieth century, there could still exist the sort of "mutual forbearance and understanding" that Du Bois had detected in the 1890s—a kind of civility and respect among individuals that county records from before the Civil War display frequently.

Israel Hill apparently reached something of a peak in population, and perhaps of prosperity, by 1920 or so. Ms. Hartwill remembered "so many houses around everywhere. It was like a little village, Israel Hill was. Everywhere you looked, there was a house"—as many as thirty at one point, she thought. The Hill's people remained unified—Elizabeth Watkins's father ran an afternoon Sunday School in the Israel Hill school building that was open to all the settlement's children—but the community never became uniform or insular. Some residents attended the First Baptist Church in Farmville, while others walked or rode to Mount Moriah Baptist Church in the opposite direction, near Tuggle—a spot named, by the way, after the white family that had resided there and dealt so frequently with the black Israelites during the first half of the nineteenth century.

Continued outmigration of ambitious young Afro-Virginians made the North seem a familiar place to many Israelites of the 1920s and 1930s. Ms. Watkins and her mother accompanied Elizabeth's elder sister to school in Philadelphia and lived there for two years; Elizabeth would gladly have stayed there rather than return to "the country." She did come home, but went on to attend high school and teachers' college at Virginia State near Petersburg. Meanwhile, Pearl Hartwill spent almost every summer in New York or New Jersey, traveling on her father's railwayman's pass. Both women had relatives and former neighbors who had moved north to work in factories—Baltimore and New York were favored destinations—or west to labor in the coalfields. In the latter 1920s, that exodus, combined with the passing of older people, was noticeably reducing the Hill's population; the neighborhood school

Elizabeth Hill Watkins was born on the edge of Israel Hill in 1908. Her white neighbors regularly drew water from her parents' well. (MELVIN PATRICK ELY)

closed for lack of clientele. By the time the African American historian Luther P. Jackson visited the area around 1940, "the better element of Negroes in Farmville" had come to look on Israel Hill with a condescending attitude which Jackson compared to that of the proslavery propagandists of old.[77]

Even so, Israel Hill's name survived locally through much of the twentieth century. The folk memory of the settlement's origins, however, had faded between the time of Du Bois's visit and the childhood years of Elizabeth Watkins and Pearl Hartwill. Ms. Watkins, sharp of wit and recall when she reminisced in 1989 about her childhood, said she had grown up knowing nothing of the community's early history. The equally articulate Ms. Hartwill, though born a few years later, believed that "most of the people" during her youth knew Israel Hill had been founded by freed slaves—yet the details had become hazy at best. The emancipator in the version Ms. Hartwill inherited was "a man from Roanoke during slavery time . . . and his name, they say, was Jack Reynolds." The passing of more than a century had shrouded the names of Richard and Judith Randolph in obscurity and left that of Jack Randolph—whose plantation called Roanoke lies nowhere near the Virginia city of that name—mutated beyond recognition.

The names of the Hill's black founders lived on. Pearl Hartwill had a Patterson grandmother, and Elizabeth Watkins's grandmother had married into the White family. Both women vividly remembered growing up with neighbors named Patterson, White, Gibbs, and Johnson (probably a variant of Johnston); two of the Gibbses whom Ms. Hartwill knew bore the given name of family founder Titus, handed down by then over the course of a hundred years or so. Like most Americans, however, neither woman knew names of her ancestors beyond two generations, nor did they realize that some of those forebears had likely numbered among Israel Hill's original settlers in 1810–11. Still, both women testified to their own and their neighbors' attachment to the Hill, and to the pride they took in the history of their race. Elizabeth Watkins told of her grandfather, state senator James W. D. Bland, and of his tragic death during Reconstruction. Pearl Hartwill recalled that even some of the Hill's expatriates in the big cities would eventually say, "Well, I'm going back to Farmville, to Israel Hill—my home," and she noted that the Hill's origins had bequeathed it the reputation of "a free place." "The house is still there now in which I was born," noted Ms. Watkins; her ambition late in life to restore the place had been frustrated by disputes with a contractor.

A turning point for many African Americans in Prince Edward had come in the late 1950s and early 1960s, when the county's white officials closed the public schools for five years rather than desegregate them. The crisis reinforced the determination of Pearl Hartwill and Elizabeth Watkins to advance the cause of the race: Ms. Watkins taught black children in a "freedom school" at the village of Prospect in northwestern Prince Edward. The quiet voice of her fellow teacher, Ms. Hartwill, took on a steely timbre as she spoke, years after that conflict, of segregationist "die-hards" who had "tried to instill within their children . . . [that] they are superior to blacks." Her retort echoed an ancient credo of her people—a worldview that clearly recognized the obstacles impeding black Americans' progress but conceded nothing to those who would block their path. "A black can be just as smart as a white," Ms. Hartwill said. "All you've got to do is to put your head to it and go for it."

The Old South, like any other long-vanished society, is distant from us, and strange. The more we learn about it, the more we realize we do not know. If the story of free Afro-Virginians in Prince Edward County teaches us anything, it is the danger of making assumptions about that past and its people based on what we see around us today, or on what we think we know about the history of other periods, or on the hubristic

"A black can be just as smart as a white," Pearl Hartwill said in 1989, echoing the attitude of her forebears on Israel Hill. "All you've got to do is to put your head to it and go for it." (MELVIN PATRICK ELY)

notion that our own society is superior to theirs in every conceivable way. It will not do, then, to implant Ms. Hartwill's late-twentieth-century thought into the mind of a person living 150 years earlier, even if the two people came from the same place and belonged to the same family. Still, it is not difficult to imagine free black men and women on Israel Hill and off, and even some of those confined in perpetual bondage, admonishing their children in slavery times to "put your head to it and go for it." That formula has been the key to African American survival and progress throughout history. If Hercules, Sam, and Phil White, Sam Strong, Milly Homes, Betty Dwin, or Phil Bowman never uttered the words, they lived lives that delivered the message, and many of their white neighbors heard it loud and clear.

Postscript: The Search for Meaning in the Southern Free Black Experience

I suspect that many readers, as they turn the last page of *Israel on the Appomattox*, will be asking three questions. Did the Israel Hill "experiment" set the tone for white-black relationships in Prince Edward County generally? How typical were the Hill and Prince Edward of Southern life before the Civil War? And what implications does this story have for race relations in our own time?

I turned to Prince Edward because of an aspect of its history that seemed anything *but* typical—the presence there of Israel Hill. I actively determined at several points in my work to keep that community at the center of my narrative, or at least to use it as a frequent point of reference within a bigger story. That the Hill itself never ceased to fascinate me argued for that approach; so did the decision of white propagandists to use Israel Hill as a featured, if grossly distorted, exhibit in their proslavery campaigns.

Yet records pertaining to this little community lay scattered throughout the mass of archives for Prince Edward County, and that made it only natural to move beyond Israel Hill—something I had wanted to do anyway. The work of Ira Berlin and other extraordinarily able scholars had laid open legislative debates and public statements of white opinion about free blacks from the Revolution to the Civil War, and the laws those expressions produced. But to examine intensively the life of a particular county, I thought, would help me see how the slaveholding regime operated day by day. I would aim to write a history of the larger community in which the Hill settlement took shape, and I would consider carefully the relationship between the two.

The rise of Israel Hill was bound to affect free black life in Prince Edward more generally. At least a quarter of all free Afro-Virginians in the county—and more than a third of them in the 1810s—lived on the Hill. Four of the six or seven most prosperous free blacks in the county during the antebellum era were Randolph manumittees, and they surely benefited from the head start that the Randolphs' bequest gave them. Nevertheless, I immediately found that other people of color in Prince Edward had been free for years before Richard Randolph's idea gave belated birth to the black Israelites' experiment. Those pioneering free blacks had been buying land, running boats, accumulating assets, and interacting with whites and slaves in all sorts of ways. They influenced Israel Hill more tellingly than the Randolphs themselves did, and they laid the groundwork for a post-Emancipation black community in which non-Israelites took on most of the leading roles.

I believe that life in Prince Edward would have been different had there been no Hill settlement—but not radically so. I certainly reject any notion that the presence of Israel Hill accounts for the flexibility toward free Afro-Virginians that many whites displayed. On the contrary, it was largely the concentration of free blacks on the Hill that drew such acts of repression as did take place, including the post–Nat Turner gun confiscation.

I have asked myself often how typical life in Prince Edward might be of Virginia or of the South. After all, I was discovering, at least locally, a divided Southern white mind: a proslavery ideology supported by most whites and a determination to reserve true citizenship exclusively for white males coexisted with considerable openness toward free African Americans in daily life. I also encountered white individuals, in limited spheres and sometimes for self-interested reasons, displaying more flexibility even toward the long-suffering slave population than I had anticipated. High-achieving free blacks, and whites who dealt civilly with them, turned out not to be outliers or anomalies in this part of Virginia, but integral players in society.

I agree with other historians who say that laws and public statements about free blacks in the Old South constitute a sordid parade of mean-spiritedness. But human *behavior* governs quality of life, whatever the abstract ideas, spoken or unspoken, that underlie it. Abundant nineteenth-century sources such as county court papers allow us to know fairly reliably whether we are looking at situations of cooperation or live-and-let-live on the one hand, or at a refusal by white Southerners to "tolerate free Negroes living among them" and at "enraged" white responses to free black self-improvement on the other.[1]

I do not doubt that there were localities in Virginia and other states in the South where whites behaved less tolerantly toward free blacks than they usually did in Prince Edward. But a new look at primary sources reveals that whites' actions in one of the most frequently cited Virginia counties have been depicted less than accurately in the historical literature.[2] My examination of documents assembled by Virginia's state government showed me further that free black nonpayment and spotty white enforcement of the discriminatory tax levied on black men in the 1850s were not confined to Prince Edward, but rather were replicated in many other localities, at least in the years for which I found records. A number of historians who have examined different issues and other places likewise challenge the idea that free Afro-Southerners before the Civil War generally felt that they lived like slaves, and have questioned whether the majority of whites had any real interest in making them feel so from day to day. Some of those studies are discussed in the essay on Sources and Interpretations that follows. Nevertheless, I suspect that many people—even those who accept the picture of free black accomplishment that I paint here—will not part easily with the idea that free African Americans lived under the heel of relentlessly hostile white neighbors. That point of view has a distinguished pedigree extending at least as far back as the 1920s.

Between the two World Wars, African American historians including Carter G. Woodson and Luther Porter Jackson took on the daunting task of conveying to a dismissive white America, and of documenting for their own people, a vitally important truth: that blacks had a history as achievers in American life. Jackson wrote that white public opinion and legislation in the South condemned free blacks to "pariah" status from the 1830s on. He added that the Commonwealth of Virginia during the decade before the Civil War set its sights on "reducing these people just as near to slavery as possible." But Jackson also insisted that free people of color had persevered against all odds, applied themselves to economic pursuits, and "prospered."[3] Jackson did note that Virginia's free black expulsion law of 1806 faced white opposition and fairly quickly became a "dead letter," that rates of manumission in Virginia cities did not wane up till the time of the Civil War, and that politicians' statements condemning free blacks "at times . . . meant nothing whatever."[4] Nevertheless, the theme of black triumph achieved against a backdrop of utter repression persisted. This thesis found echoes during the closing decades of the twentieth century, and it is not difficult to see why.[5]

In the 1950s and 1960s, black Americans carried on a heroic struggle to claim an equal place in American society. They held their own against oppression then; it stood to reason that they had done so in earlier periods. Most scholarship on slavery produced since the 1970s reflects that insight. The corollary of triumph that Luther Jackson coupled to his pariah thesis exposed the very real achievements of Afro-Americans and helped move us away from seeing their history simply as a catalogue of what was done *to* them. But nearly every historian of the Old South in modern times, including Jackson, has believed that the nature and degree of oppression that blacks faced varied over time and place. Did such variation, as Jackson seemed to imply, have no profound effect on what African Americans were able to accomplish? Greater oppression ordinarily makes achievement by the oppressed more difficult; vacillation, or apathy, or even selective benevolence on the part of the dominant group creates new opportunities for the subordinate.

I submit that the story of Israel Hill and vicinity supports this simple proposition, as do the findings of other historians. Yet some graduate thesis writers and established historians alike continue to proclaim free blacks "children of the shadows" and "strangers in the land," even if their own research shows numerous free African Americans earning a decent livelihood, gaining access to the courts, and living—as second-class citizens, to be sure—among whites who knew them well and showed little desire to apply most of the discriminatory laws. Why is it so difficult to allow that what these free black people accomplished came about *in part* because the society in which they lived, in spite of its racist ideology and draconian laws, afforded room for them to act and achieve? I can think of several reasons. Some of them are empirical, but others revolve around our present-day perceptions and needs as a society.

First, free African Americans *were* relegated to second- or third-class citizenship. White persons of the time would not have traded places with them (except, perhaps, for poor whites, themselves disfranchised in law or in effect, who may have envied the most prosperous free people of color). In a fair society, a man of Sam White's ability might well have served not only on juries, but also on the county court that governed him. He would not have had to listen as blowhards like Colonel James Madison slandered his friends and relatives—and, of course, slavery itself would not have existed.

Second, we compare the lives of free blacks not only with those of their white neighbors but also with our own. As one of my students put it, "'Free,' to me and my twenty-first-century mind, means all things are granted to you." If any of us today faced the civil disabilities and abusive political discourse that confronted free people of color before the Civil

War, we would echo our Revolutionary forebears and protest that we were being enslaved.

A third reason we hold on to the idea of free blacks as virtual slaves has to do with our changing perception of history. In a case of tragically delayed maturation, many white Americans have finally come to accept that great crimes were committed against Africans and African Americans during and after the days of slavery. Today, the average person finds it easy to assume that white oppression of blacks has been uniform in kind and intensity throughout American history—in every era, we tell ourselves, except our own.

And that brings us to a final reason I believe we gravitate to the notion of free blacks as slaves in all but name and as "children of the shadows." The idea that white supremacy developed in predictable, even inevitable fashion can at least be tested through historical research. A number of fine historians who study periods ranging from the seventeenth century up to Emancipation and beyond have challenged that deterministic idea; they find less rigidity in some eras and deepening oppression in others.[6] But we have a couple of particular social needs that I suspect remain fairly impervious to historical evidence. Almost no one today wants to risk soft-pedaling the racial oppression that has blighted American history. Beyond that concern lies another tendency that is more elusive, but in my view no less real. I observed in my first book that white Americans love to condemn the injustices of earlier eras because it makes them feel righteous in their insulated present. The theme of black triumph restores the honor of Afro-America, but by itself it does not vindicate today's *white* America. The easiest way to make today's flawed society seem fair is to declare that each black victory in the past was won not merely in the face of oppression, but against a society whose infinite capacity to oppress differentiates it utterly from our own.

Many people in our time have moved beyond seeing blacks during the era of slavery, or in any other period, as mere pawns of those who exploited them. Less easy to accept is a companion proposition: that white authorities and white neighbors, for all their moral failings and acts of callousness, left space in which free blacks *could* act as something other than slaves. I contend, however, that to accept the thesis of free black achievement that I and others put forward is also to accept a meaningful distinction between white racial ideology and actual behavior in the Old South. Most of us agree on at least one thing: white Southerners—white Americans—knew how to oppress. In many parts of the region, they had the means to re-enslave the free black population. They certainly could have intervened to prevent or obliterate the accomplishments of free Afro-Virginians such as Phil White, Booker Jackson, Sam Strong, and Milly Homes. But with all their sins of commission and omission, most white Virginians—and most white Southerners—had not the stomach, or even the desire, to do these things. As human societies often do, they deviated from the path their social ideology prescribed.

This book is in large part a narrative of African American accomplishment. At the same time, I have tried to show how white ambivalence or lassitude often, and the decent impulses of white individuals sometimes, created openings within a system whose benighted racial credo seemed to rule out any sort of flexibility. The enterprise of restoring to the black South its human complexity has been flourishing for some time now; may it continue apace, and may this book contribute to that project. Before us lies a second task, inseparable from the first: to portray all the injustices of the American past, yet at the same time to give back to the *biracial* South, too, its own boundless, often tragic complexity.

Having just expressed my unease at allowing present-day agendas to shape our view of history, I must also admit that we all draw on our own experience and common sense when we examine the past. Doing so can occasionally warn us away from imprudent conclusions.

As I studied Israel Hill and its surroundings, I thought many times of a documentary film I saw on public television, in the early 1980s, I believe, about the revival of the Ku Klux Klan among shrimpers on part of the Texas Gulf Coast; those men directed their ire against Vietnamese refugees who had begun to compete with them by operating shrimp boats of their own in that neighborhood. The scene that stays with me showed a Vietnamese captain buying gasoline for his boat from a dock operator who was active in the Klan. The Vietnamese knew exactly whom he was dealing with—there was no other source of fuel in the area—and the Klansman knew the Vietnamese knew. Each man dealt politely with the other, smiles and money were exchanged, and both went about their business.

Every time I felt inclined in this book to characterize relations between whites and free blacks as "friendly," I remembered the film about the shrimpers. The documents that past generations leave behind are often infuriatingly silent on some of the very points we urgently want to know about. In many of the black-white relationships I describe in

Israel on the Appomattox, I frankly cannot say whether the parties were "friends," even if there were a generally accepted definition of that word.[7] In some cases, the evidence points strongly toward genuine, reciprocal regard, even affection. In other situations—for instance, the business partnership between the anti–free black propagandist Colonel Madison and Afro-Virginian boatman Randolph Brandum—one can only imagine a "correct," arm's-length, workaday relationship. I do know, and hope I have shown, that free blacks and whites interacted, even cooperated, in almost every manner we can conceive of, except in the political realm and the jury box. (In North Carolina and Louisiana, in fact, people of color in some periods voted in numbers, and white politicians sought their support.)

Even as our experience of recent times shapes our understanding of history, we do well to remember that the past is like a foreign country—comprehensible, we hope, but different from the place in which we live. Each era, indeed, differs in important ways from all others. A case in point: in 1951, African American students marched out of the black high school in Farmville, staged a prolonged strike, and enlisted the NAACP in their fight for equal public school facilities, which soon became a quest for desegregation. That case became one of four decided collectively by the United States Supreme Court and known to history under the title *Brown v. Board of Education.* Eight years after the student walkout, as the actual integration of Prince Edward's public schools approached, the county's white leadership simply abolished the school system—a decision that made Prince Edward unique in all the South even at the height of Massive Resistance. The white community arranged private schooling for its own children, while black pupils and their families were left to fend for themselves.

How does the remarkable history of old Prince Edward explain this all but unbelievable twentieth-century story? I offer no answer. Only a fool would try without examining the ninety years of county history between the first Reconstruction and the second as I have tried to investigate the earlier period.

The county in 1959 was living under a social system that, for all its inequities, differed markedly from the slaveholding regime. The family names of people involved in the crisis of 1951 to 1964 only occasionally duplicate those of the folk who populate this book. Both sides during the civil rights years looked to the past as they understood it—the white leadership to the supposed horrors of Reconstruction, the blacks to the strivings of their people before and after Emancipation. But almost none of those citizens, from either race, knew the story of Israel Hill, and few if any could have imagined the measure of racial fluidity that had existed before 1865.

Israel on the Appomattox was a product of its own time in the deepest possible sense. The community's story unfolded as it did partly because the society that surrounded the Hill depended on slavery. Without slavery, of course, there could have been no Randolph will and manumission, and indeed no such category as "free Negroes." But slavery was also crucial in a less obvious way: it gave whites the luxury of recognizing *free* black individuals as skillful, upstanding, productive members of society. Bondage kept most Afro-Virginians in a netherworld of exploitation; that rendered free blacks, especially the many who lived in rural areas, essentially unthreatening in any sphere other than the theoretical realm that generated antiblack editorials, speeches, and legislation.

This book therefore tells a story not only of freedom but also of slavery—and thus of a world that differs profoundly from the one we live in, so full of its own heartbreaks. I thought I knew a great deal about cruelty to slaves before I began this project. Then I discovered descriptions of Hillery Richardson beating a slave repeatedly and mercilessly from eye to thigh and yanking out the man's teeth while compelling another slave to restrain the victim. I had read various accounts of masters and slave traders breaking up black families. But to encounter such breakups repeatedly in primary sources drove the point home more wrenchingly than ever, especially since I myself by then was the father of young children. As my friend and former colleague, Christopher Brown, once remarked, there are times when a historian, reading the evidence of what some human beings have done to others, feels the need to leave the archives reading room and go outside to breathe some clean air.

Still, along with the horrors, the history of Israel Hill, of old Prince Edward County, and of the Old South as a whole contains innumerable surprises and countless moments in which people recognize each other's humanity across the color line. Does that history therefore augur well for race relations in the future? Not necessarily, especially if I am correct in my not very uplifting suggestion that the flexibility free blacks encountered depended largely on the enslavement of other African Americans.

It will not do to romanticize the story I have told in this book. A thousand, or a hundred thousand, courteous exchanges between whites and free blacks, many of them based on respect and some even on affection, made only the most infinitesimal dent in the institution of slavery. It took the abolitionists, the Republican Party, the impetuousness of the secessionist South in 1860–61—and above all, the biracial if segregated Union Army and the black Southern men and women who lent it a hand—to bring change.

Similarly, black and white Southerners of a certain age, including the latter-day black Israelites whom I interviewed during this project, recall friendly cross-racial contacts from their youth. But those encounters did little or nothing to replace Jim Crow with some semblance of equity. It took the NAACP Legal Defense Fund, the Supreme Court—and above all, the peaceful armies of the civil rights movement—to accomplish that. In both eras, ironically, the very friendliness that could arise between members of the dominant group and the oppressed may have postponed change by encouraging white people to see their social system as less abusive than it was in fact.

The records I dug into as I prepared this book often saddened and sometimes horrified me. But those thousands of documents have also helped me see this corner of the Old South not as a machine geared to grind down free blacks—even though it deprecated and discriminated against them in many respects—nor solely as an arena of human bondage and of black strength and achievement, though it certainly was that. I also found a society in which black and white people related to one another in a stunning variety of ways. That fact may not help us predict our racial future, but along with revelations from other historians, it warns us against the easy conclusion that contempt for blacks is unvarying among whites. That realization, I confess, colors my view of our own world, whose future will likely harbor as many surprises as its past.

DOCUMENTS
SOURCES AND INTERPRETATIONS
ABBREVIATIONS AND REMARKS
NOTES
ACKNOWLEDGMENTS
INDEX

Will of Richard Randolph, 1796

To all whom it may concern, I Richard Randolph Junior of Bizarre, in the County of Cumberland, of sound mind and memory, do declare this writing, written with my own hand, and subscribed with my name, this eighteenth day of February in the twentieth year of american Independance, to be my last will and Testament, in form & substance as follows:

In the first place—To make retribution, as far as I am able, to an unfortunate race of bondmen, over whom my ancestors have usurped and exercised the most lawless and monstrous tyranny, and in whom, my countrymen (by their iniquitous Laws, in contradiction of their own declaration of rights, and in violation of every sacred Law of nature; of the inherent, unalienable & imprescriptible rights of man; and of every principle of moral & political honesty;) have vested me with absolute property:

To express my abhorrance of the Theory, as well as infamous practice of usurping the rights of our fellow creatures, equally entituled with ourselves to the enjoyment of Liberty and happiness:

To exculpate myself, to those who may perchance to think or hear of me after death, from the black crime, which might otherwise be imputed to me, of voluntarily holding the above mentioned miserable beings in the same state of abject slavery in which I found them on receiving my patrimony, at Lawful age; To impress my children with just horror at a crime so enormous & indelible, to enjure them in the last words of a fond father never to participate in it, in any the *remotest* degree, however sanctioned by Laws (formed by the tyrants themselves who oppress them,) or supported by false reasoning, used always to soil the sordid views of avarice, and the lust of power:

To declare to them and to the world, that nothing but uncontroalable necessity, forced on me by my father, (who wrongfully bound over them to satisfy the rapacious creditors of a Brother—who for this purpose, which he falsely believed to be generous—mortgaged all his slaves to british Harpies, for money to gratify pride & pamper sensuality; by which mortgage the said

Slaves being bound, I cou'd not exercise the right of ownership necessary to their Emancipation; and being obliged to keep them on my land was driven reluctantly to violate them in a general degree, (tho' I trust far less than others have done,) in order to maintain them) that nothing, I say, short of this necessity, should have forced me to an act which my soul most abhors;

For the aforesaid purposes, & with an indignation too great for utterance at the tyrants of the Earth—from the throned Despot of a whole nation, to the [more] despicable, but not less infamous petty tormentor of single wretched Slaves, whose torture constitutes his wealth and enjoyment—I do hereby declare that it is my will and desire, nay most anxious wish, that my negroes—all of them be liberated, & I do declare them by this writing, free and emancipated to all intents and purposes whatsoever, fully and freely exonerated from all future service to my heirs executors or assigns, & altogether as free as the illiberal laws will permit them to be. I mean herein to include all and every slave of which I die possessed or to which I have any claim by inheritance or otherwise.

I thus yield them up their liberty, basely wrested from them by my forefathers—& beg *humbly* beg, their forgivness, for the manifold injuries I have too often inhumanly, unjustly, & mercilessly inflicted on them, and I do further declare & it is my will, that if I shall be so unfortunate as to die possessed of any slaves (which I will not do, If I ever can be enabled to emancipate them legally,) & the said Slaves shall be liable for my fathers debts & sold for them; that in that case, five hundred pounds be raised from my other estate real or personal, as my wife shall think best, and in any manner she may choose, and applied to the purchase, at such sale, of such of the said miserable Slaves, as have been most worthy, to be judged of, by my said wife; which said Slaves I do hereby declare free as soon as they are purchased to all intents and purposes whatsoever; and in case I emancipate the said Slaves (which I shall surely do the first moment possible) I do devise, give, and bequeath unto them, the said Slaves, four hundred acres of my land to be laid off as my wife shall direct, and to be given to the heads of families, in proportion to the number of their children and the merits of the parties, as my said wife shall judge of for the best. The land to be laid off where & how my said wife shall direct, & to be held by the said slaves when allotted to them, in fee [i.e., having outright ownership with the right to bequeath]. I do likewise conjure my said wife to lend every assistance to the said Slaves thro' life, in her power, & to rear our Children up to the same practice, and leave it on them as her latest injunction—& to do every thing directed above, relative to the sd. Slaves.

I now proceed to direct the manner in which my property is to be disposed of, (having fulfilled this first and greatest duty & most anxious and Zealous wish to befriend the miserable & persecuted of whatsoever nation colors or degree) by my will as here seen written on this and another sheet of paper each signed by my own hand & with my own name and connected to gether by wafers.

Rd. Randolph, Jun'r.

In the second place I give and bequeath to my wife Judith Randolph all my personal estate remaining, of whatsoever nature animate or inanimate, in possession or in action, claimed or to be claimed by any right or title whatsoever, to her sole use and disposal forever, that is exclusive of Slaves.

I likewise devise, give, and bequeath to my said wife, all my real estate whatsoever of which I die possess'd, and also all to which I have any claim or title whatsoever, to her and to her heirs forever, in full confidence, that she will do the most [ample?] justice to our Children—by making them independant as soon as they are of age, if she remain single, or by secureing a comfortable support by settlement on them, *before* any marriage into which she may hereafter resolve to enter (which if she do do money will be the only *certain* mode of providing for them) and by educating them as well as her fortune will enable her;

The only anxiety I feel on their accounts, arises from a fear of her maternal tenderness leading her to too great an indulgence of them; against which I beg leave thus to caution her.

I now consign them to her affectionate love—desiring, that they be educated in some profession, or trade if they be incapable of a liberal profession and that they be instructed in virtue, and in the most Zealous principles of Liberty & manly independance. I dedicate them to that virtue & that liberty which I trust will protect their infancy, and of which I conjure them to be indefatigable and incorruptible supporters [thro'?] life. I request my wife frequently to read this my will to my tenderly beloved Children, that they may know something of their fathers heart when they have forgotten his person. Let them be virtuous & free the rest is vain. Finally I intreat my wife to consider the above confidence as the strongest possible proof of the estimation and ardent love which I have always uniformly felt for her, & which must be the latest acting impulse of my heart.

I hereby appoint my said wife sole executrix of this my last will and Testament—but in case I should be so unfortunate as to be left by her single & die without any other will than this, executed by me, I appoint in that case as my executors, (requesting their attention to every injunction on my wife above mentioned, relying on them to execute them & the directions in my said will (as she will other wise do:) to wit, the following most esteemed friends—My father in Law St. Geo. Tucker, my Brother, John Randolph, my friends Ryland Randolph[,] Brett Randolph, Creed Taylor, John Thompson, Alexander

Campbell, Daniel Call, and the most virtuous & incorruptible of mankind & (next to my Father in Law) my greatest Benefactor, George Wythe Chancellor of Virginia, the brightest ornament of human nature;

I rely of [sic] the aforementioned virtuous friends for the punctual execution of my will, the care and guardianship of my Children in case of the death of my wife either before or after me, (to whom, if she live, I have intrusted them, solely) & to those of them most nearly connected with me by friendship, I look for assistance to my family after my Death, in all cases of dificulty. If any among them do not choose to undertake the task imposed on them by me, I beg them not to do so from motives of Generosity or delicacy, & to excuse the liberty which, (it may appear to them least intimately acquainted with me,) I have taken in thus calling on them. In witness of all the above directions, which I again declare to be my will & Testament, drawn by me from calm reflection, I have hereunto subscribed my name & affixed my seal the day and year aforesaid.

Rd. Randolph Junr.

WILL OF BETTY DWIN, WRITTEN 1808

In the name of God, I Betty Dwin A free black woman (commonly called Betty Gambo) being of sound mind and good recollection do make and ordain this writing to be my last will and testament viz.—

I Will that my son Harry Dwin who is my slave be put apprentice to some good business untill he be twenty one years of age, at which time it is my will and desire that he shall be free.

I Will that my son Peyton Dwin be bound apprentice to some good business untill he be twenty one years of age.

It is my will and desire that after the payment of my just debts all the ballance of my money in hand or which may be due to my estate, be equally divided between my three sons Jacob, Peyton Dwin and Harry Dwin and Charles Woodson which last is intended for the benefit of my husband Gambo who is his slave; I will that three suits of my best Sunday Clothes be given to my Grand daughter Betty who is the daughter of my son Jacob and belongs to Mrs Dillon; I have a number of other children and grand children but do not will to any of them any thing in any event whatsoever. Lastly I constitute and appoint Charles Woodson exor. to this my last will and testament with power to carry into effect all the provisions therein, as well what relates to binding out my children as other things; given under my hand and Seal this 24th day of June 1808.

Her

Betty X Dwin

mark

[Dwin's "other children and grand children" may have been slaves belonging to masters she did not trust to convey a bequest as she did Charles Woodson.]

WILL OF THOMAS FORD, WRITTEN 1821

I Thomas Ford of the County of Charlott is sicke in body, bute in my perfeck sences. I firs reques my body to buried in a Cristan like manner, then I do appinte Robert Kelso my hole and sole Executers, then I request for all my jeste devets to be pad first. I reques that the hole of my land which is aboute fore hundred and sixty four acirs, it being the land whar I now live, and all the land I pursess, to be sold to the highest bidder, one half to be paid down, the other halfe twelve munts cradit, and I reques that all my household and [?] furnitur, and all my stock horses and cattle, and of every description, to be sold, and all my crop of corn, tobacco, whete, oats to be sold, and the money arisin from the land and the abuve articles to go to pay my just dats, & the balance arising after paying my jeste devets, return to the ginnorl stock. Now I sett my negroes free that is, that the ar to be sente to the free stat by my Executors, thur names is Tony, Hary, Jim, Jessy, Rilente, Shedrick, George, Ben, Sall, Fearn, Lusey, Morning, Beckky, Nelson, Sary, Daniel, and it is my request that William a free child that my Tony had, by a free woman, may go allso with his father Tony. Now after all my devets is pad, the above named negroes, must have a sefichente quontity of money oute of my genirl stock, after paying my devets, as will carry them to the frees states. Now if Sary a old negro aboute nearly seventy years of edge, her nam is above menchuned, shude not be able to go with the rest, she is to have a nuf to seporte her well, oute of my genrel stock, that is if she says she cante go with the reste, if she can go she must with the rest. Now this is my last will and testimony. I request my Exectrs and the onable corte how [who] purhaps it may com before, may siee that my laste request may be complid with. Now if there is any more required for the above negroes support at first when the gite to the friee state, the ar to have it oute of my ginrel stock, and after all my buve requests is complid with, then I give to my brother Hezekiah Ford, one thirde part of the mony that remains in my generl stock, after all the above stated mony and exspences is paid, or any other that may accur, that is resenble [reasonable] or lawful towards the above negros being card [carried] away to the frew state & not before. Then I give to my Sister Elizabeth Jones one forth parte of the money that will remane in my ginral stock after my bove requests is complied with. Then I give to my sister Rebecco Jones, one firth parte of the balanc that will remain in my ginral stock after all my bove requestes is complied with, and note [not] before. Then I give to my sister Sally Adams and to all my brothers[,] Abner Ford deceste[,] children, the balanc of any in my ginral stock, after all my bove requests is settled, to be eculd [equally] divided between sd. Sally & Abners children.

As witness my hand this 18th day of April 1821.

Thomas Ford

COLONEL JAMES MADISON

Condition of the Descendants of a Number of Emancipated Slaves,
in Prince Edward County—*Farmers' Register,* 1836

You expressed a wish (page __ [sic] vol. III,) to obtain information in relation to the history of the emancipated people of color in Prince Edward; I presume those emancipated by the late Richard Randolph more especially.

More than twenty-five years ago, I think, they were liberated, at which time they numbered about one hundred, and were settled upon small parcels of land, of perhaps 10 to twenty-five acres to each family. As long as the habits of industry, which they had acquired while slaves, lasted, they continued to increase in numbers, and lived in some degree of comfort—but as soon as this was lost, and most of those who had been many years in slavery either died, or became old and infirm, and a new race, raised in idleness and vice, sprang up, they began not only to be idle and vicious, but to diminish instead of increasing, and have continued to diminish in numbers very regularly every year—and that too, without emigration; for they have almost without exception, remained together in the same situation as at first placed, to this day. Idleness, poverty, and dissipation are the agents which continue to diminish their numbers, and to render them wretched in the extreme, as well as a great pest, and heavy tax upon the neighborhood in which they live. There is so little of industry, and so much dissipation amongst them, that it is impossible that the females can rear their families of children—and the consequence is, that they prostitute themselves, and consequently, have few children—and the operation of time, profligacy and disease, more than keep pace with any increase among them. Whilst they are a very great pest and heavy tax upon the community, it is most obvious, they themselves are infinitely worsted by the exchange from slavery to liberty—if, indeed, their condition deserves that name.

James Madison

[Comment by Edmund Ruffin, editor]

The facts stated in the foregoing communication are both interesting and important. We are greatly indebted to our esteemed and well informed correspondent for his compliance with our request, and have only to regret that he did not enter more into the details of so fair and decisive a trial of the effects of negro emancipation, made under the most favorable circumstances. In this case, the slaves who were emancipated had been trained to labor—they were abundantly provided with fixed farming capital—and they had, and their descendants still have, in addition, a continual demand for their labor, in the boating on the Appomattox—an employment which they prefer to all others, because it is the nearest to idleness. Yet with every advantage, and through a

long course of time, their prosperity and even their numbers have been dimin-
ishing, and their condition has gradually become worse. A more full experiment cannot be adduced, nor a more decisive result.

WILL OF PHILIP BOWMAN, 1842

I Philip Boman of Prince Edward County being in feeble health but of sound
mind and memory make and ordain this my last will and testament hereby
revoking all others by me heretofore make [sic]. In the first place I desire that
all my just debts be paid. I desire that all my estate after the payment of my
debts shall be paid put [sic] into the hands of James Venable for the benefit
and support of my wife Prissey to be given to her as he may think best for her
comfort and support, my wife Prissey being a slave & purchased by myself, I
will to James Venable for the purpose of her being taken care of and my
Executor is directed to pay over to the said James Venable all my estate for the
benefit of my wife as above stated. I hereby appoint James Venable my executor of this my last will and testament as witness my hand and seal this day of
May 12th 1842.

his

Philip X Boman

mark

WILL OF ANTHONY (TONY) WHITE, 1848 AND 1850

I Anthony White of the county of Prince Edward and State of Virginia, being
of sound mind and memory, do hereby make my last will and testament in
manner and form following.

Item 1st. I desire that all the perishable part of my estate after my death be
sold and my just debts be paid & funeral expences; should the perishable part
of my estate prove insufficient for that purpose, then I desire that my executors
herein after named rent out my land, except the house and lot and garden,
which I desire may be reserved as a home for my beloved wife Milly White
untill the rents shall have discharged the debts against my estate; only reserv-
ing enough for the support of my wife aforesaid.

2. After the payment of my just debts and funeral expences, I give to my
friends Booker Jackson and John Jackson in trust for the benefit and support
of my beloved wife Milly White during her life, all my estate both real and
personal of which I shall die possessed, or that shall come to me in any wise
whatsoever, for and during the term of her natural life, and after her decease I
will and desire that all my property then remaining both real and personal be
sold, and the monies arising therefrom to be equally divided between my chil-

dren to wit: Albert now belonging to Dr. Southall, and Milly Ann belonging to the heirs of the late Wm. White of James Town, & Ennis, Herculas and Salina belonging to the Allens of Missouri; but if my Trustees cannot make a full and fair title & conveyance to a purchaser of my land after the death of my wife, I then desire that the land shall be rented out and the rents divided between my said five children, my object being that my wife to have the full benefit of my estate while living, and my children after her death.

And I hereby appoint my friends Booker Jackson & John Jackson my executors of this my last will and testament, hereby revoking all others made by me. In testimony whereof I hereby set my hand and affix my seal this 9th day of September 1848.

his

Anthony X White

mark

Codicil to my will this 23d February 1850. After more reflection I will and desire after my death, and when my debts are paid as set forth in the body of my will, that if my wife should survive me, that Susan Smith be allowed to take up her abode with her, and at her death my will and desire is that twelve acres of my land on which is the house, be laid off for the said Susan Smith, to whom I will and bequeath the same, to her and her heirs forever. As witness my hand and seal this   day   1850. February 25th 1850.

his

Tony X White

mark

SOURCES AND INTERPRETATIONS

This book is based largely on a rich but underused class of primary sources: county court papers. In Virginia, the county court not only tried defendants and heard civil suits; it also served as the governing and administrative body for a particular rural locality. Its records thus contain trial records, suit papers, deeds, wills, estate accounts and inventories, patrollers' returns, processioners' reports, records of county financial transactions large and small, coroners' inquests, apprentice indentures, militia documents, guardians' accounts, Civil War muster rolls, tax records, lists of free blacks, financial records, orders to carry out various actions, records of attempts to do so, and more. Papers of the circuit (or district, or superior) court, a court of justice in the narrower sense, are also available for many counties.

The "order books" of county courts, which historians consult frequently, generally catalogue only the barest outlines of court cases. The richest categories of evidence by far are the various administrative records of county government and the courts' "ended papers" (also known as suit, loose, or dead papers). Every one of the thousands of lawsuits and hundreds of criminal charges filed in a given county generated a series of documents, which were filed as a unit when that proceeding concluded. One wonders how Ulrich B. Phillips, a pioneering historian of slavery, could write in 1918 that "court records are . . . plentiful only for the higher tribunals"; perhaps he defined the compass of the term "court record" too narrowly.[1]

The ratio of time invested to revelations unearthed is high when one examines county records. Often, a number of separate puzzle pieces—retrieved one at a time, months apart—have to be assembled to produce a picture of even one scene or event. Other cases are self-contained narrative gold mines, in which plaintiff, defendant, and various witnesses and deponents each give their version of a train of events; estate and store accounts often were submitted in evidence, and personal letters occasionally. Every one of these individual narratives is biased in its own way, but the biases tell their own stories of values and worldviews, and the historian can apply the same critical filters to these sources as to any others.

County court documents, especially the ended papers, may have been the body of evidence that the pioneering historian of Afro-America, Carter G. Woodson, had in mind in 1925 when he spoke of "unexploited sources which, for years to come, will doubtless remain unavailable."[2] In fact, not only do local court papers abound; today, more than a few of them are readily accessible. I wish I could be certain it will remain so. I write these lines in the wake of a shortsighted, devastating series of budget cuts imposed on the Library of Virginia and other archives by state legislatures across the country.

Although court papers for some counties have been destroyed by fire, flood, war, or neglect, for other localities the record is remarkably well preserved. Prince Edward County has 120 large cartons of neatly arranged documents housed in the Library of Virginia, the majority of them ended papers, county accounts, and the like for the period up to the Civil War. The library also holds formal books of wills, county court orders, and deeds, all on microfilm, and a number of original volumes including Josiah Cheadle's extraordinary plantation account ledger. (The impressionistic final chapter of this book is based on less comprehensive sources, found in a variety of places. Much of Prince Edward's archival record for the Civil War and Reconstruction years was not available in Richmond, and the county courthouse in Farmville, though staffed by efficient, hospitable professionals, is not equipped to accommodate systematic research in suit papers.)

A sizable body of secondary literature treats the free African American experience in the South. I intend here not to catalogue those many works, but rather to flesh out what I say in the Postscript about where *Israel on the Appomattox* fits into the existing scholarship or takes issue with it. I give special attention to works that examine conditions in Virginia. The Notes identify additional ideas and writings that I have tried to address in the main text of the book.

The study that most closely resembles mine is Reginald Butler's dissertation of 1989 on free Afro-Virginians in Goochland County—located, like Prince Edward, in the Piedmont, but a considerable distance away, on the north bank of the James River not far west of Richmond. Butler and I once conversed about free blacks' experience with apprenticeship, but only briefly; eager though I was to read his dissertation, I resolved to do so only after I had completed my research and written my own manuscript. When I did read Butler's thesis, I was deeply struck by the harmony between his findings and mine.

Butler devoted perhaps half his investigation to the colonial and very early national periods, a task I did not attempt, and he ended his study in the early 1830s, a generation or more before mine terminates. He carried out formidable research but made only sparing, though skillful, use of county court ended papers. Still, Butler and I asked some of the same questions, and we came up with similar answers. The eminent historian John Hope Franklin, much like

Karl Marx a century earlier, once equated "rurality" with "isolation," "social and economic backwardness," "inarticulateness," and "cultural sterility."[3] Butler emphatically rejects, as I do, the idea that free blacks in the countryside were an atomized, helpless population who lacked what it took to move to the supposedly greater freedom and opportunity afforded by towns and cities. Both of us aim to reorient a literature on Southern free blacks that long focused on the important but statistically atypical urban experience.

The similarities between Butler's findings and my own are almost beyond counting: free blacks' preference to live without dependence on whites, their sometimes successful efforts to defend themselves against aggressors by turning to the courts, widespread economic and legal dealings between them and white persons, their desirability as workers alongside whites (especially in cutting wheat), to name only a few. In both Prince Edward and Goochland, free blacks tended to ply more than one trade, and they often received wages similar to those paid to white workers.

Butler sees court-ordered apprenticeships from the late eighteenth century on as resembling at times "a form of county social welfare" that "enabled [young blacks] to strengthen their status as free persons of color." Many of Goochland's free Afro-Virginians migrated there from other places; the county court, like that in Prince Edward, readily replaced free papers that individuals said they had lost or accidentally destroyed. In both localities, manumissions continued after 1806, and liberated blacks often remained in the neighborhood as if the expulsion law did not exist. Both Butler and I recognize the prevalence of anti–free black sentiment on the level of ideology, yet we also agree that, on the level of everyday behavior, "exceptions to the rule begin to undermine the validity of the rule itself."[4]

When my own research on Prince Edward County was in its early stages, Anthony R. Miles, a student of mine at Yale, wrote a senior thesis on Fairfax County near Washington. The courts there, he found, ensured that emancipatory wills were carried out; they afforded free blacks jury trials even after the law supposedly precluded them, frequently acquitted black defendants, and administered similar punishments to those of both races whom they found guilty. The free black registration and expulsion laws were rarely enforced. Miles notes that "whites had legal power over blacks; they knew it, and when it suited them they used it." There were upticks in enforcement—for a few weeks following Nat Turner's revolt, and again as the friction between North and South intensified in the 1850s. For the most part, however, Miles concludes that "Fairfax County whites clearly did not *care* about making the law stick."[5]

Ellen D. Katz, now a professor of law, has published an article in a legal journal on free Afro-Virginians in Cumberland County, across the Appomattox from Prince Edward. She examined, among other things, every identifiable land transaction involving a free black individual and all litigation to which free Afro-Virginians were parties. Katz discovered that one in four free black households in Cumberland owned real estate by 1860. White authorities there showed remarkable apathy toward registration laws and other statutes that discriminated against free blacks; no one in Cumberland County was ever jailed for lacking free papers, Katz says. As often happened in Prince Edward, authorities in Cumberland accommodated those blacks who were emancipated after 1806 and who stayed on. Katz draws a conclusion that seems especially striking coming from a legal scholar—that "the white perceptions of free blacks embodied in the state's laws are not readily evident in the daily interactions between whites and free blacks in the county."[6]

Though Katz carried out prodigious research, her study did not include an examination of ended papers from the county and circuit courts, nor did Miles's. Moreover, though neither researcher knew much about what I was finding, Miles was my student and Katz had been at one time. It is important to review what other historians who lack that tie have to say. A number of them depict conditions similar to those I uncovered in Prince Edward County, while some draw different conclusions.

James D. Watkinson finds blacks and whites attending estate sales side by side in Lancaster County, Virginia, each buying property left by the dead of the other race. "All citizens, regardless of rank, race, or gender, availed themselves of the courts and generally received equal treatment," Watkinson adds. Free black children bound out to apprenticeships in Lancaster—in Virginia's Tidewater section, far from Prince Edward—generally learned "desirable" trades. All in all, Watkinson says, "between 1800 and 1860 race relations in Lancaster County seemed to have been, if not cordial, then certainly less fraught with tension than one might think."[7]

Several studies of localities along Virginia's Blue Ridge find significant numbers of Afro-Virginians buying land, making a living at skilled trades, moving about geographically, ignoring the expulsion law, seeking to live independent of whites, yet experiencing fair treatment in the courts. One book about Lynchburg concludes that free blacks "were generally hated as a class, although often beloved and praised as individuals."[8]

Diane Miller Sommerville demonstrates the absence of rape hysteria directed by whites against free and enslaved blacks in pre–Civil War Virginia and North Carolina; she shows that the vigorous legal defenses afforded to the few such defendants in Prince Edward County and the pivotal role played by social class in the Mary Tatum case had many counterparts in other places. Martha Hodes reveals that "white Southerners could react [to sex between black men and white women] in a way that complicates modern assumptions." She does not find "sanguine acceptance" of such contact on the part of whites, but does uncover "a measure of toleration."[9] Joshua Rothman goes even further, finding cross-racial sexual activity "ubiquitous" in Virginia before the Civil War and white citizens "only rarely" inclined to do anything about it, legally or otherwise. The "wide array of sexual activity across the color line" that whites "tolerated and accommodated," says Rothman, included "viable and supportive interracial families" and networks of kin such as those I find in Prince Edward County. Thomas E. Buckley has chronicled the fortunes of one prosperous interracial family in Campbell County not far from Lynchburg, whose "respectable" white neighbors saw the family's mulatto head as one of their own group and were prepared to attest to his status in writing.[10]

Looking at the treatment of slaves in Virginia courts, Philip J. Schwarz draws some conclusions about trials of enslaved and free blacks that parallel mine. Within a framework of unequal justice, he finds that executions and other harsh punishments diminished in number during the nineteenth century. More generally, he writes, while some jurists behaved unfairly, "the canons of the bench" and "the search for justice" produced many "acquittals, reductions of charges, and pleas [from justices to the governor] for mercy." One of Schwarz's conclusions about the slaveholding regime in Virginia reinforces the idea I present through the vignette of storekeeper Ebenezer Frothingham's nailed-down but paneless windows: "In conception, slavery was the absolute control of some human beings by others; in practice, however, it was sufficient control"—with sufficiency defined, of course, by whites.[11]

Much of Sally E. Hadden's research on slave patrols in the nineteenth century covers places other than Virginia, and much of her information about Virginia does not stem from the nineteenth century. But she finds, as I do, that patrollers came from all social classes. She gives attention to the alleged laxity, drunkenness, or somnolence of some patrols, and to white as well as black resistance to patrollers; on the whole, however, she believes patrols in the areas of the South that she studied acted more vigilantly than I suggest those in Prince Edward often did. She discovered little evidence showing how patrols interacted with free blacks, and says that, in any event, patrollers concentrated their attention on slaves.[12]

Suzanne Lebsock's influential study of women's culture in Petersburg during the decades between the Revolutionary and Civil Wars contains one chapter on free black women. Lebsock depicts the group as oppressed and mostly impoverished. Like me, she emphasizes the failure of the apprenticeship system to impart lucrative skills to most black girls who went through it. But Lebsock also finds "considerable long-term progress" over the years in property holding by free black women. She asserts that free black females, ironically, "were in some respects Petersburg's most autonomous women." They faced a shortage of potential husbands and in some cases purposefully opted out of marriage, which left many of them free from "day-by-day domination" by men.[13]

Alison Goodyear Freehling offers a persuasive account of Virginia's debate over slavery in the months after Nat Turner's rebellion. She finds persistent doubts about slavery among many white Virginians rather than a blind embrace of the idea that bondage was a positive good, and she documents thoroughly the controversy over manumission, gradual emancipation, and the fate of blacks who were free or might become so. She depicts free Afro-Virginians as active opponents of schemes to expatriate them, and notes that whites deferred to free black sentiment on this issue. William W. Freehling, too, depicts persistent discomfiture over slavery (and over the presence of the black population) in Virginia and elsewhere in the Upper South. He describes an uphill battle that proslavery "crusaders" fought, and escalated during the 1850s, to enlist hesitant fellow white Southerners in an all-out defense of the institution—an escalation apparent in the renewed disparagements of Israel Hill that I find in that decade. William G. Shade discusses the "ambivalent view of slavery" that many Virginians, especially Whigs, maintained during the antebellum period, though both parties were "proslavery" when all was said and done. He finds attitudes toward economic development in Virginia that parallel those I describe, but locates them more exclusively among city and town folk than I do.[14]

Michael L. Nicholls examines the free black experience in eight Southside Virginia counties, including Prince Edward, from the colonial period to about 1820. He notes, as I do, that few white Southsiders freed slaves during the early years after passage of the law of 1782 allowing private manumissions. Nicholls suggests that a "weakening of ties with the surrounding slaves" owing to the growing availability of free black spouses, combined with "resistance and racism of whites" in the rural Southside, prompted free blacks to migrate from there into Virginia's cities. The focus and scope of his article do not allow him to test the second part of that hypothesis by methodically examining free blacks' interactions with individual whites and with county authorities during the years from 1782 to 1820.[15]

Two studies help us appreciate that the lot of free blacks varied from locality to locality and from one period to another. In Prince Edward County as in much of the South, free people of color markedly expanded their landholdings during the 1850s, yet Brenda E. Stevenson reports a "devastating" erosion of free blacks' economic fortunes at that time in Loudoun County in northern Virginia. Stevenson says that "not a few" free black Loudouners were pushed by deprivation into crime, a phenomenon I almost never find in my own research. It may be that the presence of tobacco factories, the foundry, the warehouses, and the railroad in Prince Edward created opportunities in the 1850s that blacks in Loudoun did not encounter; other historians' findings suggest that Prince Edward's economic experience of that decade may have been more typical than that of Loudoun.[16] Stevenson adds that employers "often" declined to hire free blacks, and that white workers refused to toil alongside them. Such ostracism is not apparent in Prince Edward either before or after the rise of factories and the rest, or in Reginald Butler's Goochland County; Stevenson in fact offers little evidence that white employers and laborers excluded blacks. On the other hand, there is no reason to doubt her categorical statement that no free black person received poor aid in Loudoun except by entering the poorhouse.[17] I find Prince Edward's overseers of the poor behaving quite differently.

In some instances, it is difficult to know whether Loudoun differed from other counties, or whether Stevenson and I are reading similar evidence differently. She writes that "many free people of color hired themselves out on an annual basis like slaves." I suggest that moving from employer to employer and striking one's own best deal were in large part assertions of independence. Either point of view is defensible; perhaps there is some truth in each. Stevenson cites the widespread employment of free black women at clothes washing as evidence of economic desperation, and writes that they earned "only a few cents a day." I find two part-time or full-time washers earning and saving enough to buy lots in Farmville, one of them for $550; Loren Schweninger shows that more than three hundred washers across the Upper South purchased nearly $200,000 worth of real estate in the 1850s. Stevenson says that "many local whites actively prevented free people of color from acquiring land." Whites apparently did not attempt such a thing, and certainly did not achieve it, in Prince Edward, in Cumberland, or in other counties that have been studied.[18]

Stevenson calls the institution of apprenticeship a device to "destroy impoverished free black families by parceling out their children to strangers."[19] The system did indeed have its coercive aspects, and it discriminated against girls. At the same time, Reginald Butler and I find that, in Goochland and Prince Edward at least, black and white parents alike complained when their apprenticed children were ill-used, and that courts often listened. Those who assigned and took on free black apprentices typically knew and consulted the families, and the institution imparted useful, sometimes even lucrative skills, at least to boys. John Hope Franklin offers a similarly positive view of free black apprenticeship in North Carolina, as we shall see in a moment.

Stevenson's findings and mine do coincide on a number of points. She portrays members of multigenerational families all chipping in to help the group prosper, as the Sam White, Teny Carter, and Milly Homes households did in Prince Edward County. In Loudoun as in Prince Edward, a number of couples consisting of a black man and a white woman maintained stable relationships. And Stevenson offers two intertwined observations that apply perfectly to Israel on the Appomattox and its surroundings. Free blacks, she says, had "an array of relationships . . . with Loudoun's diverse European-American residents." Widely varying attitudes toward free Afro-Virginians existed within the white community, she adds, leading to "white factionalism on issues of race" and even to "biracial support networks."[20] Still, the overriding tone of Stevenson's work is pessimistic. At one point, she goes so far as to say that for free Afro-Virginians, living "decent, productive, 'free' lives" was "not possible" in Loudoun County, or in the rest of Virginia.[21]

A Virginia study whose tone and substance differ even more sharply from mine is Tommy L. Bogger's history of free blacks in Norfolk. Bogger says that free African Americans in that city faced "overwhelming social ostracism and racism" after a post-Revolutionary period of relative liberalism. This deterioration, he says, came about in no small part because Norfolk's economy went into depression in 1807 and remained so until the eve of the Civil War.[22] If Bogger is right, then his study illustrates how different conditions in diverse parts of the state could produce varying outcomes. Bogger examined a city rather than a rural county, and he emphasizes white immigrants' resentment of black competition—a factor that was missing in the countryside. Yet he also notes frankly that "many of the sources on free blacks" that he consulted came from those "who mentioned them . . . for the purpose of disparaging them"— and that undoubtedly shaped his findings.[23]

Much of the evidence that Bogger's research yielded qualifies his negative overall verdict, I believe. He cites various petitions in which "ordinary citizens . . . rallied" to support free blacks faced with expulsion under the law of 1806, and he says that white opinion deplored the kidnapping and selling of free blacks.[24] Bogger quotes a local newspaper effusively proclaiming white citizens' "gratitude and admiration" for black volunteer firefighters, but concludes that the praise was expressed "grudgingly." He says that white officials showed considerable support for enslaved people who sued for their freedom, but characterizes those sympathizers' exertions as expressions of white elite paternalism.[25]

Bogger vividly depicts one of Norfolk's weeklong "Ebony Festivals," which attracted elegantly dressed free blacks to "the most fashionable ballroom in the city" with the active cooperation of the mayor and other white officials; he also shows how white rioters broke up one ball in 1850.[26] The passage seems to offer compelling evidence that a middle class had developed among black Norfolkians, and that whites vehemently disagreed with one another on how to treat free blacks. Bogger himself ends up saying that "the laws are not a true gauge of the social and legal climate in which free blacks lived. . . . [Free blacks] preached even to whites, sued whites, established schools, and traveled regularly between Norfolk and northern ports. In short, they did a host of things that legal statutes said they were not to do."[27]

Historians have documented conditions in Southern states other than Virginia that should prompt us to reconsider whether the panoply of anti–free black rhetoric and legislation describes the actual treatment of free Afro-Southerners. The acquisition of real estate by thousands of free blacks in the Upper South, which continued through the 1850s, has been thoroughly documented by Loren Schweninger and others. Arthur Howington, a legal historian, concludes that Tennessee courts would not act in ways that called the institution of slavery into question, but that, short of this, they treated most blacks who came before them much as they did white defendants.[28]

In Maryland, Barbara Jeanne Fields details "a bewildering profusion of legal restrictions" on free blacks and a propensity among Baltimore's lawmen to incarcerate them. She also remarks that the oppressive laws "were not always enforced to the letter," and she expresses "a strong suspicion that many operated, not as literal rules, but as a sort of warrant for the free blacks' good behavior." Nonslaveholders depended on Maryland's numerous free blacks as a labor force, Fields says, and they successfully turned back the more extreme measures that slaveholders proposed to direct against free people of color; that conflict contributed to an irreparable split in the state's white population. Fields also describes free blacks' mostly quiet yet steadfast and often successful resistance to pressure.[29]

Day-to-day inconsistency in enforcement, and downright laxity, against a forbidding backdrop of state law were not confined to the Upper South. In a dissertation on Mobile County, Alabama, Christopher Andrew Nordmann finds considerable white tolerance of manumission, as well as nonexpulsion of emancipated blacks, general nonenforcement of the ban on free black immigration, freedom of black economic activity, successful lawsuits by free blacks against whites, and significant rates of landholding among free Afro-Alabamians, reaching new heights in the 1850s.[30]

Mobile, like New Orleans, had a "special" past as a Spanish and French colony under which a secure and recognized mulatto group emerged. Yet Gary B. Mills, a historian of "Anglo" Alabama—the greater part of the state—arrives at conclusions compatible with those of his student, Nordmann, after attempting to research the life of every free black who lived in Alabama before 1865. "Nothing has emerged thus far to support the theory that whites in Alabama hated or feared free blacks," Mills writes; "they did not fear the widow next door who was a founding member of their church or hate the barber with whom they hunted. Instead, it was the vague and theoretical mass of black freedmen that troubled them"—an anxiety fanned by "political demagogues."[31] Of course, for demagogic appeals to work, there had to be a substratum of prejudice against free blacks for them to play on.

Louisiana was home to a large population of sometimes well-off free mulatto *gens de couleur,* secured in certain rights since colonial times under Spain and France. Free people of color there, writes H. E. Sterkx, possessed "quasi-citizenship" that included the right to acquire property, file suit, and testify in court; thus they "enjoyed a better legal position than any of their counterparts in other states of the South." Manumissions were fairly numerous until they were restricted in the 1850s and then prohibited at the end of the decade; slaves "frequently" obtained liberty through lawsuits—though the quoted word, to be sure, is a relative term. A generally "permissive" attitude toward free blacks prevailed, Sterkx says, punctuated by periods of "hostility" and even violence in some localities when the North-South conflict heated up, especially at the end of the 1850s.[32]

Georgia imposed much more heavily on its small free African American population. Under the law, free blacks by the 1850s could not make contracts or file suit except through a white guardian—a restriction never introduced in Virginia or in most other places. Yet even in this particularly repressive state, Edward F. Sweat reports, "lax" law enforcement "mitigat[ed] the harshness" of the legal code during most periods. Few free blacks were prosecuted for alleged crimes, and public opinion demanded laws to guard against the false enslavement of free Afro-Georgians by "wicked white men." Moreover, some white "guardians" may have fulfilled that role in name only, giving their "wards" a free hand.[33]

Even as evidence piles up that daily practice often ignored the law, that free blacks encountered a wide variety of white behavior, and that they had room to make effective use of freedom that was no mere illusion, a very different picture of free African American life continues to thrive. This is the world described in Ira Berlin's acclaimed book, *Slaves Without Masters*. Free black life, Berlin wrote in 1974, "straddled one of hell's elusive boundaries," the border between slavery and freedom. Many if not most whites saw the free Afro-American as "an incorrigible subversive," and blacks "enraged" whites any time they improved themselves. According to Berlin, "southern whites almost uniformly feared and despised" free African Americans and "would not tolerate free Negroes living among them." Free blacks' lawyers "had little incentive to protect them"; "free Negroes rarely received justice at the hands of all-white judicial systems," and black defendants "rarely escaped . . . terrifying punishments." In sum, "whites systematically barred free Negroes from any of the rights and symbols they equated with freedom."[34]

Berlin's thesis, then, is that whites treated free blacks as though they were slaves who unfortunately had slipped the formal bonds of the peculiar institution. The state, he writes, stepped in to take the place of the masters that free Afro-Southerners lacked, and it played the role ruthlessly. He notes that free blacks resisted efforts to degrade them, and that they achieved a degree of success in a few areas—rendering the registration laws difficult to enforce, for example. But overall, Berlin and others have written, free Afro-Southerners could not fend off the onslaught of repression that deepened from one year to the next.

I need not list here the ways in which the life I find in Prince Edward County differs from this picture, and I have already mentioned a number of works by others that likewise call this stark portrayal into question. But when I launched the research for this book, I had no idea that I would find anything that did not comport with Berlin's picture of free black life. I still find his work valuable, as do the students who read it in my courses every year.

Berlin, a formidable researcher and interpreter, presents a superb compendium and analysis of anti–free black *ideology*—and there was an ample supply of that even in Prince Edward, as the writings of Colonel Madison and

Attorney Francis Watkins prove. Berlin also shows that the treatment of free blacks, at certain times and places, did turn nasty on the practical as well as the theoretical level. His book retains its place alongside other crucial works of the 1950s, 1960s, and 1970s that drew readers' attention to an American outrage: our society's methodical violation of its founding ideals as it excluded from civil life, education, and the embrace of human equality most of the relatively few blacks it did not hold in outright bondage.

Berlin has always sought to understand the big picture. In his dissertation, he set out to depict conditions across the entire Upper South; the book that followed examined the South as a whole. That approach limited the degree to which he could delve into the daily life of particular localities. The deeper local probing that Berlin's project did allow involved cities, where newspapers, justifiably, figure prominently among his sources; he has considerably less to say about life in rural counties. Just as my choice of topic and use of sources allow me to do things Berlin could not, his own approach permits him to address subjects I cannot, such as differences between white views of free blacks in the Upper South and in the Lower—although even here, I wonder whether the contrasts were greater on the level of ideology than on that of day-to-day life.

I believe that much of the content of Berlin's book calls into question his general propositions about free blacks' having been treated as virtual slaves. What I think he does show us, and vividly, is a white South that disapproved of free blacks as a concept but could never decide, or agree on, what to do about them as flesh-and-blood people. What whites did more often than not, Berlin himself says, was to let their own free black laws go unenforced even as they toughened those codes over time. Explaining that lack of enforcement, Berlin mentions free blacks' "determined opposition" and resistance.[35] The geographic sweep of his topic naturally prevents his chronicling that resistance in all its forms. For example, he quotes the law about hiring blacks out for nonpayment of taxes, but does not depict widespread nonpayment followed by nonhiring, as in Prince Edward and other localities in Virginia. He does not show us free blacks suing whites over financial matters, or in the aftermath of physical aggression.

Berlin does allow that free Afro-Southerners avoided some of the system's potential horrors, but he suggests that they did so largely by finding paternalistic white protectors.[36] I agree that this happened, but I also find a number of instances in which black men and women went toe-to-toe with aggressors before a local court. The primary sources I read tell me that cooperation between free blacks and well-to-do, influential whites did not necessarily involve condescension by the one and self-effacement on the part of the other. Religious affinities, the desire for economic gain, and simple neighborliness could count for a great deal even when individuals belonged to different races. Berlin concludes that "inability, rather than a lack of desire, accounted for much of the failure to enforce the free Negro codes."[37] Granting a large measure of inability, I and others nevertheless contend that there was in fact a *pervasive* lack of desire to enforce many of those codes most of the time. Where Berlin finds a gap between will and capacity to oppress, I find a different fissure—between laws and pronouncements about free blacks as a faceless abstraction on one side, and relations among real-life neighbors of both races on the other.

Berlin himself documents the latter dichotomy vividly, nowhere more so than in his treatment of proposals to expel or re-enslave free blacks as the crisis of the Union deepened. I, too, find a hardening of white attitudes then, and even of behavior, at least toward free Afro-Virginians who had ties to the North. But Berlin rightly notes that "a surge of popular opposition" to expulsion and re-enslavement fairly quickly proved that radical anti–free black measures "offended the sense of right of many [white] Southerners."[38] In the last lines before his Epilogue, Berlin states explicitly what I think his evidence throughout the book tends to show: that instead of forming a solid phalanx to implement the degradation of free blacks, the white South found itself engulfed in a series of "contradictions." These, I contend, the Colonel Madisons and Edmund Ruffins never could overcome.[39] In fact, Berlin does such a good job of defining those contradictions that I believe his title, *Slaves Without Masters,* and his statements about universal white loathing of free blacks, do not do justice to the remarkable complexity of his findings.

There is much else in Berlin's rich work, only two further points of which I will mention here. He believes that the very laxity—or unpredictability—of enforcement made life under the anti–free black laws even more hellish than it might have been had Afro-Southerners known what to expect at every turn. I myself, if I lived in a society with a panoply of unjust laws, would prefer that they be applied only occasionally, even capriciously, rather than consistently. But beyond that, I believe that life for free blacks in Prince Edward County was largely predictable, and spasms of enforcement neither frequent nor random nor violent. Everyone, white and black alike, seems to have understood that, most of the time, most of the truly onerous laws would not be applied. But when a Nat Turner or a John Brown came along, free blacks knew they had best exercise some caution for a while.

Finally, Berlin asserts that the white South's behavior toward free blacks before the Civil War constituted a kind of dress rehearsal for its treatment of all Afro-Southerners after Emancipation. That proposition may hold up better for urban settings, where physical segregation and competition for jobs became issues, than for the countryside—and again, much of Berlin's evidence apart from the law codes themselves comes from urban sources. Yet it is difficult to see how the flexibility, the ambivalence, the fumbling, the ubiquitous cross-racial contact, and the generally apathetic mood of many rural Southern whites before the war prepared them to impose on blacks the physical separation and the outright terrorism that subverted Reconstruction and marred the latter nineteenth century. Those enormities came in response to conditions that existed only after general Emancipation and the granting to black men of the right to vote. In my view, the enslavement of most Afro-Southerners before the war allowed many whites to deal tolerantly and confidently with the relatively few blacks who were free.

Two works on the Carolinas fall, I believe, somewhere between the Berlin thesis and the kind of picture I myself present. Both illustrate how difficult it can be, even for the most discerning scholar, to characterize a phenomenon as complex as the treatment of free blacks in the Old South.

John Hope Franklin, the distinguished historian who first made his reputation in 1943 with a nuanced study of free blacks in North Carolina, presents a deeply researched, complicated picture, yet he punctuates it with some statements that seem to underplay that very complexity. Franklin finds little white opposition to manumission or desire to expel its beneficiaries. "Often, there was no enforcement at all" of anti–free black laws in rural areas, he reports.[40] Numerous free black men voted until 1835, and even then some influential white North Carolinians defended their right to do so.

Court-ordered apprenticeships were "an effective method of training free Negro children to become proficient workers and intelligent citizens," Franklin asserts. The free black landowner gained "the respect—somewhat disquieted, perhaps" of whites, and he "could be fairly sure that the courts would stand by him during his period of possession." Franklin readily discerns the difference between proslavery rhetoric and concrete action, noting that "the seeming harsh and illiberal laws of North Carolina were often softened by those who interpreted and administered them."[41]

Yet the most oft-quoted sentence from Franklin's book is one in which he states that North Carolina's free blacks were "surrounded on all sides by a legal system which denied them the opportunity to seek a livelihood where they could and by a hostile community that often made them as unwelcome as a contagious disease." He goes on to say that discrimination and white contempt, combined with lax enforcement of the law, gave rise to a "prevalence of drunkenness and thievishness among the free Negro population," an assertion that leaves me skeptical to say the least. By the 1850s, according to Franklin, "life was becoming unbearable for the free Negro in ante-bellum North Carolina"; he even says that "a large number of free Negroes" sought to enslave or re-enslave themselves.[42]

John Hope Franklin offers a further estimate of the free black experience that others, both before and since, have stressed as well. "The amazing thing," he says, is that black North Carolinians, though beset by white enmity, "were able to acquire more than a million dollars' worth of property . . . and to have possessed several hundred slaves during the seventy-year period ending in 1860."[43]

This thesis of triumph in the face of what Luther P. Jackson called an "avalanche of laws and abuses" has proved long-lived, and not without reason. Marina Wikramanayake, a student of free black life in South Carolina, skillfully portrays, page by page, a mixture of laxity and repression in that state. Courts mitigated the practical effect of a benighted legal code; whites protested curtailment of their right to manumit slaves and "devised every conceivable means of circumventing the law." White people who defrauded or kidnapped free blacks encountered spirited opposition from members of their own race, and "many" free blacks became secure, even affluent. For much of the time up to the 1850s, "the free Negro [in South Carolina] enjoyed a long legislative respite that was denied his counterparts in the rest of the South," and lawmakers "consistently rejected all petitions against free Negroes"— observations that Ira Berlin himself endorses.

I understand this as a story of free black South Carolinians managing to make progress through their own exertions *and* because of the disharmony between white people's professed ideology and their customary behavior. Yet the writer frames her work as a chronicle of "sheer survival in adversity"; Michael P. Johnson and James L. Roark, in their own influential book on South Carolina, agree that "simply to survive as a free person of color in the slave South was no mean feat." Many free blacks, it seems to me from Wikramanayake's own evidence, accomplished much more than mere "survival," partly because the restrictions they faced, though very real and repugnant to our sense of fairness, were far less than absolute in practice.[44]

I have written in the Postscript about why the formidable achievements of free African Americans are sometimes not satisfying enough for us—why we also want the odds against free Afro-Southerners to have been nearly as prohibitive as those the slaves faced. But to depict free black lives as having been lived beneath a seamless fabric of oppression leaves much of those people's story untold. Moreover, the assumption that free blacks lived almost like slaves underrates the suffering, the resilience, and the creativity of black Americans who were enslaved in fact. Even as we recall the injustices that free blacks faced, we owe it to those millions of bondpeople to remember that they held their own in the face of oppression the likes of which few free people ever had to confront.[45]

ABBREVIATIONS
IN NOTES AND REMARKS
ON PRIMARY SOURCES

acct = account

Acts of Assembly = *Acts of the General Assembly of Virginia* [title varies slightly from session to session] (Richmond: Thomas Ritchie, various years)

admor = administrator

affi = affidavit

certf = certificate

Cheadle = Josiah T. Cheadle's tobacco sales book, 1821–57, Archives Research Services, Library of Virginia

CirCt = Circuit (or District or Superior) Court Papers (Prince Edward County, unless otherwise specified), Archives Research Services, Library of Virginia

CoCt = County Court Papers (Prince Edward County, unless otherwise specified), Archives Research Services, Library of Virginia

CW = Commonwealth (of Virginia)

DB = deed book (Prince Edward County)

deft = defendant

depo = deposition

DoT = deed of trust

Duke = Rare Book, Manuscript, and Special Collections Library, Duke University

est = estate

exor = executor

FNL = free Negro list (compiled annually by each county; here, Prince Edward County, unless otherwise specified)

Hening = William Waller Hening, ed., *The Statutes at Large; Being a Collection of All the Laws of Virginia, from the First Session of the Legislature in the Year 1619* (Richmond: Franklin Press, various years)

IH 1816 = Samuel Allen, sheriff, List of free Negroes on Israel Hill, 1816 (filed CoCt 1816, January–April)

LVA = Library of Virginia

OB = order book (Prince Edward County Court, unless otherwise specified)

OP = overseers of the poor

plff = plaintiff

Shepherd = Samuel Shepherd, ed., *The Statutes at Large of Virginia, from October Session 1792, to December Session 1806, Inclusive* (New York: AMS Press [1835] 1970)

spa = subpoena

TC/W&M = Tucker-Coleman Papers, Manuscripts and Rare Books Department, Swem Library, College of William and Mary
UNC = Southern Historical Collection, Wilson Library, University of North Carolina at Chapel Hill
UVa = Special Collections Department, University of Virginia Library
VHS = Virginia Historical Society
WB = will book (Prince Edward County)
Yale = Manuscripts and Archives Department, Sterling Memorial Library, Yale University

A Note on Citations

Court cases are cited in the abbreviated style by which they are labeled in suit papers (also known as ended or dead papers) and in order books—for example, Smith v Jones. This style is followed by the name of the court that considered the case (almost always CoCt or CirCt) and the "ended date"—the year and month the case was finally disposed of, and according to which the papers it generated were filed in county records. (The institution that I and others call the circuit court actually took somewhat different shapes and went by various formal and informal names over the years, including superior court and district court.)

At the time the research for this book was conducted, ended papers and other county documents were filed in bundles that sometimes covered two or more months; some such documents are referred to accordingly in these Notes: for example, Lewis v Royall, CoCt 1839 Mar–Apr. At this writing, Archives Research Services at the Library of Virginia plans to refile county records according to type and year/month ended, so the case given here would be filed under either 1839 Mar or 1839 Apr. This may require the researcher to spend some additional time locating certain papers referred to here. When necessary, the exact ended date of an action can be determined by seeking that case in the appropriate order book, which will begin with an index.

References to will books take the form: volume number/page number, name of document, then, in parentheses, year document was generated (if different from year of recordation)/year document was recorded. Example: WB 2/142-143, Benjamin Lawson will (1787/1789).

References to deed books take the form: volume number/page number, principal parties to transaction, then, in parentheses, year document was generated (if different from year of recordation)/year document was recorded. Example: DB 22/234–235, J. White to Steger (1837/1838).

References to order books take the form: volume number/page number, then, in parentheses, year and month of court session. Example: OB 20/311 (1822 Jun). The Notes often cite ended papers without the corresponding order book entry, because the former are generally more informative; in such instances, the order book entry can almost invariably be found according to the ended date of the action.

In some references to free Negro lists (FNLs), the year is accompanied by a notation indicating which of Prince Edward County's two districts the list covers. These districts are designated as lower district and Green's (or upper) district for years in which lists for both districts survive (1801, 1802, 1804–1807). For 1803, 1809, 1811, and 1817–1820, lists are extant only for the upper district; for 1808, 1810, 1812–1815, 1826–1856, and 1859, no lists apparently survive. A list from 1816 for the lower district is found in the property tax enumeration book for that year. The lists from 1821 through 1825 cover the entire county; those for 1824 and 1825 are located in the property tax enumeration books for those years. Lists survive also for 1857–1858 and 1860–1864; each covers the entire county. Fortunately, the bulk of Prince Edward's free Afro-Virginian population, including the black Israelites, lived in the better-documented upper district.

The Cheadle tobacco sales book is actually a ledger containing plantation records of all sorts, arranged chaotically. One agglomeration of records begins at the front of the ledger, another at the back; Josiah Cheadle numbered some pages, but this numbering covers only part of the book. In an attempt to make references to this ledger clear, I have superseded Cheadle's partial numbering. Pages designated 1st p., 2nd p., and so on are counted from the first extant page at the front of the ledger, which begins with an account of smith's work done by H. Y. Jenkins. Pages referred to as B1st p., B2nd p., and so on are counted from the back, which begins with drafts of formal letters.

In the lines below, I have attempted to identify the headings and filing schemes under which each category of Prince Edward County records will be organized after the Library of Virginia processes those papers—a project scheduled to begin shortly. A small number of documents cited in this book are difficult to categorize, and their location after refiling is thus hard to predict; nevertheless, the outline that follows should help the researcher to locate even these records.

County Court Records

Judgments

Civil suit papers, by month and year, then alphabetical by plaintiff's surname

Commonwealth or criminal causes

Grand jury presentments, by month and year
Criminal trial papers, by month and year, then alphabetical by defendant's
    surname

Tax and fiscal records (each subcategory sorted by year)

Tax enumeration books
Lists of insolvents/delinquents in land tax, property tax, county levy, and free
    black special tax
Lists of free blacks to be hired out for delinquent taxes
Patrol returns
County accounts not included under other headings such as Road and
    bridge papers
Contracts not included under other headings
Tobacco inspectors' reports
War bonds and kindred papers
Reports from county functionaries

Free Negro and slave records

Annual lists of free black residents, by year
Free black registrations and kindred documents, by year
Affidavits regarding, and requests for replacement of, free papers, by date,
    then by applicant's surname
Requests from other counties for copies of free black registrations, by date,
    then by individual's surname
Some lists of free blacks to be hired out for delinquent taxes may be filed
    under Free Negro and slave records, either as original documents or as
    photocopies

Road and bridge papers (each subcategory sorted by year)

Orders and commissioners' inquests regarding opening of roads
Highway surveyors' claims and reports
List of hands to work on roads

Fiduciary records

Estate accounts and reports, by year
Guardians' bonds not related to lawsuits, by year

Land records

Processioners' reports, by year

Bonds, commissions, and oaths

Commissions of justices of the peace and appointees of court
Apprentice indentures, by year (currently housed in the State Records
    Center, these may remain there)

Miscellaneous records

Overseers of the poor records, by year
Letters and petitions to county court, by month and year
Court orders not pertaining to specific cases and originally filed separately in
    county records may be filed under miscellaneous records, by year, though
    that remains uncertain at present
Coroner's inquests (inquisitions), by year (currently housed, and may remain,
    in the State Records Center)

Circuit (or District, or Superior) Court Records

Judgments

Civil suit papers, by month and year, then alphabetical by plaintiff's surname

Commonwealth or criminal causes

Grand jury presentments, by month and year
Criminal trial papers, by month and year, then alphabetical by defendant's
    surname

Fiduciary records

Estate accounts and reports, by year

Miscellaneous Documents

Prince Edward County Records in the form of volumes, as contrasted to loose papers, are
currently housed at the State Records Center, and they may continue to be held for viewing
there. These include Josiah T. Cheadle's ledger book and the Circuit Superior Court of
Law and Chancery minutes for 1846–70.

Microfilmed records may be viewed at the main building, LVA. These include order books, will books, deed books, land tax and personal property tax rolls, guardians' accounts, marriage bonds, index to marriage bonds, and death register, as well as manuscript United States Census returns.

Records assembled at the state level will remain in their current locations in LVA. These include governors' executive papers, legislative petitions (filed according to county of origin), Auditor of Public Accounts Records, and Bureau of Public Works papers. The Sharon Baptist Church minute book, LVA 20803, will remain available in its current location in the main building, LVA.

NOTES

CHAPTER 1: *The View from Israel Hill, 1863*

1. Israelites in army, according to FNLs, 1862 and 1863: Caesar Carter, John Clark, Isaiah Carter, Clem Carter, Patrick Cousins, John Giles, Sidney Howard, Tom Scott; and George, Rial, and Tom Johnson [Johnston]. See also "Deacon W. H. White," *Richmond Planet*, January 26, 1895; I thank Harold Forsythe for bringing this item to my attention.

2. Sam White's appearance and carriage: OB 16/688 (1811 Feb), registration of Hercules White [Sr.], Sam's father (and of three immediate members of Sam's family at five feet nine to five eleven, tall for that era); OB 17/22 (1811 Mar), registration of Molly White, Hercules White Sr.'s wife and Sam's probable mother; OB 20/311 (1822 Jul), registration of Samuel White (born c. 1798), probably Sam Senior's son; George W. Bagby, "My Uncle Flatback's Plantation," in Bagby, *The Old Virginia Gentleman and Other Sketches*, ed. Thomas Nelson Page (New York: Scribners, 1910), p. 101, brought to my attention by Brent Tarter.

3. "Beg[,] *humbly* beg": District Court WB 1/4-7, Richard Randolph will (1796/1797).

4. Accolades: *New York Evening Times*, August 31, 1854, "A Free Negro Community in Virginia," reprinted from *Baltimore Patriot*, provided to me by Frank Moore (which mentions "honorable . . . original settlers" of Israel Hill, but does not mention Sam White by name); F. N. Watkins, "The Randolph Emancipated Slaves," in *De Bow's Review* (April 1858), p. 288 ("venerable patriarch").

5. "Idle and vicious"; "nearest to idleness": James Madison, "Condition of the Descendants of a Number of Emancipated Slaves, in Prince Edward County," with editor's response, *Farmers' Register*, 4, no. 1 (1836), 3–4.

6. Honest and decent: J. D. Eggleston, typescript beginning "Richard Randolph of Bizarre . . . ," p. 2, in Eggleston papers, Mss1 Egg3966, section 30, "Slavery," VHS; and Eggleston, letter to W. M. Thornton, January 22, 1934, in folder, "Prince Edward County," second stack, General Library, LVA, courtesy of John Kneebone.

7. "Drive against the free Negro": Luther Porter Jackson, *Free Negro Labor and Property Holding in Virginia, 1830–1860* (New York and London: D. Appleton–Century, 1942), p. 3. Jackson himself offers aspects of what I am calling the other part of the story, detailing the economic progress free blacks made from 1830 to the Civil War.

8. "Prolific . . . of many good free negroes": Rip Van Winkle (pseudonym), "Farmville Then and Now," in *Farmville Herald*, August 31, 1906, p. 3.

9. Ira Berlin, *Slaves Without Masters: The Free Negro in the Antebellum South* (New York: New Press, [1974] 1992), pp. 88 ("whites would not tolerate"), 89 ("incorrigible subversive"; "enraged"), and 183 ("almost uniformly feared"). Elsewhere in his classic book, Berlin's impressive research and sensitivity to nuance yield a picture of considerable regional and individual variation in Southern whites' treatment of free African Americans.

CHAPTER 2: *Liberty and Happiness*

1. Dickey's fear: Richard Randolph, letter to St. George Tucker, July 9, 1781, TC/W&M; Frances Bland Randolph Tucker, letter to Tucker, July 14, 1781, TC/W&M (expressing concern about Tucker's horse).

2. Syphax, life and death: John Randolph, letter to St. George Tucker [c. October 1, 1781] (in which John reported that everyone was frightened for Tucker when Syphax appeared without him), and Frances B. R. Tucker, letter to St. George Tucker [c. October 1, 1781] (reporting the same incident; Syphax's "Grin"), both in TC/W&M.

3. "I wish the british"; Dickey follows campaigns: Richard Randolph, letter to St. George Tucker, July 9, 1781, TC/W&M.

4. British prisoners: James Moss petition for Revolutionary War pension, filed CoCt 1833 Aug. Role of neighborhood in war: Herbert Clarence Bradshaw, *History of Prince Edward County, Virginia, from Its Earliest Settlements Through Its Establishment in 1754 to Its Bicentennial Year* (Richmond: Dietz Press, 1955), pp. 113–25 and 130 (the quotation).

5. Military events: Bradshaw, *Prince Edward County,* pp. 117–18 and 123. Tucker's role: John Randolph, letter to St. George Tucker, July 10, 1781, TC/W&M.

6. Tarleton's raid: Bradshaw, *Prince Edward County,* pp. 125–26; Samuel Carter depo, Jenkins v Watson, CoCt 1822 Jul (Tarleton takes prisoners).

7. "Utmost distress"; preparations to flee: Frances B. R. Tucker, letter to St. George Tucker, July 14, 1781, TC/W&M; Frances Tucker, letter to St. George Tucker, March 22, 1781, TC/W&M, mentions the Tucker babies. "Flung . . . papers": John Randolph of Roanoke, *Forty-Six Autograph Letters to Harmanus Bleecker of Albany* (cited hereafter as *Letters to Bleecker*), October 10, 1818, UVa.

8. Tarleton's withdrawal and aftermath: Bradshaw, *Prince Edward County,* pp. 125–27.

9. "My faithful Servants": Frances B. R. Tucker, letter to St. George Tucker, July 14, 1781, TC/W&M. On Afro-Americans and the Revolutionary War, see Sylvia Frey, *Water from the Rock: Black Resistance in a Revolutionary Age* (Princeton: Princeton University Press, 1991).

10. Reliance on Syphax: Frances B. R. Tucker, letters to St. George Tucker, June 9, 1781, and [c. October 1, 1781], TC/W&M.

11. Syphax's family: Frances B. R. Tucker, letter to St. George Tucker, March 22, 1781, TC/W&M. "Old attendant Syphax": John Randolph, letter to Theodorick Tudor Randolph, December 13, 1813 (typescript), Grinnan family papers, Mss1 G8855 d90, VHS.

12. Syphax as waiter: Thomas Green's FNLs, 1801 and 1802 ("Waiter on Gentlemen"), and 1803 ("Waiter & Tender").

13. "Pert walk": Advertisement placed by Archer Taylor of Chesterfield in *Richmond Enquirer,* June 20, 1806, p. 4, col. 5, found amid CoCt papers, [apparently 1810] Jun–Aug.

14. Non-mortgaging of Syphax: District Court WB 1/9–13, Richard Randolph inventory (1797/1798). The Randolph inventory notes that all but five of the slaves owned by Richard Randolph at his death—Syphax [Brown Sr.], as well as Rose [Johnston] and her family—were still mortgaged to the creditors of Randolph's father. John Randolph Sr.'s will does not mention specific slaves, and I have found no postmortem appraisal of his estate. I thus cannot rule out that some or all of the five slaves not mortgaged at the time Richard died may have been so at John Senior's death, but redeemed by Richard's mother, his stepfather, or Richard himself between 1775 and 1797. Jonathan Daniels, *The Randolphs of Virginia* (Garden City, NY: Doubleday, 1972), pp. 119 and 124, says Syphax was never mortgaged; though he does not cite a source for this, it seems eminently plausible.

15. Eventful life: The two sources for Syphax Brown's age are probably both in error, falling at opposite extremes. Hampton Giles asserted in Answer, Brown v Giles, CoCt 1841 Jun, that Syphax was nearly one hundred when Israel Hill was settled in 1811; IH 1816 recorded Brown's age as forty years younger than that. The truth is probably somewhere in between: it is doubtful that Giles could have mistaken a sixty-year-old associate for a centenarian, or that he could expect to make such an assertion to a court without being contradicted by his adversary in the suit, who was Syphax Brown Sr.'s own son. By the time Richard Randolph died in 1796, Syphax Brown was known as Syphax the Elder also to differentiate him from his young grandson and namesake.

16. Richard's experiences at Princeton: Richard Randolph, letters to St. George Tucker and Frances B. R. Tucker, July 15, 1787, and to Frances, September 10, 1787, TC/W&M. One historian depicts Richard as a "chronic underachiever" because he attended more than one college, complained about William and Mary and Princeton, and never took a degree—Christopher L. Doyle, "The Randolph Scandal in Early National Virginia, 1792–1815: New Voices in the 'Court of Honour,'" *Journal of Southern History*, 69, no. 2 (May 2003), 289. In fact, many students of the time, including Thomas Jefferson, never sought a degree. Richard was chosen as a commencement speaker at Princeton and he displayed a keen intellect in his will, despite his earlier discomfiture at various schools.

17. Ellis's appearance: Billy Ellis certf of freedom, 1811, filed CoCt 1822 Aug. "Dusky Othello": John Randolph, letter to Ann Cary [Nancy Randolph] Morris, [October 31, 1814], typescript, in Nancy Randolph papers, Manuscripts and Rare Books Department, Swem Library, College of William and Mary. John seems genuinely to have believed that his allegation regarding Billy Ellis and Nancy was well founded; see John Randolph, *Letters to Bleecker*, April 18, 1815, UVa.

18. "Poor Billy": Ann C. [Nancy Randolph] Morris, letter to Edward Dillon, January 20, 1815, Dillon-Polk papers, UNC.

19. Hercules' age: IH 1816. His versatility: Entries for 1804 Mar 24 (p. 17) and 1806 Jun 7 (p. 22), in Copy of proceedings in the county court, Attorney General v Chambers's trustees, CoCt 1821 Nov; Acct of Hercules, in Allen's exors v Fowler, CoCt 1822 Jul; Acct, Nathan Dupriest to Peter Johnston, in Dupriest v Johnson, CoCt 1809 May; WB 4/354–355, Hercules White appraisal (1812) (note also that the appraisal enumerates both farm implements and tools used in carpentry and construction). Hercules' position as leader: Answer, Brown v Giles, CoCt 1841 Jun.

20. Fanny's piety: Frances B. R. Tucker, letter to St. George Tucker, July 14, 1781, TC/W&M. "The conduct and conversation": John Randolph, letter to Theodorick Tudor Randolph, December 13, 1813, Grinnan family papers, Mss1 G8855 d90, VHS.

21. "Without learning either trade or profession": Robert Dawidoff, *The Education of John Randolph* (New York: W. W. Norton, 1979), p. 78. Fanny's admonitions: recapitulated in Richard Randolph, letter to Frances B. R. Tucker, October 28, 1787, TC/W&M; Fanny apparently represented the values of Richard's natural father as having been nearly identical to those of St. George Tucker. "Be assured": Richard Randolph, letter to St. George Tucker, July 9, 1781, TC/W&M.

22. Experiments with electricity: Richard Randolph, letter to Frances B. R. Tucker [c. April 1786], TC/W&M.

23. Randolph's library: District Court WB 1/9–13, Richard Randolph inventory (1797/1798). Dick's Latin and Greek: John Randolph, letter to St. George Tucker, July 10, 1781, TC/W&M; John Randolph, letter to Theodorick Tudor Randolph, December 13, 1813, Grinnan family papers, Mss1 G8855 d90, VHS.

24. Wythe as Richard's teacher: John Randolph, letter to Theodorick Tudor Randolph, December 13, 1813, as in note 23.

25. "Nothing would advance me": William Munford, letter to John Coalter, June 13, 1790,

box I, folder 34, Brown–Coalter–Tucker Papers, Manuscripts and Rare Books Department, Swem Library, College of William and Mary. "That best of men"; "not to be deferred": Richard Randolph, letter to Frances B. R. Tucker, May 19, 1786, TC/W&M. "The brightest ornament": District Court WB 1/4–7, Richard Randolph will (1796/1797). "Neglect": Richard Randolph, letter to Frances Tucker, August 18, 1786, TC/W&M. Randolph's encomiums to Wythe were no mere tokens of a fleeting schoolboy enthusiasm, for Richard wrote them ten years apart. Professions of devotion to Wythe seem no less sincere because Richard used them as excuses for not writing his mother longer letters.

26. "Slow, sure, and imperceptible": David Brion Davis, *The Problem of Slavery in the Age of Revolution, 1770–1823* (Ithaca and London: Cornell University Press, 1975), pp. 169–70.

27. Tucker's views: St. George Tucker, *A Dissertation on Slavery: With a Proposal for the Gradual Abolition of It, in the State of Virginia* (Philadelphia: Mathew Carey, 1796), especially pp. 10 ("we were imposing"), 50 ("perfectly irreconcilable"), 51 ("fellow men"), and 77 ("submission"; "arrogance").

28. Wythe and slavery: Appomattox (pseudonym), "To the People of Virginia" (1832), published with Thomas R. Dew, *An Essay on Slavery*, 2nd ed. (Richmond, VA: J. W. Randolph, 1849); and see Imogene E. Brown, *American Aristides: A Biography of George Wythe* (Rutherford, NJ: Fairleigh Dickinson University Press, 1981), especially p. 267; John H. Russell, *The Free Negro in Virginia, 1619–1865* (Baltimore: Johns Hopkins Press, 1913), p. 98. "Appomattox" was the pseudonym of attorney and political figure Benjamin Watkins Leigh, of whom more will be said later in this book—see Joseph Clarke Robert, *The Road from Monticello: A Study of the Virginia Slavery Debate of 1832* (Durham: Duke University Press, 1941), p. 10 and p. 11, n. 12. John Chester Miller, by contrast, groups Wythe, at least in the 1770s, among those who insisted upon colonization of emancipated blacks—Miller, *The Wolf by the Ears: Thomas Jefferson and Slavery* (Charlottesville and London: University Press of Virginia, 1991), p. 21. Some have stated—without marshaling any evidence at all—that Lydia Broadnax, a mulatto servant, was the widowed Wythe's mistress, and Brown their son; see, e.g., Daniels, *Randolphs of Virginia*, pp. 216–17, and Miller, *Wolf by the Ears*, pp. 42–43. Suggestions of a sexual liaison between Wythe and Broadnax are challenged by Brown, *American Aristides*, pp. 298–304, and by Philip D. Morgan, "Interracial Sex in the Chesapeake and the British Atlantic World, c. 1700–1820," in Jan Ellen Lewis and Peter S. Onuf, eds., *Sally Hemings and Thomas Jefferson: History, Memory, and Civic Culture* (Charlottesville: University Press of Virginia, 1999), pp. 56–60.

29. In a final, tragic twist, the murderer, indicted and obviously guilty, could not be convicted. Virginia law prohibited Wythe's housekeeper, Lydia Broadnax, from testifying against him because she was black. The phrase "my greatest Benefactor" comes from Richard Randolph's will.

30. On use of the title "Citizen," see Bradshaw, *Prince Edward County*, p. 366, citing letters of both Richard and John Randolph; Judith Randolph, letter to Citizen St. George Tucker, April 22, 1799, TC/W&M; and numerous letters of John Randolph from the period in various collections. On the use of the Revolutionary calendar, see John Randolph, letter to St. George Tucker, dated "24 June [year] 21 of Indep./6 Messidor [year] 5 of Fr. Rep.," John Randolph papers, Randolph-Macon Woman's College (microfilm), UVa—Messidor being one of the months in the French Revolutionary system.

31. Wedding date of Richard and Judith: John Randolph, letter to Theodorick Tudor Randolph, December 13, 1813, Grinnan family papers, Mss1 G8855 d90, VHS. A useful attempt to untangle the Randolph family history—unfortunately lacking footnotes, but containing partial family trees—is Daniels, *Randolphs of Virginia*.

32. On Tuckahoe during Judith's childhood and youth, see Thomas Anburey, *Travels Through the Interior Parts of America,* vol. 2, p. 208, quoted in Hunter Dickinson Farish, ed., *Journal and Letters of Philip Vickers Fithian: A Plantation Tutor of the Old Dominion, 1773–1774* (Charlottesville: University Press of Virginia, 1957), p. 239, n. 20; Peter S. Randolph, letter to [Peter, Samuel, or Dabney] Carr, July 28, 1787, in "Letters from Old Trunks," *Virginia Magazine of History and Biography,* 48, no. 3 (July 1940), 238–42. On the Jeffersons' residency at Tuckahoe, see Camille Wells, "Virginia by Design: The Making of Tuckahoe and the Remaking of Monticello," *Arris: Journal of the Southeast Chapter of the Society of Architectural Historians,* 12 (2001), 44–73, especially 44–46.

33. "Most perfect": Peter S. Randolph, letter to Carr, as in note 32. Judith's erudition: Judith Randolph, letters to John Randolph, January 18, 1808 (citing Pericles), November 11, 1807, January 29, 1808 (comments on John's political battles accompanied by a disclaimer of sophistication on that subject), and March 9, 1808; Judith Randolph, letter to Citizen Saint George Tucker, April 22, 1799; all in TC/W&M. Also Judith Randolph, letter to Mary Harrison in care of Citizen Creed Taylor, February 23, 1800, Harrison family papers, Mss1 H2485 g5, VHS.

34. The rumors and their diffusion: Notes of John Marshall at Trial [sic] of Anne Cary (Mrs. Gouverneur) Morris and Richard Randolph (so titled although Nancy apparently had not been a defendant), copied from original by John Randolph Jr. (typescript), Mss2 M3567 a1, VHS; Richard Randolph, letter to St. George Tucker, March 14, 1793, Mss2 R1572 a2, VHS; St. George Tucker, "To the Public," May 5, 1793, broadside 1793:3, VHS; and Judith Randolph, letters to Eliza[beth] Pleasants, March 15, 1793, and to St. George Tucker, April 21, 1793, reproduced in the same broadside.

35. Communication between slaves and whites: Testimony of Randolph Harrison, Mrs. Randolph Harrison, Peyton Harrison, in Notes of John Marshall at Trial, VHS. Since I wrote this passage, Christopher L. Doyle has published an article which draws attention to the role blacks played in spreading information about the events at the Harrison home, and which discusses the indirect introduction of those slaves' stories into formal court testimony. For reasons detailed in this and later chapters, however, I disagree that there was something unusual about elite whites' heeding the words of blacks in matters bearing on the character of other whites. And I certainly take issue with Doyle's suggestion that Richard Randolph "underestimated the slaves' importance" in transmitting information or in any other capacity, and indeed that he exhibited "blindness" toward them; on the contrary, Randolph's will shows that he had unusual regard for the personhood and agency of blacks. See Doyle, "The Randolph Scandal," especially pp. 295–97, including n. 27 ("blindness").

36. Judith (and apparent loss of baby): Judith Randolph, letter to Mary Randolph Harrison, June 5, 1794, in Harrison family papers, Mss1 H2485 g8, VHS. "Public enquiry": Richard Randolph, letter to St. George Tucker, March 14, 1793, Mss2 R1572 a2, VHS (emphasis in original). Some have suggested that the William Randolph who accused Richard was Judith's brother of that name; yet evidence from later years suggests that Judy and her brother were on good terms, which seems unlikely had he caused her the kind of agony the Bizarre scandal entailed—Judith Randolph, letter to St. George Tucker, March 27, 1814, TC/W&M.

37. Source of money for attorneys' fee: Richard Randolph, letter to St. George Tucker, March 14, 1793, as in note 36. Except as stated, the following account of the testimony regarding Richard Randolph relies on Notes of John Marshall at Trial, VHS. Richard also hired a third attorney, Alexander Campbell.

38. Judith Randolph's deposition for the hearing repeated information she had already given St. George Tucker, which had then been included in his broadside, "To the Public," May 5, 1793, broadside 1793:3, VHS (see additional detail in note 39). Engagement to Theo, and admission of delivery: Ann C. [Nancy Randolph] Morris, letter to

John Randolph, [January 16, 1815], typescript, in Nancy Randolph papers, Manuscripts and Rare Books Department, Swem Library, College of William and Mary.

39. The influential St. George Tucker tried to help restore the reputation of Richard, who with Nancy and Judith had lived in Tucker's household during the winter before the hearing; he drew up and distributed a broadside defending the Randolphs' character and behavior—"To the Public," May 5, 1793, broadside 1793:3, VHS.

40. "Not a single negro": Hugh A. Garland, *The Life of John Randolph of Roanoke*, 13th ed. (New York: D. Appleton, 1860), vol. 1, p. 63. Although Garland gives no specific citation for this letter or for another referred to later in this chapter, I am inclined to believe the quotations are genuine. On the mortgaged slaves left by John Randolph Sr., see letter of John Randolph Jr., March 31, 1799, and supporting letter from John Wickham, reprinted in *Virginia Gazette and General Advertiser* (Richmond), April 5, 1799.

41. Randolph's mahogany desk and secretary: District Court WB 1/9–13, Richard Randolph inventory (1797/1798). On Richard's health and unexpected death: John Randolph, letter to Theodorick Tudor Randolph, December 13, 1813, Grinnan family papers, Mss1 G8855 d90, VHS; John Randolph, letter to Judith Randolph, January 20, 1816, Grinnan family papers, Mss1 G8855 d89, VHS. Richard's will: District Court WB 1/4–7, Richard Randolph will (1796/1797). Quotations in the following paragraphs are from the will except where attributed otherwise. A transcript of Randolph's will appeared in the *Virginia Magazine of History and Biography*, 34 (1926), 72–76, but it contains lacunae and various inaccuracies, some of which materially affect the sense of the document and detract from its eloquence; in an apparent concession to white Southern sensibilities, this version sometimes even bowdlerizes the forthright term "slaves" used by Randolph, rendering it as "servants."

42. Another local example of the widespread problem of "British debts" among Virginians: George Walton of Prince Edward County, whose will, like Richard Randolph's, was written in 1796 and proved in 1797, left a British debt big enough that £200 would only cover part of it (WB 3/77).

43. Here Richard the Deist seems to have heard some echoes from the Book of Common Prayer he had known as a child, in which one asks pardon for the "manifold sins and wickedness, which we, from time to time, most grievously have committed."

44. Randolph's landholdings: Thomas Green's land tax book, Prince Edward County, 1797, LVA; cf. List of Bizarre & Buffaloe Property, 1850, in WB 9/412, long after the acreage that became Israel Hill passed out of the estate's possession.

45. A few years earlier, telling St. George Tucker of his plans to free the slaves he would soon inherit, Richard is supposed to have explained, "I consider every individual thus unshackled as the source of future generations, not to say nations, of freemen"—Garland, *Life of John Randolph*, vol. 1, p. 63.

46. Companionate marriage: See Suzanne Lebsock, *The Free Women of Petersburg: Status and Culture in a Southern Town, 1784–1860* (New York and London: W. W. Norton, 1984), pp. 17–18 and 28. Frances Tucker's affectionate nature: Various letters of Frances to St. George during the Revolutionary War, such as those of March 22 and September 7, 1781, TC/W&M; John Randolph, letter to Theodorick Tudor Randolph, December 13, 1813, Grinnan family papers, Mss1 G8855 d90, VHS.

47. "Lonely hours": Judith Randolph, letter to Mary Randolph Harrison, June 5, 1794, Harrison family papers, Mss1 H2485 g8, VHS. Judy's estimate of Dick's character: Judith Randolph, letter to Elizabeth Pleasants, March 15, 1793, in St. George Tucker, "To the Public," May 5, 1793, broadside 1793:3, VHS; see also Judith Randolph, letter to St. George Tucker, April 21, 1793, in same broadside. Christopher Doyle accepts Nancy Randolph Morris's statement, written years after her bitter estrangement from Judith, that Richard had not truly loved Judy; but Judith wrote to and of Richard as if

the two enjoyed a loving union, and Dick's will emphatically asserted the same— Doyle, "The Randolph Scandal," 289.

48. Worries about Dick's associates: Frances B. R. Tucker, letter to [Col. John Banister, 1787 Feb]. An attempt by Dick to reassure Fanny: Richard Randolph, letter to Frances B. R. Tucker, April 12, 1787. Quoting Fanny's threat to die: Richard Randolph, letter to Frances Tucker, October 28, 1787. All these letters are in TC/W&M.

49. "Great & conspicuous": Richard Randolph, letter to Frances B. R. Tucker, October 28, 1787, TC/W&M.

50. Allegation of poisoning: John Randolph, letter to Judith Randolph, January 20, 1816, Grinnan family papers, Mss1 G8855 d89, VHS, in which John's error in recalling the year of his brother's death is one of the most glaring of many chronological mistakes in his letters.

51. "Iniquitous": Garland, *Life of John Randolph,* vol. 1, p. 62.

52. Judy's father: Daniels, *Randolphs of Virginia,* pp. 118–20 and 124–26.

53. Not liberating nonmortgaged slaves: District Court WB 1/9–13, Richard Randolph inventory (1797/1798), with Syphax, Rose, and Rose's children still listed.

54. Judy's financial situation: John Randolph, letter to Theodorick Tudor Randolph, December 13, 1813 (typescript), Grinnan family papers, Mss1 G8855 d90, VHS; Judith Randolph, letter to St. George Tucker, October 18, 1801, TC/W&M ("very considerable" debts); Richard Randolph, letter to St. George Tucker, March 14, 1793, Mss2 R1572 a2, VHS (tobacco crop to pay for legal costs); District Court WB 1/9–13, Richard Randolph inventory (1797/1798). John seems to say Richard had amassed more debts of his own than the estate inventory reflects.

55. Judith's sufferings: Judith Randolph, letters to Mary Randolph Harrison, June 5, 1794 ("attacks" and "affections") and September 17, 1796 ("Hope[,] the sweetest soother"), in Harrison family papers, Mss1 H2485 g2–9, VHS. "Hypochondriack": John Randolph, letter to St. George Tucker, November 14, 1809, John Randolph Papers, Randolph-Macon Woman's College (microfilm), UVa.

56. John's role in the settlement: John Randolph, letter to Theodorick Tudor Randolph, December 13, 1813, Grinnan family papers, Mss1 G8855 d90, VHS. Partial sale of slaves: District Court WB 1/10, Richard Randolph inventory (1797/1798).

57. The Browns: FNLs, Thomas Green's district, 1801, 1802, and 1803; List of free people of colour, in Green's property tax enumeration book, 1804, LVA; FNL, lower district, 1807; and Answer of Hampton Giles, Brown v Giles, CoCt 1841 Jun (in which Giles, in fact, erroneously stated that Syphax had been liberated even before his master's death). Betty Brown as midwife: Chambers acct with Watson, Allen, and Green, 1802 Sep 14 (p. 12) and 1803 Jan 17 (p. 14), in Copy of proceedings, Attorney General v Chambers's trustees, CoCt 1821 Nov; FNL, Green's district, 1811. The available records do not reveal definitively whether Betty and her son had been slaves of the Randolphs.

58. There are three slaves named Rose in the inventory of Richard Randolph's estate taken in 1797, and a couple of Rose Johnston's children also share given names with other Randolph slaves. The absence of surnames in the inventory confuses matters, as is true in virtually all slave records. Still, Rose Johnston had four children—Jacob, George, Rachel, and Hannah—born in that order; four of the five unmortgaged Randolph slaves were Rose, Jacob, George, and Rachel, who are listed in that order. Rose Johnston's youngest child, Hannah, was born around the time Richard Randolph's will was proved, and that may account for her omission from the list of unmortgaged slaves. Approximate birth dates: IH 1816; FNL, 1819; OB 16/688, 17/22, and 18/414.

59. Resettlement of Hercules et al.: Property tax enumeration books, upper district, 1799, 1802, and 1804, LVA. IH 1816 has the boys ranging in age from ten to fourteen in the year 1799; that Dick, Hercules Senior's youngest son, went with the family is a near

certainty, but this cannot be proved by the tax enumeration book, as he was only eight or nine in 1799 and therefore not taxable. For information on Judith Randolph's slaves living on the Buffalo tract in subsequent years, see Taxable property rolls, Thomas Green's (upper) district, 1803–07 and 1809–10, LVA.

60. Virginia antislavery feeling and its context: See Davis, *Problem of Slavery in the Age of Revolution*, pp. 164–65, 174–75, and 211. "So very contradictory": Quoted in Thad W. Tate Jr., *The Negro in Eighteenth-Century Williamsburg* (Williamsburg, 1965), pp. 210–11, cited in turn by Davis, p. 169. Manumission law of 1782: Hening, 11 (1782), chapter XXI, pp. 39–40. Rhetorical Society: William Bolling diary, 1795 Oct 3, Mss5:1 B 6386:1, VHS (thanks to Sarah Hughes for bringing this item to my attention).

61. The quoted phrase is found in WB 3/521, Edward Haskins will (1806/1807), and in many other Prince Edward wills of the period. Requiring purchase of additional slaves: WB 1/355, Peter Davis will (1784 and 1785/1785); WB 2/84–87, John Thomas Dejarnett will (1788/1789); WB 4/124–125, John Fowlkes will (1808).

62. "Trusty Slave Lewis": WB 2/99–100, Charles Price will (1790). Biggest slaveholder (coincidentally named Richard K. Randolph): Bradshaw, *Prince Edward County*, p. 271; Ms. United States Census, Prince Edward County, 1810.

63. Churches owning slaves: See Bradshaw, *Prince Edward County*, p. 275, confirmed by many primary documents.

64. Black population figures: Ms. Census, 1810.

65. Freedom of choice: WB 3/142–144, William Bauldwin [sic] will (1796/1799); and WB 3/243, Mary Ritchey will (1798). "To those that the said Negroes would wish": WB 3/14, Christian Baker will (1795). Slaves to remain in family (example): WB 3/179–180, Mary Booker will (1798/1800).

66. Johnson's manumission: OB 7/52 (1783 Apr). His former slaves' later residence and occupations: FNL, lower district, 1801 (which gives the family name as Johnston). Neither was Jesse Johnson motivated by guilt or affection toward slaves he had fathered; although the slaves he liberated took his family name, they were black, not mulatto.

67. Jackson manumission: WB 3/130–131, Nancy Jackson will (1798). Manumitters' responsibility to support minors: Hening, 11 (1782), chapter XXI, section 2, pp. 39–40.

68. Goode manumission: WB 3/370–372, Robert Goode will (1804), and WB 3/392, Goode appraisal (1804/1805).

69. Baker manumission: WB 3/353, Andrew Baker Sr. will (1804). On Baker himself, see Joseph D. Eggleston, two articles in *Virginia Magazine of History and Biography:* "The Minute Book of the Buffalo Circulating Library," 49, no. 2 (April 1941), 159; and "The Buffaloe Settlement and Its Makers," 49, no. 4 (October 1941), 321–22. The aftermath of the Baker manumission is discussed later in this chapter and in chapter 8.

70. Mettauer bequest: WB 4/311, Joseph Mettauer will (1811/1812); OB 22/580 (1832 Jan). On Mettauer's career: Bradshaw, *Prince Edward County*, pp. 354–55. Withholding of bequest: Mettauer's devisees v Mettauer's exors, CoCt 1835 Jul. Beneficiaries liberated: OB 20/311 (1822 Jun); OB 21/23 (1824 May); Henry Mettauer certf of freedom, 1821 Aug 22, filed CoCt 1829 Aug. It may be that Mettauer's sons settled with the former slaves for a smaller sum many years afterward.

71. Antimanumission activity: Fredrika Teute Schmidt and Barbara Ripel Wilhelm, "Early Proslavery Petitions in Virginia," *William and Mary Quarterly*, 3rd ser., 30, no. 1 (January 1973), 133–46; Davis, *Problem of Slavery in the Age of Revolution*, pp. 167–68 and 175, n. 17. On Virginia's largest mass manumission and the opposition it aroused in some quarters, see John Randolph Barden, " 'Flushed with Notions of Freedom': The Growth and Emancipation of a Virginia Slave Community, 1732–1812" (Ph.D. diss., Duke University, 1993).

72. On the genesis of the free black expulsion law, and opposition to a repeal of the right

to manumit, see Russell, *Free Negro in Virginia,* pp. 63–70, with text of the law on p. 70, n. 107.

73. Widow Baker: Copy of C. Baker's Will, in Ellis v Baker's exor and Baker, CoCt 1815 May. John Nash Sr.'s will: WB 3/225–228 (1800/1801). John Nash Jr.'s will: WB 4/273 (1811). The younger Nash did apparently employ a family of blacks freed by others—FNLs, lower district, 1802, 1804, 1805 (on which the former John Nash Jr. has now become "Sr.," his father having died by 1801), and 1806. Two of the elder Nash's children did take in the two people he had emancipated—FNL, lower district, 1801, showing Tony Boils residing on Charles Nash's land and Agnes Stith living with Elizabeth F. Smith.

74. Slaves entrusted with property: Judith Randolph, letter to St. George Tucker, March 6, 1800. Links in grapevine (example involving bondman Essex): Judith Randolph, letter to John Randolph, November 11, 1807. "Poor Johnny": Judith, letter to John, December 30, 1807. "A good nurse": Judith, letter to John, February 9, 1808. All these letters are in TC/W&M.

75. Tony's volubility in earlier times: See Frances B. R. Tucker, letter to St. George Tucker, April 18, 1787, TC/W&M (assuming, as seems likely, that the Tony referred to there is the same one who later handled horses for Richard and Judith Randolph). Missing horses: J[udith] Randolph, letter to Creed Taylor, n.d. 1798, box 1, Creed Taylor papers, UVa. Breaking horses: Judith Randolph, letter to St. George Tucker, April 22, 1799, TC/W&M. "Neglect": Judith, letter to Tucker, March 6, 1800, TC/W&M.

76. "Servants . . . inattentive": Judith Randolph to St. George Tucker, March 6, 1800, TC/W&M. Quotations regarding slaves' "discontents" and protests: Judith, letter to Tucker, October 18, 1801, TC/W&M, except for quotations involving lending or hiring to Taylor, which come from J[udith] Randolph, letter to Creed Taylor, January 10, 1801, box 1, Creed Taylor papers, UVa (emphasis in original). For other complaints about her slaves' productivity, see Judith [to Mary Harrison], November 24, 1805, Harrison family papers, Mss1 H2485 g2–9, VHS; and Judith, letter to Tucker, September 29, 1808, TC/W&M.

77. "Extreem, & repeated cruelty": Frances B. R. Tucker, letter to St. George Tucker [November? 1787], TC/W&M.

78. Information on Baker's dealings with Aaron comes mainly from Aaron v Baker's exors, CoCt 1811 Jun, especially Aaron's bill, answer of Catherine Baker, and Elliott Baker depo ("if he gave him land"). The other principal source on Aaron's quest for freedom is Ellis et al. v Baker's exors and Baker, CoCt 1815 May; see also OB 17/107. In the end, Baker himself decided to use Aaron for the last of the four years, and to credit his slave with a year's hire in return.

79. One of my students at Yale, Genevieve Preer, made an interesting suggestion: that Baker may have cited the prospective demand of the other slaves for land as a mere excuse not to give Aaron any. To my mind, the documents do not suggest this. But even if it were so, such an excuse would have sounded absurd if Baker and his auditors alike had not assumed that slaves made demands and might assert a right to equitable treatment. Another Yale student, Peter Laub, contributed significantly to the discussion of this issue. On slaves' adroitness at turning ostensible "privileges" into established rights, see Eugene D. Genovese, *Roll, Jordan, Roll: The World the Slaves Made* (New York: Vintage, 1974), pp. 30–31 and *passim.*

80. Aaron's labor contract: William Cary depo, corroborated by Catherine Baker depo, in Aaron v Baker's exors; the latter makes it clear that the employer issued his bond for Aaron's labor to Baker, not to Aaron himself.

81. "Miserable plight"; "well founded": Judith Randolph, letter to John Randolph, November 21, 1807; for an earlier expression of concern, accompanied by complaints about her slaves' behavior, see Judith, letter to St. George Tucker, October 18, 1801.

Sending boat downriver: Judith, letter to John, December 2, 1807. "Fears . . . ground-less": Judith, letter to Tucker, October 18, 1801. All these letters are in TC/W&M.

82. Hercules and mill: Allen's exors v Fowler, CoCt 1822 Jul, especially acct of "Hercules (a free negro)"; large ledger sheet of debts owed Allen & Fowler; and commissioners' report (with payments from Hercules 1806 Sep and 1807 May–Oct).

83. Carpentry: Acct, Gen. Peter Johnston to Nathan Dupriest, in Dupriest v Johnson [sic], CoCt 1809 May. Hogsheads: Copy of proceedings, Attorney General v Chambers's trustees, 1804 Mar 24 (p. 17), CoCt 1821 Nov. Wheat-cutting: Copy of proceedings, Attorney General v Chambers's trustees, 1810 Mar 30 (p. 33). At this same time, the Chambers estate was paying a white cooper $1 (6 shillings) per hogshead (1806 Feb 11 [p. 22]); that Hercules earned exactly $2 from the same buyer for an unrecorded number of hogsheads is difficult to account for by any explanation other than that Hercules had made two hogsheads and sold each for $1, the same price the white man got.

84. Hercules sells tobacco: Copy of proceedings, Attorney General v Chambers's trustees, 1806 Jun 7 (p. 22). Cf. *ibid.*, 1813 Oct 7 (p. 42) (a clear example of mixing tobacco from the Chambers plantation in the same hogshead with leaf grown by someone else). Hercules' borrowing and investments: See Francisco's admor v White's admor, CirCt 1838 Apr. On what $19 would buy, see Philip Bowman est acct with James Venable and brother, Bowman v Bowman's exor, CirCt 1847 Apr; Stokes v Anderson, CoCt 1822 Dec–1823 Mar; Rent replevy bond, Scruggs to Lewis, filed CoCt 1824 May; and Bartlett v Bartlett, CoCt 1841 Mar (annual rental on house $30); if anything, a dollar would have purchased a bit more when Hercules was producing tobacco than it would in these later years. Tobacco in the Chambers accounts in the early 1800s sold for as little as 24 shillings/cwt (1808, p. 31) and as much as 33 shillings/cwt (1807 Jan 24, p. 26); the price Hercules and Peter received—28 shillings and 6 pence—falls in the middle of that range.

85. Hercules and Backus: Randolph [sic] v Backus, CoCt 1809 Aug; Randolph's [sic] admor v Backus, CoCt 1825 Aug; White's admor v Backus, CoCt 1828 Oct, and recorded in OB 21/764 (1828 Oct). Eventual payment: WB 7/439–440, Hercules White Sr. est acct with S. Allen, deputy of Carter (1836), 1830 Mar.

86. Gun transaction: Notations on back of delivery bond, White's admor v Backus, CoCt 1828 Oct. At the time, shotguns sold for $10 to $12 at the most (WB 3/84; WB 4/3, 139, 245, and 250); they often sold for much less (WB 3/419 and 4/281). "Rifles," by contrast, typically ran from $16 to $20 (WB 3/271, 395–399, 415; WB 4/31). The new gun-licensing law of 1806: see Russell, *Free Negro in Virginia,* p. 96.

87. Hercules' complexion: OB 16/688 (1811 Feb), Hercules White registration.

88. Different appellations of Hercules: Copy of proceedings, Attorney General v Chambers's trustees, 1804 Mar 24 (p. 17) and 1810 Mar 30 (p. 33); acct of Hercules (a free Negro), n.d. (about the same time?), large ledger, and 1806 Sep, both in Allen's exors v Fowler, CoCt 1822 Jul; Randolph v Backus, CoCt 1809 Aug; OB 16/688 (1811 Feb).

89. Sy Brown's hogs: Brown v Bennett, CoCt 1809 Aug, and OB 16/415 (1809 Aug); except as indicated, the material in the following paragraphs also derives from this source. The jury decided that Brown should receive damages of £4; on realizing that the court would award him double damages, the jury accordingly altered its nominal award to £2. Brown did receive double that amount. (The point about Brown's rang-ing beyond the sphere of domestic service emerged during an exchange I had with Emily Moore.)

90. About the same time Bennett shot Brown's hogs, a white woman in the county accused a young man and his father of wounding her horse, and a dozen or so years later one white man alleged that another had killed assorted livestock belonging to him. The horse: Bradshaw v Ford, CoCt 1809 Apr–May. Numerous livestock allegedly killed: Legrand v Sweeney, CoCt 1824 May and OB 21/25 (1824 May).

Brown sued Bennett for $100 and received £4, or $13.33; but plaintiffs typically sued for unrealistically high sums. The white man who sued in the 1820s had probably lost more livestock than Syphax Brown had, and indeed received an award almost twice as high as Brown's, $25; but he had sought $300, or three times as much money as Brown had.

91. Bar on black testimony against whites: See Russell, *Free Negro in Virginia,* pp. 116–17. Black shoemaker's suit: Bartlett v Thompson, CoCt 1810 Aug. The same outcome occurred fairly often when whites sued each other, or when white merchants sued free black debtors. For contemporaneous cases in which black defendants were reported to have no goods that could be attached, see Patteson & Co v Forguson, CoCt 1810 Aug; Hart & Nimmo v Moss, CoCt 1810 Sep–Nov.

92. I examined valuations and sale prices of hogs at the time of Brown v Bennett in a large number of estate appraisals, estate accounts including estate sales, and a court case or two. Examples in which £4 would cover a dozen hogs: WB 3/465 and 4/30. Examples in which £4 would cover four or four-and-a-fraction large hogs: WB 4/24, 171, 223, and 250. Five to six hogs for £4: WB 4/27, 135, 205. Six to eight hogs: Commissioners' report per court order of 1810, Harris v Price, CoCt 1816 Jul; CW v Peter, CoCt 1816 Jul; WB 3/34, 49, 127, 150, 175, 186, 216, and 338. Eight to ten hogs: WB 4/171 (small hogs), 208, and 354 (Hercules White Sr.'s appraisal). And according to the values listed in WB 4/338, £4 would have bought fully twenty small hogs.

93. Suit for assault: Homes v Bosher, CoCt 1810 Aug.

94. Taylor: Bradshaw, *Prince Edward County,* pp. 160 and 177, and E. Lee Shepard, "Learning the Law: Private Law Schools in Antebellum Virginia," *Virginia Cavalcade,* 37, no. 4 (Spring 1988), 149–51 (Taylor's home and law school); Judith Randolph, letter to Mary Harrison, February 23, 1800, Harrison family papers, Mss1 H2485 g5, VHS ("Citizen"); A[nn] C[ary] R[andolph] to Mrs. Taylor, n.d., box 3, Creed Taylor papers, UVa ("Citizen"). Judith had intended to manumit her slaves a year earlier, but then postponed the act—Judith, letters to St. George Tucker, July 23, 1809, TC/W&M; November 3, 1809, John Randolph papers, Randolph-Macon Woman's College (microfilm), UVa; and January 27, 1810, TC/W&M.

95. John Holt Rice and founding of Union Theological Seminary: Bradshaw, *Prince Edward County,* pp. 158–60. Rice on slavery: *Ibid.,* pp. 279–80. A group manumission by Anne Rice: DB 26/306, Rice to Deans and Black (1853). Judy's close friendship with Rices: See John Holt Rice, numerous letters to Judith Randolph, in William Maxwell, *A Memoir of the Rev. John H. Rice, D. D.* (Philadelphia: J. Whetham, and Richmond: R. I. Smith, 1835); and also WB 5/98, Judith Randolph will (1816).

96. Judith's decision to manumit and depart, and Jack's lease on Bizarre: Judith Randolph, letter to St. George Tucker, January 27, 1810, TC/W&M. Renting out Buffalo tract: Judith, letter to St. George Tucker, August 12, 1810, TC/W&M.

97. Judith and John's arrangement, and division of estate of John Randolph Sr.: Judith Randolph, letters to St. George Tucker, September 29, 1808, and January 27, 1810 (two personal servants to Jack; "satisfied if [Jack] reaps the benefit"; "purchase the necessary servants"), TC/W&M. Worry about her own liability: Fragment (apparently the top three quarters of the letter), [Judith Randolph to Creed Taylor], 1810 n.d., box 1, Creed Taylor papers, UVa. In the latter document, Judith also complained to Taylor that she had sacrificed the labor of a number of these slaves to John for all the years since Richard's death.

98. Judith's manumission of Whites, Johnstons, and others: Judith Randolph, letter to court, filed in CoCt 1810 Dec–1811 Mar; OB 17/21–22 (1811 Mar); FNL, Thomas Green's (upper) district, 1811. The formal survey, and the wooded terrain: Judith Randolph, letters to St. George Tucker, January 27 and August 12, 1810, TC/W&M; Bill and answer in Brown v Giles, CoCt 1841 Jun. Value of land on Israel Hill: Land tax rolls, especially 1809–14 (microfilm), LVA; Bradshaw, *Prince Edward County,* p. 525

(premium placed on bottomlands at the time); Judith Randolph, letter to Tucker, January 27, 1810 (the diminution in land values that cultivation could cause).

One letter by Judith Randolph—to St. George Tucker, August 12, 1810, TC/W&M—discusses her renting out of the Buffalo tract to a white man for three years beginning in 1810, along with the distribution of land to the blacks, in a way that seems to cloud the chronology. But in her letter to Tucker of February 4, 1811 (TC/W&M), Judith writes of her servants having already departed, and preparing to settle the lands that were now to be theirs if not already settled in there. Thomas Green's FNL of 1811 and Judith Randolph letter to the Prince Edward County Court show that all but one of the families who would become "Israelite" landowners were free residents of Prince Edward by 1811, and that all but one of the latter were already residing on what the registrar called (whether loosely or, at that date, still accurately) Richard Randolph's land south of the Appomattox. The answer in Brown v Giles makes it appear that the settlement of Israel Hill took place over a span of some months, and perhaps even a couple of years—not surprising, since the area consisted initially of unimproved land.

99. Without bitterness: Christopher Doyle asserts that Judith felt "jealousy" over the "poverty" Richard had subjected her to. He provides no documentation for that assertion, nor any to contradict Judith's statement, quoted above, that she was carrying out the wishes of "the best of men, & most indulgent of husbands." Doyle also seems to believe that Richard's will "impoverished his wife" almost immediately, when in fact—as Richard himself had feared—almost no slaves were freed for a very long time (fourteen years) after his death; any pecuniary hardship Judy experienced before 1810 could hardly be blamed on Richard's emancipatory dream. See Doyle, "The Randolph Scandal," 301.

100. Judith's doubts about ex-slaves' prospects: Judith Randolph, letter to St. George Tucker, October 18, 1801, TC/W&M. "Emancipated by the will": See OB 26/15 (1845 Jan), Samuel Strong registration, and OB 26/395 (1850 Nov) (a man registered as having been liberated "prior to 1806" even though he was born after that date).

101. Settlers' complexions: See registrations of various Johnstons, Whites, Pattersons, Wilkersons, Browns, Carters and Brandums, including OB 16/687–688 (1811 Feb); OB 17/21–22 (1811 Mar); OB 18/414 (1816 May); OB 19/126 (1819 Jan); OB 22/183–184 (1829 Sep); Para [?] no. 9, John Brown registration, Cumberland CoCt 1811 Jan 28, filed Prince Edward CoCt 1836 Mar–Apr; H[ampton] White registration, Prince Edward CoCt 1829 Aug 17, filed CoCt 1839 May; OB 26/394–395 (1850 Nov).

102. "Those of the free Negroes": Judith Randolph, letter to St. George Tucker, February 4, 1811, TC/W&M. Carpenter Billy Ellis, who did not receive land on Israel Hill, does seem to have done work for Judith after his liberation, at least on a piecemeal basis—Ann C. [Nancy Randolph] Morris, letter to Edward Dillon, January 20, 1815, Dillon-Polk papers, UNC.

103. "My continuance": Judith Randolph, letter to St. George Tucker, October 18, 1801, TC/W&M. "A creature about me": Judith to Tucker, February 4, 1811, TC/W&M.

104. Conflagration at Bizarre: Judith Randolph, letter to St. George Tucker, April 4, 1813, TC/W&M. Judith at church: John Randolph of Roanoke, *Letters to Bleecker,* March 28, 1813, UVa.

105. House in Farmville; St. George's travails: Judith Randolph, letter to St. George Tucker, July 17, 1814, TC/W&M. St. George's fate: Randolph, *Letters to Bleecker,* June 2, 1814, UVa; and see Daniels, *Randolphs of Virginia,* pp. 233–34. Tudor's illness and death: Randolph, *Letters to Bleecker,* July 26, 1814, UVa; Judith Randolph, letter to St. George Tucker, January 4, 1816, TC/W&M; and Daniels, *Randolphs of Virginia,* pp. 234, 236–37, and 240. "From scenes of woe": Judith, letter to Tucker, March 27, 1814, TC/W&M.

106. Jack's suspicions: John Randolph, letter to Judith Randolph, January 20, 1816, Grin-

nan family papers, Mss1 G8855 d89, VHS (with the phrase, "dark insinuations . . . ,"
in Judith's hand); see also John Randolph, letter to Ann Cary [Nancy Randolph]
Morris, [October 31, 1814], typescript, in Nancy Randolph papers, Manuscripts and
Rare Books Department, Swem Library, College of William and Mary, and Ran-
dolph, *Letters to Bleecker,* April 18, 1815, UVa. Alienation between sisters: See Ann C.
Randolph, letter to Edward Dillon, January 28, 1805, Dillon-Polk papers, UNC.
Judith's illness: John Randolph, letters to Edward Cunningham, March 9 and March
19, 1816, John Randolph papers, 1806–19, Mss1 R1554 a17 and a18, VHS.

107. Judith's will, and her slaves: WB 5/98, Judith Randolph will (1816); WB 5/165–166,
Judith Randolph inventory and appraisal (1816); Judith Randolph, letter to St.
George Tucker, January 27, 1810, TC/W&M; Personal property tax rolls, Cumberland
County, 1812–1816, LVA.

108. White adolescent chooses guardian: OB 19/116 (1818 Dec). Elizabeth (Eliza), daughter of Dick and Sally White, and her survival at least until 1832: Notation on back of
decree, White v White's admor, CoCt 1832 Mar. Eliza's absence from the family, and
birth of Judith White: FNLs, 1817–1825. One wonders whether perhaps the black
Eliza White merited Judith Randolph's "protection" because Judy's son was the little
girl's biological father—a possibility that no existing evidence allows us to weigh.

CHAPTER 3: *The Promised Land*

1. "Rather flat": Thomas Hamilton depo, Perkinson v Appomattox Company, CoCt
1841 Jul–Aug. The bridle path: OB 22/309–310 (1830 May). Lack of a direct road:
Map, Prince Edward County, 1820, F232 P84 1820:1, LVA; Map of a survey for a line
of railroad from Farmville to Danville, 1837, Bureau of Public Works papers, Swem
643, LVA; and Madison's to Farmville, road report, filed in CoCt 1836 Jun–Jul.

2. Number and rough configuration of individual plots: Processioners' returns, LVA,
Allen & Boatwright, 1812, Allen & Boatwright, 1820, and William Venable, 1831;
Land tax rolls, 1809–14 (microfilm), LVA. The plat of the late Hercules White Sr.'s
tract as distributed among his four sons in the 1820s (White v White, CoCt 1825 Jun),
and the descriptions of land taken and compensated for by the South Side Railroad
in the 1850s, both discussed in later chapters, can be considered alongside current
maps of the railroad's path across Israel Hill to help refine our idea of the shape and
location of each tract there.

3. Hercules White Sr.'s family: OB 16/688 (1811 Feb); IH 1816 (which is also the most
important single source for the ages and family configurations given in the rest of this
section). One of Hercules Senior's sons, Romulus, would play little part in life on
Israel Hill; he seems to have moved away or died not long after the community was
settled. Hercules White Sr.'s age in 1811 is probably understated in OB 16/688 at
fifty-five years; that would make him at the most only fourteen or fifteen when his
son Sam was born. Sam White's age as given on IH 1816 is itself probably an underestimate. If the Ms. Census and the free black lists from the late years of Sam White's
life are correct—and, though both contain mistakes, they are remarkably consistent as
to Sam's age—he was born about 1765. Thus he would have been about forty-five
when Israel Hill was settled.

   A marriage bond for Susan and Sam White was issued in 1816, but this wedding
apparently formalized a long-standing union that had begun when both parties were
slaves; Susan's surname was White even before the bond was issued. Moreover, slaves
named Sam and Sucky (a variant of Susan which rhymes with "cookie") are listed one
immediately after the other, and close to the rest of the White family, in the appraisal
of Richard Randolph's estate in 1797.

4. The ages given for some individuals on the Israel Hill list, IH 1816, differ from ages
given in other records. For example, IH 1816 has Hampton Giles six years younger

than the Prince Edward death register for 1859 does; the list of 1816 puts Giles's wife, Phoebe, at least four years younger than the Ms. Census of 1820 does. Giles's registration as a free man in 1811 (which also records his complexion) agrees with the list of 1816. It thus seems likely that Hampton Giles was in his latter twenties in 1811, and his wife some years older.

5. Pattersons boating: FNL, 1819. Isham Patterson's registration: OB 18/414 (1816 May).
6. Rose Johnston's home: Answer, Howard v White, CoCt 1837 Jul. Rachel Johnston's marriage to Philip White Jr.: Marriage bond, 1814 Dec 7 (microfilm), LVA. Jacob Johnston: OB 16/688 (1811 Feb). George and his wife, Hannah: OB 18/414 (1816 May).
7. Registration of Rose Johnson (sic), with notation of marriage to "Ceasar": OB 17/22 (1811 Mar). In 1811, when Rose Johnston registered, Caesar was the slave of one William Randolph. One wonders whether Caesar had been a slave of Richard Randolph whom Judith and John Randolph, when forced to compromise with the creditors of Richard's estate, took care to sell to a relative who lived nearby in order that he remain near his wife, Rose.
8. My speculation about cooperation between the Wilkersons and their neighbors arises from a couple of circumstances. The men who processioned the boundaries on Israel Hill in 1812—one year after settlement began there—evinced confusion as to William Wilkerson's identity, while they seemed to know exactly who the other Israelite landowners were—Allen and Boatwright processioners' return, 1812. And a road that was proposed the following year would, according to its description, quite possibly have run across the lands of both Wilkerson and Titus Gibbs; yet the men appointed to view the proposed route, all of them neighbors of Israel Hill, detailed the damage Gibbs's land would suffer while making no mention of Wilkerson—Morton v Legrand &c., road order and report, filed CoCt 1814 Mar. Although the Wilkersons had resided somewhere on Israel Hill at least since 1811 (FNL, Green's district, 1811), there seem not to have been any physical signs at first (e.g., a dwelling or cleared fields on their own tract) that they owned a homestead there.
9. Syphax Brown's age: IH 1816; Answer, Brown v Giles, CoCt 1841 Jun. Second wife: A letter from Fanny Tucker to St. George Tucker includes greetings to Syphax from one Yarmouth; Fanny added that "she & his children are well"—March 22, 1781, TC/W&M. And years later, Syphax and Betty Brown were listed on FNL, Green's district, 1802, as living with "her" son, not theirs.
10. On the assignment of the Brown tract: Brown v Giles. Of course, neither the bill nor the answer is an objective account, but much of Hampton Giles's answer, including the story rendered here, *is* consistent with the facts that emerge from other documents. Whether it had already been decided that the tract Brown now asked for would contain fifty acres and the one originally tendered only twenty-five is not clear.
11. Belinda Giles: Registration, filed CoCt 1841 Sep–Nov, and also OB 25/8 (1841 Sep). It is not certain that Belinda Giles went directly to Petersburg in 1811. But she appears in no records for Prince Edward County or Israel Hill before 1841, at which time she registered in Prince Edward as a Randolph manumittee formerly residing in Petersburg.
12. Billy Ellis: FNLs, 1811 (Green's district), 1821, 1823–1825; Billy Ellis certf of freedom, filed CoCt 1822 Aug. Zack Ellis: FNLs, 1820–1825. Tom Ellis: FNLs, 1821–1825; Tom Ellis certf, filed CoCt 1822 Sep–Oct. All three Ellises: Abner Nash, "A list of Free Negrows and Molatters within the lower District of Prince Edward County," at end of property tax book, lower district, 1816. The Ellises' activities on the Chambers place: Copy of proceedings, Attorney General v Chambers's trustees, CoCt 1821 Nov, a number of entries 1814–19.
13. Guy Howard with Whites before manumission: Property tax enumeration book, upper district, 1799. Howard's livelihood: See Bill and answer in Howard v White,

CoCt 1837 Jul; FNLs, 1811 (Green's district) and 1817; WB 7/439–440, Hercules White Sr. est acct with S. Allen, deputy of Carter (1836), 1815 Jul (helping grow tobacco).

14. Ages of the Phil Whites: IH 1816. Phil White Sr. and the Randolphs: Richard Randolph appraisal, as above. (There are three Phils on this list, none with a surname provided. One of them, judging by his appraised value, was then a child, presumably Phil White Jr. Of the other two, one—designated as a carpenter—is listed just before Fanny; this is almost surely Phil White Sr., who indeed had a wife named Fanny.) Phil White Sr. related to Hercules White Sr.: White v White's admor, CoCt 1832 Mar, and OB 22/571–572 (1831 Dec). Hercules White at least fifty-five years old: OB 16/688 (1811 Feb); a birth date a decade earlier would jibe much more naturally with the birth dates of Hercules Sr.'s wife, Molly (born 1746 per IH 1816), and of his son Sam (born 1771 per IH 1816, or 1765 per FNLs for 1863 and the years just before that). Tax exemption: OB 18/36 (1814 Mar). The uncertainty over the relationship between the two Phil Whites arises from a legal proceeding in which the four sons of Hercules White, rather than Phil White Jr., laid uncontested claim to Phil White Sr.'s estate after he died—White v White's admor. Phil Jr. did not participate in either of two suits later filed by all the surviving sons of Hercules Sr.—White v White, OB 21/121 (1824 Nov), and CoCt 1825 Jun; White v Smith (a.k.a. White v White), 1859 Aug, CirCt papers, Prince Edward County Courthouse, Farmville.

    The impression that Phil White Sr. lived on Titus Gibbs's tract arises from the participation of Phil White in the processioning of that plot in 1812 and again in 1819–20 (Allen and Boatwright processioners' returns). White accompanied the processioners with Gibbs in the former year, and in Gibbs's stead in the latter; since Phil White Jr. was a minor in 1812 and afterward lived at Sam White's (FNLs, 1817–1825), this was presumably Phil Senior. Moreover, Phil White Sr. is listed, ostensibly on his own land, immediately before Titus Gibbs, year in and year out, on FNLs, 1817ff.—on which the families of Israel Hill are listed in a rather obvious geographic progression.

15. Phil White Jr.'s place of residence: FNLs, 1817ff. The Phil Whites as nonrecipients of land: Land tax records and processioners' returns (see Allen and Boatwright, 1812 and 1819–20; Venable and Allen, 1831). None of these documents suggests that either of the Phil Whites ever owned any land during the early years of Israel Hill; yet the revenue commissioner consistently listed Phil White Sr. as living "on his own land" on FNLs, 1817–1825.

16. Purchases of equipment and supplies: Hercules White (deceased), acct with Samuel W. and W. L. Venable, filed CoCt 1814 Mar. No sons on White's place at first: FNL, Green's district, 1811. Hinges: White purchased "Garnetts," a type of hinge in the form of a T set on its side, in which the cross of the T is attached vertically to the door frame.

17. "Means to build . . . houses": "A Free Negro Community in Virginia," *New York Evening Times,* August 31, 1854, reprinted from *Baltimore Patriot,* with thanks to Frank Moore for bringing the item to my attention; see also George W. Bagby, "My Uncle Flatback's Plantation," in Bagby, *The Old Virginia Gentleman and Other Sketches,* ed. Thomas Nelson Page (New York: Scribners, 1910), p. 100.

18. John's worries: John Randolph, letter to St. George Tucker, May 9, 1801, John Randolph papers, Randolph-Macon Woman's College (microfilm), UVa. It would be all but impossible to prove that John did not give any aid to the Israelites; but I have found no evidence that he did.

19. Residents of Hill: FNL, Green's district, 1811. Giles's chronology: Answer in Brown v Giles, CoCt 1841 Jun.

20. Log houses on Israel Hill: Demintions [sic] of a house built by P. White for Isaac Gibbs, White v Gibbs, CoCt 1833 May; Answer of Sam White in Howard v White, CoCt 1837 Jul. (The latter case refers to two separate "cabins" that the Howards lived

in. These were presumably built of logs; the first, according to Sam White, "rotted down" over the years.) "Log House" as tacit indication other houses were framed: See Camille Wells, "The Planter's Prospect: Houses, Outbuildings, and Rural Landscapes in Eighteenth-Century Virginia," *Winterthur Portfolio*, 28 (1993), 1–31.

21. Giles's statement: Answer of Giles in Brown v Giles, CoCt 1841 Jun. (Although the ended date of the suit is 1841, Giles composed his statement long before then, in 1832.) Evaluating White's use of nails: Camille Wells, personal communication.

22. Hewing and sawing: See James McDearmon affi and other documents submitted in McDearmon v Jennings, CoCt 1816 Oct, among other suit papers involving carpentry; Camille Wells, personal communication, citing Willie Graham, "Preindustrial Framing in the Chesapeake," in Alison K. Hoagland and Kenneth A. Breisch, eds., *Constructing Image, Identity, and Place: Perspectives in Vernacular Architecture,* 9 (Knoxville: University of Tennessee Press, 2003), pp. 179–96.

23. Gibbs's house: Demintions of a house, as in note 20. Sizes of other houses: See, e.g., Davis Hill depo, Clark v Holland's exors, CoCt 1809 Jun–Jul (a cabin eighteen feet square in the 1790s); Admor's acct of John Elliott est, filed CoCt 1831 Jul (a house eighteen by twenty feet, c. 1830). The statement that the living space in the houses described in these documents exceeded that of Gibbs's house is based on the assumption that those dwellings, like Gibbs's, had a room or rooms upstairs. Minimum size for houses on town lots: Herbert Clarence Bradshaw, *History of Prince Edward County, Virginia, from Its Earliest Settlements Through Its Establishment in 1754 to Its Bicentennial Year* (Richmond: Dietz Press, 1955), pp. 296 (lots in Germantown) and 297 (which speaks of "the usual terms" of authorizations for the founding of towns).

24. Howard's buildings on Hercules White's property: Bill and answer in Howard v White, CoCt 1837 Jul.

25. Phil White's stable: Phil White [debts] to Isaac Gibbs, in White v Gibbs, CoCt 1833 May. Two horses and gig: Property tax, 1830. Sam White's household: IH 1816; FNLs, 1817ff.

26. "It was the custom": James Moss Jr. depo, Price v Price's admor, CirCt 1841 Apr. White at Gibbs's processionings: Processioners' returns, Allen and Boatwright, 1812 and 1819–20.

27. Kit Strong: FNLs, 1817, 1818, and 1820. A handicapped male weaver: Enumeration book, property tax [1807], rough notes for FNL, lower district, Hambleton Evans; cf. Evans entry on formal FNL, lower district, 1807. For family configurations and ages of individuals, compare FNL, Green's district, 1811, with IH 1816.

28. White's property: WB 4/354, Hercules White appraisal (1812), on which the estate is valued at about $400; Report of devision, Hercules White estate (widow's dower), filed CoCt 1812 Nov, in which the roughly one third of White's estate allotted to his widow is valued at nearly $150; and WB 4/541–542, Hercules White est acct with Samuel Carter, admor (1814).

29. Sums owed to Hercules White: WB 4/541–542, Hercules White est acct (1814). Houses, or house, garden, and field, renting for $22 to $50 per year in 1810s and early 1820s: See, among others, John Mitchel bond in League assignee v Mitchell, CoCt 1816 Nov (though filed 1816 Dec–1817 Mar); Stokes v Anderson, CoCt 1822 Dec–1823 Mar; Rent repley bond, Scruggs to Lewis, filed CoCt 1824 May.

30. Debts owed Hercules White: His est acct, as cited in note 29. In this account, there seems to be an error of £1 to the detriment of the White estate. On the other hand, the administrator had benefited the estate by selling a hogshead of tobacco left by White for a price more than half again the amount the tobacco had been valued at in the estate appraisal (WB 4/354); thus it is unlikely that the error of £1 was deliberate. The sixteen households referred to are those marked as such on IH 1816. Hercules White may have lent money or rendered services to both Phil Whites—Jr. and Sr.;

that is, debts from "Phil White" listed separately in Hercules White's estate account may have been owed by either one household or two.

31. Prevalence of fencing: See Littleberry Jenkins depo, Clarke v Holland's exors, CoCt Jun–Jul 1809; OB 26/99 (1846 May), CW v Fore, presentment; Thomas S. Jones road report (petition), Jones v Simmons, CoCt 1824 Nov; and many other documents. Gibbs's "plantation": Morton v Legrand &c., road order and report, filed CoCt 1814 Mar.

32. Planters selling beef (example): WB 4/341, Obadiah Hurt will (1812). Hercules White's tobacco and cattle: WB 4/354, Hercules White appraisal (1812). More than twenty head: Land tax, 1815.

33. White's purchase of salt: Hercules White (deceased) acct with Samuel W. and W. L. Venable, filed CoCt 1814 Mar. Early cotton growing: WB 1/275, Waddle [sic] Carter appraisal (1782); WB 2/148, Peter Davis est acct, entry for 1786 Dec 20. Larger amounts: WB 3/493, Francis Rice Sr. will (1806); and WB 3/516, Francis Rice inventory (1807) (a parcel worth £13). Ginning and sales: Cheadle, B2nd p. bottom (early 1820s?), and B15th p. middle (1824), transactions with J. Morris's mill. Cotton to clothe slaves: Judith Randolph, letter [to Mary Harrison], November 24, 1805, Harrison family papers, Mss1 H2485 g2–9, VHS; Judith Randolph, letter to St. George Tucker, September 29, 1808, TC/W&M. White's flax and cotton wheels: WB 4/354, Hercules White appraisal (1812); H. White's estate, report of devision (widow's dower), CoCt 1812 Nov.

34. Mentions of corn and oats are beyond counting; Josiah Cheadle's account book and mill records such as those of the Dupuys, cited in later chapters, are among the many sources of information about the production, milling, and uses of corn and oats. Stands of oats and their harvesting are mentioned with some frequency both in court cases and in wills and appraisals—e.g., WB 3/505, Mary Ritchey inventory (1806); and Copy of proceedings, Attorney General v Chambers's trustees, CoCt 1821, 1820 Aug (p. 57). Small, local sales of corn: See, e.g., Cheadle, 39th p. (numbered as p. 17), 1827 Jun, with payment from Cheadle, who himself produced large quantities of corn, for six bushels of that grain. Oats from Randolph lands: Judith Randolph, letter to John Randolph, March 9, 1808, TC/W&M. Quantities of oats sold: For one example, see Guardians' accounts (microfilm), LVA, pp. 12–15, John Tuggle, guardian for Jonathan Penick (1830), credits for twenty-two bushels sold in 1830. Early wheat growing: See WB 1/240, John Crenshaw appraisal (1779); WB 1/334, William Carey appraisal (1784).

35. Larger harvests: See Allen's exors v Fowler, CoCt 1822 Jul, acct of John Kelso (figure for 1805), and memorandum booklet, entry in re Creed Taylor (1805); and also Dupriest v Johnston, CoCt 1809 May, acct of Johnston's debts to Dupriest (figure for 1806). See also plff's Narration and acct in Johns v Gibson, claiming 1,000 bushels produced on one plantation, presumably in a single year. Middling producers, with 50–120 bushels per year: See WB 3/443, James Price est acct (1806, figures for 1803 and 1804); Copy of proceedings, Attorney General v Chambers's trustees, pp. 12–13 (figure for 1802); and WB 3/516, Francis Rice inventory (1807, figures for old and new wheat that year).

36. Judith Randolph's preference for use of wheat: Judith, letter to St. George Tucker, September 29, 1808, TC/W&M. Sales of wheat to local mills (example): WB 4/179, Andrew Elliott est acct, with wheat sales of 1797, 1800, and 1801; of the local buyers listed, John Purnall, at least, certainly owned a mill (WB 6/174–177, John Purnall will [1824/1825]). Boating flour downstream from Allen & Fowler's mill: Judith Randolph, letter to John Randolph, December 13, 1807, TC/W&M. James River: See McDearmon road report, filed CoCt 1823 Dec–1824 Mar, which refers to Bent Creek, a James River town, as "the most convenient place of deposit for this section of the country &

where the neighbours generally carry their wheat and Tobacco." Given the reference to three nearby mills in the McDearmon road report, the word "wheat" may well mean "wheat flour." "Carriage" of flour to Richmond: WB 4/269, Nathaniel Lancaster est acct (1809 Jun).

37. White's transactions in wheat: Acct of Hercules, a free Negro, in Allen's exors v Fowler, CoCt 1822 Jul. Supply of corn: H. White's estate, report of devision (widow's dower), filed CoCt 1812 Nov.

38. "A small tract of land": Bill, Williams's guardian v Williamson, CoCt 1837 Jul.

39. Horses: Personal property tax, Green's district, 1812. Carpenter's tools: WB 4/354–355, Hercules White appraisal (1812).

40. The Howards: Bill in Howard v White, CoCt 1837 Jul.

41. "Valuable timber": Bill in Howard v White, CoCt 1837 Jul. Gibbs and White: Phill White to Isaac Gibbs, and Demintions of a house built by P. White for Isaac Gibbs, in White v Gibbs, CoCt 1833 May. Pattersons: WB 7/273, Isham Patterson will (1831/1832).

42. "A great favourite": Answer in Brown v Giles, CoCt 1841 Jun.

43. Location of Johnston cabin: Howard v White, CoCt 1837 Jul. Birth of sons: IH 1816. Johnston-White marriage: Marriage bond, 1814 Dec 7 (microfilm), LVA. Phil and Rachel's children who married within the Hill were Curtis, Mary, and Lucy. Curtis White and Priscilla White: Marriage bond, 1836 Sep 19 (microfilm), LVA. Priscilla was the daughter of one Jenny White, who is called Jane and listed as Priscilla's mother on FNLs, 1822 and 1823; the names Jane and Jenny were interchangeable (cf. listings for Hampton Giles's daughter on FNLs of 1811 and 1819). This Jane White lived at Sam White's and had done so for years (IH 1816); she clearly was Sam's daughter (her registration, OB 18/414 [1816 May], lists her as "Jenny"). Donaldson Gibbs and Mary White: Marriage register, 1846 May [7?], recorded among marriage bonds (microfilm), LVA. Donaldson was a member of Titus Gibbs's household—IH 1816, and subsequent FNLs. But the Prince Edward death register for 1867 states that Donaldson was the son of Peter and Jenny Gibbs; since these individuals do not appear in Titus Gibbs's household on the FNLs, one suspects that Peter Gibbs was a son of Titus who was already grown when Israel Hill was settled, and who never lived there or elsewhere in Prince Edward County but sent a son, Donaldson, to be brought up there. Sidney Howard and Lucy White: Marriage bond, 1840 Nov 16 (microfilm), LVA.

44. Hannah Gibbs and George Johnston: A conclusion based on the following evidence: Titus Gibbs is listed with a daughter, Hannah, on FNL, Green's district, 1811; she does not appear with the Gibbses on later free black lists. Rose Johnston's son George appears with a wife, Hannah, on FNLs, 1817ff. That couple tended to name their children after family members—George's mother, Rose, and George himself, for example. George and Hannah called one son Isaac, the name of Hannah Gibbs's elder brother, and they called their third son Titus, a name apparently borne by only one other individual in the history of free blacks in Prince Edward County: Titus Gibbs, Hannah Gibbs's father—FNL, 1824. William Johns[t]on and Jane White the younger: Marriage bond, 1842 Oct 4 (microfilm), LVA. William Johnston son of Hannah and George: FNLs, 1820ff. Jane White Johnston and Priscilla White White sisters: Their marriage bonds, which list "Jane White" and "Jenny White" respectively as mother of the brides; see discussion of "Jane" and "Jenny" as two names for the same woman in note 43.

45. Samuel White [Jr.] and Jane Giles: Marriage bond, 1822 Jun 17 (microfilm), LVA. The young Sam White's relationship to the elder one: No Sam White Jr. appears on the relevant free black lists; but land tax schedules, *passim*, list the elder Sam White as Sam "Sr.," even after Sam Jr. had died (details such as the suffix "Sr." on land tax schedules often became obsolete because of copying from year to year). A black-

skinned Samuel White, born c. 1798, who must be Sam Junior, is registered in OB 20/311 (1822 Jun). Sam Junior's early death: Marriage bond, David Lewis and Jane White, n.d. [c. 1827] (microfilm), LVA, which lists Jane as the widow of Samuel White. Samuel Strong and Esther White: Marriage bond, 1836 Sep 19 (microfilm), LVA. Relationship of Esther's father, Tamer (wrongly copied in Index to marriage bonds [microfilm], LVA, as "James") White, to Sam White Sr., and Sam Strong's background and age: IH 1816, and subsequent FNLs.

46. Susan (also called Susanna) and Sally as wives of Hercules Junior and Dick White, respectively: IH 1816, and subsequent FNLs. The registrations of Susanna and Sally White, OB 20/341–342 (1822 Aug) list each woman as having been born c. 1795 of already free parents, rather than as having been emancipated by Richard Randolph's will. That these women are the same Susan and Sally who had married into the Hercules White family receives circumstantial confirmation from the fact that Jane White and William [Billy] Ellis, both former slaves of Richard Randolph, registered as such on the same day as Susanna and Sally White.

47. Teny: List of all the negroes belonging to the estate of John Randolph and to St. George Tucker who are connected together, n.d., TC/W&M.

48. White and enslaved family: WB 9/374, Anthony White will (1848, codicil 1850). Purchase of wife: See Prince Edward delinquent property, 1828, filed CoCt 1829 Jun–Jul, with Tony White listed as the owner of one slave—doubtless his wife, Milly.

49. Opting out of marriage: See Suzanne Lebsock, *The Free Women of Petersburg: Status and Culture in a Southern Town, 1784–1860* (New York and London: W. W. Norton, 1984), pp. 103–11, especially 107–09. Bequests to slave spouses were legally null and void—one could not bestow property *on* property—so even a free black's will, when there is one, may not mention a slave spouse. Michael Patterson: Bureau of Refugees, Freedmen, and Adandoned Lands, List of Colored persons living together as man & wife, 1866 Feb 27, 27th p., Prince Edward County records, LVA. Another free black woman married to a slave: OB 21/262 (1825 Oct), Rhoda Epperson. Examples of free blacks owning individual slaves, probably relatives in most cases: Delinquent property tax, 1815 [for 1814, lower end?], filed CoCt 1815 Aug–Sep; Delinquent property return, 1815, filed CoCt 1816 May–Jun.

50. Endogamy among Randolph slaves: District Court WB 1/9–10, Richard Randolph inventory (1797/1798). The lack of family names, and in most cases of any designation of family relationships, makes the identification of married couples in this and similar lists less than certain. Yet for each couple I say married while Richard Randolph was alive, the appraisal lists the corresponding given names one after the other, with the man's name first. For each couple who I suggest married between 1797 and 1810, there are corresponding given names on the appraisal, but they do not appear together; this separation, along with these individuals' birth dates derived from IH 1816, indicate that these couples were not married when Dick's estate was appraised in 1797. That married couples bearing these names settled on Israel Hill in 1811 is established by FNL, Green's district, 1811; that each couple already had at least one child tends strongly to confirm that they had been married slaves of the Randolph estate before their emancipation. (I am assuming that one of the two Ampeys on the appraisal is Hampton Giles, and that "Amelia" on the appraisal is Mely Howard, whose real name, Pamelia, was often misregistered by whites as Amelia.)

51. Spouses remaining together: Guy and Mely Howard, Israelite founders but not landowners, may eventually have separated—Howard v White, CoCt 1837 Jul, in which Mely alone sued even though Guy was apparently still alive (see chapter 7). John Brown, a founding Israelite who settled on his father's land, seems to have absented himself from Israel Hill for a time owing to financial troubles, but he ultimately returned.

52. In the Hill's early years, Caty Carter lived with the elderly Phil White Sr. and his

wife, Fanny, from at least age ten until she was fifteen; a Carter boy, Otha, apparently Teny's grandson, spent approximately the same ages with Dick and Sally White's family in the early 1820s. In the middle of that decade, Sam White's grandson Oby White moved in with the Gileses at age ten. Sam's little granddaughter Sooky Valentine, who had lived for a while with her parents on Sam's land, went to stay with Phil White Jr. when her mother and father apparently separated—an unusual event on Israel Hill. Caty Carter: IH 1816; FNLs, 1817–1821. Otha Carter, from ages ten to fourteen: FNLs, 1820–1824. Oby White and Sooky Valentine: FNL, 1825; the lack of subsequent lists leaves unanswered the question of how long these two children remained in their new homes.

53. Joe Bartlett's marriage to Polly Brandum: FNLs, 1819–1825. FNL, 1819, puts Bartlett and Brandum together on Sam White's land, but wrongly calls Polly "Nancy," which in fact was her daughter's name.

54. Milly Homes: Indenture between John Bickley & Milly (a Mulatto child), Apprentices, LVA. FNLs, lower district, 1801 and 1804, classify the Homeses as black, while the list for the same district, 1802, designates them as mulattoes. Possible Indian ancestry: Helen C. Rountree, *Pocahontas's People: The Powhatan Indians of Virginia Through Four Centuries* (Norman: University of Oklahoma Press, 1990), pp. 190–91, on "Holmeses" of mixed background in the counties that included King William, from where Milly Homes had apparently come—people documented from the latter nineteenth century and "presumably" present much earlier. Bradshaw, *Prince Edward County*, p. 741, n. 7, mentions that one John "Buckley" served in the Prince Edward militia during the Revolution; this may well be the John "Bickley" to whom Milly Homes had been bound in King William County.

55. Forgason's purchase of land: DB 7/315, Womack to Ferguson (1786). White Fergusons as neighbors: Compare the deed just cited, in which Massanello Womack sold land to the black Forgasons, with DB 9/198 (1792) and 11/204 (1797), in which Alexander Ferguson sold land in the same neighborhood to Womack; and see especially DB 7/316, Davidson to Womack (1786), where Womack bought land abutting Alexander Ferguson's place on the same day he, Womack, sold the hundred acres to Jethro Forgason. Color of Forgasons: FNL, Green's district, 1806—on which, however, commissioner Thomas Green, in the one year he bothered to indicate free blacks' complexions, identified every individual on his list as mulatto; but see also registrations of "Fergusons" in OB 21/101 (1824 Oct) and OB 26/3 (1844 Nov). Forgasons as farmers: FNLs, Green's district, 1801–1807, 1809. As carpenters: FNLs, lower district, 1805 and 1806 (Charles Forgason). More Forgasons moving into carpentry: FNLs, 1817ff.

56. Evanses mulattoes: FNLs, lower district, 1801, 1802, and 1804; OB 18/81 and 83 (1814 May). Evans land purchases and sales: DB 10/156 and 157, Tyree to Charles Evans and Tyree to John Evans (1794 Jun); DB 12/201, Charles Evans to Tyree (1801); DB 16/122, Evans and Forgason to McDearmon (1816); see also McDearmon and Pariss processioners' return, filed CoCt 1812 Apr–May. Evanses connected to Forgasons: DB 16/122, as just noted. To Bartletts: DB 17/127, Bartlett to McDearmon (1819/1820). To Israel Hill: IH 1816. The Evanses' land lay a little way into the panhandle that Prince Edward County would give up in 1845; by then, the Evans heirs had long since sold their land to a white man.

57. Seller to Evanses keeps remainder of own land: Land tax, 1815 and other years. White man expands plantation: DB 7/316, Davidson to Womack (1786).

58. Fears's land: Land tax, John Morton's district, 1795. Marriage with consent: Marriage bond, James Dungey and Elizabeth Fears, 1795 Mar 2 (microfilm), LVA. Dungey's land purchase: DB 11/253 (1798). Naming of son: FNL, 1818.

59. Absalom Dungey in interracial union: District Court Order Book, 1805–31, pp. 643–44, 652–54, and 667, CW v Selby, Ferguson, Holt, Dungey, Bell, and Moss (1828 Apr and Sep, and 1829 Sep, respectively). Forgasons on Fears estate: FNLs, 1820–1822,

Forgason being joined by his children in the last year. The carpenter who moved to the Fearses' was Stephen Forgason, presumably the son of Jethro who bore that name; Absalom Fears had died by then, but his family may still have lived on the farm he left.

The Fears family: A generation after James Dungey married Elizabeth Fears, a free black man names James Fears, a blacksmith, was living in Prince Edward with a white man named William Fears; Elizabeth Fears Dungey had an uncle and a brother named William Fears. The black James Fears may have been emancipated, and perhaps fathered, by the William Fears he lived with or by someone else in the Fears family; Elizabeth Dungey was the granddaughter of a white James Fears. James and William Fears: FNL, 1817. Elizabeth Dungey's uncle: WB 3/356–357, James Fears [Sr.] will (1797/1804). Her brother William: WB 5/28, Absalom Fears will (1811/1815). As late as 1850, two free black children from the Dungey and Forgason families lived with an eighty-year-old white William Fears in a household that also included two white Selbes—members of a family that itself had a tradition of fraternizing with blacks—Ms. Census, 1850, visitation 108.

60. Slaveholding pattern: Figures derived from Ms. Census, 1810.
61. Neighbors' slaveholding: Ms. Census, 1810; the figures cited here refer only to the number of slaves held by the three families within Prince Edward County. Allen's other lands: WB 4/251–252, Archer Allen will (1811). Baker Legrand's: Legrand's est, report and division, dated 1828 Jun 16, but filed CoCt 1827 Sep–Nov. The Randolphs, of course, owned Bizarre plantation in Cumberland County.
62. Archer Allen on court since 1795: Bradshaw, *Prince Edward County,* p. 679; William Cabell Bruce, *John Randolph of Roanoke, 1773–1833* (New York: Putnam, 1922), p. 110. Archer Allen sheriff 1810–Feb 1811: Bradshaw, *Prince Edward County,* pp. 682–83. Archer Allen died soon after Israel Hill was founded, leaving several sons who themselves wielded considerable influence in county life. Dillon as intellectual: Bradshaw, *Prince Edward County,* p. 171; Dillon belonged to the Library Company of Prince Edward, which purchased books for the use of its members. Dillon as friend of John Randolph: *Ibid.,* p. 178; John Randolph, letters to Edward Cunningham, December 31, 1808, and March 19, 1816, Mss1 R1554 a3 and a18 respectively, in John Randolph Papers, 1806–19, VHS. Dillon joins county court, 1805: Bradshaw, *Prince Edward County,* pp. 209, 679.
63. Payments by, and debts to, White's estate: WB 4/541–542, Hercules White est acct with Samuel Carter (1814). Laying off dower: H. White's est, report of devision, filed CoCt 1812 Nov 17. Later claims: OB 18/35 (1814 Mar); Francisco's admor v White's admor, CoCt 1838 Apr; but see also at least one large debt to White likewise not reported until after the accounting summarized here (see discussion of George Backus's debt to White in chapter 2).
64. Situations of non-landed free blacks: FNLs, 1801–1811.
65. Judith Gibbs: IH 1816; FNL, 1817. Dick Patterson: FNL, 1811. Randolph Brandum: IH 1816. To speculate that Israelite children bearing the given name John are named after John Randolph seems incautious given both the exceeding commonness of the name and John's peripheral and sometimes even obstructive role in the emancipation.
66. Rhody through Free Clory: FNLs, lower district, 1806 and 1807. "John a free Negroe": Folder, Taxable property, lower district, John Booker, 1809. Vestiges of white uncertainty or skepticism about free black surnames crop up considerably later than this; see the reference to "a certain woman of color commonly called Patty Morton" in Mittimus, CW v Stonum, CoCt 1820 Nov.
67. On the head tax of 1813–15, see John H. Russell, *The Free Negro in Virginia, 1619–1865* (Baltimore: Johns Hopkins Press, 1913), pp. 114–15. General crackdown: See List of delinquent land, statement &c of money deposited by agent for CW in redemption of land sold in 1816, and Statement of delinquent lands by sheriff in 1815, filed CoCt

496 | Notes to Pages 73–77

1815 Aug–Sep. Warning: Ampey Brandem & others, order summoning them to Oct court, 1815, filed CoCt 1815 Oct–Dec; OB 18/319 (1815 Sep); OB 18/323 (1815 Oct), order to Zack Ellis. Identities and situations of those on the list: FNLs, Green's district, 1801 (Forgason family relationships) and 1817; DB 17/130, Evans to McDearmon (1819/1820 and 1821), compared with listing for Allen Evans on FNL, Green's district, 1807, and of Charles and Benjamin Evans on FNL, Green's district, 1803. One of the names on the list—Essex White—was borne by two men, one a member of Sam White's household, probably Sam's son, born c. 1791, and the other related to Sam White but off the Hill part of the time—IH 1816; FNLs, 1817ff.; OB 19/126 (1819 Jan), registration of the "other" Essex White, born c. 1797. I would guess that the tax delinquent was the second of these Essex Whites.

68. Hiring out: Order to hire out Ferguson & Moss, filed CoCt 1815 Oct–Dec (Moss paid his obligation); OB 18/323 (1815 Oct). There is no clear pattern that would explain why a landowner's son like Hercules White Jr. should have been even a temporary tax delinquent while the landless—and, in Sam White's words, "worthless"—Guy Howard should not; or why George Johnston would have paid his taxes while his brother Jacob for a time did not, when both were similarly situated on their mother Rose's land on Israel Hill. (All these men were within the age group that was liable for the special tax.)

69. Sheriff's list: A list of free negroes on Israel hill, addressed to Samuel Allen, sheriff (IH 1816). The list numbers the Israelites sequentially; it arrives at a final figure of 115, having skipped over the number 101. Order to bind out: OB 18/367 (1816 Feb). Registrations: OB 18/414 (1816 May). One of the four justices sitting when the hiring-out order came forth was Charles Woodson, who generally had good relations with free blacks. If Woodson voted for the order, that may illustrate the capacity of one man to react differently to free blacks in differing circumstances, or it may lend credence to the idea that the order was designed to placate other elements in the white community who were hostile toward Israel Hill. Second order to bind out children: OB 22/65 (1829 Mar). The Census of 1830 is of limited use in gauging the effects, if any, of this order, for it does not list children by name. Still, a comparison between the number of children in each household in the Census and on FNL, 1825, suggests that few if any children had been removed from the Hill by 1830.

70. Challenge to Essex White: Randolph v White, summons, CoCt filed 1819 Mar–Apr; OB19/139 (1819 Mar), with marginal notation. Registration of Essex White: OB19/126 (1819 Jan). This last document places White's birth at around 1796 or 1797; thus he is probably the Essex White who was not Sam White's son (the latter born about 1790)—IH 1816. A similar challenge to Edmund Clarke, another Israelite, is mentioned in chapter 6.

71. "Chopping"; "shins . . . bruised": Processioners' return, McDearmon and Trent, filed CoCt 1831 May. For processioners able to walk "a line [only] as far as we could follow it," see Processioners' return, Abner Watson, filed CoCt 1812 Apr–May.

72. Examples of blacks attending processionings are commonplace. For 1812, see Processioners' returns of A. Baker, p. 3 bottom, and of Thomas Mitchel et al. (James Dungey); of Morton and Pettus, p. 1 middle (Jethro Forgason); and of Allen and Boatwright (the black Israelites). For 1831, nearly a generation later: Return of William Venable, including Israel Hill. And still later: Legrand and Gunter processioners' return, 1843 Jun, with James Dungey Jr. and John Dungey.

73. Gossip at processioning: See James Gilliam depo, Price v Moore, CoCt 1821 Aug. Humorous observations: Note doggerel on Processioners' return, McDearmon and Trent, filed CoCt 1831 May.

74. "The people from this way": William Legrand, letter to court, in Farmville road by Legrand's, report, filed CoCt 1839 May. Relative distances and inconvenience: Map,

Prince Edward County, 1820, F232 P84 1820:1, VHS, compared with modern topographic (USGS) map; Madison's to Farmville, road report, filed CoCt 1836 Jun–Jul.

75. "Myry" ford: James Bondurant's road order, filed CoCt 1818 May. Fording impracticable: Madison's to Farmville, road report, as in note 74. Three inches of ice: Judith Randolph, letter to John Randolph, January 14, 1808, TC/W&M.

76. Appomattox-Roanoke scheme: Bradshaw, *Prince Edward County*, p. 295. Characteristics of Buffalo and proposal for improvement: Order for notifying Justices of motion to clear Buffalo & Bush river, filed CoCt 1811 Jun–Jul. Continued dreams of opening Buffalo in 1830s: Joseph Martin, *A New and Comprehensive Gazetteer of Virginia and the District of Columbia* (Charlottesville: Joseph Martin, 1836), p. 265.

77. Duties of road surveyors and calling out of slave workers: Grand jury presentments at monthly county court sessions, as well as court orders to and vouchers submitted by road surveyors, year in and year out, throughout CoCt Papers. Removing dead trees from road, and dealing with fences: See Grand jury presentments, CoCt 1812 Mar. Cutting down dead trees: See Presentment of Charles Woodson for leaving twenty-three dead trees within thirty feet of road, CoCt 1821 Aug. Reason for use of "causeways": James Bondurant's road order, filed CoCt 1839 May.

78. In fact, the right-of-way may have run across Israelite William Wilkerson's land as well, which lay to the west of Gibbs's. But the Wilkersons may not have settled on their own plot by 1813, for the commissioners did not mention that family in their report to the county court.

79. The road proposal and its disposition: Morton v Legrand &c., road order and report, filed CoCt 1814 Mar. It is possible that the roadway would have run as much as seven hundred yards across Gibbs's land, at ten yards width. Standard width of roads: Road report, proposal by James Foster, filed CoCt 1818 Oct (apparently thirty feet); Jones v Simmons, road report, filed CoCt 1824 Nov (thirty feet including lane fences); James Bondurant's road order, filed CoCt 1839 May; Gilliam v Lodge, filed CoCt 1843 Nov–Dec (thirty feet); Sinclair's certf [for] road, filed CoCt 1844 Oct–Dec (only twenty feet, an exception to the rule). Examples of contested motions for the opening of roads during Israel Hill's early years: Wilson Carter's writ of ad quod damnum, CoCt 1820 Jul; Hughes v Cheadle, CoCt 1822 Aug (one planter petitions for a road but is overruled after a neighbor objects).

80. Sale of twenty-five acres: DB 12/157, Dungee to Trent (1801). Value of Dungey and Fears tracts: Land tax, Green's district, 1813.

81. "Mrs. Dungey": James Gilliam and Thomas Mitchell processioners' return commencing 1823 Dec 17, filed CoCt 1824 Apr–May; OP Report, filed CoCt 1830 Jun 21. "Elizabeth Dunge's Family": FNLs, 1819ff.

82. Road petition: James Dungee's road order, filed CoCt 1816 May–Jun; OB 18/424 (1816 Jun). Other petitioners expected to prepare roadway: OB 18/28 (1814); Viewers' report of Cawthon's road, filed CoCt 1821 Mar–Apr; Thomas Tuggle road report, filed CoCt 1828 Aug. James Dungey had no slaves whom he could use to alter the road, but he did have mature sons and enough income to hire temporary labor; whether these resources were sufficient to turn the road is impossible to say in the absence of a detailed, contemporaneous map of the neighborhood.

83. Dungey's suit: Dungey v Fitzsimmons, CoCt 1818 Aug–Sep; the amount involved was a hogshead and a half. Fitzsimmons's reason for buying Dungey's tobacco is open to speculation; she does not appear as a landowner in the land tax for either of Prince Edward's two districts in 1817. That Dungey's lawsuit abated at his death was not a circumstance unique to free black plaintiffs; for an example of a similar outcome where the plaintiff was white and the defendant the executor of the late free Afro-Virginian shoemaker Ben Short, see Nash for benefit of Jones v Woodson admor of Short, CoCt 1823 May and OB 20/467 (1823 Mar).

84. Dungey's record as taxpayer: List of delinquent land (1789–1814), filed CoCt 1815 Aug–Sep. Survey of Dungey land: Dungy v Dungy, CoCt 1825 Jun. John Dungey seeks reparations: OB 23/429 and 439–440 (1836 May and June).

85. Hercules White on road details: OB 16/52 (1807 Dec) and 532 (1810 Apr). Dungey on list: James McNeil's road order, issued 1808 Feb but originally filed CoCt 1814 Jan–Mar; cf. OB 16/81 (1808 Feb). In 1809 and 1811, respectively, lists of people whose hands were to work on roadways included the names of James Epperson and Phil Evans, free black men—OB 16/285 (1809 Mar) and 16/686 (1811 Feb).

86. Information on Israelites working on the road in this and subsequent paragraphs, except as noted, is from Charles Fore's road order, filed CoCt 1819 Jul. White "labourers": See, e.g., CW v Peter Fore, warrant, filed CoCt 1810 Nov, and OB 16/640–641 (1810 Nov), CW v Fore. The records, to confuse matters further, sometimes refer to small farms as "plantations" and to yeoman farmers as "planters."

87. Men's ages: IH 1816, checked against OB 16/688 (1811 Feb; Jacob Johnston); OB 18/414 (1816 May; George Johnston, Isham Patterson); Death register, 1859 (Hampton Giles).

88. Fore's black apprentice: Peter Ferguson's indenture, 1808, Apprentices, LVA; Fore letter to court, filed CoCt 1823 Jan 18.

89. Other orders for road work on which the Israelites are included: OB 19/81 (1818 Oct), 19/199 (1819 Jul), 19/483 (1820 Nov), 21/510 (1827 Feb), and 24/288 (1839 Oct). How often the Israelites actually labored is unknown; for example, the road surveyor to whom the order of 1827 was issued later faced a misdemeanor charge for not having actually performed the work—OB 21/587 (1827 Aug). It is not clear how long these court orders regarding road work applied; how many years in succession, in other words, would hands be drawn from a given list?

90. Short's place as landmark: OB 18/611 (1817 Aug), grand jury presentment of surveyor of road from fork of road below Benja. Short's. See also listing of this case in index to the same order book; on 18/653 (1817 Nov) and 693 (1818 Mar); and in ended papers as CW v Surveyor from Short's to H. E. Watkins, and copy of rule in same case, CoCt 1818 May. Dungey's fork: See Circuit Superior Court Order Book, 1853–70, p. 329 (1864 May), in office of clerk of CirCt, Prince Edward County Courthouse, Farmville.

91. Except as noted, the discussion of this slander suit is based on Giles v White, CoCt 1813 Aug. There were several Whites called Susan, Susannah, or Sukey/Sooky—all variants of the same name—in and around Israel Hill over the years. The one who was married to Sam White is the only one I have discovered who was of legal age in 1812 and thus likely to be sued in her own right.

92. "Many persons . . . murdered": Hening, 6 (1748), chapter XXXVIII, section 3, p. 105.

93. White-Giles union: Marriage bond, Sam White Jr. and Jane Giles, 1822 Jun 17 (microfilm), LVA.

94. My account of the prosecution of Jacob Johnston comes from CW v Johnson [sic], CoCt 1814 May; and from OB 17/519 (1813 May), 17/572 (1813 Aug), 18/23 (1814 Mar), 18/72 and 18/83 (both 1814 May). A whipping might in theory have been among the penalties Johnston could suffer if convicted—see Russell, *Free Negro in Virginia*, pp. 104–05—but in practice such punishment for free persons was exceedingly rare in Prince Edward County.

95. It was the Commonwealth's attorney (the county prosecutor) who asked the county court to summon Johnston. Had a grand jury "presented" Johnston on the charge, as was the usual procedure, the presentment would have stated who had accused him. The notation at OB 18/23 that the black man had been presented by the grand jury is a careless error arising from the overwhelming prevalence of that procedure in criminal cases. Witness William L. Legrand's father and his fellow witness James Allen's

brother had done business with Hercules White; William A. Allen had also employed a free black miller, Phil Bowman (see discussion below).

96. An exception: One slave was subpoenaed on November 20, 1826, by the prosecution in CW v Howard and Giles, CoCt 1826 Nov.

97. Bartlett accusation: CW v Bartlett, CoCt 1814 May, and OB 18/63 (1814 May). Bartletts as boatmen: FNL, Green's district, 1805; "List of Free Negrows and Molatters," end of property tax enumeration booklet, lower district, 1816, CoCt records; FNLs, 1819ff. Joe Bartlett as boatman at Sam White's: FNL, 1819. Relationships of Joseph/Josiah and Henry Bartlett [the elder] to the boating Bartlett clan: FNLs, 1819–1825. Homeses at Purnall's or on Milly's own neighboring land: FNLs, 1821 and 1822. The FNLs do not show the Homeses living either at Purnall's or on their own land next door from 1817 to 1820; whether they were present from 1812 to 1816 is uncertain owing to the absence of lists for those years. Milly Homes's land purchase: DB 15/14, Goode to Homes (1812); see also DB 17/54, Purnall to Homes; 17/55, Homes to Purnall; and 18/192, Purnall to Nathan Homes (all 1820, after the Bartlett trial). Trade between Purnalls and Homeses: WB 7/106–179 [sic—pagination skips from 108 to 167], John Purnall est acct with Asa Dupuy, exor (1830), *passim;* and Asa Dupuy and Joseph Dupuy, accts, 1822–1825—Dupuy—section 4, folder 1, Mssi D9295 a94-105, VHS; both these sources refer to transactions in the early to mid-1820s, after John Purnall's death, but they almost certainly typify the general's own practices. Carpenter James Epperson and family at Woodson's: FNLs, Green's district, 1803–1807 and 1809. Woodson as guardian: OB 18/315 (1815 Sep); see also OB 16/642 (1810 Nov) and OB 18/317 (1815 Sep). Betty Dwin at Woodson's: FNLs, Green's district, 1805–1806. Dwin's family history and connection to Woodson: WB 5/341–342, Betty Dwin will (1808/1818), whence the phrase, "best Sunday Clothes." Charles Woodson later executed Betty Dwin's will and fulfilled her charge to free her son, Harry, when the boy turned twenty-one—DB 18/93, Dwin's exor to Dwin (1822).

98. Crop rejection rates: Annual tobacco inspectors' reports for warehouses, each October, in CoCt papers and OBs. Fluctuation in prices: Cheadle, 34th p., sales of 1825 Jan 17 and 1825 Aug 30. Burying distempered cattle: CW v Galespie, CoCt 1812 Apr–May.

99. Wheat harvesting and transactions by barter: Cheadle, *passim.* Masonry: Gafford's contract with Hendrick, Hendrick v Bondurant, CoCt 1824 Aug.

100. Paying blacksmith with pork: Cheadle, B18th p., upside down, top: Agreement with Daniel Y. Jenkins (1828). Buying hat: Cheadle, 2nd p. middle, 1832 Oct. Paying in wheat, oats, etc.: Cheadle, B23rd and B24th p., and 25th p. top, Smith's work by R. Fuqua, 1835 (account, interrupted, resumes at middle of 24th p.).

101. Lawsuits became epidemic: Among many examples, see record of delivery bonds filling some four pages at one court session, OB 20/618–622 (1823 Nov); delivery bonds in county court papers for 1823 Aug and 1828 Mar.

102. Merchant Martin P. Smith's lawsuit: Smith v Clarke and Patterson, CoCt 1821 Aug; OB 20/61 (1821 May); and OB 21/143 (1821 Aug).

103. Allen and deed of trust to Short: DB 14/575, Short to Holcombe, DoT (1811), with Allen as a trustee; DB 18/92–93, Samuel V. Allen to Ben Short, release (1822); OB 17/252 (1811 Dec).

104. Lawsuit: Jones assignee v White, CoCt 1822 Aug; OB 20/4–5 (1821 Mar; white men give bond), 20/59 (1821 May; legal defense), 20/358 (1822 Aug; verdict against White, with no mention of Miller Smith except in style [title] of suit). Miller Smith's age: OB20/342 (1822 Aug). Smith's occupation: FNL, 1823. Dick White's occupations: FNLs, 1817–1823. James D. Wood ships tobacco: Haskins v Wood, CoCt 1822 Aug. Thomas A. Morton as boating contractor: Legrand v Morton & Co., CoCt 1822 Aug. White's age and family: IH 1816.

105. Suit against Giles over carpentry: Guerrant v Giles, CoCt 1831 May, and OB 22/461–462 (1831 May).

106. Slave ownership on Hill: Property tax, 1834 (Sam and Phil White with two slaves each); 1838–39 (Sam with two slaves, Phil with none); 1840, 1845, 1846–49 (Sam with one slave, Phil with none); 1850 (both men slaveless).

107. Patterson's wishes: WB 7/273, Isham Patterson will (1831/1832).

108. Johnston bequest: WB 8/159, Rosa Johnson [sic] will (1838/1839). Division of Whites' land: White v White, CoCt 1825 Jun; the White brothers' decision to divide the land formally may have been prompted by the death of their widowed mother, who had continued to reside on the tract after the death of Hercules White the elder.

109. White's lawsuit: White v Gibbs, CoCt 1833 May.

110. Giles v Brown, CoCt 1818 Oct, but originally filed CoCt 1818 Nov–Dec.

111. Information about the attack on Giles's worker, and the lawsuit arising from it, comes, except as noted, from Giles v Brown, OB 21/458 (1826 Aug), 21/490 (1826 Nov), and 21/529 (1827 Mar), and in CoCt 1827 Mar. In the last-named source, writ of capias ordering arrest of John Brown, 1825 Nov 19, shows that Brown's alleged attack took place no later than November 1825; the motion for a peace bond discussed below suggests that the assault occurred in October. The statement in Giles's declaration that Brown "did shoot, and beat with switches" Giles's slave, is formulaic and perhaps not descriptive of the actual attack. Giles not a slaveowner: Personal property tax rolls, 1823, 1824, and 1825.

112. Peace bond considered: OB 21/264 (1825 Oct). Ordinarily, a peace bond was required at the behest of a single county justice. It is not clear why the entire court considered this particular request for one, or why the body postponed a decision. One could posit that the race of the two parties to the dispute contributed to the postponement; but in fact the court put itself to more trouble, not less, in this instance and besides, there is little evidence from other cases that the court was inattentive to suits or motions filed by free blacks. It may be that Giles, for some reason, took his complaint straight to the county court rather than to a single justice of the peace.

113. Brown's conviction: CW v Brown, OB 21/325 and 444 (1826 Mar and Aug), and CoCt 1826 Aug. Charles Carter is listed as residing on Israelite Teny Carter's land on FNL, upper district, 1817; this may well be the witness of that name to whom a subpoena was issued but not served in CW v Brown.

114. Charge of hogstealing: CW v Giles and Howard, CoCt 1826 Nov. James Morton as justice and sheriff: See OB 21/432 (1826 Aug); Bradshaw, *Prince Edward County,* pp. 679 and 683 (which erroneously implies Morton took on the latter office only in 1827). Stella Strong, a second potential witness, was the eighteen-year-old daughter of Kit Strong, the weaver and sometime shoemaker who, owning no land himself, had since moved to Farmville; Stella still lived on Sam White's land. The Sooky White who found herself summoned was probably the wife of Hercules White Jr. The Sooky White whom Hampton Giles's wife had sued for slander in the poisoned-cabbage episode of 1812—apparently Sam's wife—had probably died c. 1822 (cf. FNLs, 1822–1825); Susan White, likely a granddaughter of Sam White, was only fourteen when Giles and Howard were tried.

115. Carter as White's administrator: See White's admor v Backus, CoCt 1828 Oct; OB 21/764 (1828 Oct); and OB 23/323 (1835 May).

116. Allen and deed of trust to Ellis: DB 18/238, Ellis to Morton and Allen, DoT (1823); and Land tax rolls, town lots, 1824, entry for Billy Ellis, lot 54.

117. Outcome of trial: CW v Giles and CW v Howard, CoCt 1826 Nov, OB 21/481 (1826 Nov), and OB 21/484–485 (1826 Nov 21). There was a somewhat mysterious, second judicial proceeding involving (the same?) hog theft a few weeks after the acquittal, but here the county attorney declined even to present a case against the two black men—CW v Giles and Howard, CoCt 1827 Feb, and OB 21/515 (1827 Feb).

118. The suit: Giles v Brown, CoCt 1827 Mar and OB 21/529 (1827 Mar). Brown had to post bond permitting the sheriff to seize and sell his horse should he fail to make the large payment he now owed Giles—Giles v Brown and White, CoCt 1827 Sep, originally labeled "John Brown to Hampton Giles D[elivery] B[ond]"; OB 21/608 (1827 Sep).

119. Breakup of marriage: Compare Index to marriage bonds, Jenny White to Peter Valentine, 1820 (microfilm), LVA, with interlinear recordations of White, Valentine, and Sooky Valentine on FNL, 1825.

120. "Cutting down"; "irresponsible": Bill, Brown v Giles, CoCt 1841 Jun. I encountered this lawsuit earlier in my research than I otherwise would have thanks to Loren Schweninger.

121. Spinning wheels and looms: Judith Randolph, letter to John Randolph, January 18, 1808. Lathing (here called "turning"): Judith, letter to St. George Tucker, February 4, 1811; St. George Randolph, letter to Tucker, February 15, 1811. "Earn an honest subsistence": Judith, letter to Tucker, July 23, 1809. All these letters are in TC/W&M. "Industrious and economical": Branch J. Worsham depo, Burke v Rice, CirCt 1850 Apr.

122. Giles's retort: Answer, Brown v Giles, CoCt 1841 Jun.

123. The Israelites' neighbor John Tuggle, for example, was selling from $7.50 to more than $10.00 worth of timber annually, and plank worth twice that much, from the nearby Penick place, which he was administering at the time—John Tuggle, guardian's acct for Jonathan Penick (1830), credits for 1829 and 1830, Guardians' accounts, 1829–55, pp. 14–15 (microfilm), LVA.

124. Brown's ostensible death: FNLs, 1824 (with the notation "decd." interpolated above John Brown's name) and 1825 (listing Tilla Brown and family as living on John Brown's estate). As late as 1837, the feud between Giles and Brown continued: in that year, each was required to post bond guaranteeing peaceful behavior toward the other—OB 24/46 (1837 Jul).

125. Freedom from supervision: For a similar point regarding acquisition of small tracts by blacks after Emancipation, see Harold D. Woodman, "Class, Race, Politics, and the Modernization of the Postbellum South," *Journal of Southern History*, 63, no. 1 (February 1997), 22.

126. Smith earning money: WB 4/176, Andrew Elliott est acct, 1795 Dec and 1796 Dec. Smith's purchase of tract: DB 12/371 (1802/1803). By 1814, Smith was living in Charlotte County (Land tax, Green's district, 1814); his one acre was finally sold in 1821 (DB 17/276, Smith to Love).

127. Nathan Homes's second purchase of land: DB 20/198, Sharp to Homes (1829).

128. "Truck": Bill in Howard v White, CoCt 1837 Jul, in which Pamelia Howard concurred in the assumption that one acre is "ground enough for a house, garden & truck pa[t]ches." Homes women's ownership of male slaves, which no purely economic motive can explain: Lucy Homes and Milly Homes in Ms. Census, 1820. Absence of Milly Homes and family from their land: FNLs, 1817–1820.

129. An apparent example of self-purchase: DB 13/36, Chaffin to Jack (1803); see also OB 16/278 (1809 Mar).

130. "Little to set them apart": Ira Berlin, *Slaves Without Masters: The Free Negro in the Antebellum South* (New York: New Press, [1974] 1992), p. 223.

131. Limited stays with any given employer: FNLs, 1817–1825. Chaffin's move: FNL, lower district, 1805.

132. Bowman at Childress's: FNL, 1821. The contract: Bowman v Childress, CoCt 1822 May and OB 20/295 (1822 May). White laborers' contracts: Cheadle, 13th p. top, Stinson Bryant acct, in which "Elic" (Alec) Bryant, a white youth, was paid in 1833 at an annualized rate of $35; and Jones v Bowman, CoCt 1844 Jan–Mar, including the bill Jones submitted to one Robert Bowman "To hire my self for 1 year" at $55.

133. Bowman sued for assault rather than for lost wages per se, but the jurors seem to have chosen the amount of Bowman's award to correspond to the wages he should have received. Bowman's subsequent employer: FNLs, 1822–1825.

134. Edmund Young's appearance and year of birth: OB 20/448 (1823 Mar). Young's lawsuit: Young v Denton, CoCt 1814 May; OB 17/397 (1812 Aug) and OB 18/83 (1814 May). The jury initially found for the white defendant, then altered its verdict to favor Young with an award of 1 cent. One might speculate that the jury deviously issued a nominal finding for Young to prevent him from appealing their verdict—except that appeals in cases such as this were rare in that time and place. In any event, the jury's tinkering with its verdict in this way was not something that happened only when the plaintiff was black; a different jury did much the same thing in a white-against-white assault suit in 1811, after striking out first a verdict for the plaintiff and then an "opinion" that each party should pay his own costs in the suit—Fore v Connor, CoCt 1811 Apr–May.

135. Young living alone: Ms. Census, 1810. His registration as free black: OB 16/232 (1808 Nov). At Allen & Fowler's: Allen's exors v Fowler, [Commissioners'] Report, entries for 1805 Aug and Sep, CoCt 1822 Jul; one entry has the mill paying for three days' boarding for Edmund Young, which suggests that the mill was responsible for his maintenance at the time.

136. History of this abandoned tract in brief: See Justices of Prince Edward v Young, CirCt 1833 Sep. Location of tract, designated "British land": Land tax, 1820. Young farming on Buchanan and Hastie's ("British land"): FNLs, 1817ff.

137. Ben Short's apprentices: FNLs, Green's district, 1807 and 1811. Short's land: DB 14/571, Holcombe to Short (1811).

138. Financing Short's purchase: DB 14/575, Short to Holcombe, DoT (1811); Credits, 1812, in commissioners' report, p. 46, Attorney General v Chambers's Trustees, CoCt 1821 Nov.

139. Patty Bartlett's purchase: DB 15/211, Short to Bartlett (1814).

140. Bartlett's apparent absence from county shortly after purchase: Delinquent [land and] property tax for 1815, filed CoCt 1815 Aug–Sep; Persons whose land is returned as delinquent, filed CoCt 1816 Aug. Occupants of Bartlett tract: FNLs, 1821–1825; the second boatman to move onto Bartlett's land was Dancy Brown. Ben Short's heirs were Sylvia and Susannah Short.

141. Short's health failing: See the discussions in chapters 4 and 7. Providing for family and emancipating wife: WB 5/354, Benjamin Short nuncupative will (1818). Sale of land: DB 16/239, Short to Smith (1817). The pertinent deeds and other records present some slight anomalies: the deeds have Short originally buying twenty-five acres, selling one acre to Patty Bartlett and then twenty-three acres to Francis Smith, but supposedly retaining two acres—which totals twenty-six acres, not twenty-five; meanwhile, OB 18/632 (1817 Sep) says Short sold Smith twenty-one acres. Addition of free black woman, Nancy Smith, to household: FNL, 1818.

142. Ampy Brandum at White's: IH 1816 (Brandum may have arrived at White's during the years 1812–15, for which lists of inhabitants are lacking). Polly Brandum: IH 1816; FNLs, 1817–1819, the last of which erroneously lists Polly as "Nancy." Strongs former Randolph slaves: OB 26/15 (1845 Jan), renewal of registration of their son Sam, who is designated as having been emancipated by Richard Randolph's will. The Strongs' whereabouts: FNLs, Green's district, 1811 and 1817ff.

143. Jacob and Malinda Johnston, George and Nancy Patterson: FNL, 1820. Joe Bartlett joins Polly Brandum: FNL, 1819, which wrongly calls Polly "Nancy"; that this is in fact Polly Brandum is clear when one notes the names of her sons and compares the listing of 1819 with those of earlier and later years. Bartletts in Farmville: FNL, 1821. Edmund and Hannah Clark: FNLs, 1819 and 1825 (at Isham Patterson's), 1820–1824 (at Sam White's).

144. Robert Eldridge at Brown's: IH 1816. At Brown's with wife: FNLs, 1817–1819 and 1821–1823. Robert Eldridge disappears from the record after 1823, probably through death, but his wife Marga remained on the Brown place even then—FNLs, 1824–1825. The Eldridges do not appear at Brown's on the FNL of 1820; but this may be the result of an oversight by the enumerator, as one or both Eldridges appear there on the four preceding and four following years' lists. Jane Evans, who was sixty-five at Israel Hill's founding and doubtless a relative of the landowning free black Evanses, made a permanent home with the Titus Gibbs family—IH 1816, which notes Evans's age; and FNLs, 1817–1825.

145. Four short-term residents of Sam White's: FNL, 1819. Ampy Crowder at Carter's: FNL, 1817. Crowder a boatman: FNLs, 1822–1824. Two younger women: IH 1816 (Betsy Bradley, thirty-two, at Patterson's; Nancy Mettauer, twenty-three, recorded at the end of the list, just after the Gibbs family); the two women may have lived on Israel Hill longer than one year, as lists of inhabitants are lacking for 1812–15. A (young?) man, Maglane Stoner, at Giles's: FNLs, 1821–1823. Stoner was probably the son or other relative of boatman Samuel Stoner/Stonum and his wife, Sally, who lived in Farmville—CW v Salley Stonum, CoCt 1820 Nov; FNL, 1821.

146. Figures derived from IH 1816 and FNLs, 1817–1821; the figure of twenty-nine individuals at Sam White's includes Phil White Jr., his wife, and the four children born to them by 1821. The Clarks at White's: FNLs, 1820–1824. Cordial ties: WB 7/273, Isham Patterson will (1832). Strong's children: FNLs, 1819ff.

147. Brandum's movements: IH 1816, and FNLs, 1818–1825. Baker's movements: FNLs, 1819, 1820, and 1821.

148. Archer Allen's sons, favoring of William, and legacy: WB 4/251, Archer Allen will (1811), and WB 4/265, Archer Allen appraisal (1811). William Allen's plantation and his residency there: DB 14/6, Watson to Allen (1806), and 14/487, Allen to Allen (1808/1811). Number of slaves: Ms. Census, 1810, p. 240. Deputy sheriff, 1801–03: Prince Edward delinquent land, filed CoCt 1815 Aug–Sep; Leigh v Allen, CoCt 1835 Jun–Jul. Tax collector: Allen, collector, acct with county, filed CoCt 1809 Jun–Jul.

149. Allen's association with Woodson: Woodson v Allen, CoCt 1837 Aug; Allen v Woodson, CoCt 1823 Nov. Dwins at Allen's: FNL, 1817. Allen witnesses will: WB 5/341–342, Betty Dwin will (1808/1818). Allen hires Harry Dwin: Dwin's exor v Allen, CoCt 1823 May. Branch Epperson at Allen's: FNL, 1818. Allen on Bowman-Childress jury: Bowman v Childress, CoCt 1822 May, and OB 20/295 (1822 May).

150. Phil Bowman working for Allen: Details here and subsequently from Answer of James Venable, Bowman v Bowman's exor, CirCt 1847 Apr, except where another source is indicated. Allen and Bowman listed together: Ms. schedules, taxable property, upper district, 1809 and 1810; by way of comparison, see Ms. property tax schedules, 1803–10.

151. Hiring out slaves, and suing brother: Allen v Allen, CoCt 1817 May. "In Strict subjection"; plan to sell a slave: Coleman v Allen, CoCt 1820 May.

152. Beginnings of Allen's troubles, and general scope of the crisis: See Woodson v Allen, CoCt 1821 Nov; Woodson v Allen, CoCt 1823 May; and many other suits filed by the same attorney—at what appears to have been a rapid clip—in the same period. Sale of plantation: DB 17/597, Allen to Allen (1821/1822). Auction: Allen v Woodson, CoCt 1823 Nov, with charge against Charles Woodson for "Purchase at my sale" in 1821. Allen family's troubles and intrafamily suits (example): Allen v Allen, CoCt 1824 Mar. Allen's financial troubles with Charles Woodson: Woodson v Allen, CoCt 1825 Oct; and other Allen-Woodson litigation already cited. Struggling a decade later: Note dates of court actions just cited, and especially Allen's letter of August 16, 1827, in Allen v Legrand, CoCt 1829 Aug.

153. Forfeiture of slaves: Tuggle and Penick assignees v Allen, CoCt 1822 Dec–1823 Mar; Delivery bond in Allen v Legrand, CoCt 1823 May; and Woodson v Allen, CoCt 1823

Dec. Sale of Priscy Bowman: Delivery bond, Tuggle v Allen, CoCt 1822 Aug; Answer of James Venable, Bowman v Bowman's exor, CirCt 1847 Apr.

154. Bowman's agreement with Venable: Answer of James Venable, Bowman v Bowman's exor, CirCt 1847 Apr (which also details the events that followed Allen's insolvency).

155. "Very disagreeable": William A. Allen, letter to Colonel Charles Woodson, exhibit in Pearce's exor v Pearce, CoCt 1823 Nov.

156. Neighbors of Israel Hill: See Legrand's exor [William L. Legrand] v Allen, CoCt 1819 Aug; Tuggle and Penick assignees v Allen, CoCt 1821 Nov; Allen v Pearce et al., CoCt 1822 Sep; and Delivery bond, Tuggle v Allen, CoCt 1822 Aug, which led directly to the sheriff's sale of Priscy Bowman.

CHAPTER 4: *Work*

1. Two hogsheads from Hercules Junior: Document A, Commissioner Berkeley's audit of Madison's acct, 1829 Feb 12 (p. 25), Chambers's committee v Madison's exor, CirCt 1842 Apr. Seven hogsheads from Hercules Junior: Jonathan Penick acct with John Tuggle (1830), Guardians' accts, 1830 Jan (microfilm), LVA. Hercules Junior as farmer: FNLs, 1817–1825. Twenty-six cents to Samuel White for coopering: Doct E, acct of monies paid after the death of Z. Lackland, 1830 Aug 5, Sublett v Lackland, CirCt 1851 Sep. The 26-cent coopering fee corresponds to the cost of a whiskey barrel; see Major Nathaniel D. Price, acct with McDearmon & Booker, 1848 Dec, McDearmon & Booker v Price's admor, CirCt 1852 Apr. On versatility of free and enslaved Southern workmen, cf. Catherine W. Bishir, "Black Builders in Antebellum North Carolina," *North Carolina Historical Review*, 61, no. 4 (October 1984), 433.

2. Tony White as cooper: FNLs, 1822–1824. As farmer: FNLs, 1817, 1818, 1820, and 1821. As boatman: FNL, 1819. Phil Bowman: FNL, Green's district, 1811; FNLs, 1817 (at Allen's) and 1818–1819 (at Venable's); Answer of Venable in Bowman v Bowman's exor, CirCt 1847 Apr. Official free black lists understate occupational flexibility by giving only one occupation per year for most individuals; for example, they list carpentry as Billy Ellis's only occupation, even though other sources (see later in this chapter) make it clear he did other work as well. Ulrich B. Phillips drew conclusions similar to mine about the occupational versatility of rural free blacks and applied them to the entire South, but he differs from me in implying that these people's "level of attainment" in their occupations was typically mediocre—Phillips, *American Negro Slavery: A Survey of the Supply, Employment and Control of Negro Labor as Determined by the Plantation Regime* (Baton Rouge: Louisiana State University Press, [1918] 1966), pp. 436–37.

3. One pitfall in researching labor in the Old South is that documents often record payments to white persons for work that was actually done by their slaves. When one finds a payment to General John Purnall, one of the richest men in Prince Edward County, for repairing a chair, it is clear that an unnamed slave made the actual repair; but when the white person receiving the payment was a slaveholder of more modest means, the situation is ambiguous. Payment to Purnall: Owen Haskins est acct, 1810 Feb, Haskins v Ligon, CirCt 1844 Sep.

4. Dilcy and Franky: Acct and devision of S. Waltons estate, 1839, Jeter v Walton, CirCt 1842 Apr; Saml Walton est acct, 1839, Walthall v Walthall, CirCt 1848 Sep. Solomon and Moses: Henry P. Davis acct with Thweatt & Miller, 1831 Apr 4, Thweatt & Miller v Davis, CirCt 1843 Apr. Example of account with many payments to others' slaves in 1820s: Benjamin A. Thackston acct with Thweatt, Carter & Co., entries from 1826 Jan through Dec, Thweatt, Carter & Co. v Thackston, CoCt 1829 Jan–Mar. Example of frequent payments to slaves in 1840s: N. C. Read acct with Read, Carrington, & Williams, Read v Venable, CirCt 1846 Jun. On slaves' earning of

income and acquisition of property, see Loren Schweninger, *Black Property Owners in the South, 1790–1915* (Urbana: University of Illinois Press, 1990), chapter 2.

5. Example of payments to female slaves (for corn): Vouchers, Wm. Price est acct with William Price, Ingram v Price, *passim*, CirCt 1839 Sep. More than $100 for produce: "Galen," letter in *Farmers' Register*, 4, February 1, 1837, 577–79, U. B. Phillips papers, group 397, series XV, box 33, folder 335, Yale.

6. Penick transactions: Penick's guardian v Penick, CirCt 1840 Apr, as follows: Vouchers for account no. 4, from Nathan Glenn, 1825 Nov, and note from overseer Thackston (including $8.40 to one slave, at typical market rate); Vouchers for account no. 2, est of Josiah Penick to Nathaniel Penick, 1822 Jun (payment for "Tob[acc]o put in Hodshed," and *passim* (payments for corn). The Penick payment for tobacco could conceivably be read as remuneration for loading rather than growing tobacco, though the import of the transaction for the present discussion would be much the same.

7. Abram: Dupuy papers, section 10, Mss1 D9295 a681–718, VHS, *passim*. Interest: Voucher no. 38 ½, Ingram v Price, CirCt 1839 Sep; and Martin Saylor est acct with Otis Williams, curator, Saylor's exor v Williams, CoCt 1835 Nov–Dec. A payment of 13 cents: Mercer M. Booker acct with Ebenezer Frothingham, Perkinson v Booker, CirCt 1843 Apr. Below-market rates: Payment to Elliott's Billy, 1828 Dec, OP report, filed CoCt 1829 Jun. Abraham: J. Todd's Abraham, acct with F. A. Booker, 1839 Nov–Dec, Booker v Todd, CoCt 1841 Jun.

8. Business with other whites (example): James Amos est acct with David Walker, 1820 Dec, Still by Prince Edward justices v Walker, CoCt 1829 Apr–May (in which free black carpenter Claiborne Evans received a payment of $2.50 from David Walker, admor of James Amos's estate, in 1820, while Evans lived at William Jones's, per FNLs, 1820 and 1821). Payments to Farmville residents (examples): Henry M. Wheatley est acct with Josiah Perkinson, 1825 Jun ($3.50 to Joe Bartlett, shoemaker and boatman), and 1825 Aug ($2.75 to Billy Ellis), Wheatley v Wheatley's admor, CoCt 1827 Nov–1828 Jan.

9. Short hires Queen: Report, Redford's acct of 1826 Jun 3, transaction 1824 Dec 23, Attorney General v Chambers's trustees, CirCt 1842 Sep. The modest amount—$11—received from Sam Short probably reflects traits of Queen that made her less attractive as a slave—Royal F. Godsey affi, 1833, Attorney General v Chambers's trustees, CirCt 1842 Sep; but it is possible, too, that the $11 was only a partial payment for the year's hire. Sam White and Harry: Alexander Legrand est acct with Joseph Binford, 1834 Jan 1, Legrand v Legrand's admor, CoCt 1837 Jul; in 1830, Sam White's household included one adult male slave, perhaps either this hired bondman or another of similar station—Ms. Census, 1830, sheet 127. Also in the 1820s, Afro-Virginian Billy Brown hired a bondman even before Brown's own self-purchase out of slavery had been formalized—Document A, Commissioner Berkeley's audit of Madison's acct, p. 5, in Chambers's committee v Madison's exor, CirCt 1842 Apr. Brown's family remained in slavery, and the person he hired may have been one of them—Petition of Billy Brown, 1818 Dec 18, Legislative petitions, LVA. (On Brown's history, see chapter 5, note 97.)

10. Modest sums: See William Wootton est acct with William T. Wootton exor, 1828 Dec, Wootton v Wootton's heirs, CoCt 1831 Jul, with a payment of 50 cents to Dennis Evans; and Vouchers, Ingram v Price, CirCt 1839 Sep, *passim*. Phil's money: Phill's exor v Maddox, CoCt 1814 Nov (but originally filed 1815 Jan–Apr); the debtor was not found, and the sum went uncollected by Phil's white executor.

11. Ellises' work for Chambers: Copy of proceedings, Attorney General v Chambers's trustees, CoCt 1821 Nov, a number of entries, 1814–19; Report, Redford's acct, 1826 Jun 3, entries 1822–24, Attorney General v Chambers's trustees, CirCt 1842 Sep; Document A, Berkeley's audit, Chambers's committee v Madison's exor, CirCt 1842 Apr,

passim, 1820s and 1830s; James Madison acct with Flippin & Dunnington, 1839 Mar 3 and 5, Madison's trustees v Morton, CirCt 1854 Aug. Example of Billy Ellis working elsewhere: Henry M. Wheatley est acct with Josiah Perkinson admor, 1825 Aug 17, Wheatley v Wheatley's admor, CoCt 1827 Nov–1828 Jan. Tom Ellis working for Chambers while living elsewhere: Compare FNLs, 1823–1825 (at Francis Smith's) with Report, Redford's account, 1826 Jun 3, Attorney General v Chambers's trustees, as just above, entries 1823 Jul and 1824 Dec 23. Ellis's lot: Land tax, Booker's district, 1819, 1820, and 1824 (though Ellis is not listed as a grantee in Index to Deeds); DB 18/238, Ellis to Morton, DoT (1823). Example of Homeses working elsewhere: George R. Mottley acct with Wootton & Co., 1841 Jun 19, Baldwin v Wootton, CirCt 1842 Sep (Susan Homes); Littleberry Royall, note to Capt. Dupuy, 1826 Sept 6 (?), section 4, folder 2, Dupuy Papers, Mss1 D9295 a106–136, VHS; see also later discussion of the Royall–Joe Homes relationship. Homes-Dupuy mill transactions: Asa Dupuy and Joseph Dupuy, Accounts, 1822–27, Dupuy papers, Mss1 D9295 a94–156, VHS, *passim*, with deliveries to Milly Homes ordered on 1826 Mar 22 and 1827 Apr 4.

12. Services requested by a white employer for a free black: Otis Williams, letter to Dr. [J. P.] Mettauer, August 14, 1831, John Peter Mettauer Papers, Mss1 M5677 a47, VHS. For medical services to free blacks, apparently sought by the blacks themselves, see John Peter Mettauer papers, section 2, account book, Mss1 M5677 a50, VHS: [1830s?] Jun 30–Sep 3 and 1837 Oct 11 (Phil White), and 1827 Apr 28 (Joe Bartlett); Bonds and accounts due J. P. Mettauer & put into Todd & Moseley's hands, filed 1845 May 1, Mettauer v Todd, CirCt 1847 Apr (Joe Bartlett and Billy Ellis).

13. Tony White's years away from Hill: FNLs, 1822–1824. His return, FNL, 1825. Other departures from Hill (Kit Strong Sr.; Polly and Ampy Brandum): IH 1816, and FNLs, 1817–1825 and 1857–1864. Tony's wife: Three of the couple's children were owned by an Allen family in 1848—WB 9/374, Anthony White will (1848 with codicil 1850/1850); the place Tony White lived on in the 1820s was owned by Mary Allen. Technically, Tony White did not own land on Israel Hill at the time; but practically speaking, he did, as an heir to Hercules Senior—a fact that the county court would soon formalize. Location of Mary Allen's land: Land tax, 1822.

14. "Found a niche": Phillips, *American Negro Slavery*, p. 437. John H. Russell, *The Free Negro in Virginia, 1619–1865* (Baltimore: Johns Hopkins Press, 1913), asserts that free black workers did function in a competitive labor market, and that their services were more attractive to employers than those of white laborers or hired-out slaves (pp. 146–56, especially 147).

15. Disunity among carpenters: McDearmon v Jennings, especially bill, depos, and carpenters' appraisals, CoCt 1816 Oct; phrase, "was the way with workmen," in James McDearmon affi.

16. Campbell land: Cheadle, 41st p. (numbered as p. 19), 1830 May 12. Selling in Lynchburg and trips to Richmond: Cheadle, 27th p. top (numbered as p. 5), 1822 Feb 20; B2nd p., 1822 Apr, and *passim*. Shipping to Petersburg: Nathaniel D. Price depo, Cheadle v Ferguson, CirCt 1849 Sep.

17. Forgasons' occupations and residences: FNLs, Green's district, 1801–1811; lower district, 1805–1807; 1817–1825. "Itinerant": Charles Forgason, FNL, Green's district, 1805, and lower district, 1805. Residing "anywhere": Jesse Forgason, FNL, 1817; Stephen Forgason, FNLs, 1817 and 1818. Absence of some Forgasons from Prince Edward in any given year: FNLs, Green's district, 1807–1811; FNLs, 1817–1825. Sale of land: DB 17/125, Forgason to Morton (1820); DB 17/589–590, Forgason to Morton (1822); OB 20/233 (1822 Mar). (The deeds themselves convey only about three quarters of Jethro Forgason's original one hundred acres; he apparently disposed of the other quarter of his land between land tax, 1820, and land tax, 1821, but no recorded deed explains where those twenty-three-odd acres went.) Poor aid: Report of board meeting of OP, 1826 Jun 5 (not labeled), filed CoCt 1826 Aug; I have assumed that the "Jethro Fergu-

son" referred to in this report is the elder of that name, for Jethro Junior appears on no county FNL after 1820. In 1822, Jethro's son Stephen sold his scythe; perhaps he assumed that any further farming he might do would be on land, and with tools, owned by others—Stephen Forgason and John Webb's note to Thomas Trent admor, Thomas assignee v Ferguson [sic] and Webb, CoCt 1827 Mar–Apr, credit of 1822 Jul 16, "for the purchase of your [not "a"] scythe," with "your" probably referring to Forgason, though possibly to Webb. According to the same document, Stephen Forgason had had enough economic credibility in 1820–21 to join with a white man and sign a note for a $56 loan or purchase (the record does not reveal for what), and he managed to pay back more than half that amount over the next four years.

18. Forgasons' places of residence: FNLs, 1817–1825. From 1817 to 1825, no year passed in which anywhere from two to five Forgason men were not living together somewhere in Prince Edward, except for 1822, when most of them were absent from the county and perhaps residing together elsewhere. The census enumerator in 1830 recorded each Forgason man as heading an independent household even when they resided on land owned by white persons—Ms. Census, 1830, pp. 99 and 124; see also Ms. Census, 1820, sheet 155.

19. Cheadle-Forgason contract: Cheadle, B21st p.

20. Forty dollars: Westly Wilkerson's certf and Moseley's charge for repairs, 1834–36, Moseley v Woodson's admor, petition and affis, CirCt 1842 Apr. Seven dollars: Arbitrators' statement of work for Wilkinson by Davis, Davis v Wilkinson, CoCt 1835 May. Twenty-three dollars for Cheadle's other tobacco house: Cheadle, 30th and 31st pp. (numbered as pp. 8 and 9), J. T. and other Cheadles, acct with Josiah Cheadle, payments to Sheppard Thackston, 1823 Dec 21 and 1824 Jun 30, and to Thomas T. Boatwright, 1824 Feb 7, totaling $22.84, which may have included some interest on the delayed payments.

   Constructing other outbuildings generally ran between $10 and $20; even a relatively complicated structure such as a five-stall stable with an upper floor might cost as little as $25 or $30. See Depos of Hudson Wilson, James Thackston, John Smith, and Thomas Moseley, Baker v Mathews, CoCt 1811 Aug (stable appraised at $25–$40); Cheadle, 2nd p., 1826 (or perhaps 1822), agreement with E. Boles ($12.50 for a smokehouse); Jonathan Penick acct with Stephen Harvey, Harvey v Penick, CoCt 1836 Mar ($16.05 for a corn house, including "finding" [defined in text below] at one third, 1834); Bill, Redford v Todd, CoCt 1831 Oct ($10 for a meat house in 1824); Cole & Ballow's bill, Ballow v Thackston, CirCt 1849 Sep ($19 for a log corn house of eight by ten feet).

21. "Finding" as an add-on of one third to carpenters' and sawyers' fees: Charles Woodson acct with John G. Godsey, hewing and sawing, 1823, Godsey v Woodson, CoCt 1826 Mar; Bill of corn house and bill of repairs done to granary, Harvey v Penick, CoCt 1836 Mar. The fraction of a job's cost that went toward finding materials could range as low as one seventh on jobs with a high ratio of labor to materials costs; see finding as add-on of one sixth in Bill of stable, Harvey v Penick, 1834. Thirty-five dollars to white employee, Ben Roberts: Cheadle, B20th p., upside down, An agreement . . . with Ben Roberts. Fourteen dollars to white employee: Cheadle, B25th p., John Beazely account.

22. "So much money": Narration, Holt v Ligon, CoCt 1819 May, among other examples. Josiah Cheadle himself hired a white employee for most of the year 1828, but specified that he had the right to raise the cost of provisions he furnished to the man after the first two months should neighborhood prices rise—Cheadle, B20th p., upside down, agreement with Ben Roberts.

23. Deducting provisions routine: See Bills in Harvey v Penick, CoCt 1836 Mar; Cheadle, *passim;* and countless other records of the period.

24. Charles Forgason reaping: WB 4/162 and 166, Thomas Flournoy est acct with John J.

Flournoy, exor (1809), 1805 Jul and 1807 Jul. White's son: Copy of proceedings, Attorney General v Chambers's trustees, 1810 Mar 30 (p. 33), CoCt 1821 Nov. Brandum cutting hay: Caleb Baker est acct with Branch J. Worsham, 1824 Jul, Hendrick v Jones, CoCt 1825 Jun–Jul. Brandum making shoes: FNL, 1824.

25. Twelve-hour day, and pressure of weather: Cheadle, 26th p., payments for wheat, tobacco ("before frost"), and bridge work (six man-hours remunerated at 50 cents). Twelve-hour day: See also Cheadle, 16th p., payment to Charles Forgason. Harvesting by hand: Herbert Clarence Bradshaw, *History of Prince Edward County, Virginia, from Its Earliest Settlements Through Its Establishment in 1754 to Its Bicentennial Year* (Richmond: Dietz Press, 1955), pp. 342–43; Sam Bowers Hilliard, *Hog Meat and Hoecake: Food Supply in the Old South, 1840–1860* (Carbondale and Edwardsville, IL: Southern Illinois University Press, 1972), p. 164. Summer sun: Hilliard, *Hog Meat,* p. 164. "Sweating" (example): Herbert G. Gutman, *The Black Family in Slavery and Freedom, 1750–1925* (New York: Vintage, 1976), p. 398.

26. A dollar a day: Cheadle, 26th p. and *passim;* Acct for building schoolhouse, Walker's exor v Foster, CoCt 1835 May; and countless other papers in CoCt records. A dollar a bushel: Copy of proceedings, Attorney General v Chambers's trustees, CoCt 1821 Nov, p. 25, fifteen bushels of wheat, 1807; Cheadle, *passim;* Accts in Walker's exor v Foster; and many other documents. Contemporaneous example of 50 and 75 cents per day: Accts in Pryor assignee v Bowles, CoCt 1830 Mar–Apr. Pay for day laborers and for skilled carpenters remained at these levels as late as 1850, though there was sharp rise by 1860—Ms. Census, 1850 and 1860, schedule 6, Social statistics.

27. Harvest of 1822: Cheadle, 16th p. top (bottom of page missing); 17th p. top, Acct of wheat sent to mill; 25th p. middle (numbered as p. 3), J. T. and other Cheadles, acct with Josiah Cheadle [1822]; B14th p. middle, 1822 Jun 28. (Charles Forgason also spent a day and a half cutting grass, for which he was apparently paid the same rate as for harvesting grain.) Balance of the 1820s: Cheadle, 17th p. bottom, Acct of wheat made 1823; 31st p. (numbered as p. 9), J. T. and other Cheadles, acct with Josiah Cheadle [1824]; inside front cover, Payment to Sharick Fergerson [sic], 1829. Mid-1830s: Cheadle, 20th p. bottom, Acct of wheat paid hirelings for cutting 1834; 20th p. bottom, Acct for cutting, 1835. John Forgason: Cheadle, B28th p. middle, Acct of wheat made 1845, Sep 3. (A black John Forgason in the appropriate age bracket appears on FNLs, 1857, 1858, 1860, and 1861.) Cheadle, B2nd p. bottom, appears at first glance to cover 1826, but I believe this is an illusion created by Cheadle's chaotic record keeping; this record is more likely a running account of man-hours worked in the harvest of 1835, for the men listed as working are exactly the same as in the final Acct for cutting, 1835.

28. Example of an early white cutter: WB 4/176, Andrew Elliott est acct with William Womack Sr. exor, 1796 July, payment to Robert Spencer. Early instance of black-white wage parity for cutting: Two small green receipts, 1808 Jun and 1809 Jun, payments to Absalom, Foster v Foster's exors, CoCt 1843 Nov; and Abraham Foster est acct with Booker and John Foster exors, 1810 Aug, payments to white men. Example of slaves and white man cutting oats for same rate (and together?) on a plantation other than Cheadle's: Clark & Hubbard acct with Benjamin Hubbard, payments to Apperson's hands and to Thomas Smith (c. 1829), Hubbard v Clark, CirCt 1844 Apr. On rare occasions, Josiah Cheadle deviated upward or downward from the rate of $1 (or a bushel) per day, but he did not do so according to the recipients' race—Cheadle, B2nd p. bottom, payments to "Gorff" (i.e., Goff—75 cents) and Jesse Forgason (a bushel and a half), both black.

29. Charles Forgason reaping with white man: WB 4/162, Thomas Flournoy est acct, 1805 Jul. (Forgason and free black Tom Ligon [see FNLs, lower district, 1805 and 1807] were paid on July 11 for four days, the white Fowlkes and the slave on July 10 for shorter periods; the most plausible conclusion is that, for one day or so, all four men worked Flournoy's fields together.) Forgasons and whites cutting in same years:

Cheadle, 20th p. bottom, Acct for cutting, 1835 (and, in what may essentially be a duplicate record, though it seems to be marked 1826: Cheadle, B2nd p. bottom); possibly B28th p. middle, Acct of wheat made 1845, Sep 3, where John Young may be white; and the records cited in the remainder of this note. Forgasons and whites working in same year, but apparently at different periods: Cheadle, 17th p. bottom, Acct of wheat made 1823. Apparently working same days: Cf. Cheadle, 16th p. top (partial page), Wheat cutters' remuneration, 1822, with 25th p. middle (numbered as p. 3), J. T. and other Cheadles, acct with Josiah Cheadle [1822] (Jesse Forgason paid 1822 Jun 28 for three days, Guill and Black Jun 26 for one day); Cheadle, 20th p. bottom, Acct of wheat paid hirelings, 1834 (where no dates are recorded, but the total days worked by most of the cutters, including Shadrach Forgason and two or three white men, all end in "³/₄," a circumstance suggesting that all ceased working at the same time, presumably on completion of the harvest). The free black man other than the Forgasons who cut for Cheadle is recorded only by his surname, Goff—probably Dick Goff, a carpenter by trade, who in 1822 had lived on the same white man's land as Peter Forgason (FNL, 1822).

30. Whites designated "Mr.": Cheadle, 20th p. bottom, Acct for cutting, 1835. Whites with surnames only: Cheadle, 16th p. top (partial p.), Wheat cutters' remuneration, 1822; and Cheadle, 25th p. middle (numbered as p. 3), J. T. and other Cheadles, acct with Josiah Cheadle, [1822] Jun 26. All cutters with first and last names: Cheadle, 20th p. bottom, Acct of wheat paid hirelings, 1834. A white man (not a harvester) listed with given name only: Cheadle, 3rd p. middle, Acct of Archibald [Faris?], 1829.

31. Presentment of Forgason: District Court Order Book, 1805–31, CW v Selby, Ferguson, et al., pp. 643–44 (1828 Apr), 652–54 (1828 Sep, with process still not served on Forgason after five months), and 667 (1829 Sep, not prosecuted). Continued cohabitation: Ms. Census 1830, sheet 124. Forgason buys whiskey from Cheadle in 1832: Cheadle, 2nd p. middle. Stephen harvesting for Cheadle at least as early as 1822, and listed with whites: Cheadle, 16th p. top; and also Cheadle, B14th p. middle, Order to Stephen Furgerson. As late as 1835, with whites: Cheadle, 20th p. bottom, Acct for cutting 1835; and B2nd p. bottom, though entry appears to be marked 1826. The interracial couple had apparently been together for some years prior to 1828, for the number of children in Forgason's household grew in the mid-1820s without any black wife appearing alongside him on official lists (FNLs, 1822–1824). Selby, the surname of Forgason's wife, is also rendered as "Selbe," "Silby," and "Silvey" in various records. The 1840 Census includes one free black, "Stephen P. Ferguson," in this part of Virginia (Buckingham County), heading a family of fifteen which had no white members. One wonders whether this is the Stephen Forgason who had lived in Prince Edward, now separated from his white spouse by death or under pressure from whites. The middle initial inclines me to believe he is not the same man; Southside Virginians of both races were very consistent in their use or nonuse of such initials.

32. Eighty cents per bushel: Cheadle, 33rd p. (numbered as p. 11), J. T. and other Cheadles, acct with Josiah Cheadle, payment to Stephen Moseley, 1825 Oct. Differing modes of payment to cutters: Cheadle, 16th p. top, Wheat cutters and remuneration, 1822; see also Cheadle, 25th p. middle (numbered as p. 3), J. T. and other Cheadles, acct with Josiah Cheadle [1822], Jun 26 and 28. Different rates for workers' board: Ms. Census, 1850, schedule 6, Social statistics. Differential allocations for boarding, but pay not correlated with race: John Long acct [1840], Edwin Edmunds Account Book, 1838–92, UNC. By 1860, no difference in board rates according to race was reported; one wonders whether this indicates a change in actual practice—Ms. Census, 1860, schedule 6, Social statistics.

33. Various purchases by Forgasons: Cheadle, 5th p. top, Charles (including salt and ax), 1822; 29th p. bottom (numbered as p. 7), Isaac (corn), 1824 Aug 10; 35th p. top, Shadrach, 1834 (including wheat); B21st and B22nd pp., Shadrach, 1835 (including

sugar and leather); 2nd p. middle, Stephen, 1832? (whiskey). Order to "mike" (a slave?): Cheadle, 3rd p. top, 1820s? Chit from white man, and leather charged to him: Cheadle, 19th p. bottom, Enoch Brightwell acct, 1835; the same account shows Jesse Forgason making shoes and boots from leather the planter provided, for which Cheadle then billed Forgason's client.

34. Corn at 60 cents: Cheadle, 5th p. top, Charles Foggerson, 1822. Billy Bryant, a white man, once got wheat for 90 cents a bushel instead of $1—but Cheadle at one point charged Shadrach Forgason less than 70 cents. Bryant: Cheadle, 36th p. bottom (numbered as p. 14), Billy Bryant acct, (1840?) Aug 10. Forgason's discount: Cheadle, B22nd p. bottom. Charles Forgason bought bacon from Cheadle in 1822 at a shilling (16²/₃ cents) a pound, but in a different year, Shadrach Forgason regularly paid him only 9 pence—the low end of the price scale in those days. Charles's expensive bacon: Cheadle, 5th p. top, Charles Foggerson, 1822. Shadrach's cheap bacon: Cheadle, 35th p. top (numbered as p. 13), Shederick Fergerson, 1834 Mar and Apr.

35. One-dollar discrepancy: Cheadle, 35th p. top (numbered as p. 13), Shederick Fergerson acct, 1834 (the erroneous running total is $9.66). Nine-dollar (net) discrepancy: Cheadle, B21st p. (at this point, there is an error to *Cheadle's* detriment in the running total of $19.58); B22nd p. (with corrected grand total, which, however, originally read over $31); and B19th p., Shedrick Furgerson account, 1835.

36. White man overcharged for oats: Cheadle, B26th p., John P. Clark, 1843 Jan. Cheadle recoups previous year's overpayment to blacksmith—twice: Cheadle, B23rd, B24th, and B25 pp., Smith's work by R. Fuqua, 1835 (cf. 1833). Silk purchased for J. Beazely for 6.25 cents: Cheadle, B26th p. top, Acct of articles bought of James J. Morris & Co., 1836 Nov; cf. Cheadle, 26th p. (numbered as p. 4), J. T. and other Cheadles, acct with Josiah Cheadle, [1823?] Dec. The record does not show what Cheadle charged Beazely for this particular hank of silk, but he had got 13 cents from him for one hank a few months earlier: Cheadle, B25th p., John Beazely acct, 1836 Jun. Standard rate of 6 cents for hank of silk in same period: John P. Mettauer acct with Todd & Moseley, Mettauer v Todd, 1835, CirCt 1847 April.

37. Example of "hireling" referring to hired-out slave: Bond, Wilson v Smith, CirCt 1848 Apr. Cheadle's use of term: Cheadle, 20th p. bottom, Acct of wheat paid hirelings for cutting, 1834. Blacksmith: Cheadle, 18th p. bottom, B. J. H[ughes] account.

38. Fuqua Cason cutting: Cheadle, 16th p. top (partial page) [wheat cutting, 1822], Jul 8; 17th p. bottom, Acct of wheat made 1823, Nov 12, payment to "Mrs. Cason & her son Fuqua for cuting." Cason data: Ms. Census 1830, Buckingham County, pp. 296 (Fuqua) and 294 (Sally). Sally Cason's slaves (listing only those age twelve or older): Property tax, Buckingham County, 1822 and 1823.

39. Forgason hauling: Cheadle, 41st p. (numbered as p. 19), J. T. and other Cheadles, acct with Josiah Cheadle, 1829 Aug 17 and Sep 21. Faris cutting: Cheadle, 20th p. bottom, Acct of wheat paid hirelings for cutting 1834. Faris making shoes: Cheadle, inside back cover, bottom, upside down, "Made by Sill Faris 1835"; B19th p. top, "Settled with Sill Faris," 1835 Apr 18. Cutting and cart repair: Cheadle, 36th p. middle (numbered as p. 14), Billy Bryant, 1840 July.

40. Damaged a spade: Cheadle, 12th p. middle, Jim Lig [i.e., League], spade handle and blade; Cheadle docked the man 50 cents. Smiths: 1st p., Smith's work done by H. Y. Jenkins, 1822; Cheadle, 11th p., Smith's work by R. Fuqua, 1832; B21st p. top, Smith's work by Robert Fuqua; B23rd p., B24th p., and B25th p. top, Smith's work by R. Fuqua, 1835. Conflict over a road: Hughes v Cheadle, CoCt 1822 Aug. Over trees: Hughes v Cheadle, CoCt 1822 Aug. With overseers: Cason v Cheadle, CoCt 1820 Aug, and CoCt 1821 Aug–Oct; Lawson Ferguson v Cheadle, CirCt 1847 Apr; Ferguson v Cheadle, CirCt 1847 Apr; Cheadle v Ferguson, CirCt 1849 Sep. With blacksmith: Jenkins v Cheadle, CoCt 1825 Oct. With ditcher: Martin v Cheadle, CirCt 1838 Apr. With neighboring Faris family: Cheadle v Faris, 1821 Mar–Apr, especially

depos of Thomas C. Martin, C. H. Holland, and Samuel Watkins (unlabeled); John Cheadle v Faris, CoCt 1824 Mar, and OB 20/694 (1824 Mar); Cheadle v Faris, CoCt 1830 Aug; Cheadle, 25th p. middle (numbered as p. 3), J. T. and other Cheadles, acct with Josiah Cheadle, 1822, cash advanced to sheriff (payment of court costs). Alleged beating: CW v Fore (two counts: breaking fence and beating), OB 26/99 (1846 May; presentments); 118 (1846 Aug; defendant discharged on fence breaking charge); 167 (1847 May; beating charge nol-prossed).

41. "Brandy for the negroes": Cheadle, 30th p. (numbered as p. 8), J. T. and other Chea-dles, acct with Josiah Cheadle, 1824 Jun 8. Leg irons and handcuffs: 1st p., Acct of smith's work done by H. Y. Jenkins, 1822 Feb and Mar. The one court case involving both Josiah Cheadle and black defendants arose when two slaves were charged with stealing one of Cheadle's hogs; but the slaves may not have been accused by Cheadle himself (he was not called as a witness), and the defendants were found not guilty— CW v Phil and Pryor, OB 21/629 and 632 (1827 Nov); CoCt 1827 Nov.

42. Jack Bryant: Cheadle, 3rd p. middle and bottom, Accts with Bryants, 1832 (and 1822 [sic]). Alec Bryant: Cheadle, 5th p. bottom, 1832; 10th p. middle, 1833 Jan. William Bryant: Cheadle, 10th p. top, William Bryant, 1833 Feb–Apr. William Bryant's last month: Cheadle, 10th p. bottom, William Bryant acct, 1833 Mar–Apr.

43. This point was brought home to me by Carolyn Harvey, my student at Huguenot High School, in 1973–74.

44. Value of slave labor: Dodson admor v Thackston, depos of James Thackston and Ben-jamin A. Watson, CoCt 1825 Jul ($8 per hand per month in 1813); see text and notes elsewhere in this chapter for further discussion of labor rates. Luther Porter Jackson contends that slave labor was expensive in antebellum Virginia and became "well-nigh prohibitive" in the late 1850s—Jackson, *Free Negro Labor and Property Holding in Virginia, 1830–1860* (New York and London: D. Appleton–Century, 1942), pp. 61–64.

45. Increase in annual hire: [Alexander] Marshall est acct with Foster exor, additional ledger sheet, hire of slave boy Walker, CoCt 1840 Jun–Jul.

46. Manumission: WB 3/130, Nancy Jackson will (1798). Binding out: Polly (age seven), Indenture to Mary Booker, filed 1799; Keziah (age five), Indenture to Humphrey Nelson, filed 1799; Tilda (age nearly six), Indenture to James Pigg, filed 1802; all in Apprentices, LVA. Polly was bound out to a new master five years later—Polly, Indenture to Josiah Jackson, filed 1804.

47. Orphans: Chloe Richardson, Indenture to David Holt Jr., filed 1808; Tamer Richard-son, Indenture to John Foster, filed 1810 (but see Tamer's earlier indenture to David Holt Sr., filed 1807, at which time the boy apparently was not yet orphaned); all in Apprentices, LVA. (The term "orphan," by the way, was often applied to children who had lost only one parent, but I am using the word in the modern sense.) In about half the indentures for black children apprenticed before they were ten, the contract does not specify a reason for the binding out; some of these children, too, may have been orphaned. Apprenticed together with elder siblings: Crinner Richardson, Indenture to David Holt, filed 1804, with Lucy Richardson; Betsy Homes Indenture to Henry Ligon, filed 1813 (but drawn up 1810), with Mima Homes (who possibly was a cousin rather than a sister); Jincy and Sterling Matthews, Indenture to Richard Shepherd, filed 1837 (but drawn up 1836), with Len Matthews (these children were probably black, given the absence of a reading-and-writing clause in their indentures, and given the separate binding out of a mulatto girl named Rachel Matthews just a month earlier—Indenture to Stephen Godsey, 1836. In his first apprenticeship, with David Holt Sr. in 1807, Tamer Richardson joined Crinner and Lucy, who presumably were his sisters; he stayed in that home for perhaps three years. White children bound out young: See Daniel Smith's Indenture, 1804 (age six); Sally Massey's Indenture, 1805 (age seven); Morris to OP binding Nancy Miles, 1820 (age four); and Dolly Miles to Giles, 1827 (age three); all in Apprentices, LVA. Though these four children

were not identified by race in their indentures (white children never were), it is probable that at least a couple were white, and very possible that all four were.

Only half a dozen indentures of blacks are on file for the forty years before 1799. The numbers cited here refer to contracts, not individuals, as a few persons were bound out on two different occasions. A number of indentures do not specify the apprentice's age. Not all indentures were filed centrally. An example of one that was not: Washington Lewis, Indenture to Littleberry Royall, 1819, in Lewis v Royall, CoCt 1839 Mar–Apr. There may be indentures of black children whom I have not identified as black. Such errors, however, are so few that they do not appreciably alter the picture offered here.

48. "Mechanical business": WB 4/274, Andrew Johnston will (1811). Example of indenture voluntarily entered into: Indenture between John J. Flournoy, guardian of Rowland Anderson (who was white), and Mitchell M. Gallion, filed 1827, Apprentices, LVA. "Liberal Education"; "will probably depend": WB 2/142–143, Benjamin Lawson will (1787/1789). For Lawson's background, see Bradshaw, *Prince Edward County*, pp. 51, 108, 110. Some legal guardians of poor, orphaned children received the court's approval for placements they arranged without any involvement of the overseers of the poor, as Colonel Charles Woodson did for the children of his family's deceased black tenant James Epperson—OB 18/317 (Sep 1815). Example of guardian binding out white children: OB 21/228 (1825 Jul).

49. Bidy Godsey: Godsey letter to court, March 2, 1810, filed CoCt 1810 Mar; OB 16/514 (1810 Mar). Dungey's admonition: WB 11/159–160, John Dungey will (1852/1861); by the time Dungey died, his assets would be seriously depleted.

50. "The necessary qualifications": Jenny Massey, Indenture to Sherwood Massey, 1805. The indenture of Parkey League, another white girl, in 1806 called for her to be taught "all such useful & necessary things for a girl of her station"; a few years later, a new master contracted to teach Parkey to be a "spinster"—Parkey J. League, Indenture to Reaves Jordan, filed 1806; Parkey League, Indenture to James McNeal, filed 1809. Indentures of black girls with no occupation specified: Mary Ann Richardson, Indenture to Jacob Price, and Betsey Richardson, Indenture to Josiah M. Rice, both filed 1816; see also Rhoda Artis, Indenture to Mary Bishop, filed 1830, which specifies spinning "and other house work," and Chloe Richardson, Indenture to David Holt Jr., filed 1808. Three black boys were bound out to learn the occupation of a "farmer and planter," or "husbandry"; that may sound like a ploy to allow masters to use the boys as mere field hands, except that two came from the Homes family, who actually had acquired agricultural land of their own, and the third later got a new situation with a master carpenter—Archer Homes, Indenture to Daniel Glenn, filed 1814; Lewis Homes, Indenture to Peggy Bigger, 1823. Transfer: Branch League [the younger], Indenture to Samuel B. Baldwin, filed 1828, and Indenture to Henry S. Guthrey, 1833. All these documents are in Apprentices, LVA.

51. One white apprentice boy who was supposed to learn reading and writing grew up to become a master of apprentices himself, yet signed their indentures with an X— Sherrard Massey, Indenture to Thomas Johnston, 1786; William F. Massey, Indenture to Sherrard Massey, 1795; Jenny Massey, Indenture to Sherwood Massey, 1805; all in Apprentices, LVA. Some masters who could sign their names may not have known how to do much else with pen and paper. Moreover, the number of nonliterate masters cited here refers only to those who signed indentures that are on file in LVA today; there surely were others.

52. Bricklaying apprentices with $75 "freedom dues": William and Archer Homes, Indenture to Granville Nunnally, filed 1840. Twelve dollars to white boy: James Nunnally, Indenture to Granville Nunnally, filed 1834. Nunnally as contractor: See Nunnally bill to county, CoCt 1819 Jun–Jul; P. H. Jackson acct with Nunnally, Nunnally v Jackson, CirCt 1843 Apr (specifications for two-story brick "sweat house"). Twenty-

five-dollar freedom dues and $8 a year: Stephen Forgason, Indenture to Thomas M. Cobbs, filed 1841. One hundred dollars: Theophilus Scott, Indenture to Booker Jackson, filed 1840. All indentures in Apprentices, LVA. Surviving indentures include a dozen white boys and one girl who received $20 in freedom dues, and half a dozen blacks, including one girl, who were promised that much or more.

53. Overseer Armes and two boys: Cousins report of OP, filed CoCt 1851 Dec–1852 Feb. The two boys, Branch Cousins and John Hartwell Cousins, were probably black: the name Cousins appears mostly among blacks in central Virginia; one boy was assigned to a black master; and the census of 1860 lists a John H. Cousins, free black, living in neighboring Nottoway County. On the other hand, this Cousins's age differs by seven years from what one would expect from John Hartwell Cousins's apprenticeship documents, and he is not listed as plying the trade, blacksmithing, that young J. H. Cousins was sent to learn—Ms. Census, 1850, Nottoway County, family visitation 437. Master smith a free black: OB 26/155 (1847 Feb) and 456 (1851 Oct), Alexander Cousins registrations. Binding to blacksmith, with $50 freedom dues: John Homes, Indenture to Henry Y. Jenkins, filed 1835, Apprentices, LVA. Jenkins's prowess: Rip (pseudonym), "Farmville Then and Now," *Farmville Herald,* September 14, 1906, p. 3.

54. Special commissioner: Note by Asa D. Dickinson, n.d. ("suitable person"); Commissioner's report, 1848 Jul 29 (which states that Dickinson solicited "several applications" for the boy's services); Commissioner's report, 1849 Jul 14 ("could not teach"; "no man"); all in Borum v Ellington's exor, CirCt 1853 Aug.

55. The three Homeses who received desirable apprenticeships were John, William, and Archer, with indentures as in notes 52 and 53. A sixteen-year-old Israelite boy ordered to be bound out: OB 21/318 (1826 Jan).

56. The overseer who, like Purnall, lived next to the Homeses was Branch O. Scott—see WB 7/350, John Purnall est acct with Asa Dupuy, an exor (1833), 1831 May; and DB 20/335–336, Purnall's exors to Scott (1830), which defines the tract as bounded in part by Scott's own land; this, along with the listing of all Scott's lands as being in the same immediate neighborhood, means that Scott had been a neighbor of the Homeses longer than the four years that elapsed between this land purchase and his binding out of John Homes. Jacob Homes's master: Indenture to Joseph Goode, filed 1818, Apprentices, LVA. Jacob's relationship with Milly Homes: WB 8/292, Mildred Holmes will (1833/1841). Overseer Massanello Womack and Forgason indenture: Peter Ferguson, Indenture to Charles Fore, filed 1808, Apprentices, LVA. Womack's sale of land to Forgasons: DB 7/315, Womack to Ferguson (1786). Joseph Bartlett's apprenticeship with Holcombe: OB 18/77 (1814 May). Bartlett's residency near Walthall Holcombe, and the latter's sale of land to Ben Short: See the discussion in chapter 3.

57. James League Sr.'s biography and grandchildren: James League's case (petition for Revolutionary War pension), filed CirCt 1818 Apr; League's papers (pension petition), filed CoCt 1820 Sep–Oct. One League's work for Cheadle: See discussion of broken tool earlier in this chapter. Connection between the two James Leagues: List of Insolvents in the County Levy, 1809. Leagues' nonliteracy and poverty: League's papers, as above; Lucy League depo, Woodrum v Porter, CoCt 1816 Jul. Grandchildren black: FNLs, 1820ff. Additional black grandchildren: FNLs, 1819ff., especially 1819 (Molly and Becky) and 1825 (Harriet); and Ms. Census, 1810, p. 251, with two free blacks in the League household who were older than the three mulatto children James League named in his pension application.

58. Branch League the elder bound out: Indenture to Charles Farrar (to learn smithing), filed 1806, Apprentices, LVA. I infer that Branch League the elder was a relative of Branch the younger from their shared name (an unusual one) as well as from their common station in life and county of residence. I infer that the second older League apprentice, Parkey, was related to Branch the elder (probably his sister) from the fact

that both—along with one Anderson League—were bound out as orphans by a single court order—OB 15/158 (1806 May). Branch and Judith League to be bound out: OB 21/544 (1827 May). Branch's placement: Indenture to Samuel B. Baldwin, filed 1828, Apprentices, LVA. Patty's relationship with father, and probable death of Martha League: WB 6/344–345, James League [Sr.] will (in which James leaves virtually everything to his executrix-daughter Patty, and in which Martha League is not mentioned even though her siblings are). Role of Patty (Patsey) in binding Branch: League v Baldwin, CoCt 1829 Sep–Oct.

59. Aid to Patty League: OP report for 1825 and 1826, table no. 2, filed CoCt 1827 Jun–Jul; Parish of St. Patrick [OP] to J. McDearmon &c acct, 1828, filed CoCt 1828 Jun (aid to Sucky Baker for keeping Patty League); OP report, filed 1829 June, CoCt 1829 Jun–Jul (Patty League called a "pauper"). Father's estate: WB 6/344–345, James League [Sr.] will (1826).

60. Instances of complaints, rescissions, and new assignments involving black apprentices: OB 17/475 (1813 Jan); OB 17/488 (1813 Mar); OB 19/21 (1818 Jun); OB 21/496 (1826 Dec). Patty (Patsey) League's challenge: League v Baldwin, as in note 58, and in OB 22/179 (1829 Sep). Branch's placement with contractor Henry S. Guthrey, who is discussed later in this chapter: OB 23/121 (1833 May); Branch League, Indenture to Henry S. Guthrey, filed 1833, Apprentices, LVA. By 1833, the county court regarded the white Patty as the mother of the young brown man (OB 23/121).

61. Leagues' difficulties with human relations: CW v League, CoCt 1818 May (peace bond); League v Dabney, especially Andrew Porter depo, CirCt 1826 Apr (ejection from house); Lucy League depo in Woodrum v Porter, CoCt 1816 Jul (earlier dispute over land).

62. Royall, Dupuys, and Homeses: Dupuy accts, Mss1 D9295 a106–156, VHS, *passim;* John Purnall est acct book, Mss1 D9295 a899, VHS, *passim,* especially 1830 Jul 27; Asa Dupuy acct book concerning est, Mss1 D9295 a900, VHS, *passim,* especially p. 40; WB 7/349, John Purnall est acct with Asa Dupuy exor, 1830 Jul; OB 21/356 (1826 Apr).

63. Lewis: Lewis v Royall, CoCt 1839 Mar–Apr; OB 24/238 (1839 Mar) (where dismissal by consent of parties suggests either that Royall paid Lewis, or that the two reached a compromise). White apprentice discharged from indenture: Ford [alias Hawkes] v Royall, CoCt 1827 Nov; OB 21/614 (1827 Oct) and OB 625 (1827 Nov). White apprentice's appeal fails: Waddell v Royall, CoCt 1828 Sep.

64. Royall's proposal: N. D. Price OP return, CoCt 1833 Jul.

65. Examples of moving structures: John W. Rodgers affi (one of two), Shelton v King's exors, CirCt 1852 Apr; George King's bill of charges, Ballow v Thackston, CirCt 1849 Sep (two shops, each two stories and forty feet long); Sarah Baker depo, Baker v Mathews, CoCt 1811 Aug (a stable). Kiln-drying: Contract between Byassee and Redd, Byassee v Redd, CirCt 1850 Apr; "hans Hire," expense acct 1840, Ballow v Thackston, CirCt 1849 Sep; Camille Wells, personal communication.

66. The Thackstons: Dodson admor v Thackston, CoCt 1825 Jul, depos of James Thackston, John Purnall, Benjamin A. Watson, Thomas Green ("superintended"), Allen Foster ("negroe fellows"), and John Watkins, and letter, Francis Thackston to Samuel Dodson, June 19, 1813. Example of white man actively engaged in "rough" carpentry, building a tobacco barn: William Woodall (Halifax County), letter to John Woodall, September 5, 1858, John Woodall papers, Duke.

67. Woodson and Mat: Voucher no. 20, Price v Woodson admor of Price; and Statement no. 1 ("man Mat"), est acct, Price v Price's admor; both in CirCt 1841 Apr. John Thackston's crews: "hans Hire, Expence a/c 1840 [and 1841]" and "Hans Hire in 1842," Ballow v Thackston, CirCt 1849 Sep. "Drunken frolick": Reuben Boatwright depo, Ballow v Thackston, CirCt 1849 Sep.

68. House at Hampden-Sydney: Perry v Cushing, especially depos of James C. Ander-

son, Peter McVicar ("he Mr. Perry was master"), Albert G. Carter, Joshua Terry, Thomas P. Ligon, James D. Whitice, Francis M. Fortes, and Nathan A. Grubbs ("had their beds"), CoCt 1838 Nov. On predominantly black but often biracial construction crews in a neighboring state, see Catherine W. Bishir, "Black Builders in Antebellum North Carolina," *North Carolina Historical Review*, 61, no. 4 (October 1984), 423–61, with a vivid example on 456; Bishir's discussion of free black builders is on 447–54.

69. Guthrey's apprentices (in addition to Branch League): Samuel and John Richardson, Indentures to Henry S. Guthrey, filed 1833, Apprentices, LVA. One of the Richardson boys died after only a month of apprenticeship—Inquisition taken on the body of Samuel Richardson, June 28, 1833, Inquests, LVA; County of Prince Edward acct with Robert Hill, coroner, filed CoCt 1835 Jun–Jul. Richardsons' land purchase: DB 27/185, Guthrey to Richardson (1856).

70. Guthrey gave bail for Franklin when he was sued over a debt; Guthrey seems also to have paid off the merchant to whom Franklin owed money and let Franklin reimburse him later. (F. W. Smith & Co. v Franklin, especially capias and statement of acct with Franklin's bond to Guthrey for benefit of F. W. Smith Co., CoCt 1845 Sep–Dec.) Franklin manumission: DB 25/185, Robert A. Franklin to Mary J. Franklin, emancipation (1846). Living with Guthrey: Ms. Census, 1850, family visitation 212. Purchase of land: DB 27/112, Ely to Franklin (1855). Loan of money to buy and/or develop Franklin's land: DB 27/195, Franklin to Thackston, DoT (1856), securing debt of $500 to Guthrey. There were as many as three Robert Franklins in Prince Edward during these years. The name of one—found frequently in the annual reports of the overseers of the poor—always appears without a middle initial. Another, a white man about the same age as the black Franklin and, like him, a carpenter, creates confusion—Ms. Census, 1850, family visitation 579. That the Franklin whose house was shot at by a white man (see note 71) did not testify against the suspect suggests that he was the black man of that name. The store transaction documented in this note could have involved the white Robert A. Franklin, but the participation of Henry Guthrey, who clearly was close to the black Franklin, suggests to me that the suit involved the latter.

71. Damage to Franklin's house, and trial: CW v Rodgers, CoCt 1860 Nov; OB 27/363 (1860 May) and 394 (1860 Nov). Shooter's identity: Ms. Census, 1850, family visitation 431, Albert Rodgers. This was not the first time Henry Guthrey's connections with free blacks had led him to become involved in the aftermath of a violent confrontation. He had lodged a criminal complaint in 1852 when one black man shot and wounded another with a shotgun—see CW v Green (assault on Branch Roach), CoCt 1852 Sep, and OB 26/506 (1852 Sep). The fact that Roach and another free black were called to testify against Green indicates that the latter was himself black.

72. Guthrey's charges against Julius Richardson: CW v Richardson, CoCt 1860 Feb (charge of remaining in state dismissed); CW v Richardson, CoCt 1860 Nov (charge of returning after sojourn in Ohio); OB 27/336 (1859 Nov), 363 (1860 May), and 393 (1860 Nov).

73. Range of brickmasons' work: See James H. Brown acct with George R. Jeffress, Jeffress v Brown, CoCt 1826 Dec–1827 Mar; Cheadle 39th p. (numbered as p. 17), payment to Isaac Sallie, 1827 Oct; Pankey v Randolph (with occupational designation "bricklayer & plasterer"), CoCt 1822 Aug; William Penick acct with George R. Jeffries [sic], Penick v Penick, CoCt 1830 Mar–Apr; Rice v Farmville Female Seminary Association (with reference to "the bricklaying and plastering business"), CirCt 1843 Apr; P. H. Jackson acct with Granville Nunnally, Nunnally v Jackson, CirCt 1843 Apr; Nunnally bill to county, CoCt 1819 Jun–Jul; Gafford's contract with Hendrick, Hendrick v Bondurant, CoCt 1824 Aug. Brick houses and buildings: See Rice v Farmville Female Seminary Association and Nunnally v Jackson (with two-story brick "sweat

house," eighteen by fourteen feet); Notice of sale from *Richmond Whig,* 1842, in Thweatt's creditors v Thweatt (with "large brick store house"—i.e., a mercantile store), CirCt 1853 Mar.

74. Brickmaking: Josiah Chambers acct with James Madison, in Record, Venable v Goode's admor, p. 78, CirCt 1848 Sep (clay from Chambers's); Atwell v Legrand, CoCt 1823 May; Attorney C. C. Lockett's notes regarding depo of R. Hughes in Prince v Allen, on back of calculations filed with Martin & Co. v Lowry, CirCt 1852 Apr (with reference to brick kiln). Lewis: FNLs, 1823–1825.

75. Brother "& other hands": James D. Whitice depo, Perry v Cushing, 1838 Nov. Homeses and others in later years: FNLs, 1857, 1858, and 1860–1862.

76. Two loads of brick: Offset on back of Sam Strong's charges against Phil White, Strong v White, CoCt 1844 Nov.

77. Homes at King's: Martha King acct with William S. King, marked "(50)," 1848 May 1; and Mrs. Martha King acct with William S. King, 1846; both in King v King's admor, CirCt 1854 Aug. Probably for a kitchen: Chimneys for houses routinely cost anywhere from two and a half to a dozen times the amount bricklayer Homes received—see Jeffress v Brown as in note 73, and Voucher no. 54, Price v Woodson admor of Price, CirCt 1841 Apr. Lewis's pay: Lewis v Royall, CoCt 1839 Mar. A white man had received a couple of dollars more than Homes's seven for a kitchen chimney at King's two years earlier; that gap may point to discrimination, but could easily reflect a modest difference in scale between the two jobs. Black bricklayers' mobility: FNLs as follows: Llewellyn Denetty, 1821–1822 (listed as carpenter in 1822); William Harrison, 1821; William Homes (age twenty-five to thirty), 1857, 1858, and 1861; Henry Garns (age c. twenty-two), 1858; Townsend Goe (age c. twenty-four), Henry Mason (age c. fifty-seven), and Jim Seldon (age c. twenty-two), 1860. Royall a contentious figure: Homes v Royall (assault), CoCt 1835 May; OB 23/92 (1833 Mar) and 321 (1835 May).

78. Forgason and Dick Goff, carpenters, at John Boatwright's: FNLs, 1821 and 1822. Boatwright as carpentry contractor: E. Booker depo, Boatwright v Dillon, CoCt 1825 Jul (hewing and sawing); Acct of timber hewn and sawn, Boatwright v Penick's guardian, CoCt 1830 Mar–Apr; and Receipt from Boatwright, vouchers for acct no. 1, Penick's guardian v Penick, CirCt 1840 Apr. Forgason in harvest, 1822: Cheadle, 16th (partial) p. top [wheat cutters and remuneration, 1822], and 17th p. top, Acct of wheat sent to mill 1822.

79. Ellis at 91: FNL, 1857. Ellis's lot: Land tax, Booker's district, 1819 and 1820; Land tax 1824 lists the same lot, no. 54, as belonging to "Billy" Ellis, which confirms that the owner was indeed the free black Ellis and not some other. Ellis's batteau (and use of his lot to secure his payment of a debt): DB 18/238–240, Ellis to Morton, DoT (1823). Ellis's work for Chambers, 1826 to about 1832: Chambers's committee v Madison's exor, CirCt 1842 Apr, as follows: 1826 Aug 11 (p. 16); 1827 Jul 17 (p. 18); 1828 Apr 12 (p. 22); 1829 Jul 13 (p. 27); 1829 Dec 25 (p. 29); 1830 Jul 6 (p. 30); 1832 May 5 (p. 35); 1833 Jan 1 (p. 37). Carpentry and shoes: Charles A. Watkins acct with John Rice, guardian, Justices for Watkins v Rice, 1835 Oct and 1838 Jan, CirCt 1845 Sep.

80. Ellis sues: Ellis v Dennis, CoCt 1825 Dec–1826 Mar. Ellis had been eager to collect the $100 because he himself had recently been pressed to pay a smaller debt of his own to a white man with whom he had traded back and forth for a long period. Ellis's creditor eventually sued, but instructed the sheriff not to demand any bail of the black man; Ellis settled the matter before the case came to court—Williard v Ellis, CoCt 1825 Mar.

81. Smaller carpenters' tasks: John T. Ligon acct with Henry Tucker, Tucker v Ligon, CirCt 1842 Apr.

82. King jobs: King v King's admor, CirCt 1854 Aug, as follows: Acct, William S. King to Samuel Willard, 1847–49; Acct, William S. King to Edward Williams; Acct, Martha King to William S. King, 1848 May 1 (Homes's bricklaying), 1849 May 1 (Dwin's

repairs), and see also 1850 May 1 (Samuel D. Rodgers, another white man, repairing tavern lot).

83. Baker and Cody: Baker v Mathews, CoCt 1811 Aug, especially affis of Isham Rice, Hudson Wilson, Jane Baker, James Thackston, George Cardwell, and John Smith.

84. Ellis's coffins: Document A, 1826 Aug 11 (p. 16; $1.75), 1830 Jul 6 (p. 30; $2.00), and 1833 Jan 1 (p. 37; $1.25), Chambers's committee v Madison's exor, CirCt 1842 Apr; Justices for Watkins v Rice, 1838 Jan, CirCt 1845 Sep ($1.25). Fore's $1.00 coffin for a slave: Judith, Lavalette, Josiah, and Frances Penick acct with Amplias Tuggle, trustee, 1836 Nov 22, Tuggle v Penick, CirCt 1840 Apr. Paupers' coffins: Examples include Report of proceedings of board of OP of Prince Edward Co., annual meeting, 1854 Apr 10 ($2.00 or $3.00 apiece, with one entire burial complete with shroud for only $1.50); Acct of the proceedings of the Board of OP of Prince Edward County, 1845, p. 1 ($3.00 each for coffins for free blacks).

85. Coffin for Phil White Sr.: WB 7/266, Philip White est acct with John Tuggle (1831). Ellis builds and digs: Mary V. Ligon acct with James Ligon, committee, 1834 Jul 1, Ligon v Vaughan, CoCt 1839 Jun–Jul. One dollar for digging grave: Unlabeled Prince Edward County acct with Robert Hill, coffin and burial for Sally White, filed CoCt 1830 Jun–Jul.

86. Baker kinswoman's response: Jane Baker affi, Baker v Mathews, CoCt 1811 Aug. See also Smith v Cody, CoCt 1811 Nov, and OB 17/233 (1811 Nov); Baker v Matthews, CoCt 1810 Mar; Matthews v Baker, CoCt 1812 May. Baker and Cody owned little property (Property tax, 1810); Cody was the son of a recently deceased man who had been well-off, but who had left Cody only a paltry inheritance—OB 16/427 (1809 Sep).

87. Ditches as boundaries: See Farmville road by Legrands, report, CoCt 1839 May. Ditches with fences: See Gibson v Venable & Redford, CirCt 1838 Apr; Plat in Watkins v Binford, CirCt 1830 Apr/Sep. Fencing, ditching, diking as required amenities: Cheadle, B37th p. top and bottom, "for T. J. Hardy, 1857," and B37th p. ("to enable"); Commissioner's report, 1849 Jul 14, Borum v Ellington's exor, CirCt 1853 Aug ("no bid" on land without fencing); Answer and John R. Bell depo, Gibson v Raines's admor, CirCt 1849 Sep; Joseph Martin, *A New and Comprehensive Gazetteer of Virginia and the District of Columbia* (Charlottesville: Joseph Martin, 1836), p. 266, nevertheless remarked that "a large quantity [of land in Prince Edward] is unenclosed." Ditching on roads: See Court House to Farmville road report—view, filed CoCt 1850 Jan–Apr. In Farmville: See Peters & Brightwell to Farmers Bank, agreement, Flournoy's Trustee v Farmers Bank, CirCt 1855 Aug.

88. White "ditchers" as contractors selling the labor of slaves: See Cheadle, 4th p., "Delivered Price's Ditchers"; Martin v Cheadle, CirCt 1838 Apr; Guinn v Holland (where the magnitude of the job—over twelve hundred yards at three to four feet deep—and references to a couple of hired slaves by name make clear that this "ditcher" was supervising bondmen). Creeks, dikes, canals: See Holland acct with Guinn and William P. Watson depo, Guinn v Holland, CoCt 1826 Aug–Sep; Contract and description in Martin v Cheadle, CirCt 1838 Apr; Watkins v Binford, CirCt 1830 Apr; Moseley v Binford, CirCt 1840 Sep; Depos of James T. Price (one of a number of experts who used the term "wading"), Joseph Todd, Joseph Berry, Thomas Hamilton, and P. L. Ligon, Perkinson v Appomattox Company, CoCt 1841 Jul–Aug. (The paper containing the record of the last case is exceedingly fragile and disintegrating.) A vivid example of stream diversion: Plat in Watkins v Binford, CirCt 1830 Apr. Mending "Dyke on Buffalo": Executor's accts, Worsham v Booker, 1841 Jan, CirCt 1846 Sep. Tributaries of the Appomattox were dredged over distances of half to three quarters of a mile upstream from their confluences with the river. Cheadle's canal: Martin v Cheadle, CirCt 1838 Apr.

89. "Cutting a ditch": Guinn v Holland, CoCt 1826 May. Whiskey ration: Holland acct

with Guinn, Guinn v Holland, CoCt 1826 Aug–Sep. Spring: Guinn v Holland, 1826 Aug–Sep. Well: Acct, Prince Edward County with Booker Hill, filed CoCt 1856 Jul–Aug. Grave: Acct submitted by Guinn to Holland, Guinn v Holland, CoCt 1826 May. Icehouse: See [Dr. Joel W.] Dupuy's est acct with [Paulina P. Dupuy,] admor, 1856 Sep, filed CoCt 1857 Nov–1858 Jan. Well-diggers: See [Henry E.] Watkins est acct with [F. N. Watkins,] exor, 1856 Sep, filed CoCt 1857 Nov–1858 Jan; Gerald Tate Gilliam, "Occupations of Free Blacks," *Southsider*, 5, no. 1 (Winter 1986), 14.

90. Whites ditching for pay: Orphans of Thomas D. Ligon, acct with Henry N. Watkins, guardian, 1816 Jun and 1819 Dec, submitted in Ligon v Ligon, CoCt 1825 Jul; cf. Property tax 1816 (Joseph Davidson) and 1819–20 (with no mention of ditcher Solomon Davis). Rennals: Ms. Census, 1850, family visitation 730. Murphy: Cheadle, B32nd p. middle, [1857?] Oct. Whites doing their own digging: Sarah J. Blankenship depo, Hurt v Hurt, CirCt 1851 Apr, which seems to object not to the idea of whites digging their own ditches, but rather to children being put to that work in bad weather.

91. Black ditchers other than those covered in this discussion include John Cousins, William Mettauer, and Richard Dobbins—FNLs, 1820–1823 and 1825. Contract and acct of "Billy," the ditcher at Cheadle's (possibly Billy Boram; see Property tax book, lower district, 1816): Cheadle, B16th p., "Agreement with Billy"; "²/₃rd [of Billy's remuneration was] to be paid in trade & ¹/₃rd in money." Another unnamed black man—this one perhaps a slave—earned more than $9 mending a dike along Buffalo River—Executor's accts, Worsham v Booker, 1841 Jan, CirCt 1846 Sep.

92. Davis married to Jemima (Mima Homes, listed here with daughter Tempy, named after the daughter and mother of Millie Homes): FNL, 1823. Hill as ditcher: FNLs, 1821 and 1822. Land purchase: DB 17/201, Keeling to Hill (1820).

93. Origins of the Hills: Registration of Sarah and Moses Hill, OB 20/343 (1822 Aug); Sarah alias Sarah Lewis, free papers, filed CoCt 1822 Aug; Moses Hill's free pass, filed CoCt 1822 Aug. Move to Nottoway: DB 21/119–120, Hill to Keeling (1833). Hills' land transactions: DB 17/201, Keeling to Hill (1820); DB 17/327–329, Hill to Keeling (1821), a DoT with Daniel Hamblen as trustee; DB 21/119–120, Hill to Keeling (1833). Hills' possession of the land: FNL, 1822 (with actual occupancy); Land tax, 1821 (new entry for Hill), 1822 (see entries for Daniel Hamblen and Patrick H. Anderson), 1823 (Hamblen), 1824 (Hamblen and Mary Hancock); Deed, Hill to Keeling 1833, as earlier in this note. Middle names: FNL, 1822. Favorable terms: Moses Hill bought the land for a nominal $1 pending his securing of a deed of trust for the purchase price six weeks later; no payment on that deed of trust was due for three years. When the Hills finally conveyed the 160 acres to Abner W. Keeling in 1833, they received the same $380 Hill had paid for the land in 1820; Keeling immediately sold the tract to a white man for only $340. It is unlikely that Keeling bought the tract in order to sell it at a loss of nearly 10 percent. Keeling's "purchase" at $380 may really have been a return of land that Hill had never managed to pay for. If that is the case, then it is noteworthy that Moses Hill's tract had never been foreclosed on.

94. Examples of sizable mills: Depos of Thomas Good (separate mills, single wheel) and Richard Shepherd (separate mills, with quantities produced), in Perkinson v Appomattox Company, CoCt 1841 Jul–Aug. Cotton: Many examples, including Cheadle, B2nd p., cotton, and B15th p., J. Morris, 1824. Sawmills: See Lockett v Smith, CirCt 1830 Apr (sawing combined with grain and cotton processing); Thomas S. Davis's writ of ad quod damnum, CoCt 1821 Aug–Oct; and Venables' writ for mill, filed CoCt 1832 Aug–Oct (damming streams specifically to erect sawmills). Mills that ground wheat were often called "manufacturing mills." Twenty-foot dams: See Ben Borum's writ of ad quod damnum, CoCt 1814 Jan–Mar; Baker's writ for mill, CoCt 1836 May.

95. "A white man miller": John W. Wilson depo, Perkinson v Appomattox Company,

CoCt 1841 Jul–Aug. Examples of slave millers are numerous. See, e.g., WB 3/311–313, Thomas Miller appraisal (1801); Copy of record, p. 1, C. Baker's exor v A. Baker's exors, CirCt 1834 Sep; Henry Clay Bruce, *The New Man: Twenty-Nine Years a Slave; Twenty-Nine Years a Free Man* (New York: Negro Universities Press, [1895] 1969), pp. 24–25.

96. Billy Bones: Wilson v Newton, CirCt 1811 Apr/Sep. "As good as": Richard Shepherd depo, Perkinson v Appomattox Company, as in note 95. Dennis Evans: FNLs, 1821–1825. Civil War years: See Dick Davis and Sterling Johnson, FNL, 1863.

97. Among numerous examples of mill tracts, mill hands, and mill hogs from the 1780s through the 1840s, see WB 2/44–45, William Ligon will (1787/1788) (including a "home Stock of Hogs" in contrast to mill hogs); WB 3/399–400, Nathaniel Venable will (1803/1805); Copy of record, p. 1, C. Baker's exor v A. Baker's exors, CirCt 1834 Sep; Asa Dupuy and Joseph Dupuy, accts 1828–29, 1828 Dec, Mssi D9295 a137–156, VHS (J. H. Dupuy receives 740 lb. of pork "from the mill"); List of articles sold, Perkinson v Lockett, CoCt 1839 Jun–Jul; Report of commissioners (assigning hands to road surveyors), p. 1, CoCt 1846 Aug–Oct. Slave miller sleeping in mill: Among other examples, see May v Baker, CoCt 1814 May. Norms of mill operations emerge from many sources, including Cheadle; Allen v Fowler, CoCt 1822 Jul; Asa and Joseph Dupuy accts, section 4, folder 2, 1827, VHS as just above, a117–136; and especially Perkinson v Appomattox Company, CoCt 1841 Jul–Aug. It should be mentioned that the Dupuys' several millers, with whom much of the proprietors' everyday correspondence has been preserved, were white; black millers' responsibilities were similar to those recorded there.

98. Proprietors' imperfect knowledge: Dupuy accts, VHS, as in note 97, *passim*. Clients request goods directly from miller: Thomas Flournoy, note to John Cox, April 2, 1827, and Samuel Blankenship, note to Cox, April 21, 1827 (telling miller "I expect [Dupuy] will rite you himself in a few days"), both in Dupuy accts.

99. Shepherd's nonliteracy: Indentures, Amanda Walker and Bob Branch to Richard Shepherd, filed 1828, and Len, Jincy, and Sterling Matthews to Shepherd, filed 1837, both in Apprentices, LVA; Richard Shepherd depo, Perkinson v Appomattox Company, CoCt 1841 Jul–Aug. "Not being able": Bruce, *The New Man*, p. 11.

100. Michael Henchard: Thomas Hardy, *The Mayor of Casterbridge* (New York: Modern Library, [1886] 1950), pp. 167, 138. "If we had been stupid": Pierre-Jakez Helias, trans. June Guicharnaud, *The Horse of Pride: Life in a Breton Village* (New Haven and London: Yale University Press, 1978), p. 155.

101. Bowman seems to have been employed by the Venables during an earlier period, too, before working for a number of years around the time of Israel Hill's founding for William A. Allen, the owner of his wife, and then rejoining Venable.

102. Bowmans and Venables: James Venable's answer; Philip Bowman est acct with James Venable, exor (Bowman's final positive balance); and Bowman est acct with James Venable and brother (annual rent of $12 for house and lot); all in Bowman v Bowman, CirCt, 1847 Apr.

103. Tom Ellis: Property tax enumeration book, lower district, 1816; FNLs, 1821–1825. Ampy Brandum: IH 1816; FNLs, 1817–1825.

104. "Imported" shoes: The many examples of shoes that were clearly "imported"—in most cases, records of shoe sales are not so detailed—include Cheadle, 38th p. (numbered as p. 16), J. T. and other Cheadles, acct with Josiah T. Cheadle, 1826 Oct 15. "Coarse" shoes for slaves, which were often made locally, offered by stores (example): Obadiah Jenkins acct with Thweatt & Miller, 1821 Aug and Oct, Thweatt & Miller v Jenkins, CirCt 1843 Sep. Tanyards: Bradshaw, *Prince Edward County*, pp. 352 and 773–74, n. 64. George King supplies leather "to shoe . . . slaves": Attorney General v Chambers's trustees, accts, 1802 Sep 1 (p. 12), CoCt 1821 Nov. "Shoemaker Ben" (probably Short) supplies half-boots to planter: Attorney General v Chambers's trustees,

accts, 1799 May 20 (p. 4), CoCt 1821 Nov. Zack Ellis as carpenter and shoemaker: Property tax enumeration book, lower district, 1816; FNLs, 1820–1825. See also Claiborne Evans, carpenter on FNLs, Green's district, 1809, 1811, 1820–1821, and shoemaker 1822; Dennis Evans, shoemaker in Property tax enumeration book, lower district, 1816, and miller, FNLs, 1821–1825; John Moss, farmer on FNLs, Green's district, 1809, 1818, 1824–1825, and shoemaker, FNLs, 1819, 1821–1823.

105. White shoemakers: Cheadle, as follows: inside of back cover, bottom, upside down, 1835, sixteen pairs from Sill Faris; B17th p., upside down, 1827 Nov, six pairs from Baldy Faris; B19th p., 1835 Apr 18, one pair from Sill; and also Daniel Glenn testimony, CW v Joshua, OB 23/17–21 (1832 Aug). White shoemakers, 1850: Ms. Census, 1850. Horse collars: The many examples include payment to "Kelsos Gim," Attorney General v Chambers's trustees, accts, 1811 Dec 28 (p. 39), CoCt 1821 Nov, and other instances in the Chambers accts; payment to "negro," 1828 Dec, in John Tuggle, guardian's acct for Jonathan Penick (1830) (microfilm), LVA; Cheadle, 33rd p. (numbered as p. 11), J. T. and other Cheadles, acct with Josiah T. Cheadle, payment to Mike, 1826 Mar.

106. Shoe prices: Among countless examples, see Attorney General v Chambers's trustees, accts, CoCt 1821 Nov, *passim*, especially 1806 Jan 20 (p. 21), 1807 Dec 28 (p. 27), 1808 Jan 30 (p. 27), 1808 Dec 22 (p. 29), 1809 Dec 23 (p. 32), 1810 Dec 31 (p. 36), 1812 Jan 2 (p. 39), and 1820 Aug (p. 58). Also, Booker Foster acct with John Foster, Foster v Clark, *passim*, CoCt 1836 Aug–Dec. Also, Cheadle, 4th p., payment to R. Bristenne [?], n.d. [1822–32]; B17th p., upside down, Baldy Faris transactions, 1827; 14th p., Enoch Brightwell transactions, 1834; B19th p. top, Sill Faris transactions, 1835.

See also Obadiah Jenkins acct with Thweatt & Miller, Thweatt & Miller v Jenkins, CirCt 1843 Sep, as follows: 1821 Aug ("strong shoes" for customer's son at $2.00, and "course [shoes] for negroe" at same price of $2.00, all store-bought), and 1821 Oct (coarse shoes, $2.00). Ben [Short?] sells shoes for $1.75 a pair (probably including materials): Attorney General v Chambers's trustees, accts, 1797 Dec 26 (p. 43), CoCt 1821 Nov. Same man sells half-boots for nearly $2.50: Attorney General v Chambers's trustees, accts 1799 May 20 (p. 4), CoCt 1821 Nov. Understanding account entries for shoes can be confusing until one realizes that most seeming discrepancies simply reflect either the inclusion or exclusion of materials from the amount charged; leather for one pair of shoes ran about $1.00.

107. $140 debt (£42 10s): Hart & Nimmo v Moss "Mol[atto]," CoCt 1810 Sep–Nov. Tax insolvency: Order to hire out Ferguson & Moss, filed CoCt 1815 Oct. Signing name: Research into Moss's life is complicated by the presence of a white John Moss, who was having financial difficulties of his own (Ms. Census, 1810, p. 252); one or more contemporaneous suits against a John Moss may involve the white man (Watkins v Moss, CoCt 1810 Mar; Black's admor v Moss, CoCt 1812 Mar; Hart & Nimmo v Moss, CoCt 1808 Nov, but filed 1809 Mar). The white John Moss died by 1811 (notation on capias, Berryman v Moss, CoCt 1811 Aug), and John Moss the free mulatto provided, on his bond in a case tried in 1831, his own signature, which helps the historian to identify the same signature elsewhere—CW v Moss, CoCt 1831 Aug. Assault suit: Moss v Lewis, CoCt 1816 Nov. Defendant of middling rank: Ms. Census, 1810 (Robert Lewis); Ms. Census, 1820 (Robert Lewis Jr.); Robert Lewis depo and Richardson-Lewis appraisal of McDearmon house, McDearmon v Jennings, CoCt 1816 Oct.

108. Charges brought: CW v Selby, Ferguson, Holt, Dungey, Bell, and Moss, District Court OB 1805–31, pp. 643 (1828 Apr), 652–654 (1828 Sep), and 667 (1829 Sep). Continuing cohabitation, and Moss's family: Ms. Census, 1830, sheet 99; cf. FNLs, Green's district, 1805–1807 and 1809 (on which Moss's black wife is mistakenly called Lucy, perhaps by confusion with "Lizzie"), 1818–1819, and 1821–1825, with Moss's first wife absent by 1821 and a child, likely that of Moss's daughter Susannah (Sooky),

appearing in the family that same year. All six defendants were charged with "fornication," even though at least two and probably all three couples were living as husband and wife; see discussion of the Forgason-Selby union earlier in this chapter.

109. Charge against Moss, jailing, bond, and trial: CW v Moss, OB 22/514 (1831 Aug), and CoCt 1831 Aug. Moss's accuser was Lorenzo D. Scott. Henry Thweatt, signatory to Moss's bond, a county justice: Summons to justices in CW v Moss.

110. Loan to Short with signature on bond: Ben Short B[on]d to A. Cocke, and Short acct with Cocke, CoCt 1820 Jan–Mar; Short may ultimately have used the $200 to set up a workshop on the land he would buy in 1811. Short's first appearance as a resident of the land he would later own comes on the FNL compiled some two years after he received the loan—FNL, Green's district, 1807. The acct between Ben Short and Anderson Cocke may contain one error of 15 shillings—about $2.60—in Cocke's favor, partly offset by various minor errors favoring Short. Any net discrepancy was so small in the context of such substantial sums dealt in over a period of ten years that it arouses little suspicion. Cocke never sued Short for his money even when the latter made no payments for two years, and the white man claimed the remainder of the sum due him only after Short died in 1818. Another account showing substantial purchases by Short from whites, with a significant amount repaid by the black man: Nash for Jones v Woodson shff admor of Short, CoCt 1823 Mar and OB20/467 (1823 Mar).

111. Buying (in this case, 115) barrel staves: Short's est acct with Williams, filed CoCt 1820 Jan–Mar. Shoemaking again: FNL, 1817.

112. White men's visit to Short, and official acceptance of "will": WB 5/354, Benjamin Short nuncupative will (1818). Status of white visitors: Property tax, 1818 (William S. Armstead, with four slaves twelve or older), 1819 (Sharp Spencer).

113. Short's property: WB 5/371, Benjamin Short inventory (1818/1819).

114. Sylvia Short remains on land; "her land": FNLs, 1819–1822.

115. Ben Short and Matt: Benjamin Short acct with Jos. Lewis' Matthew, CoCt 1820 Jan–Mar.

116. Foster's inheritance; "good Shoe maker": WB 4/126, Abraham Foster will (1808/1809). The estate sale of Foster's father brought in some $900, a substantial but not fabulous amount (WB 6/277–278, Abraham Foster est sale (1811/1826). Small amount of land: Land tax, 1807 (Abraham Foster owned 236 acres and some land in Kentucky, which he divided among three sons). The horse (and a couple of items of furniture, which Foster, however, had to compensate his sisters for): OB 18/110–111 (1814 Jun), Foster v Foster's exors. Foster's "shop": Writ to jailer, CW v Chumley, CoCt 1825 May. Foster's apprentices: Tamer Richardson, Indenture to John Foster, filed 1810; Samuel Homes, Indenture to John Foster, filed 1817; both in Apprentices, LVA.

117. Foster enters own name in florid script: John Foster and Edmunds processioners' return, filed CoCt 1843 Jun; Copy of poor levy &c, 1850 June 3, filed CoCt 1850 May–July; and as signature in dozens of other documents. Foster in militia: Bradshaw, *Prince Edward County*, pp. 230–32; Jack Vaughan letter, filed CoCt 1849 Jun–Aug. As coroner: Bradshaw, *Prince Edward County*, p. 208; Inquest on the dead body of Negro slave Patsy, March 17, 1861, filed CoCt 1861 Jan–Apr; and many other county documents. As deputy sheriff: Jack Vaughan letter; CW v Baldwin [or Bauldin], CoCt 1849 Sep–Nov. As clerk of overseers of poor: OP report, filed 1829 June; OP [report], filed 1861 May; and other overseers' reports between those two dates. Foster and sale of slave: Oliver v Ford, CoCt 1822 Jun–Jul, including copy of Mary Dupuy's will and of John Foster, letter to Samuel C. Anderson, December 21, 1819 (referring to the slave as "the property").

118. Hiring Tamer Richardson out to brother Booker: Booker Foster acct with John Foster, 1812–23, Foster v Clark, CoCt 1836 Aug–Dec. Richardson as adult shoemaker: FNLs, 1821–1825. Homes as adult shoemaker with same residence as Richardson:

FNLs, 1821–1823. Polly Patterson's suit: Patterson v Weaver, CoCt 1825 Mar, OB 20/470 (1823 Mar), and OB 21/176 (1825 Mar). Foster belonged to Sharon Baptist Church, as did two or three members of the free black Homes clan that had supplied him with at least one of his apprentices—Sharon Baptist Church minute book, 1827–65, pp. 114–15, LVA 20803 (Foster's membership); List of colored members, including Archer Homes, 1842 Jul, a Homes man with first name blank, 1845 Apr (p. 9), and Sarah Dupuy, who, judging by her surname, may have been related to the Homeses, 1833 Jan (p. 12).

119. Jackson's origins: B. Jackson [registration], filed CoCt 1835 Sep–Oct. Jackson's purchase of lots: DB 20/518–519, Randolph to Jackson (1832), and 21/298–299, Venable's commissioners to Jackson (1832/1835); Plat and report, Watkins v Venable's heirs, CoCt 1835 Jun–Jul. Tuggles, Penicks: Judith, Lavalette, Josiah, & Frances Penick with Amplias Tuggle, trustee, 1837 May 3, and voucher no. 58, Tuggle v Penick, CirCt 1840 Apr.

120. Smith's purchase of a "spott," and its valuation: DB 12/371, Allen to Smith (1802/1803); Land tax, Green's district, 1804. Smith's sale of land: DB 17/276–277, Smith to Love (1821). Tract's location, and Smith's move: Land tax, Green's district, 1814. Twelve-dollar payment to Smith from Prince Edward County after 1830: John P. Mettauer acct with Thweatt & Miller, 1832 Jan 3, Mettauer v Thweatt & Miller, CirCt 1846 Jun.

121. Apprentice blacksmiths: Indentures, Peter Ferguson [sic] to Charles Fore, 1808; Billey Cousins to Abner Willard, filed 1812 (see also FNLs, 1821–1823); Billy Evans to Thomas Worsham, 1822; John Homes to Henry Y. Jenkins, filed 1835 (see also OB 23/353 [1835 Aug]); all indentures in Apprentices, LVA. Peter Forgason's career path later in life is unclear. The figure of five apprentices also includes the boy whom the overseers of the poor assigned to a black master in 1851, and who himself presumably was black—Cousins report of OP, filed CoCt 1851 Dec–1852 Feb; cf. OB 26/155 (1847 Feb) and 26/456 (1851 Oct). John Dungey smithing: FNL, 1820. Dungeys' son-in-law: James Fears, FNLs, 1817, 1820, 1823 ("forging"), 1824. Fears's marriage to John Dungey's sister: Rebecca H. Dungee [sic] and James Fears, marriage bond, 1822. At least a dozen free black smiths: Richard A. Gault [?], letter to attorney, CW v Redd and Scott, CoCt 1849 Nov (Henry Mettauer); Register of Doctor Sawney, CoCt 1839 Mar–Apr; Alexander Cousins, who took on the black apprentice, as above; Charles Henry Diuguid, discussed below; FNLs, 1862–1864 (John Johnson); FNL, 1863 (Charles Smith); and the five apprentices. See also one Charles, employed by a white smith, in Report of the commissioners to build small pox hospital, CoCt 1837 Jan–Mar.

122. Diuguid: Presentments, CirCt 1844 Apr; CW v Diuguid, CirCt 1846 Sep; and CW v Diuguid (so styled, but actually CW v Sheriff of Appomattox), CirCt 1847 Apr. Diuguid's "shop" seems to have been located in the portion of Prince Edward that became part of Appomattox County in 1845—see capias to sheriff of the newly established Appomattox County, 1845 Oct 9, in CW v Diuguid, as above.

123. Plantation smithy (Samuel V. Allen's place) and overseer: Joseph H. Borum depo, Allen v Thurstons admor, CoCt 1823 Dec–1824 Mar. Purnall's shop: Purnall v Winn, CoCt 1824 Sep–Nov. Purnall's blacksmiths: WB 6/174–177, John Purnall will (1824/1825). Tuggle and blacksmith: Venable v Tuggle (2 suits), CirCt 1845 Apr.

124. Cheadle's blacksmiths: Cheadle, 1st p., H. Y. Jenkins acct, 1822; 32nd p. (numbered as p. 10), J. T. and other Cheadles, acct with Josiah T. Cheadle, payment to H. Y. Jenkins, 1825 Sep 9, for 1822 and 1823; B15th p. top, accts with Jones P. Simmons, 1824; Daniel Y. Jenkins, details later in this note; 8th p. middle, acct with Charles McKinney, 1832; 11th p., Robert Fuqua acct, 1832; B21st p., Robert Fuqua acct, 1833; 12th p. middle, Tom Prince acct, 1833; B23rd p., B24th p., and B25th p. top, Robert Fuqua acct, 1835. Also, Henry Y. Jenkins v Cheadle, CoCt 1825 Oct. Daniel Jenkins and

Cheadle: Cheadle, B18th p., upside down, Agreement with Daniel Y. Jenkins, 1828. D. Jenkins hauling, and his insolvency: Faris v Jenkins, CoCt 1831 Jul.

125.   Relationship and inheritance of Jenkinses: Report of Watkins and report on widow's dower, McDearmon v Jenkins, and Answer of Henry Y. Jenkins, Thweatt & Miller v Jenkins, both in CirCt 1843 Sep; WB 6/108, Obadiah Jenkins est acct (1824) (with cash to Daniel Jenkins, 1823 Jun 9). H. Jenkins's income (example): Jenkins v Womack, CoCt 1831 Jul. H. Jenkins's prowess and prominence: Rip (pseudonym), "Farmville Then and Now," *Farmville Herald*, September 14, 1906, p. 3; Bradshaw, *Prince Edward County*, pp. 266 and 650–51. John Homes bound to Jenkins: OB 23/353 (1835 Aug).

126.   "Best . . . labourer": Bondurant acct with Featherston, draft of same (1840, in which the misspelled pronouns apparently identify the slave's sex), and Declaration (whence the quoted phrase), all in Featherston v Bondurant, CoCt 1843 May. Cooking and field labor: Ann Stiff depo, Davis v Bradley, CirCt 1839 Sep.

127.   Explicit evidence of dividing time between house and field: FNL, lower district, 1801. Free black farm women on whites' land: FNLs, 1821 and other years.

128.   Housekeeping versus specialized crafts: FNLs, lower district, 1801–1807; Gerald Tate Gilliam, "Occupations of Free Blacks," *Southsider*, 5, no. 1 (Winter 1986), 15. The annual lists of free blacks, especially before and including 1825, offer only a rough idea of the work people actually did. They do not usually show people plying more than one trade at a time, though they do at least reveal considerable shifting back and forth between occupations from year to year. The annual record categorizes many black Israelites, even the versatile Whites, simply as farmers. The revenue commissioners also noted a single occupation, or perhaps two, for each household without specifying which individuals did what. Even so, the annual lists do make clear that farming and "house work" were the most common remunerative pursuits of black Israelite women.

Revenue commissioner Thomas Green used the term "House keepers" once in nine years, applying it to an unspecified number of the women in Sam White's household on his list of 1818. That it appears, oddly, as an annotation outside the column where occupations were recorded makes one wonder whether even these women were "housekeeping" for white women; one suspects they were doing such work only for their own family. Green's lack of interest in the specifics of women's work was remedied only marginally by his successor in the 1820s.

129.   The second part of the designation "Farming &c." may indicate that the many women and girls in Teny Carter's household, too, earned some money by practicing traditionally female crafts.

130.   "House work" after 1821: Dick White household, FNL, 1823. Two of the households not listed as doing "house work" in 1821 were headed by women—Teny Carter and Rose Johnston—and the others by men with living wives; in three families, a daughter sixteen or older was also present. Seven of the eleven households were recorded as doing farming "&c."; but even if some of those et ceteras encompassed "house work," the bulk of the womanpower that helped Israelite families earn a living apparently went into agricultural pursuits.

131.   Rose Johnston's two sons established families on their parents' land during the 1810s; so did one son each of John Brown and Isham Patterson. Patterson's daughter and a daughter of Sam White did the same with their respective husbands. Yet the revenue commissioner never recorded White's married daughter or the wife of either Johnston as engaging in "house work" up through 1825, and the households of the younger Brown and of the Patterson son and daughter were so listed only once. (Jacob Johnston, George Johnston, and Syphax Brown II appear with their wives in the FNLs from 1817 on; Edmund and Hannah Patterson Clark first appear in 1819; George Patterson's household in 1820; Peter and Jane White Valentine in 1822.)

132.   Dungeys and Forgasons: FNLs, 1817–1825 (one and three years of "house work,"

respectively). Black women with small plots: FNLs, as follows: Milly Homes doing "house work," 1821–1822, but farming, 1823–1825; Sylvia Short doing "house work," 1819–1823 (Susannah Short on Sylvia's land in 1823), but Susannah farming, 1824–1825; Patty Bartlett doing "house work," 1821–1822, but farming "&c.," 1823, and simply farming, 1824–1825; see also Lucy Homes and her family of mostly females farming and residing on the five acres bought by Nathan Homes, Lucy's son, 1824–1825. Even these three households were listed as farming by 1823–24, though that designation may have included farm work done for whites; Short and Bartlett, after all, held only one acre each.

133. Records of neighboring plantations after the days of Hercules White Sr. show few transactions with people of Israel Hill; even white neighbors' estate sales seem typically to have drawn few if any Israelites. Why that should have been the case is unclear, given that other kinds of transactions did take place. (See, e.g., Penick's guardian v Penick, CirCt 1840 Apr.)

134. "House work" in 1821: FNL, 1821.

135. Betsy Lyle: Lyle testimony, CW v George, CoCt 1854 Feb.

136. Weaving and sewing by slaves (example): Attorney General v Chambers's trustees, accts, 1816 Dec (p. 52), $2 to T. T. Tuggle, CoCt 1821 Nov. "Doing sewing," "superintended": Trent E. Harrison depo, Doswell v Doswell, CirCt 1845 Sep. Bequest to Orange Johnston: WB 5/369, Rachel Pearce will (1818/1819).

137. Expected to "labour": See Bill, Holeman v Holeman, CoCt 1825 Oct. Miss Kitty: Gilliam v Martin, CirCt 1852 Aug; quotation from Richard Carter depo.

138. White women sewing with own hands: See, e.g., Nancy E. Vernon depo, I'Anson v Vernon's admor, CirCt 1848 Sep; financial accounts from Prince Edward from the first half of the nineteenth century are replete with payments to white individuals for work at traditional women's crafts. Seamstress wife of Justice George W. Clibourne: R. D. Noell depo, Mettauer v Clibourne, CirCt 1852 Aug. Clibourne's status: Bradshaw, *Prince Edward County*, pp. 210, 215, and 680; note by Asa D. Dickinson, n.d., and Dickinson's report, 1848 Jul 29, Borum v Ellington's exor, CirCt 1853 Aug. "Mrs. Young" paid by Cheadle: Cheadle, 33rd p. (numbered as p. 11), J. T. and other Cheadles, acct with Josiah T. Cheadle, 1825 Dec. A legacy from a minister to his esteemed live-in weaver: WB 4/91, Archibald McRobert will (1807).

139. Abusive husband, industrious wife: Depos of Sarah J. Blankenship, Dr. William A. Fuqua, and William Gaines Miller, in Hurt v Hurt, CirCt 1846 Sep.

140. Examples of white "grannies" attending slaves: Attorney General v Chambers's trustees, accts, 1801 Jan 6 (p. 9) and 1810 Jan 30 (p. 33), CoCt 1821 Nov, in which the first midwife mentioned is probably, and the second certainly, white. Sometimes a "granny fee" was paid for nursing someone who was not pregnant; practical nursing might even be done by a black or white male.

141. White midwives earning $2 from Chambers: Attorney General v Chambers's trustees, accts, CoCt 1821 Nov, 1801 Jan 6 (p. 9), to Betty Graves, and 1806 Mar 8 (p. 22), to Mary Johnson; receipt for $2 paid to Nancy Davis, 1836, in small bundle of vouchers (Samuel Hurt acct on top), Attorney General vs Chambers &c, CirCt 1842 Sep. Granny Patty: Attorney General v Chambers's trustees, CoCt 1821 Nov, accts, 1819 Jan (p. 55), and 1819 Dec (p. 56) (but Patty received only $2 in 1817 May [p. 53] in the same acct; her free status is indicated at 1815 Jan [p. 49]). "Negro Hannah," Betsy Hill, and white midwife Elizabeth Foster: Report of the proceedings of board of O[verseers of the] Poor of Prince Edward Co., 1854 Apr 10; Proceedings of the OP of Prince Edward Co. to May Ct 1857. Milly Homes: Asa Dupuy, admor of Thomas Walton, acct current settled by commissioners 1829 Apr 16, entry of 1827 Apr 6, filed CoCt 1831 May. The amount a midwife received depended partly on the difficulty of the particular task she performed. One woman got $3 for delivering twins; another received the higher payment when she had to attend a pregnant woman twice, the

lower when only one visit was required. Twins: Report, 1815 Oct, Vaughan and wife v Ligon, CoCt 1823 Jun–Jul. Two visits: Acct of Polly S. Fore, vouchers for acct, bundle no. 4, Penick's guardian v Penick, CirCt 1840 Apr.

142. Three dollars for slave deliveries: Ebenezer McRobert est acct with Samuel Carter, 1817 Apr and 1822 Dec, Smith and wife v McRobert, CoCt 1825 Jun, and many other sources. Family's payments for attendance to own mother and to slaves: Orphans of Elizabeth Holt, guardian's acct with John McGehee, entries for 1822–23, Rogers v Clemmons, CoCt 1841 Nov–Dec. Births to paupers: Report of the proceedings of board of O[verseers of the] Poor of Prince Edward Co., 1854 Apr 10; Proceedings of board of OP of Prince Edward Co., 1856 Apr 14; Proceedings of the OP of Prince Edward Co. returned to May Ct 1857, CoCt 1857 May; Proceedings of the Board of OP of Prince Edward Co., 1858 Apr, CoCt 1858 May.

143. Examples of enslaved midwives: Elizabeth C. Fowlkes guardian's acct with Paschal Fowlkes, 1824 July, CoCt 1841 Nov–Dec; Asa Dupuy, admor of Thomas Walton, acct current settled by commissioners, 1828 May 26, filed CoCt 1831 May. Payments to "Negro Hannah" in the 1850s (see note 141) suggest that some bondwomen continued to practice midwifery throughout the period before the Civil War. Status and pay: See, e.g., Orphans of Elizabeth Holt, guardian's acct with John McGehee, payments to K. Rice in 1822–23 and 1829, Rogers v Clemmons, CoCt 1841 Nov–Dec; see also citations in discussion of slave, free black, and white midwives in the paragraphs below. For a series of payments that seem to illustrate both the general trend and the existence of exceptions to it, see Orphans of Thomas D. Ligon, guardian's acct with Henry N. Watkins, 1813 Nov (where a $4 fee may perhaps cover two deliveries), 1815 Oct, 1817 Jan, and 1821 Dec, filed CoCt 1825 Jul.

144. King: Caleb Baker est acct with Branch Worsham, 1824 Nov, Hendrick v Jones, filed CoCt 1825 Jun–Jul; Martin Saylor est acct with James D. Wood exor, *passim,* filed CirCt 1833 Apr/Sep; J. Price est acct with William Price exor, vouchers, 1832, receipt no. 75, in Ingram v Price, CirCt 1839 Sep; Leonard W. Anderson est acct with Hugh F. Morton, 1837 Jan, Anderson v Morton, filed CoCt 1837 Jul. Elizabeth Hargrove: J. Price est acct with William Price, vouchers, receipt nos. 24, 31, and 46½. Rachel Cole: William Sublett, letter to John Lackland, February 5, 1846, Sublett v Lackland, CirCt 1851 Sep.

145. Betty Brown: Attorney General v Chambers's trustees, accts, 1802 Sep 14 (p. 12) and 1803 Jan 17 (p. 14), CoCt 1821 Nov; FNL, Green's district, 1811. Morton in Farmville: FNLs, 1817–1823; Mittimus, CW v Stonum, CoCt 1820 Nov. Essex White: FNL, 1817. The midwife called "Granny Patty" (and ultimately "old Patty") in Chambers's guardians' accts is identified as Patty Morton in at least two places in a subsequent report drawn up in 1826—Document A, 1829 Apr 4 (p. 42), Chambers's committee v Madison's exor, CirCt 1842 Apr; and Redford's acct of 1826 Jun 3, payments of 1822 Dec and 1823 Dec to "Patty Morton, Midwife," Attorney General v Chambers &c, CirCt 1842 Sep.

146. "Free Liddy": Attorney General v Chambers's trustees, accts, CoCt 1821 Nov, 1802 Sep 14 (p. 12), 1804 Feb 27 (p. 16), and 1808 Aug 1 (p. 28; the $7). Milly Homes: FNL, lower district, 1801; notes on WB 7/36ff., Thomas Walton est, 1822 Mar 25, in "Slavery," Eggleston papers, section 30, Mss1 Egg3966, VHS. Betsy Hill: Reports of OP for 1854 and 1857, as in note 141; FNL, 1857. Booker Hill and well: Acct, Prince Edward County with Booker Hill, filed CoCt 1856 Jul–Aug.

147. Israel Hill neighbors: Penick's guardian v Penick, CirCt 1840 Apr, as follows: Vouchers filed with report of commissioner Watkins, 1826 Jul, and also Vouchers for acct no. 5, n.d. and 1829 Feb (Nancy Tuggle, John Tuggle's mother per WB 8/229, Nancy Tuggle will [1839/1840]); Josiah Penick est acct with Nathaniel Penick and John Tuggle, 1820, payments to Charles Fore and "Mrs. Fore," and also Vouchers for acct no. 4, Polly S. Fore midwife's acct, as well as Vouchers filed with report of Watkins, "say

1827," payment to Polly "Ford" (i.e., Fore); Vouchers for acct no. 2, Mary S. Fore mid-wife's fees, c. 1822 (Stephen Fore's wife). Another payment to "Mrs. Fore": Alexander Legrand est acct with Joseph Binford, 1833 Dec 15, Legrand v Legrand's admor, CoCt 1837 Jul. Mary S. Fore: Josiah Chambers est acct with B. F. Wilson, doctor visits, 1832–34, Mrs. Fore midwife's acct, in Attorney General v Chambers's trustees, receipts to Chambers's trustee ... 1833 ... 1834 & 1835 (compared), CirCt 1842 Sep. One document may even hint at collaboration between a white and a black practitioner—Attorney General v Chambers's trustees, CoCt 1821 Nov, accts, 1806 Mar 8 (p. 22), an ambiguous entry involving Mary Johnson and (probably free "granny") Lydda/Liddy.

148. Chambers inquest: Report of Edward Redford under order of 1821 Dec 13, pleadings and exhibits, Attorney General v Chambers &c, CirCt 1842 Sep. "Declined": Report of trustee [Edward Redford], 1822 May 21, Attorney General v Chambers &c.

149. Physician-midwife cooperation: Josiah Chambers est acct with B. F. Wilson, doctor visits, 1832–34, in which a charge from Mary Fore for serving as midwife to a slave is entered, in Attorney General v Chambers's trustees, receipts to Chambers's trustee ... 1833 ... 1834 & 1835 (compared), CirCt 1842 Sep. Woodson impugns Durphey's competence: Durphey v Gilliam, especially William Gilliam's acct with E. M. W. Durphey, Betsy Woodson depo, and Edward Durphey, letter to Abraham Venable, November 16, 1822, CoCt 1822 Nov. Durphey eventually became the doctor for the county poorhouse, where his work may have come under less incisive scrutiny. The federal census manuscripts between 1820 and 1840 turn up only one Elizabeth (Betsy, the midwife?) Woodson, who was white and headed a household that owned twenty-five slaves in 1840.

150. Wagon drawn by team of oxen: Acct, [County with] William Routon, filed CoCt 1825 Jun–Jul. Yokes of steers: Delivery bond, Morton v Seay, filed CoCt 1828 Nov–Dec.

151. Rolling hogsheads: See, e.g., Bruce, *New Man*, p. 46; cf. Rosa Faulkner Yancey, *Lynchburg and Its Neighbors* (Richmond: J. W. Fergusson & Sons, 1935), p. 20; Camille Wells, personal communication. For slaves rolling hogsheads in Prince Edward, see Copy of proceedings, Attorney General v Chambers's trustees, Josiah Chambers acct with Watson, Allen & Green, his committee, 1809 Apr 26 (p. 30) and 1811 Mar 9 (p. 36), CoCt 1821 Nov; and John Purnall's statement in CW v Surveyor of road from Bush River to county line, CoCt 1816 Aug. (On each of the occasions mentioned in the Chambers account, a slave was awarded a quart of brandy for rolling tobacco.) A planter running wagons: Anthony Brooks, David M. Doswell, and David Ellington depos, Doswell v Doswell, CirCt 1845 Sep. Example of hauling oats (to Buckingham Court House): Accts, 1838–41, Martin v Wright's admor, CoCt 1845 May. "Running waggons": Bill, Wright v Willis's admor, CirCt 1845 Mar. Payments by merchants/wagon runners: Accts (including Willis & Wright to free black shoe-maker Booker Jackson, 1843), in Wright v Willis's admor.

152. Wheat to Farmville: David Wammack [sic], acct with T. J. and Robert Paulett, 1842, Womack v Paulett, CirCt 1855 Aug. Tobacco: *Ibid.;* Voucher no. 24, David Anderson, 1828 May, Price v Woodson, admor of Price, CirCt 1841 Apr. Same producer alternately paying to boat and to haul tobacco hogsheads to Farmville: Voucher nos. 22 and 24 (1828 May), both in Price v Woodson. Wagoning wheat to market: David M. Doswell depo, Doswell v Doswell, CirCt 1845 Sep. Cheadle wagoning: Cheadle, B27th p., McKinney & Walker acct and Moseley, Spence & Co. accts, both 1839 Apr; see also Cheadle, same p., 1843 Jan. Places on the James to which wagons from Prince Edward carried produce included Bent Creek and even Lynchburg to the west, and Cartersville at the far northern end of Cumberland County. Wheat and tobacco to a James River "place of deposit" (Bent Creek): Road report, McDearmon, filed CoCt 1823 Dec–1824 Mar. Cartersville: Nathan Dupriest, account with Peter Johnston,

Dupriest v Johnston, CoCt 1809 May. Lynchburg: David F. Womack, acct with Henry Thweatt, 1837 Jun and 1839 Jul, Thweatt v Womack, CirCt 1844 Apr; Accts, 1838–41, Martin v Wright's admor, CoCt 1845 May.

153. Wagoning tobacco to Richmond: WB 4/269, Nathaniel Lancaster est acct with John Lancaster (1810), 1806 Aug (two hogsheads wagoned from Ca Ira to Richmond—even though Ca Ira was a port on the Willis River, a navigable tributary of the James, which flows through Richmond); David Ellington depo, Doswell v Doswell, CirCt 1845 Sep; David Wammack to T. J. and Robert Paulett, 1842, Womack v Paulett, CirCt 1855 Aug. Flour: WB 4/269, Nathaniel Lancaster est acct. Charles Fore: Josiah Penick est to Nathaniel Penick and John Tuggle exors, 1820, and vouchers, 1820, 1821, 1822, all in Penick's guardian v Penick, CirCt 1840 Apr; Fore shipped to Manchester, a city immediately across the James from Richmond.

154. Products from Richmond: Acct, Stokes v Smith's estate, filed CoCt 1823 Nov–1824 Mar; Coleman Jeffress depo, Depriest v Smith, CoCt 1819 Aug; Obadiah Jenkins acct with Thweatt & Miller, 1820 Oct, Thweatt & Miller v Jenkins, CirCt 1843 Sep.

155. Six-horse covered wagons; duties and image of slave wagoners: Bruce, *New Man,* pp. 43–45. Bruce remarked on the "peculiar and characteristic dress" of the black wagoners, but unfortunately did not describe it. Possibility that slave wagoners collected money: See David M. Doswell depo, Doswell v Doswell, CirCt 1845 Sep—in which, however, the race and status of the wagoners is not stated. Another ironic responsibility did fall occasionally to the proprietor who employed an enslaved wagoner: if a dispute arose with a client, the wagon owner was on his own, since his slave teamster was legally barred from testifying on his behalf—see Winn v Pearson, CoCt 1831 Sep–Oct.

156. Duration of round trip: Bruce, *New Man,* p. 45 (thirty, sixty, or even ninety days); but see James Madison's note on list of witnesses, warrant for court, 1828 Dec 26, CW v Ellick, CoCt 1829 Jan (one week).

157. Two-horse rig: David M. Doswell depo, Doswell v Doswell, CirCt 1845 Sep. White carter: Poorhouse account with steward, credit, 1830 Dec, James Wilson carting, in OP report filed 1830 Jun 21. White wagoners: See Bill, Womack v Paulett, CirCt 1855 Aug; Bill of work and materials, Farmville road & bridge papers, filed CoCt 1852 Nov–1853 Jan (though some of these wagons may have been driven by black men for whites); and the following documents, cited in detail in several later notes: Fuqua v Trent, Depriest v Smith, Grand jury presentment of David Coleman, CW v Joseph Davis, and CW v Samuel Davis. Wagoning for scattered periods: See especially Paulin Anderson depo, Depriest v Smith, CoCt 1819 Aug; and the discussion and notes on free black wagoners that follow.

158. Valentine: Index to marriage bonds, 1820; FNLs, 1823 and 1825. Peter Forgason: FNL, 1819. Charles Forgason: Cheadle, 41st p. (numbered as p. 19), J. T. and other Cheadles, acct with J. T. Cheadle, 1829 Aug 17 and Sep 21.

159. Some wagoners' wide latitude: Answer (a white wagoner on commission, who did not collect payments himself) and Gabriel Fuqua depo, both in Fuqua v Trent, CoCt 1816 Jul; Unlabeled agreement between Ellington and Dupriest, 1817 ($15 per month plus commission; payments from clients; wagoner using proceeds), affi and depo of Pleasant Ellington, and Paulin Anderson depo (provisions from owner; "partner"), all in Depriest v Smith, CoCt 1819 Aug. On the other hand, a white wagoner found himself presented by the grand jury in 1821 "for working the waggon, while in his employ, of Wm. J. Price"—OB 20/1 (1821 Mar).

160. Repairs, care of horses, "loading," illiteracy: Answer and Rebecca Grizzle depo in Fuqua v Trent, as in note 159. "Earn't a good deal": Paulin Anderson depo, Depriest v Smith, as in note 159.

161. Planter on wagoners: N. C. Read, letter from Clarksville to N. E. Venable, September

8, 1838, Read v Venable, CirCt 1846 Jun. N. C. Read was a kinsman and business associate of Clement C. Read, whose close relationships with various Israelites and other free blacks are discussed later in this chapter.

162. White wagoner and black boy: Madison's note on list of witnesses, CW v Ellick, CoCt 1829 Jan.

163. Wagoners fight at Bartlett's: CW v Davis, especially clerk's notes on testimony, CoCt 1846 Nov. Bartlett boating: FNLs, 1821–1825. Totty and Whites: Totty acct with Perkinson and Co., 1832 Nov 12, in Perkinson v Totty, CoCt 1838 Aug–Oct; Spa to Totty, Bailey for Anderson v White, CoCt 1853 Jul. Totty and slaves: CW v Totty (five counts), OB 22/291–292 and 360–361 (1830 May and Aug); CW v Totty (receiving bag of corn from slave), CoCt 1837 Mar–Apr.

164. Patteson as merchant: OB 17/546 (1813 Jun), peddler's license of Alexander and Lilborne Patteson. Tavern owner: Patteson, Alexander, receipts for ordinary license, filed CoCt 1823 May and 1830 Jun–Jul; see also Thomas A. Legrand's road order, CoCt 1821 May; the surname was frequently spelled Patterson. Stage line: Alexander Patteson est acct with Willis P. Bocock, Lewis v Patteson, CoCt 1839 Jun–Jul; Bradshaw, *Prince Edward County*, pp. 308–09 and 310. "Wagoner for the stage": Alexander Patteson est acct with Bocock, 1839 Feb 20. Patteson's manumissions: WB 7/436, Alexander Patteson will (1836); Charles' mo[tion to remain in county], filed CoCt 1838 Jan; OB 24/130 (1838 Feb; unanimous approval of Charles's application to remain). Three years after Patteson's death, his executor still showed every intention of carrying out the subsequent emancipation of the remaining slaves—Note on Statement showing the entire amount for equal distribution, Lewis v Patteson.

165. John Cluff as wagoner: FNL, 1821. Cluff's land in Hanover: Land tax, Hanover County, 1818–25, on which the surname is spelled Clough; whether the only Hancock listed there—Joseph, with 275 acres—was the husband of either Mary or Rebecca, the records do not reveal. Six horses: Delinquents, property tax for 1821, lower district, filed CoCt 1822 Jun–Jul. Cluff-Hancock land transactions: DB 17/331, Keeling to Cluff (1821) (a deed with obvious errors in the text); DB 17/332–333, Cluff to Keeling, DoT (1821); DB 17/378–380, Cluff to Hancock, DoT (1821); DB 18/176–177, Cluff to Rebecca Hancock (1823—listing both Cluff and the Hancocks as residents of Hanover); Land tax rolls, 1822–23, entries for Patrick H. Anderson, and 1824, entry for Mary Hancock; see also OB 20/161 (1821 Oct) for a transaction involving furniture. Rebecca disposed of the tract four years after Cluff signed it over to her—DB 19/599–600, Hancock to Ellington (1827). Cluff residing there: FNL, 1821. Hancocks likely white: Marriage bond of one Rebecca Ann Hancock, 1842 Apr 25, where husband and surety are almost certainly white. Perhaps Mary Hancock had needed an unrelated man's help to secure real estate for her daughter that would not be subject to the control of Mary's husband. My wife, Naama Zahavi-Ely, played an important role in interpreting this train of events.

166. Terms of Hill's land purchase: DB 17/327–329, Hill to Keeling, DoT (1821); Land tax rolls, 1821, Moses Hill, new entry, and 1822ff., entry for Daniel Hamblen. Hill's land abutting Cluff's: Land tax rolls, 1822, entry for Patrick H. Anderson. Cheap land: Compare, e.g., DB 17/23, Keeling to Jackson (1819), a contemporaneous sale by Mary Keeling at a high enough price per acre to make clear that the terms given Moses Hill were attractive, even if one supposes that the land he bought was inferior, and that the amount of his deed of trust to Keeling represented less than the full price of the tract (assumptions for which there is no evidence). Thirteen years later, Hill—having moved away—conveyed the land back to the Keelings, who had apparently never even pressed Hill to pay the full purchase price for the tract—DB 21/119–120, Hill to Keeling (1833); see also DB 21/119 (1833), Keeling to Wootton.

167. Deneufville as coach driver: FNL, 1823. Deneufville's background: John Deneufville's certf of register, 1819, filed CoCt 1819 Sep–Oct; also John Deneufville certf of free-

dom, 1835, filed CoCt 1835 Nov–Dec (both of which identify him as a "bright mulatto" bearing the same surname as his liberator). Hostler: FNLs, 1821–1822, 1824; his designation as farming on the 1825 list, and that of several others near him on the list, is apparently a careless mistake on the part of the revenue commissioner. Lot purchase: DB 21/19, Venable's commissioners to Deneufville (1832/1833). Prosperous buyers: Plat for Abraham B. Venable est, Watkins v Venable's heirs, CoCt 1835 Jun–Jul, with lots bought by Henry Y. Jenkins, John Rice, Colonel James Madison, and Booker Jackson. Improvements to Deneufville's lot: Land tax rolls, John Deneufville, 1833 new entry, 1836 town lots, 1840 transfer from Deneufville to Read; WB 8/179–180, John Deneufville appraisal (1839). Purchase of slave: OB 21/103 (1824 Nov), deed recorded, Venable to Deneufville; see also Property tax 1835 (with one slave), 1836 (with no slave—owing to manumission of his wife?), and 1837 (ambiguous owing to a tear in the document, but may indicate ownership of one slave).

168. Read's career: Bradshaw, *Prince Edward County*, pp. 8, 20, 28, 51, 682 (founding family); 210, 211, 679, 680 (county court justice); 297, 694 (Farmville trustee); 322–23 (bank director); 168 (founding school trustee); 391 (insurance company director); 301, 518, 526–27 (tobacco manufacturer); also, Lockett v Appomattox Co. (writ of ad quod damnum), CoCt 1841 Aug (Appomattox Company). By 1850, Read would own, in addition to his commercial interests, 750 improved acres of farmland worth $13,000— Ms. Census, 1850, schedule 4, Productions of agriculture, pp. 519–20.

169. Read, White, and Gibbs: Voucher beginning "Isaac Gibbs pd Phill White," Henry M. Spencer statement, Read's bail bond for Gibbs, and account on back of Gibbs's bond to White, all in White v Gibbs, CoCt 1833 May. Read's involvement with Isaac Gibbs would continue at least into the 1840s—Warrants in CW v Johns[t]on, CoCt 1845 Jan. Witness to will: WB 9/374, Anthony White will (1848 with codicil 1850/1850).

170. Will: WB 8/148, John Deneufville will (1839). Lot in Read's hands: DB 26/615, Read to Flournoy (1854). The record does not tell what Read's dealings with Deneufville's survivors may have been. If the deed just cited is to be taken literally, Read sold the former Deneufville lot in 1854 for only $5, which may mean it was long vacant and neglected.

171. Legacy: WB 8/179–180, John Deneufville appraisal (1839).

172. Curdsville and Willis River: See Cheadle 38th–40th pp. (numbered as pp. 16–18), J. T. and other Cheadles, acct with Josiah Cheadle, various entries, 1824–26, including 1828 Jan. Ca Ira: See, e.g., WB 4/269, Nathaniel Lancaster est acct with John Lancaster (1810), 1805 Aug and 1806 Aug; Edwin Land depo, Land v Thornton, CoCt 1824 May. Willis River navigation: William E. Trout III, *The American Canal Guide: A Bicentennial Inventory of America's Historic Canal Resources,* part 5 (Freemansburg, PA: American Canal Society, 1992), p. 25.

173. Local wheat and tobacco to Farmville: Bill and answer in Taggart v Morton, CoCt 1811 Oct; Voucher no. 22, Price v Woodson, admor of Price, CirCt 1841 Apr. On Shenandoah River boats, called gundalows, see Seth C. Bruggeman, "The Shenandoah River Gundalow and the Politics of Material Reuse" (M.A. thesis, College of William and Mary, 1999), especially pp. 13–14.

174. River improvements: Bradshaw, *Prince Edward County*, p. 93 (1760s); Rip Van Winkle (pseudonym), "Farmville Then and Now," *Farmville Herald*, August 31, 1906, p. 3; Trout, *American Canal Guide*, p. 28; William E. Trout III, "A Tour Guide to Petersburg's Canal," in Trout, ed., with R. Dulaney Ward Jr., *Appomattox River Seay Stories: Reminiscences of James Washington Seay, The Last of the Appomattox River Batteaumen* (Petersburg, VA: Historic Petersburg Foundation and Virginia Canals and Navigations Society, 1992, cited hereafter as *Seay Stories*), pp. 85–87; Gerald T. Gilliam, "The Upper Appomattox Company," *Southsider*, 6, no. 2 (Spring 1987), 38–41; Appomattox Company v Southall and Lockett (regarding compensation), filed CoCt 1836 Jun–Jul; Copy of record, Goodman v Goodman, CirCt 1843 Apr; Copy of inquest, Appomattox Company and Ligon, in Perkinson v Appomattox Company, CoCt 1841 Jul–Aug.

A mistaken contemporaneous reference to Farmville as supposed "head of batteaux navigation": Joseph Martin, *A New and Comprehensive Gazetteer of Virginia and the District of Columbia* (Charlottesville: Joseph Martin, 1836), p. 266.

175. Canals at Petersburg: Trout, *American Canal Guide*, p. 28; Trout, ed., *Seay Stories, passim.* Basin's elevation; runoff: Trout, ed., *Seay Stories*, p. 22; Bradshaw, *Prince Edward County*, p. 293. Drayage to Richmond: See Acct no. 96, 1833, and voucher no. 17, Madison to Woodson, 1827 Oct, both in J. Price est acct with William Price, Ingram v Price, CirCt 1839 Sep.

176. Dimensions of batteau: Gary Dalton, "River Is Focal Point of a Happy Life," in Trout, ed., *Seay Stories*, and pp. 11 and 15 in *ibid.* James River batteaux, which may have been slightly smaller on average than Appomattox batteaux, were about two feet deep—Yancey, *Lynchburg and Its Neighbors*, p. 21, quoting "Dr. [George W.] Bagby." Capacity of batteau: Rip Van Winkle, "Farmville Then and Now," *Farmville Herald*, August 31, 1906; Bradshaw, *Prince Edward County*, pp. 292 and 294; Bill, Read, Womack & Co. v Daniel, CirCt 1837 Sep; Martin, *Gazetteer of Virginia*, p. 268; Gilliam, "Upper Appomattox Company," 42 (referring to a period of "years" ending in the early 1880s). Continued importance of flour: See Bill, Watt v Brown, CoCt 1814 May; and Read, Womack & Co. v Daniel, as above. Weight of hogsheads: Statement of amount sales of tobo. & shewing the overseer part, Cason v Cheadle, CoCt 1821 Aug–Oct; Cheadle, *passim.* Depth needed for flotation: John Fretwell depo (pp. 6–7), Perkinson v Appomattox Company, CoCt 1841 Jul–Aug. Height of cargo: Trout, ed., *Seay Stories*, p. 18. Cover over cargo: Lewis Miller, *Farmville at Appomattox River* (nineteenth-century painting), in Lewis Miller Sketch Books, vol. II (Williamsburg, VA: Abby Aldrich Rockefeller Folk Art Center), p. 11. "Tent cloths," poles: Declaration, Lightfoot v Bartlett, CirCt 1838 Sep. Canvas or oilcloth: Yancey, *Lynchburg and Its Neighbors*, p. 20 (albeit in reference to wagons).

177. Steering oars: Trout, ed., *Seay Stories*, pp. xviii and 17.

178. Shoulder pad; "hadn't lost momentum": *Ibid.*, p. 15. No one today seems to know for certain whether a batteau's two boatmen moved in unison or in alternation. The sentence quoted here suggests the former, Lewis Miller's painting the latter—though Miller also, implausibly, depicts both boatmen poling on the same side of the batteau.

179. Poles and poling: Trout, ed., *Seay Stories*, pp. 15–16.

180. Use of towpath: Dalton, "River Is Focal Point," p. 3, and Trout, "A Tour Guide to Petersburg's Canal," p. 86, in *Seay Stories*. A "hauling wall": See Trout, ed., *Seay Stories*, p. 8.

181. Coal: B. M. Hurt acct with William Seay, 1822, Venable v Seay, CoCt 1822 Mar. Salt, lime, shells: William A. Seay acct with Venable & Co., 1820 and 1821, Venable v Seay; William Seay acct with Thweatt & Miller, 1822 Mar, Thweatt & Miller v Seay, CoCt 1822 Mar. Herrings, merchandise: OB 19/252–255 (1819 Sep); Notice, Venable v Trent & Skipwith, CoCt 1819 Sep. Shells: William L. Legrand acct with Thomas A. Morton & Co., 1820 Feb, Morton & Co. v Legrand, CoCt 1821 Aug; Owen Haskins est acct, 1809 Jul, Haskins v Ligon, CirCt 1844 Sep. Shells and mortar: Camille Wells, personal communication, citing Harley McKee, *Introduction to Early American Masonry: Stone, Brick, Mortar, and Plaster* (Washington, DC: National Trust for Historic Preservation, 1973). Merchandise: Rip Van Winkle, "Farmville Then and Now," *Farmville Herald*, August 31, 1906. Oysters: CW v Samuel and William Wright, presentment, CoCt 1833 Mar; Edmund Young on FNL, 1818. Firewood: Accts with Scott & Smith, in receipts, 1847 Jan, 1847 Apr, and 1848, Flournoy v Epes, CirCt 1852 Apr.

182. Forty boats: Martin, *Gazetteer of Virginia*, p. 268; Ms. Census, 1850, schedule 5, Products of industry. Jenkins: Venable, Anderson, & Flournoy acct with James and Henry Jenkins, 1849, Jenkins v Venable, Anderson & Flournoy, CoCt 1854 May. A boat fork was presumably the forked swivel on which a batteau's steering oar pivoted. Boat-

wright: Receipt from Boatwright, vouchers for acct no. 1, Penick's guardian v Penick, CirCt 1840 Apr. Forgason: FNLs, 1821 and 1822.

183. Slaves as boatmen (examples): Drury Watson's certf, Haskins v Wood, CoCt 1822 Aug (with "Headman Aaron"); Document A for 1829 and 1832, p. 9, Chambers's Committee v Madison's exor, CirCt 1842 Apr (hiring out of Joe, a boatman); William Ranson depo and other documents, Chambers's trustee v Ransone, Currie & Co., CoCt 1845 Jun–Jul.

184. Wheat to mill: Bill, answer, and John Goode and John Roy affis, Taggart v Morton, CoCt 1811 Sep–Nov. Produce to Petersburg (examples): Bill, Watt v Brown, CoCt May 1814; Thomas T. Stegar testimony, CW v Weaver, CoCt 1832 Sep. Other white boatmen (examples): "Brown[,] Felix (a Boatman)," Ms. land tax rolls, Thomas Green's district, 1803; James B. Hilliard testimony, CW v Fox, CoCt 1840 May (with William B. Fox, white, clearly designated as a "hand," not a headman); "Wm Jones (Boatman)," H. M. Spencer & Company list of balances, 1847 Sep 1, Venable v Spencer, CirCt 1848 Apr. Cheadle, slave and white boatmen, and first names: Josiah Cheadle, letters to Messrs. Harris and Jones, February 10 and 12, February 17, May 17, July 7, and July 17, 1821, Cheadle, B5th–B6th, B8th, B10th, and B12th pp. Cheadle did list white headmen's family names at times; he confined himself to the first name particularly when the headman bore the same family name as, and presumably was a relative of, the boat's owner, whose surname Cheadle did consistently list. But there are instances, as in the letter of July 17, where one does not know whether the headman, mentioned without surname, is white or enslaved.

185. Early free black boatmen: FNLs, lower district, 1801 and 1802 (Isaac Johnston, in Jamestown, not Farmville), 1807 (David Bartlett farming); and Green's district, 1803 (Daniel Smith), 1805 (Samuel and David Bartlett boating), 1811 (Phil Bowman boating).

186. Numbers of boatmen: FNLs, 1824 and 1825, which list 87 people in boating households, or about a quarter of the people included on the list. One in 6 or 7: I am assuming that the number of boats operating out of the town in 1825 was not much smaller than the 40 that typically ran in the 1830s. I have multiplied that number by 4 rather than 3 crewmen to allow for the presence of occasional boatmen in the population, then divided the figure of about 25 free black boatmen in Prince Edward and southern Cumberland by the product, 160. These may be conservative assumptions; just a year earlier, there had been 20-some free blacks listed as boatmen in Prince Edward alone—FNL, 1823. Boatmen and families as fraction of whole free black population: FNLs, 1824 and 1825. On the former year's list, there were 87 members of boating households out of a total of about 335 persons altogether. Even in 1825, when fewer men were recorded as working on batteaux, the figure was 56 of about 346, which would mean that nearly 1 in 6 free black residents of the county belonged to a household headed by such a man. The overall population figures on the free black lists for 1824 and 1825 are approximate because those lists are drafts on which not all strikeouts, interpolations, and other notations are entirely clear. The free black lists regularly include fewer individuals than the federal Census, but I have assumed that the number of boatmen is understated on those lists in about the same proportion as the overall free black population is. Uncertainty over the number of boatmen in a given year arises because free black lists record occupations for households collectively rather than for each individual.

187. Numbers and residences of boatmen: FNLs, 1824 and 1825, cross-checked with 1821 and other years. Bartletts' houses: Davy Bartlett's neighbors and the wagoners who ate at his residence referred to it as "Bartlett's" (see discussion earlier this chapter); and Henry Bartlett rented out "his house" to a relative in 1838 (Bartlett v Bartlett, CoCt 1841 Jan–Mar).

188. "They hailed": Rip Van Winkle, "Farmville Then and Now," *Farmville Herald*, August 31, 1906.

189. Phil White Jr.'s boat: White v Trent & Skipwith, CoCt 1819 Sep. Phil's and Dick's boats: Records of the 1820 Census of manufactures. Davy Bartlett's boat: Declaration, Lightfoot v Bartlett, CirCt 1838 Sep. White-Bartlett transaction (for $40): Declaration, and John Robertson's and Joe Bartlett's bond to John White, White v Bartlett, CoCt 1837 Aug. Statistics from 1850: Ms. Census, 1850, schedule 5, Products of industry, pp. 123–25.

190. Passengers: See William C. Wells testimony, CW v Burton, CoCt 1842 Aug, which refers matter-of-factly to two men riding in batteaux as passengers from Petersburg to Farmville; Caption, Lewis Miller, *Farmville at Appomattox River* (painting); and Trout, ed., *Seay Stories*, p. 14. White passenger, 1842: Wells depo, CW v Burton. "Smith's boat," on which the witness had traveled from Petersburg, may have been captained by James Smith (FNL, 1819) or Isaac Smith (FNLs, 1819 and 1821–1825), both free blacks, or owned by a white merchant named Smith; the other free black headman involved was Jim Bartlett.

191. Venables' hogsheads to three boats: William A. Seay, acct with Venable & Co., 1821 Jan 31, Venable v Seay, CoCt 1822 Mar. On James Ellison: See FNLs, 1822–1825. (As an example of the lack of nuance in the snapshot-style official free black lists, it is worth noting that no extant FNL records Jacob Johnston as a boatman, though his brother George is so entered.)

192. Phil White and Grief Weaver owning one boat each: Records of 1820 Census of manufactures. Voyage of six batteaux, obstruction, and motions for fines: Cases of White, Weaver, Venable, and Wood, all v Trent & Skipwith, CoCt 1819 Sep, and OB 19/252–255 (1819 Sep). Within a month, the owners of Stony Point Mills decided to appeal the fine assessed against them on Phil White's complaint. They cited purely technical grounds—that White's complaint had not named the specific law the millers had violated. The other complaining boat owners had not done so, either. Yet the mill company probably did not single White out because of his race, for they let a second fine assessed on White's behalf go uncontested. More likely, the millers decided to pursue a test case and chose White simply because he happened to head the list of complainants the county court had dealt with. If the mill owners did harbor any hopes that White's color would affect their fortunes, they were disappointed. Their appeal made its way with glacial slowness through the system before the General Court of Virginia upheld the fine in Phil White's case a dozen years later—Trent & Skipwith ads White, CirCt 1831 Sep, and District Court Order Book, 1805–31, many entries, particularly p. 570 (1821 Sep). A somewhat similar action in a case involving an Appomattox River dam: Appomattox Company ads Perkinson, CirCt 1842 Apr.

193. Headmen's names recorded; bearing shippers' letters: See, e.g., Cheadle, B3rd p. bottom (two letters "By Boatman") through B12th p.; and Tobacco received 1822–24, in abstract from books of L. E. Stainback, Fowler v Booker, CoCt 1833 May. Cargo receipts from headmen: See Receipts of 1805 from Jim and Ampy, Allen's exors v Fowler, CoCt 1822 Jul. Shipper paying headman: William L. Womack affi, and also John Roy affi, Taggart v Morton, CoCt 1811 Sep–Nov. Headman-owner receiving money in Petersburg: Thomas T. Stegar testimony, CW v Weaver, CoCt 1832 Sep.

194. "Ducking": Cheadle 39th p. (numbered as p. 17), J. T. and other Cheadles, acct with Josiah Cheadle, 1827 Oct (2 hogsheads ducked); Rip Van Winkle, "Farmville Then and Now," *Farmville Herald*, August 31, 1906; see also Legrand's statement to Morton & Co., Legrand v Morton & Co., CoCt 1822 Aug. Damage "from rain or wet": Drury Watson's certf (see also Grief C. Weaver's certf), Haskins v Wood, CoCt 1822 Aug. "The dangers": Receipts of 1805 from Jim and Ampy, Allen's exors v Fowler. Unsuccessful suits against those who owned or engaged boats: Thweatt v Routon, CoCt

1823 Aug, and OB 20/572 (1823 Aug); Wilkes v Steger and Randolph, CoCt 1829 Aug, and OB 22/104–105 (1829 May) and 157 (1829 Aug); Legrand v Morton & Co., 1822 Aug. Shipper's refusal to pay upheld: Haskins v Wood, CoCt 1822 Aug. Gibbs docked: Isaac Gibbs, acct with N. E. Venable & Co., White v Gibbs, CoCt 1833 May.

195. Extremes around 1840: Depos of James Edwards (whence the quotations) and John Fretwell, Perkinson v Appomattox Co., CoCt 1841 Jul–Aug.

196. Streams changing course: Venable v Allen, CoCt 1819 Nov; DB 14/519, Nash to Redford (1811). Moored boat destroyed: Bill, Watt v Brown, CoCt 1814 May. Aqueduct destroyed: Trout, ed., *Seay Stories*, p. 26; Bradshaw, *Prince Edward County*, p. 293. "Laybys": Trout, ed., *Seay Stories*, p. 20.

197. Ice jams: Trout, ed., *Seay Stories*, p. 37 (relating a specific instance in the late nineteenth century). "Wait for a swell": Richard N. Venable and Thomas A. Morton, report of 1816 Oct 14, Board of Public Works, Box 213, LVA, cited in Gilliam, "Upper Appomattox Company," 38.

198. "A fine stream"; "the navigation of the river": Martin, *Gazetteer of Virginia*, pp. 265 and 268. "Precarious": Bradshaw, *Prince Edward County*, pp. 293 and 327. "Was stranded": Rip Van Winkle, "Farmville Then and Now," *Farmville Herald*, August 31, 1906. Complementarity of rivers and roads: Cf. Yancey, *Lynchburg and Its Neighbors*, p. 20.

199. Boat owners' fees: Cheadle, *passim;* Archibald Wright affi, Taggart v Morton, CoCt 1811 Sep–Nov; and many other documents. Boatman paid by trip (by two different employers): Isaac Gibbs, acct with N. E. Venable & Co.; Phil White, acct with Isaac Gibbs, and Gibbs, acct with White; all in White v Gibbs, CoCt 1833 May. Boatman paid by share: John Roy affi, Taggart v Morton. Provisions: Cf. Bagby, quoted in Yancey, *Lynchburg and Its Neighbors*, p. 21.

200. Duration of round trip before 1830s: Cases of White, Weaver, Venable, and Wood, all v Trent & Skipwith, CoCt 1819 Sep, and OB 19/252–255 (1819 Sep). (On this voyage, the six batteaux passed Stony Point Mills first on August 5, and then again on August 25 as they returned to Farmville; Stony Point Mills was sixteen miles or so downstream from Farmville. We do not know by how long the boats were delayed in each direction, but the impression is that the obstruction added hours or at most a day or two to the round trip.) Duration after 1830s: Using the Industrial Census of 1850, one historian reported that a batteau could take 150 hogsheads of tobacco from Farmville to Petersburg in one year; assuming the optimum 10 hogsheads per boat and no idle periods, the average duration of a round trip would have been three and a half weeks, and less when time is subtracted for loading, unloading, and weather-induced idle time—Industrial Census, 1850, Prince Edward County, pp. 123–25, cited in Gilliam, "Upper Appomattox Company," 41; my own analysis of Ms. Census, 1850, schedule 5, Products of industry, confirms Gilliam's figure of about 150 hogsheads per year. Three weeks and a day: Drury Watson's and Stainback & Booth's certfs, Haskins v Wood, CoCt 1822 Aug. Delays at mill dams: Cases against Trent & Skipwith, cited above; Read, Womack & Co. v Daniel, CirCt 1837 Sep. In both these instances, separated by nearly two decades, boats were delayed at the same company's dam at Stony Point Mills.

201. Bagby: Quoted in Yancey, *Lynchburg and Its Neighbors*, p. 21.

202. "The boatmen said": Mary Tredway, letter to W. C. Thornton, December 2, 1852, William C. Thornton papers, Duke.

203. Rum: Bill, and John Roy affi, Taggart v Morton, CoCt 1811 Sep–Nov. "Such a drun[k]ard": John Goode affi (see also John Roy affi), in same case. Fox: CW v Fox, especially testimony of John W. Netherland, Thomas Maxey, John W. French, and James B. Hilliard, CoCt 1840 May; H. S. Guthrey bill to county for $8, "reparing the window that Fox broke," filed CoCt 1841 Jun.

204. One slave killed: Coroner's inquest, Bob, 1813, LVA. Epperson: B. Epperson's affi, filed CoCt 1832 Aug–Oct. Brown: Brown v Fielder, CoCt 1827 Mar.

205. Alleged assaults by Weaver: CW v Weaver, CoCt 1826 May (alleged victim a white man); Otterson v Weaver, CoCt 1821 Aug, and OB 19/479 (1820 Nov) and 20/127 (1821 Aug) (another white man); White v Weaver, CoCt 1819 Aug (a black man); and Patterson v Weaver, CoCt 1825 Mar (a black woman). White's suit: White v Weaver, as above, and OB 19/147, 177, 234 (1819 Mar, May, and Aug). In what may have been a sign of their reconciliation, White and Weaver both filed their motions against the negligent dam owners through the lawyer who had filed, and then terminated, White's suit against Weaver. Weaver's conviction for theft: CW v Weaver, especially William Williams testimony, CoCt 1832 Sep, and CirCt 1832 Sep.

206. "Said negroe": Bond of hire for Phil, Purnall's exor v Peter Winn, CoCt 1828 Nov–Dec. Law regarding black boatmen: Acts of Assembly, 1835–36, chapter 73, pp. 49–50.

207. Thomas and Major: CW v Thomas and CW v Major, CoCt 1828 Oct, and OB 21/762 (1828 Sep) and 769 (1828 Oct). There had been a batteau headman named Major in earlier years, perhaps this same man—Wood v Trent & Skipwith, OB 19/255. Major, the codefendant in this case, was hired out to a resident of Chesterfield County, near Richmond, charged with a theft in Farmville, sixty miles or so away, and owned by a man who lived in Amelia County, which lay between the other two places; his mobility reinforces the impression that he was regularly involved in transporting cargo. That the two suspects could be thought to have "rolled" the hogshead seems unlikely, for—unlike regular wagoners or boatmen—enslaved would-be perpetrators would have to call attention to themselves by obtaining equipment and a team of animals for the project. Although the discharging of these two defendants seems straightforward, it is conceivable that the stolen goods were recovered, or paid for by the slaves' master, and the bondmen released into his custody for extralegal punishment.

208. Kit Strong Sr. an original settler of Israel Hill: FNL, Green's district, 1811. Kit Strong Jr. appears with his family at Sam White's, FNL, 1817. Theft charge: CW v Strong and Clark, CoCt 1838 Aug. I conclude that the Strong involved in these events is Kit Junior rather than Kit Senior, the weaver and shoemaker. Although Strong and Clark are not identified explicitly as boatmen in this suit, their occupation seems clear from the nature of the alleged crime; from the fact that one of the two black men was reported "down the river" when a deputy sheriff tried to serve papers on him soon afterward (see below); and from numerous payments that one Kit Strong received from William Seay in the same store accounts through which Seay paid his free black batteaumen—Wood & Dupuy v Seay, Morton & Venable v Seay, and Venable v Seay, CoCt 1822 Mar. The owner of the stolen tobacco was Clement C. Read, the good friend of free black coachman and landowner John Deneufville and the associate of several black Israelites.

209. Attorneys' lawsuit: Watkins & Flournoy v Strong & Clark, CirCt 1840 Sep. Deputy Sheriff James McDearmon stated that Strong was "no inhabitant" of the county and that Clark possessed "no effects in my bailiwick known to me"; both assertions, and especially the first, were, to put it mildly, distortions of the truth that benefited the black defendants.

210. Randolph Brandum's age: IH 1816. At Sam White's: FNLs, 1817–1819; young Brandum probably lived at White's earlier, too, in years from which FNLs do not survive. Continued dealings with Whites and Gibbses: Isaac Gibbs, acct with Phil White, White v Gibbs, CoCt 1833 May.

211. Owning boat: Plea filed 1839 Aug, Goodman v Brandon [sic], CoCt 1840 Mar. Hiring black hands: Goodman v Brandon; Bill, and bond of Madison and Brandon, Gillispie v Brandom and Madison, CoCt 1840 Mar. Transactions with leading

whites: Gillispie v Brandom and Madison (hiring the slave); Jackson v Brandon, CirCt 1840 Sep–Dec (with actual ended date Jun?); Carroll v Brandum, CoCt 1840 May; list of debts remaining to be collected in settlement, Lyle, Booker & Co., Booker v Lyle, CirCt 1847 Sep.

212. Brandum accused in Petersburg mayor's court, and ensuing developments described in following paragraphs: Goodman v Brandon, CoCt 1840 Mar, and OB 24/251, 279, 305, and 338 (1839 May, Aug, and Nov, and 1840 Mar, respectively). Homes: CW v Homes: OB23/293 and 310 (1835 Mar and May). Charges filed against Homes for hiring a runaway were dismissed, perhaps for lack of proof that he had known his hireling was an escapee.

213. One wonders whether $50 was a fair valuation of the labor Goodman had lost; the entire year's hire for another slave boatman Brandum had employed ran to $125— Bond of Madison and Brandon, Gillispie v Brandom and Madison, CoCt 1840 Mar. But we do not know how long the slave had been absent. Brandum's case as recorded in the terse, formulaic order book—that he had already paid Goodman the money under dispute—was more mundane than the one embodied in his story as recorded in the suit papers (OB 24/251 [1839 May]).

214. Short-term boating contract, early nineteenth century (example): Taggart v Morton, especially John Roy affi, CoCt 1811 Sep–Nov. "The pride of many": Rip Van Winkle, "Farmville Then and Now," *Farmville Herald,* August 31, 1906. Extended, first-refusal contract (example): Bradshaw, *Prince Edward County,* p. 294; see also penciled attorney's notes, Declaration, Legrand v Morton & Co., CoCt 1822 Aug, which state: "The boats worked for [a particular shipper] whenever he had work."

215. Patterns of boating by mercantile companies and independents: Ms. Census, 1850, schedule 5, Products of industry, pp. 123–25. Merchant avoids liability: Declaration, and attorney's penciled notes, Legrand v Morton & Co., CoCt 1822 Aug.

216. Seay and black boatmen: William A. Seay accts in the following cases: Venable v Seay, CoCt 1822 Mar; Morton & Venable v Seay, CoCt 1822 Mar; and Wood, Dupuy & Co. v Seay, CoCt 1822 Mar. Seay's collapse: In addition to the three cases just mentioned, see a volley of lawsuits against Seay concluded in CoCt roughly from fall 1826 through 1828. Deeds of trust on Seay's plantation: DB 20/33, Seay to Thweatt & Co. (1828); DB 20/231, Seay to Tredway (1829); DB 22/424, Seay to Thweatt & Miller (1839). Financial status at death: WB 9/37, William Seay appraisal (1845); WB 9/136, William Seay est acct with Rachel Seay (1846); see also Miller, Thweatt & Hudson v Seay, CirCt 1840 Apr, and Gregory v Wilson, CoCt 1848 Apr–May. Seay did make a modest and temporary comeback in the mid-1820s—Land tax, upper district, 1826, with a new building adding $1,200 to Seay's assessment.

The most striking entry in the 1820 Census for Prince Edward County is the one for William Seay's household, which had consisted only of Seay himself and two slaves in 1810 but now, according to the enumerator, included some four dozen young white men, not to mention twenty-four slaves and four free black children who may have been apprentices. Whether these whites were employees—some of them boatmen, perhaps—who were playing a part in Seay's business expansion is unknown. It is certain, though, that Seay had just acquired a 371-acre tract of land; the entrepreneur had now become a planter as well—Land tax, upper district, 1818–20, and DB 17/6, Clark to Seay (1819).

217. Gibbs's boating: Phil White, acct with Isaac Gibbs, and Isaac Gibbs, acct with White; credits in Gibbs, acct with N. E. Venable & Co.; all in White v Gibbs, CoCt 1833 May. Gibbs's income and purchases: Gibbs, acct with Venable & Co. The account explicitly includes one payment that Gibbs directed Venable to make against Gibbs's account with another merchant. That Gibbs bought at stores other than Venable's is supported also by the very irregular tempo of his purchases of staples there

and by the clear insufficiency of the quantities of those staples to sustain him for a year, even taking into account provisions he would have received from Venable during boat trips and food he may have produced on Israel Hill.

218. Merchandise and payments issued to Israelites: William A. Seay accts in Venable v Seay, Morton & Venable v Seay, and Wood, Dupuy & Co. v Seay, all CoCt 1822 Mar. Salt to Johnston: Seay acct with Wood & Dupuy, 1821 Aug 9. Romulus White, the one son of Hercules Senior who did not long remain on Israel Hill, makes most of his very rare appearances in the historical record through Seay's store accounts, receiving cash and whiskey. In less than eighteen months, William Seay paid out $150 or more to free blacks through the three merchants whose records survive; he may well have made other payments directly or through other stores, and the boatmen undoubtedly earned money from other boat owners. Occasionally, Israelites who did not belong to boating families received payments in cash or merchandise from William Seay, presumably in return for other services they had rendered or goods they had sold to him.

219. Seay's payments to White: William A. Seay acct in Wood & Dupuy v Seay, CoCt 1822 Mar. Sam White's business obligations to Seay: Summonses to garnishees in the following cases: Venable v Seay, Morton & Venable v Seay, Wood, Dupuy & Co. v Seay; and Thweatt & Miller v Seay, CoCt 1822 Mar. There were two Samuel Whites, one of them a white man who participated in Prince Edward's economy during Israel Hill's early years; that the one summoned as a potential "garnishee" in the cases surrounding William Seay's debts is the free black Sam White of Israel Hill is supported circumstantially by the juxtaposition of the Sam White in Seay's mercantile accounts with other free black Israelites, and by White's acknowledgment of the summons in Morton & Venable v Seay with an X.

220. Boatmen also farming; Johnston not appearing as boatman: FNLs, 1817–1825.

221. Population: Suzanne Lebsock, *The Free Women of Petersburg: Status and Culture in a Southern Town, 1784–1860* (New York and London: W. W. Norton, 1984), p. 280, n. 5, and p. 11.

222. Lilly conviction: CW v Lilly, CoCt 1823 Nov; OB 20/624 and 626 (Nov 1823).

223. Stabbing charge: CW v Brandon, CoCt 1842 Jan. Official's request to Worsham: R. Brandem certf, Marius Gilliam, letter to clerk of Prince Edward County, July 17, 1850, filed CoCt 1850 Oct–Nov. Brandum's age, and Worsham's assistance: IH 1816, which suggests a birth date of 1808; Randolph Brandem renewal, OB 26/394 (1850 Nov), which has Brandum at age forty in 1850.

224. "Good free negroes"; "much respected"; "those old commanders": Rip Van Winkle, "Farmville Then and Now," *Farmville Herald,* August 31, 1906.

225. "Rapid and clear": See Lewis Miller, *Farmville at Appomattox River* (painting); Trout, ed., *Seay Stories,* p. 34; see also purchase of fish hooks in William A. Seay, acct with Venable & Co., 1820 Sep 26, Venable v Seay. "Most any beautiful shaped rock" and potholes: Trout, ed., *Seay Stories,* p. 39.

226. More cleared land: Bruce, *New Man,* p. 43; Bradshaw, *Prince Edward County,* p. 525.

227. "A boatman . . . upon the waters": Plea filed 1839 Aug, Brandum v Goodman, CoCt 1840 Mar.

CHAPTER 5: *Challenges*

1. Service in War of 1812 (example): Spas to Johnson McNeil, in CW v Watkins, CoCt 1814 Mar, and in CW v Carter and CW v Faris, CoCt 1814 Mar–Apr.

2. "Bugle" and "Colours": Acct, Samuel W. and William L. Venable with Prince Edward County, CoCt 1814 Mar–Apr.

3. Protest to governor, 1811: Governor's letter to court, CoCt 1811 Apr–May. Protest to governor, 1816: Petition of sundry persons against proceedings of the court martial, CoCt 1816 Mar.

4. Lindsey's old field as battalion muster ground: See CW v Preston, CoCt 1820 Mar; and CW v Moss, CoCt 1820 May. Timing of battalion muster (which, however, seems to have varied in some years): Herbert Clarence Bradshaw, *History of Prince Edward County, Virginia, from Its Earliest Settlements Through Its Establishment in 1754 to Its Bicentennial Year* (Richmond: Dietz Press, 1955), p. 228. Short and whites charged: CW v Neighbours, Reynolds, Ritchie, and Short, presentments, in OB 17/507–508 (1813 May); the disposition of these charges is discussed in chapter 6.

Identity of Susannah Short: There seem to have been two women in Ben Short's immediate family who bore similar given names. Ben Short was listed with a wife named Susan or Sooky ("Sucky") on FNLs, Green's district, 1807, 1809, and 1811; on none of these lists is this wife listed as Susannah, though that was a common variant of Susan. By the time FNL, 1817, was compiled, Ben Short was listed without a wife; his first wife gone, presumably through death, he was now married to Sylvia, whose enslaved status explains her absence from the free black list. The Susannah Short who is listed on FNL, 1824, as farming on her own land some six years after Ben Short's death—the same land that Ben had previously left to his widow, Sylvia, in life estate—is therefore probably either Ben Short's daughter-in-law (Short did have at least one son, who is named in his nuncupative will) or his daughter by, and namesake of, his first wife. It is almost surely this Susannah Short who had been charged with selling liquor in 1813, for she was declared unable to pay her fine in 1818, long after Ben Short's first wife, Susan, apparently died.

5. Cursing at Clarke's muster ground: CW v Brookes, Brookes, and Fowlkes, presentments, CoCt 1815 Aug 21. Liquor at Lindsey's old field: CW v Lindsey, presentment, CoCt 1811 May. Liquor at muster ground of Madison and Penick: CW v Reynolds, District Court Order Book, 1805–31, pp. 439 (1813 Apr) and 471 (1815 Apr). First charge against Moss: CW v Moss, CoCt 1819 Aug; OB 19/97 (1818 Nov), 223 (1819 Aug), 389 (1820 Jun). Second charge against Moss: CW v Moss, CoCt 1820 May; OB 19/265 (1819 Nov) and 349 (1820 May). Charge that a slave sold liquor on same date in 1819: CW v Preston, CoCt 1829 Mar.

6. "Totally destitute": James Carr et al. (Deep Creek), 1831 Sep 4; see also Benjamin W. S. Cabell (Danville), 1831 Sep 21; both in Executive papers, Governor John Floyd, LVA, which also contain many communications describing the panic among ordinary citizens. Role of governor and militia leadership; "to quiet the publick mind": Exchange of letters among James [?] Davidson, John D. Macklin, and Governor Floyd, August 27–30, 1831, in Floyd Executive papers. Limiting reprisals against blacks: John Thompson Kilby (Nansemond County), September 16, 1831; see also letter of John D. Macklin, August 30, 1831, in Floyd Executive papers. Pardons of accused slaves: See William M. Dugger (Brunswick County), October 6, 1831, and "W. R.," in folder, 1831 Oct, Floyd Executive papers.

7. Dupuy's assessment: Asa Dupuy, September 19, 1831. Other three counties: William Wilson (Cumberland), September 19, 1831; Benjamin Walker et al. (Buckingham), October 13, 1831; Drury A. Bacon (Charlotte), October 7, 1831. All in Executive papers, Governor Floyd, LVA.

8. "No cause for any apprehension": William Wilson, September 19, 1831. Charlotte: Drury A. Bacon, October 7, 1831. "The slaves appear": Asa Dupuy, September 19, 1831. All in Executive papers, Governor Floyd, LVA. Alison Goodyear Freehling quotes part of Dupuy's letter, but not the part showing that the blacks in Farmville whom some whites worried about were mostly free people—see Freehling, *Drift Toward Dissolution: The Virginia Slavery Debate of 1831–1832* (Baton Rouge and London: Louisiana State University Press, 1982), p. 7. Not everyone felt as sanguine as Dupuy; "many times do I wish me and mine all in some free state," one woman wrote from Farmville in October—Unsigned (W. C. Thornton's mother?) letter to William, Rebecca and Caroline, October 31, 1831, William C. Thornton papers, Duke.

9. Woodson "convinced": Asa Dupuy, September 19, 1831, Executive Papers, Governor Floyd, LVA.

10. "In and contiguous to Farmville"; "recently there appears"; "may proceed": Dupuy, September 19, 1831, Executive papers, Governor Floyd, LVA.

11. John Rice knew at least some of the Israelites well enough that he could have distinguished them from other blacks at a distance. But in fact it is not clear whether he actually said he had seen people of Israel Hill in town, or whether Dupuy simply assumed Rice was referring to Israelites.

12. Rice complains of unlawful assemblages: CW v Keirnan, presentment, CoCt 1831 May, and OB 22/456 (1831 May); trial on counts 1–3, CoCt 1833 May. Rice failed to testify at the defendant's trial on one of the counts, so even his vigilance may have had its limits—Trial for alleged offense of 1831 Apr 17, CoCt 1833 May.

13. Rice, Gibbs, and White: Statement of Rice, White v Gibbs, CoCt 1833 May. Witnessing will: WB 8/409–410, Titus Gibbs will (1841/1842). "*Renowned in story*"; "gilt . . . buttons": W. A. [?] Parker to Colonel Bernard Peyton, September 14, 1831, in Executive papers, Governor Floyd, LVA (emphasis in the original).

14. To "quiet the minds"; two companies; "to make as little shew": Dupuy to governor, as in previous notes.

15. Orders to confiscate guns and to settle White's estate: OB 22/525 (1831 Sep 19).

16. "Some reason to apprehend": Henry E. Watkins, order to John Rice, n.d., in Report—arms etc., filed CoCt 1832 Mar–Apr.

17. "Six or eight" houses searched in upper district: Joseph Wilson, report to court, 1831 Oct 17, in Report—arms etc.

18. Gun collection: J. Rice's report, in Report—arms etc.

19. Read, Israelite customers, White, and Gibbs: White v Gibbs, *passim*, CoCt 1833 May. Read and boating: Read, Womack & Co. v Daniel, CirCt 1837 Sep. Read and Phil White: Spa to Read, White v Peters, CoCt 1838 May. Read and Tony White: WB 9/374, Anthony White will (1848/1850). Read and Deneufville: WB 8/148, John Deneufville will (1839).

20. Mrs. Chambers, the white woman who claimed the gun held by Bartlett, may have been the sometime mistress of the Josiah Chambers estate near Israel Hill, who was herself the mother of at least one mulatto child.

21. Men on patrol: OB 22/475–479 (1831 Jun); OB 23/1–5 (1832 Jun); OB 23/127–130 (1833 Jun); OB 23/244–246 (1834 Jun). Gun auction with compensation: OB 22/602 (1832 Mar).

22. "Plotting rebellion": CW v Flem, CoCt 1831 Oct. "Conspiracy": Claims, CW v Daniel, filed CoCt 1833 Jun–Jul. "Suspected of insurrection": Jail report, 1832 Apr, filed CirCt 1831 Jun–Sep/1832 Apr.

23. Assemblage of free blacks: CW v Williams, CirCt 1831 Sep (presentment), and CirCt 1833 Apr. Assemblage of slaves: CW v Beach, CirCt 1832 Apr. It is not clear whether the assemblage at Beach's had allegedly taken place before or after the Turner revolt, though the presentment came afterward; Williams's presentment alleged that the supposed assembly at his place had occurred late in September, after the Turner rising. In the months after the rebellion, yet another white man came to trial on four charges, filed *before* Turner's revolt, of having permitted unlawful assemblages of slaves, and two of having sold liquor to them illegally. Juries did convict the man on two counts of allowing bondmen to assemble, but they fined him only $5 plus costs for each offense and acquitted him on the other four counts. Presentments: CW v Keirnan, CoCt 1831 May; OB 22/456–457 (1831 May). Adjudication of presentments: CW v Keirnan, CoCt 1833 May, OB 22/630–631 (1832 May), OB 23/35 (1832 Aug) and 112 (1833 May).

24. Alleged plot: CW v Jesse, CoCt 1832 Oct; OB 23/47 (1832 Oct).

25. Registrations in aftermath of revolt: OB 22/528 (1831 Sep; replacement of lost papers),

537–538 (1831 Oct), 545 (1831 Nov), 550 (1831 Nov), and 580 (1832 Jan). In next few years: OB 23/269–270 (1834 Sep); OB 23/382 and 383 (1835 Oct). Registrations before rebellion: OB 22/149–150 (1829 Aug) and 183–184 (1829 Sep). The lawsuit, Harry v Ford, that liberated a group of slaves formerly owned by Thomas Ford in 1834 is discussed in chapter 7.

26. Phil Senior's est acct: OB 22/525 (1831 Sep). Phil Junior as guardian of children in division of Phil Senior's assets: OB 22/527 (1831 Sep); cf. notation on back of Decree, White v White, CoCt 1832 Mar. Brown's lawsuit: Brown v Giles, OB 22/578 (1831 Oct). Permanent guardian: OB 22/579 (1832 Jan). Pamelia Howard's lawsuit: Howard v White, OB 22/581 (1832 Jan).

27. Order revoking gun licenses: OB 21/483 (1826 Nov); Bradshaw, *Prince Edward County*, p. 279, mentions both gun license revocations but conveys their content inaccurately. Trial of Giles and Howard: OB 21/424–425 (1826 Nov).

28. Phony account of political meeting: "Resolutions of the Citizens of Prince Edward assembled at Israel Hill," *Richmond Enquirer*, March 27, 1827; "A Quiz!" *Richmond Enquirer*, March 30, 1827. I am much indebted to Kathryn E. Miller for locating these items on the strength of vague clues I was able to give her. Toasts to resolutions' author: Account of dinner honoring John Randolph, *Richmond Enquirer*, April 20, 1827.

29. Sam White's gun license: OB 21/523 (1827 Mar).

30. "Call Phill White": Unlabeled list of militia officers, filed CoCt 1830 Jun–Jul.

31. Young as oysterman: FNL, 1818. Oystermen in Prince Edward: Cf. CW v William Wright, "trader in oysters," presentments, CoCt 1833 Mar.

32. "Some British subject": Processioners' return [of William Scott], filed CoCt 1812 Apr–May. "The British land": Price v Woodson, CoCt 1820 Oct, especially bill, answer, Miller Woodson depo, and Richard N. Venable affi (flight of company's agent; legal reasons for failure to sell off land). Obscuring of boundaries: Processioners' return of Thomas Rice, notation for Tignal Womack's tract, filed CoCt 1812 Apr–May; William Scott processioners' return, as above.

33. Location of Young's house: Plat, Justices of Prince Edward v Young (with declarations in ejectment), CirCt 1833 Sep.

34. Perrin on British land: Woodson escheator v Young, CirCt 1820 Apr; Woodson escheator v Young, papers, CoCt 1819 Nov; Doe lessee of Thackston v Perrin, CirCt 1831 Jun. Perrin's background (he did acquire at least one slave in the 1820s): Ms. Census, 1810 and 1820 (slaveless); Spa to Perrin[']s [slave] John, 1827 Aug 20, CW v Young, CoCt 1827 Aug; Edmonds v Perrin et al., CirCt 1830 Sep; Edmonds v Perrin, delivery bond, CirCt 1831 Sep; Property tax, 1815, shows that Perrin had owned a slave in that year. Location of Colleys' residence: Land tax, lower district, 1815, Asa Cawley [sic] estate. A Young-Colley financial transaction: WB 7/104, William Colley est acct with Edmund Colley (1830). When one of the Colley clan died in 1820, Young and former Randolph slave Tom Ellis, along with a number of white craftsmen, attended the estate sale; it was a typical affair, complete with a gallon of whiskey provided for the bidders—WB 5/483, William Colley est sale (1820/1821).

35. Date Forgason joined Young: Cf. Ms. Census, Prince Edward County, 1810 (in which Young is listed alone), and FNLs, 1817ff. (on which Forgason and children are listed with him). Binding out of Betsy's children: Betsy Forgason [Jr.], Indenture to Joseph Ledbetter, filed 1806, Apprentices, LVA; FNLs, Green's district, 1807 and 1811 (Dick Forgason); Peter Forgason, Indenture to Charles Fore, 1808, Apprentices, LVA; OB 17/121 (1811 July), order to bind out Phebe Forgason; cf. FNLs, lower district, 1801–1806. Return of daughters, Phebe and Betsy/Betty: FNLs, 1817–1820 and 1825. Phebe and Betsy Junior living elsewhere: FNLs, 1821–1823. Probably Young's daughters by earlier marriage: Eliza Young (FNL, 1824; struck from FNL 1825) and Polly Young (FNLs, 1821 and 1823–1825). The two children who may have been born to

Edmund Young and Betsy Forgason are William, known as Bill or Billy, who first appears on FNL, 1817, and Jesse, who first appears in 1819.

36. Hamilton-Brown union: Index to marriage bonds, p. 24, where bride's last name is spelled Hambleton; and see FNLs, 1818 (Nancy Hamilton and daughters at Young's) and 1819 (one Nancy and daughter Eliza listed as the family of Syphax Brown [II]). Gibbs and Hamilton: WB 8/409–410, Titus Gibbs will (1841/1842). Gibbs probably a widower: FNLs, 1824–1825, on which his wife is no longer listed. Nancy the younger as Gibbs's probable heir: Nancy [Hamilton] Brown's name is struck from Brown's household on FNL, 1825, probably because she died in that year.

37. Verdict against Young would divest Perrin, too: Record of county court's judgment in Woodson v Young, 1819 Nov 5, filed with Young v Woodson (mislabeled as Woodson escheator v Young) in CirCt 1820 Apr, which awards Woodson the eight hundred acres "in the whole, part whereof is in possession of a certain John Perrin." Escheator Woodson may have been somewhat preoccupied in 1819 by the fact that he was then in the process of losing a related lawsuit. The county sheriff had beaten Woodson to the punch and already sold part of one British tract in 1815 to recover unpaid taxes on the land. When Woodson came along to claim that parcel for the public, the earlier buyer sued him, and the case began going badly for Woodson even as the latter sought to eject Young from the other British tract—Price v Woodson, CoCt 1820 Oct, OB 19/208–209 (1819 Jul) and 444 (1820 Oct) (see especially decree of 1819 Jul 21, issued just as Woodson was preparing his case against Edmund Young); Land tax, 1822, p. 55. Young and Perrin may have seemed more vulnerable to ejection because, unlike Woodson's earlier adversary, neither of them had paid a cent for the land he occupied.

38. Woodson's suit: Woodson v Young, CoCt 1819 Nov; OB 19/264–265 (1819 Nov).

39. Jurors and signatories to inquest: Compare Inquisition of escheat, Justices of Prince Edward v Young, CirCt 1833 Sep, with jury summons, Woodson v Young, as in note 38.

40. Young's appeal: Young v Woodson escheator, District Court Order Book, 1805–31 (microfilm), LVA, p. 543 (1820 Apr), and also (mislabeled as Woodson v Young) in CirCt 1820 Apr. The entire record of the suit and appeal is also found in District Court Order Book, 1804–30, pp. 418–21 (1820 Apr), in office of CirCt clerk, Prince Edward County Courthouse, Farmville.

41. Young's race known: See documents in original suit and in Young's appeal, as above. Perrin remains on land: Doe, lessee of Thackston, v Perrin (also styled Thackston lessee of Roe v Perrin), CirCt 1831 Jun.

42. Inauguration of poorhouse system: See OP report, 1825 and 1826 [and part of 1827], filed CoCt 1827 Jun–Jul. Construction of poorhouse complex: Poor house commissioners from Cunningham, contract, filed CoCt 1829 Jun–Jul, though OB 23/339 (1835 Jul) may imply that the original plan was not carried out in full. Location of complex relative to Young's house: Plat, Justices of Prince Edward v Young (with declarations in ejectment), CirCt 1833 Sep. Accusation against and trial of Young: CW v Young, OB 21/604–605 (Aug 1827); CoCt 1827 Aug. On policy toward the poor in old Virginia, see James D. Watkinson, " 'Fit Objects of Charity': Community, Race, Faith, and Welfare in Antebellum Lancaster County, Virginia," *Journal of the Early Republic,* 21, no. 1 (Spring 2001), 41–70; James D. Watkinson, "Rogues, Vagabonds, and Fit Objects: The Treatment of the Poor in Antebellum Virginia," *Virginia Cavalcade,* 49, no. 1 (Winter 2000), 16–29; and Watkinson's forthcoming book on the subject.

43. Young's accuser, Thomas Rice: Arrest warrant, CW v Young, as in note 42, to which compare list of jurors in Woodson v Young, as in note 38. One of Thomas Rice's slaves, named Billy, was summoned to testify at Young's trial. Rice may have pressed Billy to implicate Young, or the suspicion against the free black man may have originated with the slave himself. Charles Woodson, who had earlier attempted to remove

Young from the British land, was now serving as one of the county commissioners overseeing the construction of the poorhouse complex on that same tract, though Woodson apparently played no special role in the prosecution of Edmund Young for arson—Poor house commissioners from Cunningham, contract, filed CoCt 1829 Jun–Jul.

44. Witnesses and details of Young trial: CW v Young, OB 21/604–605 (Aug 1827); CoCt 1827 Aug. Attorney's suit against Young: Booker v Young, CoCt 1828 Aug. Attorney represents Young again: Fergurson [Forgason] v Goode et al., CirCt 1832 Mar.

45. Transactions with Dupuys: Joseph Dupuy, statement to Edmund Young for "1 Peck corn more than you pd for," and two notes to miller Bagby, in Asa Dupuy and Joseph Dupuy, Accts, 1828–29, section 4, folder 3, 1828, Mss1 D9295 a137–156, VHS. Apologetically: Note the wording of one instruction to the miller on January 22, 1828, to furnish Young with a half-barrel of corn (meal) on credit, "which is all I can let him have with out the money." Joseph Dupuy hardly needed to justify his decision to his employee at the mill. The quoted phrase, therefore, must have been intended either to prepare the miller for the possibility that Young would try to talk him into providing a greater quantity of meal, or else to smooth over the limitation Dupuy was imposing on a transaction with a regular customer.

46. Steward's house: Land & Fore to commissioners for poor house, agreement, filed CoCt 1828 Jun. "If we had full possession": Parish of St. Patrick to J. McDearmon &c., acct, 1828, filed CoCt 1828 Jun.

47. "Take the necessary steps": OP report, filed 1830 Jun 21. Suit against Young: Justices of Prince Edward v Young, CirCt 1833 Sep; Circuit Superior Court Order Book, 1831–37, p. 28 (1833 Sep), in office of CirCt clerk, Prince Edward County Courthouse, Farmville. Suit against Perrin: Doe, lessee of Thackston, v Perrin, CirCt 1831 Jun.

48. "Nominal wife": John A. Langhorne statement to James Madison, Justices of Prince Edward v Young, CirCt 1833 Sep.

49. Suit for assault: Fergurson [Forgason] v Goode et al., CirCt 1832 Mar. Tavern keeper: Noell v CW, CirCt 1853 Aug (permitting gambling); CW v Noell, CoCt 1857 Nov.

50. Goode's contract: OP report, 1825 and 1826 [and part of 1827], filed CoCt 1827 Jun–Jul. Length of delay: Compare CW v Young with Land & Fore to commissioners for poor house, both as earlier.

51. Young's sons and their wives: CW v Edward [sic] Young and Partheny [sic] Bigger, and CW v William Young and Elizabeth Bigger, both CoCt 1839 Nov; OB 24/180 and 302 (1838 Aug and 1839 Nov). One-year-old child: OB 26/443 (Jul 1851), registration of James Henry Bigger, then age fourteen. Deputy sheriff: E. W. Smith's notation on capias, CW v Edward Young and Parthena Bigger; the word that I read as "shut" is unclear in the original. Bigger clan: Note locations and acreages of Bigger tracts in Land tax, 1830. A subpoena in CW v Edmund Young, the poorhouse arson case, identifies Billy Young as "Edmund['s] son." Apparent identity of Ned (alias Edmund or Edward) Young as Edmund's son: Ned Young gave security for a guardian's bond entered by Ned Young in 1826—OB 21/357 (1826 May); Edmund Young "Sr." and "Jr." both appear on Delinquent property, 1831, filed CoCt 1832 Jun–Aug; Insolvents, county levy, upper district, 1841 Jun, contains a listing that reads: "Young[,] Edmund & Edward."

52. Witnesses as neighbors of free blacks: See James H. Lindsey road order, filed CoCt 1834 Jan–Mar, and contemporaneous Land tax rolls.

53. Cunningham and Womack as county justices: Bradshaw, *Prince Edward County*, p. 679. John Dungey's will: WB 11/159–160 (1852/1861). Cunningham's assistance to James Dungey's wife: Proceedings, Board of OP, 1845 Jun 2, p. 1. John M. Cunningham and Josiah Cunningham as builders of poorhouse: Poorhouse commissioners from Cunningham, contract, filed CoCt 1829 Jun–Jul. Their relationship to Newton Cunningham: WB 9/20, John M. Cunningham will (1845).

54. Second set of charges: Presentments, CW v Ned Young and Parthena Bigger, and CW v Billy Young and Betsy C. Bigger, 1841 Sep 27, CirCt. Presentments not pursued: Circuit Superior Court Order Book, 1831–37 [which actually runs to 1843], pp. 252–53 (1841 Sep, with no order to summon Young and Biggers) and index (with no additional entries for this case), in office of CirCt clerk, Prince Edward County Courthouse, Farmville.

55. Billy Young and Elizabeth (Betsy) Bigger: Ms. Census, 1860, p. 93 (with their ages); FNL, 1862, omits Betsy—who, though probably still alive and living with Young, was after all white—but lists Young and his family as living "at B[i]ggers." (Billy Young may have lived outside the county, presumably with his family, for part of the time between his marriage and 1860; see Delinquent property for 1844, George Booker, deputy sheriff, filed CoCt 1845 Mar–Apr, on which one William Young is designated as having "left Cty in Spring.") Children of Ned Young and Parthena Bigger: OB 26/443 (1851 Jul); and FNL, 1863, which, like all FNLs of that period, contains discrepancies as to ages of individuals. I believe that these are Parthena's children because the surname Bigger is found nowhere among free blacks of Prince Edward County other than in this group, and because the children of Bill and Elizabeth Bigger Young are accounted for elsewhere.

56. "Living in adultery": CW v Roberts, CoCt 1821 Mar, and CW v Sira, CoCt 1821 Aug. "Lewdly & lasciviously associating": CW v Harvey and Edwards, presentments, 1851 Oct 1, CirCt (originally filed under 1851 Sep); CW v Harvey and CW v Edwards, both CirCt 1852 Aug.

57. Reply to Ruffin: James Madison, "Condition of the Descendants of a Number of Emancipated Slaves, in Prince Edward County," with editor's response, *Farmers' Register*, 4, no. 1 (1836), 3–4.

58. Emphatic endorsement: *Lynchburg Virginian*, July 11, 1836, p. 3, courtesy of Thomas E. Buckley.

59. Colonizationists: *African Repository*, 12, no. 9 (September 1836), 287–88, courtesy of Elizabeth R. Varon. Pre–Civil War periodicals often ran opinion pieces from their ideological opposites; for another example of the *Repository*'s publication of proslavery views, see the report of a Quaker on his visits to British factories just preceding the Madison letter in the same issue.

60. Tucker: St. George Tucker, *A Dissertation on Slavery: With a Proposal for the Gradual Abolition of It, in the State of Virginia* (Philadelphia: Mathew Carey, 1796), especially pp. 86 ("hordes of vagabonds") and 90 ("a numerous . . . banditti"; "the innocent descendants"). Jefferson: Letter to Edward Coles, August 25, 1814, in Merrill D. Peterson, ed., *The Portable Thomas Jefferson* (New York: Viking Press, 1975), p. 544.

61. One in ten free persons black: Ms. Census, 1830, sheet 136, and 1840, sheet 239.

62. Free labor society: Thomas R. Dew, *Review of the Debate in the Virginia Legislature of 1831 and 1832* (Richmond: T. W. White, 1832), p. 123. "Most worthless and indolent"; "*drones* and *pests*": *Ibid.*, p. 88 (emphasis in the original).

63. To die out: George M. Fredrickson, *The Black Image in the White Mind: The Debate on Afro-American Character and Destiny, 1817–1914* (Middletown, CT: Wesleyan University Press, 1971), especially pp. 245–55 and 256–58. Fredrickson also provides an interesting discussion of antislavery people before the Civil War who likewise predicted that black extinction would follow emancipation (pp. 154–64).

64. Ohio communities: *Cincinnati Gazette*, n.d., reprinted in *Farmers' Register*, 3, no. 430 (November 1835), in Ulrich B. Phillips papers, group 387, series XV, box 25, folder 220, "Free Negroes," Yale. In diametric contrast to those who deprecated Israel Hill for its supposedly low rate of natural population increase, the Ohio article declared that the "only produce [of free blacks in the communities of that state] is children."

65. "Industrious"; "comforts and benefits": *Lynchburg Virginian*, July 11, 1836, p. 3 (emphasis in the original). Cf. the critique of Northern capitalism in George Fitzhugh, *Can-*

nibals All! Or, Slaves Without Masters, ed. C. Vann Woodward (Cambridge, MA: Belknap Press of Harvard University Press, [1857] 1960). For an interesting discussion of white Southerners' sensitivity to the abolitionists' moral strictures, see Charles Grier Sellers Jr., "The Travail of Slavery," in Sellers, ed., *The Southerner as American* (Chapel Hill: University of North Carolina Press, 1960), pp. 40–71.

66. "Truly beautiful"; "frozen yankees": George McPhail, letter to Mary V. Carrington, August 18, 1834, Carrington family papers, VHS, courtesy of Elizabeth R. Varon and Anthony Iaccarino. One George McPhail, probably the one quoted here, later became a Presbyterian minister—M. B. Williams, letter to Williana W. Lacy, December 20, 1841, p. 2, folder 6, Drury Lacy papers, UNC.

67. Supposedly largest free black population: Joseph Martin, *A New and Comprehensive Gazetteer of Virginia and the District of Columbia* (Charlottesville: Joseph Martin, 1836), p. 268. It was true that by around 1820 a high percentage—around half—of Prince Edward's sizable free Afro-Virginian population lived on their own land or in the town of Farmville rather than on some white person's plantation (see, e.g., FNL, 1823, on which between 52 and 53 percent of those listed lived on their own land, that of other free blacks, or in Farmville). Israel Hill contributed conspicuously to that figure, and on that ground alone deserved some of the attention it received as a symbol of black independence.

68. Tobacco factories: Martin, *Gazetteer of Virginia*, p. 268. Madison as tobacco manufacturer: Bradshaw, *Prince Edward County*, p. 300.

69. Black slaveowners: See Carter G. Woodson, ed., *Free Negro Owners of Slaves in the United States in 1830 Together with Absentee Ownership of Slaves in the United States in 1830* (New York: Negro Universities Press, [1924] 1968), p. 41. Bartletts and a few others: Delinquent property return, 1815, filed CoCt 1816 May–Jun. Homeses: See the discussion in chapter 3.

70. Wilkerson: FNLs, 1824 and 1825; Land tax, 1824 and 1825; Ms. Census, 1830, sheet 126. Carter: Insolvent land tax for 1827, filed CoCt 1828 Aug, which lists her property as belonging to Teny Carter Estate (Prince Edward delinquent land 1828, filed CoCt 1829 Jun–Jul, and some subsequent lists omit the "Estate"); Ms. Census, 1830, sheet 126. Dick White: Coroner's inquest, Richard White, April 17, 1826, Inquests, LVA; Coroner's Coms. [claims against county], 1826 Jun 19, filed CoCt 1826 Jul; FNL, 1825. Hercules White Jr.: OB 23/80 (1833 Feb). Phil White Sr.: WB 7/189, Philip White evaluation (1830). Patterson: OB 22/579 (1832 Jan); WB 7/273, Isham Patterson will (1831/1832). New, native generation: See OB 22/537–538 and 545 (1831 Oct and Nov); IH 1816.

71. Wilkerson's son Monroe, along with his own family and probably a sister or two, still farmed on the family tract at the close of the 1850s. Of the large Teny Carter household, a number were still in residence at that late date; they were listed as "planters," i.e., farmers—FNLs, 1857 and 1858.

72. Dick White's death: Inquest, as in note 70. His property: WB 6/345, Richard White inventory (1826); see also OB 21/407 (1826 Jul).

73. Guardianship of Dick White's daughters: OB 22/579 (1832 Jan). Several free blacks did live with a large group of slaves in the "negro quarter" that Morton maintained in Farmville, but these were grown men, not the White girls—Mittimus, CW v Ellick, CoCt 1829 Jan; Ms. Census, 1830, sheet 132. Washington White: FNLs, 1857 and 1858. The lack of extant FNLs for the years between 1825 and 1857 makes impossible any year-by-year tracing of the various Israelites' whereabouts. In those pioneering Israelite families I say were "still" living on Israel Hill in the late 1850s, some people had perhaps left and then returned. But the records that do exist suggest strongly that most, and probably all, families maintained a continuing presence there, and even Madison and other detractors never suggested otherwise.

74. Patterson's legacy: WB 7/273, Isham Patterson will (1831/1832), with Madison and his

nephew Patrick H. Jackson as witnesses, and John Tuggle as an executor. Pattersons and Clarkes in later years: FNLs, 1857ff. Pattersons in residence, early twentieth century: See chapter 9.

75. Sally White's death: Coroner's inquest, Sally White, June 15, 1829, Inquests, LVA; Coroner's bill, filed CoCt 1829 Jun–Jul; Unlabeled acct, Prince Edward County to Robert Hill, filed CoCt 1830 Jun–Jul.

76. Phil White Sr.'s legacy: WB 7/189, Philip White evaluation (1830); WB 7/266, Philip White est acct; White v White's admor, CoCt 1832 Mar, especially admor's acct. Why Phil White Jr. made no claim on Phil Senior's estate, and thus whether indeed he was the latter's son or some other relation, remain mysteries; Phil Senior's estate was divided instead among Sam, Hercules Junior, and Tony White, and the children of their brother, the late Dick White. Neighbor John Tuggle, who was white, at one point did record the value of Phil White Sr.'s estate at $1 less than its actual value. This seems to have been an honest mistake of arithmetic, in that Tuggle presumably earned a larger commission the more highly the estate he administered was valued.

77. Phil White's lot in Hampden: DB 18/56–57, Venable to White (1822); DB 19/156–157, White to Farrar (1825); Land tax, 1823–1825. There is no record of White's having built on the property; rather, he seems to have benefited from the lot's two-hundred-plus feet of frontage on the village's main street. John White's lot purchases: DB 21/324, Seay to White (1835); 21/417, Venable's guardian to White (1835/1836); 22/195, Randolph's trustee to White (1836/1838); and 22/190, Randolph's trustee to White (1837). Phil White's lot purchases: DB 21/276, John White to Phil White (and therefore not counted as a separate free black lot purchase for purposes of this discussion) (1835); 21/303, Farmville trustees to White (1835); 21/339–340, Venable's guardian to White (1835); 23/240–241, Chambers's trustee to White (1836/1841, two lots); 22/190–191, Randolph's trustee to White (1837). Phil's quick resale at $1,750 of real estate he had purchased for $285: DB 21/366, White to Venable and Proctor (1835/1836, part lot); 22/34–35, White to Peters (1835/1837). Another resale by Phil White at a profit: DB 21/497–498, White to Ely (1835). Sam White's lot purchases: DB 21/344–345, Venable's guardian to White (1835, three lots); 22/196, Randolph's trustee to White (1837/1838). Slaves, horses, and gig: Property tax, 1834.

78. Madison's, Jackson's, and Deneufville's lots: Plat, Watkins v Venable's heirs, CoCt 1835 Jun–Jul.

79. Lax enforcement of land tax: List of delinquent land, filed CoCt 1815 Aug–Sep. As the General Assembly intended, the land tax was collected more systematically from 1815 on; but sales of delinquent land remained relatively few, and seem to have occurred mainly when an owner had died or abandoned his or her land.

80. Witnessing tax sale of one's own land (examples): Venable v Bell, CoCt Sep 1834–Feb 1835; William Hill depo, Farrar v McDearmon, CirCt 1838 Apr. Delinquents predominantly absentees: See Insolvent land 1830, filed CoCt 1831 Sep–Oct 1831; Delinquent lots returned by George W. Booker, deputy sheriff, 1859, filed CoCt 1861 Jul–Dec. On tax delinquencies resulting from landowners being "so scattered over the country," see Samuel Jones depo, Allen v Allen, CirCt 1852 Aug; see also Prince Edward delinquent land, 1821, filed CoCt 1821 Aug–Oct, and Delinquent land, upper and lower ends, 1849, filed CoCt 1850 Apr.

81. Israel Hill delinquencies, 1827: Insolvent land tax for 1827, filed CoCt 1828 Aug, which also suggests Teny Carter's death by identifying her estate as the owner of the tract. Subsequent years: Prince Edward delinquent land, 1828, filed CoCt 1829 Jun–Jul; List of insolvent land tax . . . for 1829, filed with Insolvents, 1830 Jun, CoCt 1830 Jun–Jul; Land tax returned delinquent by Samuel Allen for 1830, filed CoCt 1831 Sep–Oct; Delinquent land, 1831, filed CoCt 1832 Jun–Aug. Division of Hercules White Sr.'s

land: White v White, CoCt 1825 Jun. Isham Patterson left certain other taxes unpaid as well during these several years—Insolvent tithes 1829, and Prince Edward delinquent property 1828, both filed CoCt 1829 Jun–Jul.

82. Sale of Dick White and Short acreage: Land tax delinquent sales, 1832, filed CoCt 1835 May; the record of the sales erroneously lists Dick White's holding before the auction as ten rather than twelve acres. Purchaser of Dick White's two acres departs: Delinquent lands, 1844, filed CoCt 1845 Mar–Apr; Delinquent land sales in 1845, filed CoCt 1845 Sep–Dec; the man had acquired five other small tax-delinquent parcels in Prince Edward. Sheriff's sales for 1833–34: Land tax delinquent sales ("List of all lands and lotts . . . sold for the nonpayment of the taxes due thereon"), 1833 and 1834, filed CoCt 1835 May.

83. White and Bartlett medical expenses: John Peter Mettauer papers, sec. 2 (acct book), 1827 Apr 28 and Oct 11, and [c. 1830] Jun 30–Sep 3 on p. 193, Mss1 M5677 a50, VHS.

84. Fight between White women: White v White, CoCt 1831 Nov; OB 22/297 (1830 May) and 556 (1831 Nov). This altercation is discussed in somewhat greater detail in chapter 6.

85. Madison's life is copiously documented in Prince Edward County Court records. Madison in militia: Bradshaw, *Prince Edward County,* pp. 229, 230, and 232. Educational activities: *Ibid.,* pp. 157 and 159; see also Trustees of H. S. College certificates of qualification, filed CoCt 1820 Sep–Oct. Overseer of the poor: Rezin Porter order for election, O[verseers of the] Poor, filed CoCt 1816 Jan–Apr. Farmville trustee: Bill, Randolph's exor v Seay, CirCt 1848 Apr. Political involvement: Bradshaw, *Prince Edward County,* pp. 184, 185, 188, 189, 297, 687, and 694.

86. N. Cunningham and Guthrey as active Democrats: Bradshaw, *Prince Edward County,* pp. 190, 198–99, 200, 201, 202, and 235. Breckenridge campaign: *Ibid.,* p. 377. Worsham as activist: *Ibid.,* pp. 185 and 188.

87. Read: *Ibid.,* pp. 190–91 and 673. Nunnally and Whites: "History—Farmville Baptist Church—Members. List furnished to Dr. Winston by Ben & Frank Robertson 1872," in Farmville Baptist Church record book, 1870–84, in the church office. Record of votes cast in 1840: Bradshaw, *Prince Edward County,* pp. 671–78. Charles Fore, who had been the conscientious master of an apprentice from the Forgason family, voted Democratic in 1840.

88. Dupuy switches parties: Bradshaw, *Prince Edward County,* pp. 184 and 186 (as Democrat), and p. 189 (as Whig by 1834); see also *Richmond Enquirer,* April 20, 1827 (Dupuy as Democrat), with thanks to Kathryn E. Miller. Relations between the Whites, the Robertsons, and Merit Steger are documented in chapters 7 and 8.

89. Involvement in transportation: Bradshaw, *Prince Edward County,* pp. 293, 295, 326, and 327. Owning batteau: Report of 1820 Census of manufactures. Interest in mining and a bank, and ownership of tavern: Bradshaw, *Prince Edward County,* pp. 305, 321–22, 310. Stores: Abraham Z. Venable affi, 1833 Jun 12, in Pleadings and exhibits, affis filed by Madison upon rule against him, 1833 Oct, Attorney General v Chambers's trustees, CirCt 1842 Sep; Gillispie v Brandum and Madison, CoCt 1840 Mar; Madison v Vernon, CirCt 1837 Sep. Slaves: Ms. Census, 1830, sheet 133. Land: Land tax 1836 (I am excluding a tract held by Madison in trust); DB 21/426–427, Allen to Madison, an acquisition that seems to have occurred too late to be entered in the 1836 land tax roll.

90. Steger, Read, and Robertson in tobacco business: See Bradshaw, *Prince Edward County,* pp. 300–01, and chapters 7 and 8 below.

91. Cosigning with Phil White: Bill, bond of White and Jackson, and James M. Jackson depo, all in Venable v Edmunds, CirCt 1847 Apr. Dealings with John White and Brandum: Jackson v White, CirCt 1840 Apr; Jackson v Brandum, CirCt 1840 Sep–Dec. The record does not reveal whether Jackson lent money to White and

Brandum or sold them merchandise or capital goods. Jackson would end up suing for the balance of his money, as so often happened during the stressful years after 1837, but he instructed his attorney to require no bail of the black men.

92. Tobacco industry in Farmville: This and subsequent discussion draws heavily on the Bill, answer, and depos in Daniel v Steger, CirCt 1837 Sep; other references are cited individually. The most informative depositions on the technical aspects of processing tobacco are those of William L. Lanier ("superior texture") and Joseph L. Watkins.

93. Women workers: FNLs, 1857ff. Five factories employing one third of population: Martin, *Gazetteer of Virginia*, p. 268. The number of factories grew to seven by 1837— Benjamin M. Robertson and David Bruce depos for defendant, Daniel v Steger, CirCt 1837 Sep.

94. "It is always difficult": James Madison depo, Daniel v Steger. "Stemming and twisting": David Bruce depo for plaintiff, same case. "The hands got about Farmville": David Bruce depo for defendant, same case.

95. Paying slaves: Madison acct with Venable & Venable (1837–39), Madison's trustees v Morton (MTvM), CirCt 1854 Aug; Document A, commissioner Berkeley's audit, *passim*, in Chambers's committee v Madison's exor (CCvME), CirCt 1842 Apr. Number hired out, and number owned by Chambers: Royal F. Godsey affi, 1833 Jun 11, Attorney General v Chambers's trustees, CirCt 1842 Sep; Document A in CCvME. Slave surnames: Madison to Edmunds, DoT (1839), MTvM; Document A, pp. 4–5 and 32, in CCvME. Ironically, Madison displayed his regard for black family ties in a deed of trust that in effect tendered those slaves as part of the colonel's collateral for a loan.

96. Defective warrants: CW v Lilly, CoCt 1825 Mar, and OB 21/170 (1825 Mar; warrant to call court); CW v Thomas and CW v Major, CoCt 1828 Oct, and OB 21/769 (1828 Oct).

97. Bailing Stonum: Cf. Recognizance of witnesses, CW v Stonum, CoCt 1820 Nov, and OB 19/463 (1821 Nov). Brown: Certf with twenty-five citizens' signatures accompanying petition of Billy Brown, 1825 Dec 14, Legislative petitions, LVA. Loren Schweninger writes that Billy Brown at least nominally re-enslaved himself after purchasing his freedom and seeing his petition to remain in Virginia denied by the legislature—*Black Property Owners in the South, 1790–1915* (Urbana and Chicago: University of Illinois Press, 1990), p. 47. Brown's petition of 1825 seems to say something rather different, however: that Brown purchased himself from his master, who was about to leave the state, and that Brown borrowed part of the money to do so from a second white man, whose nominal slave Brown then became while he labored to return the loan. That white man would have been entrepreneur George King, who faced a charge in 1827 of letting Brown go about as a free man, and who then formally emancipated Brown—OB 21/518 (1827 Mar) and OB 21/541 (1827 May). Neither is it clear that Brown's earlier petition to the General Assembly was actively "rejected": a legislative committee declared the black man's request to stay in Virginia "reasonable" and ordered a bill drawn up to approve it; the Assembly's failure to act may have been a simple oversight—Notation on Petition of Billy Brown, 1818 Dec 18, Legislative petitions, LVA.

98. Bad debts: Bad & Doubtfull debts due Madison, Venable & Dunnington, 1842 Aug 4, in Madison's trustees v Morton, CirCt 1854 Aug.

99. Hire of slave: Gillispie for Davis v Brandum and Madison, CoCt 1840 Mar; OB 24/298 and 321 (1839 Nov and 1840 Mar). Brandum took the oath of insolvency, in effect a declaration of bankruptcy at least as regarded this particular debt. Madison acknowledged the validity of the debt for the hire of the slave, but soon died with enormous obligations and may never have paid.

100. Madison probably also knew that Brandum and his family had moved from Israel Hill to Farmville in the 1820s, belying the colonel's charge that the Hill's population

had stagnated even without any emigration from the settlement. Brandums' move: IH 1816; FNLs, 1819 and 1821ff. Randolph Brandum seems to have enjoyed some favor with local authorities even after he was accused by a Cumberland man of illegally employing his slave, and after Brandum's business collapsed. When the black man was sued for a $300 debt in 1839, county court clerk Branch Worsham helped get the case dismissed—Carroll v Brandum, CoCt 1840 Feb; OB 24/315 (1840 Feb).

101. Madison buys plantation: DB 21/426–427, Allen to Madison (1835/1836), and 21/337–339, Madison to Allen, DoT (1835). Madison takes up residency; lack of road: James Madison road report, filed CoCt 1836 Nov. Bridle path: Tony White's motion, OB 22/309–310 (1830 May).

102. Ellis's shoemaking (for Madison as administrator of Chambers's affairs): Document A, commissioner Berkeley's audit, 1833, entries for 1826 Feb 7 and 26, Chambers's committee v Madison's exor, CirCt 1842 Apr. Assault suit: Ellis v Madison, CirCt 1838 Sep; Circuit Superior Court Order Book, 1831–37 [which actually runs to 1843], p. 144 (1838 Sep), in office of CirCt clerk, Prince Edward County Courthouse, Farmville. Cf. hung juries—but not multiple ones—in "nonracial" cases of the same period, including Burwell v Vernon, CirCt 1840 Apr; Tucker's exor v Overton, CirCt 1840 Sep. Successive hung juries in a single case, when they occurred at all, came in instances in which principles of fairness apparently competed with the perceived imperative of maintaining the slave regime. The language of complaints in assault suits was generally formulaic, listing a wide array of weapons and projectiles the alleged assailant had supposedly used, but the prominence and iteration in Ellis's complaint of "whips, cowhides, [and] switches" suggest that Madison indeed had whipped him.

103. Employing Billy Ellis: Document A, commissioner Berkeley's audit, *passim*, in Chambers's committee v Madison's exor, CirCt 1842 Apr (employing Ellis in previous years); James Madison acct with Flippin & Dunnington, 1839 Mar, in Madison's trustees v Morton (MTvM), CirCt 1854 Aug (employment after 1838). "J Johnson": James Madison acct with Venable & Venable (1837–39), 1838 Nov 10, in MTvM.

104. Allegations against Madison: Petition of Josiah Thackston et al., Attorney General v Chambers's trustees (AGvCT), CirCt 1842 Sep. Records suggest that Madison may indeed have employed several slaves of Chambers in his tobacco factory—see Madison's accts, and Chambers est acct with B. F. Wilson (with five physician's visits to Chambers slaves "at factory"), both in AGvCT; and Chambers acct with Madison, p. 71, in Record, Venable v Goode's admor, CirCt Sep 1848. Madison had become administrator of the Chambers plantation in 1825.

105. Road petition denied: James Madison road report, filed CoCt 1836 Nov; OB 23/443, 452, 464, and 491 (1836 Jun, Jul, Sep, and Nov); Madison appealed to the circuit court, with what results I have been unable to determine.

106. Tony White's road petition: OB 22/309–310 (1830 May). Other road petitions by individuals considered in same period, several of them contested and a couple aborted (all references are to OB 22, except as indicated): Rudd's to Sandy River church, 44, 57, 118, and 440 (1829 Feb–1831 Apr); Flournoy's to Court House road, 596 and 624, and OB 23/54 (1832 Mar–Nov); Scott's to Nunnally's (discontinue road), 147 and 181 (1829 Aug–Sep); Phillips for Ligon's Mill road, 239 and 247 (1829 Dec–1830 Jan); Road by Henry E. Watkins's, 423 and 528 (1831 Feb–Sep; granted and ordered to be carried out by the surveyor of the current road); From Sandy River road by Ligon's, 626 and OB 23/10-11 (1832 May–Jun); Bush River to Court House by Redd's, 383 (1830 Nov); By Ligon's mill (by Thomas C. Ligon), 535 and OB 23/40 (1831 Oct–1832 Sep); Scott's mill to Watkins's tavern, 591 (1832 Mar); also Road order in Hughes v Cheadle, CoCt 1822 Aug.

107. "Greatly embarrassed"; "notoriously insolvent": Bill, and decree of 1847 May 7, Venable v Edmunds, Cir Ct 1847 Apr. Plutarch's *Lives:* Deputy sheriff's notation on writ

of attachment, Bruce's exor v Madison et al., CirCt 1840 Sep–Dec. Plan to leave state: Bill, Chambers's committee v Madison's exor, CirCt 1842 Apr. Madison's death: Madison's est, filed CirCt 1841 Apr. Documentation of Madison's financial collapse is copious in county court records for the last few years of the colonel's life; see, e.g., in addition to the cases cited elsewhere in these notes, Spencer v Madison, CoCt 1838 May; some half a dozen suits in CoCt, 1839 Nov–1840 Feb; and Anderson & Co. v Madison (two suits), CirCt 1841 Sep.

108. Madison promotes expansion of town: See Venable v Venable, CoCt 1834 Nov (concerning the W. G. Venable addition). Diversion of funds: Bill, and decree of 1847 May 7, Venable v Edmunds, Cir Ct 1847 Apr; Morton et al. v Madison et al., 1841 Sep; see also Bill, Martin v Goode, CirCt 1844 Apr; Answer, Madison v Morton, CirCt 1847 Sep; and Venable v Goode's admor, CirCt 1848 Sep. Madison did not personally own the Chambers plantation, and his accepting official positions that fed the Chambers coffers did not in itself offend the sensibilities of the time. Madison's own records do show that, as trustee, he had bought supplies for the Chambers estate from companies in which he himself was a partner—Document A, *passim*, in Chambers's committee v Madison's exor (CCvME), CirCt 1842 Apr. $40,000: Court order in CCvME; cf. Report of commissioner Watkins, CCvME.

109. Madison's accusation and slander suit: Geohegan v Madison, CoCt 1837 May, and OB 23/436 (1836 May) and 24/28 (1837 May).

110. Lot purchases: DB 21/18, Farmville trustees to Madison (1833). Windfall sale: DB 21/20-21, Madison to Watkins (1833). Sale to Methodists: DB 21/183-185, Madison to Scott et al. (1833/1834); Deed, Madison to Trustees of church, filed CirCt 1845 Sep. Democracy in Farmville: Election of trustees for Farmville, filed CoCt 1824 Mar; Farmville trustees, report of election, filed CoCt 1835 Mar–Apr.

111. "Veriest paupers": Leigh at Virginia State Convention, 1829–30, quoted in Freehling, *Drift Toward Dissolution,* p. 75. Leigh employed by Judith Randolph (he drafted her will): "The Randolph Family," *Farmville Mercury,* September 23, 1875. Leigh employed by Madison: James Madison, letter to Benjamin Watkins Leigh, n.d., Attorney General v Chambers's trustees, CirCt 1842 Sep.

112. Few "idle" blacks: FNL, Cumberland County, 1851, LVA.

113. Prince Edward contributors to *Farmers' Register:* One of Woodson's contributions there is summarized in chapter 6; see also Bradshaw, *Prince Edward County,* p. 357, on William S. Morton. Ruffin's frustrations: See William M. Mathew, *Edmund Ruffin and the Crisis of Slavery in the Old South: The Failure of Agricultural Reform* (Athens: University of Georgia Press, 1988), especially chapter 11. "Very good"; "exhausted": Martin, *Gazetteer of Virginia,* pp. 265–66. My understanding of Ruffin also owes a good deal to the research of two of my undergraduate students at Yale, Shawn Childs and Nat Keohane; and to David F. Allmendinger Jr., *Ruffin: Family and Reform in the Old South* (New York and Oxford: Oxford University Press, 1990), and Betty L. Mitchell, *Edmund Ruffin: A Biography* (Bloomington: Indiana University Press, 1981).

114. Girdled trees: Joseph H. Borum depo in Allen v Thurston's admor, CoCt 1823 Dec–1824 Mar.

115. Jefferson's prediction: Martin, *Gazetteer of Virginia,* p. 69. William G. Shade writes that Virginia's demographic, economic, and political development had actually reattained healthy proportions by the time laments such as Martin's were issued in the 1830s—Shade, *Democratizing the Old Dominion: Virginia and the Second Party System, 1824–1861* (Charlottesville and London: University Press of Virginia, 1996), p. 6 and *passim.*

116. "Honest[,] unoffending": Certf with twenty-five citizens' signatures accompanying petition of Billy Brown, 1825 Dec 14, legislative petitions, LVA.

117. "Despised and suspected": Minutes, Virginia branch, American Colonization Society, 1823 Nov 4–1859 Feb 5, p. 30, Mss3 AM353 a1, VHS.

118. This ironic harmony among the abolitionist, colonizationist, and proslavery lines on free blacks was remarked upon many years ago by two pioneering African American historians: Carter G. Woodson, *Free Negro Heads of Families in the United States in 1830, Together with a Brief Treatment of the Free Negro* (Washington, DC: Association for the Study of Negro Life and History, 1925), pp. xxxiii–iv, and later, Luther Porter Jackson, *Free Negro Labor and Property Holding in Virginia, 1830–1860* (New York and London: D. Appleton–Century, 1942), pp. 32–33.

119. "The good conduct": J. D. Eggleston, typescript beginning, "Richard Randolph of Bizarre . . . ," p. 2, in Eggleston papers, Mss1 Egg3966, section 30, "Slavery," VHS; and Eggleston, letter to W. M. Thornton, January 22, 1934, in folder, "Prince Edward County," second stack, General Library, LVA, courtesy of John Kneebone.

120. The article of 1835 lambasting communities of manumitted blacks in Ohio included a similar tiny loophole, admitting that "two or three families" among a thousand black settlers might have improved themselves as free people—*Cincinnati Gazette*, reprinted in *Farmers' Register*, 3, no. 430 (November 1835), in U. B. Phillips papers, Yale.

CHAPTER 6: *Law and Order*

1. An alleged murder by the defendant of his own slave: CW v Andrews, OB 13/250 (1803 May). Prosecution after inconclusive inquest (Baker and Scipio): CW v Baker, CoCt 1811 Aug, and CirCt 1811 Sep; and also Coroner's acct for examination of the court (inquisition on Scipio, 1811 Aug 2), filed CoCt 1812 Jun–Aug. A third prosecution: Coroner's inquisition, Nancy, 1814 (explicit accusation), Inquests, LVA; CW v Farley, District Court OB, 1805–31, pp. 456 and 459–60 (1814 Apr); CirCt 1814 Apr (sixteen white witnesses). Cf. acquittal of aggravated assault on a slave toward end of antebellum period: CW v Cobbs, CoCt 1859 Mar; Circuit Superior Court of Law and Chancery minute book, 1846–70, 1859 Aug 12 and 13, 1860 Mar 13, LVA; but contrast conviction of James D. Shepherd, another master charged with shooting, though not killing, one of his own slaves, discussed later in this chapter.

2. Inquest over Robin, slave of Overton, submitted July 18, 1859, filed CoCt 1859 May–Sep, especially statements of Dr. J. Lyle ("flogged"), Samuel W. Bondurant ("as badly whipped"), and Giles Cockran ("a great many negroes").

3. Two-year sentence: CW v Harvey, CoCt 1831 Jun (filed 1831 Jul), and CirCt 1831 Jun–1832 Apr. Contrast an acquittal in a similar case: CW v Price, CoCt 1829 May, and CirCt 1829 Sep. One white man was required in 1859 to post a $1,000 bond to guarantee his peaceful behavior toward another man's slave—Circuit Superior Court Order Book, 1853–70, p. 241 (1859 Aug), in office of CirCt clerk, Prince Edward County Courthouse, Farmville.

4. Brandum trial: CW v Brandon [sic], CoCt 1842 Jan; OB 25/36 (1841 Dec) and 43 (1842 Jan). Non-slaveholding white witness: William Riley Wright; cf. W. R. Wright, Ms. Census, 1830, sheet 235.

5. Dudley acquitted: CW v Dudley, CoCt 1821 Mar; OB 20/10 (1821 Mar). Alleged attempted murder of "a free white man": CW v Stepney, CoCt 1829 May; OB 22/94 (1829 May). Alleged stabbing and beating: CW v Lindsey (two cases), CoCt 1833 Aug; OB 23/154 (1833 Aug).

6. Attempted rape and slave's rescue attempt: CW v Smith, CoCt 1842 May; OB 25/53 and 71 (1842 Mar and May). Serial offender: CW v Smith and Smith, in same locations.

7. Killing of Foster by Tom: CW v Tom, CoCt 1825 Nov; OB 21/274, 275, and 281–284 (1825 Nov); N. Jones et al. guard claims, filed CoCt 1826 Jul. Tom was not owned by his overseer's sister or brother-in-law; the bondman had been hired from another master, apparently for a considerable stretch of time.

8. Choked his master: CW v Will, Jacob, and Martin, CoCt 1810 Oct, and OB 16/630–633 (1810 Oct); and CW to Joseph Walker voucher, filed CoCt 1810; OB 16/632-633 (1810 Oct); County acct with Lockett, 1810, filed CoCt 1811 Jun–Jul.

9. Killing of slave traders: CW v Moses, George, and Littleton, CoCt 1834 May; and OB 23/221, 224-226, and 230-232. Ambush: CW v Scott's Simon, Wootton's Simon, and John, CoCt 1848 Aug; OB 26/254-255 and 256 (1848 Aug); Coroner's inquest, Charles A. Scott, 1848 Jul, Inquests, LVA.

10. Escapes by Miles: Cheadle, 30th p. (numbered as p. 8), 1823 Dec 26 and 1824 Jun 6; 31st p. (numbered as p. 9), 1824 Aug 16; and 41st p. (numbered as p. 19), 1830 Jun. Dupuy-Purnall escapee: Herbert Clarence Bradshaw, *History of Prince Edward County, Virginia, from Its Earliest Settlements Through Its Establishment in 1754 to Its Bicentennial Year* (Richmond: Dietz Press, 1955), p. 272. Phoebe: Martin Saylor est acct with James D. Wood, filed CirCt 1829 Aug and Dec.

11. Medical testimony: CW v Susan, CoCt 1852 Mar.

12. "Reputed poisoner": See an example from the same summer Phoebe Giles sued Sooky White, in which a white man complained to the county court that another man had sold him a slave whom he then discovered to be "of infamous character . . . a reputed poisoner"—Bill in Dejarnett v Jefferess & Hurt, CoCt 1813 Jun–Aug; but the ended date for the only suit between these parties in the corresponding OB, 17/206, is 1811 Nov. Trials of George: CW v George, OB 11/617 (1797 Nov); CW v George, CoCt 1813 Mar, and OB 17/501 (1813 Mar). Slaves accused of poisoning other slaves: CW v Renah and CW v Fanny, CoCt 1832 Aug, and OB 23/14-17; CW v Pharaoh, CoCt 1817 Feb; CW v Sy, CoCt 1833 Jun; CW v Ben, CoCt 1841 May.

13. Slaves tried for arson and acquitted or discharged, listed with the object of their alleged crime: CW v Isaac, CoCt 1815 Nov, and OB 18/333 (Peter Fore's mill house); CW v Ellick, CoCt 1829 Jan, and OB 22/41 ("a certain Building commonly called a negro quarter" in Farmville); CW v Billy, CoCt 1834 Jul, and OB 23/250 (stables); CW v Jordan, CoCt 1837 Jul (a barn); CW v Venable, CoCt 1840 Feb, and OB 24/320 (a tobacco factory); CW v Edwin, CoCt 1854 Oct (a tobacco barn and wheat house). White man accused of arson: Holland v Fore, CoCt 1817 Aug, especially unlabeled statement of Peter Fore. Whites accused of poisoning: Mary Armstead depo, Holeman v Holeman, CoCt 1825 Oct; Answer, Hurt v Hurt, CirCt 1851 Apr.

14. Padlocks (example): Samuel Baldwin est acct with Baldwin exor, 1850 Oct 25, four padlocks, filed Cir Ct 1854 Mar. Accompanying cook: Testimony, CW v Susan, CoCt 1852 Mar. Knife worth 25 cents: CW v Doctor, CoCt 1817 Jun; OB 18/592 (1817 Jun). Hogshead of tobacco: CW v Thomas and Major, CoCt 1828 Oct; OB 21/769 (1828 Oct). Watches and jewelry: CW v Dick, CoCt 1856 Feb.

15. No aggravating factors; "well laid on": CW v Joe, OB 7/75 (1783 Jun), and a number of examples in subsequent years.

16. Two slaves, three burglaries: CW v Charlton and Brister, CoCt 1823 Jul; OB 20/534-535. Watches and jewelry: CW v Dick, CoCt 1856 Feb; OB 27/150 (1856 Feb).

17. Fourteen lashes: CW v Brooks, CoCt 1815 Jan–Apr; OB 18/185 (1814 Dec) and 18/205 (1815 Mar). Tobacco theft: CW v Goins/Gowen, CoCt 1830 Dec–1831 Feb; 1831 Sep, and OB 22/529-530 (denied bail); CirCt 1831 Sep (exclusion of testimony regarding black man; sentence imposed).

18. Forgason: CW v Ferguson, OB 16/233 (1808 Nov).

19. First Lilly trial: CW v Lilly, CoCt 1823 Nov; OB 20/624 and 626 (626 refers to the court's "remiting fourteen lashes"). Lilly's acquittal: CW v Lilly, CoCt 1825 Mar, and OB 21/170 (1825 May).

20. Acquittal of stealing four hogs from two different victims: CW v Rucker, CoCt 1813 Dec; OB 17/615 (1813 Dec). Dismissal on technicality of charges in three separate hog thefts: CW v Sanker, CoCt 1823 Apr; OB 20/478 (1823 Apr). Vigorous defense (example): CW v Phil and Pryor, CoCt 1827 Nov, and OB 21/629 (1827 Nov; at least

eight white men and four slaves summoned for the defense); and, as fallout from the same case, Wilson v Garnett, CoCt 1837 Jul, and Garnett ads Wilson, CirCt 1838 Apr.

21. Five or six years' imprisonment: CW v Goolsby, CirCt 1808 Apr; CW v Maxey, CoCt 1824 Jun, and CirCt 1824 Sep (six-year sentence); CW v Fox, CoCt 1840 May, OB 24/355-356 (1840 May), and CirCt 1840 Sep.

22. Charges against Hill: CW v Hill, CoCt 1855 Nov. Background of Constable William F. Scott: CW v George, CoCt 1854 Feb (Scott family); OP v Scott, CoCt 1850 Sep (mulatto child). A good overview of Virginia's district and superior (circuit) courts is F. Thornton Miller, *Juries and Judges Versus the Law: Virginia's Provincial Legal Perspective, 1783–1828* (Charlottesville and London: University Press of Virginia, 1994), pp. 24–33.

23. Horse theft case: CW v Bradley, CoCt 1841 Aug, and OB 24/475 (1841 Aug); CoCt 1841 Nov, and OB 25/25 (1841 Nov). Jim Bradley as outsider: Bradley was arrested in Lynchburg, and at least one witness against him was summoned from there. One justice opined that constituting the court that tried Bradley as a court of oyer and terminer for trial of a free black ran contrary to the United States Constitution—OB 24/475. Whether this was a mere technical point or a principled insistence that Bradley receive a trial in the circuit court as a white man would must remain an intriguing question.

24. Alleged burglary at Forgasons': CW v Young, CoCt 1842 Aug; OB 25/95 (1842 Aug). Martha Young's background and age: Warrants in CW v Young (1842), which name the defendant's mother; cf. CW v Young (1844) just below, which does not name a parent of Martha Young, who had probably just reached the age of majority. As it had done in the initial Jim Bradley horse theft proceeding and in a burglary case against three slaves several years earlier, the court declared that it lacked jurisdiction to try the defendant. Second Young prosecution: CW v Young, CoCt 1844 Feb; OB 25/270 (1844 Feb).

25. Young's father a slave; poor aid: [Property tax] Insolvents, 1825, filed CoCt 1826 Nov (Esther Young listed as owning one slave); Table no. 2, OP Report for 1825 and 1826 [and part of 1827], filed CoCt 1827 Jun–Jul (with the unusual entry, "Easther Young & husband"); Parish of St Patrick [OP] to J. McDearmon &c., acct, 1828, filed CoCt 1828 Jun.

26. Gregory case: CW v Gregory, CoCt 1854 May; OB 27/29 (1853 Nov) and 27/59 (1854 May). Twenty-dollar fines against whites for buying corn from slaves: See CW v Winn and CW v Noell, presentments, CirCt 1830 Apr, and CirCt 1831 Sep.

27. Mettauer case: CW v Mettauer: CoCt 1853 Mar; OB 26/377 and 538 (1850 Aug and 1853 Mar).

28. Homes charges: CW v Homes and CW v Caesar, CoCt 1845 Jul; OB 26/49 (1845 Jul).

29. Presentments for receiving stolen goods from slaves (examples): CW v Patrick H. Jackson (the entrepreneur), presentment, CoCt 1832 Aug, and OB 23/23; CW v Wilkinson and Jenkins, OB 24/439 (May 1841); CW v Carter, CoCt 1841 Oct; and CW v Franklin (two gold coins), CoCt 1856 Mar. The outcome for Wilkinson and Jenkins is uncertain, but none of the other three prosecutions ended with a guilty verdict.

30. Woodson's views: Charles Woodson, letter, July 9, 1834, in *Farmers' Register*, 2, no. 4 (September 1834). This letter is quoted in Bradshaw, *Prince Edward County*, pp. 273–74, with the mistranscription of a key word (substituting "exceptionally" for "unexceptionable"). Eugene D. Genovese, *Roll, Jordan, Roll: The World the Slaves Made* (New York: Vintage, 1974), p. 643, renders the phrase in question correctly.

31. Moving about: CW v Joshua, CoCt 1832 Aug. Another similar story of slave mobility is found in CW v Peter, CoCt 1821 Apr.

32. "Sitting up with the Corps": WB 3/249-250, Thomas Jones est acct with Richard Jones (1801/1802). Wades: WB 4/40-41, Philip Wade est acct with Daniel Wade

(1806/1807). Other examples of brandy for appraisers and bidders at estate sales: WB 3/418, Cuthbert H. Rowland est acct with Zachariah Rice (1803/1805); WB 4/96, Littleberry Davis est acct with John Taggart (1804/1807); Owen Haskins est acct, 1809 Jul, Haskins v Ligon, CirCt 1844 Sep.

33. Rolling tobacco: Copy of proceedings, Attorney General v Chambers's trustees, Josiah Chambers acct with Watson, Allen & Green, his committee, 1809 Apr 26 (p. 30) and 1811 Mar 9 (p. 36), CoCt 1821 Nov. "Measuring corn": *Ibid.*, 1811 Dec 3 (p. 38). Rolling logs: WB 4/107, Richard Dowdy est acct with Robert Kelso (1808). Hog killing: Leighton A. Boaz acct with Nathaniel Venable, 1817 Feb 27, Boaz v Venable, CoCt 1822 May. "For 2 gallons . . . raising the house": Benjamin Hubbard acct with Clark & Hubbard, Hubbard v Clark, CirCt 1844 Apr. Liquor for harvesters: Zadock Lackland est acct with James Lackland, acct B, 1828 Jun 16, Sublett v Lackland, CirCt 1851 Sep; John Tuggle for Jonathan Penick, guardians' accounts, 1829–55 (microfilm), pp. 12–15, 1829 Jun; Cheadle, 5th p., fall 1832; Barnet M. Brightwell depo, Davis v Bradley, CirCt 1839 Sep.

34. Liquor to slaves at hiring out: WB 3/171, Jesse Owen est acct with Christopher Dejarnett (1798/1799), entry in 1792; WB 4/96, Littleberry Davis est acct with John Taggart (1804/1807); Ebenezer McRobert est acct with Samuel Carter, 1818 Dec 28, Smith v McRobert, CoCt 1825 Jun; Copy of proceedings, Attorney General v Chambers's trustees, Josiah Chambers acct with Watson, Allen & Green, his committee, 1805 Dec 28 (p. 21), 1807 Dec 28 (p. 27), 1809 Dec 28 (p. 32), 1810 Dec 28 (p. 36), 1811 Dec 28 (p. 39), in CoCt 1821 Nov.

35. Richardson elected sheriff: OB 26/492 (1852 Jun). Fined for liquor sales: CW v Richardson, three separate cases: CirCt 1848 Oct (originally filed 1848 Sep); CirCt 1850 Sep; CW v Richardson, CoCt 1850 Oct–Nov.

36. Read as "temperance man": Bradshaw, *Prince Edward County*, p. 270. Read before grand jury: CW v Davis, presentment, CirCt 1832 Apr.

37. Short and whites charged: Presentments, CW v Neighbours, CW v Reynolds, CW v Ritchie, and CW v Short, OB 17/507-508 (1813 May); disposition of Neighbours, Reynolds, and Short cases, OB 18/22-23 (1814 Mar), and CoCt 1814 Mar (Short and Reynolds convicted); disposition of Ritchie case, OB 18/78 (1814 May), and CoCt 1814 May. John Reynolds, a nonslaveholder, was assessed a second $30 fine for committing the same offense at a different muster ground on a different day that same spring— CW v Reynolds, District Court Order Book, 1805–31, pp. 439 (1813 Apr) and 471 (1815 Apr). Nonslaveholder: Property tax, 1815 and 1816. In a separate case of illegal liquor selling by a free black, a man known simply as Morton was charged with selling spirits outdoors in 1813—CW v Morton, presentment, CoCt 1813 Aug. Insolvency of Short and Ritchie: J. McDearmon, letter via Mr. Patterson to court, May 17, 1818, filed CoCt 1818 Jun–Jul; OB 19/22 (1818 Jun). The court "remitted" the fines of convicted liquor sellers on a few occasions—OB 17/142 and 145 (1811 Aug).

38. First charge against Moss: CW v Moss, CoCt 1819 Aug; OB 19/97 (1818 Nov), 223 (1819 Aug), 389 (1820 Jun; fine waived). Second charge against Moss: CW v Moss, CoCt 1820 May; OB 19/265 (1819 Nov) and 349 (1820 May). Cheadle neighbor convicted: CW v Faris (two counts), CoCt 1820 Mar; OB 19/326 (1820 Mar).

39. Diuguid: CW v Diuguid, CirCt 1844 Apr (two presentments), and CirCt 1846 Sep; the second count was nol-prossed (CW v Diuguid, CirCt 1847 Apr). This surname is sometimes rendered as "Duiguid" or "Dinguid." Black and white liquor defendants (James Moss and Robert Bowman, respectively): Presentments, CirCt 1841 Apr; CW v Moss, CirCt 1842 Sep; CW v Bowman, CirCt 1842 Apr.

40. Three-day gambling session with vendors: Presentments, CirCt 1837 Apr.

41. Forty dollars won or lost (example): CW v Robertson, 1834 May.

42. An apparent coerced confession: OB 17/539-541 (1813 Jun), William Fowlkes and

Edward Bradshaw testimony, CW v Anthony. Another instance: CW v Smith and CW v Ridley, CoCt 1826 Jul, and OB 21/404-405 (1826 Jul). The court convicted the abused slave anyway, against whom there was good evidence beyond the confession, but it discounted the damning testimony against a second defendant delivered by the white man who had whipped the first suspect. Allegation by enslaved witness of interrogation accompanied by coercion: Testimony—apparently of slave Titus, although attribution is not perfectly clear—in CW v Cephas, CoCt 1846 Jul.

43. Dr. Rice and slave wedding: CW v Rice, presentment, CirCt 1849 Sep, and CirCt 1850 Sep; the quotations come from Rice's affidavit replying to the charge against him. The name of the slave bride is not mentioned anywhere in the court papers. Rice minister at Hampden-Sydney Church: William S. White, *The African Preacher: An Authentic Narrative* (Philadelphia: Presbyterian Board of Publication, 1849), at http://docsouth. unc.edu/white/white.html. Benjamin Rice was the brother of John Holt Rice; the latter founded Union Theological Seminary of Virginia, befriended Judith Randolph, and was married to Anne S. Rice, who would eventually manumit a number of slaves. Benjamin Rice living in North: See Philip B. Price, *Life of the Reverend John Holt Rice, D. D.* (Richmond: Library of Union Theological Seminary in Virginia, [1886–87] 1963), p. 141. Other allegations of permitting unlawful assemblages: CW v Kidd, CoCt 1842 Nov, and OB 25/134 (1842 Nov; case dismissed); CW v Warner, CirCt 1844 Apr (fine of $17 for allowing thirty slaves to hear "negro preaching" at defendant's house); CW v Mills and Bradley, CirCt 1846 Sep (defendants acquitted).

44. On the toll of unpredictable enforcement, see Ira Berlin, *Slaves Without Masters: The Free Negro in the Antebellum South* (New York: New Press, [1974] 1992), pp. 331–34, the thrust of which, however, differs from the interpretation presented here.

45. Alleged assault on patrol: CW v Jenkins, Wheeler, Noble, Erambert, and Womack, CirCt 1851 Apr (presentments); CirCt 1852 Apr (CW v Womack), and 1852 Aug (the other four cases). Joel W. Womack a county justice: Bradshaw, *Prince Edward County*, pp. 679 and 680. The acquittals and nol-prosses came even though Hillery G. Richardson, soon to be sheriff, joined the patrolmen in giving testimony before the grand jury that presented the "rescuers."

46. Allowing slaves "to go at large": CW v Carter and CW v Williams, presentments, Cir Ct 1851 Apr 29; CW v Carter, CirCt 1852 Apr (acquittal), and 1852 Aug (conviction); CW v Williams, CirCt 1853 Mar (conviction on two counts). These convictions brought fines of $10 to $14 plus costs.

47. Sears and white alleged lawbreakers: CW v Coffee, CoCt 1833 May, OB 22/541 (1831 Nov, presentment, with patrollers Sears and Jacob Tibbs as informants), and OB 23/113 (1833 May); CW v Coleman, presentment, CoCt 1832 Nov. Sears's accusation against Robert B. Wright: CW v Wright, CoCt 1826 May. Charges against alleged rescuers, and dismissal: CW v Samuel and William Wright, presentment, CoCt 1833 Mar, and OB 23/83 (1833 Mar); CoCt 1833 May (filed separately from Sears's peace bond case against Wright group), and OB 23/114 (1833 May). Patrollers' request for peace bond, and identities of patrollers and "rescuers": Arrest warrant, patrol commission, and summons to witnesses, in CW v Wright et al., CoCt 1833 May; see also CW v Wooldridge, CoCt 1833 May. Resisting and threatening patrol in 1860: CW v Bland, presentment, CoCt 1860 Nov. Such discord among whites had very old precedents. In 1813, for example, patrollers pressed charges against three men for "protecting an unlawful assemblage of negroes" from the would-be enforcers of order—OB 17/600 (1813 Nov).

48. "All slaves[,] free negroes or mulattoes": Patrol commission in CW v Wright et al., as in note 47 (emphasis added).

49. Patrols visit Purnall's or assemble at Purnall's store: See William Dodd patrol return, recorded 1808 Jul 18, filed CoCt 1809 Jun–Jul; McGehee &c. Patroler, n.d. [1809 or

1810], filed in CoCt [1810?] Jun–Aug. Free blacks at Purnall's: FNL, lower district, 1802; and see discussions of Homes family in earlier chapters. John Purnall proprietor of "Purnall's store": Bradshaw, *Prince Edward County*, p. 310.

50. Genovese, *Roll, Jordan, Roll*, p. 22, largely endorses the "white trash" theory of patrol personnel. Sally E. Hadden, *Slave Patrols: Law and Violence in Virginia and the Carolinas* (Cambridge, MA, and London: Harvard University Press, 2001), pp. 90–104, challenges it, albeit without much reference to evidence from nineteenth-century Virginia; see pp. 103–04 for some general conclusions. For one of countless examples of how the "white trash" theory has permeated popular culture, see Alex Haley, *Roots* (Garden City, NY: Doubleday, 1976), p. 272.

51. "Patter role all Night": Paul Mullins patrol return, in Sundry claims against county, filed CoCt 1820 Jun–Jul. Mullins owned only one juvenile slave; his fellow patroller Osborne Meadows owned an enslaved woman and (presumably her own) three children. The other two patrollers do not even appear as heads of households—Ms. Census, 1820.

52. Well-established citizens on patrol: Charles Woodson patrol return, filed CoCt 1811 Jun–Jul (apparently the future militia colonel of that name); David B. McGehee and William Clark patrol returns in county levy, filed CoCt 1813 Jun (including Booker Foster, who at the time owned ten slaves older than twelve—Property tax, 1813); OB 18/259-261 (1815 Jun); OB 21/35-38 (1824 Jun); OB 21/219-222 (1825 Jun); OB 21/708-709 (1828 Jun); OB 22/119-122 (1829 Jun); and neighbors of Israel Hill enumerated in note 53. Examples from 1850s: Patrol returns of James M. Marshall, in unlabeled bundle of county accts, filed CoCt 1850 May–Jul (including Creed P. Harper, who was well established enough to serve as a road "surveyor" according to a return from him filed in the same bundle, and who would own more than $7,000 in real and personal property by 1860—Ms. Census, 1860, family visitation 75); Christopher C. Phillips, in Sundry claims v county, filed CoCt 1851 Jun (including Edmund S. Lockett, Peter Redford, and Edward G. Redford; Lockett owned 590 acres in Land tax, 1850, and planter-surveyor Edward Redford the elder had laid out the property lines on what became Israel Hill); William J. McGehee, filed CoCt 1856 Apr–Jun (including Vincent Phillips Jr.; Vincent Phillips Sr. owned $4,000 in real estate—Ms. Census, 1850, family visitation 699—and would have $35,000 worth of real and personal property by 1860—Ms. Census, 1860, family visitation 51); William J. Foster (unlabeled), filed CoCt 1857 May (including Albert G. Green, whose father, with whom Albert Jr. lived, owned $35,000 in real and personal property in 1860—Ms. Census, family visitation 462). Vincent Phillips Sr. served on the county court from 1825 to 1852, and Albert G. Green Sr. from 1845 to 1852—Bradshaw, *Prince Edward County*, pp. 679–80. See also OB 27/317 (1859 May).

53. Patrollers around Israel Hill: See Patrol returns of Josiah Penick (1809 Jan 16), Charles Fore, and Alexander Legrand Jr., all filed CoCt 1809 Jun–Jul; T. T. Tuggle Jr. (1809 Jul 17 and Aug 21) and Charles Fore [1809?], filed CoCt [1810?] Jun–Aug; Alexander Legrand Jr., filed CoCt 1811 Jun–Jul; James Anderson (1812 May 18) and L. Clarke (1812 Jun 15), filed CoCt 1812 Jun–Aug. Also: Patrol returns in county levy, 1813 Jun; Unlabeled account (county levy, 1814), filed inside Insolvents for 1814, filed CoCt 1815 Jun–Jul; Stephen Fore patrol return, in Sundry claims against County, filed CoCt 1820 Jun–Jul. (The James Allen who patrolled may have been the son either of James Allen Sr. [d. 1808] or of Archer Allen, who owned the tract of land between Israel Hill and the Appomattox River.)

54. "At least as often": See Benjamin F. Perkinson patrol return, in Sundry claims against county, filed CoCt 1820 Jun–Jul; Patrol commission to William J. Marshall, filed CoCt 1836 Jun–Jul. Dodd's schedule: William Dodd patrol returns, Mar–Jun 1813, filed 1813 Jun–Aug.

55. Gilliam's schedule: James Gilliam patrol return, filed CoCt 1813 Jun 7. One to three

outings a month: See also James Ewing patrol return, 1812 Jul 20, originally filed CoCt 1813 Jun–Aug. Five outings in December 1810: William Mathews patrol return, filed CoCt 1811 Jun–Jul. At least once a week: Patrol commission to J. J. Waddill, filed CoCt 1860 May.

56. In 1809, there had been more than a hundred patrollers: OB 16/363-365 (1809 Jun). Patrollers' hours, 1814: Unlabeled county levy, 1814, filed CoCt 1815 Jun–Jul, and copied in OB 18/259-261 (1815 Jun).

57. Two or three hours (example): James Gilliam Jr. patrol return, filed CoCt 1813 Jun 7. Eighteen to twenty-four hours: See Patrol returns of William Dodd (Mar–Jun 1813), of Thomas Rice (1813 May 17), and of James Ewing (1812 Jul 20), all in Returns of patrolling, filed CoCt 1813 Jun–Aug; Returns of William S. Davis (unlabeled) and of William Bryant (two returns), both filed CoCt 1811 Jun–Jul; Return labeled McGehee &c Patroler, CoCt [year missing; apparently 1810] Jun–Aug.

58. Patrollers' and processioners' remuneration (the former at 6¼ cents per man per hour): See County levy, 1809, filed CoCt 1809 Jun–Jul; and unlabeled County levy, 1814, filed CoCt 1815 Jun–Jul. The rate paid processioners was later raised from 50 cents to $1 per day—Processioners' return, J. McDearmon and William Trent, 7th p., Mar 14, filed CoCt 1831 May.

59. Patrolling in late afternoon and early evening (example): Simon Hughes patrol return, 1808 Dec 29, filed CoCt 1809 Jun–Jul (excepting service on December 24 and 25, the hours of which may have been atypical owing to the holiday).

60. Itineraries of patrols departing from Purnall's: William Dodd patrol return, 1808 Jul 18, filed CoCt 1809 Jun–Jul. (In a given period of twelve hours, the group visited an average of ten farms and plantations. Very approximate distances covered can be derived by taking each list of landowners whose places Dodd's patrol visited, and then finding as many of those properties as possible on Land tax rolls, 1814, the first year locations of lands are given in the lower district. Those persons who can be identified on each list of places Dodd visited lived within what appear to be ovular beats measuring nine to ten miles the long way by some six or seven miles across. My calculations allow for four to four and a half of the twelve hours spent on a given patrol to have been devoted to transit among farms and plantations.) Patrol visits its own member's property: William Dodd patrol return, 1808 Oct 18, filed CoCt 1809 Jun–Jul.

61. Aborted patrols: Jacob McGehee Jr. patrol return, 1808 Dec 19, filed CoCt 1809 Jun–Jul.

62. Cyrus Hill: Hill v Peters, CirCt 1837 Sep; Cyrus Hill registration, filed CoCt 1839 Aug (for Hill's race). Davy Smith: Smith v Robertson, CirCt 1842 Sep. A third suit for false imprisonment was filed by William "Furgerson"; this may well have been a free black man of that name who appears on FNL, 1857—Furgerson v Beazley, CoCt 1853 Jul. White man sues for false imprisonment (example): Webb v Scott, CirCt 1848 Sep; a deputy sheriff conveniently "overlooked" serving the first arrest warrant on the defendant, a constable.

63. Salaries and fees: See County levy, 1809 Jun, filed CoCt 1809 Jun–Jul, and County levies from other years; Bill, Woodson v Allen, CoCt 1837 Aug.

64. "Farm the sheriffalty": Bill, and answer of John Watson Sr., in Jenkins v Watson, CoCt 1822 Jul; Allen v Mathews, CirCt 1845 Sep, with quotations from answer of James McDearmon and William Mathews in the latter case; and Bill, Woodson v Allen, CoCt 1837 Aug.

65. Qualifications of jurors: See Jury summons, 1847 May 21, in CW v Thackston, CirCt 1847 Sep.

66. Review by governor: See Philip J. Schwarz, *Slave Laws in Virginia* (Athens and London: University of Georgia Press, 1996), p. 99.

67. Unanimity required: See OB 20/10 (1821 Mar), CW v Dudley; Exceptions and

demurrers, CW v Bradley, CoCt 1841 Nov; John H. Russell, *The Free Negro in Virginia, 1619–1865* (Baltimore: Johns Hopkins Press, 1913), p. 104.

68. Both extremes as to timing of appointment of defense attorney within the course of a single prosecution: CW v Sam, OB 18/359-360 (1816 Jan; counsel appointed declines to serve; trial postponed one month), and OB 18/368 (1816 Feb; attorney appointed on the spot when defendant again appears with no lawyer). Another appointment of a defender as the trial itself began: CW v Bob, OB 21/605 (1827 Sep). In these two cases, Sam was convicted of a reduced charge while Bob was acquitted. Another one-month continuance, granted after a defender was appointed for a defendant who had appeared without one: CW v Major, OB 21/762 (1828 Sep).

69. Twenty-five-dollar fee: CW v Booker, Will, and Beverly, OB 23/499 (1836 Dec); the fee was awarded for defending one, not all three, of the accused slaves. Expenses for defense witnesses and for jail time (example): Copy of proceedings, Josiah Chambers acct with Watson, Allen & Green, his committee, Attorney General v Chambers's trustees, CoCt 1821 Nov. A dismissive appraisal of slaves' defense attorneys, and of courts of oyer and terminer in general ("There was no jury and no appeal except to the governor. The legalistically minded authorities did, however, supply the accused with counsel, for whose services the slave's owner paid five dollars"): Douglas R. Egerton, "An Upright Man: Gabriel's Virginia and the Path to Slave Rebellion," *Virginia Cavalcade*, 43, no. 2 (Autumn 1993), 65; Douglas R. Egerton, *Gabriel's Rebellion: The Virginia Slave Conspiracies of 1800 and 1802* (Chapel Hill and London: University of North Carolina Press, 1993), p. 31.

It seems likely that some acquittals of slaves came on the understanding that the defendant's master would make restitution to the aggrieved party and chastise the slave informally after the trial was over—though I find no direct evidence of this. This speculation, however, cannot explain the strenuous effort and the money that was often invested either to convict or to defend accused slaves, exertions that would hardly seem worthwhile if the system had preferred to relegate the disciplining of these slave defendants to the plantation itself. It appears that slave acquittals often, perhaps usually, were in fact what they were in form: acquittals.

70. Acquittals at trials in which numerous witnesses were called (examples): CW v Doctor, CoCt 1817 Jun; CW v Aaron, CoCt 1829 May, and OB 22/94 (1829 May).

71. Rape trial: CW v Anderson, CoCt 1837 May; OB 24/22 and 28 (1837 May).

72. First Lilly trial: CW v Lilly, CoCt 1823 Nov; OB 20/624 and 626 (1823 Nov; 626 refers to Lilly's "dispensing with the right of examination before a called court"). Lilly's acquittal: CW v Lilly, CoCt 1825 Mar; OB 21/170 (1825 Mar). The court declared that the warrant summoning justices to assemble for the trial had "not . . . been legally issued." The county justice who had drawn up the supposedly defective warrant, and whose warrant would be similarly declared invalid in the case of accused slave tobacco thieves three years later, was Colonel James Madison, the later nemesis of Israel Hill. Dismissals and acquittals of black defendants on seemingly far-fetched technical points, as described elsewhere in this chapter and this book, were not unique to Prince Edward County; one authority finds that the Tennessee Supreme Court "did not hesitate to reverse a slave's conviction when a procedural error had been made in the trial." The author identifies this readiness with the "Due Process Model of criminal justice" as contrasted with the "Crime Control Model"—Arthur F. Howington, *What Sayeth the Law: The Treatment of Slaves and Free Blacks in the State and Local Courts of Tennessee* (New York and London: Garland, 1986), pp. 170–72.

73. Identity and background of justices newly elected 1852, and interval since prior appointments: Justices of the peace commission, filed CoCt 1852 Jun–Aug; Bradshaw, *Prince Edward County*, p. 680, and *ibid.*, pp. 319 (Giles A. Miller, business associate and apparently relative of the once prosperous merchant and county justice Anderson P. Miller), 196, 198–99, 328–29 (Robert S. Carter), 196, 199, 200, 201, 232 (John T.

Carter), 158, 194, 196, 199, 200, 201, 202, 204, 284, 328, 335, 340, 342, 345, 348, 349, 372, 375–77, 476, 687 (Thomas T. Tredway), 198, 204–05, 323–24, 376 (John A. Dalby), 388 (Charles A. Morton), 165–66, 306, 322–23, 324, 335 (H. E. Warren), 198, 204, 323, 346, 347, 372, 377 (Francis P. Wood). Some of these citations refer to activities conducted after an individual's first election to the court in 1852, since these help characterize the justices' interests and career trajectories; but I have not cited references to their activities during and after the Civil War. Reelection of court in 1856: *Ibid.*, p. 212.

74. Nash family: *Ibid.*, p. 631. Abner Nash charged: Presentments, CoCt 1811 Mar.

75. For this point, I am indebted to Gerald David Jaynes. "Principles of right": Christopher G. Memminger, quoted in Michael P. Johnson and James L. Roark, *Black Masters: A Free Family of Color in the Old South* (New York and London: W. W. Norton, 1984), p. 167.

76. The original registration law: Shepherd, 1 (1793), chapter 22, p. 238; Berlin, *Slaves Without Masters*, p. 93. Berlin suggests even greater laxity in observance of the registration system than I do, concluding that "probably few [free blacks] carried freedom papers" (p. 327).

77. Preserving registration certificates: See, e.g., Free Negroes certfs [John Jackson et al.], CoCt 1851 May renewed. Pattersons: Free Negroes certfs, filed CoCt 1851 Jun–Jul; see also Certfs of Emeline, Martha, Eliza, Patty, and Diana Lilly (the first four marked "Dead"), filed CoCt 1850 Dec–1851 Mar. Mettauer: OB 26/382 (1850 Aug). Gibbs: OB 26/444 (1851 Jul). Another replacement of a lost certificate: OB 27/172 (1856 Jun), Joseph Artis.

78. Clarke: CW v Clarke, CoCt 1822 Aug. Arrests of 1845–46: Unlabeled acct [CW with John V. Miller, constable], filed CoCt 1847 May. Before he served even one day: William Homes, OB 26/77 (1845 Dec 15); cf. date of Homes's arrest in Unlabeled acct [with John V. Miller], just cited. Blacks other than Edmund Clarke required, at least formally, to pay jailor's fees or be hired out to cover those amounts: OB 20/216 (1822 Jan), 24/270 (1839 Aug), 24/436 (1841 Apr), 25/22 (1841 Nov), 26/213 (1847 Dec), 27/347 (1859 Dec). Law requiring payment of jail fee: Shepherd, 1 (1793), chapter 22, p. 238.

79. Issuances of duplicate certificates (examples): OB 26/77 (Dec 1845), William Homes; Judy Fergusons certf &c., filed CoCt 1837 Jan–Mar, certf supposedly thrown into fire by child; Henry Cousins certf, filed CoCt 1844 Jun–Aug 1844; OB 26/231 (1848 Apr), Mary A. White; OB 26/259 (1848 Sep), Archer Richardson; OB 26/382 (1850 Aug), James Mettauer; OB 26/444 (1851 Jul), Donaldson Gibbs ("casually lost or destroyed"); see also OB 25/25 (1841 Nov), where Jesse Forgason convinced the court that his registration had never been delivered to him and was granted a new one. The arrests in 1845 and 1846, precisely because they constitute a series, might suggest a general, if temporary, increase in white vigilance—except that one particular constable made all these arrests, and there is little or nothing to suggest a pervasive rise in tension at the time.

80. Carter: Affis of Otha Carter and Daniel P. Jenkins, filed CoCt 1847 Nov; OB 26/207 (1847 Nov). Second case of employer vouching: B. Epperson's affi, filed CoCt 1832 Oct. Walden: Micajah Walden certf, filed CoCt 1848 Nov; OB 26/267 (1848 Nov). Hitchins: Ed Hitchins registration, filed CoCt 1857 Aug. Hitchins and others may, however, have suffered the major inconvenience of having to return to their former home county to secure a duplicate certificate.

81. Flurry of 1829: See OB 22/149-150 and 183-184 (1829 Aug–Sep), and also OB 22/192 and 212 (1829 Oct–Nov); it should be noted that the county's oral tradition placed the searching of Israel Hill "soon after" the Israelites were freed—Typescript beginning "Richard Randolph of 'Bizarre' . . . ," in J. D. Eggleston papers, Mss1 Egg3966, section 30, "Slavery," VHS. Flurry of 1831: OB 22/529 (1831 Sep), 537-538 (1831 Oct), 545 and 550 (both 1831 Nov), and 580 (1832 Jan); but see also OB 22/422 and 423 (1831 Feb, before the revolt).

82. Flurry of 1850–51: OB 26/394-395, 405-406, 408-411, 416, 419-422, 425, 427, 429-430, 441, and 443 (1850 Nov–1851 Jul); Free Negroes certfs [Abby Homes et al.], renewed CoCt 1851 Mar; Free Negroes certf, filed CoCt 1851 April; Free Negroes certf [John Jackson et al.], renewed CoCt 1851 May; William Homes registration, in Sundry claims v county, filed CoCt 1851 Jun; Free Negroes certfs, filed CoCt 1851 Jun–Jul.

83. Newcomer's application to register denied: OB 26/417 (1851 Feb), Catherine Jenkins.

84. Patterson: Free negroes certfs, filed CoCt 1851 Jul. Franklin: Robert A. Franklin's register, filed CoCt 1851 Aug–Oct. White and Johnston: Free negroes certf, renewed CoCt 1851 May.

85. "A free Negro who failed to register": Berlin, *Slaves Without Masters*, p. 93. Berlin himself suggests toward the end of his book that compliance with the registration law was in fact rare (pp. 327–28).

86. Law on "intruders": Shepherd, 2 (1800), chapter 70, section 6, p. 301; Russell, *Free Negro in Virginia*, p. 107.

87. "Only a few miles": Henry Thweatt depo, Lancaster v Legrand's exors, CirCt 1841 Sep. "Every body knows": Insolvent property, James McDearmon, 1825, filed CoCt 1826 Nov. Population: Bradshaw, *Prince Edward County*, p. 669. (The population held steady through 1820, then grew by about 1,500 through 1830, where it stabilized again through 1840. Part of Prince Edward was allotted to the new Appomattox County in 1845; Prince Edward's population then remained at about 12,000 through 1870.) "Bein acquainted": Abner Coffee, letter to county court, n.d., filed CoCt 1814 Mar–Apr.

88. "Seldom does it occur": Joseph Martin, *A New and Comprehensive Gazetteer of Virginia and the District of Columbia* (Charlottesville: Joseph Martin, 1836), p. 150n.; Bradshaw, *Prince Edward County*, pp. 188 and 690 (date of Congressman Thomas T. Bouldin's death).

89. Free black population per census: Ms. Census, 1830, p. 136 (475 free black persons), and 1860 (460 persons by my tally); see also Ms. Census, 1850 (470 free blacks by my tally). That the number of free blacks was no greater in 1860 than in 1830 testifies yet again to the propensity of free Afro-Virginians to move across county lines—as often as not, one assumes, to cities. Berlin cites similar discrepancies between numbers of free blacks registered and actual population figures—*Slaves Without Masters*, pp. 327–28.

90. Forgasons: Mary Fergerson, letter to Joshua Furgerson, January 14, 1837, in Judy Fergusons certf. &c., filed CoCt 1837 Jan–Mar. Charles Forgason father of Judith and Joshua: FNLs, 1819–1823.

91. Bookers and Evanses: Bouldin's admor v Booker, especially depos of Stephen C. Brown ("pursuing," "refused," "overtook"), William Booker ("in Company with," used twice), and Benjamin W. Simmons ("refused"), CoCt 1822 Jul. Booker as slaveholder: Property tax, 1813. Lawsuit for freedom: WB 4/437-438, Molly Moore will and exception (1810/1813); Maria et al. v Moore, OB 16/135 (1808 Mar) and 604 (1810 Aug); District Court Order Book, 1805–31, pp. 463–64 and 464–65 (1814 Apr). In what seems a bit of a paradox, Molly Moore, the mistress whom the slaves were suing for freedom, had named Samuel Booker as one of the executors of a will in which she attempted to parcel out those bondpeople to her heirs. Kentucky law: Berlin, *Slaves Without Masters*, p. 92. Later, when Samuel Booker followed his family westward, his creditor William Bouldin sallied forth a second time and "overtook" Booker, brandishing a court order that authorized the seizure of the latter's horse and gig. Bouldin offered to hire the black Evanses out to Booker—as though he, Bouldin, owned their labor or had any control of them now that they had moved west. Samuel Booker would have none of it, and settled his debt with Bouldin on other terms. Samuel Booker took pains afterward to deny that he had actively assisted or hired the Evanses, and for a very self-interested reason: Bouldin had gone on to sue Booker to recover the value of the blacks' labor that he, Bouldin, had supposedly lost. That the Evanses had not

been employees of Booker is in fact true. Yet it is clear that the two families had traveled westward in concert, cooperated with one another, and stayed in touch after reaching Kentucky.

92. Hitchins: Hitchins certf, renewed CoCt 1856 Mar; Ed Hitchins registration, filed CoCt 1857 Aug; OB 28/64 (1863 Jul). See also the discussion in chapter 7, note 75.

93. Mobility among river counties (examples): John White on FNL, Cumberland County, 1861, LVA; Frank and Jim Lipscomb and David Mayho [Mayo], Sheriff insolvents, upper district [1841], filed CoCt 1842 Jun–Jul (cf. FNLs, Cumberland County, 1851 and 1861, LVA). One in six; continued immigration: Ms. Census, 1850. This is a conservative figure, for I have omitted from the ranks of immigrants some seventeen whose birthplace is ambiguous or unknown, as well as those manumitted by Richard Randolph's will, who alone would have added another twenty-five names to the list of arrivals from outside the county (in this case, from Cumberland). Overseers of the poor in counties of central Virginia did prove ever ready to expel paupers, whether black or white, who arrived from other jurisdictions and looked as if they might eventually seek support from public funds—Report of board meeting of OP, 1826 Jun 5; Payment to Samuel A. Moore, Report of proceedings of board of OP, 1854; OP of Appomattox v OP of Prince Edward, CirCt 1854 Mar; Payment to constable James Mickle, and notation regarding six paupers from Appomattox County, both in Proceedings of the OP, filed CoCt 1857 May.

94. Accusation of stealing pants: CW v Littleton Smith ("late of Petersburg"), CoCt 1850 May. The figure of 40 percent represents an important phenomenon in that the county court explicitly accepted these people as residents, but it is the fraction of urbanites among those who *turned in old registrations;* in the 1850 Census, the thirteen or fourteen free blacks from Richmond-Manchester or Petersburg represented one in six of all those (other than Randolph manumittees) born outside Prince Edward— still a significant number—and 3 percent of all free Afro-Virginians in the county.

95. Deneufville was one of at least eight and probably more immigrants from distant eastern Virginia. Of those registered newcomers over the years whose former free papers remain on file among county court papers, half or more had light skin; only a quarter of those newcomers whose color we know were "black" or "dark." That ratio may only mean that some people of light complexion came with assets obtained partly from white fathers and therefore felt more confident about registering with county authorities. In the 1850 Census, the color discrepancy was small between those born outside the county other than Randolph manumittees (about 30 percent "mulatto") and those either born inside Prince Edward or manumitted by Randolph (22 percent "mulatto").

96. Protest of overseers of the poor: Lancaster County OP, 1821, cited in James D. Watkinson, " 'Fit Objects of Charity': Community, Race, Faith, and Welfare in Antebellum Lancaster County, Virginia," *Journal of the Early Republic,* 21, no. 1 (Spring 2001), 58, n. 31.

97. Failure of attempts to enslave or expel blacks: Berlin, *Slaves Without Masters,* pp. 371–80 ("a surge," "injustice," pp. 375–76; "horror," p. 377).

98. "Oftentimes": Luther Porter Jackson, "Manumission in Certain Virginia Cities," *Journal of Negro History,* 15, no. 3 (July 1930), 313.

99. Frothingham burglary: CW v Smith and CW v Ridley, CoCt 1826 Jul; OB 21/404-405 (1826 Jul).

100. Jackson's mother: Quoted in Edward L. Ayers, *Vengeance and Justice: Crime and Punishment in the 19th-Century American South* (New York and Oxford: Oxford University Press, 1984), p. 18. The seminal (and a controversial) book on honor in the Old South is Bertram Wyatt-Brown, *Southern Honor: Ethics and Behavior in the Old South* (New York and Oxford: Oxford University Press, 1982). Other important treatments of the subject include Ayers, *Vengeance and Justice,* chapter 1, "Honor and Its

Adversaries"; and Kenneth S. Greenberg, *Honor & Slavery* (Princeton: Princeton University Press, 1996).

101. Paternalistic protectors: See Berlin, *Slaves Without Masters,* pp. 338–40.

102. Allen: William A. Allen v James Allen (two cases), CoCt 1817 May and Aug, respectively. Foster: Foster v Nunnally, CoCt 1819 Aug.

103. "All the phacilities": John Tuggle depo, 1832 Nov 19, Price v Price, CirCt 1836 Sep. Eighty-one days: Robert Wooldridge to jailor, acct, jailing of Morris, filed CoCt 1833 Jun–Jul.

104. "Lawyer" the horse: Cheadle, 21st and 23rd pp., smith's work by R. Fuqua. "Become too fond": Vincent Phillips, letter to A. W. Womack, March 19, 1849, Womack v Phillips, CirCt 1851 Sep.

105. "Worth taking relatives": James Oakes, *The Ruling Race: A History of American Slave-holders* (New York: Vintage, 1982), pp. 171–72. The exact number of legal actions involving slander or assault that were initiated in Prince Edward County is all but impossible to specify, in part because some suits or charges were filed but never recorded in the order books after proceedings terminated at a relatively early stage. To add all those to the total would require opening and examining each of the tens of thousands of documents preserved in county records, rather than merely the thousands I have read. The more than two hundred relevant cases I am familiar with include the suits and criminal proceedings involving slander and assault that are apparent from the county court order books; a number of actions not recorded there that I have identified in the ended papers of the county court; and still others of which I am aware through ended papers in the circuit court. Although this body of material is not exhaustive, I believe it offers at least a representative picture. I thank Jackson Sasser for helping me systematize information on suits and prosecutions for assault as recorded in county court OBs.

106. "Did not desire . . . money": Depos of Thomas H. Campbell (whence the quotation) and Louis C. Bouldin, Flournoy v Harper, CirCt 1855 Mar. See also OB 20/494 (1823 May), Anderson v Gregg, release.

107. Woodson's alleged attacks: CW v Woodson, CoCt 1823 Nov; Woodson v Holland, as follows. Woodson's slander suit: Woodson v Holland, especially Anderson Lumpkin depo ("give . . . the cow hide"), attorneys' notes ("If the Holiday hills"; the attempted whipping), and Augustus Watkins depo ("in a pregnant state"), CoCt 1824 Nov; OB 21/118 (1824 Nov). The second slander suit: Woodson v Glenn, CoCt 1825 Aug; cf. reference to Glenn's role in spreading the story about Woodson in Watkins depo, Woodson v Holland. Woodson's economic status: Property tax, 1823 and 1824 (with two slaves older than twelve).

108. Suits in 1850s: See Price v Allen, CirCt 1851 Sep; Parrish v Whiteman, CirCt 1852 Aug. The aggregate number of slander suits given here is a minimum. There may have been others which, though filed in complete earnest, never proceeded far enough through the legal process to enter the order books, and which I did not encounter in my examination of the loose court papers.

109. A planter and a prosperous yeoman suing for slander: Cheadle v Hurt, CoCt 1814 May, but originally filed 1814 Jun–Jul, and the related case of Cheadle v Perkins, CoCt 1815 Aug, OB 18/305 (an instance complicated by the fact that the alleged slanderer was a woman); John M. Price v Dupuy, CoCt 1825 Aug (cf. Price in Property tax, 1825). Suits by men of middling or modest means: Smith v Cody, CoCt 1811 Nov; Fowler v Hurt, CoCt 1814 May, filed 1814 Jun–Jul (cf. Property tax, 1815–17, for Fowler); Perkinson v Hamblen, CoCt 1817 Mar (cf. Property tax, 1817); William Price v Moore, CoCt 1821 Aug (cf. Land tax and Property tax, 1820); Farrar v Gordon, CoCt 1834 May (Farrar not listed in Land Tax, 1830). Plain man sues planter: Farrar v Trent, CoCt 1834 May and OB 23/238 (1834 May) (also OB 23/161 [1833 Aug], with Trent's appointment to county court); the plaintiff lost the suit and had to pay more

than $100 in costs. Plain men suing others of their class for slander: Cheshire v Allen, CirCt 1811 Apr and Sep (cf. Property tax, 1810, in which Cheshire does not even appear); Joseph M. Price v Allen, CirCt 1851 Sep (cf. Property tax, 1850).

110. Stealing sheep: Vaughan v Dungans, CoCt 1834 May. Tobacco: James v Andrews, CoCt 1812 Nov. Bacon: Deshazer v Jackson, CoCt 1810 Nov. Money: Cheshire v Allen, CirCt 1811 Apr/Sep. Burning mills: Holland v Fore, CoCt 1817 Aug; Ellington v Jackson, CoCt 1826 May. Burning dwelling: Price v Allen, as in note 109. Adultery: Mickle v Richardson, CoCt 1821 Mar. "Sent to the Penitentiary": Parrish v Whiteman, CirCt 1811 Apr and Sep. Against this background, Phoebe Giles's slander suit against Sooky White appears a bit less unusual than it might otherwise, except that women generally sued through their husbands or fathers.

111. Post-Revolutionary suits decided in a single fourteen-month period: OB 7/16 (1782 Aug); 57, 59, and 60 (1783 May); and 129 (1783 Oct). Prosperous men or their sons: Baker v Nash, CoCt 1811 Mar, filed 1811 May. Planter: Dillon v Spaulding, OB 18/398 (1816 Mar). Merchants: Fore v Connor, 1811 Mar?, filed CoCt 1811 Apr–May; Fore v McDearmon, OB 18/220 (1815 Mar); Frothingham v Wells, CirCt 1830 Apr. Constable: McDearmon v Fore, OB 16/530 and 561 (1810 Mar and May); see also CW v Fore, CoCt 1810 Mar, which makes clear that James McDearmon, though a minor, was old enough to be serving as a constable at the time of the alleged assault by Fore. Brick contractor: Royall v Scott, CoCt 1834 May, and OB 23/237—an instance of a man suing his social superior (cf. Land tax and Property tax, 1834, in which Littleberry Royall has one slave older than twelve and no land, while Branch O. Scott has twenty-one bondpeople, expensive inanimate possessions, and fifteen hundred acres of land). This list of suits for assault is not exhaustive.

112. Dismissed by plaintiff at his own cost upon reaching accommodation (examples): Key v Porter, CoCt 1811 Jan; Baker v Nash, CoCt 1811 Mar, filed 1811 May; Furguson v Webb, CoCt 1819 Nov–Dec.

113. Cheadle assaulted: CW v Fore, presentment, OB 26/99 (1846 May); CoCt 1847 May. Complaints of assault by men of standing: Presentments, CirCt 1845 Apr (complainant: Merit B. Allen); CW v Walker, presentment, CirCt 1849 Sep (Don Pedro Taylor); CW v Nunnally, CoCt 1819 Aug (Booker Foster); Presentments, CirCt 1850 Sep (James B. Ely). Schoolmaster: Presentments, CoCt 1827 Aug. Some grand jury informants were recorded as having been "sent for," others were designated as "voluntary informers," and still others were not described at all. It is unclear how many of those who reported assaults on themselves did so at all involuntarily, but presumably it was easy enough to avoid implicating another person if one so wished.

114. Homes shooting: CW v Brown, OB 27/57 (1854 May); the prosecution went no further. Franklin case: CW v Rodgers, CoCt 1860 Nov. For some reason, county and circuit court records from the 1840s on reflect a shift among people of both races away from filing civil suits in cases of assault and toward pressing criminal complaints before the grand jury.

115. Richards case: CW v Richards, CoCt 1839 Mar; OB 24/203 (1838 Nov) and 238 (1839 Mar). Richards a shoemaker: FNL, 1823. Porter case: CW v Porter, OB 24/203 (1838 Nov) and 329 (1840 Mar). One Fanny Cousins, who may have been a free black woman, had unsuccessfully sued Abner Willard for assault many years earlier— Cousins v Willard, CoCt 1814 May.

116. Bowman: Bowman v Armes, CirCt 1839 Sep.

117. Patterson's suit: Patterson v Weaver, CoCt 1825 Mar; OB 20/470 (1823 Mar), 576 and 592 (both 1823 Aug; non-suited and reinstated); OB 21/176-177 (1825 Mar). On economic standing of witness Thomas C. Spencer, see Spencer, letter to Martin Pearce, May 17, 1823, Pearce's Exor v Pearce, CoCt 1823 Nov. Patterson's stature: OB 21/260 (1825 Sep).

118. Three figures: Hubbard v Beasley, OB 16/256 (1808 Nov; $130; victim a minor, though

age not specified); Overstreet v Dowell, OB 18/337 (1815 Nov; award of $110, by referees); Wright v Webb, OB 19/146 (1819 Mar; $370); Silvey/Selby v Morgan, OB 20/29-30 (1821 Mar; $250; woman victim); Anderson v Gregg, CoCt 1823 May, and OB 20/494 (1823 May; $100); Royall v Scott, CoCt 1834 May ($180).

119. Token awards to whites: Knight v Walton, OB 16/30 (1807 Nov), for 12½ cents; McDearmon v Fore, OB 16/530 and 561 (1810 Mar and May)—although defendant Fore was fined $10 in a criminal case that may have arisen from the same event (CW v Fore, CoCt 1810 Mar); Nunnally v Farmer, CoCt 1811 Mar; Fore v Connor, CoCt 1811 Mar?, filed 1811 Apr–May. Two additional, later examples of what 1-cent awards or fines meant to juries, this time in criminal trials: Jury verdicts in CW v Carwiles, CoCt 1859 May–Sep; CW v Thomas H. Harper, CoCt 1859 May. When a jury believed that two parties to a suit were equally to blame for an altercation, it might express "an opinion [that] each man shall pay his own cost" for the suit. If jurors reached such a conclusion, however, they decided, or were instructed, to render instead a verdict for the plaintiff, awarding him only a penny—See Nunnally v Farmer and Fore v Connor.

120. Similar awards to white men: Martin v Preston, CoCt 1819 May ("many blows"); Holland v Fore, OB 20/26 (1821 Mar); Jackson v Bayne, CoCt 1824 Nov, and OB 21/115 (1824 Nov); Pettus v Faulkner, OB 21/129 (1824 Nov, though a new trial was granted; Faulkner also paid a $6 fine when found guilty in a criminal trial of assaulting Pettus—CW v Faulkner, CoCt 1824 May).

121. Denouement of case: Delivery bond, Patterson v Weaver, CoCt 1826 Oct, originally filed CoCt 1826 Aug–Sep. Anderson represents black clients: White v White's admor, CoCt 1832 Mar; Howard v White, CoCt 1837 Jul; Anderson depo, Wilson v Garnett, CoCt 1837 Jul; Petition, and letter of Nathaniel Venable Sr. to Anderson, August 15, 1831, both in Jacob v Purcell, CoCt 1838 May; Bowman v Armes, CirCt 1839 Sep.

122. Anderson after hogstealing case: Anderson v Giles and Howard, CoCt 1828 May. Anderson arranges payment from white client: Bailey for Anderson v White, CoCt 1853 May, filed 1853 Jul. (Bailey, as it happened, was suing Phil White over a debt. Anderson arranged officially, before filing the lawsuit, to have first call on any money he won for the white client, hence the style "Bailey for benefit of Anderson.") Anderson gives bond for Hill: CW v Hill, CoCt 1855 Nov.

123. Artis's suit: Artis v Totty, CoCt 1836 Mar; OB 23/362 (1835 Aug, in which the plaintiff is called Mary Artis) and 418 (1836 Mar). Totty and Whites: Totty acct with Perkinson and Co., 1832 Nov 12, in Perkinson v Totty, CoCt 1838 Aug–Oct; Spa to Totty, Bailey for Anderson v White, CoCt 1853 Jul. Artis's age: Free negroes certified, filed CoCt 1851 April. Poor aid to Artis: OP report, filed CoCt 1861 May. An additional suit for assault, in 1814, involved a plaintiff who may have been a free black woman; see note 124.

124. Homes's suit: Homes v Owen, CoCt 1818 Apr, filed 1818 May. This was not the Archer Homes who later became an apprentice bricklayer; this plaintiff may well have been the latter's father. One additional assault suit in the 1810s may have been filed by a free black: one Fanny Cousins sued a white man, though she apparently did not follow up and the action was terminated at Cousins's cost in 1814—Cousins v Willard, CoCt 1814 May; OB 18/85 (1814 May). I find no free black Fanny Cousins in the documents I have examined. (On one FNL only, that of 1821, there is a woman named Fanny, enumerated without a surname, resident on a property—that of John Clarke—where one other free black among several who lived there bears the family name Cousins.) But Cousins was a surname found particularly among Afro-Virginians; a number lived in neighboring Nottoway and Cumberland Counties, and Fanny Cousins may have been one of them.

125. Ebenezer Frothingham: White v Frothingham, CoCt 1827 Nov; OB 21/494 (1826

Nov), 529, 549, and 635 (1827 Mar, May, and Nov). Frothingham whipping a boy (whose race is not clear from the record): Brisbane F. Anchram depo, Frothingham v Wells, CirCt 1830 Apr.

126. Zack Ellis: Ellis v Madison, CirCt 1838 Sep. Branch Roach's probable arrival in county: OB 25/151-152 (1843 Feb). Roach's suit: Roach v Hudson, CirCt 1840 Jan, filed 1840 Apr. Alleged shooting of Roach: CW v Green, CoCt 1852 Sep, and OB 26/506 (1852 Sep); Roach's black alleged assailant was acquitted. Whether free blacks' success rate in suits against whites for assault is one in five or one in six depends on whether Zack Ellis's wresting of $10 from Colonel James Madison is counted as a victory. There were eighteen or nineteen such suits in Prince Edward during the half century preceding the Civil War.

127. Cyrus Hill's suit: Hill v Peters, CirCt 1837 Sep. Peters's birthplace: OB 24/14 (1837 Apr). His profession: Ms. Census, 1850, and numerous OP reports. Davy Smith's marriage: Susan White, Index to marriage bonds, 1836 Jun 30, LVA. Smith's suit: Smith v Robertson, CirCt 1842 Sep. Robertson backs boat purchase: Bond in White v Joe Bartlett, CoCt 1837 Aug. Robertson and stolen horse: CW v Bradley, CoCt 1841 Nov.

128. Jacksons: Jackson v Jackson, CirCt 1845 Apr. James Jackson, the free black: Charles E. Chappell's list of hands to work on road, filed CoCt 1850 Jan–Apr, and FNL, 1858; the James Jackson who sued Booker Jackson signed his letter to dismiss with an X, which among other evidence rules out his being James M. Jackson, the entrepreneur, brother of Patrick Jackson, and nephew of James Madison.

129. Putrefied corpses: Coroner's inquests, Child found at Farmville (1841), and Mary Frances Lindsey (1841), Inquests, LVA. One victim in 1841 was apparently white; the race of the other could not be determined. Other unsolved homicides: Inquests, Wade's Negro (1797); Unknown Mulatto (man, 1798); Benjamin Lowdon, 1797; William Hill Sr., 1810; Lucy, Negro girl, 1820.

130. "Honor" displayed by slave duelists: Newspaper in Lee County, quoted in Henry Howe, *Historical Collections of Virginia* (Charleston, SC: Babcock, 1845), p. 351, courtesy of Brent Tarter. On "honor" among slaves, see John C. Willis, "From the Dictates of Pride to the Paths of Righteousness: Slave Honor and Christianity in Antebellum Virginia," in Edward L. Ayers and John C. Willis, eds., *The Edge of the South: Life in Nineteenth-Century Virginia* (Charlottesville and London: University Press of Virginia, 1991), pp. 37–55.

131. Slaves using guns: See Nicolas W. Proctor, *Bathed in Blood: Hunting and Mastery in the Old South* (Charlottesville and London: University Press of Virginia, 2002), pp. 119–32 and chapter 7, especially pp. 162–63.

132. Murder on boat: CW v Isham, OB 17/541-543 (1813 Jun); Coroner's inquest, Bob, 1813, Inquests, LVA. Isaac "shamed," then killed: CW v Peter, CoCt 1821 Apr; that Peter struck Isaac from behind was not held against him by the court in light of Isaac's provocations. Free black witnesses: The record of Peter's trial includes testimony from a woman named Joyce, labeling her as a slave. But Claibourne and "Joice" are referred to as a unit in the defense attorney's notes; Joyce is called "Alexander Patterson's Joesy" in at least one court document; Claibourne Humbles and Joice Dunscomb are both listed as living at Alexander Patteson's in 1819–22; and Dunscomb's first name is spelled "Joicy" (cf. "Joesy") on FNL, 1822. It seems clear that this is the Joyce who testified at Peter's trial. Alexander Patteson went on to free his slaves by deed and by will, and even as early as 1821 he may have behaved in ways that left some whites unsure which blacks on his place were free and which enslaved.

133. Killing of Edie: CW v Langhorne, CoCt 1857 Feb; Circuit Superior Court of Law and Chancery minute book, 1846–70, 1857 Mar 13–17, LVA. See also Bradshaw, *Prince Edward County*, pp. 587–88.

134. Swinney and Wright: CW v Swinney, CoCt 1815 Jul and OB 18/265-267, especially testimony of Joshua Coffee and Benjamin Franklin; CirCt 1816 Aug/Sep.

135. "To the Public": Document labeled "Papers in Sam Morris' care and Wm Guthrey certificate 1841," unsigned [issued by Guthrey], n.d. [1841 Apr], box 8, folder 79, Hubard family papers, UNC.

136. Furgerson stabbing: Presentments, CirCt 1836 Sep 26. Edmund Furgerson's race: The presentment carefully identifies Jesse Forgason, but not Edmund Furgerson, as black; this suggests that the latter was white. Neither the records of this prosecution nor other county documents note Edmund W. Furgerson's race, nor does he appear in proximate censuses. Index to marriage bonds does note an Edmund "Foggerson" marrying Martha Bryant, apparently a white woman, in 1834. At the time of the alleged assault, Edmund had recently cut grain on the Penick plantation near Israel Hill, and he signed a receipt for his pay with an X—but we have seen that men of both races did such work, and that more than a few whites lacked literacy—Penick account with Amplias Tuggle, trustee, 1836 Jul 13, in Tuggle v Penick, CirCt 1840 Apr. Furgerson was charged the following year with having stolen a saddle; his prosecution was discontinued, apparently after he departed from Prince Edward—CW v Ferguson [sic], CoCt 1837 Jul; CirCt 1838 Sep and 1839 Sep. Jesse Forgason was a son of Jethro Forgason Sr.

137. Rutledge: CW v Whorley [and Rutledge], CoCt 1847 Nov; OB 26/208 (1847 Nov; not prosecuted). Rutledge's race: He had been a potential witness in another criminal trial in which the victims, the defendant, and the other witness were all free blacks—CW v Young, CoCt 1842 Aug; OB 25/95 (1842 Aug). Witness Thomas Worley white: Ms. Census, 1850, family visitation 129; Ms. Census, 1860, family visitations 552 and 553 (two of same name). The better-off Worley's economic status, at least as of 1860: Ms. Census, schedule 4, Productions of Agriculture, pp. 479–80 (with only twenty acres of land, producing very little). Rutledge never faced prosecution; the deputy sheriff either could not locate him in Prince Edward, or perhaps did not care to.

138. Stonum-Moss confrontation: CW v Stonum, CoCt 1820 Nov, and OB 19/458 and 463 (1820 Nov); CirCt 1821 Apr and Sep, and District Court Order Book, 1805–31, p. 555. Moss's occupation: FNL, 1824. Stonum son's apprenticeship: OB 20/153 (1821 Sep). Surname rendered as "Stoner"; Stonum's husband a boatman: FNL, 1821. One of those present at the confrontation, Betsy Gibbs, may have been a kinswoman, possibly an older daughter or daughter-in-law, of Israelites Titus and Amy Gibbs. The background of the altercation may have been even more complex than it appears at first glance. The surname of Sally's husband, Samuel, was often rendered as "Stoner," and there was a white Samuel Stoner who was well-off and did business in Prince Edward, though he lived in another county. Maybe Sally did have kin who seemed to her, at least, "so rich they could buy Mrs Cook"—and who were white to boot. See Stoner assignee v Cunningham, CirCt 1832 Sep; Cunningham v Johnston, CirCt 1837 Apr; Delivery bond, Johnston v Cunningham, CirCt 1838 Sep.

139. Conflict between White women: White v White, CoCt 1831 Nov; OB 22/297 (1830 May) and 556 (1831 Nov). The lawsuit had to be formally styled "Tony White v Hercules White and Wife." Tony's spouse was disqualified from suing on two counts— she was a married woman, and a slave. The former disability apparently prevented Susannah White, though free, from being sued except through her husband. Milly White's enslaved status meant further that her husband ended up suing ostensibly for having been "deprived of her labor." The two witnesses called to the trial were Amy White, Sam's daughter, and Stella, daughter of Kit Strong. Stella would soon be called to testify also in the hogstealing trial of Hampton Giles and Guy Howard.

140. Stabbing of Strong: CW v Howard, CoCt 1843 Aug; OB 25/221 (1843 Aug). Sale of boat: Strong v White, CoCt 1845 May. Strong marriage to Esther White (daughter of Tamer White, who was a son of Sam White): Marriage bond, 1836, LVA. Howard marriage to Lucy White: Index to marriage bonds, 1840, LVA. Backgrounds of principals and witnesses: IH 1816; FNLs, 1817–1825 and 1857ff. Whites' promissory bonds

to Strong: Strong v White, CoCt 1844 Nov; Strong v White and White, CoCt 1844 Jul. Strong's other financial dealings (example): Seay v Strong, CoCt 1845 Nov. Citations for Strong's land transactions in subsequent years appear in chapter 8, note 60. Those summoned as witnesses were Phil White Jr. and two of his sons, Sam Strong himself, Sidney Howard's elder brother, another granddaughter of Sam White, and one Christopher Strong, who was either the father or brother of Sam, the victim (both men bore the same name). The same county justice who witnessed the signing of the Whites' last bond to Sam Strong would issue the arrest warrant for Sidney Howard the very next day.

141. Johnston-Gibbs altercation: CW v Johnson [sic], CoCt 1845 Jan; OB 26/16 (1845 Jan). Ages, backgrounds, and later residences of parties: IH 1816, and FNLs, 1817–1825 and 1857ff. County justice (Clement C. Read) friendly with Gibbs: Capias and vouchers, White v Gibbs, CoCt 1833 May. William Johnston's mother, Hannah, was Titus and Amy Gibbs's daughter and the elder sister of Isaac Gibbs; Hannah had married Rose Johnston's son George, and William was their middle son. Closeness of Johnston and Gibbs families: William Johnston's parents named one younger son after his grandfather, Titus Gibbs, and another after his uncle, Isaac Gibbs. Gibbs and Johnston still residing on Israel Hill five years later: Ms. Census, 1850, family visitations 442 and 444.

142. Price of shotgun (example): Martha Moseley acct with Miller, Thweatt & Hudson, 1837 Nov, Moseley v Venable, Thweatt &c., CirCt 1850 Sep. "Persons carrying . . . weapons": Sharon Baptist Church minute book, 1827–65, p. 25, LVA 20803. "Going armed": CW v Shepherd, CoCt 1852 Nov. Others charged with concealing weapons: CW v Colley, presentment, CirCt 1847 Apr; CW v Scott, CirCt 1848 Apr; CW v Casey (or Cary), CoCt 1848 May, and OB 26/222 (1848 Mar); CW v Crute, CoCt 1859 Jul.

143. "Revolving pistols": CW v Casey, as in note 142. Arrest precipitated by menacing others: CW v Colley, as in note 142; CW v Shepherd, CoCt 1852 Nov. Shotgun murder: CW v Shepherd, CoCt 1855 Feb; CirCt 1855 Aug (first trial 1855 Mar). Victim and shooter related: James D. Shepherd, examination for lunacy, CoCt 1861 Jan–Apr. Other shootings or attempted shootings include: CW v Walton, presentment, CoCt 1834 Nov; CW v Craddock, CoCt 1833 May, and CirCt 1833 Apr and Sep; CW v O'Brien, CirCt 1852 Apr; CW v Haskins, CoCt 1855 Nov.

144. Hercules White Sr.: Notation on back of delivery bond, White's admor v Backus, CoCt 1828 Oct. Short: WB 5/371, Benjamin Short inventory (1819). Dick White: WB 6/345, Richard White inventory (1826). Phil White Sr.: WB 7/18, Philip White appraisal (1830). Gun licenses: OB 19/413 (1820 Aug; Samuel Short); 19/437 (1820 Sep; Tony White); 20/519 (1823 Jun; John Brown); 21/361 (1826 May; Nathan Homes); 21/523 (1827 Mar; Sam White).

145. Strong, White, and shotgun: Strong v White, CoCt 1845 May. Alleged assault on Roach, with acquittal of defendant: CW v Green, CoCt 1852 Sep. We have no details on William Green, except that he must indeed have been black. His purported victim and another free black witness whom the court summoned could not have testified against Green had he been white.

146. Whites attack other whites with knives (examples): CW v Holeman, CoCt 1824 Jun; CW v Walker, CirCt 1851 Apr; CW v Hamilton, CoCt 1858 Apr. White-on-white homicides using dirks: CW v Gibson, CoCt 1811 Aug; CW v Chumley, CoCt 1825 May. Using rock: CW v Armes, CoCt 1812 Sep–Nov. Bartlett acquittal in slaying of Rial Allen, with Ben and John White providing bail: OB 26/460 (1851 Nov).

147. Taylor's attack: CW v Taylor, CoCt 1853 Feb–Apr and 1853 Aug–Sep; Taylor ads CW, CirCt 1854 Mar (on original docketing, ended papers: "1853 Mar"). Clibourne's health: R. D. Noell depo, Mettauer v Clibourne, CirCt 1852 Aug; Commissioner's report, 1849 July 14, in Borum v Ellington's exor, CirCt 1853 Aug. Taylor appealed the county's attempt to collect this fine; the result is not entirely clear from the record.

148. Homes's alleged threats: CW v Homes, CoCt 1857 May. William Homes was required to post a six-month peace bond.

149. Abuse by men other than husbands (example): CW v Berry, CoCt 1827 Sep–Nov, and CoCt 1829 Nov. Repeated beatings: CW v Nunnally, CoCt 1822 Aug. "Frequently driven": CW v Hill, CoCt 1826 Aug. Stabbing: CW v Waddell, CoCt 1840 Jan. Patching and stitching: CW v Sullivan, CoCt 1853 Oct, and CirCt 1854 Mar; Dr. Dillon, OP acct with A. S. Dillon, and Acct, guardian of the poor for services rendered, both filed CoCt 1854 Jun–Jul.

150. Rape of daughters: CW v Harrison, District Court Order Book, 1805–31, pp. 570–71 (1821 Sep); Harrison ads CW, CirCt 1821 Sep.

151. Thirteen men and married couple: Goins v Watkins et al., CirCt 1832 Sep.

152. Whipping of Stafford Gibbs: Gibbs v Robinson et al., CirCt 1812 Apr and Sep; Gibbs won an award of $50 against his assailants. Other alleged group assaults: CW v Valentine et al., CoCt 1839 Jul, and OB 24/264 (two defendants, after three accused initially); Ellington v Mottley, CoCt 1826 Aug, and OB 21/447 (four defendants); CW v Hawkins et al., OB 21/103 (1824 Nov) and 169 (1825 Mar; seven defendants); CW v Bayne, Keeling, et al., presentments, CoCt 1826 Mar, and OB 21/325 (ten defendants).

153. Randolph Brandum complained of what, in effect, was a false arrest perpetrated by a group of Cumberland County men after he employed an absconded slave, but he did not allege that the whites had beaten him.

154. White folklore implies that the search or searches for stolen property that are supposed to have taken place on Israel Hill did not include violence against persons; there is no evidence that similar searches were repeated in later periods, except perhaps when guns were confiscated after the Nat Turner rebellion. Whites did perpetrate many violent acts of punishment or revenge against slaves, of course; but those assaults, however one-sided, were ordinarily carried out by individual masters and overseers. The poorly documented activities of posses and slave patrols doubtless encompassed exceptions, yet mob violence against slaves, had it occurred, might very well have been recorded owing to complaints by masters of the enslaved victims. On mob attacks elsewhere in the South, see David Grimsted, *American Mobbing, 1828–1861* (New York and Oxford: Oxford University Press, 1998), especially chapters 3–5.

155. James Shepherd's longer imprisonment: CW v Shepherd, CirCt 1855 Aug. Sentence for shooting slave: CW v Shepherd, CoCt 1860 Jul 30; Circuit Superior Court of Law and Chancery minute book, 1846–70, 1860 Aug 15 and 16, LVA. "Attempt to cut the throat" of a relative and to stab several slaves; insanity: James D. Shepherd, examination for suspected lunacy, especially statement of John J. Allen (whence the quotation), filed CoCt 1861 Jan–Apr.

156. Hillery Richardson's wealth: H. G. Richardson est, appraisal (1861), filed CoCt 1861 Jul–Dec. Stabbing: CW v Richardson, 1845 Jun; OB 26/41 (1845 Jun). Peace bond: CW v Richardson, and CW v Cobbs, both filed CoCt 1853 Aug–Sep. As barbarous master: Testimony of John V. Miller et al., CW v William (murder), CoCt 1861 Dec 19; and see the discussion in chapter 9.

157. Fore's land: Land tax, upper district, 1815, filed CoCt 1815 Jan–Mar. Shooting (Garland): CW v Fore, CoCt 1810 Nov; OB 16/640-641 (1810 Nov); CirCt 1811 Apr. Shooting (Saunders): CW v Fore, CoCt 1817 Jul, and OB 18/593-595 (1817 Jul); CirCt 1817 Sep. Stabbing: CW v Fore (attack on Wilson Hix), CoCt 1817 Oct, OB 18/641-642 (1817 Oct), and CirCt 1818 Apr. Attack on male slaves: Dabney v Fore and Guill, CoCt 1819 Mar, especially depos of Mace C. Spencer and Pitman Spencer; OB 19/150 (1819 Mar); Fore delivery bond to Dabney, CoCt 1819 May; Fore and his friend were required to pay a large judgment to the slaves' owner. Mill-burning accusation: Holland v Fore (slander), CoCt 1817 Aug. Fore Jr. disturbing worship: CW v P. Fore Jr.,

CoCt 1819 May. Setting dogs on slave, and running feud: W. Holland v Fore, and J. Holland v Fore, CoCt 1821 Mar, as well as OB 20/26 (1821 Mar), 617 (1823 Nov), and 688 (1824 Mar) (the Fores had to pay over $70 in damages and costs); Fore v Holland, CoCt 1823 Dec–1824 Mar (boundary dispute). See also CW v Fore (peace bond toward Woodson), CoCt 1818 Feb, and Woodson v Fore, CoCt 1819 Mar. Ready as Fore might be to use violence against others, no construction of honor prevented him from following up on a physical altercation by filing suit against an adversary—Fore v Connor, 1811 Mar?, filed CoCt 1811 Apr–May; Fore v Richard McDearmon, District Court Order Book, 1805–31, p. 570 (1821 Sep).

158. Earlier assaults on McDearmons: McDearmon (minor) v Fore, OB 16/561 (1810 May); CW v Fore (assault on Constable James McDearmon), CoCt 1810 Mar. Later arrest by McDearmon: Fore v Richard McDearmon, as in note 157. Shooting at store: Unlabeled summary of testimony, CW v Fore (Saunders shooting), as in note 157.

159. From behind tree: CW v Fore (shooting of Garland). Verbal threats: CW v Fore, shootings of Garland and of Saunders. Fore's drunkenness: Holland v Fore (slander); CW v Fore (Saunders shooting). References for all these cases are in note 157.

160. Free black neighbors: Land tax, Green's district, 1814; Land tax, upper district, 1815, filed CoCt 1815 Jan–Mar. Free blacks at Fore's: FNLs, 1819 and 1821.

161. Land purchase: DB 17/358, Jackson to Weaver; 371, Weaver to Bayne, DoT; and 372, Weaver to Venable, DoT (all 1821). Hiring slaves: Copy of proceedings, Attorney General v Chambers's trustees, entries for sundry bonds, 1820 n.d. (p. 57) and 1821 n.d. (p. 58), CoCt 1821 Nov. Weaver selling "groceries": CW v Weaver "& Co.," CirCt 1830 Sep, and District Court Order Book, 1805–31, pp. 643 (1827 Apr) and 686 (1830 Sep).

162. Suits for debt and assault: Otterson v Weaver, CoCt 1821 Jun, and OB 20/77 (1821 Jun); Otterson v Weaver, CoCt 1821 Aug, OB 19/479 (1820 Nov), and OB 20/127 (1821 Aug). Charged with assault against Reuben Seay: CW v Weaver, CoCt 1826 May, and OB 21/359 (1826 May). Weaver seems to have been jailed at least briefly after his arrest. He suffered arrest for breach of the peace in 1826, and when a deputy sheriff tried to serve papers on him in another case in 1830, the deputy was "kept off by force of armes." Breach of peace: Joseph Woodson, constable, lower district, acct with CW, 1826 Jun, filed CoCt 1826 Oct–Nov. "Kept off": Notation on al. caps., Doyne's admor v Weaver, CoCt 1830 Mar.

163. Weaver steals $50: CW v Weaver, especially William Williams depo, CoCt 1832 Sep; OB 23/41 (1832 Sep); CirCt 1832 Sep.

CHAPTER 7: *Worldviews*

1. William B. Smith, "The Persimmon Tree and the Beer Dance," *Farmers' Register,* 6 (April 1838), 58–61. Much of this article is reprinted in Jay B. Hubbell, "A Persimmon Beer Dance in Ante-Bellum Virginia," *Southern Literary Messenger,* 5, no. 5 (November–December 1943), 461–66. Smith may have allowed scenes he had witnessed or heard about elsewhere to influence details of his vignette; he said he was writing several years after the event.

2. Fly whisk: Grey Gundaker, personal communication.

3. "Marking" or "mocking": Grey Gundaker, personal communication.

4. "The skin, the odor": Walter White, *A Man Called White* (New York: Viking, 1948), p. 4.

5. Differences pervaded by commonalities: For a discussion of cultural interaction between white and black Virginians in an earlier period, see Mechal Sobel, *The World They Made Together: Black and White Values in Eighteenth-Century Virginia* (Princeton: Princeton University Press, 1987).Three dollars: WB 4/264, John Simmons est acct with Joel and John Simmons (1811), 1807 Apr 16. Name Doctor bestowed at birth: Josiah Chambers est acct with [Dr.] B. F. Wilson, 1832–34, receipts to Chamber's [sic]

trustee from 1833 from 1st. Octr. & for 1834 & 1835 (compared), and elsewhere, all in Attorney General v Chambers's trustees, CirCt 1842 Sep.

6. Ben Short and Matt: Benjamin Short acct with Jos. Lewis's Matthew, filed CoCt 1820 Jan–Mar. Distance between Matt's and Short's residences: Land tax roll, lower district, 1818, and Pythagorean theorem. Smith's fees: Smith for Ligon v Phillips's admor, CoCt 1821 Aug.

7. "Not . . . more than 48"; "45 or 50": CW v Surveyor of road from Bush River to county line, CoCt 1816 Aug. Seven children: Amended bill, Jenkins v Watson, CoCt 1822 Jul.

8. "3 hours after night"; "an hour before day"; "day light down": Isaac's testimony, CW v Joshua, OB 23/17-21 (Aug 1832). "Next morning": Isaac Kirk testimony, CW v Samuel Davis, CoCt 1846 Nov. Series of references to time "by sun": CW v Solomon, OB 21/394-397 (1826 Jun); Mary J. Tatum testimony, CW v George, CoCt 1854 Feb. Ownership of timepieces by tax insolvents: Delinquent property 1848, James Leigh, filed CoCt 1849 May (cf. other returns of delinquent property tax from the same decade, such as Delinquent property 1849, upper end, filed CoCt 1850 Apr). More than eight hundred timepieces: Estimate of tax, 1853, filed CoCt 1853 Aug–Sep. As civil war loomed: Erastus P. Davis testimony, CW v Trent, CoCt 1861 Feb.

9. Jackson's watch and clock: Property tax, 1843ff. Deneufville's watch: WB 8/179-180, John Deneufville appraisal (1839). Richardson children: Milley's certf, filed CoCt 1809 Dec–1810 Feb; Notation of Godfry's birth on back of [Milly] Richardson's certf, 1820 Apr, filed CoCt 1843 Aug–Oct; for a similar phenomenon in the same clan, see OB 22/143 (1829 Aug). Artis: Rhoda Artis certf of freedom, 1811 Aug 20, filed CoCt 1818 Jun–Jul. Cousins boys: Cousins report of OP, filed CoCt 1851 Dec–1852 Feb.

10. Law against teaching groups; literacy rate, 1850: John H. Russell, *The Free Negro in Virginia, 1619–1865* (Baltimore: Johns Hopkins Press, 1913), pp. 143–45. Schools (examples): Davis v Fuqua, CoCt 1826 Mar (tuition $15); Articles of agreement for running of a school, Williams v Price's admor, CoCt 1830 May, and James Gilliam depo in Price v Moore, CoCt 1821 Aug; Dance v Scott, CoCt 1852 Sep–Nov (tuition $15 for "English scholars," $25 for "Latin scholars"). On girls' schooling by 1810s, see Andrews's admor v Walthall, p. 21, CirCt 1842 Apr. Prince Edward also had girls' boarding schools and boys' academies. Girls: Joseph Martin, *A New and Comprehensive Gazetteer of Virginia and the District of Columbia* (Charlottesville: Joseph Martin, 1836), pp. 268 and 269; see Female Collegiate Institute v Thackston, CoCt 1844 Aug, and Hawkins v Farmville Seminary, CirCt 1845 Apr. Boys: C. Edward Burrell's Centennial history, 1926, in Mrs. Judson Dowdy and Historic Committee, scrapbook, 1961, Farmville Baptist Church, in the church office; Martin, *Gazetteer,* p. 269.

11. "Purports" explained: CW v John [sic—should read Thomas] Harper and CW v Oliver, both in CoCt 1859 May. Schooling for poor whites: See OB 21/267 (1825 Oct); School commissioners, letter of Charles Woodson, filed CoCt 1836 Jan–Feb. Attendance: James D. Watkinson, personal communication based on his research into treatment of the poor in antebellum Virginia; see also Watkinson, " 'Fit Objects of Charity': Community, Race, Faith, and Welfare in Antebellum Lancaster County, Virginia, 1817–1860," *Journal of the Early Republic,* 21, no. 1 (Spring 2001), 67–68.

12. Ewing "[did] not understand": John Whitehead testimony, CW v Ewing, CoCt 1825 May. Ewing's status: Property tax, 1820–21; Land tax, 1821. Captain Stevens's inadequacies: George W. Bradley and B. J. Worsham depos, Williams v Stevens, CirCt 1853 Mar. Stevens's German birth may have contributed to his impairment in writing English—Ms. Census, 1850, family visitation 434.

13. Schoolmaster: Thomas George, letter to Lyddal Bacon, in Bacon v George, CoCt 1823 Mar. "Abscratt": Fowler v Booker, CoCt 1833 May. "Holy and soly": WB 1/339, William Cary will (1784).

14. "Eye exnowledg": Endorsement on notice to Thomas B. McGehee, 1830 Dec 16,

Watson v Watson, CoCt 1831 Aug. "Exnokleg": Endorsement on spa, Brown v Brown, CoCt 1840 Aug–Oct. "Actngle": Endorsement on spa to George W. Pulliam, Jackson v Bayne, CoCt 1824 Nov. Bruces: Henry Clay Bruce, *The New Man: Twenty-Nine Years a Slave, Twenty-Nine Years a Free Man* (New York: Negro Universities Press, [1895] 1969), pp. 25–27.

15. Lorenzo Scott: Ingram v Price, CirCt 1839 Sep, as follows: voucher no. 14 in bundle, "Esta. J. Price with Wm. Price his Exor, Vouchers" (this voucher apparently written entirely by Scott); and receipts 76 and 95 in bundle, "Esta. Jno. Price with Charles Woodson, the Exor, Vouchers" (all 1832 and 1833). Curtis White signature: Bond, Strong v White, CoCt 1844 Jul. Sam Strong and wife: DB 27/422, Strong to Homes (1859); WB 11/116, Samuel Strong will (1860). (DBs and WBs contain copies of original documents, and do not indicate infallibly whether parties signed or made their mark; for example, John Dungey marked his will with an X, but DB 28/48 suggests—mistakenly, I think—that he signed that deed.) Robert Franklin: Franklin acct with F. W. Smith Co., Smith & Co. v Franklin, CoCt 1845 Oct; Bond, with assignment by Franklin to Price, in Price assignee of Franklin v Scott, CirCt 1844 Apr. Philip White III's signature will be discussed and documented in chapter 8.

16. Free black letters: Samuel Richardson and Mary Fergerson, letters to Joshua Ferger-son, January 14, 1837, in Judy Ferguson's certf &c., filed CoCt 1837 Jan–Mar. The jus-tice of the peace who endorsed the accompanying affidavit certified that Samuel Richardson's signature on that document was genuine, though the body of the affi-davit itself is written in the justice's hand; the two personal letters are written in the same hand as Richardson's signature on the affidavit.

17. Early appearance of dialect features: See, e.g., Indenture of Cata [Caty] Wilson to James Graham Jr., Apprentices, LVA; see also Robert Dawidoff, *The Education of John Randolph* (New York: W. W. Norton, 1979), pp. 41–44. Sociolinguists now con-sider some attributes of white Southern speech to have originated after the Civil War; these include the shift of some vowels to diphthongs, so that, for example, *bid* becomes *bee-uhd* and *mess* sounds like *may-uhss*. But the features outlined here are copiously documented for many decades before that.

18. "Spelt as he generally talks": William S. King depo, Williams v Stevens, CirCt 1853 Mar. Mocock; spelling book: WB 2/186, Henry Young est acct, Elizabeth Young, executrix, pp. 190 and 187, respectively.

19. "Horse Pittle": Prince Edward County to E. J. Erambert, small pox, two vouchers, filed CoCt 1853 Aug–Sep.

20. "The Nomination": OB 23/41, CW v Weaver (1832 Sep). White writers would later put forms such as *enduring* (for *during*) into the mouths of black comic characters.

21. "O-fella": Author's interview with Reginald Othello White Sr., Farmville, Va., March 19, 1992; I have no doubt the pronunciation was a long-standing one. The pro-nunciation of a certain slave's name as "Cupit," though reflected in the spelling of a document written by a white man, may have originated among Cupid and his fellow slaves, but it may also represent the kind of linguistic influence that flowed across the color line in both directions. "Perkinson hoe"; "Mr Miller Iron": Ben Hawkins depo, Perkinson v Hamblen, CoCt 1817 May. "Mrs Woodson sister": Notes regarding testi-mony of Wilson Hix, Woodson v Holland, CoCt 1824 Nov. "Col Charles Woodson place": Reuben Brightwell affi, Moseley v Woodson's admor, CirCt 1842 Apr.

22. "Jasse Jinnings Bell": McDearmon v Jennings, CoCt 1816 Oct; the word "Bell" is cap-italized in the original. Pronunciation of "Hercules": Josiah Chambers acct with Wat-son, Allen & Green, his committee, 1806 Jun 7 (p. 22) and 1810 Mar 30 (p. 33), in Attorney General v Chambers's trustees, CoCt 1821 Nov (spelled "Herculass"); William A. Seay acct with Venable & Co., 1820 Oct 21 and June 11, in Venable v Seay, CoCt 1822 Mar (as "Herculas"); WB 9/374, Anthony White will (1848/1850; as "Her-culas"); Delinquent lands, 1846, filed CoCt 1847 Jan–Apr; Ms. Census, 1850, family

visitation 445 (as "Herculus"); FNLs, 1857ff. In at least some words, syllables that get secondary stress and a long vowel in standard English received no stress in the white and black speech of Prince Edward County, so that the vowel in that syllable became a shwa. Thus, *Ambrose* could be spelled and pronounced *Ambrous*, and *faro*, the game of chance, was pronounced *farra* (written *Farrer*); the pronunciation of the second syllable of *nigra* (for *Negro*), mentioned earlier, conforms even more specifically to this pattern than it does to that of *window/winda*.

23. Dr. Smith's renditions of slave songs sung at the persimmon beer dance contain examples of *he* (for *his*), *de*, and the like (though he spelled *he* as *hi'*). One slave's recorded testimony contains the phrase, "you done tell your master"—Testimony of Amanda, CW v Frank, CoCt 1855 Mar. The construction may be underrepresented in the documentary record for both blacks and whites.

24. "A thinking" at Hampden-Sydney: Joseph Fuqua testimony, p. 43, in CW v Langhorne, CoCt 1857 Feb. "The Springs": R. W. Martin, letter to Joel Watkins, 1833, in McGlasson v Martin, CirCt 1837 Apr.

25. "I have three negroes": Wootton letter to court, March 18, 1811, filed CoCt 1811 Mar. "You was an advocate": Colonel William Bentley, letter to John Randolph, March 27, 1799, published by Randolph in *Virginia Gazette and General Advertiser,* April 5, 1799. "As we was talking": P. Flagg, letter to George Watson, May 7, 1849, Taylor v Flagg, CirCt 1853 Mar. "David M. Doswell": Thomas Doswell affi, Doswell v Doswell, CirCt 1845 Sep. "I believes"; "I now lives": One copy of Samuel F. Moses in Venable & Allen plat and report, and deed of Watson to Allen & Allen, both in Venable v Allen, CoCt 1819 Nov. "Some people trys": Woodson v Holland, CoCt 1824 Nov.

26. "Never gave no account": Charles Woodson interrogatory in Anderson Lumpkin depo, Woodson v Holland, CoCt 1824 Nov. "Them very words": Adam Bell testimony, p. 40, CW v George, CoCt 1854 Feb.

27. Legacy: WB 2/38, Bartholomew Zachery will (1786).

28. Poem: William Branch Jr., quoted in Herbert Clarence Bradshaw, *History of Prince Edward County, Virginia, from Its Earliest Settlements Through Its Establishment in 1754 to Its Bicentennial Year* (Richmond: Dietz Press, 1955), pp. 277–78.

29. Thomas Ford's ex-slaves: Registrations, OB 23/269-270 (1834 Sep): nineteen registered, of whom fourteen freed by will of T. Ford. The color of each of Ford's slaves is carefully recorded, except for the eight born between the writing of his will and his death. It cannot be ruled out that some of the latter were of mixed race and fathered by Ford, but only if Ford waited until very late in life, and *after* he decided on a mass manumission, to beget them. Only two of Ford's older slaves—Shedrick and Fanny, about twenty-six and twenty-one years old, respectively, at Ford's death—were "yellow." Fanny had a "yellow" baby by the time the Ford manumission took place.

30. Ford: WB 7/330, Thomas Ford will (1821/1830); Harry v (Hezekiah) Ford, CoCt 1834 Aug.

31. Many point to names: See, e.g., discussions of names and naming in Ira Berlin, "From Creole to African: Atlantic Creoles and the Origins of African-American Society in Mainland North America," *William and Mary Quarterly,* 3rd ser., 52, no. 2 (April 1996), 251–52; David Brion Davis, review of Ira Berlin, *Many Thousands Gone: The First Two Centuries of Slavery in North America* (1998), in *American Historical Review,* 104, no. 4 (October 1999), 1286 ("comic, animal-like names"); Gary B. Nash, *Forging Freedom: The Formation of Philadelphia's Black Community, 1720–1840* (Cambridge, MA, and London: Harvard University Press, 1988), pp. 80–87; Douglas R. Egerton, *Gabriel's Rebellion: The Virginia Slave Conspiracies of 1800 and 1802* (Chapel Hill and London: University of North Carolina Press, 1993), p. 20; and Peter Rachleff, *Black Labor in Richmond, 1865–1890* (Urbana and Chicago: University of Illinois Press, 1989), p. 22. For a popular depiction of the naming of slaves for whites' amusement, note the scene in the television miniseries *Roots* set at the Annapolis slave market in

1767, in which factor John Carrington asks customer John Reynolds, "Do you fancy the classics, sir? 'Tis all the fashion here on the Bay to have Psyches and Caesars and Hectors running about the place—a whole pantheon of nymphs and satyrs, a delightful conceit"—William Blinn, M. Charles Cohen, Ernest Kinoy, and James Lee, screenwriters, *Roots,* 1977, VHS cassette, vol. 2, 1977. For an extensive scholarly discussion of naming among slaves, see Herbert G. Gutman, *The Black Family in Slavery and Freedom, 1750–1925* (New York: Vintage, 1976), chapter 6.

32. Israelite Titus Gibbs was presumably named after the apostle Paul's assistant rather than the Roman emperor who destroyed Jerusalem.

33. Susannah Forgason: CW v Martha Young, CoCt 1842 Aug.

34. Wills: WB 8/292, Mildrid Holmes [sic] will (1841); WB 9/374, Anthony White will (1850); see also WB 6/345, Richard White inventory (1826). Sam White called Samuel (examples): Summons to garnishees, Morton & Venable v Seay, CoCt 1822 Mar; Bail bond in Anderson v Clark & White, CoCt 1840 Mar; Randolph's commissioners v Samuel White et al., CoCt 1843 Mar. The Phil Whites called Philip (examples): OB 18/36 (1814 Mar); OB 26/222 (1843 Aug); writs in Hobson Trustee v White, filed CirCt 1846 Sep (order 1846 Aug?). Davy Bartlett called David (example): Lyle & Co v Bartlett, CoCt 1843 May.

35. "Mr. Phil White": Accts, Smith & Co. v White, CoCt 1844 Mar. "Mr. Robert Franklin": Franklin account with F. W. Smith Co., Smith & Co. v Franklin, CoCt 1845 Sep–Dec; though there was also a white Robert A. Franklin in the county, the man named in these store accounts appears to be the free black man of that name. Edmund Wiltse of this store may have been a native of New York (Ms. Census, 1860, family visitation 275), and one might therefore attribute his application of "Mr." to free blacks to a non-Southern upbringing; but in fact the phrase "Mr. Phil White" appears in at least two different hands in these accounts.

36. Two younger Hercules Whites: See IH 1816 (born c. 1803); and FNLs, 1857 and 1858 (born c. 1840). Gaius Williard: Williard v Ellis, CoCt 1825 Jan–Mar. Justices Augustus Watson and Augustus Watkins are abundantly documented in county records. Augustus Reynolds: Summons and recognizance, CW v Betty, CoCt 1815 Sep, filed CoCt 1815 Oct–Dec. Augustus Patteson: WB 7/436, Alexander Patteson will (1836). Augustus Erambert: Witness summons, CW v Jones, CirCt 1848 Apr. Augustus J. Price: CW v Price, CoCt 1855 Nov–Dec. Augustus F. Anderson leads slave patrol: Spa to Augustus Anderson in CW v Flowers, CoCt 1843 Nov; Unlabeled patrol accounts of Anderson, filed CoCt 1850 May–Jul.

37. Caesar Smart: WB 4/276, Additional inventory of Archer Allen est (1811). Two younger Caesars: IH 1816 (born to Phil Junior and Rachel Johnston White c. 1812); and FNLs, 1857ff. (born c. 1838 to Curtis, Rachel Johnston White's son, and Priscilla White). Caesar White in late nineteenth century: Author's interview with Elizabeth Hill Watkins, Prospect, Va., July 26, 1989.

38. Virago: Delivery bond, Mathews v Hughes, CoCt 1822 Dec–1823 Mar. Cupid: Attachment, Venable v Seay, CoCt 1822 Mar. Neptune the elder and the younger: Carter v Mettauer, CoCt 1831 Jun–Jul. Venus Homes: See FNL, 1821. White Romulus: OB 23/192 (1833 Dec), line 3. Achilles Puryear: OB 24/244 (1839 Apr).

39. Lucy, Patsey et al.: Price v Walthall, CoCt 1823 Sep–Oct.

40. Christmas: Report, Carter v Carter, CoCt 1841 Jun. Champion: Champion's testimony, CW v Simon (Scott's), Simon (Wootton's), and John, CoCt 1848 Aug.

41. Burton brothers: CW v Burton, CoCt 1842 Aug. Green: FNL, 1811. Clay: Dupuy mill records, section 4, folder 3, 1828, Mssi D9295 a137-156, VHS. Dred: WB 4/73, Richard Burke inventory (1807). Mourning Sweeney: See William Pattesons road report, filed CoCt 1814 Jan–Mar (though this dating may be incorrect), and many other county documents. Blizzard Magruder: Prince Edward delinquent land, 1817, filed CoCt 1817 Sep–Nov, and many other documents. Barshebea Allen: OB 17/536 (1813 May).

42. Boaz: James McNeil's road order, 1808, which, however, was filed in CoCt 1814 Jan–Mar. A certain slave, a doctor, constitutes the exception that proves the rule about interracial biblical names: he bore a name from the Bible—Pharaoh—that no white mother would likely give her son—CW v Pharaoh, CoCt 1817 Feb. Magdalen: Est of Mrs. Magdalen Venable, appraisement [sic], filed CoCt 1856 Sep–Dec. Ketturah and Masurah: Sophia W. Harrison will (1824/1825), in Matthews v Harrison's admor, CirCt 1852 Apr. Kittura: Ellington v Harrison, CirCt 1854 Aug.

43. Allen: DB 21/426-427, Allen to Madison (1835/1836). America, wife of James Mickle: Mickle v Richardson, CoCt 1821 Mar. Missouri: Ellington v Harrison, CirCt 1854 Aug; Ms. Census, 1850, family visitations 295 and 305; Ms. Census, 1860, family visitation 64. Indiana: Williams v Stevens, CirCt 1853 Mar. A white Indiana, named 1842: Ms. Census, 1850, family visitation 340.

44. Allen's slaves: WB 4/265-267, Archer Allen appraisal (1811). Donaldson Gibbs and Wilson Carter were born not long after the manumission, but these men's given names are not clearly associated with the white social elite.

45. Blacks with middle names (examples): OB 26/15 and 16 (1845 Jan).

46. Purnall slaves with surnames: WB 7/213, John Purnall appraisal (1831). Dupuy as John Purnall's "friend and nephew": WB 6/174-177, John Purnall will (1824/1825). Dupuy slaves named: Report: Negroes belonging to est of Asa Dupuy, appraisal, 1858, Dupuy v Dupuy's exor, Oct–Dec 1858. Dupuy administers estate: Commissioners' report, Neal v Walton, CoCt 1831 May. On Dupuy's plantation, the daughter of one enslaved mother acquired a surname from her free black father, and the same thing certainly happened in other places from time to time. Purnall slave Franky as mother to Milly Homes's granddaughter: John Purnall appraisal, as above; and Dupuy v Purnall, est of General John Purnall, Report: Allotment of Negroes belonging to estate between widow & heirs, CoCt 1828 Jul; and see also Eggleston v Dupuy, CoCt 1848 Apr–May, by which time Franky's daughter Milly had twice made Franky a grandmother.

47. Uncertain whites use slave surnames: Caleb Baker est acct with Branch J. Worsham, exor, credit 1824 Oct, in Hendrick v Jones, CoCt 1825 Jun–Jul ("Ivan alias Jones"); James Madison to John H. Edmunds and James W. Dunnington, DoT (1839), in Madison's Trustees v Morton, CirCt 1854 Aug ("Jack [Dandridge]"). See also Nunnally v Nunnally, CirCt 1838 Apr (where Lucy Wade's surname appears once in parentheses). Not surprisingly, slaves whose masters allowed them to sell their own labor tended to use surnames openly as they moved through the world of free people—see, for example, Circuit Superior Court Order Book, 1853–70, pp. 159 (1857 Mar), 188–89 (1858 Mar), and 200 (1858 Aug), in office of CirCt clerk, Prince Edward County Courthouse, Farmville.

48. A given white person in later years might still find it vaguely novel that an Afro-Virginian carried two names, styling a court case, say, Phil White v Trent & Skipwith (CoCt 1819 Sep) where last names alone were the norm (Smith v Jones, for instance).

49. Bruce on slave traders: Bruce, *New Man*, pp. 47–48. "Road is thronged": John Randolph of Roanoke, *Forty-Six Autograph Letters to Harmanus Bleecker of Albany*, October 10, 1818, UVa (cited hereafter as *Letters to Bleecker*).

50. Slave sale in Buckingham; "the greater portion": Charles L. Christian depo, Raine v Wilson & Lockett, CirCt 1845 Sep. Virginians and Alabamians: John P. Williams depo, Hocker v Cobbs, CirCt 1851 Apr.

51. Expert valuations of slaves (example): Statement to show the value of each negro &c., report of Commissioner Watkins, Michaux & Watson v Williams, CirCt 1854 Aug. Valuations of categories (example): Depos of P. H. Jackson et al., Michaux & Totty v Williams, CirCt 1854 Aug. "A negro lad" in lieu of interest: Obadiah Jinkins depo, Holland v Jones, CoCt 1815 Oct–Dec. Woman and child as security for loan: Bill and answer, Blanton v Blanton, CoCt 1832 Feb–Mar.

52. Boy, three, and girl, six: Howson Clark depo, Clark v Burke, CirCt 1845 Sep. Auction of four-year-old: WB 9/136, William Seay est acct (1846).

53. "Buy him a little Negro": John Boatwright depo, Cox v Legrand, CoCt 1826 Apr–May.

54. Knowledge of others' slaves (examples): Wyatt Whitehead depo, Preston v Thackston, CirCt 1846 Jun; Mary Vaughan depo, Rice's exor v Lewelling, CoCt 1824 Mar–Apr; E. M. Mettauer and John W. Rodgers depos, Shelton v King's exors, CirCt 1852 Apr; Testimony, CW v Peter, CoCt 1821 Apr. Recognized even at a distance; differentiating within a group (example): Irby Hudson depo, 1832 August, Doswell v Doswell, CirCt 1845 Sep.

55. "Did not think [it] proper": Robert A. Thackston depo, Thackston v Thackston, CoCt 1835 Aug. Attempt to avoid loss of slave (example): Jackson by Labby v Smith et al., CirCt 1847 Apr, especially bill and Pleasant Partin depo.

56. "Sold to the Highest bidder": WB 3/512, Richard D. Pincham will (1806/1807).

57. Tobacco chewing: "Colo. Rice" depo, James Dillon's will case, filed CirCt 1844 Apr. Mole Hill: Legrand's est, report and division, dated 1828 Jun 16, but filed CoCt 1827 Sep–Nov. "From time immemorial": William S. Lacy, letter to Sister Bess [Dewey], February 7, 1863, box 2, folder 15b, Drury Lacy papers, UNC. Hard Times: Charles Baldwin depo, I'Anson v Vernon's admor, CirCt 1848 Sep.

58. Sleeping in same room: Testimony of Martha C. Selby, Wyatt, and Tom, CW v Joshua, OB 23/17-21 (1832 Aug). Whites rent lot just vacated by "old Patty": John Vawter est acct with William Gilliam, Woodson v Vawter, CoCt 1841 Jun. (The name Patty was written over the original Sally, or vice versa; but either way the tenant was black.) White v Wright, CoCt 1842 Aug–Oct. The wording of the Wrights' bond to White makes the transaction sound like a sale, but the sum promised, $25, is unrealistically low for a house and lot. The occupant up till then was apparently a free black woman.

59. Shoemaker: Daniel Glenn testimony, CW v Joshua, OB 23/17-21 (1832 Aug); see also CoCt 1832 Aug.

60. Frostbitten foot: Samuel Hurt testimony, Inquest on the dead body of negro slave Patsy, March 17, 1861, filed CoCt 1861 Jan–Apr. Gravely ill woman unable to go to "the quarter": Peyton R. Berkeley depo, Gilliam v Martin, CirCt 1852 Aug.

61. Picking boils: William Doswell depo ("foul disorder") and Stephen D. Rowlett depo ("If she had known"), in Dejernatt v Miller, agent of Perkinson, CoCt 1831 Jun–Jul.

62. Colley and Selina: CW v Colley, CirCt 1847 Apr, presentment; CoCt 1847 May, and OB 26/168-170 (1847 May), with testimony; CirCt 1849 Sep, and CirCt 1849 Oct (filed Sep—a separate charge of carrying a concealed weapon). After being convicted and sentenced to two years in jail, Colley was granted a new trial and acquitted, perhaps in no small part because most potential witnesses were blacks whose testimony against him was inadmissible. Colley slaveless: He does not appear in Property tax, 1847, and neither of the two Colleys who do owned any slaves. A dozen years after Colley's trial, a white man was presented by the grand jury for "committing fornication with Betsy a negro woman slave"—Circuit Superior Court Order Book, 1853–1870, p. 185 (1858 Mar), in office of CirCt clerk, Prince Edward County Courthouse, Farmville.

63. Documented cases of white women with black or mulatto male partners include the five who were charged with cohabiting (or "fornicating") with free black men, discussed earlier; Martha League, Elizabeth Dungey, and the sister-in-law of the "other" Charles Woodson, also discussed earlier; "a free white woman" who bore a daughter of mixed race—OB 24/290 (1839 Oct); a white woman who was admitted to the poorhouse with her mulatto children—Annual report of OP, 1853 Mar 31, filed 1853 Aug 15, entered CoCt 1853 Sep; and the mother of Betsy Lyle, discussed later in this chapter.

64. Complaint of cohabitation first: Answer of Chambers's committee, Nelson, Allen, and Thackston, Attorney General v Chambers's trustees, CirCt 1842 Sep. "Improperly there": [Creed Taylor's] notation on notes by defendant Thackston's counsel in same case, and those notes themselves; and see other documents in same case; all in Attorney General v Chambers's committee, same location as the other Chambers case cited here. For a well-researched discussion that finds the color of the parties more of the essence in cases of interracial adultery than I do, see Thomas E. Buckley, S.J., *The Great Catastrophe of My Life: Divorce in the Old Dominion* (Chapel Hill and London: University of North Carolina Press, 2002), chapter 4. For evidence that seems to confirm my picture of babies' race as a forensic clue, see John Hope Franklin, *The Free Negro in North Carolina, 1790–1860* (Chapel Hill: University of North Carolina Press, 1943), p. 38.

65. One interracial relationship that did produce a documented bastard child involved a free black woman and a white man who shirked his responsibility. See the discussion of the Betsy Lyle case later in this chapter.

66. Murder of Nancy Morgan: CW v Solomon, CoCt 1826 Jul, and OB 21/392-397; CW v Hill, CoCt 1826 Jul, and OB 21/397-403, especially testimony of Nathaniel Hill, John Martin, Moseley Johnson, Bowler Brizendine, William Childress, and Benjamin Boatwright; CirCt 1826 Sep. Location of crime: Land tax, 1826, homes of William Brightwell, Nathaniel Hill, and Benjamin Boatwright. Leg irons and jail time: Gallion et al. acct to county (guard claims), and Prince Edward County acct with Gallion & Jones, both filed CoCt 1827 Jun–Jul. White witnesses with black family members or relatives were James League and "Shed" (presumably Sherwood) Selbe; it was the latter who had been charged with allowing blacks to visit him—CW v Silvey [sic], OB 19/410 (1820 Aug), and CoCt 1820 Nov–Dec.

67. "Vilest white persons"; "disgraceful"; "privately organized bands": Russell, *Free Negro in Virginia*, p. 127.

68. "As black a negro": Benjamin W. Womack testimony, OP v Scott, CoCt 1850 Sep.

69. Betsy Lyle case: OP v Scott, CoCt 1850 Sep, particularly testimony of B. W. Womack and Watkins Dupuy. Lyle's employment: Lyle testimony, CW v George, CoCt 1854 Feb. Census taker: Ms. Census, 1850, family visitation 207. Legal definition of blackness: Ira Berlin, *Slaves Without Masters: The Free Negro in the Antebellum South* (New York: New Press, [1974] 1992), p. 99, citing Hening, 12 (1785), p. 184.

70. Processionings: Legrand and Gunter processioners' return, 1843 Jun. Dungeys and Gilliams: DB 20/316-317, Absalom Dungey to Gilliam (1830); 21/282-283, Gilliam to John Dungey (1835). Dungey-Gilliam purchases on same day: DB 26/5-6, Elam to Dungey (1850); DB 26/6-7, Elam to Gilliam (1850). Elam and Dungey contest road: H. G. Richardson &c. road order, filed CoCt 1836 Jun–Jul. Toward the end of the 1820s, Absalom Dungey twice mortgaged his part of the family's land, but he paid back that money to the white mortgagees within a year or two—DB 20/71, Dungey to Richardson (Smith, trustee), DoT (1828), and 20/316, Richardson's trustee (Byrd Smith) to Dungey, release (1830); DB 20/57-58, Dungey to Morgan, DoT (1828), and 20/324, Morgan to Dungey, release (1830). Absalom then sold his thirty-five acres of land to one of the Gilliams, but his brother John bought back thirty-five acres—apparently the same tract—a few years later (see documentation at head of note).

71. Stephen Forgason's household: Ms. Census, 1830, sheet 124 (Stephen "Furgerson"). Selbes slaveless: Ms. Census, 1820 and 1830. Becky Forgason, 19, at Sherwood Selbe's: FNL, 1857. Accusation against Selbes: CW v Selvey, OB 19/410 (1820 Aug) and 469 (1820 Nov). (The family name was sometimes spelled Selby or Silvey.)

72. Williams's move to Prince Edward: Williams v Saylor's exors, CirCt 1838 Sep (background in New York: Sullivan D. Hubbell and Peter Himrod depos; schoolteaching: James S. Allen depo; "had tried with negroes": Joseph Binford depo). Free blacks at

Williams's: Otis Williams, letter to Dr. [J. P.] Mettauer, August 14, 1831, John Peter Mettauer papers, Mss1 M5677 a47, VHS. Prosecution of Williams: CW v Williams, CoCt 1842 Oct. Williams's struggles with his wife's family over the legacy of her now dead uncle may have encouraged some to believe him guilty (Williams v Saylor's exors).

73. For an astute discussion of "personalism" in dealings between whites and blacks in old Virginia, see Suzanne Lebsock, *The Free Women of Petersburg: Status and Culture in a Southern Town, 1784–1860* (New York and London: W. W. Norton, 1984), chapter 5. Another warning against pigeonholing whites as friendly or unfriendly to blacks is the case of C. E. Chappell, a white man who conducted business transactions on Phil White's behalf, yet who also gave information to the grand jury in 1850 that led to the presentment of three men for allowing slaves to go at large and trade as free people—OB 26/376 (1850 Aug). Chappell is discussed later in this chapter.

74. Nathan Homes buys land: DB 18/192, Purnall to Homes (1820), and DB 20/198, Sharp to Homes (1829). Homes's "friend" tries to fleece him: Bell v Sharp and Homes, CoCt 1837 Jul, especially answer, and depos of John W. Redd and Samuel V. Watkins. Bell's assets: Land tax 1830; Ms. Census, 1830, p. 114.

75. Expulsion of Homes's new wife and stepchildren sought: OP report, filed CoCt 1836 May. Homeses remaining together: FNL, 1857. On this FNL, Nathan Homes's name is immediately followed by those of Susan Homes (the new wife the overseers of the poor had worried about had been named Susan Hitchins) and of sixteen-year-old Martha Homes, presumably the couple's daughter. Nathan's name is preceded by that of Edward Hitchins, thirty, who apparently had been one of the children Susan had brought with her when she married Nathan Homes. Ms. Census, 1860, family visitation 130, lists shoemaker Nathan and Susan Homes together, with five children, on $300 worth of real estate.

76. Penick's behavior: Penick's guardian v Penick, CirCt 1840 Apr (Tuggles and Penicks as relatives: Amplias Tuggle depo; Jonathan's schooling: Vouchers for account no. 4; "dissipation and recklessness": Charles Woodson depo); Penick's trustee v Penick &c., and Penick v Raine (especially plaintiff's letter to dismiss bill), both in CirCt 1836 Apr; Penick v Penick, CirCt 1838 Apr, and John Tuggle depo, Penick v Penick, CirCt 1840 Apr; Jones v Penick, CirCt 1852 Apr. Some further background is found in Penick's guardian v Penick's exors, CirCt 1838 Apr.

77. Legrand's family and personal history: Lancaster v Legrand's exors, CirCt 1841 Sep. His complaints against the county: Farmville road by Legrand's, report, filed CoCt 1839 May. Cutting off bridle path: Davis v Legrand, especially Davis's petition for road, CoCt 1822 Nov. Stolen horse: CW v Maxey, CoCt 1824 Jun. Father's trade with White: Rights & credits, 1826 Dec 8, in Legrand's est, report and division, dated 1828 Jun 16, but filed CoCt 1827 Sep–Nov.

78. Charges against Patterson and Gregory: CW v Patterson and CW v Gregory, both OB 20/170-171 (1821 Nov), 240, 280, 351 (1822 Aug; summonses redirected to Buckingham), and 402. One wonders whether the William Gregory who informed on Michael Patterson to the grand jury was related to Thomas Gregory, whom the same grand jury presented for disturbing worship. There is a twelve-year age discrepancy between the earlier registrations of Michael Patterson—OB 19/21 (1818 Jun); OB 20/86 (1821 Jun); OB 21/515 (1827 Feb)—and two later ones—OB 22/212 (1829 Nov); OB 23/269 (1834 Sep). I find no other evidence that there may have been two Michael Pattersons, and inconsistencies between the last two registrations call into question the year of birth that they cite. In any event, the Michael Patterson born c. 1797 and emancipated by Richard Randolph's will is the only one who would have been old enough to face charges in 1821.

79. Development of Patterson case: CW v Patterson, apart from the foregoing: CoCt

1823 Mar; OB 20/458 (1823 Mar; dismissal). Development of Gregory case: CW v Gregory (disturbing worship), apart from the foregoing: CoCt 1823 Aug; OB 20/170 (1821 Nov), 402, 458, 483, and 562-563 (1823 Aug; conviction). Patterson's marriage: List of colored persons living together as man & wife, 1866 Feb 27 (compiled by Freedmen's Bureau), Prince Edward County Records, LVA. "Snaped a pistol": CW v Gregory, CoCt 1823 Aug; OB 20/267 (1822 May), 273 (1822 May), 351 (1822 Aug), 402, 458, 483, 564 (1823 Aug; the conviction).

80. "Three cuts": Ebenezer Frothingham testimony, CW v Smith, OB 21/404-405 (1826 Jul); and see same trial, CoCt 1826 Jul.

81. McDearmon and Evans heirs: DB 16/122, Evans to McDearmon (1816); DB 17/119, Goff to McDearmon (1819/1820); DB 17/127, Bartlett to McDearmon (1819); DB 17/130, Evans to McDearmon (1819); DB 20/22, Evans to McDearmon (1828).

82. Census taker: Ms. Census, 1860, family visitations 751–52 (sheep rustlers) and 673 (Young and Bigger).

83. Howard-White dispute: Howard v White, CoCt 1837 Jul; OB 24/59 (1837 Jul); see also OB 22/581 (1832 Jan). Mely Howard's suit also challenged Sam White's very right to inherit his father's land: since he and his brothers had been born out of wedlock, she said, they were not lawful heirs to Hercules White the elder, who had left no will. This was a mere legalism concocted, no doubt, by Mely's lawyer rather than by Howard herself. Hercules White, as a slave, could not have been legally married at the time his children were born.

84. Congregation crystallizing: See C. Edward Burrell's Centennial history, 1926, in Mrs. Judson Dowdy and Historic Committee, scrapbook, 1961, Farmville Baptist Church. To the liquor question, Sam White may have brought the zeal of a convert; if he was the "S. White" who bought two gallons of brandy for Christmas 1820, then he apparently had been less punctilious in earlier life than he later became—William A. Seay, acct with Wood & Dupuy, Wood & Dupuy v Seay, CoCt 1822 Mar.

85. "The sabbath": Sally [Lyle, of Charlotte County], letter to Williana Lacy, June 7, 1835, folder 3, Drury Lacy papers, UNC.

86. Seay and Weaver: CW v Weaver, CoCt 1826 May. Sam White may also have had an ulterior motive for depicting Mely Howard as a servant: to assert in yet another way that she had no claim to any White land despite having lived there for years.

87. Howards in later years: FNLs, 1857, 1861, and 1862; see also lists for 1858, 1860, 1863, and 1864. The sons were Beverly and Sidney Howard, who are listed with their parents Guy and Mely on FNLs for 1825 and earlier. Mary Jane Howard, twenty, at Phil White's: FNL, 1862. She was almost surely Guy and Mely Howard's granddaughter; there was no other free black Howard family in Prince Edward, and Mary Jane, then fifteen, had been listed just above the Howards of Israel Hill on FNL, 1857.

88. Opening courthouse: OB 24/47 (1837 Jul). A revival: Sharon Baptist Church minute book, 1827–65, LVA 20803, especially pp. 46–47 and 52–56 (fall 1837). Camp meetings: CW v Reynolds and Reynolds, CirCt 1811 Sep; Cheadle, 14th p. top, E. Brightwell acct; Thomas Ellington testimony, CW v Colley, OB 26/168 (1847 May). Evening prayer meetings: "Colo. Rice" depo, sheet 3, p. 2, James Dillon's will case, filed CirCt 1844 Apr. Baptists in private homes: C. Edward Burrell's Centennial history, 1926, p. 1, in scrapbook, 1961, Farmville Baptist Church.

89. "Peeping wistfully": John T. Watkins, letter to the editor of the *Farmville Journal*, October 16, 1856, box 14, folder 147, Hubard family papers, UNC. For earlier concerns about what appear to have been similar problems, see S. H. Lyle [Charlotte County?], letter to Williana Lacy, August 15, 1835, box 1, folder 3, Drury Lacy papers, UNC. Cumberland slaves: List of colored members, Sharon Baptist Church minute book, LVA, in early pages and continued following p. 115. The Briery congregation also owned and hired out slaves; see Green v Warden, CoCt 1844 Nov, and Green v Webb, CoCt 1845 Sep–Dec.

90. Wavering commitments: See, e.g., Sharon Baptist Church minute book, LVA, p. 31 (1830 Jun), with appointment of a committee "to admonish all delinquent members of the duty & importance of a regular & punctual attendance to Church meetings." "Personal experience": Martin, *Gazetteer,* p. 267. "Convicted": See, e.g., "Deacon W. H. White," *Richmond Planet,* January 26, 1895, courtesy of Harold Forsythe. Archer Homes's baptism: Sharon Church minute book, List of colored members, p. 24 (1842 Jul), following p. 115 of minute book proper. Homes's age: OB 22/580 (1832 Jan).

91. Receiving experience: Sharon Baptist Church minute book, LVA, pp. 38 and 42. Only rarely were such events explicitly recorded by Sharon's secretary; in these two instances, the people whose experience was received were probably white. "Received by experience" at Farmville Baptist: *Religious Herald,* 12, no. 23 (1836 Dec 23), p. 199, col. 5, Virginia Baptist Historical Society.

92. "21 white members": *Religious Herald,* 12, no. 23 (1836 Dec 23), p. 199, col. 5. Peter Winston church clerk: Burrell's Centennial history, in Farmville Baptist Church scrapbook, 1961. The Whites as first members: Two loose sheets in Farmville Baptist Church Record Book, 1870–84: "Written in 1872 P.[eter] W.[inston]," and "History— Farmville Baptist Church—Members—List furnished to Dr. Winston by Ben Robertson 1872"; in the church office.

93. Sharon as mother church: Bradshaw, *Prince Edward County,* p. 254. Sharing church buildings: See Martin, *Gazetteer,* p. 269. Communing with Methodists: Sharon Church minute book, LVA, p. 77 (1838 Jul). Specific sins: Sharon minute book, *passim* (backgammon, p. 38; adultery [a slave woman], p. 16; fighting, p. 44; carrying dirk, p. 25; illegitimate child, pp. 83–85; communing with Methodists, p. 77). "Disorderly" slaves: *Ibid.,* p. 76. Christine Leigh Heyrman writes that blacks in the South overall were less likely than whites to be accused in church of misconduct, but "far more likely to be expelled" if convicted—Heyrman, *Southern Cross: The Beginnings of the Bible Belt* (New York: Knopf, 1997), p. 69. Heyrman (pp. 159 and 301, n. 57) and Donald G. Mathews find that disciplinary action by congregations became less frequent over time—Mathews, *Religion in the Old South* (Chicago and London: University of Chicago Press, 1977), p. 100. But Sharon Church recorded such actions fairly often through the 1840s, with a decrease in the 1850s.

94. "Religious melancholy": "Colo. Rice" depo (and Francis N. Watkins depo), James Dillon's will case, filed CirCt 1844 Apr.

95. Before turn of century: CW v Arnol [sic], OB 11/602 (1797 Nov; "disorderly behavior"). Intoxication clearly linked to disturbing worship: CW v Weaver, OB 18/450 (1816 Aug; presentment), and CoCt 1817 Sep–Nov; OB 18/648 (1817 Nov; three presentments); CW v Ligon, CoCt 1818 Aug, presentment, and OB 19/171 (1819 May).

96. Defacing with knife: CW v Price, CoCt 1858 Nov. Beating minister: CW v McDearmon, OB 22/344 and 351 (1830 Aug—two charges) and 392 (1830 Nov). Pistol and drawn knife: CW v J. Giles, CW v G. Giles, and CW v Beard, all CoCt 1833 Aug. Student: CW v Foster, CirCt 1846 Jun. Verser: CW v Verser, two counts, OB 25/305 (1844 Aug; presentment); CoCt 1844 Nov, and OB 26/6 (1844 Nov); CoCt 1845 Mar, and OB 26/27 (1845 Mar). Other cases: CW v J. Cavender and CW v F. Cavender, CoCt 1818 Nov, and OB 19/108 (1818 Nov); CW v P. Fore Jr. and CW v S. Fore, CoCt 1819 May; CW v Ralls and CW v Atwell, 1847 Sep, presentments, and CirCt 1851 Sep. Twenty-five-dollar fine and costs: CW v Ligon and CW v Weaver, as in note 95. On harassment of preachers, see Heyrman, *Southern Cross,* pp. 230–32.

97. "Baptist preachings": John Randolph, *Letters to Bleecker,* April 22, 1813, UVa.

98. Giving bond for Phil White: Strong v White, CoCt 1844 Nov, and OB 26/9 (1844 Nov); and again in Randolph's commissioners v White and White, CirCt 1841 Aug, filed 1841 Sep. Robertson and church: "History—Farmville Baptist Church—Members— List furnished to Dr. Winston by Ben Robertson 1872"; Burrell's Centennial history,

in scrapbook, 1961, Farmville Baptist Church (on the Sunday School). (One wonders whether there had been a Sunday School for blacks in Farmville even before there was one for whites.) The horse theft: CW v Bradley, discussed in chapter 6.

99. Purchase of lots: DB 21/324, Seay to White (1835); DB 22/338, Seay to Robertson (1838). John N. Robertson as cosigner: White v Bartlett, CoCt 1837 Aug–Sep; Joe Bartlett's creditor in this instance was fellow free black John White. John N. and Ben Robertson: DB 22/338 (1838), Seay to Robertson, in which the two bought a lot jointly. Robertson's eventual lawsuit: Robertson v Bartlett, CoCt 1843 Jul.

100. Chappell a coachmaker: Ms. Census, 1850, schedule 5, Products of industry, p. 122. Chappell as Phil White's "agent," and the quotation: White for Marker v Wrights, CoCt 1842 Aug–Oct. See also White v Steger, CoCt 1843 Mar, in which the notation of a credit of $70 on the back of Steger's note to Sam White seems to be in Chappell's handwriting. Sale of Chappell's lots: DB 22/179, Chappell to Phillips (1837); DB 23/74-75, Chappell to Gregg (1840); DB 23/96-97, Chappell to Robertson (1840); Land tax, town lots, 1840 and 1841. Financial free fall: DB 23/75-78, Chappell to Flournoy (1840).

101. "As any Yankee": Judith Randolph, letter to John Randolph, March 9, 1808, TC/W&M. General Peter Johnston of Prince Edward was a potential contender for John's seat in Congress—J[ohn] R[andolph] to [Edward Dillon?], January 7, 1809, Dillon-Polk papers, UNC. "Best esteemed and most applauded": Philip V. Fithian, letter to Reverend Enoch Green, December 1, 1773, in Hunter Dickinson Farish, ed., *Journal and Letters of Philip Vickers Fithian, 1773–1774: A Plantation Tutor of the Old Dominion* (Charlottesville: University Press of Virginia, 1957), p. 27.

102. "Very Persevering People": Wyatt Whitehead depo, Preston v Thackston, CirCt 1846 Jun.

103. "Turned gentlemen and merchants": "Testimony, dem[urre?]r & joinder," Ewing v Ewing, CoCt 1838 Mar.

104. "Industrious and economical"; "adding to [their] property": Branch J. Worsham depo, Burke v Rice, CirCt 1850 Apr.

105. "[Men] of capital": David Bruce depo for plff, Daniel v Steger, CirCt 1837 Sep.

106. Phil White Jr. requires bail: Capias, 1832 Sep 20, in White v Gibbs, CoCt 1833 May. Hiring slave: Jackson v Boatwright and Nunnally, CoCt 1843 May. Booker Jackson's slaves: Property tax, 1841–46 (one slave), 1847–48 (two slaves), 1849 (three slaves age twelve or older), and 1850 (two slaves). The thesis that free blacks became economically "indispensable," especially in the country districts, appears in Luther Porter Jackson, *Free Negro Labor and Property Holding in Virginia, 1830–1860* (New York and London: D. Appleton–Century, 1942), pp. 101 and 195. He also asserts that slave labor in Virginia was expensive in the years he studied—pp. 61–64.

107. Ben White's IOU: Anderson v White, CirCt 1837 Sep. In the end, as happened to men of both races, Ben White was unable to pay off the bond he had signed, and he faced a lawsuit.

108. By the mid-1840s, a lot in Farmville might be taxed at less than 50 cents annually, or at several dollars if it was highly developed. The personal property tax bill on a slave generally ran between 40 and 50 cents a year; the tax, if any, on a watch or clock was typically 25 cents, but very few free blacks owned one.

109. The county set the levy as low as 15 or 20 cents or as high as 85 cents in a few exceptional years. The archaic terms "tithe" and "tithable" in county levy records are synonyms for "taxable male." The county's overseers of the poor also seem to have authorized a "poor levy" each year, but the charge per man was only 20 or 30 cents. See discussion in OP report, filed CoCt 1830 Jun 21, and other OP reports.

110. Curtis White: Insolvent tithes [upper district, 1837], filed CoCt 1838 Jun 18 with Delinquents for parish levy, 1837, lower end; and Sheriff, insolvents, upper district

[1841], filed CoCt 1842 Jun, which also includes sometime black Israelite "Mike" Patterson.

111. "Free Negroes . . . For Hire": Free Negroes, filed CoCt 1825 May. "To be sold for taxes": List of Free Negroes, filed CoCt 1847 Jan–Apr. People sometimes called the specific tax a head tax or poll tax—"poll" being simply an old word for head.

112. Hiring-out laws: Hening, 11 (1782), chapter XXI, section 3, pp. 39–40; Acts of Assembly, 1814, chapter XX, p. 61, and 1820, chapter XXXII, section 2, p. 26; *Code of Virginia*, 1849 (Richmond: William F. Ritchie, 1849), title 30, chapter 107, para. 15, p. 468.

113. Specific tax $2.50: See Delinquent property tax, upper end, 1815, filed CoCt 1815 Oct–Dec, with "poll tax" obligation listed for several individuals. Nonpayment in 1814: Insolvent property tax, 1814, filed CoCt 1814 Sep–Dec. Hiring out, 1815: Ampey Brandem & others, summons to 1815 Oct CoCt, and Order to hire out Ferguson & Moss, both filed CoCt 1815 Oct–Dec. Orders to hire out, 1820s and 1830s: OB 21/200 and 208 (1825 May); OB 23/10 (1832 Jun). Other free blacks, such as Michael Patterson and Kit Strong in the county levy of 1820, not having paid initially, proceeded to do so and have their names removed from the rolls of nonpayers—see County levy insolvents (tithes), 1820, filed CoCt 1821 Jun.

114. Twenty Israelites or children of Israelites per year: Insolvent tithes [upper district, 1837], filed CoCt 1838 Jun 18 with Delinquents for parish levy, 1837, lower end; Sheriff, insolvents, upper district [1841], filed CoCt 1842 Jun. That the younger generation were simply more numerous than their fathers in itself tended to amplify their presence among the ranks of nontaxpayers.

115. List of Free negroes to be hired for Taxes, CoCt 1844 Dec. (While he was at it, the writer even collated from the county's land tax rolls a list of every tract on Israel Hill and a couple of Israelite-owned lots in Farmville, without regard to whether the owners had paid the land tax or not.) Nonpayment of taxes had become so widespread by 1844 that one deputy sheriff drew up a list of delinquents that he titled simply, "A list of free persons of collour"—Artist [sic], John, John Brown, and others, free negroes, filed CoCt 1844 Jan–Mar.

116. Orders to hire out, 1840s: OB 25/151-152 (1843 Feb), 74 names to hire out; OB 25/270-271 (1844 Feb), 76 names; OB 26/12 (1844 Nov), 75 names; OB 26/16 (1845 Jan), 13 names; OB 26/88 (1846 Mar), about 80 names; OB 26/162 (1847 Apr), 103 names; OB 26/233 (1848 Apr), about 100 names; OB 26/285 (1849 May), nearly 50 names. Delinquents in levy, upper district, 1842: Insolvents, 1843 [sic], list of insolvent tithes returned by Nat Watkins, filed CoCt 1843 Jul. Delinquents in levy, upper district, 1843: Insolvents, 1843, list of delinquent tithes returned by Nathl Watkins, filed CoCt 1844 Jun–Aug; there is a fourth name, that of Nathan Wilkerson, which is followed by an illegible notation and is not counted in the enumerator's running totals (thus Wilkerson in all likelihood was not offered for hire).

117. On a document from 1848, the names of eight out of twenty-two black men are not followed by the notation "no Bidder"; but of those eight, one was quite possibly a white man erroneously listed as "of Co[lor]," and another who was indeed black had died in the spring of the year before the list was drawn up—Insolvents, 1848 Jun, filed CoCt 1848 Jun–Oct. Possible white man: Pettus Ferguson, here marked "of Co." Dead man (Thomas Jefferson): See Tredway, Sheriff, to P. E. County, acct, filed CoCt 1847 Jun–Aug. Similarly, a delinquent list of 1845 carries as nonpayers at least two Israelites, Dick White and Isham Patterson, who had been dead for many years; additional obvious examples appear over the years, and others may lurk undetected— Free persons of colour, list of free negroes who have not paid their taxes of 1845, filed CoCt 1846 Jan–Apr. Another long list of nonpayers with extensive annotation in the form of strikeouts, whose meaning is not clear, but which may indicate those who paid, died, or moved away, is Free negroes to be hire [sic] out, filed CoCt May.

118. Documents attending March 1852 order: Compare court order and lists in Free Negroes, order of 1852 Mar to hire them out, filed CoCt 1852 Jun–Aug. The court order listed fifty-six black delinquents for 1850 and forty-six for 1851. Many lists of tax delinquents have no annotations at all regarding bids or hiring out and thus offer no conclusive evidence one way or the other. But the direct evidence we do have leads me to suspect that these lists, too, did not result in the hiring out of black nonpayers. See, e.g., a notation of supposed offering of black delinquents for hire entered as an apparent cosmetic afterthought: OB 27/119 (1855 May). Orders to hire out from mid-1850s through Civil War: OB 27/105 (1855 Feb), 214 (1857 Apr), 313–314 (1859 May), and 406 (1861 Mar); OB 28/46 (1863 Apr, with some 130 names) and 104 (1864 Apr).

119. Nonpayment and non–hiring out across Virginia: Auditor of Public Accounts, inventory no. 413, Delinquent free Negro taxpayer lists, 1851–52, LVA; Norfolk County, 1851 May 31, offers a vivid example of the phenomena described here. Sheriff hires out one man: William W. Lamb, letter to Robert Johnston, May 12, 1851, filed with list for 1850 submitted by city of Norfolk. Between one twelfth and one quarter: Henrico County, 1851 May 31; Richmond County (which is nowhere near the city of Richmond), 1852 Apr 30 (for tax year 1851). "Go through all the forms": W. Chilters [?], letter to C. M. Castleman (Alexandria), May 20, 1851 (emphasis in the original); see also Prince George County, 1852 April 30, and Fairfax County, 1853 Mar 31. There are some reports in the state auditor's files that one conceivably could read as including not all of a county's delinquent free blacks but only those on whom no one bid, there having been other men who were hired out; I read most of these papers, however, as saying that those blacks who remained delinquent after sometimes energetic efforts to collect from them did not face hiring out except in the most formalistic sense. A number of reports make it absolutely clear that a particular county drew up an exhaustive list of black delinquents, but that not one of those men was hired out—see Spotsylvania County, 1851 Apr 31 [sic]; Loudoun County, 1851 May 31; Frederick County, 1852 Feb 28; Alexandria County, 1852 Dec 31; and Norfolk County, 1851 May 31. All reports cited in this note are in Auditor of Public Accounts, inventory no. 413, LVA. I have seen no reports on free black tax delinquencies in state auditor's papers beyond 1853; the incidence of hiring out as an enforcement measure may have changed during those years.

120. Sheriff's commission on insolvents: See, e.g., Delinquents, Free Negroes, 1852, 1853, List of Free Negroes delinquent for nonpayment of . . . levy, filed CoCt 1856 Apr–Jun.

121. Tax exemptions: Phil White Sr., Prince Edward delinquent taxable property, 1814, filed CoCt 1814 Sep–Dec; Rhoda Epperson, OB 21/262 (1825 Oct), an exemption that applied both to Epperson and her husband, who was apparently a slave (see Delinquents 1821, List of insolvent property returned . . . 1821, filed CoCt 1822 Jun–Jul).

122. Moral effect of taking master's property: I am indebted for this idea to the work of Eugene D. Genovese.

123. A county official reported toward the end of the 1820s that between eighteen and forty-six people per year had received poor aid in Prince Edward during the previous three decades; free blacks, he wrote, had been among that number in slightly fewer than one third of those years—usually only one black in a given year, but as many as four in 1807—Report relative to the poor of St. Patrick's Parish, Prince Edward County, in Auditor of Public Accounts, entry 739, annual reports: checklists, overseers of the poor, 1800–30, box 1, LVA, with thanks to James D. Watkinson. That report seems to have understated the case. It overlooked, for example, even recent instances of aid to free blacks.

124. Aid to Forgason and to Young and husband, and also to Patty League, white guardian of her black nephew Branch League: Report of board meeting of OP, 1826 Jun 5, filed CoCt 1826 Aug; OP report for 1825 and 1826, filed CoCt 1827 Jun–Jul; Parish of St.

Patrick [OP] acct with J. McDearmon, filed CoCt 1828 Jun (see Esther Young and family on FNL, 1825). Esther Young's husband was apparently a slave, perhaps belonging technically to his wife; in the overseers' reports, he is mentioned after her and then not by name, and he does not appear on the free black lists.

125. Wool hat: OP report, filed CoCt 1830 Jun 21, which also records $4 in aid to one free black, Tom Baker, for nursing another. Coffins in 1860: Annual report of OP to CoCt 1860 May. John White: Report of proceedings of board of OP, 1854 Apr 10, filed CoCt 1854 Jun–Jul. Thirty dollars for house rent, etc.: Proceedings of OP, returned to CoCt 1857 May. Zack Ellis: Proceedings of board of OP, annual meeting 1859 Apr 11, filed CoCt 1859 May–Sep. One hundred dollars: OB 27/365 (1860 May). Other instances of aid to free blacks: OB 21/716 (1828 Jul) and OB 22/26 (1828 Dec).

126. "Mrs. Dungy" receives aid: OP report, filed CoCt 1830 Jun 21.

127. Ned Young as guardian: OB 21/357 (1826 May).

128. Slave selling goods and work: OP report, 1829 June, filed CoCt 1829 Jun–Jul. Homes: Proceedings of board of OP, annual meeting 1859 Apr 11, filed CoCt 1859 May–Sep; Annual report of OP to CoCt 1860 May.

129. "Worthy"; "consent & go": John Foster, in Report relative to the poor of St. Patrick's parish, as in note 123.

130. Self-sustaining; vegetables, corn, and clothing; "Bread and water"; no "ardent spirits": Parish of St. Patrick [OP] acct with J. McDearmon, filed CoCt 1828 Jun. Tobacco: Proceedings of board of OP, annual meeting 1859 Apr 11, filed CoCt 1859 May–Sep. One dollar per person per year: OP report, filed CoCt 1830 Jun 21.

131. Fourteen inmates: Parish of St. Patrick [OP] acct with J. McDearmon, filed CoCt 1828 Jun.

132. Estate pays for care (one of the more vivid of countless examples): Appraisal, Moses Tredway, filed CoCt 1861 Jan–Apr. Slave adrift (example): "Old Betty," J. H. Martin, letter to Dr. S. B. Wilson, April 14, 1850, filed CoCt 1850 Jan–Apr. Ostensible manumission: Bagby petition to court, 1822 Mar 20. Fine levied: CW v Thweatt, CoCt 1852 Nov; CirCt 1854 Aug. The overseers of the poor might try to recover costs from a master, but it seems the public generally ended up absorbing the expenses of caring for such bondpeople—OP v Womack, CoCt 1845 Mar. Slaves in poorhouse: Annual report of OP, 1853 Mar 31, filed 1853 Aug, entered CoCt 1853 Sep; OP report, filed CoCt 1854 Jun 19; Proceedings of board of OP, 1858 Apr, filed CoCt 1858 May. See also the discussion of Priscy Bowman below, as well as the names of other blacks who may have been slaves but who are not identified explicitly as such, in OP reports from the 1850s.

133. Whites as likely to work in fields: See Annual report of OP to CoCt 1860 May, and other overseers' reports.

134. Plan of complex and residences: Poorhouse commissioners from Cunningham, contract, filed CoCt 1829 Jun–Jul.

135. "Little code"; "the Paupers": Parish of St. Patrick [OP] acct with J. McDearmon, filed CoCt 1828 Jun. Other counties: James D. Watkinson, "Rogues, Vagabonds, and Fit Objects: The Treatment of the Poor in Antebellum Virginia," *Virginia Cavalcade*, 49, no. 1 (Winter 2000), p. 24.

136. Insanity: See, among many instances, Oregon [John Arregon], certf of recovery, filed CoCt 1852 Jun–Aug; Isaac Evans, certf of justices, filed CoCt 1853 Oct 16 (released to father's care); William F. Scott, constable's voucher for Nash and Thackston, lunatics, filed CoCt 1860 May (expenses; lack of hospital capacity). Free blacks: Acct, Prince Edward County to H. A. Clark, filed CoCt 1860 May; Lemuel Johnson, J. J. Flournoy's jailor's account, filed CoCt 1860 May.

137. Smallpox, 1836–37: Report of the commissioners to build small pox hospital, filed CoCt 1837 Jan–Mar. Later measures: Prince Edward County to H. W. Wall, in county accts, filed 1848 Jun[–Oct] (more than $40 for treating a black smallpox

patient) County to James T. Price, in county accts, filed CoCt 1848 Jun[–Oct] (another hospital); County to E. J. Erambert, smallpox, two vouchers to county, filed CoCt 1853 Aug–Sep (a "Horse Pittle"); E. J. Erambert [hospital account], allowed by CoCt 1853 Nov; Small pox certf by H. S. Guthrey et al., filed CoCt 1856 Apr–Jun (yet another hospital). Vaccinations: Prince Edward County acct with B. C. Peters, filed CoCt 1854 Jun–Jul.

138. Trends in 1850s: In addition to documents cited in other notes for this discussion, see Copy of poor levy [OP report], filed Co Ct 1850 Jun 3; Copy of poor levy [OP report], filed CoCt 1851 Jun 2. Inmates not working: See, e.g., Annual report of OP, 1852, filed CoCt 1852 Jul. Receipts and expenses, 1859: Proceedings of board of OP, annual meeting 1859 Apr 11, filed CoCt 1859 May–Sep. By 1857, the overseers were calling for the poorhouse system to be phased out, and the county court agreed, though the institution continued to exist for the time being—Report by OP to CoCt, approved 1857 Nov 16.

139. Judith Forgason: Annual report of OP, 1855 Mar 31, filed CoCt 1855 Jun. "Unmanageable": Proceedings of OP, returned to CoCt 1857 May. "Too lazy to work": Proceedings of board of OP, annual meeting 1859 Apr 11, filed CoCt 1859 May–Sep. "Nothing but [sit] & sleep": OP annual report, filed CoCt 1861 May.

140. Bowman case: Bowman v Bowman's exor, CirCt 1847 Apr. Philip Bowman's will: WB 8/409 (1842).

141. Aid in 1854: Report of proceedings of board of OP, 1854 Apr 10, filed CoCt 1854 Jun–Jul. Following year: Annual report of OP, 1855 Mar 31, filed CoCt 1855 Jun. The aid went to aid "negro woman Priscy" through James Venable. Surely there was only one needy black woman named Priscy at Venable's place: Phil Bowman's widow.

142. Bowman at poorhouse: Proceedings of board of OP of Prince Edward County, 14 April 1856, filed CoCt 1856 Apr–Jun; Proceedings of OP, returned to CoCt 1857 May; Proceedings of the board of OP of Prince Edward County, 1858 Apr, filed CoCt 1858 May. Bowman's death: Proceedings of board of OP, annual meeting 1859 Apr 11, filed CoCt 1859 May–Sep.

143. Some forty slaves freed: WB 4/437–438, Molly Moore will and exception (1810/1813); Maria et al. v Moore, OB 16/135 (1808 Mar) and 604 (1810 Aug); District Court Order Book, 1805–31, pp. 463–64 and 464–65 (1814 Apr). Inclusion of "black" individuals in court decision: OB 18/71 (1814 May).

144. Baldwin manumission: WB 3/233, Thomas Baldwin will (1797/1801), and WB 3/235, Thomas Baldwin appraisal (1801). The latter document lists two slave children not explicitly freed in Baldwin's will, but other evidence suggests that these, too, were to be emancipated—Nathaniel Venable Sr., letter to Samuel C. Anderson, August 15, 1831, in Jacob v Purcell, CoCt 1838 May. Jacob's suit: Jacob v Purcell; see also copy of John Gosling's will among these papers, and at WB 3/127 (1798/1799).

145. Jacob withdraws suit: Jacob v Purcell, OB 24/157 (1838 May). Death of Baldwin's heir Hannah Gosling, possibly after she had essentially freed Jacob: OB 21/189 (1825 Mar), in which Hannah's widower consented to have Jacob's suit continue though his wife, the defendant, had died. Here Jacob is called "a man of colour" as though he were free, but Hannah's husband is also referred to as "the present holder" of Jacob—though perhaps in a technical sense only. See also WB 8/20, James Purcil/Purcell will (1837), and 8/57–58, James Purcell appraisal (1838), both of which name slaves left by James Purcell, husband of Hannah Baldwin Gosling till her death. Jacob does not appear on either list.

146. Charge of concealing or destroying will: CW v Ford, CoCt 1834 Jan; OB 23/179 (1833 Nov) and 196 (1834 Jan; acquittal). It is not clear at what point the concealment or destruction was alleged to have happened; the accusation, lodged in 1833, seems to refer to an event that had occurred much earlier. Hezekiah's accuser, Woodson, had earlier fulfilled Betty Dwin's wish that her son and nominal slave be liberated.

Hezekiah's appointment as curator of estate: OB 22/388 (1830 Nov); and docketing, Ford v Ford (case labeled "Thomas Ford's Will"), CoCt 1831 Nov. Hiring out the slaves: WB 7/390-391, Thomas Ford est acct (1834/1835).

147. Slaves' defense of will's validity: OB 22/514 (1831 Aug) and 544 (1831 Nov); Circuit Superior Court Order Book, 1831-37, p. 20 (1833 Apr), in office of CirCt clerk, Prince Edward County Courthouse, Farmville. Slaves filing suit for their freedom: Petition of plffs, 1830 Nov 17, and order of 1830 Nov 18, Harry et al. v Ford, CoCt 1834 Aug. Subpoenas: Ford v Ford (case labeled "Thomas Ford's Will"), CoCt 1831 Nov.

148. Summoning of witnesses to authenticate the will: OB 22/514 (1831 Aug); Rule against witnesses, Ford v Ford (case labeled "Thomas Ford's Will"), CoCt 1831 Nov. These witnesses' testimony: OB 22/544 (1831 Nov); and Robert Morton's affi, in Ford v Ford ("Thomas Ford's Will"), CoCt 1831 Nov. Court's acceptance of the will: Docketing notations on Ford v Ford ("Thomas Ford's Will"), and OB 22/544 (1831 Nov).

149. Ages of Harry and the other slaves: OB 23/269-270 (1834 Sep). Legislators' wish: See Alison Goodyear Freehling, *Drift Toward Dissolution: The Virginia Slavery Debate of 1831–1832* (Baton Rouge and London: Louisiana State University Press, 1982), chapter 6, especially pp. 177–88; see also [state delegate] P. H. Bolling, letter to Robert T. Hubard, February 12, 1832, p. 3, box 6, folder 57, Hubard family papers, UNC.

150. A list of jurors in the first trial of Harry et al. v Ford, in March 1834, is found in OB 23/214. Juror John Walthall's complaints about Williams and Rice: Presentments, CirCt 1831 Sep; Presentments, CirCt 1849 Sep. There may have been two or even three John Walthalls in the vicinity at one time or another, but county records make no gesture toward distinguishing among them; that suggests that only one man who bore the name lived within Prince Edward, and that he was the one who appeared before grand juries in that county. (WB 4/473, Patience Walthall will [1813]; WB 7/311, Thomas Walthall will [1824/1832]; and see John Walthall—apparently the same individual—in Ms. Census, Prince Edward County, 1830, 1840, and 1850, with a John E. Walthall in 1830 in Cumberland County and a John Walthall in Cumberland in 1850.) Joseph Binford charges tannery owner and tavern keeper George King with allowing slave to go at large: OB 21/518 (1827 Mar), presentments.

151. Other transactions involving Tuggle and men of Israel Hill: Accts included in Strong v White, CoCt 1844 Nov. The accounts from 1844 happen to have survived because they were entered in evidence in a lawsuit; there is every reason to believe that similar transactions between Tuggle and his neighbors on Israel Hill occurred over the previous years. Tuggle as administrator of estate of Phil White Sr.: OB 22/525 (1831 Sep); White v White's admor, CoCt 1832 Mar, as well as OB 22/571-572 (1831 Dec) and 619 (1832 Mar). Tuggle designated executor of Patterson's will: WB 7/273 (1832). Reuben Seay and organization of congregation: C. Edward Burrell's Centennial history, 1926, in Mrs. Judson Dowdy and Historic Committee, scrapbook, 1961, Farmville Baptist Church, in church office; and two loose papers in Farmville Baptist Church record book, 1870–84, in church office, "Written in 1872 P.[eter?] W.[inston?]—Data furnished 1872 by Ben Robertson," and "History—Farmville Baptist Church—Members. List furnished to Dr. Winston by Ben Robertson 1872." Thomas A. Legrand, juror at Young trial, a minister: Bradshaw, *Prince Edward County*, pp. 256 and 260. John Stephens/Stevens's business with Hercules White: WB 4/541-542, Herculas White est acct. Stevens trading with slave: CW v Stevens, presentment and ended papers, CirCt 1834 Sep.

152. Free blacks on jurors' land: FNLs, 1821 and 1823 (juror Joseph A. Watson); FNL, 1822 (juror Nathan Fowlkes). Location of Scott's land: Land tax, 1831; WB 7/350, John Purnall est acct (1833), entry for 1831 May. Binding out: John Homes indenture (1835), in Apprentices, LVA.

153. Tuggle on patrol: Patrollers' returns of Alexander Legrand, 1811 Jan and Feb, and of Alexander Legrand Jr., 1810 Dec, both filed CoCt 1811 Jun–Jul; Patrollers' returns of

T. T. Tuggle Jr., 1809 Jul 17 and Aug 21, and also Patrollers' return of Charles Fore, all filed CoCt Jun–Aug [year missing; there are indications that it is actually 1810, though these returns were filed under a different year in the loose papers]. (This almost surely was the John Tuggle whom the Census of 1810 lists as a young man; the other, probably young John's father, was more than forty-five years old. It was the same, younger John who went on to do business with people of Israel Hill; the elder of the name apparently died during the 1820s.) Tuggle's testimony against Short: CW v Short, OB 17/508 (1813 May); CoCt 1814 Mar. Tuggle's slaves: Ms. Census, 1830, sheet 127; Property tax, 1830, including Penick slaves Tuggle controlled as trustee. Steadily adding: Cf. Ms. Census, 1840.

154. Hung jury: OB 23/214 (1834 Mar).

155. New trial, with jury list: OB 23/264 (1834 Aug); Spas in Harry v Ford, CoCt 1834 Aug. The "repeaters" were Joseph Watson, John Walthall, and Joseph Binford; the latter two were those who complained about other whites' dealings with blacks. George King had also taken on at least two poor boys, one of them white and the other a free black Bartlett, as apprentice tanners. Black apprentice: Bartlett's indenture to George King (1796), Apprentices, LVA; FNLs, upper district, 1803 and 1804. White apprentice: Cressy's indenture to G. King, Apprentices, LVA. King was unusual in having had apprentices of both races; most others who took on more than one indentured child stuck with one color or the other.

156. Juror Robert Morgan and Dungey: Henry and Robert Morgan, in Land tax, 1829, p. 15; DB 20/57-58, Dungey to Morgan, DoT (1828); DB 20/324, Morgan to Dungey, release (1830). George King had had a free black apprentice. John Walthall, George King, and Charles Baldwin had served on one jury in Homes v Royall—OB 23/92 (1833 Mar). Robert Morgan and James Ewing had served as jurors both in CW v Brown (OB 21/444 [1826 Aug]) and in one of the trials of Jacob v Purcell (OB 21/444 and 447 [1826 Aug]).

157. Allen serves papers: Order, 1830 Nov 18, and capias, in Harry v Ford, CoCt 1834 Aug. James Ewing rivals Samuel Allen as the most surprising juror by modern standards. He had been summoned by Hezekiah Ford as a witness when Hezekiah had contested his late brother's last testament, though we do not know whether Ewing actually bolstered Hezekiah's case in any way—Spas, Ford v Ford (case labeled "Thomas Ford's Will"), CoCt 1831 Nov. Ewing was elected foreman of the jury in the second trial of Harry v Ford. Another juror, Robert Morgan, had owed emancipator Thomas Ford $50 when the latter died; that money would help resettle Ford's manumitted slaves in free territory, should the dead man's will be carried out—WB 7/390, Thomas Ford est acct (1834/1835).

158. An example of Allen's involvement in seizing and selling a slave (and then seizing him from the new owner!): Hart & Nimmo v Wood et al., CoCt 1812 Nov. Samuel Allen's involvement with Giles and Brown: Spas to Guy and Amelia [sic] Howard, 1826 Aug 30 and Nov 19, in Giles v Brown, CoCt 1827 March; Delivery bond, John Brown to Hampton Giles, 1827 May 21, and accompanying documents, Giles v Brown and White, CoCt 1827 Sep, as well as OB 21/608 (1827 Sep); and Summons to justices, CW v Howard and Giles, CoCt 1826 Nov, in which Justice Samuel V. Allen also figures. Samuel Allen as administrator of White's estate: Notations on back of delivery bond in White's admor v Backus et al., CoCt 1828 Oct; OB 23/323 (1835 May), and OB 24/97 (1837 Oct); WB 7/439-440, Hercules White Sr. est acct with S. Allen, deputy of Carter (1836).

159. The verdict: Back of Declaration, Harry v Ford, CoCt 1834 Aug; OB 23/264 (1834 Aug).

160. Award to ex-slaves: Capias (the $12,000), declaration (the $5,000), and back of declaration (the verdict and award), Harry v Ford; see also OB 23/264 (1834 Aug).

161. Lack of money to resettle ex-slaves: Petition of Ryland, 1835 Jan 23, Legislative petitions, LVA, with thanks to James D. Watkinson. The ex-slaves' registration as free persons: OB 23/269-270 (1834 Sep).

162. Under Virginia case law, children born to an enslaved woman before the effective date of a will emancipating her were indeed slaves—Russell, *Free Negro in Virginia,* p. 87, n. 174. But the hung jury in the first Ford trial, the second panel's apparent dissension over a cash award to the black plaintiffs, and the sometimes idiosyncratic behavior of other juries in suits involving slaves who sought freedom suggest that gut feelings played at least as great a role in this Ford panel's deliberations as fine points of law did.

CHAPTER 8: *Progress and Struggle*

1. Jenkins: Venable, Anderson, & Flournoy acct with James and Henry Jenkins, 1849, in Jenkins v Venable, Anderson, & Flournoy, CoCt 1854 May. Foundry: Document C, Nunnally settlement with Cole, in Cole v Nunnally, CirCt 1847 Apr. Foundry's location: Gross's Branch bridge order, filed CoCt 1859 Jan–Apr.

2. Definition and organization of "factory": Middleton v Baber, CirCt 1852 Apr, inventory ("Coach Factory"), and spa and injunction (the different shops within the "factory"). "Boot and shoe factory": Joseph Martin, *A New and Comprehensive Gazetteer of Virginia and the District of Columbia* (Charlottesville: Joseph Martin, 1836), p. 268. Tailoring: Ms. Census, 1850, schedule 5, Products of industry, p. 124, quoted in Virginia G. Redd, "C. H. Erambert, Photographer," *Southsider,* 7, no. 1 (Winter 1988), 6; see also Blanton's exors v Erambert, CirCt 1855 Mar.

3. Farmville's population and rank: Martin, *Gazetteer,* pp. 266 and 268 ("one of the finest"). Merchants purchasing from New York: See Downer & Co. v Mottley, CirCt 1839 Apr. "Negro Clothing": Sundry papers filed before Commissioner Dunnington, sales of property under deed of 1839 Nov 12, transaction of 1839 Dec 1, and receipt from Flippin & Dunnington, 1839 Dec 1, in Chambers deeds, both in Madison's trustees v Morton, CirCt 1854 Aug. Coach manufacture and sales: Middleton v Baber, CirCt 1852 Apr, and CirCt 1855 Mar; Newhall & Pardee v Baber, Middleton, & Baker, CirCt 1855 Mar. "Commission-merchants": Michaux & Vaughan v Steger, CirCt 1847 Apr; see also Rowlett v Jackson, CirCt 1850 Sep.

4. Buying provisions locally: Eagle Hotel to Mary Tredway, nine transactions involving pots of butter, in bundle, Receipts, 1847 Apr, Flournoy v Epes, CirCt 1852 Apr. Payments to slaves (among many examples): Edwin Edmunds acct book, 1838–92, Bettie Venable acct, 1856, payments to Peyton and to Lucy, p. 2; 1857 Dec 26, p. 7, payments to thirteen slaves; undated, [1857?] Jul, and p. 39, with many payments to slaves, UNC. The practice of paying slaves for extra work seems to have continued well into the Civil War years—Edwin Edmunds acct book, 1838–92, p. 133, Memorandum 1863, with payments up to 50 cents a day (in inflated Confederate money) to slaves for cutting and hilling tobacco, weeding corn, and plowing; p. 220, "Negros Corn for 1864," $1.50 per barrel of corn.

5. Sales to Deep South: Depos, Hairston v Berkeley, CirCt 1846 Jun; Wilson F. Dillon, letter to William Dillon, June 4, 1838, and R. C. Dillon, letter to B. Worsam [sic], August 25, 1847, both in Dillon v Dillon, CirCt 1847 Sep. Quotations and figures regarding slave sales: R. H. DeJarnette, letter to F. N. Watkins, n.d. ("southern judgment and taste"), and memo of J. B. Oliver's testimony ("pay Millener bills"; prices of clothing and slaves), both in Rudd v Dejarnett, CirCt 1848 Apr.

6. Blowing a horn: Rip (pseudonym), "Farmville Then and Now," *Farmville Herald,* September 14, 1906, p. 3. "A negro quarter": Mittimus, CW v Ellick, CoCt 1829 Jan, in which the owner of the "quarter" in question was a tobacco manufacturer. "Over-

seers": Daniel v Steger, CirCt 1837 Sep; and see Currie v Steger, CirCt 1833 Apr and Sep.

7. White employees and owners: Daniel v Steger, CirCt 1837 Sep, especially depos of Thomas Nash, William C. Moore, Thomas T. Steger (room, board, laundry), and Henry B. Scott (twisting in lower room).

8. "Sometimes the hand from the Mill": Robert Shepherd depo, Jones v Blanton, CirCt 1845 Apr.

9. "Considered the temptation"; "running the River": Abraham Z. Venable affi, 1833 Jun 12, Attorney General v Chambers's trustees, CirCt 1842 Sep.

10. Desire to reduce competition; scarcity and prices of workers: Daniel v Steger, CirCt 1837 Sep, especially depos of Patrick H. Jackson ("experienced labourers"), William L. Lanier, and David Bruce.

11. Far from own masters: See slaves of Farrar & Meadow, Hilliard Hill & Co., and other firms, resident in Farmville, in James M. McNutt and F. P. Wood, [Order] To divide hands in Farmville, filed CoCt 1857 Jun–Aug.

12. Roberts-Artis case: CW v Artis, CoCt 1858 Dec. Artis's age and occupations: FNLs, 1857ff. Law permitting certfs of non-Negro identity: Acts of Assembly, 1832–33, chapter 80, p. 51.

13. Forty-acre addition: See Venable v Venable, CoCt 1834 Nov. Second addition: See Document F, Acct of sales of lots from Chambers land, 1836 Apr, Chambers's committee v Madison's exor, CirCt 1842 Apr. Plan of new courthouse: Thackston &c. account with county, CoCt 1832 Nov. Armchairs: Prince Edward County acct to James D. Wood ("6 Arm Chairs"), filed CoCt 1831 Nov–1832 Jan.

14. Diagram of cemetery: Back of Bill of exceptions, CW v Moss, CoCt 1847 Jun–Aug; the diagram actually pertains to a separate, adjacent prosecution, CW v Richardson.

15. Rations on Allen plantation: Hill v Allen, CirCt 1846 Sep. Forgason's corn meal and wheat purchases: Cheadle, 35th p. (numbered as p. 13), Shederick Fergerson acct, 1834. Forgason's family size: Ms. Census, 1830, sheet 124. Forgason was married and at the time had either no children at all or none old enough to have eaten much of these foods. The Allen document also records the amount of pork issued to the same group of fifteen slaves; but the amount is so low that it seems likely there was an additional, untallied source of meat, rendering comparisons impossible.

16. White's store account: Smith & Co. v White, CoCt 1844 Mar.

17. "Natural good taste": Harriet Martineau, in Walter Brownlow Posey, ed., *Alabama in the 1830s as Recorded by British Travellers, Birmingham-Southern College Bulletin,* 31, no. 4 (December 1938), p. 34, brought to my attention by Melissa Ann Mullins. Marriages: Marriage bonds, Curtis White and Priscilla White (Sam's granddaughter), 1836 Sep 19; Sidney Howard and Lucy White, 1840 Nov 16; Donaldson Gibbs (Titus's grandson) and Mary White (copied from Marriage register), 1846 May [7?] (all microfilm), LVA.

18. "Hardness of the times": Jacob W. Holt, letter to John B. Williams, January 10, 1843, in Williams v Holt, CirCt 1845 Apr. "Grate falling off": Anderson P. Miller affi, Betts v Burke, CirCt 1844 Apr. "Every body . . . pressed": (Sister) Mary, letter to William C. Thornton, December 21, 1842, William C. Thornton papers, Duke; see also S. Goodwin, letter to William [Thornton], April 13, 1842, in same collection. "Heaviest pressure": Valuation of Mrs. Rudd's Negroes 1845, in Rudd v Dejarnatt, CirCt 1848 Apr. See also Paulina, letter to Williana [W. Lacy], November 24, 1842, p. 3, folder 6, Drury Lacy papers, UNC, referring twice to "these hard times," once with the phrase underscored.

19. Merchant Henry Thweatt's failure: Thweatt's creditors v Thweatt, especially notice of sale from *Richmond Whig,* CirCt 1853 Mar; see also various actions with Thweatt's firm as plaintiff or defendant in CirCt 1838 Apr. Using trading company as bank:

Read v N. A. Venable, CirCt 1850 Apr, especially answer of Nathaniel E. Venable and William M. Watkins depo. John Rice: Ely v Rice, CirCt 1843 Apr (takes oath of insolvent); Delinquent lands, 1845, filed CoCt 1846 Jan–Apr; Land tax, town lots, 1845.

20. Beverly Howard and Robert Giles: List of debts due est of Edward Booker, Worsham v Booker, CirCt 1846 Sep. The round figures suggest that Howard and Giles signed the notes not to cover goods they had purchased, but rather to secure money to invest. Hampton Giles: Blanton v Giles, CoCt 1838 Nov.

21. Steger as merchant sues boatman Henry Bartlett: Steger & Wootton v Bartlett, CoCt 1838 May. Bartlett as boatman: FNLs, 1821–1825 (there were two boatmen named Henry Bartlett). Steger bails White: Capias, Gauldin v White, CoCt 1839 May. Steger bails Brandum: Capias, Goodman v Brandon [sic], CoCt 1840 Mar.

22. Steger's purchase of lots: DB 23/2, S. White to Steger (1840, two lots). Steger also acquired, for a token $1.00, two lots that free black John White had purchased on credit; one assumes that Steger thereby took on also the obligation to pay for those lots—DB 22/233 and 244, J. White to Steger (1837). Sam White sues Steger: White v Steger, CoCt 1843 Mar. Steger declares insolvency: Moseley v Nash and Steger, CoCt 1843 Mar; and Bill in Michaux and Vaughan v Steger, CirCt 1847 Apr. Suits against Steger and his firm: See CoCt 1841 Aug; CoCt 1842 Dec–1843 May, and 1843 Nov. Sam White's own difficulties: One account lists a debt of $3.50 from one Samuel White as uncollectable in 1843, but it is not clear whether this refers to Sam White of Israel Hill—List of balances due Willis & Wright, Wright v Willis's admor, CirCt 1855 Mar. The same account lists a larger debt of free black Henry Bartlett, whom Steger sued, as uncollectable.

23. Uncollectable debts: See Bad & Doubtfull debts due Madison, Venable, & Dunnington, 1842, in Madison's trustees v Morton, CirCt 1854 Aug; Balance sheets: List of balances due to and from Read, Venable, & Spencer, in Read v Venable, CirCt 1846 Jun. Brandum as boat owner: Plea, Goodman v Brandon, CoCt 1840 Mar. Brandum's town lot is referred to in DB 22/234-235, J. White to Steger (1837/1838), but never appears in Land tax; perhaps he possessed the lot in common with someone else who was the owner of record. Brandum's losses: Goodman v Brandon; Carroll v Brandum, CoCt 1840 May; Jackson v Brandon, CirCt 1840 Jun, filed 1840 Sep–Dec.

24. Strong's transactions with Phil White and Tuggle: Strong v White, CoCt 1844 Nov. Strong as boat owner, and sale of boat to John White: Strong v White, CoCt 1845 May. Strong's approximate birth date: Cf. IH 1816 with OB 26/16 (1845 Jan), between which there is a three-year discrepancy. Financial trouble for Strong: See Seay v Strong, CoCt 1845 Nov. Strong's boating business: Ms. Census, 1850, schedule 5, Products of industry, p. 125.

25. John White as noted boatman: Rip Van Winkle (pseudonym), "Farmville Then and Now," *Farmville Herald,* August 31, 1906, p. 3. Pressures on John White: Morgan & Croxton v White, CoCt 1837 Aug; Morton v White, CoCt 1839 Jan, filed 1839 Mar–Apr; Bad & Doubtfull debts due Madison et al., in Madison's trustees v Morton, CirCt 1854 Aug; Jackson v White, CirCt 1840 Apr (in which the plaintiff's waiving of bail suggests White's continued good reputation); Barksdale v White, CirCt 1853 Mar. White as "good" debtor later in decade, while others "doubtful": Settlement, Lyle, Booker & Co., Booker v Lyle, CirCt 1847 Sep. Most lucrative boating concern: Ms. Census, 1850, schedule 5, Products of industry, p. 125. Award to White in his lawsuit: White v Trustees of Upper Appomattox Company, Circuit Superior Court Order Book, 1853–70, p. 149 (1856 Aug), in office of CirCt clerk, Prince Edward County Courthouse, Farmville. John White's career is difficult to research because there were at least two, and perhaps three, men of that name in the same generation. Compare John White, born c. 1806, in Sam White's household on Israel Hill, IH

1816; John White, born c. 1799, only five feet four inches tall, OB 26/425 (1851 Apr); and John White, also born c. 1799, five feet eleven, OB 27/188 (1856 Sep) and OB 27/424 (1861 Sep).

26. Ben White and merchant Henry Thweatt borrow $110: Wood v White and Thweatt, CirCt 1841 Sep. Merchants' suits against Ben White: Anderson v White, CirCt 1837 Sep; Wood v White and Thweatt, and Morton & Venable v White, CoCt 1842 Mar–Apr, in which the one debt may have been incurred to pay the other; Lyle, Booker & Co. v White, CoCt 1843 Nov. The memory of at least one creditor proved long indeed; in the 1850s, when Ben White got back on his feet financially, the man went to court and forced White to pay up—Anderson v White, CirCt 1852 Apr. White as boat owner: Ms. Census, 1850, schedule 5, Products of industry, p. 123. Apprentice: OB 26/407 (1851 Jan). As depot hand: FNLs, 1857 and 1858.

27. David Bartlett's purchase of boat: Lightfoot v Bartlett, CirCt 1838 Sep.

28. Milly Homes: WB 8/292, Mildrid Holmes [sic] will (1841). Division of Homes land: OB 25/7 (1841 Sep); DB 23/246, Homes agreement (1841).

29. Brandum gives bail: Morton v White, CoCt 1839 Jan, filed 1839 Mar–Apr. White gives bail: Bail bond, Flournoy assignee v Bartlett, CoCt 1850 May.

30. Strong and Whites: Strong v C. White and P. White, CoCt 1844 Jul; Strong v White, CoCt 1844 Nov, as well as OB 25/276 (1844 Mar) and OB 26/9 (1844 Nov). The debts in question totaled about $68. Phil and John White: White v White, CoCt Oct–Nov 1850; White v White, CoCt 1853 May, OB 26/350 and 550 (1850 Mar and 1853 May); see also White v White, Superior Court Order Books, 1831–47 and 1847–58, pp. 112 (1851 Apr 28) and 311 (1856 Mar 19), respectively, involving a town lot. White and Bartlett: White v Bartlett, CoCt 1837 Aug. (This Bartlett debt was the one his white security [cosigner] ended up having to pay.)

31. Phil White as farmer and boatman: FNLs, 1817–1825. Sale of parcels at profit: DB 21/366, White to Venable and Proctor (1835/1836), and DB 21/497-498, White to Ely (1835); cf. DB 21/276, J. White to P. White (1835), and DB 21/303, Trustees of Farmville to White (1835). Improvement and resale of third part lot, and White's suit for $45: White v Peters, CoCt 1838 May, and OB 24/162 (1838 May); DB 22/34-35, White to Peters (1835/1837); cf. DB 21/303, as above. At about the same time, the county court named Phil White to administer the estate of his Israelite neighbor George Patterson; the security required by law was given by John Tuggle—OB 24/178 (1838 Jul).

32. Litigation over Randolph lots: See Copy of deed, Randolph's exors to White, 1846, in White v Hilliard, CirCt 1855 Aug, which also outlines the General Assembly's intervention in 1846; Randolph's commissioners v J. and P. White, CirCt 1841 Aug, originally filed CirCt 1841 Sep; Randolph's commrs v S. White et al. (including a crucial explanatory document, Plffs' letter, dated November 26, 1846, and, obviously, added later), and Same v J. White et al., both CoCt 1843 Mar, and then Randolph's commissioners v Phil and John White (with John Tuggle's participation) at CirCt 1844 Sep; and see also P. White v J. White, Superior Court Order Book, 1831–47, p. 331 (1846 Jun 20). On the deed of trust involving Phil White and John Tuggle, see, in addition, OB 25/7 (1841 Sept) and DB 23/141, J. White to P. White, DoT (1841). On the confusion over Randolph lots, see also at least nine suits with Randolph's commissioners as plaintiffs, in CirCt 1844 Apr; McDearmon v Randolph's commissioners, CirCt 1845 Sep; Randolph's exor v Seay, and Same v Preston, CirCt 1848 Apr; and Randolph's exor v Madison's admor, CirCt 1848 Apr.

33. White, Robertson, and Chambers lots: Venable v Edmunds, CirCt 1847 Apr (in which Madison's nephew, James M. Jackson, deposed that he had paid the cost of the lot when Madison's creditor had presented White's bond for payment); and Morton et al. v Madison et al., CirCt 1841 Sep.

34. "Went to him"; "he said his price": Malcolm Currie depo, White v Hilliard, CirCt 1855 Aug. Age and description of Philip White III: Cf. OB 26/222 (1843 Aug) and

Philip White Jr. certf, filed CoCt 1855 Jun–Oct on the one hand; and, on the other, FNL, 1824 (the first such list the younger Phil appears on).

35. Suit over rent for land: Hobson trustee of Randolph v White (especially Bond, Phil White to Fred Hobson), CirCt 1846 Sep. A suit by a lawyer, Phil perhaps involved because he had given security for another man's bond: Anderson v Clarke and White, CoCt 1840 Mar. Suit by laborer: Barley for Anderson v White, CoCt 1853 May, filed 1853 Jul; OB 26/115 (1846 Aug) and 550 (1853 May).

36. Phil White sells lots: DB 24/10-11, White's trustee (Tuggle) to Barksdale (1842/1843); DB 25/51-52, White's trustee to Daniel (1842/1845). Phil's loss: Cf. DB 23/240-241, Chambers's trustee to P. White (1836/1841). Building on Rachel White's land: Land tax, 1844, Rachel White. Sam White, too, sold off another lot, apparently the last he owned, in 1849—DB 25/510, White to Currie (1849).

37. White's debt to store: Smith & Co. v White, CoCt 1844 Mar; OB 25/284 (1844 Mar). Insolvency: White v Hilliard, CirCt 1855 Aug. Surrender of lot: DB 25/450-451, White to Vaughan (1849), which—apparently unlike the schedule of surrendered property that White gave the sheriff—specified that the lot White lost was unimproved.

38. White's fight to regain lot: White v Hilliard, especially bill, answer of Hilliard, court's note on docketing page (advising plaintiff how to amend bill), amended bill, Malcolm Currie depo, Marcus J. McGlasson depo ("he had a deed"; according to McGlasson's deposition, White went on to say that the unimproved lot was the one he had surrendered), and decree, CirCt 1855 Aug; Superior Court Order Book, 1847–58, pp. 279–80 (1855 Aug 16). Return of lot to White: DB 27/95-96, Vaughan et al. to P. White (1855). Sale of lot to Patsy Short: DB 27/191-192, White to Short (1855/1856).

39. Jackson's additional lots: DB 22/447, Angle (alias Angel) to Jackson (1840—for $1,500, with house); DB 27/272, Venable's trustee to Jackson (1855/1857). Boots bring $5 to $8: William Willis acct with Willis and Wright, 1843 Feb, in Wright v Willis's admor, CirCt 1855 Mar; Receipt from Martin & Co.'s attorney, 1850 Sep 19, in Martin & Co. v Lowry, CirCt 1852 Apr. Jackson's signature and apparent literacy/numeracy: Cf. his signature in Scott indenture to Jackson (1840), Apprentices, LVA, with signature and handwritten text of Voucher no. 58, Tuggle v Penick, CirCt 1840 Apr (Jackson's bill to Tuggle). Examples of Jackson's sales of goods and services: Wright v Willis's admor, CirCt 1855 Mar, especially William Willis acct, Willis & Wright acct with B. Jackson, 1843, and cf. George B. Wright acct with Willis & Wright, 1843, with list of balances due Willis & Wright, 1843; Willis Blanton est acct with James Blanton, report of special commissioner Watkins, in Blanton v Blanton's exor, CirCt 1855 Aug; Edwin Edmunds acct book, 1838–92, p. 9, check on Farmer's Bank to B. Jackson, 1858 Oct 18, UNC. Production in Jackson's shop: Ms. Census, 1850, schedule 5, Products of industry, p. 122. Luther Porter Jackson asserts that Booker Jackson "discontinued shoemaking to operate a livery stable" sometime in the 1850s—Jackson, *Free Negro Labor and Property Holding in Virginia, 1830–1860* (New York and London: D. Appleton–Century, 1942), pp. 219–20.

40. Jackson sues whites: Jackson v Flood, CoCt 1841 Jul; Jackson v Dillon, CoCt 1843 Jan, filed 1843 Mar–Apr, and Delivery bond and other papers for Jackson v Dillard [i.e., Dillon], CoCt 1844 Oct.

41. Jackson's sales to whites (examples): J. M. C. Venable acct with William H. Venable, guardian, 1851, filed CoCt 1856 Sep–Dec; [R. J.] Overton acct with [J. M.] Overton, guardian, 1853 May, filed CoCt 1856 Jul–Aug; J. P. Binford est acct with [J. B.] Ely, 1854 Feb (with a payment to Sam Strong in 1854 Mar), filed CoCt 1858 Feb–Apr; [E. B.] Miller est acct with [T.] Clark, 1855 Mar 2, filed CoCt 1856 Jul–Aug; [J. W.] Dupuy est acct [with Paulina P. Dupuy], 1856 Nov, filed CoCt 1857 Nov–1858 Jan; [H. E.] Watkins est acct [with F. N. Watkins], 1856 Sep, filed CoCt 1857 Nov–1858

Jan; Miles H. Cary acct with Cary, guardian, 1856 Oct, filed CoCt 1858 May; J. W. Morton est acct [with J. T. Morton], 1856 Dec 31, filed CoCt 1857 Feb–Apr; J. M. Williamson est acct with Hughes, 1858 Feb, filed CoCt 1858 Oct–Dec. Jackson's marriage and family: Sarah H. Jackson registration, and document titled "Booker Jacksons Family," both in Free negroes' certfs renewed, filed CoCt 1851 May. Jackson's sons join business: FNLs, 1858 and 1861. "Another worthy citizen": Rip, "Farmville Then and Now," *Farmville Herald,* September 14, 1906, p. 3.

42. Slave hiring: Jackson v Boatwright and Nunnally, particularly defts' bond to Jackson, CoCt 1843 May. Another transaction involving a temporary "negro hire" from one "Jackson," who may be Booker, is listed in Family or joint acct, Willis Blanton est acct with James Blanton, report of special commissioner Watkins, Blanton v Blanton's exor, CirCt 1855 Aug. "Booker Jackson corner" as landmark: Road report of Farmville hands, filed CoCt 1848 Nov 20.

43. Tony White's death: Ms. Census, 1850, Mortality. White's will: WB 9/374, Anthony White will (1848 with codicil 1850/1850); the codicil simplified White's will considerably and retained the Jacksons as executors. Half brother: Cf. parents listed on Booker Jackson's registration (from Charlotte Co., surrendered by Jackson to clerk in Prince Edward on registering there), filed CoCt 1835 Sep–Oct, with those on John Jackson's registration, in Free negroes' certfs, renewed, filed CoCt 1851 May.

44. Road repair: Court House to Farmville road report—view, filed CoCt 1850 Jan–Apr. Clerk's office: Clerk's office report, to build office on courthouse square, filed CoCt 1855 Nov–Dec.

45. Identity and background of justices newly elected in 1852: See the discussion and citations in chapter 6.

46. Read as bank president: Ms. Census, 1860, family visitation 411. Joel Womack and free blacks: See WB 9/374, Anthony White will (1848 with codicil 1850/1850); Spas in White v Gibbs, CoCt 1833 May; justices trying CW v Johnson [sic], CoCt 1845 Jan–Mar; justice issuing warrants and trying CW v Bradley, CoCt 1841 Aug; Curtis White's bond of indebtedness, Strong v White, CoCt 1844 Jul. Womack and "rescue" of slaves: CW v Womack, CirCt 1851 Apr (presentment), and CirCt 1852 Apr.

47. Clem Read as manufacturer: Clem Carter, Nathaniel Howard, et al., FNL, 1860; Herbert Clarence Bradshaw, *History of Prince Edward County, Virginia, from Its Earliest Settlements Through Its Establishment in 1754 to Its Bicentennial Year* (Richmond: Dietz Press, 1955), pp. 301 and 518. Robertson as inspector: See Robertson, inspector bond, filed CoCt 1850 Oct–Nov. Read and Farmville warehouse: Nathaniel A. Venable declaration, Read v Lyle, CirCt 1850 Sep. Curtis and Hercules White employed at "warehouse": FNLs, 1860 and 1861.

48. The federal census in 1850 and 1860 asked local enumerators to state the average weekly wage earned by a "female domestic." The local respondent in Prince Edward entered a confused—and confusing—entry in 1850 whose tentativeness may suggest that the idea of paying housemaids, however familiar to the people who formulated the census return, meant little to residents of Prince Edward County. In 1860, however, the county's census officer clearly entered a weekly figure of $2; perhaps the phenomenon of paid domestics was indeed taking hold by then—Ms. Census, 1850 and 1860, schedule 6, Social statistics.

FNL, 1861, has a separate designation, "housekeeper," applied to three women, which is difficult to interpret. One of the Harriet Whites—there were two by that name on Israel Hill, one the daughter of Hercules White Jr., and the other a generation younger—received a payment of $18.75 from Henry Guthrey in 1858. Each woman's occupation was listed during that period as "domestic," but the one who received the payment obviously did work other than keeping her own house—[M. F.] Miller est acct with [H. S.] Guthrey, 1858 Jun, filed CoCt 1859 Jan–Apr. The two Harriet Whites: FNL, 1860; cf. Hercules White family on IH 1816. Record keeping on the lists for the last antebellum years and for wartime became wildly erratic; the number of women tallied as performing "domestic" work fell as low as two in 1861. Fewer than twenty servants: Ms. Census, 1860.

49. As with those doing "domestic" work, the number of washers fluctuates extremely on county free black lists for those years, from nine up to thirty-four. For occupations presented in a more systematic way, see Ms. Census, 1860.

50. Actual numbers of factory workers: Ms. Census, 1860.

51. "Live principally": Ms. Census, 1860, pp. 49 and 50. Factory and warehouse workers; "farmers" and "planters": FNLs, 1857–1861. Occupations of Israelites: Ms. Census, 1860, pp. 105–08. Population figures tallied from Ms. Census, 1850 and 1860.

52. Nonpayment in 1840s: Delinquent lands for 1845 [sic, actually 1844], Dickinson, deputy sheriff, filed CoCt 1845 Mar–Apr; Delinquent lands for 1845, filed CoCt 1846 Jan–Apr; Delinquent lands for 1846, filed CoCt 1847 Jan–Apr; Delinquent land, Upper end, for 1847, filed CoCt 1848 Apr–May. Sales in 1845: Delinquent land sales in 1845, filed CoCt 1845 Sep–Dec. Johnston sons' inheritance: WB 8/159, Rosa Johnson [sic] will (1838/1839). Sale of Johnston land: Delinquent lands, list of sales by sheriff, 1850, filed CoCt 1850 Oct–Nov.

53. Original families in residence: FNLs, 1857ff. Even though the revenue commissioner often omitted individual free blacks' places of residence, his lists explicitly document the presence of members of most of the original Hill families for each of the years 1857–61. No member of the Patterson-Clarke family is specifically listed as living on Israel Hill in 1860, but the particular placement of boatman Tom Clarke and his wife on the list suggests that they did live there that year. The residency of members of the Brown family cannot be proved from these lists, although Sam Brown and his wife appear to have been on the Hill in 1861, and an adolescent named Nathan Brown may have been there in 1857. The very least that these incomplete records demonstrate is that all the original families were represented on the Hill during most years from 1857 through 1861, and that most families were represented in all years. Some individuals from families who had never received land likewise resided on Israel Hill in that late period.

54. Israel Hill tracts not enumerated: Ms. Census, 1850 and 1860, schedule 4, Productions of agriculture.

55. Jacob Johnston on Israel Hill: FNLs, 1857, 1861, and 1862, specify that Jacob Johnston, his wife, and other Johnstons were living on the Hill; the same is probably true of the other years after 1857 for which free black lists have survived, but the enumerator often omitted individuals' place of residence in those years. "Consists of 350 acres": Ms. Census, 1860, page with family visitations 781–87.

56. "Make out very well": Foster, Report relative to the poor of St. Patrick's parish, Prince Edward County, in Auditor of Public Accounts, entry 739, annual reports: checklists, OP, 1800–30, box 1, LVA, with thanks to James D. Watkinson.

57. Payment to Gibbs: [B. W.] Womack est acct with [A. D.] Dickinson, 1855 Oct 15, filed CoCt 1857 Nov–1858 Jan; Gibbs was listed soon after that as a farmer on Israel Hill (FNL, 1857). Payment to "Patterson for fixing clock": WB 10/63, Judith L. Penick and her children, acct with George D. Saunders, trustee (1853), 1851 Jan.

58. Places of residence: FNLs, 1857–1861.

59. John White's last tract to Phil: DB 27/330, J. White to P. White (1856/1858).

60. Black "recovery" of lots: DB 26/396-397, Peters to Homes (1853/1854; lot sold by Sam White four years earlier); DB 26/446, Daniel to Strong (1854; lot sold by Phil White a dozen years earlier). Strong's purchases: DB 26/391 and 446-447, Morton to Strong, Daniel to Strong, and Flournoy to Strong (all 1854); DB 26/635-636, Dalby to Strong (1854/1855); Jacob W. Morton est acct with Joseph T. Morton, 1855 Feb 20, filed CoCt 1856 Apr–Jun (the Morton-Strong transaction). Resale of Strong's lot: DB 27/422, Strong to Homes (1859). Strong's part lot to one of the Henry Bartletts: DB 28/447,

Strong's exor to Bartlett (1863). Strong's will: WB 11/116, Samuel Strong will (1860). Strong's executor: Strong will; Strong, Samuel, executor's bond, filed CoCt 1860 Jun–Sep.

61. Franklin's land: DB 27/112, Ely to Franklin (1855). Franklin's residence on that land: FNLs, 1857 (listing him still there a year after he mortgaged the tract), 1858–1861, 1863, and 1864; DB 27/195, Franklin to Thackston, DoT (1856). Valued at $800: Ms. Census, 1860, family visitation 825. This was the development that Franklin apparently financed through a $500 loan from his associate, the contractor Henry Guthrey—DB 27/195.

62. Homes purchases: DB 26/396-397, Peters to Homes (1853/1854); DB 27/231-232, Wright to Brown and Homes (1857, two part lots), Maria Brown being listed also under the name Maria Homes in Index to Deeds; DB 27/422, Strong to Homes (1859); DB 28/346-347 and 404-405, both of them Ely to Homes (1862 and 1863); DB 28/471-472, Peters to Homes (1863).

63. Eliza Evans's lot purchase: DB 25/524-525, Ely to Evans (1850). Dennis Evans's purchase: DB 25/500, Stanton to Evans (1850). Eliza's and Dennis's approximate ages and occupations: FNLs, 1857–1861. Dennis Evans repairs clerk's office lot: Evans [claim], 1853 Nov allowed, filed CoCt 1853 Oct–1854 Jan, and Richardson acct with Prince Edward County, filed CoCt 1854 Jun–Jul; another payment to Evans is in [F. S.] Sampson est acct with [W. S.] Walker [and C. Sampson], 1854, filed CoCt 1857 Jun–Aug. An additional Evans purchase of two part lots, accomplished through white trustees in order to deny Rhoda Evans's husband any control over the tracts: DB 26/157, Dunnington to Bruce for Evans (1852).

64. Acquisition of land by blacks in the 1850s: Jackson, *Free Negro Labor;* Loren Schweninger, *Black Property Owners in the South, 1790–1915* (Urbana and Chicago: University of Illinois Press, 1990), pp. 71–79.

65. An estate sale: Venable, Magdalen, acct of estate sale, with M. Homes's purchase of a pair of blankets, filed CoCt 1856 Sep–Dec. Public events: See earlier example of Phil White at auction of town lot. County work to blacks: Parish of St. Patrick [OP] to J. McDearmon &c acct, 1828, 1827 Nov, filed CoCt 1828 Jun (Charles Forgason, $4); County accts, 1853, Evans [claim], 1853 Nov allowed, filed CoCt 1853 Oct–1854 Jan (Dennis Evans, $3); and Richardson with P. E. County, acct, filed CoCt 1854 Jun–Jul. Hill's $15: Acct, Prince Edward County with Booker Hill, filed CoCt 1856 Jul–Aug. Two unnamed free blacks helped Branch Worsham move into the new county clerk's office in 1856; they were well paid, but received only one day's employment—Acct, Prince Edward County to B. J. Worsham, 1856 Mar, filed CoCt 1856 Apr–Jun. Hill's property: Ms. Census, 1860, family visitation 598. Hill won and lost sizable amounts in lawsuits during the same years—Circuit Superior Court Order Book, 1853–70, pp. 144 (1856 Aug), 188 (1858 Mar), 245 (1859 Aug), and 271–72 (1860 Mar), in office of CirCt clerk, Prince Edward County Courthouse, Farmville. Thornton Evans: Day book and journal by E. W. Hubard, 1862, pp. 11–12 and *passim,* box 34, folder 474, Hubard family papers, UNC; Ms. Census, Campbell County, family visitation 482, which shows the only Thornton Evans in Virginia as a mulatto carpenter.

66. Henry Cousins's petition: Cousins, Henry, to court, letter, and order to bind, August 16, 1858, filed CoCt 1858 Jun–Sep; DB 27/409-410, Cousins to Musgrove (1858, for some reason binding out only four of the Cousins children). Cousins's race: Ms. Census, 1860, Amelia County, family visitation 152 (Cousins was a farm hand, age forty). Musgrove as merchant: CW v Musgrove & Woodson, presentment, CirCt 1854 Aug. Musgrove had a history of involvement with Cousinses; he had undertaken half a dozen years earlier to teach Branch Cousins the saddler's trade—Cousins report of OP, filed CoCt 1851 Dec–1852 Feb. Rescission and generous "severance" payments (late examples, from a neighboring county): John Valentine apprenticeship (with bond [against becoming a public charge?] to be deducted, however), Minute book 3,

Nottoway County Court, pp. 312 and 323 (1859 Aug and Oct) (cf. William and Archer Homes, Indenture to Granville Nunnally, filed 1840, Apprentices, LVA); and Nottoway minute book 3, pp. 297 and 304 (1859 Apr and May), LVA.

67. A will of 1804 written by one woman and witnessed by three others offers the striking exception that proves the rule—WB 4/353, Mary Maddox will (1804/1812). A male ordinary keeper's delivery bonds cosigned by his fellow tavern owner Sarah Pearson in 1851 stand out almost as prominently, as does a woman's signature on a petition to change the route of a road, even though that kind of issue affected female landholders. Delivery bonds: CW v Don P. Taylor, two delivery bonds, CirCt 1851 Apr. Road petition: Redd's to Meherrin depot, petition to change road, filed CoCt 1859 Jan–Apr.

68. Richmond and Danville: See R.&D. R. road in Prince Edward, qualification of commissioners, filed CoCt 1854 May; Commissioners' reports on land to be taken for Richmond & Danville R. R., filed CoCt 1854 Jun–Jul. On the R&D and the South Side Railroad, see also Bradshaw, *Prince Edward County*, pp. 329–33.

69. Compensation for land, and amounts of land conveyed: Certfs of valuation of land to be taken by South Side Rail Road Company, filed CoCt 1851 Apr–May and 1851 Dec–1852 Feb. The aggressive administrator of Judith Randolph's estate went to court and got the rate for Randolph land raised from $15 to $38, partly, no doubt, because the land lay on the very edge of Farmville—[Certfs for] Randolph, Judith, CoCt 1852 Mar 15; Judith Randolph [condemnation certf], filed CoCt 1852 Mar–May. Conveyances of land by Israelites, Dungeys: DB 26/128-130 and 144-145 (1851). Many whites got compensation ranging between $4.50 and $9.00. The black Israelites and the Dungeys received $3.00 to $8.00 an acre, with one exception at $2.00: the John Brown tract, probably the least well maintained and productive of the Hill plots that the railroad crossed.

70. Number of cars and speeds: Annual report of the railroad companies made to the Board of Public Works, year ending 1859 Sep 3 [though Whitworth's footnote says 1895, an error], p. 390, quoted in William Maphis Whitworth Jr., "Cumberland County, Virginia, in the Later Antebellum Period, 1840–1860" (M.A. thesis, University of Richmond, 1991), p. 163. Length of trip to Petersburg: *Richmond Whig*, May 7, 1859 [footnote says 1895], cited in *ibid.*, p. 164.

71. Prosecutions and fines: CW v South Side Rail Road Company (three cases), CoCt 1857 Nov–1858 Jan, 1858 Nov, and 1861 Jul–Dec.

72. Road petitions involving Prospect depot: T. T. Tredway, Hunt's Gate to Prospect, road report, and Hunt's Gate to Prospect Depot, Womack's motion for road, both filed CoCt 1857 Sep–Oct; Lindsey's road, filed CoCt 1858 Apr. Pamplin: Baker's to Pamplins, petition for road, filed CoCt 1853 Feb–Apr. Meherrin; "point of access": Redd's to Meherrin depot, petition, filed CoCt 1859 Jan–Apr. Polling places: Election districts, petitions, filed CoCt 1861 Jan–Apr.

73. Boatmen haul stone: "Deacon W. H. White," *Richmond Planet*, January 26, 1895, courtesy of Harold Forsythe. Some forty batteaux: Ms. Census, 1850, schedule 5, Products of industry.

74. "Was in the habit": Depo of Julius, CW v Jim, CoCt 1858 Oct.

75. Railway's use of slaves: CW v Jim, CoCt 1858 Oct. Employment of free blacks: FNLs, 1857, 1858 (with Elick Wilkerson living with Ben White), 1861, and 1863; "Deacon W. H. White," *Richmond Planet*, January 26, 1895. Ben White apparently remained connected to the Israel Hill community also through a Wilkerson boy who lived with him for a time while he worked for the South Side line.

76. "The Jew Goodcup": George King [Jr.?] depo, Gilliam v Martin, CirCt 1852 Aug.

77. "Sundry Indians": OB 22/57 (1829 Mar). "Poor Irish Behoys": William C. Flournoy's notice to John Jones and William H. Word, filed CirCt 1847 Apr.

78. "Shanty": CW v Jim, CoCt 1858 Oct, especially depos of Robert V. Davis and Will (a slave). "Shantee": Brown v Moore, CoCt 1852 Dec. Interracial visiting: Testimony of

Walthall's Armstead and Mike Walden, Coroner's inquisition over Margaret and Elizabeth Walden, 1853, Inquests, LVA.

79. "Irishman" and blacks: Bill of work and materials, abutment, Prince Edward side, Farmville road and bridge report, filed CoCt 1852 Nov–1853 Jan.

80. Failure to pay taxes: Delinquent property 1852, upper end, filed CoCt 1853 May–Jun; Insolvents, 1853 Aug court, upper end, filed CoCt 1853 Aug–Sep (with a couple of Italians as well as Irishmen); contrast Delinquent property 1853, 1854, upper end, filed CoCt 1854 Apr, and Delinquents 1858, 1859, filed CoCt 1859 May.

81. An alleged brawl: CW v Flemming and CW v Lary, both in CoCt 1853 May–Jun. Sale of liquor: CW v Neligan, CoCt 1853 Nov; CW v Neligan (liquor), CirCt 1854 Mar. Sullivan allegedly attacks wife: CW v Sullivan, CoCt 1853 Oct, and CirCt 1854 Mar; see also Dr. Dillon, OP acct, and Acct, guardian of the poor for services rendered to Mrs. M. Sullivan, both filed CoCt 1854 Jun–Jul, and Report of board of OP, 1854 Apr 10, filed CoCt 1854 Jun–Jul. Neither the circuit court ended papers nor that court's minute book seems to contain any indication of the outcome of the Sullivan prosecution.

82. Shooting, and testimony in dialect: CW v O'Brien, CoCt 1852 Feb (with summary of testimony), and CirCt 1852 Apr.

83. Charge, testimony, and verdict in trial of Cephas: CW v Cephas, CoCt 1846 Jul.

84. Further testimony at trial of Cephas: CW v Cephas, CoCt 1846 Jul. "Wonderful art": Charles F. Adams, ed., *The Works of John Adams*, II, p. 428, cited in Tom Hatley, *The Dividing Paths: Cherokees and South Carolinians Through the Era of Revolution* (New York and Oxford: Oxford University Press, 1993), p. 75, courtesy of David Preston. One of Joel Elam's own slaves was called to appear as a witness for the prosecution at Cephas's trial.

85. Mary Jane Franklin (Bartlett): DB 25/185, Franklin to Franklin (1846) (her manumission); OB 26/180 (1847 Jun) (application to remain denied, three fourths of court not agreeing).

86. Presentments of spring 1850, dated Apr 26, May 1, and May 3, CirCt 1850 Apr. Tally of presentments and processes: filed with CW v Cole, CirCt 1852 Aug. Woodson: See the notes that follow. Isaac Coles: CW v Isaac, OB 26/377 (1850 Aug), and CoCt 1851 Nov. The Isaac N. Cole presented by the earlier grand jury on several charges appears to have been a different man from Isaac Coles, the free black.

87. Cabinetmaking with George Clibourne; petition for waiver: Petition of Jesse Woodson, 1848 Feb 7, Legislative petitions, Prince Edward County, LVA, with thanks to James D. Watkinson; the legislature's response to Woodson's petition apparently is not indicated on the extant copy. Jesse Woodson's liberation: Tarlton Woodson letter to court, May 17, 1847, filed CoCt 1847 May. His registration: OB 26/167 (May 1847).

88. Isaac Coles's manumission: OB 26/164 (1847 May). Icey Coles's manumission, paid for by Isaac from Pennsylvania: DB 26/87, Venable to Coles (1851); OB 26/449 (1851 Aug).

89. Conclusion of Woodson case: CW v Woodson, CirCt 1851 Sep. Woodson's popularity: Petition of Woodson, as in note 87, and accompanying letter of Samuel C. Anderson to Benjamin W. Womack, February 3, 1847 [apparently corrected to read 1848]. Woodson's name does not appear in Ms. Census, 1860.

90. Bartlett trial: CW v Bartlett, OB 26/350 and 400 (1850 Mar and Nov); CoCt 1850 Nov. The Patsy Bartlett jury included Henry McKinney, who, three months before he voted to acquit her, had reported free black Henry Mettauer for buying chickens from a slave. McKinney apparently based his judgments in such instances on the facts as he saw them rather than simply on the color of a suspect or defendant.

91. Dispositions of the gambling and liquor-selling cases are found in CirCt 1850 Apr and Sep, where they make up the bulk of the criminal cases, and also in CW v Noell (two counts) and CW v Taylor, CirCt 1851 Apr; CW v Lowry, CW v Noell, and CW

v Andrews (four counts), CirCt 1851 Sep; CW v Anderson & Hines (ten counts), CirCt 1852 Apr; and CW v Worsham (two counts), CirCt 1853 Aug. (Four of the sixteen presentments for selling liquor to slaves led to guilty verdicts. The conviction rate for selling liquor to slaves was low in this instance partly because the witness who had incriminated one store on ten counts left the county before trial. Yet even if those ten charges are eliminated from the tally, the conviction rate for gambling offenses still exceeded that for selling spirits to slaves.) Assault conviction: CW v Samuel A. Smith, CirCt 1851 Sep. One tavern owner paid a remarkable $100 fine and served some time in jail for permitting gambling, and county authorities spent the formidable sum of $95 pursuing another man for running a faro game. Fined, jailed: Noell v CW, CirCt 1853 Aug. Pursuit: CW v Worsham (count no. 1), CirCt 1853 Aug.

92. Homes prosecution: CW v Homes, CoCt 1856 Aug. Alleged white accomplice: CW v Hines, CoCt 1856 Jul. At least two white individuals had faced similar charges in earlier years—CW v Christian, CoCt 1837 Nov, and CirCt 1838 Apr (allegation of "stealing" slave, in which the latter pretty clearly cooperated); CW v Otis Williams, CoCt 1842 Oct; both cases ended in acquittal or dismissal.

93. "The free Negro": Carter G. Woodson, ed., *Free Negro Owners of Slaves in the United States in 1830 Together with Absentee Ownership of Slaves in the United States in 1830* (New York: Negro Universities Press, [1924] 1968), p. viii.

94. "Do many . . . know"; "free negroism": *Federal Union*, May 26, 1857, group 387, series XV, box 25, folder 220, "Free Negroes," Ulrich B. Phillips papers, Yale. Ira Berlin writes that "newspapers throughout the South avidly spread" stories of the few self-enslavements by free blacks—*Slaves Without Masters*, p. 367; that doubtless accounts for the attention this law has received from historians. (On more radical schemes for re-enslaving free blacks and the Southern white public's sweeping rejection of them, see *ibid.*, pp. 370–80.) Prince Edward's county court took note of, and then proceeded to ignore, another law passed in Richmond that required free blacks selling agricultural products to secure a statement from a "respectable" white person certifying that the goods had not been stolen—OB 27/297 (1858 Dec), with no subsequent entries implementing the new law.

95. Self-enslavement: Caesar, ex parte, Circuit Superior Court of Law and Chancery minute book, 1846–70, 1858 Mar 18 and Aug 12, LVA; Circuit Superior Court Order Book, 1853–70, pp. 191 (1858 Mar), 200 (1858 Aug), 211 (1858 Aug), 226 (1859 Mar), and 246 (1859 Aug), in office of CirCt clerk, Prince Edward County Courthouse, Farmville. Fewer than two dozen: John H. Russell, *The Free Negro in Virginia, 1619–1865* (Baltimore: Johns Hopkins Press, 1913), p. 109.

96. Careful inquests: Sophia Langhorne, 1852; Margaret and Eliza Walden, 1853; and James Cabell, 1858; all in Inquests, LVA. Micajah Walden a boatman: Ms. Census, 1850, family visitation 371. A boat owner: Ms. Census, 1850, schedule 5, Products of industry, p. 125.

97. Walden fire and living situation: Coroner's inquisition, Margaret and Eliza Walden, 1853, Inquests, LVA. One white man had entered the house during the fire's early stages, but for some reason did not go upstairs, where the girls turned out to be—Charles Erambert testimony.

98. John Coakley as shoemaker: Cokeley [sic] to Chambers's trustee, in Receipts to Chambers's trustee from 1833 . . . 1834 & 1835 (compared), 1833 Oct 22, Attorney General v Chambers's trustees, CirCt 1842 Sep; Penick acct with Amplias Tuggle, 1837 Jun 30, voucher no. 64, Tuggle v Penick, CirCt 1840 Apr. Coakley's age: Ms. Census, 1850, family visitation 609. Theophilus Scott a shoemaker: FNL, 1861. Sarah Mitchell, one of the free black women present: FNLs, 1858ff.; the discussion in the inquest of when or whether a white person was summoned suggests that the second woman in attendance, Lizzie Pollard, was also black. Coakley's death: Coroner's inquisition, December 20, 1858, Inquests, LVA; County levy, 1861 May, payment to A. S. Dillon,

filed CoCt 1861 May–Jun. One of the black women said Coakley also dropped his remaining $9 or $10 on Scott's floor—her way of explaining how such a large sum ended up in her pocket. Pauper's burial: Table C, Annual report of OP, filed CoCt 1860 May. Before he came home to find Coakley, Theo Scott had spent the evening at "the dancing School"; whether he had been watching, dancing, or simply meeting someone there we do not know.

99. Gregory rape case: CW v Jim, CoCt 1858 Oct, but originally filed Nov; OB 27/281 (1858 Aug; appointment of counsel and continuance), 283 (1858 Sep 20, the appearance at which Gregory cut Jim), and 288 (1858 Oct); Bradshaw, *History of Prince Edward County*, p. 285. Gregory's assault on Jim: CW v Gregory, CoCt 1858 Nov; OB 27/288 (1858 Oct) and 292 (1858 Nov). Jim's owner, Robert V. Davis, had an obvious vested interest in the outcome of the case: a conviction would cost him a good worker. But his readiness to seek fair play for a bondman seems to have transcended dollars and cents; a few months later he would make a formal complaint and become a witness against a former county justice who assaulted another man's slave—CW v Cobbs, CoCt 1859 Mar; Bradshaw, *Prince Edward County*, pp. 679–80 (former justice). On the relative infrequency of executions of slaves for alleged rapes of white women, see data in Philip J. Schwarz, *Twice Condemned: Slaves and the Criminal Laws of Virginia, 1705–1865* (Baton Rouge: Louisiana State University Press, 1988), pp. 209–10. Schwarz does dismiss the "legend of the absence of rapes by slaves" (p. 208, n. 18); and he writes of "a real rise in the use of capital punishment for attempted rape" during the antebellum period (p. 209), though the overall rate for the period 1823–65 did not exceed one execution in the state every two years or so.

100. Tatum's rape charge: CW v George, CoCt 1854 Feb. Mary Tatum's age: OB 27/44 (1854 Feb). Other acquittals of slave defendants charged with rape: Diane Miller Sommerville, "The Rape Myth in the Old South Reconsidered," *Journal of Southern History*, 61, no. 3 (August 1995); Diane Miller Sommerville, "The Rape Myth Reconsidered: The Intersection of Race, Class, and Gender in the American South, 1800–1877" (Ph.D. diss., Rutgers University, 1995). William F. Scott's callousness toward Betsy Lyle after she gave birth bespoke no special antipathy toward blacks; he would later give bail for free black Booker Hill after being required, in his role as constable, to arrest Hill on a hogstealing charge—CW v Hill, CoCt 1855 Nov.

101. "The great truth": *Augusta Daily Constitutionalist*, March 30, 1861, quoted in James M. McPherson, *Ordeal by Fire: The Civil War and Reconstruction* (New York: Knopf, 1982), p. 131.

102. On Virginia liberalism, its limits, and its chronology, see Robert McColley, *Slavery and Jeffersonian Virginia* (Urbana: University of Illinois Press, 1964). On the persistence of moral doubts about slavery, see Alison Goodyear Freehling, *Drift Toward Dissolution: The Virginia Slavery Debate of 1831–1832* (Baton Rouge and London: Louisiana State University Press, 1982); William W. Freehling, *The Road to Disunion: Secessionists at Bay, 1776–1854* (New York and Oxford: Oxford University Press, 1990); William G. Shade, *Democratizing the Old Dominion: Virginia and the Second Party System, 1824–1861* (Charlottesville and London: University Press of Virginia, 1996); Charles Grier Sellers Jr., "The Travail of Slavery," in Sellers, ed., *The Southerner as American* (Chapel Hill: University of North Carolina Press, 1960), pp. 40–71. For general assessments of liberalism and its boundaries, see David Brion Davis, *The Problem of Slavery in the Age of Revolution, 1770–1823* (Ithaca and London: Cornell University Press, 1975), pp. 164–84 and 196–212, and John Chester Miller, *The Wolf by the Ears: Thomas Jefferson and Slavery* (Charlottesville and London: University Press of Virginia, 1991).

103. Baldwin's "conscientious scruples": Nathaniel Venable Sr., letter to Samuel C. Anderson, August 15, 1831, in Jacob v Purcell, CoCt 1838 May. "That freedom to which": WB 3/353-356, Andrew Baker Sr. will (1804).

104. "In the manner of a free person": WB 6/326, Martin Pearce will (1824/1826).

105. "Old and faithful negroes": WB 6/310, Francis Watkins Sr. will (1826). A Professor [Rev. John D. Paxton], in *Richmond Family Visitor,* June 24, 1826, p. 4, in typescript, Eggleston Papers, section 30, "Negroes," Mss1 Egg3966, VHS (emphasis in the original).

106. Free blacks at Patteson's: FNLs, 1819–1822. Manumission: WB 7/436, Alexander Patteson will (1836), and OB 24/79 (1837 Aug). Patteson had freed at least one slave before he wrote his will—OB 23/44 (1832 Oct). Manumitted slave applies to stay: Charles' mo[tion], filed CoCt 1838 Feb. Execution of will: Patteson est acct, Lewis v Patteson, CoCt 1839 Jun–Jul. Three years after Patteson's death, his executor still showed every intention of carrying out the emancipation of the remaining slaves—Note on Statement showing the entire amount for equal distribution, Lewis v Patteson.

107. Emaline's manumission: OB 24/450 (1841 Jun); Emaline's motion to summon justices, filed CoCt 1841 Aug (but dated Jul); Emaline, a free person of colour, filed CoCt 1842 Jun–Jul; OB 25/78 (1842 Jun; approval of application; posting of notice for two months). Relationship to C. E. Chappell: DB 23/75-78, Chappell to Flournoy (1840). Henry Chappell emancipation: DB 27/159-160, Vaughan to Chappell, (1856); technically, William Chappell conveyed Henry Chappell to another party by a deed of trust which, when paid off by Henry's own labors, would result in his liberation. Richard G. Chappell was declared insane and committed to the state hospital in Staunton half a dozen years after he helped free Emaline; there is no apparent connection between the two events—WB 9/139, Chappell's certf (1846).

108. Ellington's legacy to Nelson and Henry: Borum v Ellington's exor, CirCt 1853 Aug, particularly Report, 1847 Sep ("prefer[red] to do so"); Note by Asa D. Dickinson, n.d. ("shabbily dressed"). Henry's suit for the missing payment: Henry v Perkinson's admor, CirCt 1855 Mar. Henry's intention to leave: OB 27/49 (1854 Mar). Henry remains in county: FNL, 1857. Henry was first apprenticed to cabinetmaker and county justice George Clibourne, and then, when Clibourne's health failed, to builder Henry Guthrey.

109. Except as noted, this account of the suit by the thirteen slaves comes from two sources: Randolph's Administrator v Cloe [sic] et al., Virginia Supreme Court of Appeals, Order Book 20, pp. 416 (1859 Feb 10 and 11) and 431–432 (1859 Mar 2), LVA; and WB 10/487-489, Inventory of Judith Randolph est after sale of Bizarre and Buffalo tracts (1858).

110. Alternatively, Aaron and Jinsey may have been among the other slaves from the estate of John Randolph Sr., apart from the two personal servants, whom John Randolph of Roanoke had held on to in 1810—Fragment, [Judith Randolph to Creed Taylor], 1810 n.d., box 1, Creed Taylor papers, UVa; see the discussion in chapter 2. District Court WB 1/9-13, Richard Randolph inventory (1797/1798), lists no Jinsey (or Virgin or Virginia) and no Aaron, though their absence from the inventory may simply mean that neither was born by 1797. And neither name appears on the list of five slaves whom Judith owned at her death—WB 5/165-166 (1816), Judith Randolph inventory.

111. Hunter Marshall's election as judge: Circuit Superior Court Order Book, 1853–70, p. 182 (1858 Mar), in office of CirCt clerk, Prince Edward County Courthouse, Farmville.

112. The court records for Nottoway from these years have not survived. According to local tradition, they were destroyed by Union soldiers at the end of the Civil War.

113. Cumberland sequestration: See also Judith Randolph, Inventory, p. 2, filed CoCt 1858 Jun 12.

114. Manumission of Asa Hawkes, 1859: Nottoway minute book 3, pp. 325 and 327 (1859 Nov 3 and Dec 14), LVA.

115. Porter presents options: WB 5/571, Andrew Porter will (1821).

116. Randolph slaves in Ohio: Frank F. Mathias, "John Randolph's Freedmen: The

Thwarting of a Will," *Journal of Southern History*, 39, no. 2 (May 1973), 263–72; "Slaves' Descendants Stay Angry Over Bizarre Event" (Associated Press), *Richmond Times-Dispatch*, February 21, 1993.

117. "Paradoxical regard"; survey of free blacks: Alison Freehling, *Drift Toward Dissolution*, pp. 220–21.

118. "Remove from our country": Minutes, Virginia branch, American Colonization Society (cited hereafter as Minutes, VaACS), 1823 Nov 4–1859 Feb 5, p. 19, Mss3 AM353 a1, VHS.

119. "The same influence"; "with other men": *Richmond Commercial [Compiler?]*, [Decem?]ber 17, 1828, in Minutes, VaACS. "Elevat[ing]": Minutes, VaACS, p. 19. "Respectable members": Minutes, VaACS, p. 31. "Health and comfort": Minutes, VaACS, p. 8. Consent of free blacks (example): Board of managers, Richmond city hall, 1835 Apr 10, VaACS. See also Marie Tyler-McGraw, "The American Colonization Society in Virginia, 1816–1832: A Case Study in Southern Liberalism" (Ph.D. diss., George Washington University, 1980).

120. "Against the mischievous and reckless": Annual meeting, 1851 Feb 13, Minutes, VaACS. "Spontaneously liberating": Newspaper clipping incorporated into minutes, 1855 Feb 9, Minutes, VaACS. Colonizationists' laments: Elizabeth R. Varon, *We Mean to Be Counted: White Women and Politics in Antebellum Virginia* (Chapel Hill and London: University of North Carolina Press, 1998), pp. 64 and 66. Late advent of "positive good" thesis: See Alison Freehling, *Drift Toward Dissolution*.

121. Granddaughter of John Morton, Revolutionary veteran: Unlabeled document, filed CoCt 1838 Aug–Oct. Patty Morton's will: WB 7/369-370 (1834).

122. Anne Rice's library: WB 12/138-140, Acct of est sale, Anne S. Rice (1867/1868). Rice's earlier manumissions: Marion Harland (Mary Virginia Terhune), *Marion Harland's Autobiography: The Story of a Long Life* (1910), pp. 100–01, cited in Varon, *We Mean to Be Counted*, p. 64. Manumission of 1853: DB 26/306-307, Rice to Deans and Black (1853). (Rice's manumitted slaves in 1853 belonged to the Black and Deans families.) Liberia: Bradshaw, *Prince Edward County*, p. 280.

123. Ampy Brandum at Watson's: FNLs, 1817–1825. John Watson's mass emancipation: Circuit Court WB, 1833–99, pp. 67–69, John Watson will and disposition of contest by relatives (1854/1856); 70 and 79 (acct of est sale, and est acct, both of which show Watson had died in 1855); 73–74 (inventory and appraisal, showing number of Watson slaves as of 1856 Oct); 87–90 (est acct, itemizing expenses of transporting ex-slaves). See also Bradshaw, *Prince Edward County*, pp. 280–82; *The African Repository*, 34, no. 6 (June 1858), 191, brought to my attention by Elizabeth R. Varon; Circuit Superior Court Order Book, 1853–70, p. 143 (1856 Aug); and, for the remote aftermath, Chancery Order Book, CirCt, 1859–72, p. 153 (1864 Mar); both of the latter books in office of CirCt clerk, Prince Edward County Courthouse, Farmville. Some of Watson's slaves sought to remain in Virginia rather than emigrate; see OB 27/255 (1858 Feb) and 262–63 (1858 Apr).

124. "To which our policy": Quoted from unnamed newspaper in Henry Howe, *Historical Collections of Virginia* (Charleston, SC: Babcock, 1845), p. 351.

125. Catherine Baker's bequest, and the challenge to it: Ellis et al. v Baker's exor and Baker, in CoCt 1815 May, including copy of C. Baker's will, and of marriage contract (wrongly labeled "Baker's Will"). The distribution of money to slaves was to take place after provision was first made for Baker's two handicapped bondpeople. On slave Rose's infirmity, see Baker letter to court, filed CoCt 1814 Mar–Apr.

126. Baptist condemnation of profiteering: Minute book, James River Association, 1832–50, twelfth annual session, Buckingham County, 1844 Jul 29, p. 1, [Virginia?] Baptist Historical Society, cited in William Maphis Whitworth Jr., "Cumberland County, Virginia, in the Later Antebellum Period, 1840–1860" (M.A. thesis, Univer-

sity of Richmond, 1991), p. 172. Read on slave prices: Michaux & Totty v Williams, CirCt 1854 Aug.

127. "Liberia a Swindle": "Liberty not worth having," article from *Farmville Journal* reprinted in *African Repository*, 34, no. 6 (June 1858), 191, courtesy of Elizabeth R. Varon.

128. New York City: *New-York Evening Times*, August 31, 1854, reprinted from *Baltimore Patriot*, courtesy of Frank Moore.

129. F. N. Watkins, letter to Edmund Ruffin, October 2, 1854, printed under the title "The Randolph Emancipated Slaves: Statistics of Population, Morals and Comfort of Negroes—Slaves and Emancipated," in *DeBow's Review*, 24 (New Series, vol. 4) (April 1858), 285–90. Watkins, ironically, had served as the court-appointed auditor who exposed many of the financial misdeeds of the late Colonel James Madison, the man to whom Ruffin had issued a similar assignment two decades earlier—Report of Commissioner Watkins, Chambers's committee v Madison's exor, CirCt 1842 Apr.

130. The eminent historian: See Ulrich Bonnell Phillips, *American Negro Slavery: A Survey of the Supply, Employment and Control of Negro Labor as Determined by the Plantation Regime* (Baton Rouge: Louisiana State University Press, [1918] 1966), p. 437.

131. Watkins's purchase of land: Delinquent land sales in 1845, filed CoCt 1845 Sep–Dec. Watkins's audit of estate: WB 7/439-440, Hercules White Sr. est acct with S. Allen, deputy of Carter (1836). Watkins's review of Chambers lot sales: Report of commissioner Watkins, as well as Document F, in Chambers's committee v Madison's exor, CirCt 1842 Apr. Watkins had also acted as trustee when free Afro-Virginian John White gave a deed of trust on a lot he owned in Farmville—DB 23/141-142, White to White, DoT (1841).

132. Two criminal cases involving free blacks with Randolph connections, not residents of Israel Hill—and, like Howard and Johnston, not convicted—were those in which boatmen Kit Strong Jr. and Dick Clark faced prosecution for allegedly stealing a hogshead of tobacco in 1838, and in which the prosecution of Randolph Brandum for wounding a slave with a knife in 1841 was aborted.

133. "Rotten borough": Watkins, "Randolph Emancipated Slaves," 289; see also "The Randolph Family," *Farmville Mercury*, September 23, 1875.

134. Prosecutions of free blacks in 1859–60: CW v Richardson, CW v Franklin, and CW v Minnis, all CoCt 1860 Feb; OB 27/336 (1859 Nov). There are two sets of documents on the Minnis case in CoCt 1860 Feb. The court soon confirmed Minnis's free status but required her to pay a fee for the interval she had spent in jail—OB 27/347; 1859 Dec). It is unknown whether any fee was actually collected. Minnis's child: Table C, annual report of OP to May court 1860, CoCt 1860 May.

135. Mary Jane Franklin (Bartlett): DB 25/185, Franklin to Franklin (1846) (her manumission); OB 26/180 (1847 Jun; application to remain denied, three fourths of court not agreeing); OB 26/460 (1851 Nov; application to remain with children), 462 (1851 Nov; application to register for sole purpose of leaving state), and 471 (1852 Feb; further consideration of application to remain in state); Bartlett &c., order to summon justices, CoCt 1856 Aug, and OB 27/182 (1856 Aug; permission to remain again refused, but granted to Henry Chappell); CW v Franklin, CoCt 1856 Nov (charge of unlawfully remaining nol-prossed); OB 27/194 (1856 Nov; official description of Franklin granted her by court); CW v Franklin, CoCt 1860 Feb (presentment of 1859 Nov 21 for remaining in state dismissed). Robert Franklin remains: OB 27/193 (1856 Nov); FNLs, 1860, 1861, 1863, and 1864.

136. Charges against Richardson: OB 26/180 (1847 Jun; Richardson's original registration); CW v Richardson, CoCt 1856 Jul, OB 27/158 (1856 May), and OB 27/180 (1856 Jul; charge of remaining followed by granting of registration); CW v Richardson, CoCt 1860 Feb (charge of remaining in state dismissed); CW v Richardson, CoCt 1860 Nov

(charge of returning after sojourn in Ohio); OB 27/336 (1859 Nov), 363 (1860 May), 378 (1860 Jul), and 393 (1860 Nov). The charge lodged against Richardson in November 1859 was dismissed after the black man was not found; but Guthrey complained again a few months later, and Richardson was arrested on November 16, 1860. Grand jury's call to expose undocumented free blacks: OB 27/158 (1856 May). Free blacks from other counties denied entry: OB 27/186 (1856 Sep), 27/233 (1857 Sep), and 27/303 (1859 Feb). Henry Guthrey's role in pursuing unregistered free blacks is ambiguous. He gave information to the grand jury that returned presentments against Julius Richardson, Mary Franklin, and Henry Homes in 1856. Yet Guthrey also bailed Homes out of jail in the very same case—OB 27/171 and 180 (1856 Jun and Jul).

137. Colleys: CW v Stephen F. Colley and CW v Susan Colley, both CoCt 1860 Feb. While all this went on, local people still reacted calmly to other traditional forms of black-white interaction. The post–John Brown grand jury had also included in its sweep one white man whom it charged with having sold liquor to slaves, but a jury found the defendant not guilty on one of the charges, and the Commonwealth nol-prossed the other—CW v Deshazor (two cases), CoCt 1860 May.

138. Enumerator's verdict: T. B. McRobert, note in Ms. Census, 1860, page containing family visitations 781–87.

139. Slave Peter and alleged attack with stone: CW v Peter, Nottoway minute book 3, pp. 304–05, 311, and 314 (1859 Jun 3, Jul 7, and Aug 4), LVA.

140. Arson prosecution: CW v Mary, Nottoway minute book 3, p. 361, 1860 Jun 7. "Nest" of whites: Ms. Census, 1860, family visitations 751–52.

141. Shooting at Franklin's house: CW v Rodgers, CoCt 1860 Nov. Shooting slave: CW v Shepherd, CoCt 1860 Jul 30; Circuit Superior Court of Law and Chancery minute book, 1846–70, 1860 Aug 15 and 16, LVA.

142. Substantial payments to groups of slaves, and to some free blacks: [H. E.] Watkins est acct [with F. N. Watkins], 1856 Dec (two entries), 1857 Jan, and 1857 Feb ($190 for corn; a payment to Booker Jackson), filed CoCt 1857 Nov–1858 Jan; Henry E. Watkins est acct with [Francis N.] Watkins, 1858 Dec, filed CoCt 1859 Dec–1860 Apr. The label "decline and fall" is actually applied, in quotation marks, to the Israel Hill story in the Watkins letter published in *DeBow's Review*, 289.

143. Matilda White's death: Coroner's inquisition, 1858 May, Inquests, LVA. Dick White's daughter: See FNL, 1819; White v White's admor, OB 22/571-572 (1831 Dec). Matilda back on Israel Hill: FNL, 1858. Burial at public expense: Coroner's inquisition, Matilda White; Annual report of OP, filed CoCt 1860 May.

144. Aid to Zack Ellis, and his death: Proceedings of board of OP, annual meeting 1859 Apr 11, filed CoCt 1859 May–Sep; Annual report of OP to CoCt 1860 May. Ellises' ages: FNL, 1857.

145. Hampton Giles's death: WB 11/33-34, Hampton Giles will (1859). Giles's two marriages; children and grandchildren of first marriage on Israel Hill after Giles's death: Cf. FNLs, 1825 and 1857ff.

146. Dungey's prosperity: Ms. Census, 1850, schedule 4, Productions of agriculture, pp. 513–14. In the year before this census, Dungey owned one horse, three milch cows, two working oxen, four other cattle, seven sheep, and fourteen swine; he produced 50 bushels of wheat, 30 of oats, 150 of corn, 1800 pounds of tobacco, 30 bales of ginned cotton at 400 pounds each, 15 pounds of wool, and various garden crops. Dungey's bequests: WB 11/159-160, John Dungey will (1852/1861). His property at death: WB 11/187, John Dungey appraisal (1861), also filed in CoCt 1861 May–Jun; Dungey's debts at his death exceeded $450. Sale of land: DB 28/48, Dungey to Carter (1859). Securing debts: DB 28/184-185, Dungey to Cunningham, DoT (1860/1861).

147. Strong's death and legacy: WB 11/116, Samuel Strong will (1860). James (Jim) Daniel White: FNL, 1861. One Fanny Strong—Sam's widow bore that name—traded

actively in town lots for many years after the Civil War; see deeds in which she is listed as a grantor in Index to deeds (microfilm), LVA. Another free black entrepreneur, John White, seems to have died three years after Sam Strong, during the war; white physician and investor in real estate B. C. Peters gave a substantial bond of $2,000 as administrator of the estate of one John White—OB 28/42 (1863 Mar).

148. Tony White's will: WB 9/374, Anthony White will (1848 and codicil 1850/1850).

149. Susan White's marriage to Davy Smith in 1836, and identity of her mother: Index to marriage bonds, LVA. A Jane White as daughter of Sam: IH 1816. David (Davy) Smith absent by 1850: He appears in Ms. Census for 1840 (p. 27, stamped 232), listed as having a wife of the age bracket that would include the Susan Smith who appears in Ms. Census, 1850 (family visitation 446, though entered erroneously as 456); but by 1850, this or another David Smith, forty-five, is listed in a separate household—Census, family visitation 456. (Susan Smith lived with one Nancy Strong in 1850, who was doubtless related to the Strongs of Israel Hill and Farmville. David Smith had once sued a white man, probably a deputy sheriff, for assaulting and tying him, but had dropped the suit—Smith v Robertson, CirCt 1842 Sep, related in chapter 6. Timing of Davy Smith's death or departure: Smith is listed in Delinquents, county levy, lower end, 1850, in Sundry claims v county, filed CoCt 1851 Jun; but he appears on no extant list for subsequent years. (He may have died somewhat earlier than 1850. Deaths were not always taken into account right away in records of tax delinquencies.)

150. The Whites' lawsuit: White v Smith (a.k.a. White v White), CirCt ended papers, 1859 Aug, Prince Edward County Courthouse, Farmville (but now located in LVA?). Susan Smith still on Israel Hill: FNLs, 1860 (Sukey Smith, listed as forty-five years old), 1861 (Susan Smith, listed as forty-seven and designated specifically as living on Israel Hill), and 1864 (Sukey Smith, listed as forty-eight). The judge to whom the suit was addressed was Hunter H. Marshall, the administrator of Judith Randolph's estate, who at that very time was being successfully sued by Aaron and the other Randolph slaves who claimed their freedom on grounds of having belonged to John Randolph, and of having been covered by John's emancipatory will.

151. White's guardianship and signature: Smith, Harriot, guardian bond, 1860 Feb 19 and 20, filed CoCt 1859 Dec–1860 Apr. By this time, White was called Phil or Philip Junior, his grandfather having been dead for years. Census, 1850, family visitation 447, reports Phil White "Jr." [III] as being, like the rest of his father's family, unable to read and write; the enumerator seems to have assumed too much (or rather, too little) in this instance. There is a deed from 1856 in which one of the Philip Whites conveys a lot; the deed book indicates that the seller signed rather than made a mark—DB 27/191-192, White to Short (1855/1856). But the deed books contain transcriptions and not actual deeds, and in at least one other instance a deed book from the period indicates a signature was entered by a person I know to have been nonliterate. The deed on which a signature is indicated was executed before Howell Warren, the same JP before whom Philip White III most definitely did sign his name in 1860, so it is at least conceivable that Warren in the latter year was seeing Phil III sign a document not for the first time, but rather for the second.

CHAPTER 9: *Appomattox and the New Birth of Freedom*

1. Saylor clan: Williams v Saylor's exors, CirCt 1838 Sep, *passim;* note places of origin of the many answers filed in the case. Moving between Virginia and North (example): Answer of Charles C. Hudson and certf of service of papers on him, Mettauer v Thweatt & Hudson, CirCt 1852 Aug. Ely from Connecticut: Ms. Census, 1860, family visitation 330. Frothingham from Connecticut: WB 7/96, Ebenezer Frothingham

will (1830). Dupuy's wife from Massachusetts: Virginia G. Redd, "Emily Howe duPuy: Northern School Teacher/Southern Slave Owner," *Southsider*, 5, no. 3 (Summer 1986), 51–65, citing Carrol Franklin Adams, "A New England Teacher in Southside Virginia: A Study of Emily Howe, 1812–1883" (M.A. thesis, University of Virginia, 1954); Ms. Census, 1850, family visitation 535. Woodson's mother from New York: Herbert Clarence Bradshaw, *History of Prince Edward County, Virginia, from Its Earliest Settlements Through Its Establishment in 1754 to Its Bicentennial Year* (Richmond: Dietz Press, 1955), p. 839; Catherine G. Obrion, "Charles Woodson Collection," http://spec.lib.vt.edu/mss/woodsonc.html. "Go to the South" (example): John Simmons depo, Jones v Ritchie, CirCt 1853 Mar.

2. Election results: Bradshaw, *Prince Edward County*, p. 377.

3. Sale of county war bonds: Order for the purchase of arms; Arms &c paper filed 1861 Feb by Mr. Southall; Bond, 1861 Jan 21; all filed in CoCt 1861 Jan–Apr. An act of the General Assembly had authorized counties to issue such bonds. Crowded court session: William C. Flournoy resolutions, filed CoCt 1861 Apr 15; OB 27/412 (1861 Apr 15).

4. Readiness for war: Lewis Coleman "and many others," telegram to Lieutenant Governor Montague, April 20, 1861, Governor John Letcher Executive papers, LVA; see also E. P. Jones tender of 109th regiment, Apr 20, in same collection. "Special police force": OB 27/405 (1861 Feb). Four charged with crimes: Presentments, 1861 May 20, CoCt 1861 May, and OB 27/415-416 (1861 May); CW v Durham, CoCt 1861 Jul, and OB 27/419 (1861 Jul; dismissal on recommendation of prosecutor). The two men accused of receiving stolen goods, Durham and Grant, may have left the county before their trials. The equipment allegedly stolen by the free blacks had belonged to Benjamin Peters, the white man who had bought a lot from Phil White and sold Robert Franklin's daughter to him.

5. Difficulty selling bonds: Report on blue document labeled "County bonds $7500.00, January Court 1861," in bundle, "War material—1861–1865; Bonds—county—Lists of free negroes, etc.," Prince Edward County Court papers, LVA. Old Dominion Rifles: W. M. Boyd, letter to governor, and telegram to same, both April 18, 1861. "Take muskets": William R. Weisiger, letter to governor, April 20, 1861. Governor reports on appropriation: Draft message of Governor Letcher to Virginia Convention, April 20, 1861. "Ten thousand stand": Draft telegram, George W. Munford, secretary of Commonwealth, to Governor J. W. Ellis, April 20, 1861. All these documents, except for the one noted, are in Governor John Letcher Executive papers, LVA.

6. "For every five or ten thousand"; "even fight": Daniel H. Flournoy, letter to governor, April 22, 1861. "Expressed . . . a willingness": E. R. Turnbull, letter to governor, April 20, 1861. Offers of services of writers' own slaves: See George Gilmer (n.p.), letter to governor; J. Henry Epes Jr. (Louisa County), notation on back of letter from William Overton to governor; George B. Hammatt (Clarksville), letter to governor; all April 22, 1861. Suggestion to raise corps of slaves for service: See letters or telegrams to governor from John Taylor (Culpeper County), April 22; John H. Lee (Orange Court House), April 22; C. R. Mason (Staunton), April 20; David G. Potts (Petersburg), April 20; G. T. Pace (Danville), April 22; and also Charles L. Crockett (Wytheville). Offers to forgo compensation for service of writers' slaves: See letters to governor from E. R. Turnbull (Brunswick County) and J. Ralls Abell (Albemarle County), both April 20. All this correspondence is in Letcher Executive papers, LVA.

7. "The free colored population": *Richmond Dispatch*, April 22, 1861, quoted in Michael John Studenka, "The Myths Exposed: The Downfall of the Tidewater's Slaveowning Aristocracy During the Civil War" (Senior honors thesis, Department of History, College of William and Mary, 1996), pp. 31–32.

8. "One hundred (100) free negroes": James R. Branch, telegram to Thomas Branch, April 22, 1861, Letcher Executive papers, LVA. I thank Yaakov Aronson for directing my attention to the Letcher correspondence.

9. "Press . . . free men of color": Samuel Booth and others, letter to governor, April 22, 1861, Letcher Executive papers, LVA.

10. Free black labor draft: Ordinance to provide for the enrollment and employment of free negroes in the public service, Virginia Convention, 1861 Jul 1, filed with Free negroes enrollment, CoCt 1861 Sep 2. Draft of Israelites and others: Confederate Army impressment orders (11225), 1861 Nov, UVa. Virginia's legislators did try to encourage free blacks to volunteer; according to the Enrollment Act of 1861, Afro-Virginian workers would be drafted only if voluntary enlistments proved insufficient. Both the Confederate and the Union drafts of white men would operate on the same principle.

11. "Have families": J. Bankhead Magruder to George Deas, August 9, 1861, United States War Department, *The War of the Rebellion: A Compilation of the Official Records of the Union and Confederate Armies* (Washington, DC: Government Printing Office, various dates of publication), series I, vol. IV, p. 573, an appeal brought to my attention by Studenka, "The Myths Exposed," pp. 31–32.

12. Afro-Virginians helping Union: See Report of Lieutenant Franklin Ellis, June 8, 1862, vol. XI/1, p. 1000 ("many free negroes . . . messages in cipher"); A. Pleasanton to R. B. Marcy, August 15, 1862, XI/3, pp. 377–78; James A. Hardie to General Burnside, December 12, 1862, XXI, p. 109; George G. Meade to H. W. Halleck, September 6, 1863, XXIX/2, pp. 158–59; John C. Babcock to A. A. Humphreys, July 9, 1864, XL/3, p. 98 (free black "agent"); Atherton H. Stevens Jr. to William P. Shreve, November 6, 1864, XLII/1, p. 684 ("true as steel"); Henry A. Wise to General Hill, May 30, 1862, XI/3, p. 562 ("dangerous"; "good river pilots"); all in *War of the Rebellion,* series I.

13. Modification of free black labor draft: Act to amend and reenact an ordinance to provide for the enrollment and employment of free negroes in the public service, passed by the [Virginia state] convention July 1, 1861, passed February 12, 1862, filed with Free negroes enrollment, CoCt 1861 Sep 2.

14. Ninety-six free black men enrolled: Free negroes enrollment, filed CoCt 1861 Sep 2. Men serving as of 1862: FNL, 1862. Cumberland free blacks to hospital: Free Negroes detailed to Farmville Hospital, 1862, Cumberland County Court papers, LVA. Hospital's location and capacity: Bradshaw, *Prince Edward County,* p. 392. Requisition of 1863: J. F. Gilmer to R. E. Lee, March 9, 1863, LI/2, pp. 682–83, *War of the Rebellion,* series I. Like most other county enumerations of free blacks, Prince Edward's list of draft-eligible men was probably incomplete; at least two or three free men in the targeted age bracket who ended up working for the army in 1862 were not included in the preliminary enrollment—John Artis, Ben Bartlett, and Sam Bartlett, FNL, 1862.

15. Numbers, identities, and recorded ages of free blacks in army service: FNLs, 1862–1864.

16. Bob Webber as Israelite farmer, and in Army: FNLs, 1861–1863; at the time Webber was listed by the revenue commissioner in early 1863, he was presumably working locally. Webber rape case: OB 28/34, 38, and 43 (1863 Jan–Mar), CW v Watt. William H. White: "Deacon W. H. White," *Richmond Planet,* January 26, 1895, with thanks to Harold Forsythe. It is difficult to pinpoint William H. White's place in the network of Israel Hill. The *Planet*'s article says he was born in 1838 to a boatman father, belonged as a young man to the "First Baptist Church of Farmville," which presumably means Farmville Baptist, and worked in factories not long before the war. Phil White Jr.'s son Curtis was a boatman, belonged to that congregation, and had a son named William Henry who worked in a factory before the Enrollment Act took effect—but that individual was born in 1845 and supposedly died nearly thirty years before the *Planet* offered its profile of "Deacon" William Henry White, an Israel Hill native who was then still very much alive—Death register, Prince Edward County, 1866 (microfilm), LVA.

17. Clem Read and Newton Cunningham: County bonds &c., order of court, CoCt 1861

Jun; Cunningham died later in 1861, however. Read's crucial role in awarding aid to soldiers' families: Orders for provisions and clothing, 1861 to 1865, Prince Edward County Court papers, LVA.

18. Richardson's account of attack, including "cut me down" and "knocked [William] down": Hillery G. Richardson affi, CW v William (assault), CoCt 1861 Sep.

19. Richardson's wealth: Ms. Census, 1860, family visitation 420; H. G. Richardson est appraisal (1861), filed CoCt Jul–Dec. "Very badly whipped": Thomas D. Morgan testimony, CW v William (murder), CoCt 1861 Dec 19.

20. "What I heard"; "the skin": John P. Mettauer testimony. "Cruelly whipped": Creed Taylor testimony. Eyes and teeth: Richard V. Leach testimony. All in CW v William (murder).

21. "He dreaded the pain"; "diseased state": John P. Mettauer testimony. "I would as soon": B. C. Peters testimony. "Very cruel": John V. Miller testimony. Salt water; teeth: Elick's testimony. All in CW v William (murder).

22. "He whipt all of us": Dick's testimony. "Master was in the habit"; "threaten[ed] to kill": John's testimony. Both in CW v William (murder).

23. "I intend to cut": John's testimony, CW v William (murder).

24. Verdict and sentence: CW v William (murder), CoCt as above; OB 27/432-433 (1861 Dec).

25. Reformism in Confederacy: See Bell Irvin Wiley, "The Movement to Humanize the Institution of Slavery During the Confederacy," *Emory University Quarterly*, 5 (December 1949), 207–20; and Bell Irvin Wiley, *Southern Negroes, 1861–1865* (New Haven and London: Yale University Press, [1938] 1965), pp. 166–72.

26. A court had required Richardson even while he served as sheriff to give bond pledging to keep the peace toward a fellow white citizen, and he had once been formally charged with stabbing a white man, though that case was dismissed—CW v Richardson, CoCt 1853 Aug–Sep; CW v Richardson, CoCt 1845 Jun.

27. Refugees: OB 28/6 (1862 Aug). Tobacco interfering with food production: See Governor John Letcher, Proclamation to limit tobacco production (Ms.), 1863 Mar 16, Governor John Letcher Executive papers, LVA; and also A list of persons engaged in the cultivation of tobacco in Prince Edward County 1863, Prince Edward County Court papers, LVA.

28. Excess currency: See Governor John Letcher, Message to General Assembly (Ms.), March 11, 1863, Letcher Executive papers, LVA. Prices, November 1864: WB 12/3-4, Catherine Fears appraisal (1864). Read and aid committees: See Orders for provisions and clothing—1861–65, and Payments—Dunnington to committee for supplies to soldiers, 1861–64, both in Prince Edward County Court papers, LVA.

29. Federal designs on Farmville and High Bridge: Samuel Jones to General Jenkins, May 4, 1863, XXV/2, p. 775; G. E. Pickett to Braxton Bragg, May 7, 1864, LI/2, p. 898; Report of U.S. Grant of operations 1864 Mar–1865 May, XXXIV/1, p. 47; all in *War of the Rebellion*, series I. High Bridge data: Notes on photograph by T. H. O'Sullivan, "High Bridge, Crossing the Appomattox, near Farmville, on South Side Railroad, Va." (1865), file 165-SB-98, National Archives and Records Administration.

30. Requisitioning of slaves: Negroes to work on fortifications, 1863, Cumberland County Court papers, LVA. One of the slaveowners who did not reply to the first requisition was a free black man—Ellen D. Katz, "African-American Freedom in Antebellum Cumberland County, Virginia," *Chicago-Kent Law Review*, 70 (1995), 964. "Disloyal sentiments"; "a faithfull citizen": Citizens of Farmville and Prince Edward County, letter to Governor William Smith, received May 6, 1864, Smith Executive papers, LVA, courtesy of Antoinette Van Zelm. Permitting a hundred slaves to gather: Circuit Superior Court Order Book, 1853–70, pp. 323 (1863 Mar) and 329 (1864 Mar; acquittal), in office of CirCt clerk, Prince Edward County Courthouse, Farmville.

31. Bagby piece: George W. Bagby, "My Uncle Flatback's Plantation," in Bagby, *The Old Virginia Gentleman and Other Sketches,* ed. Thomas Nelson Page (New York: Scribners, 1910), pp. 99–101, courtesy of Brent Tarter. Bagby's background: Ritchie Devon Watson Jr., "George W. Bagby Jr.," in John T. Kneebone et al., *Dictionary of Virginia Biography,* 1 (Richmond: Library of Virginia, 1998), 278–80; Ritchie Devon Watson Jr., "George William Bagby," in Steven H. Gale, ed., *Encyclopedia of American Humorists* (New York and London: Garland, 1988), pp. 18–21.

32. Encounters with white and black Union soldiers: S. W. Paulett, reminiscences of service in Company F, 18th Virginia Regiment, in Charles Edward Burrell, *A History of Prince Edward County, Virginia, from Its Formation in 1753, to the Present* (Richmond: Williams Printing Co., 1922), pp. 158–60 (originally published in *Farmville Herald,* 1897).

33. Black teamsters: H. E. Davies Jr. to H. C. Weir, April 14, 1865, XLVI/1, p. 1147, *War of the Rebellion,* series I. High Bridge: A. A. Humphreys to General Webb, April 7, 1865, XLVI/3, p. 622; A. A. Humphreys to General Webb, April 10, 1865, XLVI/1, p. 674 (burning of four spans); E. O. C. Ord to John A. Rawlins, April 26, 1865, XLVI/1, pp. 1161–62; Itinerary of 2nd Corps, Army of the Potomac, Richmond Campaign, XLVI/1, p. 76; Report of George G. Meade, April 30, 1865, XLVI/1, p. 604; Fitzhugh Lee to R. E. Lee, April 22, 1865, XLVI/1, pp. 1302–03; all in *War of the Rebellion,* series I. Also photograph by T. H. O'Sullivan, "High Bridge, Crossing the Appomattox," file 165-SB-98, National Archives, showing four spans destroyed. The meeting between Lee and the Confederate officials reputedly took place at the home of Patrick Jackson, tobacco manufacturer and nephew of the long dead Colonel James Madison—James L. White, *Farmville Herald,* July 9, 1897, reprinted in Burrell, *History of Prince Edward County,* pp. 185–86.

34. Yankees fording river: F. Harwood to J. C. Duane, April 20, 1865, XLVI/1, p. 652; George G. Meade to General Humphreys, April 7, 1865, XLVI/3, p. 625; both in *War of the Rebellion,* series I. Fighting at Farmville: James L. White, reprinted in Burrell, *History of Prince Edward County,* pp. 186–87 (this account refers to the partial evacuation of the town by civilians, though it also says erroneously that there were few shots fired in or near Farmville). Further sources on fighting at Farmville: George G. Meade to T. S. Bowers, April 30, 1865, XLVI/1, pp. 604–05; Itinerary of 21st Pennsylvania Cavalry, 3rd Brigade, 2nd Division, Army of the Potomac, Richmond Campaign, XLVI/1, p. 120; A. A. Humphreys to General Webb, April 10, 1865, XLVI/1, pp. 674–75, and April 21, 1865, XLVI/1, pp. 683–84; George Crook to J. W. Forsyth, April 18, 1865, XLVI/1, p. 1142; Walter R. Robbins to R. F. Stockton, May 25, 1865, XLVI/1, p. 1151 (especially vivid on the repulse of the Union forces); J. H. Lathrop to H. B. Scott, April 25, 1865, XLVI/1, pp. 1168–69; W. N. Pendleton to W. H. Taylor, April 10, 1865, XLVI/1, pp. 1281–82; James H. Lane to Joseph A. Engelhard, April 10, 1865, XLVI/1, p. 1286 (Union artillery fire); Fitzhugh Lee to R. E. Lee, April 22, 1865, XLVI/1, p. 1303 (fighting in streets of Farmville); all in *War of the Rebellion,* series I.

35. Union Army bridges Appomattox: F. Harwood to J. C. Duane, April 20, 1865, XLVI/1, p. 652; I. Spaulding to J. C. Duane, June 14, 1865, XLVI/1, pp. 643–44; both in *War of the Rebellion,* series I. Union casualties: Frederick H. Dyer, *A Compendium of the War of the Rebellion* (New York and London: Thomas Yoseloff, 1959), part 2, p. 964. Black troops with Ord: E. O. C. Ord to John A. Rawlins, April 26, 1865, XLVI/1, pp. 1162–63, *War of the Rebellion,* series I.

36. Grant's correspondence with Lee from Farmville: Letters of April 7 and 8, 1865, in Report of U.S. Grant of operations 1864 Mar–1865 May, XXXIV/1, pp. 54–55. Union movements through Farmville: See Itineraries of the Army of the Potomac, Sheridan's Cavalry Command, and the Army of the James, Richmond Campaign, XLVI/1, pp. 76ff. Garrisoning of town: See *ibid.,* 1st Brigade, 3rd Division, XLVI/1, p. 83; T. S. Bowers to George G. Meade, April 11, 1865, XLVI/3, pp. 703–04. Tending Confeder-

ate wounded: Thomas A. McParlin to George D. Ruggles, August 21, 1865, XLVI/1, p. 612 (Union medical officers); McParlin to J. K. Barnes, April 12, 1865, XLVI/3, pp. 719–20 (Confederate surgeons). All these items in *War of the Rebellion*, series I.

37. Foraging party: J. F. Sutton to S. P. Corliss, April 10, 1865, XLVI/1, p. 755, *War of the Rebellion*, series I. "Guards of protection": James L. White, reprinted in Burrell, *History of Prince Edward County*, p. 187. Cavalry to stop plundering: Letters of M. M. Cannon, Francis C. Barlow, and George D. Ruggles, April 24, 1865, XLVI/3, pp. 921–22, in *War of the Rebellion*, series I.

38. Church bells: James L. White, reprinted in Burrell, *History of Prince Edward County*, p. 187. Apple and peach trees: Journal of Captain Jed. Hotchkiss, April 8, 1865, XLVI/1, p. 520, *War of the Rebellion*, series I.

39. "Hailed with universal Joy": EBS (or EBJ?), letter to "Wife" [no further identification of either party], January 17, 1865, Ezekiah and John Harding papers, Duke.

40. Fannie Berry: Workers of the Writers' Program of the Work Projects [sic] Administration in the State of Virginia, *The Negro in Virginia* (Winston-Salem: John F. Blair, [1940] 1994), p. 233; Leon F. Litwack, *Been in the Storm So Long: The Aftermath of Slavery* (New York: Vintage, 1980), pp. 171–72.

41. William H. White: "Deacon W. H. White," *Richmond Planet*, January 26, 1895, with thanks to Harold Forsythe.

42. "Negroes commenced"; "the custom": Edwin Edmunds acct book, 1838–92, p. 23, 1865 Apr 19, UNC. Rations: Ration reports, 1865 Aug 31–1867 Dec 31, Prince Edward County, Records of Assistant Commissioner of the State of Virginia, Bureau of Refugees, Freedmen, and Abandoned Lands (BRFAL), National Archives (microfilm), courtesy of Gregory P. Downs. Legitimization Act: J. Tivis Wicker, "Virginia's Legitimization Act of 1866," *Virginia Magazine of History and Biography*, 86, no. 3 (July 1978), 340–41.

43. Freedmen's Bureau registry: List of colored persons living together as man & wife 1866 Feb 27, Prince Edward County Court papers, LVA.

44. Hospital; attributes of schools: Gregory P. Downs, personal communication based on research for his study, "Better a Wedge Than a Beam: Integration in the Missionary Schools of Reconstruction Virginia" (Senior essay, Department of History, Yale University, 1993); the rest of the items in this note also came to me from Downs, citing Records of the Superintendent of Education, State of Virginia, Bureau of Refugees, Freedmen, and Abandoned Lands, National Archives (microfilm; cited hereafter as BRFAL—Ed.). Black teachers: School report, 1868 Apr. Numerous schools: School reports, 1868 Aug. "Colored people are anxious": Captain Stuart Barnes, report, November 30, 1865. Sources of funds for schools: See School reports, 1868 Feb, Apr, and Aug. "No open hostility": Major J. R. Stone, 1866 Oct. "Some interest": Lieutenant Colonel J. Jordan, n.d. [1866 Aug]. School enrollment: School reports for Prince Edward County, 1865 Jul–1866 Jun.

45. Wavering white support: School reports, 1868 Jun, Oct, and Nov, BRFAL—Ed., courtesy of Gregory P. Downs. "For a Southern lady": J. C. Currier, letter to Mr. Ponnis, March 16, 1869, American Missionary Association Archives, Amistad Research Center, Tulane University, New Orleans (microfilm), courtesy of Downs.

46. Howell Warren as JP: Justices of the peace commissions, 1852, filed CoCt 1852 Jun–Aug. Warren as Conservative: Bradshaw, *Prince Edward County*, pp. 429 and 430.

47. Decline of Bureau schools: School reports, 1869 Nov–1870 Jul, BRFAL—Ed., courtesy of Gregory P. Downs. Public school attendance: Bradshaw, *Prince Edward County*, p. 490. On the subsequent history of public schooling in the county, see Kara Miles Turner, " 'It Is Not at Present a Very Successful School': Prince Edward County and the Black Educational Struggle, 1865–1995" (Ph.D. diss., Duke University, 2001).

48. "Had no liberty": James L. White, reprinted in Burrell, *History of Prince Edward*

County, p. 187. Civil power to "mayor": George D. Ruggles to commanding officer, 2nd Corps, April 21, 1865, XLVI/3, p. 878, *War of the Rebellion,* series I.

49. "Imps of hell": William R. Hatchett, letter to Allen & Eliza, September 20, 1866, in Correspondence 1792–1859 (despite letter's date), Hatchett family papers, box 17-E, Duke. "Rite to vote"; "I am a friend": W[illiam] Woodall, letter to Brother [John Woodall], September 15, 1867, John Woodall papers, Duke. William was writing from nearby Halifax County to his brother in Prince Edward in 1867, when blacks were first allowed to vote.

50. Continued native white influence, and Watkins's role: Bradshaw, *Prince Edward County,* pp. 421–23 and 680.

51. James Bland: Ervin L. Jordan Jr., "James William D. Bland," in Sara B. Bearss et al., eds., *Dictionary of Virginia Biography,* 2 (Richmond: Library of Virginia, 2001), pp. 8–10; Richard McIlwaine, *Memories of Three Score Years and Ten* (New York and Washington, DC: Neale Publishing Co., 1908), p. 233; Luther Porter Jackson, *Negro Officeholders in Virginia, 1865–1895* (Norfolk: Guide Quality Press, 1945), pp. 3–4; Author's interview with Elizabeth Hill Watkins, Prospect, Va., July 26, 1989. Tazewell Branch: Lynda J. Morgan, "Tazewell Branch," in Bearss et al., *Dictionary of Virginia Biography,* 2, pp. 195–96; *New Commonwealth* (Farmville), September 8, 1870, quoted in Asa Dupuy Watkins, "Reconstruction," in *Today and Yesterday in the Heart of Virginia* (Farmville: *Farmville Herald,* 1935), p. 168; Jackson, *Negro Officeholders,* p. 5; Bradshaw, *Prince Edward County,* pp. 431–35. W. D. Evans: OB 26/409 (1851 Jan); Bradshaw, *Prince Edward County,* pp. 429, 438, 688, and 695.

52. Samuel Bolling: Jackson, *Negro Officeholders,* pp. 4–5; W. E. Burghardt Du Bois, "The Negroes of Farmville, Virginia: A Social Study," *Bulletin of the Department of Labor,* 14 (January 1898), 17; Lynda J. Morgan, "Samuel P. Bolling," in Bearss et al., *Dictionary of Virginia Biography,* 2, pp. 69–71. Du Bois is the one source who explicitly reports the purchase of the plantation and the hiring of Bolling's ex-master.

53. "Who thinks for himself": *New Commonwealth,* September 8, 1870, quoted in Watkins, "Reconstruction," p. 168. "Wholesome influence": McIlwaine, *Memories,* p. 233. Deputy sheriff: Watkins, "Reconstruction," in *Today and Yesterday,* p. 168. Republican dissension: Bradshaw, *Prince Edward County,* pp. 431–35. "Fusion" ticket in Farmville: *Ibid.,* pp. 429–30.

54. Assassination plan: Watkins, "Reconstruction," p. 168; Bradshaw, *Prince Edward County,* pp. 435 and 799, n. 77.

55. Intimidation and ballot box stuffing: Bradshaw, *Prince Edward County,* pp. 436 and 799, n. 78. Democratic dominance: *Ibid.,* p. 439.

56. Sharon Church: Burrell, *History of Prince Edward County,* p. 233.

57. Booker Jackson: Circuit Superior Court of Law and Chancery minute book, 1846–70, LVA, 1869 Aug 16 (appointment as trustee); Bradshaw, *Prince Edward County,* pp. 451–52. Trustees of black Baptist congregation: Bradshaw, *Prince Edward County,* p. 448. (A twentyish man, also named Caesar White, was almost surely too young to be the church trustee mentioned in the records. Although a man could serve as trustee of a church of which he was not a member, I think it unlikely that this was true of Caesar White, as the annals of the Farmville Baptist Church say that Curtis White stayed on but say nothing of Caesar's having done so.) Curtis White remains at Farmville Baptist: C. Edward Burrell's Centennial history, p. 3, in Mrs. Judson Dowdy and Historic Committee, scrapbook, 1961, Farmville Baptist Church, in church office. In an intriguing twist, the original Farmville Baptist property, outgrown and sold by its congregation in the 1850s, now passed into the hands of Caesar White and his fellow black trustees—*Farmville Herald,* 1936 [Nov?] 27, front page, Farmville Baptist Church scrapbook, Burrell, *History of Prince Edward County,* p. 221.

58. McIlwaine reminiscences: McIlwaine, *Memories,* pp. 232–34.

59. Black individuals remaining with whites: Bradshaw, *Prince Edward County,* p. 452;

Burrell, Centennial history, p. 3. Nannie Carter's identity: Cf. IH 1816 (on which a "Nancy" Carter of the appropriate age is included in Teny Carter's household) and FNL, 1864.

60. Whites' estrangement, and divorce case: White v White, CirCt ended papers, 1868 Mar, Prince Edward County Courthouse (but now located in LVA?), including answer of Jemima White and depos of Jennie Johnson (wife's alleged threat to kill White), Ottaway Lipscomb ("nearly white"), Mary Ann Lipscomb ("John was a great big . . ."), Elizabeth Morton (according to whom Jemima White had said she had "never before washed a niggers shirt" and "did not think she ought to sleep with as black a nigger as [John White] was"), Gilbert Mason (disturbance at church meeting), Isham Beach (on suborning false statement). John W. White on town council: Bradshaw, *Prince Edward County*, pp. 429 and 695. Some whites provided a ready audience for a drama such as that of the White divorce. One of them, recording depositions in that suit, purposely and prominently included malapropisms in the testimony of two black deponents. The counsel who later became governor of Virginia was Philip W. McKinney.

61. Death of Philip White III: Register of deaths, 1866, p. 59.

62. Multiple lots: See deeds listed in Index to deeds. Bartlett as washer: FNL, 1864.

63. "Some two or three miles west": "The Randolph Family," reprinted from *Richmond Whig* in *Farmville Mercury*, September 23, 1875. Reworkings and embroiderings of F. N. Watkins's letter in *DeBow's Review* include the *Whig* correspondent's "traditions of the vicinage" for Watkins's "annals of the parish" in the first paragraph, and descriptions of personalities and relationships within the Randolph-Tucker family; the *Whig*'s reference to Israel Hill as a "rotten borough" is taken directly from the *DeBow's* article. The *Whig* piece even followed the Baltimore writer's lead in depicting Israel Hill from the supposed vantage point of the railroad tracks. Most houses not visible from tracks: Major J. E. Weyss, map of Farmville, 1867, Map F232 P84 1867:1, VHS; Author's inspection of area. Overgrown countryside: Henry Clay Bruce, *The New Man: Twenty-Nine Years a Slave; Twenty-Nine Years a Free Man* (New York: Negro Universities Press, [1895] 1969), pp. 43, 46, 49, 50–51.

64. Real estate ownership: Du Bois, "Negroes of Farmville," 29–30. Valuation of real estate: *Ibid.*, 4 (county) and 6 (town). Home ownership: *Ibid.*, 26. Blacks, who made up two thirds of the county's population in the mid-1890s, owned less than one tenth of the land; but they owned one eighth of the county's land and buildings as measured by value, and their total holdings were growing steadily in both relative and absolute terms.

Alexander Bruce, a Scottish-born tobacco entrepreneur who was murdered in 1869, named at least two and perhaps three Afro-Virginian citizens as beneficiaries of his will, which the black Israelites' old associate Clement Read witnessed. Each beneficiary was to receive a house and lot of Bruce's that he or she was already living in; those named in the will may have been renting those quarters up to that time, or perhaps they were recipients of Bruce's largesse even before he died. Bruce bequest: WB 12/182, Alexander Bruce will (1869). Bruce's murder: CW v Jackson, Circuit Superior Court of Law and Chancery minute book, 1846–70, 1869 Aug. Bruce's alleged killer seems to have belonged to the clan of Patrick Jackson, entrepreneur and nephew of the late Colonel James Madison. Ms. Census, 1860, family visitation 267, lists among boarders at a hotel in Farmville one A. Bruce, fifty-five, tobacconist, born in Scotland, with $5,000 in real estate and $16,000 in personal property.

65. School and literacy: Du Bois, "Negroes of Farmville," 12–14; p. 17 refers to annual school sessions as running sometimes even less than six months. Sending children away: *Ibid.*, 36. Nearly a decade after Du Bois's visit, black school attendance and school completion remained at low levels—W. T. B. Williams, "Local Conditions

Among Negroes, III: Prince Edward County, Virginia," *Southern Workman,* 35, no. 4 (April 1906), 239–44.

66. Woodworking factory; "often seen working"; blacks hiring whites: Du Bois, "Negroes of Farmville," 20. Black emigration: *Ibid.,* 5 and 8–9.

67. Domestic service: *Ibid.,* 20–21 (quotation on p. 21). There is one apparent inconsistency within Du Bois's article concerning women's options for employment; cf. p. 23 with p. 19 and table on p. 28.

68. Poor, "comfortable," and "well-to-do": *Ibid.,* 28–29. "New figure among Negroes": *Ibid.,* 17. Help from former masters: *Ibid.,* 18.

69. Variety of black businesses: *Ibid.,* 17–19. "The economic importance": *Ibid.,* 21–22.

70. Lynching: *Ibid.,* 23. Black neighborhoods: *Ibid.,* 34. "Slums": *Ibid.,* 37. Interracial marriages: *Ibid.,* 12.

71. Home ownership and renting; emigration; descendants remaining; bringing in spouses (and also the phenomenon of late marriages and bachelorhood): *Ibid.,* 31–33. Living conditions on the Hill: *Ibid.,* 32–34 (quotations at pp. 33 and 34).

72. Du Bois's conclusions: *Ibid.,* 34 ("Instead of . . . dependence") and 38 ("peculiar hopefulness").

73. Social-intellectual life in 1890s: *Ibid.,* 34–37.

74. Hartwill reminiscences: Author's interview with Pearl Walker Hartwill, Israel Hill, August 1, 1989. Christmas: Author's interview with Elizabeth Hill Watkins, Prospect, Va., July 26, 1989. Subsequent notes will attribute material from the Hartwill and Watkins interviews only where the text leaves some ambiguity.

75. Israel Hill school, attendance, and dropouts: Hartwill and Watkins interviews. The school moved into a somewhat larger building, still on the Hill, during its latter years.

76. "Little bit of money": Hartwill interview.

77. Destinations: Hartwill and Watkins interviews; Author's interview with Reginald Othello White Sr., Farmville, March 19, 1992. "Better element": Luther Porter Jackson, *Free Negro Labor and Property Holding in Virginia, 1830–1860* (New York and London: D. Appleton–Century, 1942), p. 126, n. 41.

Postscript: The Search for Meaning in the Southern Free Black Experience

1. "Tolerate free Negroes"; "enraged": Ira Berlin, *Slaves Without Masters: The Free Negro in the Antebellum South* (New York: New Press, [1974] 1992), pp. 88–89.

2. Luther Porter Jackson writes of "a number of meetings" of "citizens" in Northampton and Accomack Counties on Virginia's Eastern Shore, who he says "planned and waged a campaign to drive free Negroes from the state" over a nine-year period. He deems this "one of the most blatant examples of community lawlessness" directed against free Afro-Virginians. Jackson cites a petition from Accomack to the General Assembly, filed in 1834—Jackson, *Free Negro Labor and Property Holding in Virginia, 1830–1860* (New York and London: D. Appleton–Century, 1942), p. 24.

   The events that petition actually narrates are repugnant, yet significantly different from what Jackson reports and implies—Petition of John G. Joynes, 1834 Dec 31, Legislative Petitions, Accomack County, LVA. The "meetings" were not large gatherings of "citizens" clamoring for action over nearly a decade, but rather sessions of the county overseers of the poor in 1825 and 1826. That body decided in the former year to apprehend and sell into slavery one black man who had remained in Virginia more than a year after his liberation without receiving permission; the idea was that this "one example" would produce an exodus of free blacks without "the painful necessity of taking further measures." The detainee was discharged once he agreed to leave the state, and "several hundred" other blacks reportedly left, too.

   A few months later, the overseers of the poor momentarily overcame their supposed desire to avoid painful necessities and resolved to sell *all* blacks who remained in violation of the law of 1806 after three more months; no attempt was made to implement that decision, however. Finally, in 1826, the board actually sold eight free blacks—but then the county court gave permission to one of them to sue to recover his freedom. Abel P. Upshur, later one of Virginia's political stars and a defender of slavery, represented the man (who may already have been living out of state at the time), and a local jury found in his favor. A further plan by the overseers of the poor to sell several free blacks per month appears to have fallen by the wayside.

The story shows vividly that there was at least one county in Virginia that behaved in a more hard-nosed fashion than Prince Edward did, but it does not sustain Jackson's portrait of a prolonged mass movement of vigilantes ousting free blacks wholesale. Indeed, the train of events in Accomack displays the ambivalence that even intolerant people might feel: the very board of overseers that set out to make examples of certain free blacks apparently claimed (and perhaps felt it had to claim) that it did not, in general, wish "again to subject to slavery those who had been once emancipated."

3. See Jackson, *Free Negro Labor,* pp. 3 ("pariah"), 31 ("reducing these people"), and 33 ("prospered"). Jackson attributed free blacks' economic progress both to their own efforts and to "the general upward movement in the state" from 1830 to 1860. The "favorable economic conditions" Jackson posited (p. ix) were tempered by two economic depressions during the period, one of which—that beginning in 1837—took many Virginians years to recover from. Later, having first stated that "Virginia swung over to the proslavery ranks about 1830" (p. 7), Jackson makes a remark that the story of Israel Hill, I think, confirms: questions about slavery persisted in Virginia after 1831 to such an extent, he says, that proslavery hard-liners felt the need, not merely for laws degrading free blacks, but also for "a campaign of proslavery education and the formulation of a proslavery philosophy" (p. 9).

4. See Luther Porter Jackson, "Manumission in Certain Virginia Cities," *Journal of Negro History,* 15, no. 3 (July 1930), 278–314, especially 298 ("dead letter") and 313 ("at times").

5. Free African Americans "were feared and considered threats and subversives," one historian writes in her Introduction to a popular book of the 1990s about a formidable free family, the Maddens of Virginia. "They were intimidated, restricted by law, and discriminated against, but they survived, and endured, and among their numbers were many of the free workers, farmers, skilled craftsmen, and small businessmen of antebellum Virginia"—Ann L. Miller, Introduction to T. O. Madden Jr., *We Were Always Free: The Maddens of Culpeper County, Virginia: A 200-Year Family History* (New York: Vintage, 1993), p. xxx.

6. On the development of white supremacy as dependent on concrete conditions and historical contingencies, see, among other works, Ira Berlin, "From Creole to African: Atlantic Creoles and the Origins of African-American Society in Mainland America," *William and Mary Quarterly,* 3rd ser., 53, no. 2 (April 1996), 251–88; T. H. Breen and Stephen Innes, *"Myne Owne Ground": Race and Freedom on Virginia's Eastern Shore, 1640–1676* (New York and Oxford: Oxford University Press, 1980); Edmund S. Morgan, *American Slavery, American Freedom: The Ordeal of Colonial Virginia* (New York and London: W. W. Norton, 1975); Peter H. Wood, *Black Majority: Negroes in Colonial South Carolina from 1670 Through the Stono Rebellion* (New York and London: W. W. Norton, 1974); and George M. Fredrickson, *White Supremacy: A Comparative Study in American and South African History* (Oxford and New York: Oxford University Press, 1981).

7. My friend and fellow historian Brent Tarter recently reinforced my wariness about the word "friendly." Brent offered me a vivid reminiscence of life with his grandfather,

a New Deal Democrat in Texas who employed African Americans, supervised public housing where some of them lived, dealt civilly with them—and considered them, like poor whites, irresponsible and inferior to himself.

Sources and Interpretations

1. "Court records": Ulrich Bonnell Phillips, *American Negro Slavery: A Survey of the Supply, Employment and Control of Negro Labor as Determined by the Plantation Regime* (Baton Rouge: Louisiana State University Press, [1918] 1966), p. 514.

2. "Unexploited sources": Carter G. Woodson, *Free Negro Heads of Families in the United States in 1830, Together with a Brief Treatment of the Free Negro* (Washington, DC: Association for the Study of Negro Life and History, 1925), p. xxxiv. Much later, Reginald Dennin Butler wrote that he had found ended papers "helpful," and that they needed to be given "greater attention" by researchers—Butler, "Evolution of a Rural Free Black Community: Goochland County, Virginia, 1728–1832" (Ph.D. diss., Johns Hopkins University, 1989), p. 405.

3. "Rurality," etc.: John Hope Franklin, *The Free Negro in North Carolina, 1790–1860* (Chapel Hill: University of North Carolina Press, 1943), pp. 5–6 and 19.

4. See Butler, "Evolution of a Rural Free Black Community," especially pp. 189 ("social welfare"), 192 ("strengthen their status"), and 36–37 ("exceptions").

5. Anthony R. Miles, "Purgatory of Color: The Legal vs. the Social Status of Free Blacks in Antebellum Fairfax County, Virginia" (Senior essay, African and African American Studies, Yale University, 1993), especially pp. 22 (emancipatory wills), 27 (jury trials), 33 ("whites had legal power"), and 37 ("did not *care*"—emphasis in the original). I have found at least one free black defendant in Prince Edward receiving a jury trial late in the antebellum period—OB 26/400 (1850 Nov).

6. Ellen D. Katz, "African-American Freedom in Antebellum Cumberland County, Virginia," *Chicago-Kent Law Review,* 70 (1995), 927ff., especially 960 (one in four households owning land), 952–53 (no one jailed for lacking free papers), 949–51 (expulsion statute), and 933 ("the white perceptions").

7. James D. Watkinson, " 'Fit Objects of Charity': Community, Race, Faith, and Welfare in Antebellum Lancaster County, Virginia, 1817–1860," *Journal of the Early Republic,* 21, no. 1 (Spring 2001), 41–70, especially pp. 52 ("All citizens"), 69 ("desirable" trades), and 49 ("between 1800 and 1860").

8. Skilled trades; economic success; "hated . . . beloved": Ted Delaney and Phillip Wayne Rhodes, *Free Blacks of Lynchburg, Virginia, 1805–1865* (Lynchburg: Warwick House Publishing for Southern Memorial Association, 2001); quotation from p. 15. Moving about; ignoring expulsion law; living independently; treated fairly in court: J. Susanne Simmons, "Children of the Shadows: The Free Negroes of Augusta County and Staunton" (paper submitted to the Regional Studies Seminar, James Madison University, 1996). Similar conclusions about a county on the edge of the Blue Ridge: Sherrie S. McLeroy and William R. McLeroy, *Strangers in Their Midst: The Free Black Population of Amherst County, Virginia* (Bowie, MD: Heritage Books, 1993).

9. Absence of rape myth: Diane Miller Sommerville, "The Rape Myth in the Old South Reconsidered," *Journal of Southern History,* 61, no. 3 (August 1995); and Diane Miller Sommerville, "The Rape Myth Reconsidered: The Intersection of Race, Class, and Gender in the American South, 1800–1877" (Ph.D. diss., Rutgers University, 1995). "White Southerners could react": Martha Hodes, *White Women, Black Men: Illicit Sex in the Nineteenth-Century South* (New Haven and London: Yale University Press, 1997); quotations at pp. 1–3.

10. "Ubiquitous": Joshua Rothman, *Notorious in the Neighborhood: Sex and Families Across the Color Line in Virginia, 1787–1861* (Chapel Hill and London: University of North

Carolina Press, 2003); quotations at pp. 4–5. Interracial family: Thomas E. Buckley, S.J., "Unfixing Race: Class, Power, and Identity in an Interracial Family," *Virginia Magazine of History and Biography*, 102, no. 3 (July 1994), 349–80.

11. Philip J. Schwarz, *Slave Laws in Virginia* (Athens and London: University of Georgia Press, 1996), especially pp. 79–80 ("canons"; "search for justice"; "acquittals") and 95 ("in conception"). See also Schwarz's *Twice Condemned: Slaves and the Criminal Laws of Virginia, 1705–1865* (Baton Rouge: Louisiana State University Press, 1988).

12. See Sally E. Hadden, *Slave Patrols: Law and Violence in Virginia and the Carolinas* (Cambridge, MA, and London: Harvard University Press, 2001).

13. Suzanne Lebsock, *The Free Women of Petersburg: Status and Culture in a Southern Town, 1784–1860* (New York and London: W. W. Norton, 1984), especially pp. 103 ("considerable long-term progress"; "day-by-day domination") and 90 ("were in some respects").

14. See Alison Goodyear Freehling, *Drift Toward Dissolution: The Virginia Slavery Debate of 1831–1832* (Baton Rouge and London: Louisiana State University Press, 1982). Persistent discomfiture over slavery: William W. Freehling, *The Road to Disunion: Secessionists at Bay, 1776–1854* (New York and Oxford: Oxford University Press, 1990), especially pp. 119–210 and 564 ("crusaders"). "Ambivalent view of slavery": William G. Shade, *Democratizing the Old Dominion: Virginia and the Second Party System, 1824–1861* (Charlottesville and London: University Press of Virginia, 1996), p. 13; see also p. 12 ("proslavery") and pp. 6 and 40 (economic attitudes and development).

15. See Michael L. Nicholls, "Passing Through This Troublesome World: Free Blacks in the Early Southside," *Virginia Magazine of History and Biography*, 92, no. 1 (January 1984), 50–70; quotations at p. 69.

16. Brenda E. Stevenson, *Life in Black and White: Family and Community in the Slave South* (New York and Oxford: Oxford University Press, 1996), pp. 296–98 ("devastating" erosion) and 317–18 ("not a few"). The economic progress of free blacks in much of the South during the 1850s is discussed in sources noted above; in Loren Schweninger, *Black Property Owners in the South, 1790–1915* (Urbana: University of Illinois Press, 1990); in Ira Berlin, *Slaves Without Masters: The Free Negro in the Antebellum South* (New York: New Press, [1974] 1992), pp. 343–45; and in sources cited in note 28.

17. Stevenson, *Life in Black and White*, pp. 289–90 (absence of opportunities for skilled jobs) and 316 (lack of poor aid). Stevenson provides only two examples, separated by four decades, of whites seeking to exclude free blacks from employment.

18. *Ibid.*, pp. 294 ("many free people"; "only a few cents"), 292 (supposed degradation of clothes washers), and 296 ("many local whites"). Washers' purchases of real estate: Schweninger, *Black Property Owners*, p. 78. On the subject of washers and others who did lowly jobs, Stevenson herself notes at one point that "most black real estate owners, male and female, were 'laborers' of one sort or another" (p. 298).

19. Stevenson, *Life in Black and White*, pp. 295–96 and 316 ("destroy . . . families").

20. *Ibid.*, pp. 298–99 (multigenerational families), 304 (mixed couples), 269–70 ("array of relationships"), 272 ("white factionalism"), and 271 ("biracial support networks").

21. "Decent, productive, 'free' ": *Ibid.*, p. 278. Stevenson seems ambivalent as to the character of relations between slaves and free blacks. On the one hand, she writes that white anxiety and pressure produced a "consistent strain" between the two black communities; yet elsewhere, she reports that "the marital, blood, cultural, and even criminal connections that Loudoun's free people of color had with the slave community bound the two groups tightly to one another" (pp. 268 and 318).

22. Tommy L. Bogger, *Free Blacks in Norfolk, Virginia, 1790–1860: The Darker Side of Freedom* (Charlottesville and London: University Press of Virginia, 1997), particularly pp. 1 ("overwhelming") and 3 (steady decline).

23. "Many of the sources": *Ibid.*, p. 4.

24. *Ibid.*, particularly pp. 68 ("ordinary citizens") and 99 (deplored kidnapping).

25. *Ibid.*, particularly pp. 88 (firefighters), 95–98 (support for parties suing for freedom), and 101 ("paternalism"). Bogger asserts that white attorneys stopped representing black clients in civil suits against whites around 1805 (pp. 61 and 93–94); this did not happen in Prince Edward or in other localities of which I am aware.

26. "Ebony Festivals": *Ibid.*, pp. 153–54.

27. "Laws . . . not a true gauge": *Ibid.*, pp. 170–71.

28. Acquisition of land: Schweninger, *Black Property Owners in the South;* Edward F. Sweat, *Economic Status of Free Blacks in Antebellum Georgia* (Atlanta: Southern Center for Studies in Public Policy, Clark College, 1974), pp. 10–19; cf. Luther Porter Jackson, *Free Negro Labor and Property Holding in Virginia, 1830–1860* (New York and London: D. Appleton–Century, 1942), *passim.* Tennessee courts: Arthur F. Howington, *What Sayeth the Law: The Treatment of Slaves and Free Blacks in the State and Local Courts of Tennessee* (New York and London: Garland, 1986).

29. Barbara Jeanne Fields, *Slavery and Freedom on the Middle Ground: Maryland During the Nineteenth Century* (New Haven and London: Yale University Press, 1985); quotations at p. 35.

30. See Christopher Andrew Nordmann, "Free Negroes in Mobile County, Alabama" (Ph.D. diss., University of Alabama, 1990).

31. Gary B. Mills, "Miscegenation and the Free Negro in Antebellum 'Anglo' Alabama: A Reexamination of Southern Race Relations," *Journal of American History,* 68, no. 1 (June 1981), 16–34; quotation at p. 32.

32. H. E. Sterkx, *The Free Negro in Ante-Bellum Louisiana* (Rutherford, Madison, and Teaneck, NJ: Fairleigh Dickinson University Press, 1972), especially pp. 171 ("quasi-citizenship"; "enjoyed"), 138 ("frequently"), and 196 ("permissive"; "hostility").

33. Edward F. Sweat, *Free Blacks and the Law in Antebellum Georgia* (Atlanta: Southern Center for Studies in Public Policy, Clark College, 1976), especially pp. 3 and 11 (guardianship), 2 ("lax"; "mitigat[ed]"), 31 (few prosecutions), 17 ("wicked white men"), and 11–12 (free hand).

34. Ira Berlin, *Slaves Without Masters,* especially pp. xiv ("straddled"), 89 ("incorrigible"; "enraged"), 183 ("southern whites"), 88 ("would not tolerate"), 335 ("had little incentive"; "rarely received justice"; "rarely escaped"), and 316 ("whites systematically barred"). In a formidable synthetic-interpretive work on slavery in this country, Berlin in 1998 modified his earlier statements about the lives of free blacks, mainly by incorporating nuances that recent scholarship, including his own, had yielded, and by giving much greater weight to free blacks' own creative responses to their surroundings. Nevertheless, his basic thesis on the treatment of free blacks, which he has always said varied in different parts of the South, remains similar to that of the earlier book. He emphasizes "new forms of dependency [that] emerged even more quickly than the old ones could be liquidated," "ostracism and discrimination" directed by whites against free blacks, and "new forms of subordination that equated free blacks with slaves"—Ira Berlin, *Many Thousands Gone: The First Two Centuries of Slavery in North America* (Cambridge, MA, and London: Belknap Press of Harvard University Press, 1998), especially pp. 224–27 and, on the Upper South specifically, pp. 282–89; quotations from pp. 284–85. See also Berlin's stimulating *Generations of Captivity: A History of African-American Slaves* (Cambridge, MA, and London: Belknap Press of Harvard University Press, 2003), especially pp. 119–23, 182–84, and 224–25.

35. "Determined opposition": Berlin, *Slaves Without Masters,* p. 327; see also pp. 205–06. Berlin's dissertation: Ira Berlin, "Slaves Who Were Free: The Free Negro in the Upper South, 1776–1861" (Ph.D. diss., University of Wisconsin, 1970).

36. Paternalistic protectors: Berlin, *Slaves Without Masters,* pp. 338–40.

37. "Inability": *Ibid.*, p. 330.

38. "Surge"; "offended": *Ibid.*, pp. 375–76. Alison Goodyear Freehling, *Drift Toward Dissolution,* shows that a similar white aversion to forcible expulsion had prevailed in Virginia even in the aftermath of the Nat Turner rebellion.

39. "Contradictions": Berlin, *Slaves Without Masters,* p. 380.

40. "Often . . . no enforcement": Franklin, *Free Negro in North Carolina,* p. 198.

41. *Ibid.,* pp. 129–30 ("an effective method"), 150–51 ("the respect"; "fairly sure"), and 94 ("seeming harsh and illiberal").

42. *Ibid.,* pp. 162 ("surrounded on all sides"), 190 (crime), 195 ("prevalence of drunkenness"), 210 ("life . . . unbearable"), and 219 ("a large number").

43. "The amazing thing": *Ibid.,* p. 162.

44. "Avalanche": Jackson, *Free Negro Labor,* p. 33. South Carolina: Marina Wikramanayake, "The Free Negro in Ante-Bellum South Carolina" (Ph.D. diss., University of Wisconsin, 1966), especially pp. 47 ("devised every . . . means"), 127 ("many" free blacks secure), 221–22 ("long legislative respite"; "consistently rejected"), and 29 ("sheer survival"); see also Wikramanayake, *A World in Shadow: The Free Black in Antebellum South Carolina* (Columbia: University of South Carolina Press for South Carolina Tricentennial Commission, 1973). Berlin's concurrence: Berlin, *Slaves Without Masters,* pp. 194–95. On free mulattoes in South Carolina who achieved far more than simple survival, see Michael P. Johnson and James L. Roark, *Black Masters: A Free Family of Color in the Old South* (New York and London: W. W. Norton, 1984), and Johnson and Roark, eds., *No Chariot Let Down: Charleston's Free People of Color on the Eve of the Civil War* (Chapel Hill and London: University of North Carolina Press, 1984). These authors depict the prosperity some free blacks attained as a counterpoint to what they see as "the degraded circumstances of most free Negroes" in South Carolina—*Black Masters,* p. xii, whence also the phrase beginning "simply to survive."

45. I say *few* free people had to face the hardships that slaves confronted because some free blacks were kidnapped and sold into slavery, even though many Southern whites condemned that practice vociferously. See Carol Wilson, "Freedom at Risk: The Kidnapping of Free Blacks in America, 1780–1865" (Ph.D. diss., West Virginia University, 1991), which, however, deals in large part with blacks kidnapped from free states and then sold into bondage in the South. Not surprisingly, the author finds it impossible to say with any precision how widespread the phenomenon of kidnapping was.

ACKNOWLEDGMENTS

Working in the archives at the Library of Virginia in the 1990s carried with it a great privilege: one instantly joined an informal but cordial band of brethren and sisters engaged in a common enterprise. The makeup of the group changed from week to week and from year to year as academic researchers from afar came and went, but the esprit held steady, year in and year out. The core around whom this remarkable structure formed consisted of the library's own John Kneebone and Brent Tarter. Largely thanks to them, I got to know more fellow historians at the old Virginia State Library, and over the lunch table at nearby restaurants, than I have in any other place outside the departments of history and African American studies to which I have belonged.

The element of the Library of Virginia experience that most revived one's faith in human nature was the eagerness of each researcher to pass on any discovery that seemed potentially useful to another. To thank those who have treated me warmly and shared information is to risk leaving someone out. I nevertheless want to recognize Yaakov Aronson, Thomas E. Buckley, Reginald D. Butler, Harold Forsythe, Sarah Hughes, Anthony Iaccarino, Jeffrey Kerr-Ritchie, Cynthia A. Kierner, Suzanne Lebsock, L. Jeffrey Perez, Tatiana van Riemsdijk, Loren Schweninger, and James Sidbury. Graduate students at Yale and William and Mary—most of them professional historians by now—who shared information on Prince Edward County that they had come across while doing their own research at the Library or elsewhere include Lynn Nelson, Antoinette Van Zelm, Elizabeth R. Varon, and Nancy A. Moll.

The staff of the state archives graciously adapted to my presence in the reading room for stretches of time so lengthy that I could almost have claimed legal domicile. Several staffers actively helped me find material, decipher handwriting, or place my findings in context, and they made innumerable photocopies for me. J. Christian Kolbe and Minor Weisiger were there from beginning to end; Wendy Clark, Robert Clay, Grace Lessner, and Jennifer Davis McDaid likewise helped and encouraged me on many occasions.

John Hopewell took an active interest in my work and gave me a tour of the inner sanctum in which county records are processed. I received numerous valuable tips from the aforementioned Messrs. Tarter and Kneebone, and from James D. Watkinson, whose research on the treatment of the poor in old Virginia has been of great value to me and others. State archivist Conley Edwards was an ever cordial host; he and Lyndon Hart went out of their way to accommodate my research. Lyn Hart and Carl Childs helped me describe my sources and their locations in ways we hope will make it easy for future researchers to track down specific documents.

At the Virginia Historical Society (VHS), the estimable Frances Pollard got me started on this project, along with Howson Cole and Waverly Winfree; Frances helped me again toward the end. Nelson Lankford made me feel welcome at the society. I thank the VHS for a Mellon Research Grant that allowed me to begin my work. In the Manuscripts and Rare Books Department, Earl Gregg Swem Library, College of William and Mary, Margaret Cook and her staff, including Susan A. Riggs, offered extraordinary hospitality and active, deeply knowledgeable help. I am grateful also to Alan Zoellner, Hope Yelich, and Bettina Manzo of Swem Library.

A number of people in Prince Edward County contributed generously to this project. James Ghee told me how to find Israel Hill on the ground, and he gave me the names and telephone numbers of Marie E. Bowery De Laney, Pearl Walker Hartwill, and Elizabeth Hill Watkins. Mrs. De Laney kindly shared with me some material she had collected. Mmes Hartwill and Watkins welcomed me into their homes and answered my many questions about their early life on Israel Hill.

Ceile Dunlap overwhelmed me with her generosity, methodically gathering information on the Farmville Baptist Church and on the descendants of Israel Hill's White family. Mrs. Dunlap also put me in touch with Reginald O. White Sr., a man of Israelite stock, who granted me a lengthy interview. The staff of Farmville Baptist Church gave me work space and permission to review their congregation's nineteenth-century minute book. Virginia G. Redd and John M. Osborn shared their expertise in local history, and Bid Wall of the *Farmville Herald* provided information on Prince Edward County in the late nineteenth century.

Frank L. Overton, clerk of circuit court for Prince Edward County, and his assistants, Machelle J. Eppes, Jessica Sayer Hayes, and Lynnette Coe, received me hospitably at the courthouse, and Mr. Overton granted me permission to use county records. Circuit court clerks James W. King, Stuart B. Fallen, and Imogene W. Tunstall of Nottoway, Charlotte, and Cumberland Counties, respectively, gave me similar permission; Mr. King and Ms. Tunstall offered their advice as well.

I have been aided efficiently at a number of institutions whose archival collections I have used. I would like to recognize the Rare Book, Manuscript, and Special Collections Library, Duke University (Janie C. Morris and Eleanor Mills); the Southern Historical Collection, Manuscripts Department, Wilson Library, University of North Carolina at Chapel Hill (John White and Rachel Canada); the Special Collections Department, Alderman Library, University of

Virginia (Regina Rush and Ervin Jordan); the Virginia Baptist Historical Society (Darlene Slater); the Manuscripts and Archives Department, Sterling Memorial Library, Yale University (William Massa); the Rockefeller Library, Colonial Williamsburg Foundation; the William Smith Morton Library, Union Theological Seminary and Presbyterian School of Christian Education (Paula Youngman Skreslet); and the Longwood University Library.

A number of people helped me locate pictures. I thank Petie Bogan-Garrett, Elizabeth M. Gushee, Marianne McKee, and Carolyn Parsons at the Library of Virginia; Teresa Roane of the Valentine Museum; Heather W. Milne at the Museum of the Confederacy; William E. Trout III; Robert S. Dietz at the Dietz Press; Ruth Mitchell of the Maryland Historical Society; Sylvia Inwood at the Detroit Institute of Arts; and Catherine H. Grosfils in the Audiovisual Library of the Colonial Williamsburg Foundation.

Yale University offered crucial support for my research through a Morse Fellowship, a Senior Faculty Fellowship, several A. Whitney Griswold Faculty Research Grants from the Whitney Humanities Center, a John F. Enders Research Grant, a major research award from the Program in African and African American Studies, and the Heyman Prize for Scholarly Publication and Research from Yale College. Sue Roberts and Susan Steinberg of Sterling Memorial Library at Yale purchased microfilms of Prince Edward and Cumberland County Court records. I am grateful for the moral and intellectual support I received at Yale during the early stages of this project from John W. Blassingame, Richard H. Brodhead, Nancy Cott, William Cronon, David Brion Davis, John Mack Faragher, Gerald David Jaynes, Howard Lamar, Harry Miskimin, and David Montgomery.

The National Endowment for the Humanities aided me with a Summer Stipend and a Travel to Collections Grant, as did the College of William and Mary with two Summer Research Grants. The College's Lyon Gardiner Tyler Department of History provided a Tyler Faculty Research Grant and other funds in support of my work. A Fulbright Senior Scholar Grant afforded me some time for writing; I thank Emily Budick of the American Studies program at the Hebrew University in Jerusalem for helping to make that fellowship possible and for seeing to my welfare while we were colleagues.

Many students have read chapters in manuscript, and a number have contributed useful insights; several of these people are acknowledged in the Notes. Susan A. Kern kindly presented comments in writing. Jackson Sasser helped me identify secondary writings on free blacks, and he compiled data on trials and suits for assault as recorded in the microfilmed order books of the Prince Edward County Court. Gregory P. Downs shared the abundant information on Prince Edward that he had gathered during his work on schooling for blacks and whites in Virginia during the early post–Civil War years.

Kathryn E. Miller read many chapters, commented helpfully on one in particular, and discussed with me at length the secondary literature on free

African Americans. Taking up some slender leads I gave her, Katy also conducted an inventive, intrepid, and ultimately successful search for the "Israel Hill Resolutions."

A number of fellow historians and others helped me in various ways. Lynda J. Morgan provided helpful advice early on; Elizabeth Regosin and Marie Tyler-McGraw shared with me their findings on related subjects. Frank Moore sent me an example of the myth of Israel Hill's decline and fall as published in the North; Fran Heiner lent me a useful history of the Watkins family. Preston and John Nowlin made me aware of a controversy in 1799 surrounding John Randolph's views about slavery, and Richard Kremer raised a point that led me to include in this book a discussion of Virginia's self-enslavement law of 1856. Steven Fraser offered an important suggestion about the organization of the book.

At William and Mary, Grey Gundaker and Camille Wells replied eruditely to my queries on specific points; Camille pursued several issues as persistently as if they pertained to her own project rather than to that of an associate. Chandos Michael Brown asked a critical question that helped shape a chapter of this book. Scott Reynolds Nelson discussed sources of illustrations with me and gave me a compact disc that made it much easier to navigate the multivolume *War of the Rebellion.* James P. Whittenburg tendered good advice and lent me a computer when mine broke down in the home stretch.

No could have been more generous than Edward L. Ayers, Gerald David Jaynes, Ellen D. Katz, John T. Kneebone, James M. McPherson, Nancy Weiss Malkiel, Carol Sheriff, and Brent Tarter, all of whom were patient enough to read the entire manuscript and offer astute comments. Larry J. Griffin wrote a helpful critique of one crucial chapter.

C. Vann Woodward offered an unforgettable professional and personal example. He spent his career laying bare the exploitative character of the society that had produced him, and his work led me into the serious study of history. He also shared with me memories of his youth in Arkansas. These confirmed an insight that informed his work—that thoroughgoing racial *separation* was one thing racial *oppression* had never managed to produce. Vann's avid interest in my efforts to recover the story of Israel on the Appomattox encouraged me greatly.

I thank my literary agent, Richard Balkin, for doing his job skillfully and for making a useful editorial suggestion early on. I am grateful to Jane Garrett, my editor at Alfred A. Knopf, for her astounding patience and for wise counsel when it mattered most. With dedication and skill, Jane, her assistant, Emily Owens, copyeditor Ann Adelman, production editor Ellen R. Feldman, designer Anthea Lingeman, and cover designer Peter Mendelsund transformed my manuscript into a book.

My family has provided much encouragement and practical support. My brother, Gordon, has followed this enterprise with active and gratifying interest from the beginning. My son, Oren, and my daughter, Kinneret, have offered the best sort of companionship and have grown up along with this project; if the book turns out half as well as the children have, I will be a happy man.

My wife's parents, Amotz Zahavi and Avishag Kadman-Zahavi, have likewise provided good company as well as abundant concrete assistance. I wrote most of this book in their home and in other quarters supplied by them; during the year I maintained an office in their apartment, Avishag offered me tea, cake, and fascinating conversation every afternoon.

The contributions of my wife, Naama Zahavi-Ely, have been too numerous to list. Naama believed, from the first moment and unwaveringly, that this project had a future. She enthusiastically moved back and forth between New Haven and Richmond as I conducted my research. She explored the upper Appomattox River with me and the children, took genuine interest in each archival discovery I made, and talked me through moments of discouragement. Naama provided much technical guidance and helped me untangle some thorny issues that the sources raised; she read two versions of the full manuscript and commented astutely.

I thank my mother, Vivien, for offering practical help at every turn. On three separate occasions she located summer lodgings in Richmond to make my research there possible, and she took me and my family in during other seasons. She "carried" me, as Virginians used to put it, to and from the Library of Virginia numerous times and assisted me in many additional ways.

But I dedicate this book to her for other reasons entirely. She and my father brought me up in abundant love, and with just the right amount of attentiveness. That would have been more than enough, but my mother is a born teacher as well. I remember vividly a hundred specific moments when I learned something from her—to form numbers with a pencil, tie my shoes, cook my lunch; to follow city politics; to place Richmond's streets on a mental map in order to pass the test for my taxi driver's license; to write an English sentence worth reading. Above all, my mother taught me by word and deed that the equality of all people is a moral fact, not a mere slogan. That lesson underlies everything I do as a historian and as a citizen of the world.

M. P. E.
Williamsburg, Virginia

INDEX

Page numbers in *italics* refer to illustrations; page numbers after 475 refer to notes.